Less managing. More teaching. Greater learning.

INSTRUCTORS...

Would you like your **students** to show up for class more **prepared**? *(Let's face it, class is much more fun if everyone is engaged and prepared...)*

Want ready-made application-level **interactive assignments**, student progress reporting, and auto-assignment grading? *(Less time grading means more time teaching...)*

Want an **instant view of student or class performance** relative to learning objectives? *(No more wondering if students understand...)*

Need to **collect data and generate reports** required for administration or accreditation? *(Say goodbye to manually tracking student learning outcomes...)*

Want to **record and post your lectures** for students to view online?

With **McGraw-Hill's *Connect*™ Plus Marketing,**

INSTRUCTORS GET:

- Interactive Applications – **book-specific interactive assignments** that require students to APPLY what they've learned.

- Simple **assignment management**, allowing you to spend more time teaching.

- **Auto-graded** assignments, quizzes, and tests.

- **Detailed Visual Reporting** where student and section results can be viewed and analyzed.

- Sophisticated **online testing** capability.

- A **filtering and reporting** function that allows you to easily assign and report on materials that are correlated to accreditation standards, learning outcomes, and Bloom's taxonomy.

- An easy-to-use **lecture capture** tool.

Want an online, **searchable version** of your textbook?

Wish your textbook could be **available online** while you're doing your assignments?

 ### Connect™ Plus Marketing eBook

If you choose to use *Connect™ Plus Marketing*, you have an affordable and searchable online version of your book integrated with your other online tools.

Connect™ Plus Marketing eBook offers features like:

- Topic search
- Direct links from assignments
- Adjustable text size
- Jump to page number
- Print by section

 Want to get more **value** from your textbook purchase?

Think learning marketing should be a bit more **interesting**?

 ### Check out the STUDENT RESOURCES section under the *Connect™* Library tab.

Here you'll find a wealth of resources designed to help you achieve your goals in the course. You'll find things like **quizzes, PowerPoints, and Internet activities** to help you study. Every student has different needs, so explore the STUDENT RESOURCES to find the materials best suited to you.

International Marketing

International Marketing

fifteenth edition

Philip R. Cateora
FELLOW, ACADEMY OF INTERNATIONAL
BUSINESS UNIVERSITY OF COLORADO

Mary C. Gilly
UNIVERSITY OF CALIFORNIA, IRVINE

John L. Graham
UNIVERSITY OF CALIFORNIA, IRVINE

McGraw-Hill Irwin

The McGraw-Hill Companies

McGraw-Hill
Irwin

INTERNATIONAL MARKETING

Published by McGraw-Hill/Irwin, a business unit of The McGraw-Hill Companies, Inc., 1221 Avenue of the Americas, New York, NY, 10020. Copyright © 2011, 2009, 2007, 2005, 2002, 1999, 1996, 1993, 1990, 1987, 1985, 1983, 1979, 1975, 1971 by The McGraw-Hill Companies, Inc. All rights reserved. No part of this publication may be reproduced or distributed in any form or by any means, or stored in a database or retrieval system, without the prior written consent of The McGraw-Hill Companies, Inc., including, but not limited to, in any network or other electronic storage or transmission, or broadcast for distance learning.

Some ancillaries, including electronic and print components, may not be available to customers outside the United States.

This book is printed on acid-free paper.

1 2 3 4 5 6 7 8 9 0 DOW/DOW 1 0 9 8 7 6 5 4 3 2 1 0

ISBN 978-0-07-352994-3
MHID 0-07-352994-X

Vice president and editor-in-chief: *Brent Gordon*
Editorial director: *Paul Ducham*
Publisher: *Doug Hughes*
Executive editor: *John Weimeister*
Director of development: *Ann Torbert*
Development editor: *Sara Knox Hunter*
Editorial assistant: *Heather Darr*
Vice president and director of marketing: *Robin J. Zwettler*
Marketing manager: *Katie Mergen*
Marketing specialist: *Meredith Desmond*
Vice president of editing, design, and production: *Sesha Bolisetty*

Senior project manager: *Bruce Gin*
Buyer II: *Debra R. Sylvester*
Interior designer: *JoAnne Schopler*
Senior photo research coordinator: *Jeremy Cheshareck*
Photo researcher: *David Tietz, Editorial Image, LLC*
Senior media project manager: *Greg Bates*
Media project manager: *Cathy L. Tepper*
Cover design: *JoAnne Schopler*
Interior design: *JoAnne Schopler*
Typeface: 10/12 Times New Roman
Compositor: MPS Limited, a Macmillan Company
Printer: R. R. Donnelley

Library of Congress Cataloging-in-Publication Data

Cateora, Philip R.
    International marketing / Philip R. Cateora, Mary C. Gilly, John L. Graham. — 15th ed.
        p. cm.
    Includes index.
    ISBN-13: 978-0-07-352994-3 (alk. paper)
    ISBN-10: 0-07-352994-X (alk. paper)
    1. Export marketing. 2. International business enterprises. I. Gilly, Mary C. II. Graham, John L. III. Title.
HF1416.C375 2011
658.8'4—dc22

2010020200

To Nancy

To the people who led me down this
career path:

Richard Burr, Trinity University

Tom Barry, Southern Methodist University

Betsy Gelb, University of Houston

To Geert Hofstede

ABOUT THE AUTHORS

Philip R. Cateora

Professor Emeritus, The University of Colorado at Boulder. Received his Ph.D. from the University of Texas at Austin where he was elected to Beta Gamma Sigma. In his academic career at the University of Colorado he has served as Division Head of Marketing, Coordinator of International Business Programs, Associate Dean, and Interim Dean. His teaching has spanned a range of courses in marketing and international business, from fundamentals through the doctoral level. He received the University of Colorado Teaching Excellence Award and the Western Marketing Educator's Association's Educator of the Year Award.

Professor Cateora has conducted faculty workshops on internationalizing principles of marketing courses for the AACSB and participated in designing and offering similar faculty workshops under a grant by the Department of Education. In conjunction with these efforts, he co-authored *Marketing: An International Perspective,* a supplement to accompany principles of marketing texts. Professor Cateora has served as consultant to small export companies as well as multinational companies, served on the Rocky Mountain Export Council, and taught in management development programs. He is a Fellow of the Academy of International Business.

Mary C. Gilly

Professor of Marketing at the Paul Merage School of Business, University of California, Irvine. She received her B.A. from Trinity University in San Antonio, Texas; her M.B.A. from Southern Methodist University in Dallas, Texas; and her Ph.D. from the University of Houston. Dr. Gilly has been at UCI since 1982 and has served as Vice Dean, Associate Dean, Director of the Ph.D. Program and Faculty Chair in the school of business, as well as the Associate Dean of Graduate Studies for the campus. She has been on the faculties of Texas A&M University and Southern Methodist University and has been a visiting professor at the Madrid Business School and Georgetown University. Professor Gilly has been a member of the American Marketing Association since 1975 and has served that organization in a number of capacities, including Marketing Education Council, President, Co-Chair of the 1991 AMA Summer Educators' Conference, and member and chair of the AMA–Irwin Distinguished Marketing Educator Award Committee. She currently serves as Academic Director for the Association for Consumer Research. Professor Gilly has published her research on international, cross-cultural, and consumer behavior topics in *Journal of Marketing, Journal of Consumer Research, Journal of Retailing, California Management Review*, and other venues.

John L. Graham

Professor of International Business and Marketing at the Paul Merage School of Business, University of California, Irvine. He has been Associate Dean and Director, UCI Center for Citizen Peacebuilding; Visiting Scholar, Georgetown University School of Business; Visiting Professor at Madrid Business School in Spain; and Associate Professor, University of Southern California. Before beginning his doctoral studies at UC Berkeley, he worked for a division of Caterpillar Tractor Co. and served as an officer in the U.S. Navy Underwater Demolition Teams. Professor Graham is the author (with William Hernandez Requejo) of *Global Negotiation: The New Rules*, Palgrave-Macmillan, 2008; (with N. Mark Lam) of *China Now, Doing Business in the World's Most Dynamic Market,* McGraw-Hill, 2007; (with Yoshihiro Sano and James Hodgson, former U.S. Ambassador to Japan) of *Doing Business with the New Japan,* Rowman & Littlefield, 4th edition, 2008; and editor (with Taylor Meloan) of *Global and International Marketing,* Irwin, 2nd edition, 1997. He has published articles in publications such as *Harvard Business Review, Journal of Marketing, Journal of International Business Studies, Strategic Management Review, Journal of Consumer Research, Journal of International Marketing*, and *Marketing Science.* Excerpts of his work have been read into the *Congressional Record,* and his research on business negotiation styles in 20 cultures was the subject of an article in the January 1988 issue of *Smithsonian.* His 1994 paper in *Management Science* received a citation of excellence from the Lauder Institute at the Wharton School of Business. He was selected for the 2009 International Trade Educator of the Year Award, given by the North American Small Business International Trade Educators' Association.

PREFACE

At the start of the last millennium, the Chinese were the pre-eminent international traders. Although a truly global trading system would not evolve until some 500 years later, Chinese silk had been available in Europe since Roman times.

At the start of the last century the British military, merchants, and manufacturers dominated the seas and international commerce. Literally, the sun did not set on the British Empire.

At the start of the last decade, the United States had surged past a faltering Japan to retake the lead in global commerce. The American domination of information technology has since been followed by the political upheaval of 9/11 and the economic shocks of 2001 and 2008. China started that decade as the largest military threat to the United States, and at the decade's end, it has become a leading, often difficult trading partner.

What surprises do the new decade, century, and millennium hold in store for all of us? Toward the end of the last decade, natural disasters and wars hampered commerce and human progress. The battle to balance economic growth and stewardship of the environment continues. The globalization of markets has certainly accelerated through almost universal acceptance of the democratic free enterprise model and new communication technologies, including cell phones and the Internet. Which will prove the better, Chinese gradualism or the Russian big-bang approach to economic and political reform? Will the information technology boom of the previous decade be followed by a demographics bust when American baby boomers begin to try to retire after 2012? Or will NAFTA and the young folks in Mexico provide a much needed demographic balance? Ten years out the debate about global warming should be settled—more data and better science will yield the answers. Will the economic tsunami of 2008–2009 evolve into something even worse? What unforeseen advances or disasters will the biological sciences bring us? Will we conquer AIDS/HIV in Africa? Will weapons and warfare become obsolete?

International marketing will play a key role in providing positive answers to all these questions. We know that trade causes peace and prosperity by promoting creativity, mutual understanding, and interdependence. Markets are burgeoning in emerging economies in eastern Europe, the Commonwealth of Independent States, China, Indonesia, Korea, India, Mexico, Chile, Brazil, and Argentina—in short, globally. These emerging economies hold the promise of huge markets in the future. In the more mature markets of the industrialized world, opportunity and challenge also abound as consumers' tastes become more sophisticated and complex and as the hoped for rebound in purchasing power provides consumers with new means of satisfying new demands.

With the recent downturn in the industrialized countries and the continued growth in emerging markets has come a new competitive landscape, one vastly different from that earlier period when United States multinationals dominated world markets. From the late 1940s through the 1960s, multinational corporations (MNCs) from the United States had little competition; today, companies from almost all the world's nations vie for global markets. Fareed Zakaria reported:

> "During the last two years, 124 countries grew their economies at over 4 percent a year. That includes more than 30 countries in Africa. Over the last two decades, lands outside the industrialized West have been growing at rates that were once unthinkable. While there have been booms and busts, the overall trend has been unambiguously upward. Antoine van Agtmael, the fund manager who coined the term 'emerging markets,' has identified the 25 companies most likely to be the world's next great multinationals. His list includes four companies each from Brazil, Mexico, South Korea, and Taiwan; three from India, two from China, and one each from Argentina, Chile, Malaysia, and South Africa. This is something much broader than the much-ballyhooed rise of China or even Asia. It is the rise of the rest—the rest of the world."[1]

The economic, political, and social changes that have occurred over the last decade have dramatically altered the landscape of global business. Consider the present and future impact of the following:

- The ever-present threat of global terrorism as represented by the September 11, 2001, attacks

- Major armed conflicts in sub-Saharan Africa and the Middle East

- The potential global recession emanating from the United States

- The emerging markets in eastern Europe, Asia, and Latin America, where more than 75 percent of the growth in world trade over the next 20 years is expected to occur

- The reunification of Hong Kong, Macau, and China, which finally puts all of Asia under the control of Asians for the first time in over a century

- The European Monetary Union and the successful switch from local-country currencies to one monetary unit for Europe, the euro

- The rapid move away from traditional distribution structures in Japan, Europe, and many emerging markets

- The growth of middle-income households the world over

- The continued strengthening and creation of regional market groups such as the European Union (EU),

[1]Fareed Zakaria, "The Rise of the Rest," *Newsweek,* May 3, 2008.

the North American Free Trade Area (NAFTA), the Central American Free Trade Area (CAFTA), ASEAN Free Trade Area (AFTA), the Southern Cone Free Trade Area (Mercosur), and the Asia-Pacific Economic Cooperation (APEC)

- The successful completion of the Uruguay Round of the General Agreement on Tariffs and Trade (GATT) and the creation of the World Trade Organization (WTO), the latter now including China and Taiwan

- The restructuring, reorganizing, and refocusing of companies in telecommunications, entertainment, and biotechnology, as well as in traditional smokestack industries around the world

- The continuing integration of the Internet and cell phones into all aspects of companies' operations and consumers' lives

These are not simply news reports. These changes affect the practice of business worldwide, and they mean that companies will have to constantly examine the way they do business and remain flexible enough to react rapidly to changing global trends to be competitive.

As global economic growth occurs, understanding marketing in all cultures is increasingly important. *International Marketing* addresses global issues and describes concepts relevant to all international marketers, regardless of the extent of their international involvement. Not all firms engaged in overseas marketing have a global perspective, nor do they need to. Some companies' foreign marketing is limited to one country; others market in a number of countries, treating each as a separate market; and still others, the global enterprises, look for market segments with common needs and wants across political and economic boundaries. All, however, are affected by competitive activity in the global marketplace. It is with this future that the fifteenth edition of *International Marketing* is concerned.

Emphasis is on the strategic implications of competition in different country markets. An environmental/cultural approach to international marketing permits a truly global orientation. The reader's horizons are not limited to any specific nation or to the particular ways of doing business in a single nation. Instead, the book provides an approach and framework for identifying and analyzing the important cultural and environmental uniqueness of any nation or global region. Thus, when surveying the tasks of marketing in a foreign milieu, the reader will not overlook the impact of crucial cultural issues.

The text is designed to stimulate curiosity about management practices of companies, large and small, seeking market opportunities outside the home country and to raise the reader's consciousness about the importance of viewing international marketing management strategies from a global perspective.

Although this revised edition is infused throughout with a global orientation, export marketing and the operations of smaller companies are also included. Issues specific to exporting are discussed where strategies applicable to exporting arise, and examples of marketing practices of smaller companies are examined.

New and Expanded Topics in This Edition

The new and expanded topics in this fifteenth edition reflect issues in competition, changing marketing structures, ethics and social responsibility, negotiations, and the development of the manager for the 21st century. Competition is raising the global standards for quality, increasing the demand for advanced technology and innovation, and increasing the value of customer satisfaction. The global market is swiftly changing from a seller's market to a buyer's market. This is a period of profound social, economic, and political change. To remain competitive globally, companies must be aware of all aspects of the emerging global economic order.

Additionally, the evolution of global communications and its known and unknown impacts on how international business is conducted cannot be minimized. In the third millennium, people in the "global village" will grow closer than ever before and will hear and see each other as a matter of course. An executive in Germany can routinely connect via VoIP (Voice over Internet Protocol) to hear and see his or her counterpart in an Australian company or anywhere else in the world. In many respects (time zone differences is a prominent exception), geographic distance is becoming irrelevant.

Telecommunications, the Internet, and satellites are helping companies optimize their planning, production, and procurement processes. Information—and, in its wake, the flow of goods—is moving around the globe at lightning speed. Increasingly powerful networks spanning the globe enable the delivery of services that reach far beyond national and continental boundaries, fueling and fostering international trade. The connections of global communications bring people all around the world together in new and better forms of dialogue and understanding.

This dynamic nature of the international marketplace is reflected in the number of substantially improved and expanded topics in this fifteenth edition, including the following:

- A deeper look at the causes of cultural differences

- The Internet and cell phones and their expanding role in international marketing

- Negotiations with customers, partners, and regulators

- Evolving global middle-income households

- Bottom-of-the-pyramid markets

- World Trade Organization
- Free trade agreements
- Multicultural research
- Qualitative and quantitative research
- Country-of-origin effects and global brands
- Industrial trade shows
- A growing emphasis on both consumer and industrial services
- Trends in channel structures in Europe, Japan, and developing countries
- Ethics and socially responsible decisions
- Green marketing
- Changing profiles of global managers

Structure of the Text

The text is divided into six parts. The first two chapters, Part 1, introduce the reader to the environmental/cultural approach to international marketing and to three international marketing management concepts: domestic market expansion, multi-domestic marketing, and global marketing. As companies restructure for the global competitive rigors of the 21st century, so too must tomorrow's managers. The successful manager must be globally aware and have a frame of reference that goes beyond a country, or even a region, and encompasses the world. What global awareness means and how it is acquired is discussed early in the text; it is at the foundation of global marketing.

Chapter 2 focuses on the dynamic environment of international trade and the competitive challenges and opportunities confronting today's international marketer. The importance of the creation of the World Trade Organization, the successor to GATT, is fully explored. The growing importance of cell phones and the Internet in conducting international business is considered, creating a foundation on which specific applications in subsequent chapters are presented.

The five chapters in Part 2 deal with the cultural environment of global marketing. A global orientation requires the recognition of cultural differences and the critical decision of whether it is necessary to accommodate them.

Geography and history (Chapter 3) are included as important dimensions in understanding cultural and market differences among countries. Not to be overlooked is concern for the deterioration of the global ecological environment and the multinational company's critical responsibility to protect it.

Chapter 4 presents a broad review of culture and its impact on human behavior as it relates to international marketing. Specific attention is paid to Geert Hofstede's study of cultural values and behavior. The elements of culture reviewed in Chapter 4 set the stage for the in-depth analyses in Chapters 5, 6, and 7 of business customs and the political and legal environments. Ethics and social responsibility are presented in the context of the dilemma that often confronts the international manager, that is, balancing corporate profits against the social and ethical consequences of his or her decisions.

We have reorganized Part 3 of the book into four chapters on assessing global market opportunities. As markets expand, segments grow within markets; as market segments across country markets evolve, marketers are forced to understand market behavior within and across different cultural contexts. Multicultural research, qualitative and quantitative research, and the Internet as a tool in the research task are explored in Chapter 8.

Separate chapters on economic development and the Americas (Chapter 9); Europe, Africa, and the Middle East (Chapter 10); and the Asia Pacific Region (Chapter 11) reflect the evolving marketing organizations of many multinational companies in response to the costs of travel and communications across time zones, as well as the steady creation and growth of regional market groups in all three regions. The discussions in all three chapters include details about both established and emerging markets present in each region.

The strategic implications of the dissolution of the Soviet Union and the emergence of new independent republics, the shift from socialist-based to market-based economies in Eastern Europe, and the return of South Africa and Vietnam to international commerce are examined. Attention is also given to the efforts of the governments of China and India and many Latin American countries to reduce or eliminate barriers to trade, open their countries to foreign investment, and privatize state-owned enterprises.

These political, social, and economic changes that are sweeping the world are creating new markets and opportunities, making some markets more accessible while creating the potential for greater protectionism in others.

In Part 4, Developing Global Marketing Strategies, planning and organizing for global marketing is the subject of Chapter 12. The discussion of collaborative relationships, including strategic alliances, recognizes the importance of relational collaborations among firms, suppliers, and customers in the success of the global marketer. Many multinational companies realize that to fully capitalize on opportunities offered by global markets, they must have strengths that often exceed their capabilities. Collaborative relationships can provide technology, innovations, productivity, capital, and market access that strengthen a company's competitive position.

Chapters 13 and 14 focus on product and services management, reflecting the differences in strategies between consumer and industrial offerings and the growing importance in world markets for both consumer and business services. Additionally, the discussion on the development of global offerings stresses the importance of approaching the adaptation issue from the viewpoint of building a standardized product/service platform that can be adapted to reflect cultural differences. The competitive importance in today's global market of quality, innovation, and technology as the keys to marketing success is explored.

Chapter 15 takes the reader through the distribution process, from home country to the consumer in the target country market. The structural impediments to market entry imposed by a country's distribution system are examined in the framework of a detailed presentation of the Japanese distribution system. Additionally, the rapid changes in channel structure that are occurring in Japan, as well as in other countries, and the emergence of the World Wide Web as a distribution channel are presented. We also have redistributed key material from a previous chapter on exporting logistics to this and other related sections of the book.

Chapter 16 covers advertising and addresses the promotional element of the international marketing mix. Included in the discussion of global market segmentation are recognition of the rapid growth of market segments across country markets and the importance of market segmentation as a strategic competitive tool in creating an effective promotional message. Chapter 17 discusses personal selling and sales management and the critical nature of training, evaluating, and controlling sales representatives.

Price escalation and ways it can be lessened, countertrade practices, and price strategies to employ when the dollar is strong or weak relative to foreign currencies are concepts presented in Chapter 18.

In Part 5, Chapter 19 is a thorough presentation of negotiating with customers, partners, and regulators. The discussion stresses the varying negotiation styles found among cultures and the importance of recognizing these differences at the negotiation table.

Pedagogical Features of the Text

The text portion of the book provides thorough coverage of its subject, with a subject emphasis on the planning and strategic problems confronting companies that market across cultural boundaries.

The use of the Internet as a tool of international marketing is stressed throughout the text. On all occasions in which data used in the text originated from an Internet source, the Web address is given. Problems that require the student to access the Internet are included with end-of-chapter questions. Internet-related problems are designed to familiarize the student with the power of the Internet in his or her research, to illustrate data available on the Internet, and to challenge the reader to solve problems using the Internet. Many of the examples, illustrations, and exhibits found in the text can be explored in more detail by accessing the Web addresses that are included.

Current, pithy, sometimes humorous, and always relevant examples are used to stimulate interest and increase understanding of the ideas, concepts, and strategies presented in emphasizing the importance of understanding cultural uniqueness and relevant business practices and strategies.

Each chapter is introduced with a Global Perspective, a real-life example of company experiences that illustrates salient issues discussed in the chapter. Companies featured in the Global Perspectives range from exporters to global enterprises.

The boxed Crossing Borders, an innovation of the first edition of *International Marketing*, have always been popular with students. They reflect contemporary issues in international marketing and can be used to illustrate real-life situations and as the basis for class discussion. They are selected to be unique, humorous, and of general interest to the reader.

The book is presented in full color, allowing maps to depict of geographical, cultural, and political boundaries and features more easily. Color also allows us to better communicate the intricacies of international symbols and meanings in marketing communications. New photographs of current and relevant international marketing events are found throughout the text—all in color.

The Country Notebook—A Guide for Developing a Marketing Plan, found in Part 6, Supplementary Material, is a detailed outline that provides both a format for a complete cultural and economic analysis of a country and guidelines for developing a marketing plan.

In addition to The Country Notebook, the fifteenth edition comprises a selection of short and long cases located online at www.mhhe.com/cateora15e. The short cases focus on a single problem, serving as the basis for discussion of a specific concept or issue. The longer, more integrated cases are broader in scope and focus on more than one marketing management problem; new cases focus on services, marketing, and marketing strategy. The cases can be analyzed using the information provided. They also lend themselves to more in-depth analysis, requiring the student to engage in additional research and data collection.

Supplements

We have taken great care to offer new features and improvements to every part of the teaching aid package. Following is a list of specific features:

- **Instructor's Manual and Test Bank.** The Instructor's Manual, prepared by the authors, contains lecture notes or teaching suggestions for each chapter. A section called Changes to This Edition is included to help instructors adapt their teaching notes to the fifteenth edition. A case correlation grid at the beginning of the case note offers alternative uses for the cases.

The Test Bank is also available on the Online Learning Center for ease of use. The Test Bank contains more than 2,000 questions, including true/false, critical thinking, and essay formats. Computerized testing software with an online testing feature is also available.

- **Videos.** The video program has been revised for the fifteenth edition and contains footage of companies, topics videos, and unique training materials for international negotiations. Teaching notes and questions relevant to each chapter in the text are available in the Instructor's Manual and at the Web site.

- **PowerPoint slides.** This edition has PowerPoint slides for both the instructor and students. The PowerPoint presentation that accompanies *International Marketing*, fifteenth edition, contains exhibits from the text and other sources.

- **Web site:** www.mhhe.com/cateora15e. Included on the site are instructor resources such as downloadable files for the complete Instructor's Manual, PowerPoint slides, test bank, and links to current events and additional resources for the classroom. Instructors can also link to PageOut to create their own course Web site. For students, our site provides links to Web sites, Cases, an interactive version of the Country Notebook, online quizzing, and chapter PowerPoint Slides.

Acknowledgments

The success of a text depends on the contributions of many people, especially those who take the time to share their thoughtful criticisms and suggestions to improve the text.

We would especially like to thank the following reviewers who gave us valuable insights into this revision:

Gregory J. Benzmiller
College of Management School for Professional Studies, Regis University

Larry Carter
Idaho State University

Anindya Chatterjee
Slippery Rock University of Pennsylvania

Dr. Dharma deSilva
CIBA, Barton School of Business, Wichita State University

David E. Foster
Montana State University

Debbie Gaspard
Southeast Community College

Jamey Halleck
Marshall University

Maxwell K. Hsu
University of Wisconsin-Whitewater

James W. Marco
Wake Technical Community College

James M. Maskulka
Lehigh University

Zahir A. Quraeshi
Western Michigan University

William Renforth
Angelo State University

Camille Schuster
California State University San Marcos

Nancy Thannert
Robert Morris University

Bronis Verhage
Georgia State University

Srdan Zdravkovic
Bryant University

We appreciate the help of all the many students and professors who have shared their opinions of past editions, and we welcome their comments and suggestions on this and future editions of *International Marketing*.

A very special thanks to Paul Ducham, John Weimeister, Sara Hunter, Heather Darr, Katie Mergen, Bruce Gin, and JoAnne Schopler from McGraw-Hill/Irwin, whose enthusiasm, creativity, constructive criticisms, and commitment to excellence have made this edition possible.

Philip R. Cateora
Mary C. Gilly
John L. Graham

WALKTHROUGH

A quick look at the new edition

International Marketing by Cateora, Gilly, and Graham has always been a pioneer in the field of international marketing. The authors continue to set the standard in this edition with new and expanded topics that reflect the swift changes of an expanding competitive global market, as well as increased coverage of technology's impact on the international market arena.

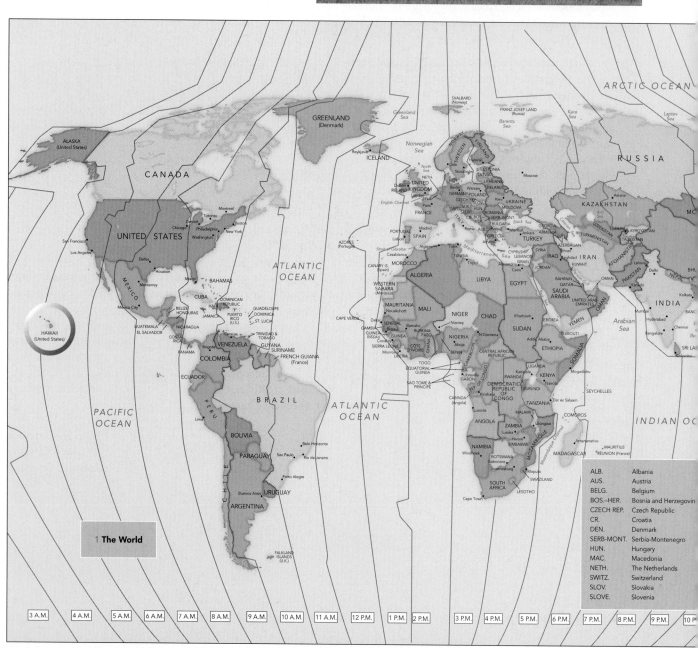

1 The World

ALB.	Albania
AUS.	Austria
BELG.	Belgium
BOS.–HER.	Bosnia and Herzegovina
CZECH REP.	Czech Republic
CR.	Croatia
DEN.	Denmark
SERB-MONT.	Serbia-Montenegro
HUN.	Hungary
MAC.	Macedonia
NETH.	The Netherlands
SWITZ.	Switzerland
SLOV.	Slovakia
SLOVE.	Slovenia

3 A.M. 4 A.M. 5 A.M. 6 A.M. 7 A.M. 8 A.M. 9 A.M. 10 A.M. 11 A.M. 12 P.M. 1 P.M. 2 P.M. 3 P.M. 4 P.M. 5 P.M. 6 P.M. 7 P.M. 8 P.M. 9 P.M. 10 P.

Global Marketing on the Web at Marriott

The Internet today is the most global of any media invented so far, having leapfrogged television and radio—which may yet become global some day but are far from doing so. It is the only medium that approaches true global reach. The power of the Internet results from its many unique attributes. It is unique in its ability to:

- Encompass text, audio and video in one platform.
- Operate in a dialogue versus monologue mode.
- Operate simultaneously as mass media and personalized media.
- Build global "communities," unconfined by national borders.

These attributes make it the most powerful medium on earth, unparalleled in its ability to communicate, especially to a global world. It is an international marketer's dream.

However, leveraging these characteristics in an effective manner requires dealing with various substantive issues. These issues include:

- Major differences in Internet adoption rates across the globe ranging from greater than 70 percent adoption in North America to less than 2 percent for the continent of Africa. This difference greatly influences the role of the Web as part of the marketing mix in international markets. Even for advanced EU economies, the variability of adoption is great, ranging from 88 percent in the Netherlands to 49 percent in Belgium. The average for the entire continent of Africa is around 1 percent (see www.internetworldstats.com).

- Unique issues caused by technology including broadband versus narrow-band, which drive what products and services can be marketed and how. In the narrow-band world, highly graphic and video-based Web sites are not viable. An example is the elaborate photo tours of hotels on www.Marriott.com, which download quickly on broadband connections but take inordinately long on narrow band. Therefore, a site designed for one market can be ineffective in another.

Renaissance is a Marriott-owned hotel brand. It uses various media to lead customers to its all-important Web sites, including print, television, Internet, and outdoor. Three 2-page print ads are directed toward U.K., Middle Eastern, and Chinese customers, and each of them lists the Web site addresses—the first two citing www.renaissancehotels.co.uk, and the last noting www.renaissancehotels.com.cn. Even though the same Web site ultimately serves customers in both the United Kingdom and the Middle East, the ad presentation is adapted to the more conservative dress appropriate in the latter region. Finally, you can see how the campaign is also used on the streets of Shanghai. Ask your classmates what "Be fashionable" translates into on the latter two ads.

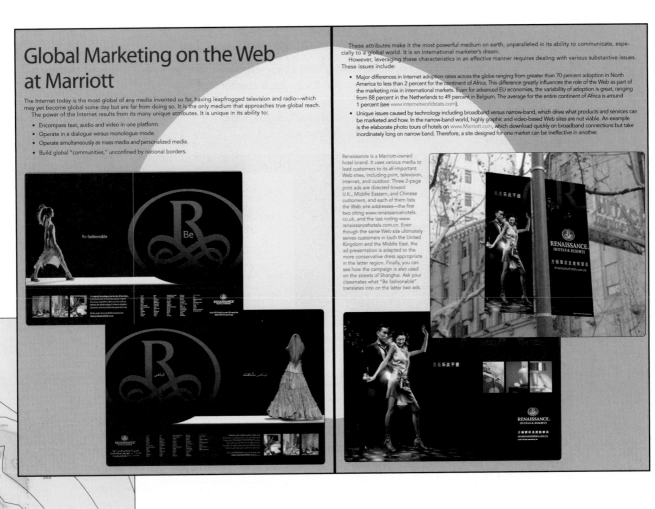

4-Color Design

New color maps and exhibits allow for improved pedagogy and a clearer presentation of international symbols and cultural meanings in marketing and advertising. In addition, photos that depend on full color for maximum impact easily bring many global examples to life. This visually stimulating combination works together to make the text material reader-friendly and accessible for both instructors and students.

Chapter Openers

A Chapter Outline provides students an at-a-glance overview of chapter topics, while Chapter Learning Objectives summarize the chapter's goals and focus. Each chapter is introduced with a Global Perspective, a real-life example of company experiences that illustrates significant issues discussed in the chapter. Companies featured in the Global Perspective vignettes range from exporters to global enterprises.

PART ONE

Chapter 1

The Scope and Challenge of International Marketing

CHAPTER OUTLINE

Global Perspective: Global Commerce Causes Peace

The Internationalization of U.S. Business

International Marketing Defined

The International Marketing Task

- Marketing Decision Factors
- Aspects of the Domestic Environment
- Aspects of the Foreign Environment

Environmental Adaptation Needed

The Self-Reference Criterion and Ethnocentrism: Major Obstacles

Developing a Global Awareness

Stages of International Marketing Involvement

- No Direct Foreign Marketing
- Infrequent Foreign Marketing
- Regular Foreign Marketing
- International Marketing
- Global Marketing

The Orientation of International Marketing

CHAPTER LEARNING OBJECTIVES

What you should learn from Chapter 1:

LO1 The benefits of international markets

LO2 The changing face of U.S. business

LO3 The scope of the international marketing task

LO4 The importance of the self-reference criterion (SRC) in international marketing

LO5 The increasing importance of global awareness

LO6 The progression of becoming a global marketer

Global Perspective

GLOBAL COMMERCE CAUSES PEACE

Global commerce thrives during peacetime. The economic boom in North America during the late 1990s was in large part due to the end of the Cold War and the opening of the formerly communist countries to the world trading system. However, we should also understand the important role that trade and international marketing play in producing peace.

Boeing Company, America's largest exporter, is perhaps the most prominent example. Although many would argue that Boeing's military sales (aircraft and missiles) do not exactly promote peace, over most of the company's history, that business has constituted only about 20 percent of the company's commercial activity. Up until 2002, of Boeing's some $60 billion in annual revenues, about 65 percent came from sales of commercial jets around the world and another 15 percent from space and communications technologies. Unfortunately, these historical numbers are being skewed by U.S. military spending and the damage done to tourism by terrorism.[1] Even so, the company still counts customers in more than 90 countries, and its 158,000 employees work in 70 countries. The new 787 Dreamliner includes parts from around the world, including Australia, France, India, Italy, Japan, Russia, and Sweden.[2] Its more than 12,000 commercial jets in service worldwide carry about one billion travelers per year. Its NASA Services division is the lead contractor in the construction and operation of the 16-country International Space Station, first manned by an American and two Russians in the fall of 2000. The Space and Intelligence Systems Division also produces and launches communications satellites affecting people in every country.

All the activity associated with the development, production, and marketing of commercial aircraft and space vehicles requires millions of people from around the world to work together. Moreover, no company does more[3] to enable people from all countries to meet face-to-face for both recreation and commerce. All this interaction yields not just the mutual gain associated with business relationships but also personal relationships and mutual understanding. The latter are the foundation of global peace and prosperity.

Another class of companies that promotes global dialogue and therefore peace is the mobile phone industry. During 2007 the number of mobile phone subscribers exceeded 3.0 billion, and this number is expected to grow beyond 4.5 billion by 2012. Nokia (Finland), the market leader, is well ahead of the American manufacturers Motorola and Apple, Samsung (S. Korea), LG (S. Korea), and Sony Ericsson (Japan/Sweden).

Individuals and small companies also make a difference—perhaps a subtler one than large multinational companies, but one just as important in the aggregate. Our favorite example is Daniel Lubetzky's company, PeaceWorks. Mr. Lubetzky used a fellowship at Stanford Law School to study how to foster joint ventures between Arabs and Israelis. Then, following his own advice, he created a company that combined basil pesto from Israel with other raw materials and glass jars supplied by an Arab partner to produce the first product in a line he called Moshe & Ali's Gourmet Foods. The company now sells four different product lines in 5,000 stores in the United States and has its headquarters on Park Avenue in New York, as well as business operations in Israel, Egypt, Indonesia, Turkey, and Sri Lanka. Again, beyond the measurable commercial benefits of cooperation between the involved Arabs, Israelis, and others is the longer-lasting and more fundamental appreciation for one another's circumstances and character.

International marketing is hard work. Making sales calls is no vacation, even in Paris, especially when you've been there 10 times before. But international marketing is important work. It can enrich you, your family, your company, and

[1] Circa 2011, approximately half of Boeing's business is defense related (http://www.boeing.com).

[2] W.J. Hennigan, "Dreamliner is Causing Nightmares for Boeing," *Los Angeles Times*, October, 15, 2009, pp. B1–2.

[3] The European commercial aircraft manufacturer Airbus is beginning to catch up, employing 57,000 people around the world (http://www.airbus.com, 2008).

PART TWO

Chapter 6

The Political Environment:

A CRITICAL CONCERN

CHAPTER OUTLINE

Global Perspective: World Trade Goes Bananas

The Sovereignty of Nations

Stability of Government Policies

- Forms of Government
- Political Parties
- Nationalism
- Targeted Fear and/or Animosity
- Trade Disputes

Political Risks of Global Business

- Confiscation, Expropriation, and Domestication
- Economic Risks
- Political Sanctions
- Political and Social Activists and Nongovernmental Organizations
- Violence, Terrorism, and War
- Cyberterrorism and Cybercrime

Assessing Political Vulnerability

- Politically Sensitive Products and Issues
- Forecasting Political Risk

Lessening Political Vulnerability

- Joint Ventures
- Expanding the Investment Base
- Licensing
- Planned Domestication
- Political Bargaining
- Political Payoffs

Government Encouragement

CHAPTER LEARNING OBJECTIVES

What you should learn from Chapter 6:

LO1 What the sovereignty of nations means and how it can affect the stability of government policies

LO2 How different governmental types, political parties, nationalism, targeted fear/animosity, and trade disputes can affect the environment for marketing in foreign countries

LO3 The political risks of global business and the factors that affect stability

LO4 The importance of the political system to international marketing and its effect on foreign investments

LO5 The impact of political and social activists, violence, and terrorism on international business

LO6 How to assess and reduce the effect of political vulnerabililty

LO7 How and why governments encourage foreign investment

Global Perspective

WORLD TRADE GOES BANANAS

Rather than bruising Chiquita Bananas, the wrath of politics instead hammered Prosciutto di Parma ham from Italy, handbags from France, and bath oils and soaps from Germany. These and a host of other imported products from Europe were all slapped with a 100 percent import tariff as retaliation by the U.S. government against European Union banana-import rules that favored Caribbean bananas over Latin American bananas. Keep in mind that no bananas are exported from the United States, yet the United States has been engaged in a trade war over the past seven years that has cost numerous small businesses on both sides of the Atlantic millions of dollars. But how can this be, you ask? Politics, that's how!

One small business, Reha Enterprises, for example, sells bath oil, soaps, and other supplies imported from Germany. The tariff on its most popular product, an herbal foam bath, was raised from 5 percent to 100 percent. The customs bill for six months spiraled to $37,783 from just $1,851—a 1,941 percent tax increase. For a small business whose gross sales are less than $1 million annually, it was crippling. When Reha heard of the impending "banana war," he called everyone—his congressperson, his senator, the United States Trade Representative (USTR). When he described his plight to the USTR, an official there expressed amazement. "They were surprised I was still importing," because they thought the tariff would cut off the industry entirely. That was their intention, which of course would have meant killing Reha Enterprises as well.

In effect, he was told it was his fault that he got caught up in the trade war. He should have attended the hearings in Washington, just like Gillette and Mattel, and maybe his products would have been dropped from the targeted list, just as theirs were. Scores of European products, from clothing to stoves to glass Christmas ornaments, dolls, and ballpoint pens, that were originally targeted for the retaliatory tariffs escaped the tariff. Aggressive lobbying by large corporations, trade groups, and members of Congress got most of the threatened imported products off the list. The USTR had published a list of the targeted imports in the Federal Register, inviting affected companies to testify. Unfortunately, the Federal Register was not on Reha's reading list.

In that case, he was told, he should have hired a lobbyist in Washington to keep him briefed. Good advice—but it doesn't make much sense to a company that grosses less than $1 million a year. Other advice received from an official of the USTR included the off-the-record suggestion that he might want to change the customs number on the invoice so it would appear that he was importing goods not subject to the tariff, a decision that could, if he were caught, result in a hefty fine or jail. Smaller businesses in Europe faced similar problems as their export business dried up because of the tariffs.

How did this banana war start? The European Union imposed a quota and tariffs that favored imports from former colonies in the Caribbean and Africa, distributed by European firms, over Latin American bananas distributed by U.S. firms. Chiquita Brands International and Dole Food Company, contending that the EU's "illegal trade barriers" were costing $520 million annually in lost sales to Europe, asked the U.S. government for help. The government agreed that unfair trade barriers were damaging their business, and 100 percent tariffs on selected European imports were levied. Coincidentally, Chiquita Brands' annual political campaign contributions increased from barely over $40,000 in 1991 to $1.3 million in 1998.

A settlement was finally reached that involved high tariffs on Latin America bananas and quotas (with no tariffs) on bananas from Europe's former colonies. But the bruising over bananas continued, and not in a straightforward way! In 2007 the issue shifted to banana bending. That is, bananas from Latin America tend to be long and straight, while those from the non-tariff countries are short and bent. Because the latter are not preferred by the shippers or retailers (the bendier ones don't stack as neatly and economically), the bananas from the former colonies were still not preferred. And new regulations were adopted by the European Commission that mandated that bananas must be free from "abnormal curvature of the fingers." So the bendy banana producers threatened to renege on the whole agreement. Circa 2007 everyone involved found this prospect very unappealing.

The tale does have a happy ending though. In 2009, after marathon meetings among all parties in Geneva, the 16-year banana split was finally healed: The EU cut import tariffs on bananas grown in Latin America by U.S. firms.

Sources: "U.S. Sets Import Tariffs in Latest Salvo in Ongoing Battle over Banana Trade," *Minneapolis Star Tribune*, March 4, 1999; Timothy Dove, "Hit by a $200,000 Bill from the Blue," *Time*, February 7, 2000, p. 54; Jeremy Smith, "EU Heading for Trade Crunch over Bananas," *Reuters*, November 14, 2007.

Crossing Borders Boxes

These invaluable boxes offer anecdotal company examples. These entertaining examples are designed to encourage critical thinking and guide students through topics ranging from ethical to cultural to global issues facing marketers today.

CROSSING BORDERS 13.3

Seeds of Fashion: Eastern vs. Western Counter-Culture Movements and A Look at the Gothic Lolitas of Harajuku, Japan

Where do new ideas come from? Since its origin, the Gothic Lolita subculture of Harajuku has continued to fascinate people around the world. This group is just one example of the counterculture fashion movements that have emerged from the Harajuku district of Japan, each group identified by a specific look that conveys a visual message. Gothic Lolita fashion infuses Victorian-era clothing with elements of Goth and Japanese anime to create a unique form of dress. Adherents take notes from the *Gothic & Lolita Bible* (a quarterly magazine with an estimated circulation of 100,000) and rely on their distinctive appearance to proclaim their subcultural identity. As in other counterculture movements, youth's fantasies of liberation, rebellion, and revolution have become embedded in the cultural mode of a changing nation.

By examining the fashion of the Harajuku, we can gain a more in-depth understanding of group affiliation and construction of self in counterculture movements. Definitive of a counterculture, the Gothic Lolita's in-group behavior and fashion evokes opposition and displays a symbolic rebellion against mainstream Japanese culture. These attitudes are reflected in norm-breaking and attention-grabbing styles.

In the past, youth subcultures generally have emerged from Western society and diffused globally. But the Harajuku subculture began in the East and is moving West, marking a shift in the cultural current. The Harajuku subculture is also an example of the difference between Eastern and Western counterculture movements. Whereas maturity in Western cultures is associated with authority and individuality, in Confucian Japan, maturity is the ability to cooperate with a group, accept compromises, and fulfill obligations to society. Therefore, rebellion in Japanese youth culture means rebellion against adulthood as well. Rather than engaging in sexually provocative or aggressive behaviors to emphasize their maturity and independence, as occurs among Western rebels, Japanese Gothic Lolitas display

themselves in a childlike and vulnerable manner to emphasize their immaturity and inability to meet the social responsibilities and obligations of adulthood.

Japanese women in an ad for Angelic Pretty fashions appearing in the Gothic & Lolita Bible

Likely because of this refusal to cooperate with social expectations, mainstream Japan views the subculture as selfish, especially considering its indulgent consumption behaviors. Unlike contemporary Western youth cultures, such as punk and grunge, the Gothic Lolita subculture does not condemn materialism or other aspects of modern consumer culture. Instead, one outfit (as seen in accompanying photo) can cost as much as $300–$1000! Because personal consumption is regarded as both antisocial and immoral in Japanese society, the subculture opposes normative social values by indulging in conspicuous consumption.

Most participants (aged 13–30 years) are students or have jobs that require them to wear a uniform everyday. On Sundays, they feel they have reached the time they can truly be themselves. Their lifestyle is frowned upon, making it very common to see teenagers carrying bags with their "harajuku outfit" on the train and changing at the park so their parents never see their outfits. Other wear the clothing as their normal daily dress, but the vast majority save it for Sundays, when they congregate at Jingu Bridge and Yoyogi Park to show off their fashions, hang out, and meet others like them. Some go just to have their pictures taken by the subculture' magazine photographers, who search for shots of new trends, or by tourists.

Source: Kristen San Jose, working paper, Paul Merage School of Business, University of California, Irvine, 2010.

When analyzing a product for a second market, the extent of adaptation required depends on cultural differences in product use and perception between the market the product was originally developed for and the new market. The greater these cultural differences between the two markets, the greater the extent of adaptation that may be necessary.

When instant cake mixes were introduced in Japan, the consumers' response was less than enthusiastic. Not only do Japanese reserve cakes for special occasions, but they prefer the cakes to be beautifully wrapped and purchased in pastry shops. The acceptance of instant cakes was further complicated by another cultural difference: many Japanese homes do not have ovens. An interesting sidebar to this example is the company's attempt to correct for that problem by developing a cake mix that could be cooked in a rice cooker, which all Japanese homes have. The problem with that idea was that in a Japanese kitchen,

---

PART SIX

cases 3 ASSESSING GLOBAL MARKET OPPORTUNITIES

OUTLINE OF CASES

NEW Cases

New cases accompany the fifteenth edition, enlivening the material in the book and class discussions while broadening a student's critical thinking skills. These cases bring forth many of the topics discussed in the chapters and demonstrate how these concepts are dealt with in the real world.

CASE 3-5 A Sea Launch Recovery?

CIRCA 2008

Sea Launch engineers say the three-week round-trip journey across the Pacific Ocean is the most rewarding part of their jobs. The cruise is the culmination of nearly two months of work preparing the rocket, payload, and launch teams for the mission. Prior to operations at Home Port, about 18 months goes into the planning, flight design, and logistics. "It's really nice to know most of the reviews are over and we're finally ready to launch," said Bill Rajeevan, mission director for the company's next flight.

More than 300 people take the trip to the company's equatorial launch site about 1,400 miles south of Hawaii. The crew includes workers from several nations, including Ukraine, Russia, Norway, the Philippines, and the United States. Ukraine-based Yuzhnoye and Yuzhmash build the Zenit 3SL rocket's first and second stages, while Energia of Russia manufactures the Block DM-SL upper stage for the rocket. Norwegian ship officers manage marine operations, and Filipino deckhands work on both the Sea Launch Commander and the Odyssey launch platform. U.S. employees from the Boeing Co. fill management roles and provide the flight design, payload fairing, and satellite adapter. Astrotech, a contractor, oversees processing of customer payloads inside a clean room at the company's Payload Processing Facility at Home Port in Long Beach, California.

After 27 missions in nine years of business, Sea Launch is thriving in the do-or-die commercial launch industry. The company's Zenit 3SL rocket has suffered three setbacks in that time. Two were total failures. The rocket's success rate places it among the top tier of heavy-lift launchers on the commercial market, and the company's launch backlog seems to confirm that. Sea Launch

is already booking payloads for launch in the future. Next year is sold out, according to company officials.

Sea Launch Home Port is a decommissioned U.S. Navy facility on the tip of a manmade peninsula at the Port of Long Beach. The Sea Launch buildings are all left over from the Navy except for the Payload Processing Facility, which the company built in the late 1990s. The company's port is home to two one-of-a-kind vessels—the Sea Launch Commander and the Odyssey launch platform. The Sea Launch Commander carries about 240 people, ranging from rocket technicians and corporate leaders to chefs and helicopter pilots. The Commander houses a state-of-the-art launch control center divided between two sections designed for Ukrainian and Russian engineers and American engineers and managers. The cavernous rocket assembly and checkout hall is located on the command ship's lower deck and stretches nearly the entire length of the vessel. The facility is capable of supporting two simultaneous launch campaigns using staging and integration compartments and a fueling cell. Giant cranes inside the high bays lift rocket stages, which sits on Russian-gauge rails on the floor integration room floor. The rocket's ground support equipment inside the Sea Launch Commander is virtually identical to hardware used for Zenit launches at the Baikonur Cosmodrome in Kazakhstan, according to Sea Launch officials.

The Sea Launch Commander was specially constructed for Sea Launch at a Scotland shipyard by the maritime unit of Kvaerner, then a leading Norwegian industrial company. Measuring 656 feet long and 105 feet wide, the command ship was outfitted with more than 600 tons of rocket support equipment in Russia before sailing to Long Beach in 1998. The massive ship's crew quarters are home to Sea Launch's international employees during their stay in the United States.

The Sea Launch Commander and the Odyssey platform are seen here docked at Home Port.

Credit: Chris Miller/SpaceflightNow

A Wealth of Supplements

Global Perspectives

At the beginning of each chapter, Global Perspectives give examples of current company experiences in global marketing. Illustrating chapter concepts, these profiles help students to combine the theory they read about with real-life application.

Online Learning Center

Numerous resources available for both instructors and students are online at www.mhhe.com/cateora15e. Instructor resources include downloadable versions of the Instructor's Manual, PowerPoint presentation, and Instructor Notes to accompany the videos. Student study tools include Chapter Quizzes, PowerPoint International Resource Links, Cases, and the Country Notebook Online with an interactive component so students can complete this popular marketing plan project online.

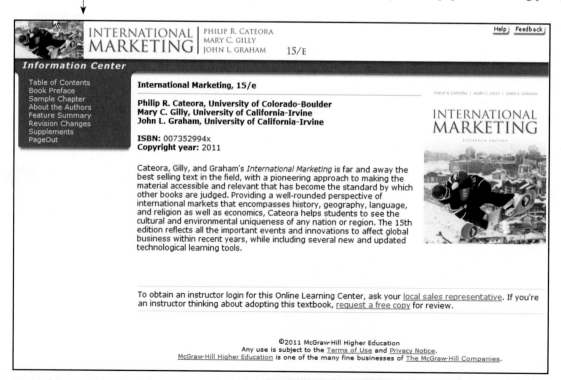

McGraw-Hill *Connect Marketing*

**Less Managing.
More Teaching.
Greater Learning.**

 McGraw-Hill *Connect Marketing* is an online assignment and assessment solution that connects students with the tools and resources they'll need to achieve success.

McGraw-Hill *Connect Marketing* helps prepare students for their future by enabling faster learning, more efficient studying, and higher retention of knowledge.

McGraw-Hill *Connect Marketing* features

Connect Marketing offers a number of powerful tools and features to make managing assignments easier, so faculty can spend more time teaching. With *Connect Marketing*, students can engage with their coursework anytime and anywhere, making the learning process more accessible and efficient. *Connect Marketing* offers you the features described below.

Simple assignment management With *Connect Marketing,* creating assignments is easier than ever, so you can spend more time teaching and less time managing. The assignment management function enables you to:

- Create and deliver assignments easily with selectable end-of-chapter questions and test bank items.
- Streamline lesson planning, student progress reporting, and assignment grading to make classroom management more efficient than ever.
- Go paperless with the eBook and online submission and grading of student assignments.

Smart grading When it comes to studying, time is precious. *Connect Marketing* helps students learn more efficiently by providing feedback and practice material when they need it, where they need it. When it comes to teaching, your time also is precious. The grading function enables you to:

- Have assignments scored automatically, giving students immediate feedback on their work and side-by-side comparisons with correct answers.
- Access and review each response; manually change grades or leave comments for students to review.
- Reinforce classroom concepts with practice tests and instant quizzes.

Instructor library The *Connect Marketing* Instructor Library is your repository for additional resources to improve student engagement in and out of class. You can select and use any asset that enhances your lecture. The *Connect Marketing* Instructor Library includes:

- *eBook*
- *PowerPoint slides*
- *Video clips*
- *Test Bank files*
- *Quizzes*

Student study center The *Connect Marketing* Student Study Center is the place for students to access additional resources. The Student Study Center:

- Offers students quick access to lectures, practice materials, eBooks, and more.
- Provides instant practice material and study questions, easily accessible on the go.
- Gives students access to the Personalized Learning Plan described below.

Student progress tracking *Connect Marketing* keeps instructors informed about how each student, section, and class is performing, allowing for more productive use of lecture and office hours. The progress-tracking function enables you to:

- View scored work immediately and track individual or group performance with assignment and grade reports.

- Access an instant view of student or class performance relative to learning objectives.
- Collect data and generate reports required by many accreditation organizations, such as AACSB.

McGraw-Hill Connect Plus Marketing McGraw-Hill reinvents the textbook learning experience for the modern student with *Connect Plus Marketing*. A seamless integration of an eBook and *Connect Marketing, Connect Plus Marketing* provides all of the *Connect Marketing* features plus the following:

- An integrated eBook, allowing for anytime, anywhere access to the textbook.
- Dynamic links between the problems or questions you assign to your students and the location in the eBook where that problem or question is covered.
- A powerful search function to pinpoint and connect key concepts in a snap.

In short, *Connect Marketing* offers you and your students powerful tools and features that optimize your time and energies, enabling you to focus on course content, teaching, and student learning. *Connect Marketing* also offers a wealth of content resources for both instructors and students. This state-of-the-art, thoroughly tested system supports you in preparing students for the world that awaits.

For more information about Connect, go to www.mcgrawhillconnect.com, or contact your local McGraw-Hill sales representative.

Tegrity Campus: Lectures 24/7
Tegrity Campus is a service that makes class time available 24/7 by automatically capturing every lecture in a searchable format for students to review when they study and complete assignments. With a simple one-click start-and-stop process, you capture all computer screens and corresponding audio. Students can replay any part of any class with easy-to-use browser-based viewing on a PC or Mac.

Educators know that the more students can see, hear, and experience class resources, the better they learn. In fact, studies prove it. With Tegrity Campus, students quickly recall key moments by using Tegrity Campus's unique search feature. This search helps students efficiently find what they need, when they need it, across an entire semester of class recordings. Help turn all your students' study time into learning moments immediately supported by your lecture.

To learn more about Tegrity watch a 2-minute Flash demo at http://tegritycampus.mhhe.com.

Assurance of Learning Ready
Many educational institutions today are focused on the notion of *assurance of learning*, an important element of some accreditation standards. International Marketing is designed specifically to support your assurance of learning initiatives with a simple, yet powerful solution.

Each test bank question for International Marketing maps to a specific chapter learning outcome/objective listed in the text. You can use our test bank software, EZ Test and EZ Test Online, or in *Connect Marketing* to easily query for learning outcomes/objectives that directly relate to the learning objectives for your course. You can then use the reporting features of EZ Test to aggregate student results in similar fashion, making the collection and presentation of assurance of learning data simple and easy.

AACSB Statement
The McGraw-Hill Companies is a proud corporate member of AACSB International. Understanding the importance and value of AACSB accreditation, International Marketing, 15e recognizes the curricula guidelines detailed in the AACSB standards for business accreditation by connecting selected questions in the test bank to the six general knowledge and skill guidelines in the AACSB standards.

The statements contained in International Marketing, 15e are provided only as a guide for the users of this textbook. The AACSB leaves content coverage and assessment within the purview of individual schools, the mission of the school, and the faculty. While International Marketing, 15e and the teaching package make no claim of any specific AACSB qualification or evaluation, we have within International Marketing, 15e labeled selected questions according to the six general knowledge and skills areas.

McGraw-Hill Customer Care Contact Information

At McGraw-Hill, we understand that getting the most from new technology can be challenging. That's why our services don't stop after you purchase our products. You can e-mail our Product Specialists 24 hours a day to get product-training online. Or you can search our knowledge bank of Frequently Asked Questions on our support Web site. For Customer Support, call **800-331-5094**, e-mail hmsupport@mcgraw-hill.com, or visit www.mhhe.com/support. One of our Technical Support Analysts will be able to assist you in a timely fashion.

BRIEF CONTENTS

PART ONE

AN OVERVIEW

PART TWO

THE CULTURAL ENVIRONMENT OF GLOBAL MARKETS

PART THREE

ASSESSING GLOBAL MARKET OPPORTUNITIES

PART FOUR

DEVELOPING GLOBAL MARKETING STRATEGIES

PART FIVE

IMPLEMENTING GLOBAL MARKETING STRATEGIES

PART SIX

SUPPLEMENTARY MATERIAL

LIST OF CROSSING BORDERS BOXES

Global Perspective

GLOBAL COMMERCE CAUSES PEACE

Global commerce thrives during peacetime. The economic boom in North America during the late 1990s was in large part due to the end of the Cold War and the opening of the formerly communist countries to the world trading system. However, we should also understand the important role that trade and international marketing play in producing peace.

Boeing Company, America's largest exporter, is perhaps the most prominent example. Although many would argue that Boeing's military sales (aircraft and missiles) do not exactly promote peace, over most of the company's history, that business has constituted only about 20 percent of the company's commercial activity. Up until 2002, of Boeing's some $60 billion in annual revenues, about 65 percent came from sales of commercial jets around the world and another 15 percent from space and communications technologies. Unfortunately, these historical numbers are being skewed by U.S. military spending and the damage done to tourism by terrorism.[1] Even so, the company still counts customers in more than 90 countries, and its 158,000 employees work in 70 countries. The new 787 Dreamliner includes parts from around the world, including Australia, France, India, Italy, Japan, Russia, and Sweden.[2] Its more than 12,000 commercial jets in service worldwide carry about one billion travelers per year. Its NASA Services division is the lead contractor in the construction and operation of the 16-country International Space Station, first manned by an American and two Russians in the fall of 2000. The Space and Intelligence Systems Division also produces and launches communications satellites affecting people in every country.

All the activity associated with the development, production, and marketing of commercial aircraft and space vehicles requires millions of people from around the world to work together. Moreover, no company does more[3] to enable people from all countries to meet face-to-face for both recreation and commerce. All this interaction yields not just the mutual gain associated with business relationships but also personal relationships and mutual understanding. The latter are the foundation of global peace and prosperity.

Another class of companies that promotes global dialogue and therefore peace is the mobile phone industry. During 2007 the number of mobile phone subscribers exceeded 3.0 billion, and this number is expected to grow beyond 4.5 billion by 2012. Nokia (Finland), the market leader, is well ahead of the American manufacturers Motorola and Apple, Samsung (S. Korea), LG (S. Korea), and Sony Ericsson (Japan/Sweden).

Individuals and small companies also make a difference—perhaps a subtler one than large multinational companies, but one just as important in the aggregate. Our favorite example is Daniel Lubetzky's company, PeaceWorks. Mr. Lubetzky used a fellowship at Stanford Law School to study how to foster joint ventures between Arabs and Israelis. Then, following his own advice, he created a company that combined basil pesto from Israel with other raw materials and glass jars supplied by an Arab partner to produce the first product in a line he called Moshe & Ali's Gourmet Foods. The company now sells four different product lines in 5,000 stores in the United States and has its headquarters on Park Avenue in New York, as well as business operations in Israel, Egypt, Indonesia, Turkey, and Sri Lanka. Again, beyond the measurable commercial benefits of cooperation between the involved Arabs, Israelis, and others is the longer-lasting and more fundamental appreciation for one another's circumstances and character.

International marketing is hard work. Making sales calls is no vacation, even in Paris, especially when you've been there 10 times before. But international marketing is important work. It can enrich you, your family, your company, and

[1] Circa 2011, approximately half of Boeing's business is defense related (http://www.boeing.com).

[2] W.J. Hennigan, "Dreamliner is Causing Nightmares for Boeing," *Los Angeles Times*, October, 15, 2009, pp. B1–2.

[3] The European commercial aircraft manufacturer Airbus is beginning to catch up, employing 57,000 people around the world (http://www.airbus.com, 2010).

During the past 50 years, world trade (exports of merchandise and commercial services) has declined three times: in 1973 by −3.1 percent after the OPEC oil crisis, in 1982 by −.3 percent, and in 2009 by −12.0 percent following the financial debacle of 2008. World trade grew at its fastest rate, 12.5 percent, in 2000. Even after the terrorist attacks on September 11, 2001, trade continued to grow until the global financial crisis began in 2008. We thought the temporary circumstance of a partial solar eclipse over Manila Bay in January 2009 was aptly symbolic of the times—especially, of the huge decline in container traffic during 2009–2010.[4]

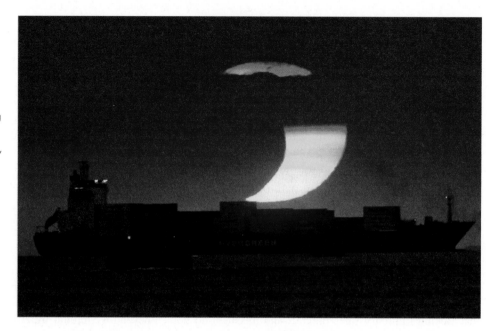

your country. And ultimately, when international marketing is done well, by large companies or small, the needs and wants of customers in other lands are well understood, and prosperity and peace are promoted along the way.[5]

Sources: http://www.boeing.com and http://www.peaceworks.com—both are worth a visit; mobile phone sales data are available at http://www.gartner.com (all accessed in 2010).

LO1

The benefits of international markets

Never before in American history have U.S. businesses, large and small, been so deeply involved in and affected by international business. A global economic boom, unprecedented in modern economic history, has been under way as the drive for efficiency, productivity, and open, unregulated markets sweeps the world. Powerful economic, technological, industrial, political, and demographic forces are converging to build the foundation of a new global economic order on which the structure of a one-world economic and market system will be built.

When we wrote those words ten years ago to open the eleventh edition of this book, the world was a very different place. The nation was still mesmerized by the information technology boom of the late 1990s. Most did not visualize the high-tech bust of 2001 or the Enron and WorldCom scandals. No one could have imagined the September 11, 2001, disasters, not even the perpetrators. The wars in Afghanistan and Iraq were not on the horizon. The major international conflict grabbing headlines then was the series of diplomatic dustups among China, Taiwan, and the United States. Who could have predicted the disruptions associated with the 2003 SARS outbreak in Asia? The great Indian Ocean tsunami of 2004 was perhaps impossible to anticipate. Oil priced at more than $100 per barrel was also unthinkable then—the price seemed to have peaked at about $40 per barrel in late 2000.[6] We wrote about the promise of the space program and the international

---

[4]Ronald D. White, "Shipping Industry in Deep Water," *Los Angeles Times*, July 8, 2009, pp. B1–2.

[5]In response to criticisms of globalization catalyzed by the riots in Seattle in 1999, a growing literature argues for trade as a fundamental cause of peace. For a variety of such arguments, see Jagdish Bhabwati, *In Defense of Globalization* (Oxford: Oxford University Press, 2004); Thomas L. Friedman, *The World Is Flat* (New York: Farrar, Straus, and Giroux, 2005); Clifford J. Schultz III, Timothy J. Burkink, Bruno Grbac, and Natasa Renko, "When Policies and Marketing Systems Explode: An Assessment of Food Marketing in the War-Ravaged Balkans and Implications for Recovery, Sustainable Peace, and Prosperity," *Journal of Public Policy & Marketing* 24, no. 1 (2005), pp. 24–37; William Hernandez Requejo and John L. Graham, *Global Negotiation: The New Rules* (New York: Palgrave Macmillan, 2008), Chapter 13.

[6]Niel King Jr., Chip Cummings, and Russell Gold, "Oil Hits $100, Jolting Markets," *The Wall Street Journal,* January 3, 2008, pp. A1, A6.

space station, whose future is now clouded by the demise of the space shuttle program and NASA budget cuts.

Through all these major events, American consumers had continued to spend, keeping the world economy afloat. Layoffs at industrial icons such as United Airlines and Boeing and a generally tough job market did not slow the booming American housing market until the fall of 2007. Lower government interest rates had yielded a refinancing stampede, distributing the cash that fueled the consumer spending, which finally began flagging in early 2008. Then in September and October of that year, the housing bubble burst, and the world financial system teetered on collapse. The ever faithful American consumer stopped buying, and world trade experienced its deepest decline in more than 50 years, a drop of 12.0 percent. And seeing into the future is harder now than ever. Most experts expect global terrorism to increase, and the carnage in Bali, Madrid, London, and Mumbai seem to prove the point. Finally, as the global economy tries to recover, international trade tensions take on new importance. Competition from new Chinese companies continues to raise concerns in the United States. Brazilian and Indian multinationals are stepping up competitive pressures as well, particularly as their and other emerging economies fared better during the most recent global downturn.[7] Perhaps the best news in these rather glum times is that we have not experienced a dramatic nationalistic rise of trade protectionism, as in the 1930s.[8] Additionally, the steady growth of the U.S. trade and balance of payments deficits dramatically abated during 2009, along with American consumer spending.

International marketing is affected by and affects all these things. For the first time in history, McDonald's has pulled out of international markets in both Latin America and the Middle East.[9] Slow economies, increasing competition, and anti-Americanism have

Trade also is easing tensions between Taiwan and China[10] and among North Korea,[11] its close neighbors, and the United States. Here a rail link between North and South Korea has opened for the first time in nearly 60 years to provide transportation of raw materials and managers from the South, bound for a special economic development zone at Kaesong in the North.[12]

[7]"Counting Their Blessings," *The Economist*, January 2, 2010, pp. 25–28.

[8]Moises Naim, "It Didn't Happen," *Foreign Policy*, January/February 2010, pp. 95–96.

[9]Richard Gibson, "McDonald's Swings to Loss on Sale of Restaurants," *The Wall Street Journal*, July 24, 2007.

[10]Patrick Smith, "Taiwan and China Dance Ever Closer," *BusinessWeek*, November 10, 2008, p. 58; "Reunification by Trade," *The Economist*, August 8, 2009, pp. 37–38.

[11]"North Korea Fully Opens Border Crossing," Associated Press, March 17, 2009.

[12]Bruce Wallace, "2 Trains Cross Korean Border," *Los Angeles Times*, May 17, 2007, p. A4; Moon Ihlwan, "A Capitalist Toehold in North Korea," *BusinessWeek*, June 11, 2007, p. 45; Associated Press, "North Korea Says It Gave Nuclear-Program List to U.S.," January 4, 2008.

impacted sales in both regions. Indeed, the salient lesson for those involved in international commerce is to expect the unexpected. Any executive experienced in international business will verify that things never go as planned in global commerce. You still have to plan and forecast, but markets, particularly international ones, are ultimately unpredictable. The natural fluctuations in markets are best managed through building strong interpersonal and commercial relationships and broad portfolios of businesses. Flexibility means survival.

Perhaps now, more than ever, whether or not a U.S. company wants to participate directly in international business, it cannot escape the effects of the ever-increasing number of North American firms exporting, importing, and manufacturing abroad. Nor can it ignore the number of foreign-based firms operating in U.S. markets, the growth of regional trade areas, the rapid growth of world markets, and the increasing number of competitors for global markets.

Nations grow a little closer together. The European Parliament votes to start discussions with Turkey about joining the European Union. Trade is beginning to bridge the religious divide between Christian Europe and Muslim Asia Minor. Despite this positive vote, European equivocation is pushing Turkey toward building stronger trade links with its Arab neighbors. Ultimately, this may be a positive turn of events if Turkey is finally invited to join the European Union.[13]

Of all the events and trends affecting global business today, four stand out as the most dynamic, the ones that will influence the shape of international business beyond today's "bumpy roads" and far into the future: (1) the rapid growth of the World Trade Organization and regional free trade areas such as the North American Free Trade Area and the European Union; (2) the trend toward the acceptance of the free market system among developing countries in Latin America, Asia, and eastern Europe; (3) the burgeoning impact of the Internet, mobile phones, and other global media on the dissolution of national borders; and (4) the mandate to manage the resources and global environment properly for the generations to come.

Today most business activities are global in scope. Technology, research, capital investment, and production, as well as marketing, distribution, and communications networks, all have global dimensions. Every business must be prepared to compete in an increasingly interdependent global economic and physical environment, and all businesspeople must be aware of the effects of these trends when managing either a domestic company that exports or a multinational conglomerate. As one international expert noted, every American company is international, at least to the extent that its business performance is conditioned in part by events that occur abroad. Even companies that do not operate in the international arena are affected to some degree by the success of the European Union, the export-led growth in South Korea, the revitalized Mexican economy, the economic changes taking place in China, military conflicts in the Middle East, and climate change.

The challenge of international marketing is to develop strategic plans that are competitive in these intensifying global markets. For a growing number of companies, being international is no longer a luxury but a necessity for economic survival. These and other issues affecting the world economy, trade, markets, and competition are discussed throughout this text.

---

[13]"Looking East and South," *The Economist*, October 31, 2009, pp. 57–58.

CROSSING BORDERS 1.1   What Do French Farmers, Chinese Fishermen, and Russian Hackers Have in Common?

They can all disrupt American firms' international marketing efforts.

Thousands of supporters and activists gathered recently to show support for a French sheep farmer on trial for vandalizing a local McDonald's. Jose Bove has become an international legend of antiglobalization. Leader of the French Peasant Confederation, he has demonized the fast-food chain as the symbol of American trade "hegemony" and economic globalization. He and nine other farmers served six weeks in jail and paid fines for partially destroying the restaurant. Most recently, Bove has been thrown in jail again, this time for 10 months, for damaging fields of genetically modified rice and corn.

Local fishermen demanded suspension of the reclamation and dredging of a bay near Hong Kong, where Disney has built Hong Kong Disneyland. The fishermen claimed that the work has plunged water quality near the site to levels much worse than predicted, killing huge numbers of fish. The spokesman for the fishermen claims they have lost some $30 million because of depleted and diseased fish stocks.

St. Petersburg has, in a decade, become the capital of Russian computer hackers. These are the same folks that are reputed to have invaded Microsoft's internal network. Russia's science city has become the natural hub for high-tech computer crime. Dozens of students, teachers, and computer specialists hack into computers, seeing themselves as members of an exciting subculture that has flourished since the fall of communism. Programs are copied on the black market; the latest Windows pirate always arrives in Russia months before it appears in the West. Yes, fines and prison terms are consequences if caught. But computers are readily accessible at universities and increasingly in homes.

Sources: Agnes Lam, "Disney Dredging Killing Fish," *South China Morning Post*, November 5, 2000, p. 4; John Tagliabue, "Activist Jailed in Attack on Modified Crops," *The New York Times*, February 27, 2003, p. 6; "Citi Expands Denial of Summer Breach," *American Banker*, December 28, 2009, p. 8; Ben Worthen, "Private Sector Keeps Mum on Cyber Attacks," *The Wall Street Journal*, January 19, 2010, p. B4.

The Internationalization of U.S. Business

LO2

The changing face of U.S. business

Current interest in international marketing can be explained by changing competitive structures, coupled with shifts in demand characteristics in markets throughout the world. With the increasing globalization of markets, companies find they are unavoidably enmeshed with foreign customers, competitors, and suppliers, even within their own borders. They face competition on all fronts—from domestic firms and from foreign firms. A huge portion of all consumer products—from CD players to dinnerware—sold in the United States is foreign made. Sony, Norelco, Samsung, Toyota, and Nescafé are familiar brands in the United States, and for U.S. industry, they are formidable opponents in a competitive struggle for U.S. and world markets.

Many familiar U.S. companies are now foreign controlled or headed in that direction. When you drop in at a 7-Eleven convenience store or buy Firestone tires, you are buying directly from Japanese companies. Some well-known brands no longer owned by U.S. companies are Carnation (Swiss), *The Wall Street Journal* (Australian), and the all-American Smith & Wesson handgun that won the U.S. West, which is owned by a British firm. The last U.S.-owned company to manufacture TV sets was Zenith, but even it was acquired by South Korea's LG Electronics, Inc., which manufactures Goldstar TVs and other products. Pearle Vision, Universal Studios, and many more are currently owned or controlled by foreign multinational businesses (see Exhibit 1.1). Foreign investment in the United States is more than $23.4 trillion.[14] Companies from the United Kingdom lead the group of investors, with companies from the Netherlands, Japan, Germany, and Switzerland following, in that order.

Other foreign companies that entered the U.S. market through exporting their products into the United States realized sufficient market share to justify building and buying manufacturing plants in the United States. Honda, BMW, and Mercedes are all manufacturing

---

[14]http://www.bea.gov (accessed June 2010).

Exhibit 1.1
Foreign Acquisitions of
U.S. Companies

Sources: Compiled from annual
reports of listed firms, 2010.

U.S. Companies/Brands	Foreign Owner
Firestone (tires)	Japan
Ben & Jerry's (ice cream)	U.K.
CITGO	Venezuela
Burger King (fast food)	U.K.
Random House (publishing)	Germany
The Wall Street Journal	Australia
Oroweat (breads)	Mexico
Smith & Wesson (guns)	U.K.
RCA (televisions)	France/China
Chef America ("Hot Pockets" and other foods)	Switzerland
Huffy Corp. (bicycles)	China
Swift & Company (meatpacking)	Brazil
Barneys New York (retailer)	Dubai
Columbia Pictures (movies)	Japan
T-Mobile	Germany
Budweiser	Belgium
Frigidaire	Sweden
Church's Chicken	Bahrain
Genentech	Switzerland

in the United States. Investments go the other way as well. Ford bought and sold Volvo; PacifiCorp acquired Energy Group, the United Kingdom's largest electricity supplier and second-largest gas distributor; and Wisconsin Central Transportation, a medium-sized U.S. railroad, controls all U.K. rail freight business and runs the Queen's private train via its English, Welsh & Scottish Railway unit. It has also acquired the company that runs rail shuttles through the Channel Tunnel. Investments by U.S. multinationals abroad are nothing new. Multinationals have been roaming the world en masse since the end of World War II, buying companies and investing in manufacturing plants. What is relatively new for U.S. companies is having their global competitors competing with them in "their" market, the United States. One of the more interesting new entrants is Chivas USA, a Mexican-owned soccer team that will play its matches in southern California.

Once the private domain of domestic businesses, the vast U.S. market that provided an opportunity for continued growth must now be shared with a variety of foreign companies

Along with NAFTA have come two of Mexico's most prominent brand names. Gigante, one of Mexico's largest supermarket chains, now has several stores in southern California, including this one in Anaheim. On store shelves are a variety of Bimbo bakery products. Grupo Bimbo, a growing Mexican multinational, has recently purchased American brand-named firms such as Oroweat, Webers, and Mrs. Baird's Bread.

CROSSING BORDERS 1.2   *Blanca Nieves, La Cenicienta, y Bimbo* (Snow White, Cinderella, and Bimbo)

Bimbo is a wonderful brand name. It so well demonstrates the difficulties of marketing across borders. In *Webster's Dictionary* "bimbo" is defined as ". . . a term of disparagement, an attractive, but empty-headed person, a tramp."

Meanwhile, in Spain, Mexico, and other Spanish-speaking countries, the word "bimbo" has no pejorative meaning. Indeed, it is often simply associated with the little white bear logo of Bimbo brand bread. Bimbo is the most popular brand of bread in Mexico and, with the North American Free Trade Agreement (NAFTA), is stretching its corporate arms north and south. For example, the Mexican firm most recently acquired Bestfoods American brands, Mrs. Baird's Bread, the most popular local brand in Dallas, Texas, and Fargo, the most popular bread brand in Argentina. And you can now see 18-wheelers pulling truckloads of Bimbo products north on Interstate 5 toward Latino neighborhoods in Southern California and beyond.

Perhaps Bimbo is the reason the city leaders in Anaheim so feared Gigante's entrance into their city. Gigante, the Mexican-owned supermarket chain, features Bimbo buns, tomatillos, cactus pears, and other Latino favorites. Gigante already had three stores in Los Angeles County. But it was denied the city's permission to open a new market near the "Happiest Place on Earth." One has to wonder if Disneyland, Anaheim's biggest employer, may have been fretting over the juxtaposition of the Bimbo brand and its key characters, blonde, little, all-American Alice and her cinema sisters. Actually, a better case can be made that the Gigante–Anaheim imbroglio was more a matter of a mix of nationalism, xenophobia, and even racism. The city council eventually was forced to allow Gigante to open.

American firms have often run into similar problems as they have expanded around the world. Consider French nationalism. French farmers are famous for their protests—throwing lamb chops at their trade ministers and such. Or better yet, Culture Minister Jack Lang's comments about the U.S. Cartoon Network: "We must fight back against this American aggression. It is intolerable that certain North American audiovisual groups shamelessly colonize our countries."

Consider our own fear and loathing of "Japanese colonization" in both the 1920s and the 1980s. This apparent xenophobia turned to racism when Americans stoned Toyotas and Hondas but not Volkswagens and BMWs or when we decried Japanese takeovers of American firms and ignored Germany's gorging on the likes of Bankers Trust, Random House, and Chrysler.

PEMEX's current ban on American investments in the oil and gas industry in Mexico is a good example of nationalism. However, when British Petroleum buying ARCO is no problem, but Mexican cement giant CEMEX buying Houston's Southdown is, that's racism at work.

A cruel irony regarding Gigante's problems in Anaheim is well revealed by a quick drive around Tijuana. During the last decade, the change in Tijuana's retail facade has been remarkable. In this border town, after NAFTA, McDonalds, Costco, Smart & Final, and other American brands now dominate the signage.

Sources: John L. Graham, "Blanca Nieves, La Cenicienta, y Bimbo," *La Opinion*, February 22, 2002, p. C1 (translated from the Spanish); Clifford Kraus, "New Accents in the U.S. Economy," *The New York Times*, May 2, 2007, pp. C1, C14; "Grupo Bimbo," *American Lawyer*, April 2009, pp. 38–40.

and products. Companies with only domestic markets have found increasing difficulty in sustaining their customary rates of growth, and many are seeking foreign markets in which to expand. Companies with foreign operations find that foreign earnings are making an important overall contribution to total corporate profits. A four-year Conference Board study of 1,250 U.S. manufacturing companies found that multinationals of all sizes and in all industries outperformed their strictly domestic U.S. counterparts. They grew twice as fast in sales and earned significantly higher returns on equity and assets. Furthermore, U.S. multinationals reduced their manufacturing employment, both at home and abroad, more than domestic companies. Another study indicates that despite the various difficulties associated with internationalization, on average, firm value is increased by global diversification.[15] Indeed, at least periodically, profit levels from international ventures exceed those from domestic operations for many multinational firms.[16]

---

[15]John A. Doukas and Ozgur B. Kan, "Does Global Diversification Destroy Firm Value?" *Journal of International Business Studies* 37 (2006), pp. 352–71.

[16]Justin Lahart, "Behind Stocks' Run at Record," *The Wall Street Journal*, April 25, 2007, pp. C1–2.

Exhibit 1.2
Selected U.S. Companies and Their International Sales

Source: Compiled from annual reports of listed firms, 2010.

Company	Global Revenues (billions)	Percent Revenues from Outside the U.S.
Walmart	$401.2	24.6%
Ford Motor	146.3	51.9
General Electric	182.5	53.7
CitiGroup	52.8	74.8
Hewlett-Packard	118.4	68.2
Boeing	60.9	38.9
Intel	37.6	85.4
Coca-Cola	31.9	77.0
Apple	36.5	46.0
Starbucks	10.4	20.8

Exhibit 1.2 illustrates how important revenues generated on investments abroad are to U.S. companies. In many cases, foreign sales were greater than U.S. sales, demonstrating the global reach of these American brands. Apple's performance has been most impressive, with total revenues exploding from just $6 billion in 2003 to $24 billion in 2007. Meanwhile, the company maintained its traditional level of more than 40 percent revenues from outside the United States.

Companies that never ventured abroad until recently are now seeking foreign markets. Companies with existing foreign operations realize they must be more competitive to succeed against foreign multinationals. They have found it necessary to spend more money and time improving their marketing positions abroad because competition for these growing markets is intensifying. For firms venturing into international marketing for the first time and for those already experienced, the requirement is generally the same: a thorough and complete commitment to foreign markets and, for many, new ways of operating.

International Marketing Defined

International marketing is the performance of business activities designed to plan, price, promote, and direct the flow of a company's goods and services to consumers or users in more than one nation for a profit. The only difference between the definitions of domestic marketing and international marketing is that in the latter case, marketing activities take place in more than one country. This apparently minor difference, "in more than one country," accounts for the complexity and diversity found in international marketing operations. Marketing concepts, processes, and principles are universally applicable, and the marketer's task is the same, whether doing business in Dimebox, Texas, or Dar es Salaam, Tanzania. Business's goal is to make a profit by promoting, pricing, and distributing products for which there is a market. If this is the case, what is the difference between domestic and international marketing?

A Citibank branch in the heart of Brazil on a rainy day in 2008. The address on the Avenida Paulista is 1776—how American! One of the world's great multinational corporations barely survived the financial debacle of October 2008. Perhaps its red, white, and blue umbrella logo protected it from "adverse weather" on Wall Street? Indeed, during the past two years, its international operations have performed much better than its domestic ones. In particular, emerging markets such as China, India, and Brazil proved relatively resilient during the global financial crisis that began in 2008.

The answer lies not with different concepts of marketing but with the environment within which marketing plans must be implemented. The uniqueness of foreign marketing comes from the range of unfamiliar problems and the variety of strategies necessary to cope with different levels of uncertainty encountered in foreign markets.

Competition, legal restraints, government controls, weather, fickle consumers, and any number of other uncontrollable elements can, and frequently do, affect the profitable outcome of good, sound marketing plans. Generally speaking, the marketer cannot control or influence these uncontrollable elements but instead must adjust or adapt to them in a manner consistent with a successful outcome. What makes marketing interesting is the challenge of molding the controllable elements of marketing decisions (product, price, promotion, distribution, and research) within the framework of the uncontrollable elements of the marketplace (competition, politics, laws, consumer behavior, level of technology, and so forth) in such a way that marketing objectives are achieved. Even though marketing principles and concepts are universally applicable, the environment within which the marketer must implement marketing plans can change dramatically from country to country or region to region. The difficulties created by different environments are the international marketer's primary concern.

The International Marketing Task

LO3

The scope of the international marketing task

The international marketer's task is more complicated than that of the domestic marketer because the international marketer must deal with at least two levels of uncontrollable uncertainty instead of one. Uncertainty is created by the uncontrollable elements of all business environments, but each foreign country in which a company operates adds its own unique set of uncontrollable factors.

Exhibit 1.3 illustrates the total environment of an international marketer. The inner circle depicts the controllable elements that constitute a marketer's decision area, the

Exhibit 1.3
The International Marketing Task

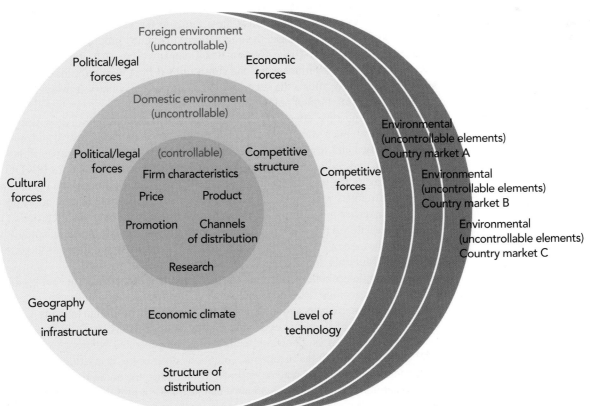

second circle encompasses those environmental elements at home that have some effect on foreign-operation decisions, and the outer circles represent the elements of the foreign environment for each foreign market within which the marketer operates. As the outer circles illustrate, each foreign market in which the company does business can (and usually does) present separate problems involving some or all of the uncontrollable elements. Thus, the more foreign markets in which a company operates, the greater is the possible variety of foreign environmental factors with which to contend. Frequently, a solution to a problem in country market A is not applicable to a problem in country market B.

Marketing Decision Factors

The successful manager constructs a marketing program designed for optimal adjustment to the uncertainty of the business climate. The inner circle in Exhibit 1.3 represents the area under the control of the marketing manager. Assuming the necessary overall corporate resources, structures, and competencies that can limit or promote strategic choice, the marketing manager blends price, product, promotion, channels-of-distribution, and research activities to capitalize on anticipated demand. The **controllable elements** can be altered in the long run and, usually, in the short run to adjust to changing market conditions, consumer tastes, or corporate objectives.

The outer circles surrounding the marketing decision factors represent the levels of uncertainty created by the domestic and foreign environments. Although the marketer can blend a marketing mix from the controllable elements, the **uncontrollable elements** are precisely that; the marketer must actively evaluate and, if needed, adapt. That effort—the adaptation of the marketing mix to these environmental factors—determines the outcome of the marketing enterprise.

Aspects of the Domestic Environment

The second circle in Exhibit 1.3 represents the aspects of the **domestic environment uncontrollables**. These include home-country elements that can have a direct effect on the success of a foreign venture: political and legal forces, economic climate, and competition.

A political decision involving domestic foreign policy can have a direct effect on a firm's international marketing success. For example, the U.S. government placed a total ban on trade with Libya to condemn Libyan support for terrorist attacks, imposed restrictions on trade with South Africa to protest apartheid, and placed a total ban on trade with Iraq, whose actions were believed to constitute a threat to the national security of the United States and its allies. In each case, the international marketing programs of U.S. companies, whether IBM, Exxon, or Hawg Heaven Bait Company, were restricted by these political decisions. The U.S. government has the constitutional right to restrict foreign trade when such trade adversely affects the security or economy of the country or when such trade is in conflict with U.S. foreign policy.

Conversely, positive effects occur when changes in foreign policy offer countries favored treatment. Such were the cases when South Africa abolished apartheid and the embargo was lifted and when the U.S. government decided to uncouple human rights issues from foreign trade policy and grant permanently normalized trade relations (PNTR) status to China, paving the way for its entry into the World Trade Organization (WTO). In both cases, opportunities were created for U.S. companies. Finally, note that on occasion, companies can exercise a controversially high degree of influence over such legislation in the United States. Recall that it is Congress's responsibility to regulate business, not vice versa. Indeed, in the case of PNTR for China, companies with substantial interests there, such as Boeing and Motorola, lobbied hard for the easing of trade restrictions.

The domestic economic climate is another important home-based uncontrollable variable with far-reaching effects on a company's competitive position in foreign markets. The capacity to invest in plants and facilities, either in domestic or foreign markets, is to a large extent a function of domestic economic vitality. It is generally true that capital tends to flow toward optimum use; however, capital must be generated before it can have mobility. Furthermore, if internal economic conditions deteriorate, restrictions against foreign investment and purchasing may be imposed to strengthen the domestic economy.

Competition within the home country can also have a profound effect on the international marketer's task. For more than a century, Eastman Kodak dominated the U.S. film market and could depend on achieving profit goals that provided capital to invest in foreign markets. Without having to worry about the company's lucrative base, management had the time and resources to devise aggressive international marketing programs. However, the competitive structure changed when Fuji Photo Film became a formidable competitor by lowering film prices in the United States, opening a $300 million plant, and soon gaining 12 percent of the U.S. market. Since then, the acceptance of digital photography, with Canon, from Japan, leading the market, has further disrupted Kodak's domestic business. As a result, Kodak has had to direct energy and resources back to the United States. Competition within its home country affects a company's domestic as well as international plans. Inextricably entwined with the effects of the domestic environment are the constraints imposed by the environment of each foreign country.

Aspects of the Foreign Environment

In addition to uncontrollable domestic elements, a significant source of uncertainty is foreign environment uncontrollables. (depicted in Exhibit 1.3 by the outer circles). A business operating in its home country undoubtedly feels comfortable in forecasting the business climate and adjusting business decisions to these elements. The process of evaluating the uncontrollable elements in an international marketing program, however, often involves substantial doses of cultural, political, and economic shock.

A business operating in a number of foreign countries might find polar extremes in political stability, class structure, and economic climate—critical elements in business decisions. The dynamic upheavals in some countries further illustrate the problems of dramatic change in cultural, political, and economic climates over relatively short periods of time. A case in point is China, which has moved from a communist legal system in which all business was done with the state to a transitional period while a commercial legal system develops. In this transitional phase, new laws are passed but left to be interpreted by local authorities, and confusion often prevails about which rules are still in force and which rules are no longer applicable.

For example, commercial contracts can be entered into with a Chinese company or individual only if that company or person is considered a "legal person." To be a legal person in China, the company or person must have registered as such with the Chinese government. To complicate matters further, binding negotiations may take place only with "legal representatives" of the "legal person." So if your company enters into negotiations with a Chinese company or person, you must ask for signed legal documents establishing the right to do business. The formalities of the signature must also be considered. Will a signature on a contract be binding, or is it necessary to place a traditional Chinese seal on the document? Even when all is done properly, the government still might change its mind. Coca-Cola had won approval for its plan to build a new facility to produce product for its increasing Chinese market share. But before construction began, the Chinese parliament objected that Coca-Cola appeared to be too successful in China, so negotiations continued delaying the project. Such are the uncertainties of the uncontrollable political and legal factors of international business.

The more significant elements in the uncontrollable international environment, shown in the outer circles of Exhibit 1.3, include political/legal forces, economic forces, competitive forces, level of technology,[17] structure of distribution, geography and infrastructure, and cultural forces.[18] These forces constitute the principal elements of uncertainty an international marketer must cope with in designing a marketing program. Although each will be discussed in depth in subsequent chapters, consider the level of technology and political/legal forces as illustrations of the uncontrollable nature of the foreign environment.

The level of technology is an uncontrollable element that can often be misread because of the vast differences that may exist between developed and developing countries.

---

[17]Shih-Fen S. Chen, "Extending Internationalization Theory: A New Perspective on International Technology Transfer and Its Generalization," *Journal of International Business Studies* 36 (2005), pp. 231–45.

[18]Laszlo Tihany, David A. Griffith, and Craig J. Russell, "The Effect of Cultural Distance on Entry Mode Choice, International Diversification, and MNE Performance: A Meta-Analysis," *Journal of International Business Studies* 36, no. 3 (2005), pp. 270–83.

CROSSING BORDERS 1.3

Mobile Phones, Economic Development, and Shrinking the Digital Divide

Wedged between stalls of dried fish and mounds of plastic goods, a red shipping container is loaded with Coca-Cola bottles. The local distributor for Soweto market, located in a tatty corner of Zambia's capital city, Lusaka, sells all its stock every few days. A full load costs 10m kwacha (about $2,000). In cash, this amount can be hard to get hold of, takes ages to count, and—being 10 times the average annual wage—is tempting to thieves. So Coca-Cola now tells its 300 Zambian distributors to pay for deliveries not in cash but by sending text messages from their mobile phones. The process takes about 30 seconds, and the driver issues a receipt. Far away computers record the movement of money and stock. Coca-Cola is not alone. Around the corner from the market, a small dry-cleaning firm lets customers pay for laundry using their phones. So do Zambian petrol stations and dozens of bigger shops and restaurants.

This is just one example of the many innovative ways in which mobile phones are being used in the poorest parts of the world. Anecdotal evidence of mobile phones' ability to boost economic activity is abundant: They enable fishermen or farmers to check prices at different markets before selling produce and make it easier for people to look for jobs and prevent wasted journeys. Mobile phones reduce transaction costs, broaden trade networks, and substitute for costly physical transport. They are of particular value when other means of communication (such as roads, post, or fixed-line phones) are poor or nonexistent.

This importance can be hard for people in affluent countries to understand, because the ways in which mobile phones are used in low-income countries are so different. In particular, phones are widely shared. One person in a village buys a mobile phone, perhaps using a microcredit loan. Others then rent it out by the minute; the small profit margin enables its owner to pay back the loan and make a living. When the phone rings, its owner carries it to the home of the person being called, who then takes the call. Other entrepreneurs set up as "text message interpreters," sending and receiving text messages (which are generally cheaper than voice calls) on behalf of their customers, who may be illiterate. So though the number of phones per 100 people is low by affluent-world standards, they still make a big difference.

Yet mobile phone technologies also can be controversial. Chinese authorities imposed a blackout on communications (Internet access, international phone service, and text messaging) in the northwest region of Xinjiang province in the wake of ethnic violence in the area in July 2009. The government there said it severed communications to ease tensions that it claims were inflamed by social networking sites and text messages.

Sources: *The Economist*, "Economics Focus, Calling across the Divide," March 12, 2005, p. 74; Bruce Meyerson, "Skype Takes Its Show on the Road," *BusinessWeek*, October 29, 2007, p. 38; Andrew Jacobs, "China Restores Text Messaging in Xinjiang," *The New York Times*, January 18, 2010, p. A9.

A marketer cannot assume that understanding of the concept of preventive maintenance for machinery is the same in other countries as in the United States. Technical expertise may not be available at a level necessary for product support, and the general population may not have an adequate level of technical knowledge to maintain equipment properly. In such situations, a marketer will have to take extra steps to make sure that the importance of routine maintenance is understood and carried out. Furthermore, if technical support is not readily available, local people will have to be specially trained, or the company will have to provide support.

Political and legal issues face a business, whether it operates at home or in a foreign country. However, the issues abroad are often amplified by the "alien status" of the company, which increases the difficulty of properly assessing and forecasting the dynamic international business climate. The alien status of a foreign business has two dimensions: It is alien in that foreigners control the business and in that the culture of the host country is alien to management. The alien status of a business means that, when viewed as an outsider, it can be seen as an exploiter and receive prejudiced or unfair treatment at the hands of politicians, legal authorities, or both. Political activists can rally support by advocating the expulsion of the "foreign exploiters," often with the open or tacit approval of authorities. The Indian government, for example, gave Coca-Cola the choice of either revealing its secret formula or leaving the country. The company chose to leave. When it was welcomed

Masai tribesmen in Tanzania with their cell phones. Competition is fierce among carriers in burgeoning markets like Tanzania. Both Celtel and Vodacom provide paint for local stores and houses. Here you see the bright Celtel yellow and red, which goes nicely with the colorful garb of local customers. Vodacom blue is at a disadvantage there. We imagine the ear lobe "carrying case" makes it easy to hear the ring but hard to dial!

back several years later, it faced harassment and constant interference in its operations from political activists, often inspired by competing soft drink companies.

Furthermore, in a domestic situation, political details and the ramifications of political and legal events are often more transparent than they are in some foreign countries. For instance, whereas in the United States, each party in a dispute has access to established legal procedures and due process, legal systems in many other countries are still evolving. In many foreign countries, corruption may prevail, foreigners may receive unfair treatment, or the laws may be so different from those in the home country that they are misinterpreted. The point is that a foreign company is foreign and thus always subject to the political whims of the local government to a greater degree than a domestic firm. Google's conflicts with the Chinese government regarding censorship and confidentiality are pertinent here.[19]

Political/legal forces and the level of technology are only two of the uncontrollable aspects of the foreign environment that are discussed in subsequent chapters. The uncertainty of different foreign business environments creates the need for a close study of the uncontrollable elements within each new country. Thus, a strategy successful in one country can be rendered ineffective in another by differences in political climate, stages of economic development, level of technology, or other cultural variations.

Environmental Adaptation Needed

To adjust and adapt a marketing program to foreign markets, marketers must be able to interpret effectively the influence and impact of each of the uncontrollable environmental elements on the marketing plan for each foreign market in which they hope to do business. In a broad sense, the uncontrollable elements constitute the culture; the difficulty facing the marketer in adjusting to the culture lies in recognizing its impact. In a domestic market, the reaction to much of the environment's (cultural) impact on the marketer's activities is automatic; the various cultural influences that fill our lives are simply a part of our socialization, and we react in a manner acceptable to our society without consciously thinking about it.

The task of cultural adjustment, however, is the most challenging and important one confronting international marketers; they must adjust their marketing efforts to cultures to which they are not attuned. In dealing with unfamiliar markets, marketers must be aware of the frames of reference they are using in making their decisions or evaluating the potential of a market, because judgments are derived from experience that is the result of

---

[19] Sharon LaFraniere, "China at Odds with Future in Internet Fight," *The New York Times*, January 17, 2010, p. 6.

acculturation in the home country. Once a frame of reference is established, it becomes an important factor in determining or modifying a marketer's reaction to situations—social and even nonsocial.

For example, time-conscious Americans are not culturally prepared to understand the culturally nuanced meaning of time to Latin Americans. Such a difference must be learned to avoid misunderstandings that can lead to marketing failures. Such a failure occurs every time sales are lost when a "long waiting period" in the outer office of a Latin American customer is misinterpreted by an American sales executive. Cross-cultural misunderstandings can also occur when a simple hand gesture has a number of different meanings in different parts of the world. When wanting to signify something is fine, many people in the United States raise a hand and make a circle with the thumb and forefinger. However, this same hand gesture means "zero" or "worthless" to the French, "money" to the Japanese, and a general sexual insult in Sardinia and Greece. A U.S. president sent an unintentional message to some Australian protesters when he held up his first two fingers with the back of his hand to the protesters. Meaning to give the "victory" sign, he was unaware that in Australia, the same hand gesture is equivalent to holding up the middle finger in the United States.

Cultural conditioning is like an iceberg—we are not aware of nine-tenths of it. In any study of the market systems of different peoples, their political and economic structures, religions, and other elements of culture, foreign marketers must constantly guard against measuring and assessing the markets against the fixed values and assumptions of their own cultures. They must take specific steps to make themselves aware of the home cultural reference in their analyses and decision making.[20]

The Self-Reference Criterion and Ethnocentrism: Major Obstacles

LO4

The importance of the self-reference criterion (SRC) in international marketing

The key to successful international marketing is adaptation to environmental differences from one market to another. Adaptation is a conscious effort on the part of the international marketer to anticipate the influences of both the foreign and domestic uncontrollable factors on a marketing mix and then to adjust the marketing mix to minimize the effects.

The primary obstacles to success in international marketing are a person's **self-reference criterion (SRC)** and an associated ethnocentrism. The SRC is an unconscious reference to one's own cultural values, experiences, and knowledge as a basis for decisions. Closely connected is ethnocentrism, that is, the notion that people in one's own company, culture, or country know best how to do things. Ethnocentrism was particularly a problem for American managers at the beginning of the 21st century because of America's dominance in the world economy during the late 1990s. Ethnocentrism is generally a problem when managers from affluent countries work with managers and markets in less affluent countries. Both the SRC and ethnocentrism impede the ability to assess a foreign market in its true light.

When confronted with a set of facts, we react spontaneously on the basis of knowledge assimilated over a lifetime—knowledge that is a product of the history of our culture. We seldom stop to think about a reaction; we simply react. Thus, when faced with a problem in another culture, our tendency is to react instinctively and refer to our SRC for a solution. Our reaction, however, is based on meanings, values, symbols, and behavior relevant to our own culture and usually different from those of the foreign culture. Such decisions are often not good ones.

To illustrate the impact of the SRC, consider misunderstandings that can occur about personal space between people of different cultures. In the United States, unrelated individuals keep a certain physical distance between themselves and others when talking or in groups. We do not consciously think about that distance; we just know what feels right without thinking. When someone is too close or too far away, we feel uncomfortable and either move farther away or get closer to correct the distance. In doing so, we are relying on our SRC. In some cultures, the acceptable distance between individuals is substantially

---

[20] Emily Maltby, "Expanding Abroad? Avoid Cultural Gaffes," *The Wall Street Journal*, January 19, 2010, p. B5.

less than that which is comfortable for Americans. When someone from another culture approaches an American too closely, the American, unaware of that culture's acceptable distance, unconsciously reacts by backing away to restore the proper distance (i.e., proper by American standards), and confusion results for both parties. Americans assume foreigners are pushy, while foreigners assume Americans are unfriendly and literally "standoffish." Both react according to the values of their own SRCs, making both victims of a cultural misunderstanding.

Your self-reference criterion can prevent you from being aware of cultural differences or from recognizing the importance of those differences. Thus, you might fail to recognize the need to take action, you might discount the cultural differences that exist among countries, or you might react to a situation in a way offensive to your hosts. A common mistake made by Americans is to refuse food or drink when offered. In the United States, a polite refusal is certainly acceptable, but in Asia or the Middle East, a host is offended if you refuse hospitality. Although you do not have to eat or drink much, you do have to accept the offering of hospitality. Understanding and dealing with the SRC are two of the more important facets of international marketing.

Ethnocentrism and the SRC can influence an evaluation of the appropriateness of a domestically designed marketing mix for a foreign market. If U.S. marketers are not aware, they might evaluate a marketing mix based on U.S. experiences (i.e., their SRC) without fully appreciating the cultural differences that require adaptation. Esso, the brand name of a gasoline, was a successful name in the United States and would seem harmless enough for foreign countries; however, in Japan, the name phonetically means "stalled car," an undesirable image for gasoline. Another example is the "Pet" in Pet Milk. The name has been used for decades, yet in France, the word *pet* means, among other things, "flatulence"— again, not the desired image for canned milk. Both of these examples were real mistakes made by major companies stemming from their reliance on their SRC in making a decision.

When marketers take the time to look beyond their own self-reference criteria, the results are more positive. A British manufacturer of chocolate biscuits (cookies, in American English), ignoring its SRC, knew that it must package its biscuits differently to accommodate the Japanese market. Thus, in Japan, McVitie's chocolate biscuits are wrapped individually, packed in presentation cardboard boxes, and priced about three times higher than in the United Kingdom—the cookies are used as gifts in Japan and thus must look and be perceived as special. Unilever, appreciating the uniqueness of its markets, repackaged and reformulated its detergent for Brazil. One reason was that the lack of washing machines among poorer Brazilians made a simpler soap formula necessary. Also, because many people wash their clothes in rivers, the powder was packaged in plastic rather than paper so it would not get soggy. Finally, because the Brazilian poor are price conscious and buy in small quantities, the soap was packaged in small, low-priced packages. Even McDonald's modifies its traditional Big Mac in India, where it is known as the Maharaja Mac. This burger features two mutton patties, because most Indians consider cows sacred and don't eat beef. In each of these examples, had the marketers' own self-reference criteria been the basis for decisions, none of the necessary changes would have been readily apparent based on their home-market experience.

The most effective way to control the influence of ethnocentrism and the SRC is to recognize their effects on our behavior. Although learning every culture in depth and being aware of every important difference is almost humanly impossible, an awareness of the need to be sensitive to differences and to ask questions when doing business in another culture can help you avoid many of the mistakes possible in international marketing. Asking the appropriate question helped the Vicks Company avoid making a mistake in Germany. It discovered that in German, "Vicks" sounds like the crudest slang equivalent of "intercourse," so it changed the name to "Wicks" before introducing the product.

Be aware, also, that not every activity within a marketing program is different from one country to another; indeed, there probably are more similarities than differences. For example, the McVitie's chocolate biscuits mentioned earlier are sold in the United States in the same package as in the United Kingdom. Such similarities, however, may lull the marketer into a false sense of apparent sameness. This apparent sameness, coupled with the self-reference criterion, is often the cause of international marketing problems. Undetected similarities do not cause problems; however, the one difference that goes undetected can create a marketing failure.

To avoid errors in business decisions, the knowledgeable marketer will conduct a cross-cultural analysis that isolates the SRC influences and maintain vigilance regarding ethnocentrism. The following steps are suggested as a framework for such an analysis.

1. Define the business problem or goal in home-country cultural traits, habits, or norms.
2. Define the business problem or goal in foreign-country cultural traits, habits, or norms through consultation with natives of the target country. Make no value judgments.
3. Isolate the SRC influence in the problem and examine it carefully to see how it complicates the problem.
4. Redefine the problem without the SRC influence and solve for the optimum business goal situation.

An American sales manager newly posted to Japan decided that his Japanese sales representatives did not need to come into the office every day for an early morning meeting before beginning calls to clients in Tokyo. After all, that was how things were done in the United States. However, the new policy, based on both the American's SRC and a modicum of ethnocentrism, produced a precipitous decline in sales performance. In his subsequent discussions with his Japanese staff, he determined that Japanese sales representatives are motivated mostly by peer pressure. Fortunately, he was able to recognize that his SRC and his American "business acumen" did not apply in this case in Tokyo. A return to the proven system of daily meetings brought sales performance back to previous levels.

The cross-cultural analysis approach requires an understanding of the culture of the foreign market as well as one's own culture. Surprisingly, understanding one's own culture may require additional study, because much of the cultural influence on market behavior remains at a subconscious level and is not clearly defined.

Developing a Global Awareness

LO5

The increasing importance of global awareness

Opportunities in global business abound for those who are prepared to confront myriad obstacles with optimism and a willingness to continue learning new ways. The successful businessperson in the 21st century will have global awareness and a frame of reference that goes beyond a region or even a country and encompasses the world.[21] To be globally aware is to have (1) tolerance of cultural differences and (2) knowledge of cultures, history, world market potential, and global economic, social, and political trends.

Tolerance for cultural differences is crucial in international marketing. Tolerance is understanding cultural differences and accepting and working with others whose behaviors may be different from yours. You do not have to accept as your own the cultural ways of another, but you must allow others to be different and equal. For example, the fact that punctuality is less important in some cultures does not make them less productive, only different. The tolerant person understands the differences that may exist between cultures and uses that knowledge to relate effectively.

A globally aware person is knowledgeable about cultures and history. Knowledge of cultures is important in understanding behavior in the marketplace or in the boardroom. Knowledge of history is important because the way people think and act is influenced by their history. Some Latin Americans' reluctance toward foreign investment or Chinese reluctance to open completely to outsiders can be understood better if you have a historical perspective.

Global awareness also involves knowledge of world market potentials and global economic, social, and political trends. Over the next few decades, enormous changes will take place in the market potentials in almost every region of the world, all of which a globally

---

[21] Gary A. Knight and Daekwan Kim, "International Business Competence and the Contemporary Firm," *Journal of International Business Studies* 40, no. 2 (2009), pp. 255–73.

aware person must continuously monitor. Finally, a globally aware person will keep abreast of global economic, social, and political trends, because a country's prospects can change as these trends shift direction or accelerate. The former republics of the Soviet Union, along with Russia, eastern Europe, China, India, Africa, and Latin America, are undergoing economic, social, and political changes that have already altered the course of trade and defined new economic powers. The knowledgeable marketer will identify opportunities long before they become evident to others. It is the authors' goal in this text to guide the reader toward acquiring global awareness.

Global awareness can and should be built into organizations using several approaches. The obvious strategy is to select individual managers specifically for their demonstrated global awareness. Global awareness can also be obtained through personal relationships in other countries. Indeed, market entry is very often facilitated through previously established social ties. Certainly, successful long-term business relationships with foreign customers often result in an organizational global awareness based on the series of interactions required by commerce. Foreign agents and partners can help directly in this regard. But perhaps the most effective approach is to have a culturally diverse senior executive staff or board of directors. Unfortunately, American managers seem to see relatively less value in this last approach than managers in most other countries.

Stages of International Marketing Involvement

LO6

The progression of becoming a global marketer

Once a company has decided to go international, it has to decide the degree of marketing involvement and commitment it is prepared to make. These decisions should reflect considerable study and analysis of market potential and company capabilities—a process not always followed.[22] Research has revealed a number of factors favoring faster internationalization: (1) Companies with either high-technology and/or marketing-based resources appear to be better equipped to internationalize than more traditional manufacturing kinds of companies;[23] (2) smaller home markets and larger production capacities appear to favor internationalization;[24] and (3) firms with key managers well networked internationally are able to accelerate the internationalization process.[25] Many companies begin tentatively in international marketing, growing as they gain experience and gradually changing strategy and tactics as they become more committed.[26] Others enter international marketing after much research and with fully developed long-range plans, prepared to make investments to acquire a market position and often evincing bursts of international activities.[27] One study suggests that striking a balance between the two approaches may actually work best,[28] with a variety of conditions and firm characteristics to be evaluated.

Regardless of the means employed to gain entry into a foreign market, a company may make little or no actual market investment—that is, its marketing involvement may be limited to selling a product with little or no thought given to the development of market control. Alternatively, a company may become totally involved and invest large sums of

---

[22]Protiti Dastidar, "International Corporate Diversification and Performance: Does Firm Self-Selection Matter?" *Journal of International Business Studies* 40, no. 1 (2009), pp. 71–85.

[23]Chiung-Hui Tseng, Patriya Tansuhaj, William Hallagan, and James McCullough, "Effects of Firm Resources on Growth in Multinationality," *Journal of International Business Studies* 38 (2007), pp. 961–74.

[24]Terence Fan and Phillip Phan, "International New Ventures: Revisiting the Influences behind the 'Born-Global' Firm," *Journal of International Business Studies* 38 (2007), pp. 1113–31.

[25]Susan Freeman and S. Tamer Cavusgil, "Toward a Typology of Commitment States among Managers of Born-Global Firms: A Study of Accelerated Internationalization," *Journal of International Marketing* 15 (2007), pp. 1–40.

[26]Marian V. Jones and Nicole E. Coviello, "Internationalisation: Conceptualising an Entrepreneurial Process of Behaviour in Time," *Journal of International Business Studies* 36, no. 3 (2005), pp. 284–303.

[27]Elizabeth Maitland, Elizabeth L. Rose, and Stephen Nicholas, "How Firms Grow: Clustering as a Dynamic Model of Internationalization," *Journal of International Business Studies* 36 (2005), pp. 435–51.

[28]Harry G. Barkema and Rian Drogendijk, "Internationalizing in Small, Incremental or Larger Steps?" *Journal of International Business Studies* 38 (2007), pp. 1132–48.

money and effort to capture and maintain a permanent, specific position in the market. In general, one of five (sometimes overlapping) stages can describe the international marketing involvement of a company. Although the stages of international marketing involvement are presented here in a linear order, the reader should not infer that a firm progresses from one stage to another; quite to the contrary, a firm may begin its international involvement at any one stage or be in more than one stage simultaneously. For example, because of a short product life cycle and a thin but widespread market for many technology products, many high-tech companies, large and small, see the entire world, including their home market, as a single market and strive to reach all possible customers as rapidly as possible.

No Direct Foreign Marketing

A company in this stage does not actively cultivate customers outside national boundaries; however, this company's products may reach foreign markets. Sales may be made to trading companies as well as foreign customers who directly contact the firm. Or products may reach foreign markets via domestic wholesalers or distributors who sell abroad without the explicit encouragement or even knowledge of the producer. As companies develop Web sites on the Internet, many receive orders from international Internet users. Often an unsolicited order from a foreign buyer is what piques the interest of a company to seek additional international sales.

Infrequent Foreign Marketing

Temporary surpluses caused by variations in production levels or demand may result in infrequent marketing overseas. The surpluses are characterized by their temporary nature; therefore, sales to foreign markets are made as goods become available, with little or no intention of maintaining continuous market representation. As domestic demand increases and absorbs surpluses, foreign sales activity is reduced or even withdrawn. In this stage, little or no change is seen in the company organization or product lines. However, few companies fit this model today, because customers around the world increasingly seek long-term commercial relationships. Furthermore, evidence suggests that financial returns from such short-term international expansions are limited.

The first two stages of international marketing involvement are more reactive in nature and most often do not represent careful strategic thinking about international expansion. Indeed, putting strategic thinking on the back burner has resulted in marketing failures for even the largest companies.

The consensus of researchers and authors[29] in this area suggests three relatively distinct approaches to strategic decisions in firms involved in international markets:[30]

1. Regular foreign marketing
2. Multidomestic or international marketing
3. Global marketing

Next we discuss each of the three stages (and their associated strategic orientations) in turn.

Regular Foreign Marketing

At this level, the firm has permanent productive capacity devoted to the production of goods and services to be marketed in foreign markets. A firm may employ foreign or domestic overseas intermediaries, or it may have its own sales force or sales subsidiaries in important foreign markets. The primary focus of operations and production is to service domestic market needs. However, as overseas demand grows, production is allocated for foreign markets, and products may be adapted to meet the needs of individual foreign markets. Profit expectations from foreign markets move from being seen as a bonus in addition to regular domestic profits to a position in which the company becomes dependent on foreign sales and profits to meet its goals.

---

[29]A seminal paper in this genre is by Yorum Wind, Susan P. Douglas, and Howard V. Perlmutter, "Guidelines for Developing International Marketing Strategy," *Journal of Marketing*, April 1973, pp. 14–23.

[30]Christian Geisler Asmussen, "Local, Regional, or Global? Quantifying MNE Geographic Scope," *Journal of International Business Studies* 40, no. 7 (2009), pp. 1192–205.

Meter-Man, a small company (25 employees) in southern Minnesota that manufactures agricultural measuring devices, is a good example of a company in this stage.[31] In 1989, the 35-year-old company began exploring the idea of exporting; by 1992 the company was shipping product to Europe. Today, one-third of Meter-Man's sales are in 35 countries, and soon the company expects international sales to account for about half of its business. "When you start exporting, you say to yourself, this will be icing on the cake," says the director of sales and marketing. "But now I say going international has become critical to our existence." Recently Meter-Man was purchased by Komelon, Inc., a larger, more diversified international company with operations in Washington state, South Korea, China, and Europe.

International Marketing

Companies in this stage are fully committed to and involved in international marketing activities. Such companies seek markets all over the world and sell products that are a result of planned production for markets in various countries. This planning generally entails not only the marketing but also the production of goods outside the home market. At this point, a company becomes an international or multinational marketing firm.

The experience of Fedders, a manufacturer of room air conditioners, typifies that of a company that begins its international business at this stage.[32] Even though it is the largest manufacturer of air conditioners in the United States, the firm faced constraints in its domestic market. Its sales were growing steadily, but sales of air conditioners (the company's only product) are seasonal, and thus, domestic sales at times do not even cover fixed costs. Furthermore, the U.S. market is mature, with most customers buying only replacement units. Any growth would have to come from a rival's market share, and the rivals, Whirlpool and Matsushita, are formidable. Fedders decided that the only way to grow was to venture abroad.

Fedders decided that Asia, with its often steamy climate and expanding middle class, offered the best opportunity. China, India, and Indonesia were seen as the best prospects. China was selected because sales of room air conditioners had grown from 500,000 units to more than 4 million in five years, which still accounted for only 12 percent of the homes in cities like Beijing, Shanghai, and Guangzhou. The company saw China as a market with terrific growth potential. After careful study, Fedders entered a joint venture with a small Chinese air conditioner company that was looking for a partner; a new company, Fedders Xinle, formed. The company immediately found that it needed to redesign its product for this market. In China, air conditioners are a major purchase, seen as a status symbol, not as a box to keep a room cool, as in the United States. The Chinese also prefer a split-type air conditioner, with the unit containing the fan inside the room and the heat exchanger mounted on a wall outside. Because Fedders did not manufacture split models, it designed a new product that is lightweight, energy efficient, and packed with features, such as a remote control and an automatic air-sweeping mechanism.

The joint venture appears to be successful, and the company is exploring the possibility of marketing to other Asian markets and maybe even back to the United States with the new product that it developed for the Chinese market. As Fedders expands into other markets and makes other commitments internationally, it continued to evolve as an international or multinational company. Finally, Fedders's successes internationally made it an attractive acquisition candidate, and in 2008 it was purchased by a French firm, Airwell, that has distributors in over 80 countries around the world.

Global Marketing

At the global marketing level, the most profound change is the orientation of the company toward markets and associated planning activities. At this stage, companies treat the world, including their home market, as one market. Market segmentation decisions are no longer focused on national borders. Instead, market segments are defined by income levels, usage patterns, or other factors that frequently span countries and regions. Often this transition from international marketing to global marketing is catalyzed by a company's crossing the threshold at which more than half its sales revenues comes from abroad. The best people in the company begin to seek international assignments, and the entire

---

[31]See http://www.komelon.com for its Meter-Man product line and other details.
[32]See http://www.airwell-fedders.com for details about the company.

For $500,000 you can now buy a four-bedroom house in Orange County—in China!

The homes are designed by Southern California architects and built with American features but are located in a new development an hour's drive north of Beijing. The country road can be icy and is lined by fields and populated by trucks and sheep. The landscape is a far cry from palm-ringed golf courses and "Surfin' USA." A bit after Sun City, another half-built gated community, the tidy homes of Orange County come into view. Finally, you drive through a stone portal, past advertisements showing men fly-fishing in cowboy hats and such, and pull up before the impressive mansions of Watermark-Longbeach, the epicenter of *faux* L.A. in China. Says homeowner Nasha Wei, a former army doctor turned business-woman, "I liked it immediately—it is just like a house in California." By the way, in other neighborhoods around Beijing, you can also buy a large home in a development of French villas called "Palais de Fortune" or an eco-friendly Toronto-designed home in "Maple Town."

Apparently, in France, the waves can actually be better than in California. Check out the 60-footers at Belharra Reef off St. Jean de Luz. Or hang ten along the surfwear shops nearby in the hamlet of Hossegor in southwest France. They're all there: Roxy, Rip Curl Girl, Billabong, and Quicksilver Boardriders Club. And the kids in the neighborhoods and sidewalk cafés are decked out in Volcom sweatshirts, Vans sneakers, and jeans.

The $5-billion plus surfwear industry, rooted in Orange County, California, has established a beachhead in Europe. So many U.S. surfwear companies have international headquarters, subsidiaries, and stores in Pays Basque that it has a new nickname: *la petite Californie.* "This is the best place to observe the market," says Petra Holtschneider, who recently organized the first Action Sports Retailer trade show in the area. "So if you're not here, you're not getting it."

Finally, perhaps the scariest OC exports are the television programs about the place. First it was Fox's *The OC,* then MTV's *Laguna Beach: The Real Orange County,* which has now morphed into *Newport Harbor: The Real Orange County.* The latter is now showing an entirely new generation of Europeans the latest kinds of misbehavior going on in "paradise" while influencing teen fashions globally. And there's a British spin-off in the works, *Alderley Edge, Cheshire.* Perhaps it will make its way back to the United States in the form of "educational TV"— those British accents make them sound so smart!

Sources: Elisabeth Rosenthal, "North of Beijing, California Dreams Come True," *The New York Times,* February 3, 2003, p. A3; Leslie Earnest, "Riding a French New Wave," *Los Angeles Times,* May 11, 2003, p. C1; Cristina Kinon, "The Laguna Effect: MTV's Sexy Soaps Are Changing the Face of Fashion, Mags, and the Way Teens Speak," *New York Daily News,* August 13, 2007, p. 33; Alyssa Abkowitz, "The Surfin' CEO," *Fortune International (Europe),* July 20, 2009, p. 17.

operation—organizational structure, sources of finance, production, marketing, and so forth—begins to take on a global perspective.

The example of Coca-Cola's transition from international to global is instructive. Coca-Cola had actually been a global company for years; the mid-1990s organizational redesign was the last step in recognizing the changes that had already occurred. Initially, all international divisions reported to an executive vice president in charge of interna-tional operations, who, along with the vice president of U.S. operations, reported to the president. The new organization consists of six international divisions. The U.S. business unit accounts for about 20 percent of profits and has been downgraded to just part of one of the six international business units in the company's global geographic regions. The new structure does not reduce the importance of the company's North American busi-ness; it just puts other areas on an equal footing. It represents the recognition, however, that future growth is going to come from emerging markets outside the United States.

International operations of businesses in global marketing reflect the heightened com-petitiveness brought about by the globalization of markets, interdependence of the world's economies, and the growing number of competing firms from developed and developing countries vying for the world's markets. *Global companies* and *global marketing* are terms frequently used to describe the scope of operations and marketing management orientation of companies in this stage.

As the competitive environment facing U.S. businesses becomes more internationalized— and it surely will—the most effective orientation for many firms engaged in marketing in another

North of Beijing, China, a new development is being marketed as Orange County, China. The gardens and stucco and tile exteriors are all intended to replicate the Mediterranean look and feel of homes in Newport Beach, California.

country will be a global orientation.[33] This orientation means operating as if all the country markets in a company's scope of operations (including the domestic market) were approachable as a single global market and standardizing the marketing mix where culturally feasible and cost effective. It does not, however, mean a slavish adherence to one strategic orientation. Depending on the product and market, other orientations may make more marketing sense. For example, Procter & Gamble may pursue a global strategy for disposable diapers but a multidomestic strategy in Asian markets for detergents.

The Orientation of *International Marketing*

Most problems encountered by the foreign marketer result from the strangeness of the environment within which marketing programs must be implemented. Success hinges, in part, on the ability to assess and adjust properly to the impact of a strange environment. The successful international marketer possesses the best qualities of the anthropologist, sociologist, psychologist, diplomat, lawyer, prophet, and businessperson.

In light of all the variables involved, with what should a textbook in foreign marketing be concerned? It is the opinion of the authors that a study of foreign marketing environments, people, and cultures[34] and their influences on the total marketing process is of primary concern and is the most effective approach to a meaningful presentation. Our views are supported by the most recent ranking of countries on their extent of globalization—see Exhibit 1.4.[35] Yes, the United States is near the top of the list, and most of the "Global Top 20" are small countries. However, the key conclusion to be drawn from the graph is the dominance of "technological connectivity" for

[33] Amar Gande, Christoph Schenzler, and Lemma W. Senbet, "Valuation of Global Diversification," *Journal of International Business Studies* 40, no. 9 (2009), pp. 1515–32.

[34] Tricia Bisoux, "Trade Secrets: An Interview with Caterpillar CEO, Jim Owens," *BizEd*, September/October 2009, pp. 20–27; Udo Zander and Lena Zander, "Opening the Grey Box: Social Communities, Knowledge and Culture in Acquisitions," *Journal of International Business Studies* 41, no. 1 (2010), pp. 27–37.

[35] "Measuring Globalization," *Foreign Policy*, November/December 2007, pp. 68–77.

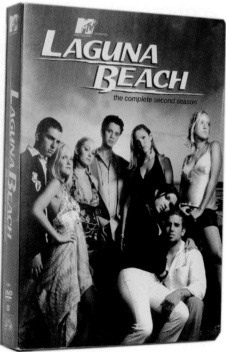

Orange County has also come to France in the form of the southern California surfing culture and clothiers. The OC's Quiksilver opened its European headquarters in southwest France in 1984. Last year, European sales amounted to over $1 billion. Part of the firm's success in Europe can be attributed to hiring local nationals in key marketing positions. Maritxu Darrigrand, former French women's surfing champion, is now Quiksilver's marketing director for Europe. The OC has also come to the U.K. as *Laguna Beach: The Real Orange County*. The MTV program brings California beach culture—clothes, music, and misbehavior—to Europe.

Exhibit 1.4
Foreign Policy's Global Top 20

The countries that top the charts in trade, travel, technology, and links to the rest of the world

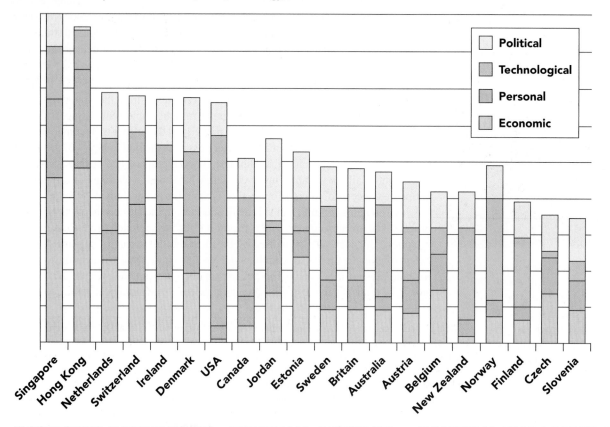

ECONOMIC INTEGRATION:

Trade and foreign direct investment

TECHNOLOGICAL CONNECTIVITY:

Internet users, Internet hosts, and secure servers

PERSONAL CONTACT:

International travel and tourism, international telephone traffic, and remittances and personal transfers (including worker remittances, compensation to employees, and other person-to-person and non-governmental transfers)

POLITICAL ENGAGEMENT:

Membership in international organizations, personnel and financial contributions to U.N. peacekeeping missions, international treaties ratified, and governmental transfers

Source: *Foreign Policy*, November/December 2007, pp. 68–77. Copyright 2007 by *Foreign Policy*. Reproduced with permission of *Foreign Policy* via Copyright Clearance Center.

America. In particular, notice that as a country, the United States is weakest on the "personal contact" dimension. Compared with folks in other countries, Americans generally do not experience foreign environments. This lack is the gap our book focuses on.

Consequently, the orientation of this text can best be described as an environmental/cultural approach to international strategic marketing. By no means is it intended to present principles of marketing; rather, it is intended to demonstrate the unique problems of international marketing. It attempts to relate the foreign environment to the marketing process and to illustrate the many ways in which culture can influence the marketing task. Although marketing principles are universally applicable, the cultural environment within which the marketer must implement marketing plans can change dramatically from country to country. It is with the difficulties created by different environments that this text is primarily concerned.

The text addresses issues relevant to any company marketing in or into any other country or groups of countries, however slight the involvement or the method of involvement. Hence this discussion of international marketing ranges from the marketing and business practices of small exporters, such as a Colorado-based company that generates more than

50 percent of its $40,000 annual sales of fish-egg sorters in Canada, Germany, and Australia, to the practices of global companies such as Motorola, Avon, and Johnson & Johnson, all of which generate more than 50 percent of their annual profits from the sales of multiple products to multiple country-market segments all over the world.

The first section of *International Marketing* offers an overview of international marketing, including a discussion of the global business environment confronting the marketer. The next section deals exclusively with the uncontrollable elements of the environment and their assessment, followed by chapters on assessing global market opportunities. Then, management issues in developing global marketing strategies are discussed. In each chapter, the impact of the environment on the marketing process is illustrated.

Space prohibits an encyclopedic approach to all the issues of international marketing; nevertheless, the authors have tried to present sufficient detail so that readers will appreciate the real need to do a thorough analysis whenever the challenge arises. The text provides a framework for this task.

Summary

The internationalization of American business is accelerating. The globalization of markets and competition necessitates that all managers pay attention to the global environment. International marketing is defined as the performance of business activities, including pricing, promotion, product, and distribution decisions, across national borders. The international marketing task is made more daunting because environmental factors such as laws, customs, and cultures vary from country to country. These environmental differences must be taken into account if firms are to market products and services at a profit in other countries.

Key obstacles facing international marketers are not limited to environmental issues. Just as important are difficulties associated with the marketer's own self-reference criteria and ethnocentrism.

Both limit the international marketer's abilities to understand and adapt to differences prevalent in foreign markets. A global awareness and sensitivity are the best solutions to these problems, and they should be nurtured in international marketing organizations.

Three different strategic orientations are found among managers of international marketing operations. Some see international marketing as ancillary to the domestic operations. A second kind of company sees international marketing as a crucial aspect of sales revenue generation but treats each market as a separate entity. Finally, a global orientation views the globe as the marketplace, and market segments are no longer based solely on national borders—common consumer characteristics and behaviors come into play as key segmentation variables applied across countries.

Key Terms

International marketing	Domestic environment	Foreign environment	Self-reference criterion (SRC)
Controllable elements	uncontrollables	uncontrollables	Global awareness
Uncontrollable elements			

Questions

1. Define the key terms listed above.
2. "The marketer's task is the same whether applied in Dimebox, Texas, or Dar es Salaam, Tanzania." Discuss.
3. How can the increased interest in international marketing on the part of U.S. firms be explained?
4. Discuss the four phases of international marketing involvement.
5. Discuss the conditions that have led to the development of global markets.
6. Differentiate between a global company and a multinational company.
7. Differentiate among the three international marketing concepts.
8. Prepare your lifelong plan to be globally aware.
9. Discuss the three factors necessary to achieve global awareness.
10. Define and discuss the idea of global orientation.
11. Visit the Bureau of Economic Analysis homepage (http://www.bea.doc.gov). Select the section "International articles" and find the most recent information on foreign direct investments in the United States. Which country has the highest dollar amount of investment in the United States? Second highest?

Chapter 2

The Dynamic Environment of International Trade

CHAPTER OUTLINE

CHAPTER LEARNING OBJECTIVES

What you should learn from Chapter 2:

LO1 The basis for the reestablishment of world trade following World War II

LO2 The importance of balance-of-payment figures to a country's economy

LO3 The effects of protectionism on world trade

LO4 The several types of trade barriers

LO5 The provisions of the Omnibus Trade and Competitiveness Act

LO6 The importance of GATT and the World Trade Organization

LO7 The emergence of the International Monetary Fund and the World Bank Group

Global Perspective

TRADE BARRIERS—AN INTERNATIONAL MARKETER'S MINEFIELD

We all know the story about U.S. trade disputes with Japan. Japan has so many trade barriers and high tariffs that U.S. manufacturers are unable to sell in Japan as much as Japanese companies sell in the United States. The Japanese claim that "unique" Japanese snow requires skis made in Japan, and U.S. baseballs are not good enough for Japanese baseball. Even when Japan opened its rice market, popular California rice had to be mixed and sold with inferior grades of Japanese rice. And, at this writing, the Japanese government continues to exclude American beef from the Japanese diet based on disputes about mad cow disease.[1]

However, the Japanese are not alone; every country seems to take advantage of the open U.S. market while putting barriers in the way of U.S. exports. The French, for example, protect their film and broadcast industry from foreign competition by limiting the number of American shows that can appear on television, the percentage of American songs broadcast on radio, and the proportion of U.S. movies that can be shown in French theaters. Most recently, France launched its own "French" version of CNN with strong governmental financial support. Not only do these barriers and high tariffs limit how much U.S. companies can sell, they also raise prices for imported products much higher than they sell for in the United States.

Another trade protection tactic even involved Britain's Supreme Court of Judicature, which has finally answered a question that has long puzzled late-night dorm-room snackers: What, exactly, is a Pringle? With citations ranging from Baroness Hale of Richmond to Oliver Wendell Holmes, Lord Justice Robin Jacob concluded that legally it is a potato chip. The decision is bad news for Procter & Gamble U.K., which now owes $160 million in value-added taxes to the state. It is thus good news for Her Majesty's Revenue and Customs—and for fans of no-nonsense legal opinions. It is also a reminder, as conservatives in the United States attack Justice Sonia Sotomayor for not being a "strict constructionist," of the pointlessness of such labels. In Britain, most foods are exempt from the value-added tax (VAT), but potato chips (known there as crisps) and "similar products made from the potato, or from potato flour" are taxable. Procter & Gamble, in what could be considered a strict constructionist plea, argued that Pringles are about 40 percent potato flour but also contain corn, rice, and wheat and therefore should not be considered potato chips or "similar products." Rather, they are "savory snacks."

The VAT and Duties Tribunal disagreed, ruling that Pringles, marketed in the United States as "potato chips," are taxable. "There are other ingredients," the Tribunal agreed, but a Pringle is "made from potato flour in the sense that one cannot say that it is not made from potato flour, and the proportion of potato flour is significant being over 40 percent."

Barriers to trade, whatever form they take, both tariff and nontariff, are one of the major issues confronting international marketers. Nations continue to use trade barriers for a variety of reasons: some rational, some not so rational. Fortunately, tariffs generally have been reduced to record lows, and substantial progress has been made on eliminating nontariff barriers. And work continues around the world to further reduce these pesky hurdles to peace and prosperity.

Sources: Adapted from Todd G. Buchholz, "Free Trade Keeps Prices Down," *Consumers' Research Magazine*, October 1995, p. 22; Tomas Kellner, "What Gaul!" *Forbes*, April 28, 2003, p. 52; Jonathan Lynn, "WTO Negotiators to Tackle Obstacles to Farm Deal," *Reuters News*, January 3, 2008; Adam Cohen, "The Lord Justice Hath Ruled: Pringles Are Potato Chips," *The New York Times*, June 1, 2009.

[1]See James Day Hodgson, Yoshihiro Sano, and John L. Graham, *Doing Business in the New Japan, Succeeding in America's Richest Foreign Market* (Boulder, CO: Rowman & Littlefield, 2008) for the complete story.

Exhibit 2.1
Top Ten 2009 U.S. Trading
Partners ($ billions,
merchandise trade)

Source: http://www.census.gov/
foreign-trade/top, 2010.

Country	Total Trade	Exports	Imports	Balance
Canada	$429.6	$204.7	$224.9	$−20.2
China	366.0	69.6	296.4	−226.5
Mexico	305.5	129.0	176.5	−47.5
Japan	147.1	51.2	95.9	−44.7
Germany	114.6	43.3	71.3	−28.0
United Kingdom	93.2	45.7	47.5	−1.8
South Korea	67.9	28.6	39.2	−10.6
France	60.6	26.5	34.0	−7.5
Netherlands	48.4	32.3	16.1	+16.2
Taiwan	46.8	18.4	28.4	−10.0

Yesterday's competitive market battles were fought in western Europe, Japan, and the United States; now competitive battles have extended to Latin America, eastern Europe, Russia, China, India, Asia, and Africa as these emerging markets continue to open to trade. More of the world's people, from the richest to the poorest, will participate in the world's growing prosperity through global trade. The emerging global economy brings us into worldwide competition, with significant advantages for both marketers and consumers. Marketers benefit from new markets opening and smaller markets growing large enough to become viable business opportunities. Consumers benefit by being able to select from the widest range of goods produced anywhere in the world at the lowest prices.

Bound together by burgeoning international communications media and global companies, consumers in every corner of the world are demanding an ever-expanding variety of goods and services. As Exhibit 2.1 illustrates, world trade is an important economic activity. Because of this importance, the inclination is for countries to attempt to control international trade to their own advantage. As competition intensifies, the tendency toward protectionism gains momentum. If the benefits of the social, political, and economic changes now taking place are to be fully realized, free trade must prevail throughout the global marketplace. The creation of the World Trade Organization (WTO) is one of the biggest victories for free trade in decades.

This chapter briefly surveys the United States's past and present role in global trade and some concepts important for understanding the relationship between international trade and national economic policy. A discussion of the logic and illogic of protectionism, the major impediment to trade, is followed by a review of the General Agreement on Tariffs and Trade (GATT) and its successor, the World Trade Organization (WTO), two multinational agreements designed to advance free trade.

The Twentieth to the Twenty-First Century

At no time in modern economic history have countries been more economically interdependent, have greater opportunities for international trade existed, or has the potential for increased demand existed than now, at the opening of the 21st century. This statement remains true even with due regard to the global financial crisis that began in 2008. In contrast, in the preceding 100 years, world economic development was erratic.

The first half of the 20th century was marred by a major worldwide economic depression that occurred between two world wars that all but destroyed most of the industrialized world. The last half of the century, while free of a world war, was marred by struggles between countries espousing the socialist Marxist approach and those following a democratic capitalist approach to economic development. As a result of this ideological split, traditional trade patterns were disrupted.

After World War II, as a means to dampen the spread of communism, the United States set out to infuse the ideal of capitalism throughout as much of the world as possible. The Marshall Plan to assist in rebuilding Europe, financial and industrial development assistance to rebuild Japan, and funds channeled through the Agency for International Development and other groups designed to foster economic growth in the underdeveloped world

LO1

The basis for the reestablishment of world trade following World War II

Even though the John Deere tractors lined up for shipment from its Waterloo, Iowa, plant appear impressive, the Hyundai cars stacked up by the water in Ulsan, South Korea, headed for the United States dwarf their numbers. The juxtaposition of the two pictures aptly reflects the persistence of America's broader merchandise trade deficit.

were used to help create a strong world economy. The dissolution of colonial powers created scores of new countries in Asia and Africa. With the striving of these countries to gain economic independence and the financial assistance offered by the United States, most of the noncommunist world's economies grew, and new markets were created.

The benefits of the foreign economic assistance given by the United States flowed both ways. For every dollar the United States invested in the economic development and rebuilding of other countries after World War II, hundreds of dollars more returned in the form of purchases of U.S. agricultural products, manufactured goods, and services. This overseas demand created by the Marshall Plan and other programs[2] was important to the U.S. economy because the vast manufacturing base built to supply World War II and the swelling labor supply of returning military created a production capacity well beyond domestic needs. The major economic boom and increased standard of living the United States experienced after World War II were fueled by fulfilling pent-up demand in the United States and the demand created by the rebuilding of war-torn countries of Europe and Asia. In short, the United States helped make the world's economies stronger, which enabled them to buy more from us.

In addition to U.S. economic assistance, a move toward international cooperation among trading nations was manifest in the negotiation (1986–1994) of the General Agreement on Tariffs and Trade (GATT). International trade had ground to a halt following World War I when nations followed the example set by the U.S. passage of the Smoot-Hawley Act (1930), which raised average U.S. tariffs on more than 20,000 imported goods to levels in excess of 60 percent. In retaliation, 60 countries erected high tariff walls, and international trade stalled, along with most economies. A major worldwide recession catapulted the world's economies into the Great Depression when trade all but dried up.[3]

Determined not to repeat the economic disaster that followed World War I, world leaders created **GATT**, a forum for member countries to negotiate a reduction of tariffs and other barriers to trade. The forum proved successful in reaching those objectives. With the ratification of the Uruguay Round agreements, the GATT became part of the World Trade Organization (WTO) in 1995, and its 117 original members moved into a new era of free trade.

---

[2]The Organization for Economic Cooperation and Development (OECD) was a direct result of the Marshall Plan.

[3]David M. Kennedy, Lizabeth Cohen, and Thomas A. Bailey, *The American Pageant*, 13th ed. (Boston: Houghton Mifflin, 2006).

World Trade and U.S. Multinationals

The rapid growth of war-torn economies and previously underdeveloped countries, coupled with large-scale economic cooperation and assistance, led to new global marketing opportunities. Rising standards of living and broad-based consumer and industrial markets abroad created opportunities for American companies to expand exports and investment worldwide. During the 1950s, many U.S. companies that had never before marketed outside the United States began to export, and others made significant investments in marketing and production facilities overseas.

At the close of the 1960s, U.S. multinational corporations (MNCs) were facing major challenges on two fronts: resistance to direct investment and increasing competition in export markets. Large investments by U.S. businesses in Europe and Latin America heightened the concern of these countries about the growing domination of U.S. multinationals. The reaction in Latin American countries was to expropriate direct U.S. investments or to force companies to sell controlling interests to nationals. In Europe, apprehension manifested itself in strong public demand to limit foreign investment. Concerns, even in Britain, that they might become a satellite with manufacturing but no determination of policy led to specific guidelines for joint ventures between British and U.S. companies. In the European Community, U.S. multinationals were rebuffed in ways ranging from tight control over proposed joint ventures and regulations covering U.S. acquisitions of European firms to strong protectionism laws.

The threat felt by Europeans was best expressed in the popular book *The American Challenge*, published in 1968, in which the French author J. J. Servan-Schreiber wrote:

> Fifteen years from now it is quite possible that the world's third greatest industrial power, just after the United States and Russia, will not be Europe but American Industry in Europe. Already, in the ninth year of the Common Market, this European market is basically American in organization.[4]

Servan-Schreiber's prediction did not come true for many reasons, but one of the more important was that American MNCs confronted a resurgence of competition from all over the world. The worldwide economic growth and rebuilding after World War II was beginning to surface in competition that challenged the supremacy of American industry. Competition arose on all fronts; Japan, Germany, most of the industrialized world, and many developing countries were competing for demand in their own countries and looking for world markets as well. Countries once classified as less developed were reclassified as newly industrialized countries (NICs). Various NICs such as Brazil, Mexico, South Korea, Taiwan, Singapore, and Hong Kong experienced rapid industrialization in select industries and became aggressive world competitors in steel, shipbuilding, consumer electronics, automobiles, light aircraft, shoes, textiles, apparel, and so forth. In addition to the NICs, developing countries such as Venezuela, Chile, and Bangladesh established state-owned enterprises (SOEs) that operated in other countries. One state-owned Venezuelan company has a subsidiary in Puerto Rico that produces canvas, cosmetics, chairs, and zippers; there are also Chilean and Colombian companies in Puerto Rico; in the U.S. state of Georgia, a Venezuelan company engages in agribusiness; and Bangladesh, the sixth largest exporter of garments to the United States, also owns a mattress company in Georgia.

In short, economic power and potential became more evenly distributed among countries than was the case when Servan-Schreiber warned Europe about U.S. multinational domination. Instead, the U.S. position in world trade is now shared with other countries. For example, in 1950, the United States represented 39 percent of world gross national product (GNP), but by 2010, it represented less than 25 percent. In the meantime, however, the global GNP grew much larger, as did the world's manufacturing output—all countries shared in a much larger economic pie. This change was reflected in the fluctuations in the growth of MNCs from other countries as well. Exhibit 2.2 reflects the dramatic changes between 1963 and 2009. In 1963, the United States had 67 of the world's largest industrial corporations. By 1996, that number had dropped to a low of 24, while Japan moved from having 3 of the largest to 29 and South Korea from 0 to 4. And following the great economic boom in the late 1990s in the United States, 36 of the largest companies were American, only 22 Japanese, and none were Korean. Most recently, GAZPROM, the Russian natural

---

[4]J. J. Servan-Schreiber, *The American Challenge* (New York: Atheneum Publishers, 1968), p. 3.

Exhibit 2.2

The Nationality of the World's 100 Largest Industrial Corporations (size measured by annual revenues)

Source: "2009 Global 500," *Fortune*, http://www.fortune.com, 2010.

	1963	1979	1984	1990	1996	2000	2005	2009
United States	67	47	47	33	24	36	33	30
Germany	13	13	8	12	13	12	15	14
Britain	7	7	5	6	2	5	10	6
France	4	11	5	10	13	11	10	10
Japan	3	7	12	18	29	22	12	10
Italy	2	3	3	4	4	3	3	5
Netherlands– United Kingdom	2	2	2	2	2	2	1	1
Netherlands	1	3	1	1	2	5	2	1
Switzerland	1	1	2	3	5	3	4	1
Luxembourg								1
Belgium		1	1	1		1		1
Norway							1	1
Finland								1
Brazil		1		1				1
Canada		2	3					
India			1					
Kuwait			1					
Mexico		1	1	1	1		1	1
Venezuela		1	1	1	1			
South Korea			4	2	4		1	4
Sweden			1	2				
South Africa			1	1				
Spain					2		1	3
Russia								2
China						2	1	5
Malaysia								1

gas giant, was the first eastern European entrant into the top 100 global firms, ranking number 52 in the most recent *Fortune* list.[5] The decline in Japanese and increase in Chinese companies' rankings are prominent as well.

Another dimension of world economic power, the balance of merchandise trade, also reflected the changing role of the United States in world trade. Between 1888 and 1971, the United States sold more to other countries than it bought from them; that is, the United States had a favorable balance of trade. By 1971, however, the United States had a trade deficit of $2 billion that grew steadily until it peaked at $160 billion in 1987. After that, the deficit in merchandise trade declined to $74 billion in 1991 but began increasing again and by 2007 had surpassed $700 billion. With the continued weakness in the U.S. dollar, the trade deficit began to abate some in the fall of 2007.[6] The positive consequence of the global financial crisis that began in 2008 in the United States was the halving of the U.S. trade deficit during 2009 from its high in 2007.

The heightened competition for U.S. businesses during the 1980s and early 1990s raised questions similar to those heard in Europe two decades earlier: how to maintain the competitive strength of American business, to avoid the domination of U.S. markets by foreign MNCs, and to forestall the "buying of America." In the 1980s, the United States saw its competitive position in capital goods such as computers and machinery erode sharply. From 1983 to 1987, almost 70 percent of the growth of the merchandise trade deficit was in capital goods and automobiles. At the time, those were America's high-wage, high-skill industries. But U.S. industry got a wake-up call and responded by restructuring its industries, in essence, "getting lean and mean." By the late 1990s, the United States was once again holding its own in capital goods, particularly with trade surpluses in the high-tech category.

---

[5]"GASPROM Eyes 10% of French Gas Market in 4–5 Years," *Dow Jones International News*, January 3, 2008.

[6]Elizabeth Price and Brian Blackstone, "U.S. Trade Deficit Shrinks—Rising Prices Dampen Demand for Imports, Could Fuel Inflation," *The Wall Street Journal Asia*, November 12, 2007, p. 9.

Among the more important questions raised in the 1980s were those concerning the ability of U.S. firms to compete in foreign markets and the fairness of international trade policies of some countries. Trade friction revolved around Japan's sales of autos and electronics in the United States and Japan's restrictive trade practices. The United States, a strong advocate of free trade, was confronted with the dilemma of how to encourage trading partners to reciprocate with open access to their markets without provoking increased protectionism. In addition to successfully pressuring Japan to open its markets for some types of trade and investment, the United States was a driving force behind the establishment of the WTO.

By the last decade of the 20th century, profound changes in the way the world would trade were already under way. The continuing integration of the countries of the European Union, the creation of NAFTA[7] and the American Free Trade Area (AFTA), and the rapid evolution of the Asia-Pacific Economic Cooperation Conference (APEC) are the beginnings of global trading blocks that many experts expect to dominate trade patterns in the future. With the return of Hong Kong in 1997 and Macao in 2000 to China, all of Asia is now controlled and managed by Asians for the first time in 400 years. During the decades since World War II, the West set the patterns for trade, but increasingly, Asia will be a major force, if not the leading force.

Beyond the First Decade of the Twenty-First Century

The unprecedented and precipitous growth of the U.S. economy in the late 1990s slowed dramatically in the last few years, and of course dramatically so in 2009. Growth in most of the rest of the world has followed suit, with the exception of China. The Organization for Economic Cooperation and Development (OECD) estimates that the economies of member countries will expand an average of 3 percent annually for the next 25 years, the same rate as in the past 25 years. Conversely, the economies of the developing world will grow at faster rates—from an annual rate of 4 percent in the past quarter century to a rate of 6 percent for the next 25 years. Their share of world output will rise from about one-sixth to nearly one-third over the same period. The World Bank estimates that five countries—Brazil, China,[8] India, Indonesia, and Russia—whose share of world trade is barely one-third that of the European Union will, by 2020, have a 50 percent higher share than that of the European Union. As a consequence, economic power and influence will move away from industrialized countries—Japan, the United States, and the European Union—to countries in Latin America, eastern Europe, Asia, and Africa.

This shift does not mean that markets in Europe, Japan, and the United States will cease to be important; those economies will continue to produce large, lucrative markets, and the companies established in those markets will benefit. It does mean that if a company is to be a major player in the 21st century, now is the time to begin laying the groundwork. How will these changes that are taking place in the global marketplace impact international business? For one thing, the level and intensity of competition will change as companies focus on gaining entry into or maintaining their position in emerging markets, regional trade areas, and the established markets in Europe, Japan, and the United States.

Companies are looking for ways to become more efficient, improve productivity, and expand their global reach while maintaining an ability to respond quickly and deliver products that the markets demand. For example, large Chinese state-owned companies are investing heavily in developing economies. Nestlé is consolidating its dominance in global consumer markets by acquiring and vigorously marketing local-country major brands. Samsung of South Korea has invested $500 million in Mexico to secure access to markets in the North American Free Trade Area. Whirlpool, the U.S. appliance manufacturer, which secured first place in the global appliance business by acquiring the European division of the appliance maker N. V. Philips, immediately began restructuring itself into its version of a global company. These are a few examples of changes that are sweeping multinational companies as they gear up for the rest of the 21st century.

---

[7]Jenalia Moreno, "Trade Tariffs End, Making NAFTA a Milestone," *Houston Chronicle*, January 2, 2008.

[8]"Fear of the Dragon," *The Economist*, January 9, 2010, pp. 73–74.

Global companies are not the only ones aggressively seeking new market opportunities. Smaller companies are using novel approaches to marketing and seeking ways to apply their technological expertise to exporting goods and services not previously sold abroad. A small midwestern company that manufactures and freezes bagel dough for supermarkets to bake and sell as their own saw opportunities abroad and began to export to Japan. International sales, though small initially, showed such potential that the company sold its U.S. business to concentrate on international operations. Other examples of smaller companies include Nochar Inc., which makes a fire retardant it developed a decade ago for the Indianapolis 500. The company now gets 32 percent of its sales overseas, in 29 countries. The owner of Buztronics Inc., a maker of promotional lapel buttons, heard from a friend that his buttons, with their red blinking lights, would "do great" in Japan. He made his first entry in exporting to Japan, and after only a year, 10 percent of Buztronics sales came from overseas. While 50 of the largest exporters account for 30 percent of U.S. merchandise exports, the rest come from middle- and small-sized firms like those just mentioned. The business world is weathering a flurry of activity as companies large and small adjust to the internationalization of the marketplace at home and abroad.

Balance of Payments

LO2

The importance of balance-of-payment figures to a country's economy

When countries trade, financial transactions among businesses or consumers of different nations occur. Products and services are exported and imported, monetary gifts are exchanged, investments are made, cash payments are made and cash receipts received, and vacation and foreign travel occur. In short, over a period of time, there is a constant flow of money into and out of a country. The system of accounts that records a nation's international financial transactions is called its **balance of payments**.

A nation's balance-of-payments statement records all financial transactions between its residents and those of the rest of the world during a given period of time—usually one year. Because the balance-of-payments record is maintained on a double-entry bookkeeping system, it must always be in balance. As on an individual company's financial statement, the assets and liabilities or the credits and debits must offset each other. And like a company's statement, the fact that they balance does not mean a nation is in particularly good or poor financial condition. A balance of payments is a record of condition, not a determinant of condition. Each of the nation's financial transactions with other countries is reflected in its balance of payments.

A nation's balance-of-payments statement presents an overall view of its international economic position and is an important economic measure used by treasuries, central banks, and other government agencies whose responsibility is to maintain external and internal economic stability. A balance of payments represents the difference between receipts from foreign countries on one side and payments to them on the other. On the plus side of the U.S. balance of payments are merchandise export sales; money spent by foreign tourists; payments to the United States for insurance, transportation, and similar services; payments of dividends and interest on investments abroad; return on capital invested abroad; new foreign investments in the United States; and foreign government payments to the United States.

On the minus side are the costs of goods imported, spending by American tourists overseas, new overseas investments, and the cost of foreign military and economic aid. A deficit results when international payments are greater than receipts. It can be reduced or eliminated by increasing a country's international receipts (i.e., gain more exports to other countries or more tourists from other countries) and/or reducing expenditures in other countries. A balance-of-payments statement includes three accounts: the **current account**, a record of all merchandise exports, imports, and services plus unilateral transfers of funds; the *capital account*, a record of direct investment, portfolio investment, and short-term capital movements to and from countries; and the official *reserves account*, a record of exports and imports of gold, increases or decreases in foreign exchange, and increases or decreases in liabilities to foreign central banks. Of the three, the current account is of primary interest to international business.

The *current account* is important because it includes all international merchandise trade and service accounts, that is, accounts for the value of all merchandise and services

Exhibit 2.3
U.S. Current Account by
Major Components, 2009
($ billions)

Exports	
Goods	$ 1046
Services	509
Income receipts	561
Imports	
Goods	−1563
Services	−371
Income payments	−472
Unilateral current transfers, net	−130
Current account balance	−420

imported and exported and all receipts and payments from investments and overseas employment.[9] Exhibit 2.3 gives the current account calculations for the United States in 2009.

Since 1971, the United States has had a favorable current account balance (as a percentage of GDP) in only a few years—see Exhibit 2.4. The imbalances resulted primarily from U.S. demand for oil,[10] petroleum products, cars, consumer durables, and other merchandise. Indeed, the merchandise trade deficit for 2009 was $517 billion, a mega improvement over the two previous years.[11] Still, such imbalances have drastic effects on the balance of payments and therefore the value of U.S. currency in the world marketplace. Factors such as these eventually require an adjustment through a change in exchange rates, prices, and/or incomes. In short, once the wealth of a country whose expenditures exceed its income has been exhausted, that country, like an individual, must reduce its standard of living. If its residents do not do so voluntarily, the rates of exchange of its money for foreign monies decline, and through the medium of the foreign exchange market, the purchasing power of

[9]"Financial Globalization and U.S. Current Account Deficit," *US Fed News,* January 3, 2008.
[10]Terence Poon, "China to Steady Prices Amid Inflation Worries," *The Wall Street Journal,* January 10, 2008.
[11]www.bea.gov.

Exhibit 2.4
U.S. Current Account Balance (% of GDP)

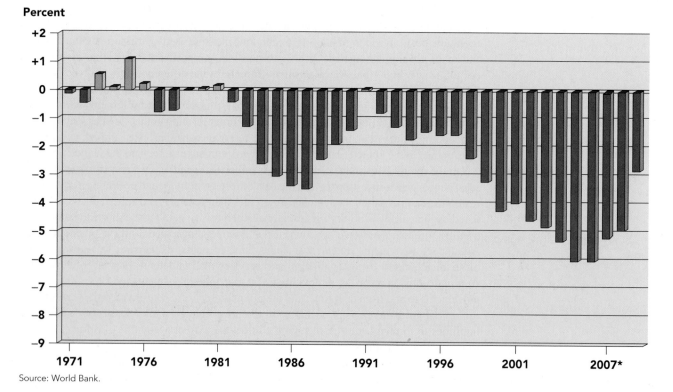

Source: World Bank.

Exhibit 2.5

What Would One U.S. Dollar Buy?

Source: *The Wall Street Journal*, 2010.

	1985	**1988**	**1992**	**1995**	**1999**	**2000**	**2005**	**2010**
British pound	0.86	0.54	0.56	0.63	0.62	0.68	0.57	0.63
French franc	9.6	5.4	5.29	4.95	6.49	7.28		
Japanese yen	250.23	123.7	126.7	93.96	102.58	112.21	112.3	89.9
Swiss franc	2.25	1.29	1.41	1.18	1.58	1.68	1.31	0.96
Euro			1.01	0.90	0.92	1.08	0.79	0.71
Mexico peso	0.37	2.28	3.12	6.45	9.43	9.47	10.8	13.0

foreign goods is transferred from that country to another. As can be seen in Exhibit 2.5, the U.S. dollar strengthened against most of the other major currencies during the 1990s but has weakened during the last decade.

As the U.S. trade deficit has grown, pressures have begun to push the value of the dollar to lower levels. And when foreign currencies can be traded for more dollars, U.S. products (and companies) are less expensive for the foreign customer and exports increase, and foreign products are more expensive for the U.S. customer and the demand for imported goods is dampened. Likewise, investments in dollar-denominated equities and such investment goods become less attractive. Indeed, the dollar itself becomes less useful as a global currency.[12]

Protectionism

LO3

The effects of protectionism on world trade

International business executives understand the reality that this is a world of tariffs, quotas, and nontariff barriers designed to protect a country's markets from intrusion by foreign companies.[13] Although the World Trade Organization has been effective in reducing tariffs, countries still resort to measures of **protectionism**.[14] Nations utilize legal barriers, exchange barriers, and psychological barriers to restrain the entry of unwanted goods. Businesses work together to establish private market barriers, while the market structure itself may provide formidable barriers to imported goods. The complex distribution system in Japan, as will be detailed in Chapter 15, is a good example of a market structure creating a barrier to trade. However, as effective as it is in keeping some products out of the market, in a legal sense, it cannot be viewed as a trade barrier.

Protection Logic and Illogic

Countless reasons to maintain government restrictions on trade are espoused by protectionists, but essentially all arguments can be classified as follows: (1) protection of an infant industry, (2) protection of the home market,[15] (3) need to keep money at home, (4) encouragement of capital accumulation, (5) maintenance of the standard of living and real wages, (6) conservation of natural resources, (7) industrialization of a low-wage nation, (8) maintenance of employment and reduction of unemployment, (9) national defense, (10) increase of business size, and (11) retaliation and bargaining. Economists in general recognize as valid only the arguments regarding infant industry, national defense, and industrialization of underdeveloped countries. The resource conservation argument becomes increasingly valid in an era of environmental consciousness[16] and worldwide shortages of raw materials and agricultural commodities. A case might be made for temporary protection of markets with excess productive capacity or excess labor when such protection could facilitate an orderly transition. Unfortunately such protection often becomes long term and contributes to industrial inefficiency while detracting from a nation's realistic adjustment to its world situation.

---

[12] Mark Whitehouse, "Foreign Investors View Dollar as 'Refuge Currency' Despite Recent Tumult," *The Wall Street Journal*, August 20, 2007, p. A2.

[13] Tor Korneliussen and Jorg Blasius, "The Effects of Cultural Distance, Free Trade Agreements, and Protectionism on Perceived Export Barriers," *Journal of Global Marketing* 21, no. 3 (2008), pp. 217–30.

[14] "The Nuts and Bolts Come Apart," *The Economist*, March 28, 2009, pp. 79–80.

[15] Alistair MacDonald and Cecilie Rohwedder, "U.K. Officials, Workers Troubled by Foreign Takeovers," *The Wall Street Journal*, January 20, 2010, p. B6.

[16] John Carey, "Global Warming, Suddenly the Climate in Washington Is Changing," *BusinessWeek*, June 27, 2005, p. 91.

CROSSING BORDERS 2.1   Trade Barriers, Hypocrisy, and the United States

The United States thinks of itself as the leader in free trade and frequently brings actions against nations as unfair trade partners. Section 301* of the Omnibus Trade and Competitiveness Act authorizes the U.S. government to investigate and retaliate against specific foreign trade barriers judged to be unfair and to impose up to 100 percent tariffs on exports to the United States from guilty nations unless they satisfy U.S. domestic demands. But critics in many countries say the United States is hypocritical in some of the stances taken, since it is just as guilty of protecting its markets with trade barriers. A Japanese government study alleges that the United States engages in unfair trade practices in 10 of 12 policy areas reviewed in the study. Notably, the United States imposes quotas on imports, has high tariffs, and abuses antidumping measures. Are the critics correct? Is the United States being hypocritical when it comes to free trade? You be the judge.

The United States launched a Section 301 investigation of Japanese citrus quotas. "The removal of Japan's unfair barriers could cut the price of oranges for Japanese consumers by one-third," said the U.S. trade representative. Coincidentally, the United States had a 40 percent tariff on Brazilian orange juice imports when the investigation was initiated.

The United States brought a 301 case against Korea for its beef import quotas even though the United States has beef import quotas that are estimated to

cost U.S. consumers $873 million annually in higher prices. Another 301 case was brought against Brazil, Korea, and Taiwan for trade barriers on footwear even though the United States maintains tariffs as high as 67 percent on footwear imports.

Can you believe that we have two phone book–sized volumes of the U.S. customs code that include restrictions on such innocuous items as scissors, sweaters, leather, costume jewelry, tampons, pizzas, cotton swabs, ice cream, and even products we do not produce, such as vitamin B12? We also have restrictions on more sensitive products such as cars, supercomputers, lumber, and every type of clothing imaginable. Would-be Latin American exporters find hundreds of their most promising export products, such as grapes, tomatoes, onions, steel, cement, asparagus, and shoes, on the customs list. Visit www.usitc.gov/tata/index.htm and select the Interactive Tariff Database to see some other examples.

So, is the U.S. as guilty as the rest or not?

*Section 301, a provision of U.S. trade law, enables the U.S. government to take action against countries deemed to have engaged in "unreasonable, unjustifiable, or discriminatory" practices that restrict U.S. commerce.

Sources: Abstracted from James Bovard, "A U.S. History of Trade Hypocrisy," *The Wall Street Journal*, March 8, 1994, p. A10; Brian Hindley and Fredrik Erixon, "Dumping Protectionism," *The Wall Street Journal*, November 1, 2007, p. 12; "Chinese Dumping Duties," *Steel Times International*, October 2009, p. 4.

To give you some idea of the cost to the consumer, consider the results of a recent study of 21 protected industries. The research showed that U.S. consumers pay about $70 billion per year in higher prices because of tariffs and other protective restrictions. On average, the cost to consumers for saving one job in these protected industries was $170,000 per year, or many times the average pay (wages and benefits) for manufacturing workers. Unfortunately, protectionism is politically popular, particularly during times of declining wages[17] and/or high unemployment, but it rarely leads to renewed growth in a declining industry. And the jobs that are saved are saved at a very high cost, which constitutes a tax that consumers unknowingly pay.

Trade Barriers

LO4

The several types of trade barriers

To encourage development of domestic industry and protect existing industry, governments may establish such barriers to trade as tariffs and a variety of **nontariff barriers** including, quotas, boycotts, monetary barriers, and market barriers. Barriers are imposed against imports and against foreign businesses. While the inspiration for such barriers may be economic or political, they are encouraged by local industry. Whether or not the barriers are economically logical, the fact is that they exist.

Tariffs. A **tariff**, simply defined, is a tax imposed by a government on goods entering at its borders. Tariffs may be used as revenue-generating taxes or to discourage the importation of goods, or for both reasons. Tariff rates are based on value or quantity or a

---

[17]Jane Sasseen, "Economists Rethink Free Trade," *BusinessWeek*, February 11, 2008, pp. 32–33.

CROSSING BORDERS 2.2

Underwear, Outerwear, Sony Playstations, and Pointed Ears—What Do They Have in Common?

What do underwear, outerwear, Sony Playstations, and pointed ears have in common? Quotas, that's what!

Call the first one the Madonna Effect. Madonna, the pop star, affected the interpretation of outerwear/underwear when the ever-vigilant U.S. Customs Service stopped a shipment of 880 bustiers at the U.S. border. The problem was quota and tariff violations. The shipper classified them as underwear, which comes into the United States without quota and tariff. Outerwear imports, however, have a quota, and the Customs official classified the fashion item inspired by Madonna as "outerwear" and demanded the appropriate quota certificates.

"It was definitely outerwear. I've seen it; and I've seen the girls wearing it, and they're wearing it as outerwear." It took the importer three weeks to obtain sufficient outerwear quota allowances to cover the shipment; by that time, several retailers had canceled their orders.

Call the second the Video/Computer Effect. EU officials originally classified Sony's Playstation a video game and thus subject to a higher tariff than it would be if it were classified as a computer, which was Sony's desired classification. The Court of First Instance ruled that "it is intended mainly to be used to run video games," thus subject to millions of euros in customs duties as a video game. The appeals court sided with Sony on a technical error and reversed the decision.

It really did not make much difference, because EU customs classifications were set to change six months later to allow computers and games consoles into the European Union with zero tariff.

Call the third the Vulcan Effect. EU officials applied the Vulcan death grip to *Star Trek* hero Spock. Likenesses of the pointy-eared Spock and other "nonhuman creatures" have fallen victim to an EU quota on dolls made in China. The EU Council of Ministers slapped a quota equivalent to $81.7 million on nonhuman dolls from China—but it left human dolls alone.

British Customs officials are in the unusual position of debating each doll's humanity. They have blacklisted teddy bears but cleared Batman and Robin. And though they turned away Spock because of his Vulcan origins, they have admitted *Star Trek*'s Captain Kirk. The Official Fan Club for *Star Trek* said the Customs officials "ought to cut Spock some slack" because his mother, Amanda, was human. But Britain's Customs office said, "We see no reason to change our interpretation. You don't find a human with ears that size."

Sources: Rosalind Resnick, "Busting Out of Tariff Quotas," *North American International Business* (now published as *International Business*), February 1991, p. 10; Dana Milbank, "British Customs Officials Consider Mr. Spock Dolls to Be Illegal Aliens," *The Wall Street Journal*, August 2, 1994, p. B1; "EU Rejects Sony Customs Claim," (Salt Lake City) *Deseret News*, October 6, 2003.

combination of both. In the United States, for example, the types of customs duties used are classified as follows: (1) ad valorem duties, which are based on a percentage of the determined value of the imported goods; (2) specific duties, a stipulated amount per unit weight or some other measure of quantity; and (3) a compound duty, which combines both specific and ad valorem taxes on a particular item, that is, a tax per pound plus a percentage of value. Because tariffs frequently change, published tariff schedules for every country are available to the exporter on a current basis.[18] In general, tariffs:

Increase	Inflationary pressures.
	Special interests' privileges.
	Government control and political considerations in economic matters.
	The number of tariffs (they beget other tariffs via reciprocity).
Weaken	Balance-of-payments positions.
	Supply-and-demand patterns.
	International relations (they can start trade wars).
Restrict	Manufacturers' supply sources.
	Choices available to consumers.
	Competition.

In addition, tariffs are arbitrary, are discriminatory, and require constant administration and supervision. They often are used as reprisals against protectionist moves of trading partners.

---

[18]The entire Harmonized Tariff Schedule of the United States can be downloaded or accessed via an interactive tariff database at http://www.usitc.gov; select the Harmonized Tariff Schedule.

Exhibit 2.6
Types of Nontariff Barriers

Specific Limitations on Trade
Quotas
Import licensing requirements
Proportional restrictions of foreign to domestic goods
   (local-content requirements)
Minimum import price limits
Embargoes

Customs and Administrative Entry Procedures
Valuation systems
Antidumping practices
Tariff classifications
Documentation requirements
Fees

Standards
Standards disparities
Intergovernmental acceptances of testing methods
   and standards
Packaging, labeling, marking standards

Governmental Participation in Trade
Government procurement policies
Export subsidies
Countervailing duties
Domestic assistance programs

Charges on Imports
Prior import deposit requirements
Administrative fees
Special supplementary duties
Import credit discriminations
Variable levies
Border taxes

Others
Voluntary export restraints
Orderly marketing agreements

Source: Reprinted from A. D. Cao, "Nontariff Barriers to U.S. Manufactured Exports," *Journal of World Business,* Vol. 15, p. 94. Copyright © 1980, with permission from Elsevier.

In a dispute with the European Union over pasta export subsidies, the United States ordered a 40 percent increase in tariffs on European spaghetti and fancy pasta. The European Union retaliated against U.S. walnuts and lemons. The pasta war raged on as Europe increased tariffs on U.S. fertilizer, paper products, and beef tallow, and the United States responded in kind. The war ended when the Europeans finally dropped pasta export subsidies. Less developed countries are increasingly voicing complaints about American and European tariffs on agricultural products.[19]

Quotas and Import Licenses.   A quota is a specific unit or dollar limit applied to a particular type of good. Great Britain limits imported television sets; Germany has established quotas on Japanese ball bearings; Italy restricts Japanese motorcycles; and the United States has quotas on sugar, textiles, and, of all things, peanuts. Quotas put an absolute restriction on the quantity of a specific item that can be imported. When the Japanese first let foreign rice into their country, it was on a quota basis, but since 2000 the quotas have been replaced by tariffs.[20] Even more complicated, the banana war between the United States and the European Union resulted in a mixed system wherein a quota of bananas is allowed into the European Union with a tariff, then a second quota comes in tariff-free. In early 2010, as *Avatar* dominated cinema around the world, China ordered its movie houses to limit showings to the 3D version only.[21] Like tariffs, quotas tend to increase prices.[22] The U.S. quotas on textiles are estimated to add 50 percent to the wholesale price of clothing.

As a means of regulating the flow of exchange and the quantity of a particular imported commodity, countries often require import licenses. The fundamental difference between quotas and import licenses as a means of controlling imports is the greater flexibility of import licenses over quotas. Quotas permit importing until the quota is filled; licensing limits quantities on a case-by-case basis.

[19]Allan Odhiambo, "EAC States in Row over Wheat Import Tariffs," *All Africa,* August 30, 2007.
[20]See the USA Rice Federation's Web site for details, http://www.usarice.com; also see Hodgson et al., *Doing Business in the New Japan.*
[21]Ian Johnson, "China's Homegrown Movies Flourish," *The Wall Street Journal,* January 20, 2010, pp. B1, B4.
[22]Peter T. Leach, "Is China Losing Its Edge?" *Journal of Commerce,* December 3, 2007.

CROSSING BORDERS 2.3   Crossing Borders with Monkeys in His Pants

Robert Cusack smuggled a pair of endangered pygmy monkeys into the United States—in his pants! On June 13, 2002, a U.S. Fish and Wildlife Service special agent was called to Los Angeles International Airport after Cusack was detained by U.S. Customs on arrival from Thailand. Officials soon also discovered that Cusack had four endangered tropical birds and 50 protected orchids with him. "When one of the inspectors opened up his luggage, one of the birds flew out," tells one official. "He had to go catch the bird." After finding the other purloined birds and exotic flowers, the inspectors asked, "Do you have anything else you should tell us about?" Cusack answered, "Yes, I have monkeys in my pants." The monkeys ended up in the Los Angeles Zoo, and the smuggler ended up in jail for 57 days. He also paid a five-figure fine.

Similarly, Wang Hong, a Chinese exporter, pleaded guilty to smuggling sea turtles into the United States. He didn't have them in his pants; instead, the sea turtle "parts" came in the form of shells and violin bows, among other things.

Smuggling isn't just a game played by sneaking individuals. Multinational companies can also get into the act. During the last year alone, convictions have come down for smuggling cell phones into Vietnam, cigarettes into Iraq and Canada, and platinum into China. In perhaps the biggest ever corporate case, after a nine-year lawsuit, Amway Corporation agreed to pay the Canadian government $38.1 million to settle charges it had avoided customs duties by undervaluing merchandise it exported from the United States to Canadian distributors over a six-year period. As long as there have been trade barriers, smuggling has been a common response. Indeed, Rudyard Kipling wrote some 100 years ago:

Five and twenty ponies trotting through the dark—
Brandy for the Parson, 'baccy for the clerk;
Laces for a lady, letters for a spy;
And watch the wall, my darling, while the Gentlemen go by!

Sources: "Amway Pays $38 Million to Canada," *Los Angeles Times*, September 22, 1989, p. 3; Patricia Ward Biederman, "Smuggler to Pay for Pocketing Monkeys," *Los Angeles Times*, December 19, 2002, p. B1; "Chinese National Pleads Guilty of Smuggling Protected Sea Turtles," *Associated Press*, January 3, 2008; Raymond Fisman, "Measuring Tariff Evasion and Smuggling," *NBER Reporter*, No. 3, 2009, pp. 8–10.

Voluntary Export Restraints.   Similar to quotas are the **voluntary export restraints (VERs)** or *orderly market agreements* (OMAs). Common in textiles, clothing, steel, agriculture, and automobiles, the VER is an agreement between the importing country and the exporting country for a restriction on the volume of exports. For many years Japan had a VER on automobiles to the United States; that is, Japan agreed to export a fixed number of automobiles annually. When televisions were still manufactured in the United States, Japan signed an OMA limiting Japanese color television exports to the United States to 1.56 million units per year. However, Japanese companies began to adjust their strategies by investing in television manufacturing in the United States and Mexico, and as a result, they regained the entire market share that had been lost through the OMA, eventually dominating the entire market. A VER is called voluntary because the exporting country sets the limits; however, it is generally imposed under the threat of stiffer quotas and tariffs being set by the importing country if a VER is not established.

Boycotts and Embargoes.   A government boycott is an absolute restriction against the purchase and importation of certain goods and/or services from other countries. This restriction can even include travel bans, like the one currently in place for Chinese tourists; the Beijing government refuses to designate Canada as an approved tourism destination. Officials in Beijing have not been forthcoming with explanations, even after three years of complaints by and negotiations with their Canadian counterparts, but most believe it has to do with Canada's unrelenting criticism of Chinese human rights policies.[23] An embargo is a refusal to sell to a specific country. A public boycott can be either formal or

---

[23]"Canada Threatens China with WTO Action over Tourism Ban," *Agence France-Presse*, January 8, 2008.

NYK Line (Nippon Yusen Kaisha) brings automobiles from Japan to Aqaba, Jordan, on the Red Sea for delivery to other countries in the area, but not for neighboring Israel. Because of the Arab boycott of Israel, separate shipments of cars are made to the adjacent port of Eilat.

informal and may be government sponsored or sponsored by an industry. The United States uses boycotts and embargoes against countries with which it has a dispute. For example, Cuba[24] and Iran still have sanctions imposed by the United States. Among U.S. policymakers, there is rising concern, however, that government-sponsored sanctions cause unnecessary harm for both the United States and the country being boycotted without reaching the desired results. It is not unusual for the citizens of a country to boycott goods of other countries at the urging of their government or civic groups. Nestlé products were boycotted by a citizens group that considered the way Nestlé promoted baby formula in less developed countries misleading to mothers and harmful to their babies.

Monetary Barriers.

A government can effectively regulate its international trade position by various forms of exchange-control restrictions. A government may enact such restrictions to preserve its balance-of-payments position or specifically for the advantage or encouragement of particular industries. Two such barriers are blocked currency and government approval requirements for securing foreign exchange.

Blocked currency is used as a political weapon or as a response to difficult balance-of-payments situations. In effect, blockage cuts off all importing or all importing above a certain level. Blockage is accomplished by refusing to allow an importer to exchange its national currency for the sellers' currency.

Government approval to secure foreign exchange is often used by countries experiencing severe shortages of foreign exchange. At one time or another, most Latin American and East European countries have required all foreign exchange transactions to be approved by a central minister. Thus, importers who want to buy a foreign good must apply for an exchange permit, that is, permission to exchange an amount of local currency for foreign currency.

The exchange permit may also stipulate the rate of exchange, which can be an unfavorable rate depending on the desires of the government. In addition, the exchange permit may stipulate that the amount to be exchanged must be deposited in a local bank for a set period prior to the transfer of goods. For example, Brazil has at times required funds to be deposited 360 days prior to the import date. This requirement is extremely restrictive because funds are out of circulation and subject to the ravages of inflation. Such policies cause major cash flow problems for the importer and greatly increase the price of imports. Clearly, these currency-exchange barriers constitute a major deterrent to trade.

Standards.

Nontariff barriers of this category include standards to protect health, safety, and product quality. The standards are sometimes used in an unduly stringent or discriminating way to restrict trade, but the sheer volume of regulations in this category is a problem in itself. A fruit content regulation for jam varies so much from country to country that one agricultural specialist says, "A jam exporter needs a computer to avoid one or another country's regulations." Different standards are one of the major disagreements between the United States and Japan. The size of knotholes in plywood shipped to Japan can determine whether or not the shipment is accepted; if a knothole is too large, the shipment is rejected because quality standards are not met. Other examples include the following: In the Netherlands, all imported hen and duck eggs must be marked in indelible ink with the country of origin; in Spain, imported condensed milk must be labeled to show fat content if it is less than 8 percent fat; and in the European Union, strict import controls have been placed on beef and beef products imported from the United Kingdom because of mad cow disease. Add to this list all genetically modified foods,

[24]Cornelia Dean, "Cuba After the Embargo," *The New York Times News Service, Edmonton Journal,* January 6, 2008, p. E8.

Cracker Jack invented the toy-with-candy promotion back in 1912. However, the Italian chocolatier Ferrero took things much further. Its milk chocolate Kinder eggs contain "sopresas" that kids enjoy in 37 countries around the world. The product is unavailable in the United States because of concerns about choking hazards. The product pictured is produced in Argentina for sale in Mexico, and it includes a warning label regarding kids under three years of age. Cracker Jack has had to eliminate many of the cool little toys it put in the packages for the same reason. Nestlé introduced a product similar to Kinder eggs in the U.S. market in the late 1990s but had to withdraw it for safety reasons. Wonderball is the latest version, but it has edible chocolate figures inside. See www.ferrero.com.ar and www.crackerjack .com for more details. Toys must be larger than the diameter of the plastic tube pictured on the right to meet the U.S. safety standard.

which are meeting stiff opposition from the European Union as well as activists around the world.

The United States and other countries require some products (automobiles in particular) to contain a percentage of "local content" to gain admission to their markets. The North American Free Trade Agreement (NAFTA) stipulates that all automobiles coming from member countries must have at least 62.5 percent North American content to deter foreign car makers from using one member nation as the back door to another.

Antidumping Penalties.   Historically, tariffs and nontariff trade barriers have impeded free trade, but over the years, they have been eliminated or lowered through the efforts of the GATT and WTO. Now there is a new nontariff barrier: antidumping laws that have emerged as a way of keeping foreign goods out of a market. Antidumping laws were designed to prevent foreign producers from "predatory pricing," a practice whereby a foreign producer intentionally sells its products in the United States for less than the cost of production to undermine the competition and take control of the market. This barrier was intended as a kind of antitrust law for international trade. Violators are assessed "antidumping" duties for selling below cost and/or "countervailing duties" to prevent the use of foreign government subsidies to undermine American industry. Many countries have similar laws, and they are allowed under WTO rules.

Recent years have seen a staggering increase in antidumping cases in the United States. In one year, 12 U.S. steel manufacturers launched antidumping cases against 82 foreign steelmakers in 30 countries. In September 2009, the U.S. imposed antidumping duties of 35 percent on tires imported from China, despite President Barack Obama's agreement with other G20 leaders "to avoid protectionist measures at a time of great economic peril" in April of that year.[25] Many economists felt that these antidumping charges were unnecessary because of the number of companies and countries involved; supply and demand could have been left to sort out the best producers and prices. And of course, targeted countries have complained as well. Nevertheless, antidumping cases are becoming de facto trade barriers. The investigations are very costly, they take a long time to resolve, and until they are resolved, they effectively limit trade. Furthermore,

---

[25]"Economic Vandalism," *The Economist*, September 19, 2009, p. 13.

the threat of being hit by an antidumping charge is enough to keep some companies out of the market.

Domestic Subsidies and Economic Stimuli. Agricultural subsidies in the United States and Europe have long been the subject of trade complaints in developing countries. However, the economic doldrums beginning in 2008 triggered new, huge, domestic bailout packages in the larger economies for banks and auto makers, to name just a couple. Developing countries complained that such subsidies of domestic industries gave companies in those countries unfair advantages in the global marketplace. Smaller countries defended themselves with a variety of tactics; for example, Malaysia limited the number of ports that could accept inbound goods, Ecuador increased tariffs on 600 types of goods, and Argentina and 15 other countries asked the WTO to examine whether stimuli and bailouts were "industrial subsidies," in which case, under WTO rules, trading partners have the right to retaliate.[26] Similarly, the U.S government complained about Chinese policies, including continuing currency controls, tax breaks on exports, and requirements that force government entities to buy Chinese products.[27]

Easing Trade Restrictions

Lowering the trade deficit has been a priority of the U.S. government for a number of years. Of the many proposals brought forward, most deal with fairness of trade with some of our trading partners instead of reducing imports or adjusting other trade policies. Many believe that too many countries are allowed to trade freely in the United States without granting equal access to U.S. products in their countries. Japan was for two decades the trading partner with which we had the largest deficit and which elicited the most concern about fairness. The Omnibus Trade and Competitiveness Act of 1988 addressed the trade fairness issue and focused on ways to improve U.S. competitiveness. At the turn of the century, China took over from Japan as America's number one "trade problem," as can be seen in Exhibit 2.1.

The Omnibus Trade and Competitiveness Act

LO5

The provisions of the Omnibus Trade and Competitiveness Act

The *Omnibus Trade and Competitiveness Act of 1988* is many faceted, focusing on assisting businesses to be more competitive in world markets as well as on correcting perceived injustice in trade practices.[28] The trade act was designed to deal with trade deficits, protectionism, and the overall fairness of our trading partners. Congressional concern centered on the issue that U.S. markets were open to most of the world but markets in Japan, western Europe, and many Asian countries were relatively closed. The act reflected the realization that we must deal with our trading partners based on how they actually operate, not on how we want them to behave. Some see the act as a protectionist measure, but the government sees it as a means of providing stronger tools to open foreign markets and to help U.S. exporters be more competitive. The bill covers three areas considered critical in improving U.S. trade: market access, export expansion, and import relief.

The issue of the openness of markets for U.S. goods is addressed as *market access*. Many barriers restrict or prohibit goods from entering a foreign market. Unnecessarily restrictive technical standards, compulsory distribution systems, customs barriers, tariffs, quotas, and restrictive licensing requirements are just a few. The act gives the U.S. president authority to restrict sales of a country's products in the U.S. market if that country imposes unfair restrictions on U.S. products. Furthermore, if a foreign government's procurement rules discriminate against U.S. firms, the U.S. president has the authority to impose a similar ban on U.S. government procurement of goods and services from the offending nation.

---

[26]Carol Matlack, "The New Protectionsim," *BusinessWeek*, June 22, 2009, pp. 22–23.
[27]Pete Engardio, "Beijing Bolsters the Barriers," *BusinessWeek*, July 6, 2009, p. 26.
[28]Caroline Baum, "China Isn't a Currency Manipulator," *Today* (Singapore), June 20, 2007, p. 35.

The billboard overlooking a busy shopping district in Beijing proclaims the importance of China's space technology to all passersby. Meanwhile, Boeing and Hughes have had to pay $32 million in a settlement with the U.S. government for allegedly giving the Chinese sensitive space technology in the middle 1990s. The restrictions on technology sales have rendered American high-tech firms less competitive in international markets even beyond China, such as Canada.

Besides emphasizing market access, the act recognizes that some problems with U.S. export competitiveness stem from impediments on trade imposed by U.S. regulations and export disincentives. Export controls, the Foreign Corrupt Practices Act (FCPA), and export promotion were specifically addressed in the *export expansion* section of the act. Export licenses could be obtained more easily and more quickly for products on the export control list. In addition, the act reaffirmed the government's role in being more responsive to the needs of the exporter. Two major contributions facilitating export trade were computer-based procedures to file for and track export license requests and the creation of the National Trade Data Bank (NTDB) to improve access to trade data.

Export trade is a two-way street: We must be prepared to compete with imports in the home market if we force foreign markets to open to U.S. trade. Recognizing that foreign penetration of U.S. markets can cause serious competitive pressure, loss of market share, and, occasionally, severe financial harm, the *import relief* section of the Omnibus Trade and Competitiveness Act provides a menu of remedies for U.S. businesses adversely affected by imports. Companies seriously injured by fairly traded imports can petition the government for temporary relief while they adjust to import competition and regain their competitive edge.

The act has resulted in a much more flexible process for obtaining export licenses, in fewer products on the export control list, and in greater access to information and has established a basis for negotiations with India, Japan, and other countries to remove or lower barriers to trade. However, since a 1999 congressional report (accusing China of espionage regarding defense technology), restrictions on exports of many high-tech products have again been tightened for national security reasons.[29]

As the global marketplace evolves, trading countries have focused attention on ways of eliminating tariffs, quotas, and other barriers to trade. Four ongoing activities to support the growth of international trade are GATT, the associated WTO, the International Monetary Fund (IMF), and the World Bank Group.

General Agreement on Tariffs and Trade

LO6

The importance of GATT and the World Trade Organization

Historically, trade treaties were negotiated on a bilateral (between two nations) basis, with little attention given to relationships with other countries. Furthermore, they tended to raise barriers rather than extend markets and restore world trade. The United States and 22 other countries signed the *General Agreement on Tariffs and Trade (GATT)* shortly after World War II.[30] Although not all countries participated, this agreement paved the way for the first effective worldwide tariff agreement. The original agreement provided a process to reduce tariffs and created an agency to serve as watchdog over world trade. The GATT's agency director and staff offer nations a forum for negotiating trade and related issues. Member nations seek to resolve their trade disputes bilaterally; if that fails, special GATT panels are set up to recommend action. The panels are only advisory and have no enforcement powers.

The GATT treaty and subsequent meetings have produced agreements significantly reducing tariffs on a wide range of goods. Periodically, member nations meet to reevaluate trade barriers and establish international codes designed to foster trade among members.

---

[29]Elaine Kurtenbach, "China Says Bids Due from Three Global Nuclear Power Companies," *Associated Press*, February 25, 2005.

[30]Florence Chong, "As GATT Turns 60, Crean Pledges to Revive the Great Struggle for World Trade Liberalization," *The Australian*, January 2, 2008, p. 17.

According to the U.S. government, you can't call it a "catfish" unless it's grown in America. Vietnamese are producing filets in flooded rice paddies at about $1.80 a pound at wholesale. American fish farmers are charging about $2.80. Neither consumers nor ichthyologists can tell the difference between the Asian and American fish, but Uncle Sam has stepped in anyway. The congressional claim on the "catfish" name has forced the United States to stifle its own protests about Europeans claiming exclusive rights to the name "herring." (©Tom McHugh/Photo Researchers, Inc.)

In general, the agreement covers these basic elements: (1) trade shall be conducted on a nondiscriminatory basis; (2) protection shall be afforded domestic industries through customs tariffs, not through such commercial measures as import quotas; and (3) consultation shall be the primary method used to solve global trade problems.

Since GATT's inception, eight "rounds" of intergovernmental tariff negotiations have been held. The most recently completed was the Uruguay Round (1994), which built on the successes of the Tokyo Round (1974)— the most comprehensive and far-reaching undertaken by GATT up to that time. The Tokyo Round resulted in tariff cuts and set out new international rules for subsidies and countervailing measures, antidumping, government procurement, technical barriers to trade (standards), customs valuation, and import licensing. While the Tokyo Round addressed nontariff barriers, some areas that were not covered continued to impede free trade.

In addition to market access, there were issues of trade in services, agriculture, and textiles; intellectual property rights; and investment and capital flows. The United States was especially interested in addressing services trade and intellectual property rights, since neither had been well protected. On the basis of these concerns, the eighth set of negotiations (Uruguay Round) was begun in 1986 at a GATT Trade Minister's meeting in Punta del Este, Uruguay, and finally concluded in 1994. By 1995, 80 GATT members, including the United States, the European Union (and its member states), Japan, and Canada, had accepted the agreement.

The market access segment (tariff and nontariff measures) was initially considered to be of secondary importance in the negotiations, but the final outcome went well beyond the initial Uruguay Round goal of a one-third reduction in tariffs. Instead, virtually all tariffs in 10 vital industrial sectors with key trading partners were eliminated. This agreement resulted in deep cuts (ranging from 50 to 100 percent) in tariffs on electronic items and scientific equipment and the harmonization of tariffs in the chemical sector at very low rates (5.5 to 0 percent).

An important objective of the United States in the Uruguay Round was to reduce or eliminate barriers to international trade in services. The *General Agreement on Trade in Services (GATS)* was the first multilateral, legally enforceable agreement covering trade and investment in the services sector. It provides a legal basis for future negotiations aimed at eliminating barriers that discriminate against foreign services and deny them market access. For the first time, comprehensive multilateral disciplines and procedures covering trade and investment in services have been established. Specific market-opening concessions from a wide range of individual countries were achieved, and provision was made for continued negotiations to liberalize telecommunications and financial services further.

Equally significant were the results of negotiations in the investment sector. *Trade-Related Investment Measures (TRIMs)* established the basic principle that investment restrictions can be major trade barriers and therefore are included, for the first time, under GATT procedures. As a result of TRIMs, restrictions in Indonesia that prohibit foreign firms from opening their own wholesale or retail distribution channels can be challenged. And so can investment restrictions in Brazil that require foreign-owned manufacturers to buy most of their components from high-cost local suppliers and that require affiliates of foreign multinationals to maintain a trade surplus in Brazil's favor by exporting more than they sell within.

Another objective of the United States for the Uruguay Round was achieved by an agreement on *Trade-Related Aspects of Intellectual Property Rights (TRIPs)*. The TRIPs agreement establishes substantially higher standards of protection for a full range of intellectual property rights (patents, copyrights, trademarks, trade secrets, industrial designs, and semiconductor chip mask works) than are embodied in current international agreements, and it provides for the effective enforcement of those standards both internally and at the border.

The Uruguay Round also includes another set of improvements in rules covering antidumping, standards, safeguards, customs valuation, rules of origin, and import licensing. In each case, rules and procedures were made more open, equitable, and predictable, thus leading to a more level playing field for trade. Perhaps the most notable achievement of the Uruguay Round was the creation of a new institution as a successor to the GATT—the World Trade Organization.

World Trade Organization[31]

At the signing of the Uruguay Round trade agreement in Marrakech, Morocco, in April 1994, U.S. representatives pushed for an enormous expansion of the definition of trade issues. The result was the creation of the **World Trade Organization (WTO)**, which encompasses the current GATT structure and extends it to new areas not adequately covered in the past. The WTO is an institution, not an agreement as was GATT. It sets many rules governing trade among its 148 members, provides a panel of experts to hear and rule on trade disputes among members, and, unlike GATT, issues binding decisions. It will require, for the first time, the full participation of all members in all aspects of the current GATT and the Uruguay Round agreements, and, through its enhanced stature and scope, provide a permanent, comprehensive forum to address the trade issues of the 21st century global market.

All member countries will have equal representation in the WTO's ministerial conference, which will meet at least every two years to vote for a director general, who will appoint other officials. Trade disputes, such as that swirling around genetically modified foods, are heard by a panel of experts selected by the WTO from a list of trade experts provided by member countries. The panel hears both sides and issues a decision; the winning side will be authorized to retaliate with trade sanctions if the losing country does not change its practices. Although the WTO has no means of enforcement, international pressure to comply with WTO decisions from other member countries is expected to force compliance. The WTO ensures that member countries agree to the obligations of all the agreements, not just those they like. For the first time, member countries, including developing countries (the fastest growing markets of the world), will undertake obligations to open their markets and to be bound by the rules of the multilateral trading system.

The World Trade Organization provision of the Uruguay Round encountered some resistance before it was finally ratified by the three superpowers: Japan, the European Union (EU), and the United States. A legal wrangle among European Union countries centered on whether the EU's founding treaty gives the European Commission the sole right to negotiate for its members in all areas covered by the WTO.

In the United States, ratification was challenged because of concern for the possible loss of sovereignty over its trade laws to WTO, the lack of veto power (the U.S. could have a decision imposed on it by a majority of the WTO's members), and the role the United States would assume when a conflict arises over an individual state's laws that might be challenged by a WTO member. The GATT agreement was ratified by the U.S. Congress, and soon after, the European Union, Japan, and more than 60 other countries followed. All 117 members of the former GATT supported the Uruguay agreement. Since almost immediately after its inception on January 1, 1995, the WTO's agenda has been full with issues ranging from threats of boycotts and sanctions and the membership of Iran[32] and Russia.[33] Indeed, a major event in international trade during recent years is China's

---

[31]See http://wto.org.

[32]Tom Wright, "WRTO to Open Talks on Iran's Membership," *International Herald Tribune*, May 27, 2005, p. 1.

[33]"Mexico Backs Russia's WTO Bid, Welcomes Russian Energy Investment," *Agence France-Presse*, June 21, 2005.

2001 entry into the WTO. Instead of waiting for various "rounds" to iron out problems, the WTO offers a framework for a continuous discussion and resolution of issues that retard trade.

The WTO has its detractors, but from most indications it is gaining acceptance by the trading community. The number of countries that have joined and those that want to become members is a good measure of its importance. Another one is its accomplishments since its inception: It has been the forum for successful negotiations to opening markets in telecommunications and in information technology equipment, something the United States had sought for the last two rounds of GATT. It also has been active in settling trade disputes, and it continues to oversee the implementation of the agreements reached in the Uruguay Round. But with its successes come other problems: namely, how to counter those countries that want all the benefits of belonging to WTO but also want to protect their markets. Indeed, the latest multilateral initiative, dubbed the "Doha Round" for the city of Qatar where the talks began in 2001, has been stalled with little progress.[34]

Skirting the Spirit of GATT and WTO

Unfortunately, as is probably true of every law or agreement, since its inception there have been those who look for loopholes and ways to get around the provisions of the WTO. For example, China was asked to become a member of the WTO, but to be accepted it had to show good faith in reducing tariffs and other restrictions on trade. To fulfill the requirements to join the WTO, China reduced tariffs on 5,000 product lines and eliminated a range of traditional nontariff barriers to trade, including quotas, licenses, and foreign exchange controls. At the same time, U.S. companies began to notice an increase in the number and scope of technical standards and inspection requirements. As a case in point, China recently applied safety and quality inspection requirements on such seemingly benign imported goods as jigsaw puzzles. It also has been insisting that a long list of electrical and mechanical imports undergo an expensive certification process that requires foreign companies but not domestic companies to pay for on-site visits by Chinese inspection officials. Under WTO rules, China now must justify the decision to impose certain standards and provide a rationale for the inspection criteria. In 2009, the WTO ruled Chinese restrictions on imports of movies, music, and books to be illegal. The ruling is subject to appeal, but if affirmed, it will create huge opportunities for companies such as Apple and its' iTunes.[35]

The previously mentioned antidumping duties are becoming a favorite way for nations to impose new duties. Indeed, following the example of the United States, the region's most prolific user of antidumping cases, Mexico and other Latin American countries have increased their use as well. The WTO continues to fight these new, creative barriers to trade.

Finally, frustrated with the slow progress of the most recent round of WTO trade negotiations, several countries are negotiating bilateral trade agreements.[36] For example, the United States has signed free-trade agreements with Peru, Colombia, Panama, and South Korea.[37] The European Union is engaged in similar activities with South American countries. Perhaps most notable, China and Taiwan have begun free trade talks.[38] South Korea and India[39] have also signed a free trade pact as have five East African countries.[40] To the

---

[34]John W. Miller, "Blame Goes Global at WTO," *The New York Times*, December 3, 2009.

[35]Don Lee, "A Win for U.S. Media in China," *Los Angeles Times*, August 13, 2009, pp. B1, B4.

[36]Jayant Menon, "Dealing with the Proliferation of Bilateral Free Trade Agreements," *World Economy* 32 (October 2009), pp. 1381–407.

[37]http://www.ustr.gov, 2010.

[38]Ting-I Tsai, "China, Taiwan Set Stage for a Landmark Pact on Trade," *The Wall Street Journal–Eastern Edition*, December 19, 2009, p. A19.

[39]Kanga Kong, "Trade Accord with India Will Cut or Eliminate Tariffs," *The Wall Street Journal–Eastern Edition*, August 8, 2009, p. A9.

[40]"It Really May Happen," *The Economist*, January 2, 2010, p. 36.

17. Discuss the evolution of world trade that led to the formation of the WTO.

18. Visit www.usitc.gov/taffairs.htm (U.S. Customs tariff schedule) and look up the import duties on leather footwear. You will find a difference in the duties on shoes of different value, material composition, and quantity. Using what you have learned in this chapter, explain the reasoning behind these differences. Do the same for frozen and/or concentrated orange juice.

19. The GATT has had a long and eventful history. Visit www.wto.org/wto/about/about.htm and write a short report on the various rounds of GATT. What were the key issues addressed in each round?

Chapter **3**

History and Geography:

THE FOUNDATIONS OF CULTURE

CHAPTER LEARNING OBJECTIVES

What you should learn from Chapter 3:

LO1 The importance of history and geography in understanding international markets

LO2 The effects of history on a country's culture

LO3 How culture interprets events through its own eyes

LO4 How long-past U.S. international policies still affect customer attitudes abroad

LO5 The effect of geographic diversity on economic profiles of a country

LO6 Why marketers need to be responsive to the geography of a country

LO7 The economic effects of controlling population growth and aging populations

LO8 Communication infrastructures are an integral part of international commerce

Global Perspective

BIRTH OF A NATION—PANAMA IN 67 HOURS

The Stage Is Set

June 1902 — The United States offers to buy the Panama Canal Zone from Colombia for $10 million.

August 1903 — The Colombian Senate refuses the offer. Theodore Roosevelt, angered by the refusal, refers to the Colombian Senate as "those contemptible little creatures in Bogotá." Roosevelt then agrees to a plot, led by secessionist Dr. Manuel Amador, to assist a group planning to secede from Colombia.

October 17 — Panamanian dissidents travel to Washington and agree to stage a U.S.-backed revolution. The revolution is set for November 3 at 6:00 p.m.

October 18 — A flag, constitution, and declaration of independence are created over the weekend. Panama's first flag was designed and sewn by hand in Highland Falls, New York, using fabric bought at Macy's.

Philippe Jean Bunau-Varilla, a French engineer associated with the bankrupt French–Panamanian canal construction company and not a permanent resident in Panama, is named Panama's ambassador to the United States.

A Country Is Born

Tuesday, November 3 — Precisely at 6:00 p.m., the Colombian garrison is bribed to lay down their arms. The revolution begins, the U.S.S. *Nashville* steams into Colón harbor, and the junta proclaims Panama's independence.

Friday, November 6 — By 1:00 p.m., the United States recognizes the sovereign state of Panama.

Saturday, November 7 — The new government sends an official delegation from Panama to the United States to instruct the Panamanian ambassador to the United States on provisions of the Panama Canal Treaty.

Wednesday, November 18 — At 6:40 p.m., the Panamanian ambassador signs the Panama Canal Treaty. At 11:30 p.m., the official Panamanian delegation arrives at a Washington, DC, railroad station and is met by their ambassador, who informs them that the treaty was signed just hours earlier.

The Present

1977 — The United States agrees to relinquish control of the Panama Canal Zone on December 31, 1999.

1997 — Autoridad del Canal de Panama, the canal authority that will assume control from the U.S. Panama Canal Commission, is created.

1998 — Panama gives a Chinese company the right to build new port facilities on both the Pacific and Atlantic sides, to control anchorages, to hire new pilots to guide ships through the canal, and to block all passage that interferes with the company's business.

January 1, 2000 — "The canal is ours" is the jubilant cry in Panama.

January 17, 2000 — The Pentagon sees a potential Chinese threat to the Panama Canal.

July 2002 — China pressures Panama to extend diplomatic recognition to China and drop recognition of Taiwan.

2005 — The Panama Canal is expected to reach maximum capacity by 2010. The administrative board proposes a $5 billion expansion to add a parallel set of locks in response to the threat of a competing project to build canals or "multimodal" systems across Mexico's Tehuantepec isthmus. Either expand or "run the risk of eventually becoming just a regional canal."

2010 — A project to double the capacity of the canal begins, scheduled to be completed in 2014.

This story is a good illustration of how history and geography can affect public and political attitudes in the present and far into the future. To the Panamanians and much of Latin America, the Panama Canal is but one example of the many U.S. intrusions during the early 20th century that have tainted U.S.–Latin American relations. For the United States, the geographical importance of the Panama Canal for trade (shipping between the two coasts via the canal is cut by 8,000 miles) makes control of the canal a sensitive issue, especially if that control could be potentially hostile. That a Chinese-owned company has operational control of both the Pacific and Atlantic ports and could pose an indirect threat to the Panama Canal Zone concerns the U.S. government. The recent history of U.S. conflict with China and the history of

Western domination of parts of China create in the minds of many an adversarial relationship between the two countries. Furthermore, some wonder if Panama would be reluctant to ask the United States to intervene at some future date, perhaps fearing that the Americans might stay another 98 years. Although the probability of China sabotaging the canal is slim at best, historical baggage makes one wonder what would happen should U.S. relations with China deteriorate to the point that the canal were considered to be in jeopardy.

Sources: Bernard A. Weisberger, "Panama: Made in U.S.A.," *American Heritage*, November 1989, pp. 24–25; Juanita Darling, "'The Canal Is Ours' Is Jubilant Cry in Panama," *Los Angeles Times*, January 1, 2000, p. A1; C.J. Scchexayder, "Spain–Mexico Team Outbids Panama Canal Competitors," *Engineering News-Record*, January 4, 2010, p. 11.

LO1

The importance of history and geography in understanding international markets

Here we begin the discussion of the Cultural Environment of Global Markets. *Culture* can be defined as a society's accepted basis for responding to external and internal events. To understand fully a society's actions and its points of view, you must have an appreciation for the influence of historical events and the geographical uniqueness to which a culture has had to adapt. To interpret behavior and attitudes in a particular culture or country, a marketer must have some idea of a country's history and geography.

The goal of this chapter is to introduce the reader to the impact of history and geography on the marketing process. The influence of history on behavior and attitudes and the influence of geography on markets, trade, and environmental issues are examined in particular.

Historical Perspective in Global Business

History helps define a nation's "mission," how it perceives its neighbors, how it sees its place in the world, and how it sees itself. Insights into the history of a country are important for understanding attitudes about the role of government and business, the relations between managers and the managed, the sources of management authority, and attitudes toward foreign corporations.

To understand, explain, and appreciate a people's image of itself and the attitudes and unconscious fears that are reflected in its view of foreign cultures, it is necessary to study the culture as it is now as well as to understand the culture as it was—that is, a country's history.

History and Contemporary Behavior

LO2

The effects of history on a country's culture

Most Americans know the most about European history, even though our major trading partners are now to our west and south. Circa 2008, China became a hot topic in the United States. It was back in 1776 as well. In a sense, American history really begins with China. Recall the Boston Tea Party: Our complaint then was the British tax and, more important, the British prohibition against Yankee traders dealing directly with merchants in Canton. So it is worthwhile to dwell for a few moments on a couple of prominent points in the history of the fast burgeoning market that is modern-day China. James Day Hodgson, former U.S. Labor Secretary and Ambassador to Japan, suggests that anyone doing business in another country should understand at least the encyclopedic version of the people's past as a matter

1000 First millennium ends; Y1K problem overblown—widespread fear of the end of the world proved unfounded
1000 Vikings settle Newfoundland
1004 Chinese unity crumbles with treaty between the Song and the Liao, giving the Liao full autonomy; China will remain fractured until the Mongol invasion in the 13th century (see 1206)

1025 Navy of Cholas in southern India crushes the empire of Srivijaya in modern Myanmar to protect its trade with China
1054 Italy and Egypt formalize commercial relations
1066 William the Conqueror is victorious over Harold II in the Battle of Hastings, establishing Norman rule in England and forever linking the country with the continent

1081 Venice and Byzantium conclude a commercial treaty (renewed in 1126)
1095 First of the crusades begins; Pope Urban II calls on Europe's noblemen to help the Byzantines repel the Turks; the crusaders' travel, stories, and goods acquired along the way help increase trade across Europe and with the Mediterranean and Asia; eighth major crusade

ends—Syria expels the Christians
1100 Japan begins to isolate itself from the rest of the world, not really opening up again until the mid-19th century (see 1858)
1100 China invents the mariner's compass and becomes a force in trade; widespread use of paper money also helps increase trade and prosperity

of politeness, if not persuasion.[1] As important examples we offer a few perhaps surprising glimpses of the past that continues to influence U.S.–Asia trade relations even today.

First Opium War and the Treaty of Nanjing (1839–1842).

During the early 1800s, the British taste for tea was creating a huge trade deficit with China. Silver bullion was flowing fast in an easterly direction. Of course, other goods were being traded, too. Exports from China also included sugar, silk, mother-of-pearl, paper, camphor, cassia, copper and alum, lacquer ware, rhubarb, various oils, bamboo, and porcelain. The British "barbarians" returned cotton and woolen textiles, iron, tin, lead, carnelian, diamonds, pepper, betel nuts, pearls, watches and clocks, coral and amber beads, birds' nests and shark fins, and foodstuffs such as fish and rice. But the tea-for-silver swap dominated the equation.

Then came the English East India Company's epiphany: opium. Easy to ship, high value to volume and weight ratios, and addicting to customers—what a great product! At the time, the best opium came from British India, and once the full flow began, the tea-caused trade deficit disappeared fast. The Emperor complained and issued edicts, but the opium trade burgeoned. One of the taller skyscrapers in Hong Kong today is the Jardine-Matheson Trading House.[2] Its circular windows are reminiscent of the portholes of its clipper-ship beginnings in the opium trade.

In 1836 some high-ranking Chinese officials advocated legalizing opium. The foreign suppliers boosted production and shipments in anticipation of exploding sales. Then the Emperor went the opposite direction and ordered the destruction of the inventories in Canton (now known as Guangzhou). By 1839 the trade was dead. The British responded by sinking junks in the Pearl River and blockading all Chinese ports.

The "magically accurate" British cannon pointed at Nanjing yielded negotiations there in 1842. The Chinese ceded Hong Kong and $21 million pounds to the British. Ports at Xiamen, Fuzhou, Ningbo, and Shanghai were opened to trade and settlement by foreigners. Hong Kong thus became the gateway to a xenophobic China, particularly for the past 50 years. Perhaps most important, China recognized for the first time its loss of great power status.

Ultimately the Opium War became about foreign access to Chinese trade, and the treaty of Nanjing really didn't settle the issue. A second Opium War was fought between 1857 and 1860. In that imbroglio, British and French forces combined to destroy the summer palace in Beijing. Such new humiliations yielded more freedoms for foreign traders; notably, the treaty specifically included provisions allowing Christian evangelism throughout the realm.

Taiping Rebellion (1851–1864).

One consequence of the humiliation at the hands of foreigners was a loss of confidence in the Chinese government. The resulting disorder came to a head in Guangxi, the southernmost province of the Empire. The leader of the uprising was a peasant who grew up near Guangzhou. Hong Xiuquan aspired to be a

---

[1]James Day Hodgson, Yoshihiro Sano, and John L. Graham, *Doing Business in the New Japan, Succeeding in America's Richest Foreign Market* (Latham, MD: Rowman & Littlefield, 2008).

[2]In a very interesting paper, the authors argue that choices made by Jardine's and Swire's (trading houses) in Asia today, for example, are an outgrowth of strategic choices first in evidence more than a century ago! See Geoffrey Jones and Tarun Khanna, "Bringing History (Back) into International Business," *Journal of International Business Studies* 37 (2006), pp. 453–68.

1100 Inca Empire in the Andes begins to develop, eventually encompassing about 12 million people until its destruction by the Spanish in 1553; cities specialize in certain farming and trade with others for what they don't make

1132 Corporate towns in France grant charters by Henry I to protect commerce

1189 German merchants conclude treaty with Novgorod in Russia

1200 Islam is introduced by spice traders to Southeast Asia

1200 More than 60,000 Italian merchants work and live in Constantinople

1206 Genghis Khan becomes the Great Khan, controlling most of northern China; after his death in 1227, the Khan

clan conquers much of Asia by midcentury and promotes trade and commerce, reviving the ancient Silk Road that linked Chinese and Western traders

1215 The Magna Carta, a pact between the English king and his subjects, is signed by King John, who becomes subject to the rule of law

1229 German merchants sign trade treaty with the Prince of Smolensk in Russia

1252 First gold coins issued in the West since the fall of Rome, in Florence

1269 England institutes toll roads

1270 Venetian Marco Polo and his father travel through Asia and the Middle East, becoming the first European

civil servant but failed the required Confucian teachings–based exam. When in Guangzhou for his second try at the exam, he came in contact with Protestant Western missionaries and later began to have visions of God.

After flunking the exam for a fourth time in 1843, he began to evangelize, presenting himself as Christ's brother. In the next seven years, he attracted 10,000 followers. In 1851, he was crowned by his followers as the "Heavenly King" of the "Heavenly Kingdom of Peace." Despite their adopted label, they revolted, cut off their pigtails in defiance of the ruling Manchus, and began to march north. With the fervor of the religious zealots they were, they fought their way through the capital at Nanjing and almost to Tianjing by 1855.

But then things started to unravel. Chinese opposition forces organized. Because foreigners appreciated neither Hong's interpretation of the scriptures, nor his 88 concubines, nor his attacks on Shanghai, they formed another army against him. Hong took his own life just before the final defeat and the recapture of Nanjing.

Estimates of the death toll from the Taiping Rebellion stand between 20 and 40 million people. We repeat: 20–40 million Chinese lives were lost. By contrast, "only" 2 million were killed in the 1949 Communist Revolution. The Taiping Rebellion is the single most horrific civil war in the history of the world. Surely Hong Xiuquan was insane. Other rebellions also occurred in China during this time; the Muslim one in the northwest is most notable (1862–78). However, based on these events in the mid-1800s, it is easy to see why the Chinese leadership has remained wary of foreign influences in general, and religious movements in particular, even today.[3]

History and Japan.
Trade with Japan was a hot topic in the United States in both the 1850s and the 1980s. Likewise, unless you have a historical sense of the many changes that have buffeted Japan—seven centuries under the shogun feudal system, the isolation before the arrival of Commodore Perry in 1853, the threat of domination by colonial powers, the rise of new social classes, Western influences, the humiliation of World War II, and involvement in the international community—you will have difficulty fully understanding its contemporary behavior. Why do the Japanese have such strong loyalty toward their companies? Why is the loyalty found among participants in the Japanese distribution systems so difficult for an outsider to develop? Why are decisions made by consensus? Answers to such questions can be explained in part by Japanese history (and geography).

Loyalty to family, to country, to company, and to social groups and the strong drive to cooperate, to work together for a common cause, permeate many facets of Japanese behavior and have historical roots that date back thousands of years. Historically, loyalty and service, a sense of responsibility, and respect for discipline, training, and artistry were stressed to maintain stability and order. **Confucian philosophy**, taught throughout Japan's history, emphasizes the basic virtue of loyalty "of friend to friend, of wife to husband, of child to parent, of brother to brother, but, above all, of subject to lord," that is, to country.

---

[3]N. Mark Lam and John L. Graham, *Doing Business in China Now, the World's Most Dynamic Marketplace* (New York: McGraw-Hill, 2007).

traders to establish extensive links with the region
1279 Kublai Khan unites China and creates the Yuan (Origin) dynasty; by the time he dies in 1294, he has created a unified Mongol Empire extending from China to eastern Europe
1300 The early stirrings of the Renaissance begin in Europe as people are exposed to other cultures, primarily through merchants and trade; trade fairs are held in numerous European cities

1315 A great famine hits Europe, lasting two years, more widespread and longer than any before
1348 The Plague (the Black Death) kills one-fourth to one-third of the population in Europe (25 million people) in just three years, disrupting trade as cities try to prevent the spread of the disease by restricting visitors; it likely started in Asia in the 1320s; massive inflation took hold, because goods could only be obtained

locally; serfs were in high demand and began moving to higher wage payers, forever altering Europe's labor landscape
1358 German Hanseatic League officially forms by the Hansa companies of merchants for trade and mutual protection, eventually encompassing more than 70 cities and lasting nearly 300 years
1375 Timur Lang the Turk conquers lands from Moscow to Delhi

1381 English rioters kill foreign Flemish traders as part of the 100,000-strong peasant rebellion against Richard II, which was led by Wat Tyler in a failed attempt to throw off the yoke of feudalism
1392 England prohibits foreigners from retailing goods in the country
1400 Koreans develop movable-type printing (see 1450)

A fundamental premise of Japanese ideology reflects the importance of cooperation for the collective good. Japanese achieve consensus by agreeing that all will unite against outside pressures that threaten the collective good. A historical perspective gives the foreigner in Japan a basis on which to begin developing cultural sensitivity and a better understanding of contemporary Japanese behavior.

History Is Subjective

LO3

How culture interprets events through its own eyes

History is important in understanding why a country behaves as it does, but history from whose viewpoint? Historical events always are viewed from one's own biases and self-reference criteria (SRC), and thus, what is recorded by one historian may not be what another records, especially if the historians are from different cultures. Historians traditionally try to be objective, but few can help filtering events through their own cultural biases.[4]

Our perspective not only influences our view of history but also subtly influences our view of many other matters. For example, maps of the world sold in the United States generally show the United States at the center, whereas maps in Britain show Britain at the center, and so on for other nations.

A crucial element in understanding any nation's business and political culture is the subjective perception of its history. Why do Mexicans have a love–hate relationship with the United States? Why were Mexicans required to have majority ownership in most foreign investments until recently? Why did dictator General Porfírio Díaz lament, "Poor Mexico, so far from God, so near the United States"? Why? Because Mexicans see the United States as a threat to their political, economic, and cultural sovereignty.

Most citizens of the United States are mystified by such feelings. After all, the United States has always been Mexico's good neighbor. Most would agree with President John F. Kennedy's proclamation during a visit to Mexico that "Geography has made us neighbors, tradition has made us friends." North Americans may be surprised to learn that most Mexicans "felt it more accurate to say 'Geography has made us closer, tradition has made us far apart.'"[5]

Citizens of the United States feel they have been good neighbors. They see the Monroe Doctrine as protection for Latin America from European colonization and the intervention of Europe in the governments of the Western Hemisphere. Latin Americans, in contrast, tend to see the Monroe Doctrine as an offensive expression of U.S. influence in Latin America. To put it another way, "Europe keep your hands off—Latin America is only for the United States," an attitude perhaps typified by former U.S. President Ulysses S. Grant, who, in a speech in Mexico in 1880, described Mexico as a "magnificent mine" that lay waiting south of the border for North American interests.

United States Marines sing with pride of their exploits "from the halls of Montezuma to the shores of Tripoli." To the Mexican, the exploit to which the "halls of Montezuma"

---

[4]An example of such biases is the differing perceptions of Turkey by European Union members in deciding on Turkey's membership in the EU. See "Which Turkey?" *The Economist*, March 17, 2005.

[5]For an insightful review of some of the issues that have affected relations between the United States and Mexico, see John Skirius, "Railroad, Oil and Other Foreign Interest in the Mexican Revolution, 1911–1914," *Journal of Latin American Studies*, February 2003, p. 25.

1404   Chinese prohibit private trading in foreign countries, but foreign ships may trade in China with official permission
1415   Chinese begin significant trading with Africa through government expeditions—some believe they sailed to North America as well in 1421
1425   Hanseatic city of Brugge becomes the first Atlantic seaport to be a major trading center

1427   Aztec Empire is created by Itzcotl; it will encompass about 6 million people before its destruction in 1519
1430   Portuguese Prince Henry the Navigator explores west African coast to promote trade
1441   Mayan Empire collapses as the city of Mayapán is destroyed in a revolt
1450   Renaissance takes hold in Florence, its traditional birthplace

1450   Gutenberg Bible is first book printed with movable type; the ability to mass produce books creates an information revolution
1453   Byzantine Empire is destroyed as Muhammad II sacks Constantinople (renaming it Istanbul)
1464   French royal mail service established by Louis XI
1470   Early trademark piracy committed by Persians

who copy mass-produced Chinese porcelain to capitalize on its popularity in foreign countries
1479   Under the Treaty of Constantinople, in exchange for trading rights in the Black Sea, Venice agrees to pay tribute to the Ottoman Empire
1482   English organize a postal system that features fresh relays of horses every 20 miles

The Monumento de Los Niños Heroes honors six young cadets who, during the Mexican–American War of 1847, chose death over surrender. The Mexican–American War is important in Mexican history and helps explain, in part, Mexico's love–hate relationship with the United States. *(© Dave G. Houser/Corbis)*

refers is remembered as U.S. troops marching all the way to the center of Mexico City and extracting as tribute 890,000 square miles that became Arizona, California, New Mexico, and Texas (see Exhibit 3.1). A prominent monument at the entrance of Chapultepec Park recognizes *Los Niños Heroes* (the boy heroes), who resisted U.S. troops, wrapped themselves in Mexican flags, and jumped to their deaths rather than surrender. Mexicans recount the heroism of *Los Niños Heroes*[6] and the loss of Mexican territory to the United States every September 13, when the president of Mexico, the cabinet, and the diplomatic corps assemble at the Mexico City fortress to recall the defeat that led to the "*despojo territorial*" (territorial plunder).

The Mexican Revolution, which overthrew the dictator Díaz and launched the modern Mexican state, is particularly remembered for the expulsion of foreigners—most notably North American businessmen who were the most visible of the wealthy and influential entrepreneurs in Mexico.

---

[6]When the United Nations recommended that all countries set aside a single day each year to honor children, Mexico designated April 30 as "Dia de Los Niños." Interestingly, this holiday often coincides with Saint Patrick's Day celebrations, which include recognition of the San Patricios, the Irish-American battalion that fought with the Mexicans in the Mexican–American War. See Carol Sowers, "El Dia de Los Niños Adds International Touch to Celebration," *Arizona Republic*, April 29, 2005.

1488 Bartolomeu Dias sails around the coast of Africa; this, along with the voyages of Christopher Columbus, ushers in the era of sea travel

1492 Christopher Columbus "discovers" the New World

1494 Portugal and Spain divide the unexplored world between them with the Treaty of Tordesillas

1500 Rise of mercantilism, the accumulation of wealth by the state to increase power, in western Europe; states without gold or silver mines try to control trade to maintain a surplus and accumulate gold and silver; Englishman Thomas Mun was one of the great proponents in 1600, who realized that the overall balance of trade was the important factor, not whether each individual trade resulted in a surplus

1500 Slave trade becomes a major component of commerce

1504 Regular postal service established among Vienna, Brussels, and Madrid

1520 First chocolate brought from Mexico to Spain

1521 Mexico is conquered by Hernán Cortés after Aztec ruler Montezuma is accidentally killed

1522 Magellan's expedition completes its three-year sail around the world; it is the first successful circumnavigation

1531 Antwerp stock exchange is the first exchange to move into its own building, signifying its importance in financing commercial enterprises throughout Europe and the rising importance of private trade and commerce; Antwerp emerges as a trading capital

1532 Brazil is colonized by the Portuguese

1534 English break from the Catholic Church, ending its dominance of politics and trade throughout Europe, as Henry VIII creates the Church of England

1553 South American Incan Empire ends with conquest by Spanish; the Incas had created an extensive area of trade, complete with an infrastructure of roads and canals

Exhibit 3.1

Territorial Expansion of
United States from 1783

The United States expanded
westward to the Pacific through
a series of financial deals,
negotiated settlements, and
forcible annexations. The
acquisition of territory from
Mexico began with the Battle
of San Jacinto in 1836, when
Texas staged a successful revolt
against the rule of Mexico and
became The Republic of Texas—
later to join the Union in 1845.
The Mexican War (1846–1848)
resulted in Mexico ceding
California and a large part of the
West to the United States.

Source: From *Oxford Atlas of the
World*, 10th ed., 2002. Reprinted with
permission of Philip Maps.

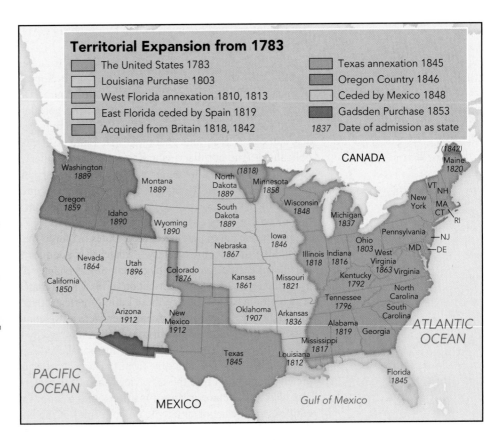

Territorial Expansion from 1783

- The United States 1783
- Louisiana Purchase 1803
- West Florida annexation 1810, 1813
- East Florida ceded by Spain 1819
- Acquired from Britain 1818, 1842
- Texas annexation 1845
- Oregon Country 1846
- Ceded by Mexico 1848
- Gadsden Purchase 1853
- *1837* Date of admission as state

Manifest Destiny and the Monroe Doctrine

Manifest Destiny and the Monroe Doctrine were accepted as the basis for U.S. foreign policy during much of the 19th and 20th centuries.[7] Manifest Destiny, in its broadest interpretation, meant that Americans were a chosen people ordained by God to create a model society. More specifically, it referred to the territorial expansion of the United States from the Atlantic to the Pacific. The idea of Manifest Destiny was used to justify the U.S. annexation of Texas, Oregon, New Mexico, and California and, later, U.S. involvement in Cuba, Alaska, Hawaii, and the Philippines. Exhibit 3.1 illustrates when and by what means the present United States was acquired.

The **Monroe Doctrine**, a cornerstone of early U.S. foreign policy, was enunciated by President James Monroe in a public statement proclaiming three basic dicta: no further European colonization in the New World, abstention of the United States from European

[7]Some say even into the 21st century. See "Manifest Destiny Warmed Up?" *The Economist*, August 14, 2003. Of course, others disagree. See Joseph Contreras, "Roll Over Monroe: The Influence the United States Once Claimed as a Divine Right in Latin America is Slipping away Fast," *Newsweek International*, December 10, 2007.

1555 Tobacco trade begins after its introduction to Europe by Spanish and Portuguese traders

1557 Spanish crown suffers first of numerous bankruptcies, discouraging cross-border lending

1561 Via Dutch traders, tulips come to Europe from Near East for first time

1564 William Shakespeare is born; many of his plays are stories of merchant traders

1567 Typhoid fever, imported from Europe, kills two million Indians in South America

1588 Spanish Armada defeated by British, heralding Britain's emergence as the world's greatest naval power; this power will enable Britain to colonize many regions of the globe and lead to its becoming the world's commercially dominant power for the next 300 years

1596 First flush toilet is developed for Britain's Queen Elizabeth I

1597 Holy Roman Empire expels English merchants in retaliation for English treatment of Hanseatic League

1600 Potatoes are brought from South America to Europe, where they quickly spread to the rest of world and become a staple of agricultural production

1600 Japan begins trading silver for foreign goods

1600 Britain's Queen Elizabeth I grants charter to the East India Company, which will dominate trade with the East until its demise in 1857

1601 France makes postal agreements with neighboring states

1602 Dutch charter their own East India Company, which will dominate the South Asian coffee and spice trade

1607 British colony of Jamestown built

political affairs, and nonintervention by European governments in the governments of the Western Hemisphere.

After 1870, interpretation of the Monroe Doctrine became increasingly broad. In 1881, its principles were evoked in discussing the development of a canal across the Isthmus of Panama. Theodore Roosevelt applied the Monroe Doctrine with an extension that became known as the **Roosevelt Corollary**. The corollary stated that not only would the United States prohibit non-American intervention in Latin American affairs, but it would also police the area and guarantee that Latin American nations met their international obligations. The corollary sanctioning American intervention was applied in 1905 when Roosevelt forced the Dominican Republic to accept the appointment of an American economic adviser, who quickly became the financial director of the small state. It was also used in the acquisition of the Panama Canal Zone from Colombia in 1903 and the formation of a provisional government in Cuba in 1906.

The manner in which the United States acquired the land for the Panama Canal Zone typifies the Roosevelt Corollary—whatever is good for the United States is justifiable. As the Global Perspective at the beginning of this chapter illustrates, the creation of the country of Panama was a total fabrication of the United States.[8]

According to U.S. history, these Latin American adventures were a justifiable part of our foreign policy; to Latin Americans, they were unwelcome intrusions in Latin American affairs. This perspective has been constantly reinforced by U.S. intervention in Latin America since 1945 (see Exhibit 3.2). The way historical events are recorded and interpreted in one culture can differ substantially from the way those same events are recorded and interpreted in another. From the U.S. view, each of the interventions illustrated in Exhibit 3.2 was justified. A comparison of histories goes a long way in explaining the differences in outlooks and behavior of people on both sides of the border. Many Mexicans believe that their "good neighbor" to the north is not reluctant to throw its weight around when it wants something. Suspicions that self-interest is the primary motivation for good relations with Mexico abound.[9]

History viewed from a Latin American perspective explains how a national leader, under adverse economic conditions, can point a finger at the United States or a U.S. multinational corporation and evoke a special emotional, popular reaction to divert attention away from the government in power. As a case in point, after the U.S. House of Representatives voted to censure Mexico for drug corruption, President Ernesto Zedillo came under pressure to

LO4

How long-past U.S. international policies still affect customer attitudes abroad

---

[8]For an interesting discussion of how past U.S. foreign interventions affect attitudes about U.S. involvement in Iraq, see "Anti-Americanism: The View from Abroad," *The Economist*, February 17, 2005.

[9]Many Latin Americans' elation with the Bush administration's first-term pronouncements that the United States was looking south "not as an afterthought but as a fundamental commitment"—that a region "too often separated by history or rivalry and resentment" should prepare itself for the start of a "new era" of cooperation—soon became disappointment as the war on terror turned U.S. attention away from Latin America. Marcela Sanchez, "Bush, Looking Every Which Way but South," *Washington Post*, January 6, 2005.

1609 Dutch begin fur trade through Manhattan
1611 Japan gives Dutch limited permission to trade
1612 British East India Company builds its first factory in India
1620 *Mayflower* sails for the New World
1620 Father of the Scientific Revolution, Francis Bacon, publishes *Novum Organum*, promoting inductive reasoning

through experimentation and observation
1625 Dutch jurist Hugo Grotius, sometimes called the father of international law, publishes *On the Laws of War and Peace*
1636 Harvard University founded
1637 Dutch "tulip mania" results in history's first boom-bust market crash
1651 English pass first of so-called Navigation Acts to restrict Dutch trade by forcing

colonies to trade only with English ships
1654 Spain and Germany develop hereditary land rights, a concept that will help lead to the creation of great wealth in single families and thus to the development of private commercial empires
1687 Apple falling on Newton's head leads to his publication of the law of gravity
1694 The Bank of England is established; it offers loans to

private individuals at 8 percent interest
1698 First steam engine is invented
1719 French consolidate their trade in Asia into one company, the French East India Company; rival British East India Company maintains its grip on the region's trade, however, and French revert to individual company trading 60 years later

Exhibit 3.2
U.S. Intervention in Latin America Since 1945

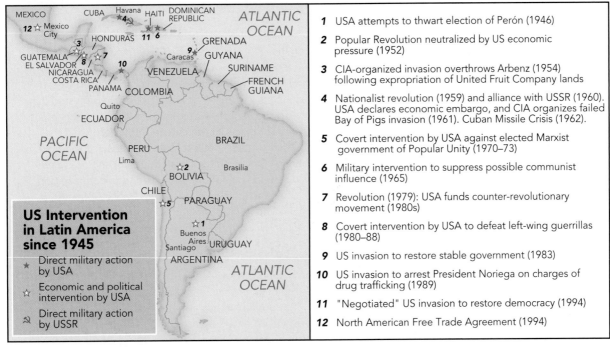

1   USA attempts to thwart election of Perón (1946)

2   Popular Revolution neutralized by US economic pressure (1952)

3   CIA-organized invasion overthrows Arbenz (1954) following expropriation of United Fruit Company lands

4   Nationalist revolution (1959) and alliance with USSR (1960). USA declares economic embargo, and CIA organizes failed Bay of Pigs invasion (1961). Cuban Missile Crisis (1962).

5   Covert intervention by USA against elected Marxist government of Popular Unity (1970–73)

6   Military intervention to suppress possible communist influence (1965)

7   Revolution (1979): USA funds counter-revolutionary movement (1980s)

8   Covert intervention by USA to defeat left-wing guerrillas (1980–88)

9   US invasion to restore stable government (1983)

10 US invasion to arrest President Noriega on charges of drug trafficking (1989)

11 "Negotiated" US invasion to restore democracy (1994)

12 North American Free Trade Agreement (1994)

US Intervention in Latin America since 1945

★   Direct military action by USA

☆   Economic and political intervention by USA

☭   Direct military action by USSR

Source: From *Oxford Atlas of the World*, 10th ed., 2002. Reprinted with permission of Philips Maps.

take a hard stand with Washington. He used the anniversary of Mexico's 1938 expropriation of the oil industry from foreign companies to launch a strong nationalist attack. He praised the state oil monopoly Pemex as a "symbol of our historical struggles for sovereignty." Union members cheered him on, waving a huge banner that read: "In 1938 Mexico was 'decertified' because it expropriated its oil and it won—today we were decertified for defending our dignity and sovereignty." Apparently Venezuelan President Hugo Chavez was listening, based on his more recent nationalization of foreign oil company assets in the Orinoco River Basin[10] and his recent renaming of the country the Bolivarian Republic of Venezuela.[11]

---

[10]"Venezuela: Spirit of the Monroe Doctrine," *Washington Times*, June 10, 2007, p. B5; Brian Ellsworth, "Oil at $100, Venezuela's Chavez Faces Industry Slump," *Reuters*, January 4, 2008.

[11]"Venezuela: Chavez's New Currency Targets Inflation," *Tulsa World*, January 1, 2008, p. A6.

1725   Rise of Physiocrats, followers of the economic philosopher François Quesnay, who believed that production, not trade, created wealth and that natural law should rule, which meant producers should be able to exchange goods freely; movement influenced Adam Smith's ideas promoting free trade

1740   Maria Theresa becomes empress of the Holy Roman Empire (until 1780); she ends serfdom and strengthens the power of the state

1748   First modern, scientifically drawn map, the Carte Géométrique de la France, comprising 182 sheets, was authorized and subsequently drawn by the French Academy; Louis XV proclaimed that the new map, with more accurate data, lost more territory than his wars of conquest had gained

1750   Benjamin Franklin shows that lightning is a form of electricity by conducting it through the wet string of a kite

1750   Industrial Revolution begins and takes off with the manufacture, in 1780, of the steam engine to drive machines—increased productivity and consumption follow (as do poor working conditions and increased hardships for workers)

1760   Chinese begin strict regulation of foreign trade to last nearly a century when they permit Europeans to do business only in a small area outside Canton and only with appointed Chinese traders

1764   British victories in India begin Britain's dominance of India, Eastern trade, and trade routes

1764   British begin numbering houses, making mail delivery more efficient and providing the means for the development of direct mail merchants centuries later

CROSSING BORDERS 3.1 | Microsoft Adapts Encarta to "Local History"

Adapting to the local culture is an important aspect of strategy for many products. Understanding a country's history helps achieve that goal. Microsoft has nine different editions reflecting local "history" to be sure that its Encarta multimedia encyclopedia on CD-ROM does not contain cultural blunders. As a consequence, it often reflects different and sometimes contradictory understandings of the same historical events. For example, who invented the telephone? In the U.S., U.K., and German editions, it is Alexander Graham Bell, but ask the question in the Italian edition, and your answer is Antonio Meucci, an Italian-American candle maker whom Italians believe beat Bell by five years. For electric light bulbs, it is Thomas Alva Edison in the United States, but in the United Kingdom, it is the British inventor Joseph Swan. Other historical events reflect local perceptions. The nationalization of the Suez Canal, for example, in the U.S. edition is a decisive intervention by superpowers. In the French and U.K. editions, it is summed up as a "humiliating reversal" for Britain and France—a phrase that does not appear in the U.S. edition.

Although Microsoft is on the mark by adapting these events to their local historical context, it has, on occasion, missed the boat on geography. South Korean ire was raised when the South Korean island of Ullung-do was placed within Japan's borders and when the Chon-Ji Lake, where the first Korean is said to have descended from heaven, was located in China. And finally, an embarrassed Microsoft apologized to the people of Thailand for referring to Bangkok as a commercial sex center, assuring the women's activists group that protested that the revised version would "include all the great content that best reflects its rich culture and history."

Microsoft also bows to political pressure. The government of Turkey stopped distribution of an Encarta edition with the name Kurdistan used to denote a region of southeastern Turkey on a map. Hence Microsoft removed the name Kurdistan from the map. Governments frequently lobby the company to show their preferred boundaries on maps. When the border between Chile and Argentina in the southern Andes was in dispute, both countries lobbied for their preferred boundary, and the solution both countries agreed to was—no line.

But our fun stories about changes to Encarta must come to an end, because the online encyclopedia has itself become a topic of history. Microsoft folded the entire Encarta operation without explanation in 2009; most analysts agree Wikipedia simply did it in.

Sources: Kevin J. Delaney, "Microsoft's Encarta Has Different Facts for Different Folks," *The Wall Street Journal*, June 25, 1999, p. A1; "Why You Won't Find Kurdistan on a Microsoft Map of Turkey," *Geographical*, November 1, 2004; Nick Winfield, "Microsoft to Shut Encarta as Free Sites Alter Market," *The Wall Street Journal*, March 31, 2009, p. B3.

These leaders might be cheered for **expropriation** or confiscation of foreign investments, even though the investments were making important contributions to their economies. To understand a country's attitudes, prejudices, and fears, it is necessary to look beyond the surface of current events to the inner subtleties of the country's entire past for clues. Three comments by Mexicans best summarize this section:

> History is taught one way in Mexico and another way in the United States—the United States robbed us but we are portrayed in U.S. textbooks as bandits who invaded Texas.

> We may not like gringos for historical reasons, but today the world is dividing into commercial blocks, and we are handcuffed to each other for better or worse.

> We always have been and we continue to be a colony of the United States.

1773 Boston Tea Party symbolizes start of American Revolution; impetus comes from American merchants trying to take control of distribution of goods that were being controlled exclusively by Britain
1776 American Declaration of Independence proclaims the colonies' rights to determine their own destiny, particularly their own economic destiny
1776 Theory of modern capitalism and free trade expressed by Adam Smith in *The Wealth of Nations*; he theorized that countries would only produce and export goods that they were able to produce more cheaply than could trading partners; he demonstrates that mercantilists were wrong: It is not gold or silver that will enhance the state, but the *material* that can be purchased with it
1783 Treaty of Paris officially ends the American Revolution following British surrender to American troops at Yorktown in 1781
1787 U.S. Constitution approved; it becomes a model document for constitutions for at least the next two centuries; written constitutions will help stabilize many countries and encourage foreign investment and trade with them
1789 French Revolution begins; it will alter the power structure in Europe and help lead to the introduction of laws protecting the individual and to limited democracy in the region

Geography and Global Markets

Geography, the study of Earth's surface, climate, continents, countries, peoples, industries, and resources, is an element of the uncontrollable environment that confronts every marketer but that receives scant attention.[12] The tendency is to study the aspects of geography as isolated entities rather than as important causal agents of the marketing environment. Geography is much more than memorizing countries, capitals, and rivers. It also includes an understanding of how a society's culture and economy are affected as a nation struggles to supply its people's needs within the limits imposed by its physical makeup. Thus, the study of geography is important in the evaluation of markets and their environment.

LO5

The effect of geographic diversity on economic profiles of a country

This section discusses the important geographic characteristics a marketer needs to consider when assessing the environmental aspects of marketing. Examining the world as a whole provides the reader with a broad view of world markets and an awareness of the effects of geographic diversity on the economic profiles of various nations. Climate and topography are examined as facets of the broader and more important elements of geography. A brief look at Earth's resources and population—the building blocks of world markets—completes the presentation on geography and global markets.

Climate and Topography

Altitude, humidity, and temperature extremes are climatic features that affect the uses and functions of products and equipment. Products that perform well in temperate zones may deteriorate rapidly or require special cooling or lubrication to function adequately in tropical zones. Manufacturers have found that construction equipment used in the United States requires extensive modifications to cope with the intense heat and dust of the Sahara Desert. A Taiwanese company sent a shipment of drinking glasses to a buyer in the Middle East. The glasses were packed in wooden crates with hay used as dunnage to prevent breakage. The glasses arrived in shards. Why? When the crates moved to the warmer, less humid climate of the Middle East, the moisture content of the hay dropped significantly and shriveled to a point that it offered no protection.

LO6

Why marketers need to be responsive to the geography of a country

Within even a single national market, climate can be sufficiently diverse to require major adjustments. In Ghana, a product adaptable to the entire market must operate effectively in extreme desert heat and low humidity and in tropical rainforests with consistently high humidity. Bosch-Siemens washing machines designed for European countries require spin cycles to range from a minimum spin cycle of 500 rpm to a maximum of 1,600 rpm: Because the sun does not shine regularly in Germany or in Scandinavia, washing machines must have a 1,600 rpm spin cycle because users do not have the luxury of hanging them out to dry. In Italy and Spain, however, clothes can be damp, because the abundant sunshine is sufficient to justify a spin cycle speed of 500 rpm.

Different seasons between the northern and southern hemispheres also affect global strategies. JCPenney had planned to open five stores in Chile as part of its expansion into countries below the equator. It wanted to capitalize on its vast bulk buying might for its North American, Mexican, and Brazilian stores to provide low prices for its expansion into South America. After opening its first store in Chile, the company realized that the plan was

---

[12]The importance of geography in understanding global challenges that exist today is discussed in Harm J. DeBlij, *Why Geography Matters* (New York: Oxford University Press, 2005).

1792 Gas lighting introduced; within three decades, most major European and U.S. cities will use gas lights

1804 Steam locomotive introduced; it will become the dominant form of transport of goods and people until the 20th century, when trucks and airplanes become commercially viable

1804 Napoleon crowns himself emperor, overthrowing the French revolutionary government, and tries to conquer Europe (after already occupying Egypt as a means of cutting off British trade with the East), the failure of which results in the redrawing of national boundaries in Europe and Latin America

1807 Robert Fulton's steamboat is the first to usher in a new age of transport when his *Clermont* sails from New York to Albany

1807 French Napoleonic Code issued and eventually becomes a model of civil law adopted by many nations around the world

1807 U.S. President Thomas Jefferson bans trade with Europe in an effort to convince warring British and French ships to leave neutral U.S. trading ships alone

1810 Frenchman Nicolas Appert successfully cans food and prevents spoilage

CROSSING BORDERS 3.2

Innovation and the Water Shortage, from Fog to Kid Power

When you live in Chungungo, Chile, one of the country's most arid regions with no nearby source of water, you drink fog. Of course! Thanks to a legend and resourceful Canadian and Chilean scientists, Chungungo now has its own supply of drinkable water after a 20-year drought. Before this new source of water, Chungungo depended on water trucks that came twice a week.

Chungungo has always been an arid area, and legend has it that the region's original inhabitants used to worship trees. They considered them sacred because a permanent flow of water sprang from the treetops, producing a constant interior rain. The legend was right—the trees produced rain! Thick fog forms along the coast. As it moves inland and is forced to rise against the hills, it changes into tiny raindrops, which are in turn retained by the tree leaves, producing the constant source of rain. Scientists set out to take advantage of this natural phenomenon.

The nearby ancient eucalyptus forest of El Tofo Hill provided the clue that scientists needed to create an ingenious water-supply system. To duplicate the water-bearing effect of the trees, they installed 86 "fog catchers" on the top of the hill—huge nets supported by 12-foot eucalyptus pillars, with water containers at their base. About 1,900 gallons of water are collected each day and then piped into town. This small-scale system is cheap (about one-fifth as expensive as having water trucked in), clean, and provides the local people with a steady supply of drinking water.

In sub-Saharan Africa, inventive folks have come up with a new way to bring water up from wells. A life-changing and life-saving invention—the PlayPump water system—provides easy access to clean drinking water, brings joy to children, and leads to improvements in health, education, gender equality, and economic development in more than 1,000 rural villages in South Africa, Swaziland, Mozambique, and Zambia. The PlayPump systems are innovative, sustainable, patented water pumps powered by children at play. Installed near schools, the PlayPump system doubles as a water pump and a merry-go-round. The PlayPump system also provides one of the only ways to reach rural and peri-urban communities with potentially life-saving public health messages. Please see the accompanying pictures of a new solution to one of humankind's oldest problems.

Sources: "Drinking Fog," *World Press Review*; "Silver Lining," *The Economist*, February 5, 2000, p. 75; "UNESCO Water Portal Weekly Update No. 89: Fog," April 15, 2005, http://www.unesco.org/water/news/newsletter/89.shtml; http://www.playpumps.org, 2008; Aliah D. Wright, "Dive into Clean Water," *HRMagazine* 54, no. 6 (2009), p. 4.

---

not going to work—when it was buying winter merchandise in North America, it needed summer merchandise in South America. The company quickly sold its one store in Chile; its expansion into South America was limited to Brazil.[13]

Mountains, oceans, seas, jungles, and other geographical features can pose serious impediments to economic growth and trade. For example, mountain ranges cover South America's west coast for 4,500 miles, with an average height of 13,000 feet and a width of 300 to 400 miles. This natural, formidable barrier has precluded the establishment of commercial routes between the Pacific and Atlantic coasts. South America's natural barriers inhibit both national and regional growth, trade, and communication. Geographic hurdles have a direct effect on a country's economy, markets, and the related activities of

---

[13]Miriam Jordan, "Penney Blends Two Business Cultures," *The Wall Street Journal*, April 5, 2001.

1810   Following Napoleon's invasion of Spain and Portugal, Simón Bolivar begins wars of independence for Spanish colonies in Latin America, leading to new governments in Bolivia, Columbia, Ecuador, Peru, and Venezuela
1814   First practical steam locomotive is built by George Stephenson in England, leading to the birth of railroad transportation

in 1825 with the first train carrying 450 passengers at 15 miles per hour
1815   Napoleon defeated at Battle of Waterloo and gives up throne days later
1815   British build roads of crushed stone, greatly improving the quality and speed of road travel
1817   David Ricardo publishes *Principles of Political Economy and Taxation*, in which he

proposes modern trade theory: Comparative advantage drives trade; countries will produce and export goods for which they have a *comparative* advantage as opposed to Adam Smith's *absolute* advantage (see 1776)
1821   Britain is first to adopt gold standard to back the value of its currency
1823   U.S. President James Monroe promulgates the doctrine bearing his name that

declares the Americas closed to colonization in an attempt to assert U.S. influence over the region
1837   Reign of Britain's Queen Victoria begins; she oversees the growth of the British Empire and Britain's emergence as an industrial power (she dies in 1901)
1837   Electronic telegraph begins wide commercial use, transmitting information, including production orders, swiftly

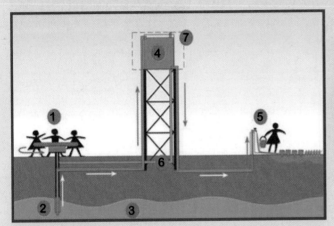

While children have fun spinning on the PlayPump merry-go-round, (1) clean water is pumped (2) from underground (3) into a 2,500-liter tank, (4) standing seven meters above the ground. A simple tap (5) makes it easy for adults and children to draw water. Excess water is diverted from the storage tank back down into the base hole (6). The water storage tank (7) provides rare opportunities to advertise to outlying communities. All four sides of the tank are leased as billboards, with two sides for consumer advertising and the other two sides for health and educational messages. The revenue generated from this unique model pays for pump maintenance. Capable of producing up to 1,400 liters of water per hour at 16 rpm from a depth of 40 meters, it is effective up to a depth of 100 meters. See http://www. playpumps.org. *(right: © Frimmel Smith/PlayPump)*

communication and distribution in China, Russia, India, and Canada as well. As countries seek economic opportunities and the challenges of the global marketplace, they invest in infrastructure to overcome such barriers. Once seen as natural protection from potentially hostile neighbors, physical barriers that exist within Europe are now seen as impediments to efficient trade in an integrated economic union.

For decades the British resisted a tunnel under the English Channel—they did not trust the French or any other European country and saw the channel as protection. But when they became members of the European Union, economic reality meant the channel tunnel had to be built to facilitate trade with other EU members. Now you can take a bullet train through the Chunnel, but even a decade after it opened, its finances are still a bit shaky,[14] and recently, undocumented workers have tried to walk the underwater route to reach England.[15]

---

[14]Robert Lea, "Chunnel Rail Link Firm Heads for a Multi-Billion Break-Up," *Evening Standard*, November 1, 2007, p. 28.
[15]"Illegals in the Chunnel," *Daily Express*, January 4, 2008, p. 39.

1839 Process for recording negative images on paper is introduced in England, the precursor to modern film technology
1841 Briton David Livingstone begins 30 years of exploring in Africa
1842 Hong Kong ceded to Britain with the Treaty of Nanjing following the Opium War; the city will become a financial and trading center for Asia

1844 Chinese open five ports to U.S. ships
1847 First government-backed postage stamps issued by United States, leading to more certain and efficient communication by post
1848 John Stuart Mill publishes *Principles of Political Economy*, completing the modern theory of trade by stating that gains

from trade are reflected in the strength of the *reciprocal* demand for imports and exports and that gains would come from better terms of trade (see 1817)
1848 The Communist Manifesto, by Germans Karl Marx and Friedrich Engels, is issued; it will become the basis for the communist movements of the 20th century

1851 First international world's fair held in London, showcasing new technology
1856 Declaration of Paris recognizes the principle of free movement for trade, even in wartime—blockades could only extend along the enemy's coast; it also establishes the practice of allowing the accession to treaties of nations other than the original signatories

This advertisement provides the only time we have seen a human vomiting to market a product. The product advertised treats altitude sickness. The billboard appears in the Lima, Peru, airport, targeting tourists traveling from sea level to Cuzco and Machu Picchu (pictured in the scenic background). Cuzco, the old Inca capital, rises more than 11,000 feet in altitude, and many foreign tourists visiting there suffer this particular sort of *tourista*.

From the days of Hannibal, the Alps have served as an important physical barrier and provided European countries protection from one another. But with the EU expansion, the Alps became a major impediment to trade. Truck traffic between southern Germany and northern Italy, which choked highways through some of Switzerland's most treacherous mountain roads and pristine nature areas, was not only burdensome for all travelers but becoming economically unacceptable. The solution, the 21-mile Loetschberg Tunnel, which opened in 2007, burrows under the Alps and trims the time trains need to cross between Germany and Italy from a three-and-a-half-hour trip to less than two hours. By 2014, the 36-mile Gotthard Tunnel will provide additional rail coverage for the area and be the world's longest rail tunnel.

Geography, Nature, and Economic Growth

Always on the slim margin between subsistence and disaster, less-privileged countries suffer disproportionately from natural and human-assisted catastrophes.[16] The Haitian earthquake disaster of 2010 is perhaps the prominent example. Climate and topography coupled with civil wars, poor environmental policies, and natural disasters push these countries further into economic stagnation. Without irrigation and water management, droughts, floods, and soil erosion afflict them, often leading to creeping deserts that reduce the long-term fertility of the land.[17] Population increases, deforestation, and overgrazing intensify the impact of

---

[16]"Asia's Tsunami: Helping the Survivors," *The Economist*, January 5, 2005.

[17]See Map 2, "Global Climate," in the World Maps section for a view of the diversity of the world's climate. The climatic phenomenon of El Niño wreaks havoc with weather patterns and is linked to crop failures, famine, forest fires, dust and sand storms, and other disasters associated with either an overabundance or a lack of rain.

1857 Russia and France sign trade treaty
1858 Ansei Commercial Treaties with Japan open the formerly closed country to trade with the West (treaties follow "opening" of Japan to the West by American Matthew Perry in 1854)
1860 The Cobden Treaty aims to create free trade by reducing or eliminating tariffs between Britain and France; also

leads to most-favored-nation status in bilateral agreements and eventually to multilateral agreements
1860 Passports are introduced in the United States to regulate foreign travel
1866 The principle of the electric dynamo is found by German Werner Siemens, who will produce the first electric power transmission system

1866 The trans-Atlantic cable is completed, allowing nearly instant (telegraphic) communication between the United States and Europe
1869 Suez Canal completed after 11 years of construction; the canal significantly cuts the time for travel between Europe and Asia, shortening, for example, the trip between Britain and India by 4,000 miles

1869 First U.S. transcontinental rail route is completed, heralding a boon for commerce; first commercially viable typewriter patented; until computer word processing becomes common more than a century later, the typewriter enables anyone to produce documents quickly and legibly
1873 United States adopts the gold standard to fix the international value of the dollar

drought and lead to malnutrition and ill health, further undermining these countries' abilities to solve their problems. Cyclones cannot be prevented, nor can inadequate rainfall, but means to control their effects are available. Unfortunately, each disaster seems to push developing countries further away from effective solutions. Countries that suffer the most from major calamities are among the poorest in the world.[18] Many have neither the capital nor the technical ability to minimize the effects of natural phenomena; they are at the mercy of nature.

As countries prosper, natural barriers are overcome. Tunnels and canals are dug and bridges and dams are built in an effort to control or to adapt to climate, topography, and the recurring extremes of nature. Humankind has been reasonably successful in overcoming or minimizing the effects of geographical barriers and natural disasters, but as they do so, they must contend with problems of their own making. The construction of dams is a good example of how an attempt to harness nature for good has a bad side. Developing countries consider dams a cost-effective solution to a host of problems. Dams create electricity, help control floods, provide water for irrigation during dry periods, and can be a rich source of fish. However, there are side effects; dams displace people (the Three Gorges Dam in China will displace 1.3 million people[19] while attracting tourists[20]), and silt that ultimately clogs the reservoir is no longer carried downstream to replenish the soil and add nutrients. Similarly, the Narmada Valley Dam Project in India will provide electricity, flood control, and irrigation, but it has already displaced tens of thousands of people, and as the benefits are measured against social and environmental costs, questions of its efficacy are being raised. In short, the need for gigantic projects such as these must be measured against their social and environmental costs.

As the global rush toward industrialization and economic growth accelerates, environmental issues become more apparent. Disruption of ecosystems, relocation of people, inadequate hazardous waste management, and industrial pollution are problems that must be addressed by the industrialized world and those seeking economic development.[21] The problems are mostly byproducts of processes that have contributed significantly to economic development and improved lifestyles. During the last part of the 20th century, governments and industry expended considerable effort to develop better ways to control nature and to allow industry to grow while protecting the environment.[22]

Social Responsibility and Environmental Management

Nations, companies, and people reached a consensus during the close of the last decade: Environmental protection is not an optional extra; it is an essential part of the complex process of doing business. Many view the problem as a global issue rather than a national issue and as one that poses common threats to humankind and thus cannot be addressed by nations in isolation. Of special concern to governments and businesses are ways to stem the tide of pollution and to clean up decades of neglect.

---

[18]"Water Shortage Fears in Darfur Camps," *All Africa*, December 10, 2007; "Northern Vietnam Likely to Face Water Shortages," *Xinhua News Agency*, January 4, 2008.

[19]Anita Chang, "China: Three Gorges Dam Impact Not That Bad," *Associated Press*, November 22, 2007.

[20]"Tourist Arrivals to Three Gorges Dam Hit New High in 2007," *Asia Pulse*, January 8, 2008.

[21]Sandy Bauers, "Big Wake-Up to Global Warming," *Philadelphia Inquirer*, December 24, 2007, p. D1.

[22]Visit http://www.gemi.org for information on the Global Environmental Management Initiative, an organization of U.S. multinational companies dedicated to environmental protection. Also see Keith Bradsher, "Hong Kong Utilities Agree to Pollution-Linked Rates," *The New York Times*, January 10, 2008, p. C4.

1875   Universal Postal Union created in Switzerland to provide for an international mail service
1876   Alexander Graham Bell is granted a patent for the telephone, which will revolutionize communications
1880   Thomas Edison creates first electric power station, after inventing the electric light in 1878, which lights New York City and starts a revolution in

culture and business—making a truly 24-hour day and paving the way for electronic machines
1881   Zoopraxiscope, which shows pictures in motion, is developed
1884   The basis for establishing standard time and measuring the longitude of any spot in the world is created with the designation of Greenwich,

England, as the prime meridian (0° longitude)
1886   American Federation of Labor founded, becoming a model for workers around the world to unite against management and gain higher pay and better working conditions
1901   Italian Guglielmo Marconi sends the first radio message; the radio could

be said to spark the start of globalization because of the speed with which information is able to be transmitted
1903   First successful flight of an airplane, piloted by Orville Wright, takes place at Kitty Hawk, North Carolina
1904   First vacuum tube is developed by John Fleming, allowing alternating current to become direct current and

Two kinds of economic progress, one with great collateral damage and one with much less. Large trucks are dwarfed by the 185-meter sluice gates of the Three Gorges Dam. China began filling the reservoir in a major step toward completion of the world's largest hydroelectric project. The level is expected to reach 135 meters (446 feet), inundating thousands of acres, including cities and farms along the Yangtze River. The second picture depicts Mongolian men as they view a small section of a huge solar energy project in their region. Perhaps still an eyesore for the locals, at least it is relatively energy efficient. (AP/Wide World Photos)

Companies looking to build manufacturing plants in countries with more liberal pollution regulations than they have at home are finding that regulations everywhere have gotten stricter. Many governments are drafting new regulations and enforcing existing ones. Electronic products contain numerous toxic substances that create a major disposal problem in landfills where inadequate disposal allows toxins to seep into groundwater. The European Union, as well as other countries, has laws stipulating the amount and types of potentially toxic substances it will require a company to take back to recycle. A strong motivator is the realization that pollution is on the verge of getting completely out of control.

China is now the world's top polluter in almost all respects.[23] By 2020 its **greenhouse-gas emissions** will be more than double the closest rival, the United States. An examination of rivers, lakes, and reservoirs in China revealed that toxic substances polluted 21 percent and that 16 percent of the rivers were seriously polluted with excrement. China has 16 of the world's 20 most polluted cities.[24] The very process of controlling industrial wastes leads to another and perhaps equally critical issue: the disposal of hazardous waste, a byproduct of pollution controls. Estimates of hazardous wastes collected annually exceed 300 million tons; the critical issue is disposal that does not simply move the problem elsewhere. Countries encountering increasing

---

[23]Sharon Begley, "Leaders of the Pack," *BusinessWeek*, November 30, 2009, pp. 46–51.

[24]Jim Yardley, "Consultant Questions Beijing's Claim of Cleaner Air," *The New York Times*, January 10, 2008, p. A3.

helping create widespread use of the radio

1913 Assembly line introduced by Henry Ford; it will revolutionize manufacturing

1914 The first war to involve much of the world begins with the assassination of Archduke Francis Ferdinand and lasts four years; construction of Panama Canal is completed, making trade faster and easier

1917 Lenin and Trotsky lead Russian revolution, creating a living economic model that will affect trade (adversely) for the rest of the century

1919 First nonstop trans-Atlantic flight completed, paving the way for cargo to be transported quickly around the globe

1920 League of Nations created, establishing a model

for international cooperation (though it failed to keep the peace)

1923 Vladimir Zworykin creates first electronic television, which will eventually help integrate cultures and consumers across the world

1929 Great Depression starts with crash of U.S. stock market

1930 Hawley-Smoot Tariff passed by U.S. Senate,

plunging the world deeper into the Great Depression

1935 Radar developed in Britain; it will allow travel on ships and planes even when there is no visibility, enabling the goods to keep to a transport schedule (eventually allowing the development of just-in-time and other cost-saving processes)

Exhibit 3.3

A Comparison of Greenhouse-Gas Emission Rates and Pledges for Reductions

Source: Intergovernmental Panel on Climate Change

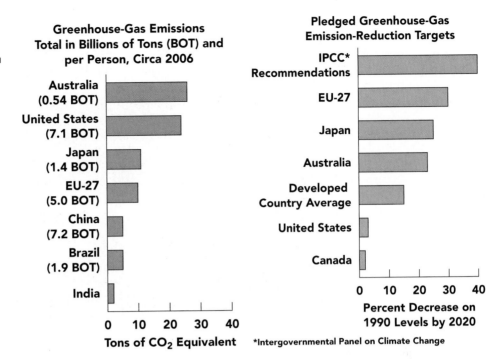

Greenhouse-Gas Emissions Total in Billions of Tons (BOT) and per Person, Circa 2006

Australia (0.54 BOT)
United States (7.1 BOT)
Japan (1.4 BOT)
EU-27 (5.0 BOT)
China (7.2 BOT)
Brazil (1.9 BOT)
India

0   10   20   30   40
Tons of CO$_2$ Equivalent

Pledged Greenhouse-Gas Emission-Reduction Targets

IPCC* Recommendations
EU-27
Japan
Australia
Developed Country Average
United States
Canada

0   10   20   30   40
Percent Decrease on 1990 Levels by 2020

*Intergovernmental Panel on Climate Change

difficulty in the disposal of wastes at home are seeking countries willing to assume the burden of disposal. Waste disposal is legal in some developing countries as governments seek the revenues that are generated by offering sites for waste disposal. In other cases, illegal dumping is done clandestinely. A treaty among members of the Basel Convention that required prior approval before dumping could occur was later revised to a total ban on the export of hazardous wastes by developed nations. The influence and leadership provided by this treaty are reflected in a broad awareness of pollution problems by businesses and people in general.[25]

Governments, organizations, and businesses are becoming increasingly concerned with the social responsibility and ethical issues surrounding the problem of maintaining economic growth while protecting the environment for future generations. However, the commitment made by governments and companies varies dramatically around the world. For example, with one of the highest pollution rates on a per capital basis, the United States lags behind almost all major competitors in agreeing to greenhouse emission standards (see Exhibit 3.3).[26] The Organization for Economic Cooperation and Development, the United Nations, the European Union, and international activist groups are undertaking programs to strengthen environmental policies.[27] In many ways China, because it has the most urgent and greatest pollution problems, is leading the charge in new green technology.[28] Many large

---

[25]For a comprehensive view of OECD programs, including environmental issues, visit http://www.oecd.org.

[26]"Closing the Gaps," *The Economist*, December 5, 2009, pp. 18–19.

[27]William C. Clark, "Science and Policy for Sustainable Development," *Environment*, January–February 2005.

[28]Shai Oster, "World's Top Polluter Emerges as Green-Technology Leader," *The Wall Street Journal*, December 15, 2009, online.

1938   American Chester Carlson develops dry copying process for documents (xerography), which, among other things, will enable governments to require that multiple forms be filled out to move goods
1939   World War II begins with German invasion of Poland; over 50 million people will die

1943   The first programmable computer, Colossus I, is created in England at Bletchley Park; it helps to crack German codes
1944   Bretton Woods Conference creates basis for economic cooperation among 44 nations and the founding of the International Monetary Fund to help stabilize exchange rates

1945   Atomic weapons introduced; World War II ends; United Nations founded
1947   General Agreement on Tariffs and Trade signed by 23 countries to try to reduce barriers to trade around the world
1948   Transistor is invented; it replaces the vacuum tube, starting a technology revolution

1949   People's Republic of China founded by Mao Zedong, which will restrict access to the largest single consumer market on the globe
1957   European Economic Community (EEC) established by Belgium, France, West Germany, Italy, Luxembourg, and the Netherlands, the precursor to today's European Union

Here in São Paulo, Shell sells two kinds of fuel: alcohol made primarily from sugarcane and gasoline made from dirtier fossil fuels. Flexible-fuel engines in Brazilian cars can burn either kind of fuel or any mixture of the two. Although the price per liter is quite different, so is the mileage per liter. Brazilians make their choice of fuel based on the kind of driving they anticipate, city versus highway.

multinational companies such as Petrobras,[29] Walmart,[30] and Nike are not only cleaning up their own operations around the world but also pushing their suppliers to do the same.

The issue that concerns everyone is whether economic development and protection for the environment can coexist. **Sustainable development** is a joint approach among those (e.g., governments, businesses, environmentalists, and others) who seek economic growth with "wise resource management, equitable distribution of benefits and reduction of negative effects on people and the environment from the process of economic growth." Sustainable development is not about the environment or the economy or society. It is about striking a lasting balance between all of these. More and more companies are embracing the idea of sustainable development as a "win–win" opportunity.[31] Responsibility for protecting the environment does not rest solely with governments, businesses, or activist groups; however, each citizen has a social and moral responsibility to include environmental protection among his or her highest goals.[32] This idea is particularly a problem in the United States, where consumers are often more interested in style than in sustainability,[33] public opinion polls favor growth over the environment,[34] and

---

[29]Jose Sergio Gabrielli de Azevedo, "The Greening of Petrobras," *Harvard Business Review*, March 2009, pp. 43–47.

[30]Adam Aston, "Wal-Mart's Green Stock," *BusinessWeek*, May 25, 2009, p. 44.

[31]Visit http://www.oecd.org, the OECD Web site, for a directory and complete coverage of sustainable development.

[32]Visit http://www.webdirectory.com for the *Amazing Environmental Organization Web Directory*, a search engine with links to an extensive list of environmental subjects.

[33]Burt Helm, "Nike Goes Green, Very Quietly," *BusinessWeek*, June 22, 2009, p. 56.

[34]"Who Cares?" *The Economist*, December 5, 2009, p. 15.

1961   Berlin Wall is erected, creating Eastern and Western Europe with a physical and spiritual barrier
1964   Global satellite communications network established with INTELSAT (International Telecommunications Satellite Organization)
1965   *Unsafe at Any Speed* published by Ralph Nader, sparking a revolution in

consumer information and rights
1967   European Community (EC) established by uniting the EEC, the European Coal and Steel Community, and the European Atomic Energy Community
1971   First microprocessor produced by Intel, which leads to the personal computer; communist China joins the

United Nations, making it a truly global representative body
1971   United States abandons gold standard, allowing the international monetary system to base exchange rates on perceived values instead of ones fixed in relation to gold
1972   One billion radios on the planet

1973   Arab oil embargo jolts industrial world into understanding the totally global nature of supply and demand
1980   CNN founded, providing instant and common information the world over, taking another significant step in the process of globalization started by the radio in 1901

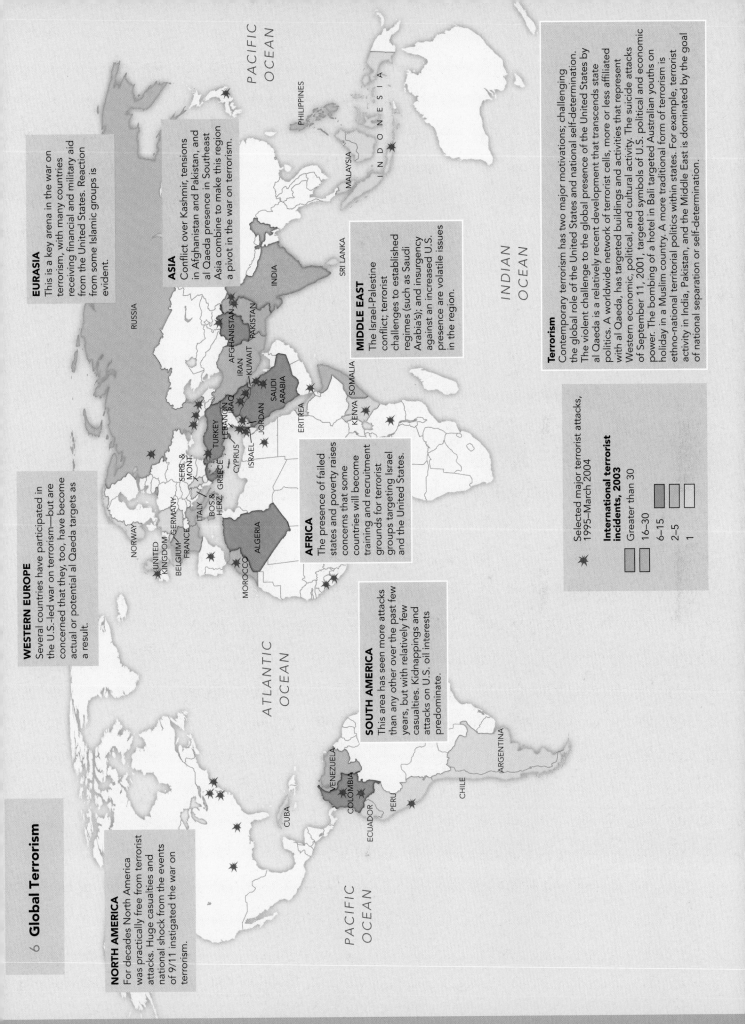

6 Global Terrorism

NORTH AMERICA
For decades North America was practically free from terrorist attacks. Huge casualties and national shock from the events of 9/11 instigated the war on terrorism.

WESTERN EUROPE
Several countries have participated in the U.S.-led war on terrorism—but are concerned that they, too, have become actual or potential al Qaeda targets as a result.

SOUTH AMERICA
This area has seen more attacks than any other over the past few years, but with relatively few casualties. Kidnappings and attacks on U.S. oil interests predominate.

EURASIA
This is a key arena in the war on terrorism, with many countries receiving financial and military aid from the United States. Reaction from some Islamic groups is evident.

ASIA
Conflict over Kashmir, tensions in Afghanistan and Pakistan, and al Qaeda presence in Southeast Asia combine to make this region a pivot in the war on terrorism.

MIDDLE EAST
The Israel-Palestine conflict; terrorist challenges to established regimes (such as Saudi Arabia's); and insurgency against an increased U.S. presence are volatile issues in the region.

AFRICA
The presence of failed states and poverty raises concerns that some countries will become training and recruitment grounds for terrorist groups targeting Israel and the United States.

Terrorism
Contemporary terrorism has two major motivations; challenging the global role of the United States and national self-determination. The violent challenge to the global presence of the United States by al Qaeda is a relatively recent development that transcends state politics. A worldwide network of terrorist cells, more or less affiliated with al Qaeda, has targeted buildings and activities that represent Western economic, political, and cultural activity. The suicide attacks of September 11, 2001, targeted symbols of U.S. political and economic power. The bombing of a hotel in Bali targeted Australian youths on holiday in a Muslim country. A more traditional form of terrorism is ethno-national territorial politics within states. For example, terrorist activity in India, Pakistan, and the Middle East is dominated by the goal of national separation or self-determination.

Selected major terrorist attacks, 1995–March 2004

International terrorist incidents, 2003
Greater than 30
16–30
6–15
2–5
1

PACIFIC OCEAN

ATLANTIC OCEAN

INDIAN OCEAN

RUSSIA

INDONESIA

PHILIPPINES

MALAYSIA

INDIA

SRI LANKA

AFGHANISTAN

PAKISTAN

IRAN

KUWAIT

IRAQ

SAUDI ARABIA

JORDAN

LEBANON

ISRAEL

CYPRUS

TURKEY

GREECE

SERB. & MONT.

BOS. & HERZ.

ITALY

FRANCE

BELGIUM

GERMANY

UNITED KINGDOM

NORWAY

MOROCCO

ALGERIA

ERITREA

SOMALIA

KENYA

CUBA

VENEZUELA

COLOMBIA

ECUADOR

PERU

CHILE

ARGENTINA

PACIFIC OCEAN

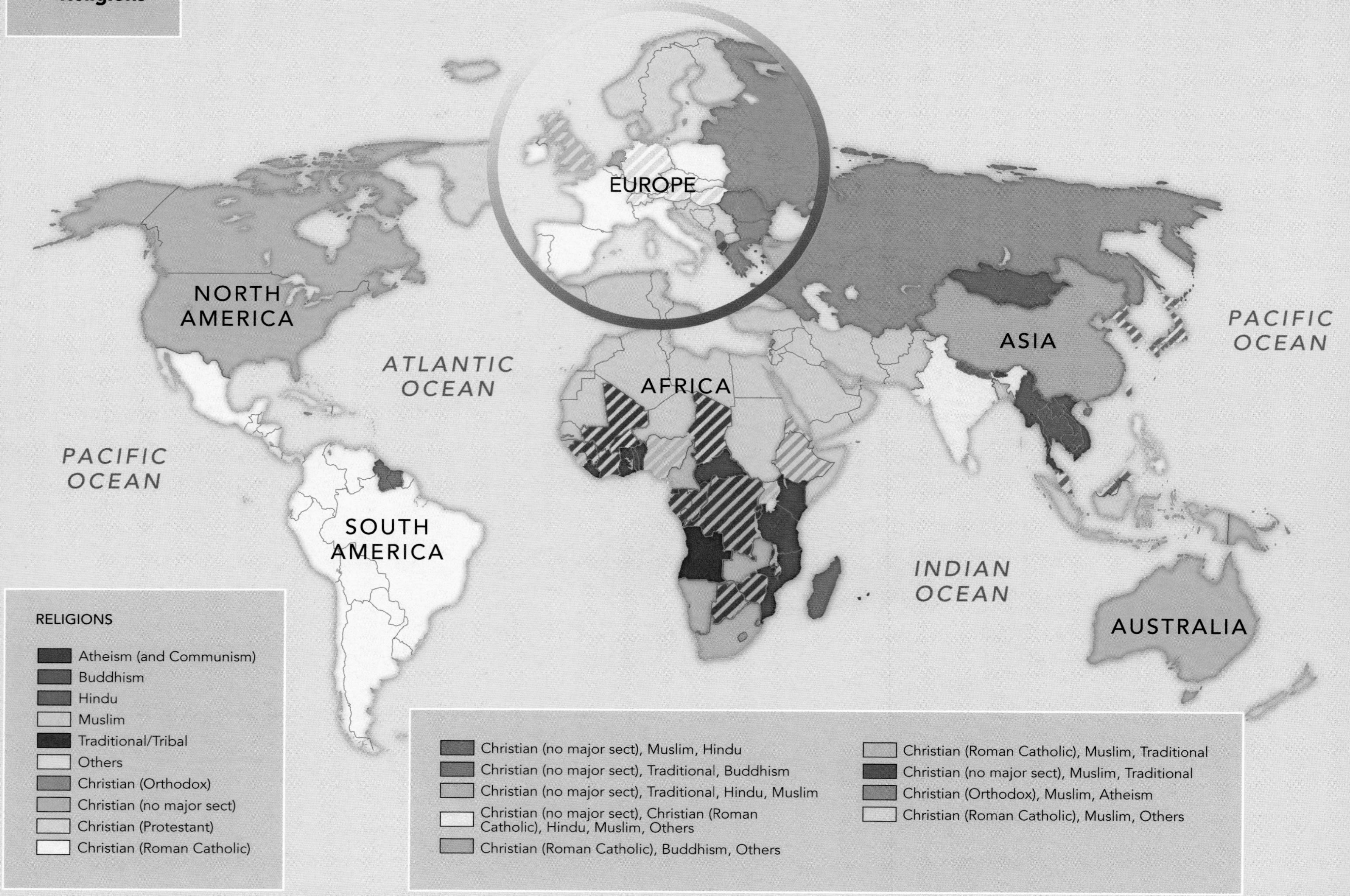

PACIFIC OCEAN

NORTH AMERICA

ATLANTIC OCEAN

SOUTH AMERICA

EUROPE

AFRICA

ASIA

AUSTRALIA

INDIAN OCEAN

RELIGIONS

Atheism (and Communism)

Buddhism

Hindu

Muslim

Traditional/Tribal

Others

Christian (Orthodox)

Christian (no major sect)

Christian (Protestant)

Christian (Roman Catholic)

Christian (no major sect), Muslim, Hindu

Christian (no major sect), Traditional, Buddhism

Christian (no major sect), Traditional, Hindu, Muslim

Christian (no major sect), Christian (Roman Catholic), Hindu, Muslim, Others

Christian (Roman Catholic), Buddhism, Others

Christian (Roman Catholic), Muslim, Traditional

Christian (no major sect), Muslim, Traditional

Christian (Orthodox), Muslim, Atheism

Christian (Roman Catholic), Muslim, Others

Trade flow
The circling paths of trade between continents show just how inter-connected the world's economies truly are. The richest countries, such as those in North America, western Europe, and the Far East, trade mostly with each other, exchanging different varieties of similar goods such as automobiles. However, trade also flows between higher- and lower-income regions. In those cases, the high-income countries typically provide more complex goods, such as electronic equipment, while low-income countries provide primary goods such as minerals. Smaller, poorer countries are more likely to be dependent on exporting a single commodity, such as coffee or petroleum. In general, poor, labor-abundant countries tend to export labor-intensive goods, such as textiles and shoes, and the countries rich in arable land will export foods such as grains.

AUSTRALIA

ASIA

NORTH AMERICA

EUROPE

AFRICA

SOUTH AMERICA

World economies

High income

Upper-middle income

Lower-middle income

Low income

No income data

World merchandise trade
(in billions of U.S. dollars)

Greater than 200

101–200

31–100

5–30

Less than 5

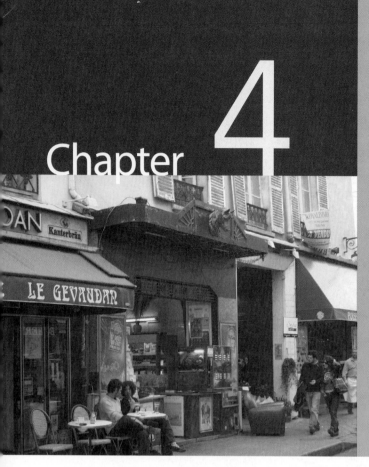

Chapter 4

Cultural Dynamics in Assessing Global Markets

CHAPTER LEARNING OBJECTIVES

What you should learn from Chapter 4:

LO1 The importance of culture to an international marketer

LO2 The origins of culture

LO3 The elements of culture

LO4 The impact of cultural borrowing

LO5 The strategy of planned change and its consequences

Global Perspective

EQUITIES AND eBAY—CULTURE GETS IN THE WAY

Two trillion dollars! That's about 200 trillion yen. Either way you count it, it's a lot of money. American brokerage houses such as Fidelity Investments, Goldman Sachs, and Merrill Lynch rushed new investment products and services to market in Japan to try to capture the huge capital outflow expected from 10-year time deposits, then held in the Japanese postal system. Liberalization of Japan's capital markets in recent years now gives Japanese consumers more freedom of choice in their investments. Post office time deposits still yield about a 2 percent return in Japan, and bank savings yields have been around 0. By American e-trading standards, that means an electronic flood of money moving out of the post offices and into the stock markets. Right?

However, Japan is not America. There is no American-style risk-taking culture among Japanese investors. The volume of stock trading in Japan is about one-sixth that of the United States. In Japan, only 12 percent of household financial assets are directly invested in stocks and a mere 2 percent in mutual funds. In contrast, about 55 percent of U.S. households own stock. Says one analyst, "Most of the population [in Japan] doesn't know what a mutual fund is." So will the flood be just a trickle? And what about online stock trading? Internet use in Japan has burgeoned—there are now some 88 million users in Japan. That's about the same percentage as in the United States. But the expected deluge into equities has been a dribble. Merrill Lynch and others are cutting back staff now as fast as they built it just a couple of years ago.

Making matters worse, for the Japanese, the transition into a more modern and trustworthy securities market has not been a smooth one. In 2005, an astounding transaction took place on the Tokyo Stock Exchange (TSE); instead of placing a small order of 1 share for 610,000 yen of J-Com, a trader with Mizuho Securities Co. mistakenly placed a sell order for 610,000 shares for 1 yen. Mizuho ended up losing 40 billion yen ($344 million) due to a simple computer glitch that ultimately led to the resignation of TSE president Takuo Tsurushima. Ouch!

A French firm is trying to break through a similar aversion to both e-trading and equities in France. That is, only about 32 million people use the Internet in France, and one-third of that number own stocks. The French have long shied away from stock market investments, seeing them as schemes to enrich insiders while fleecing novices. After the Enron (2001) and Lehman Bros. (2008) debacles in the United States, you could almost hear the chortling in the sidewalk cafés there. But even in France, investment preferences are beginning to change, especially since the real estate market has turned. At the same time, the liberalization of Europe's financial services sector is bringing down transaction costs for institutional and retail investors alike.

eBay, the personal online auction site so successful in the United States, is running into comparable difficulties in both Japan and France. The lower rate of Internet use in France is just part of the problem. For the Japanese, it is embarrassing to sell castoffs to anyone, much less buy them from strangers. Garage sales are unheard of. In France, eBay founder Pierre Omidyar's country of birth, the firm runs up against French laws that restrict operations to a few government-certified auctioneers.

Based on our knowledge of the differences in these cultural values between the United States and both Japan and France, we should expect a slower diffusion of these high-tech Internet services in the latter two countries. E-trading and e-auctions have both exploded on the American scene. However, compared with those in many other countries, U.S. investors are averse to neither the risk and uncertainties of equity investments nor the impersonal interactions of online transactions.

Sources: William D. Echikson, "Rough Crossing for eBay," *Business-Week E.Biz*, February 7, 2000, p. EB48; Sang Lee, "Japan and the Future of Electronic Trading," *Securities Industry News*, November 5, 2007; *World Development Indicators*, World Bank, 2010.

LO1

The importance of culture to an international marketer

Culture deals with a group's design for living. It is pertinent to the study of marketing, especially international marketing. If you consider the scope of the marketing concept—the satisfaction of consumer needs and wants at a profit—the successful marketer clearly must be a student of culture. For example, when a promotional message is written, symbols recognizable and meaningful to the market (the culture) must be used. When designing a product, the style, uses, and other related marketing activities must be made culturally acceptable (i.e., acceptable to the present society) if they are to be operative and meaningful. In fact, culture is pervasive in all marketing activities—in pricing, promotion, channels of distribution, product, packaging, and styling—and the marketer's efforts actually become a part of the fabric of culture. How such efforts interact with a culture determines the degree of success or failure of the marketing effort.

The manner in and amount which people consume, the priority of needs and wants they attempt to satisfy, and the manner in which they satisfy them are functions of their culture that temper, mold, and dictate their style of living. Culture is the human-made part of human environment—the sum total of knowledge, beliefs, art, morals, laws, customs, and any other capabilities and habits acquired by humans as members of society.[1]

Markets constantly change; they are not static but evolve, expand, and contract in response to marketing effort, economic conditions, and other cultural influences. Markets and market behavior are part of a country's culture. One cannot truly understand how markets evolve or how they react to a marketer's effort without appreciating that markets are a result of culture. Markets are the result of the three-way interaction of a marketer's efforts, economic conditions, and all other elements of the culture. Marketers are constantly adjusting their efforts to cultural demands of the market, but they also are acting as *agents of change* whenever the product or idea being marketed is innovative. Whatever the degree of acceptance, the use of something new is the beginning of cultural change, and the marketer becomes a change agent.

This is the first of four chapters that focus on culture and international marketing. A discussion of the broad concept of culture as the foundation for international marketing is presented in this chapter. The next chapter, "Culture, Management Style, and Business Systems," discusses culture and how it influences business practices and the behaviors and thinking of managers. Chapters 6 and 7 examine elements of culture essential to the study of international marketing: the political environment and the legal environment.

This chapter's purpose is to heighten the reader's sensitivity to the dynamics of culture. It is neither a treatise on cultural information about a particular country nor a thorough marketing science or epidemiological study of the various topics. Rather, it is designed to emphasize the importance of cultural differences to marketers and the need to study each country's culture(s) and all its origins and elements, as well as point out some relevant aspects on which to focus.

Culture's Pervasive Impact

Culture affects every part of our lives, every day, from birth to death, and everything in between.[2] It affects how we spend money and how we consume in general. It even affects how we sleep. For example, we are told that Spaniards sleep less than other Europeans, and Japanese children often sleep with their parents. You can clearly see culture operating in the birthrate tables in Exhibit 4.1. When you look across the data from the three countries, the gradual declines beginning in the 1960s are evident. As countries move from agricultural to industrial to services economies, birthrates decline. Immediate causes may be government policies and birth control technologies, but a global change in values is also occurring. Almost everywhere, smaller families are becoming favored. This

---

[1]An interesting Web site that has information on various cultural traits, gestures, holidays, language, religions, and so forth is www.culturegrams.com.

[2]A most important summary of research in the area of culture's impact on consumption behavior is Eric J. Arnould and Craig J. Thompson, "Consumer Culture Theory (CCT): Twenty Years of Research," *Journal of Consumer Research* 3, no. 2 (March 2005), pp. 868–82.

Exhibit 4.1
Birthrates (per 1,000 women)

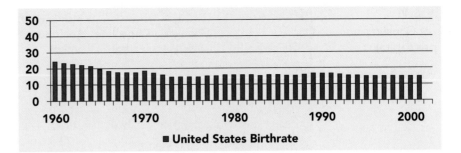

■ United States Birthrate

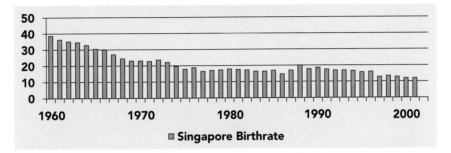

■ Singapore Birthrate

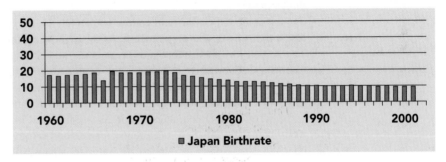

■ Japan Birthrate

cultural change now leads experts to predict that the planet's population may actually begin to decline after 2040 unless major breakthroughs in longevity intervene, as some predict.

But a closer look at the tables reveals even more interesting consequences of culture. Please notice the little peaks in 1976 and 1988 in the Singapore data. The same pattern can be seen in birthrate data from Taiwan. Those "extra" births are not a matter of random fluctuation. In Chinese cultures, being born in the Year of the Dragon (12 animals—dogs, rats, rabbits, pigs, etc.—correspond to specific years in the calendar) is considered good luck. Such birthrate spikes have implications for sellers of diapers, toys, schools, colleges, and so forth in successive years in Singapore. However, culture-based superstitions[3] have an even stronger influence on the birthrates in Japan, as shown in Exhibit 4.1. A one-year 20 percent drop in Japanese fertility rates in 1966 was caused by a belief that women born in the Year of the Fire Horse, which occurs every 60 years, will lead unhappy lives and perhaps murder their husbands. This sudden and substantial decline in fertility, which has occurred historically every 60 years since Japan started keeping birth records, reflects abstinence, abortions, and birth certificate fudging. This superstition has resulted in the stigmatization of women born in 1966 and had a large impact on market potential for a wide variety of consumer goods and services in Japan. It will be interesting to see how technological innovations and culture will interact in Japan in 2026, the next Year of the Fire Horse.[4]

---

[3]We know that superstitions can influence other kinds of consumers judgments as well. See Thomas Kramer and Lauren Block, "Conscious and Nonconscious Components of Superstitious Beliefs in Judgment and Decision Making," *Journal of Consumer Research* 34, no. 2 (2008), pp. 783–93.

[4]Robert W. Hodge and Naohiro Ogawa, *Fertility Change in Contemporary Japan* (Chicago: University of Chicago Press, 1991).

Exhibit 4.2
Patterns of Consumption
(annual per capita)

Source: EuroMonitor International,
2010.

Country	Cut Flowers (stems)	Chocolate (kg)	Fish and Seafood (kg)	Dried Pasta (kg)	Wine (L)	Tobacco (sticks)
France	81	3.9	6.2	5.7	26.9	845 (−25%)*
Germany	120	7.8	4.6	5.9	21.5	1,019 (−34%)
Italy	87	2.6	8.8	18.5	26.2	1,532 (−11%)
Netherlands	125	4.8	25.0	2.7	20.7	837 (−11%)
Spain	33	2.0	20.2	3.9	10.3	2,133 (−8%)
United Kingdom	48	10.5	12.4	1.5	18.2	754 (−15%)
Japan	110	1.1	38.2	1.5	4.7	1,875 (−16%)
United States	75	5.0	5.2	3.1	6.9	1,106 (−12%)

*Five-year growth rate.

Culture's influence is also illustrated in the consumption data presented in Exhibit 4.2. The focus there is on the six European Union countries, but data from the two other major markets of affluence in the world—Japan and the United States—are also included. The products compared are those that might be included in a traditional (American) romantic dinner date.

First come the flowers and candy. The Dutch are the champion consumers of cut flowers, and this particular preference for petals will be explored further in the pages to come. The British love their chocolate. Perhaps the higher consumption rate there is caused by Cadbury's[5] advertising, or perhaps the cooler temperatures have historically allowed for easier storage and better quality in the northern countries. At least among our six EU countries, per capita chocolate consumption appears to decline with latitude.

In Europe, the Dutch, then Spaniards, are the most likely to feast on fish. Both are still well behind the Japanese preference for seafood. From the data in the table, one might conclude that being surrounded by water in Japan explains the preference for seafood. However, what about the British? The flat geography in England and Scotland allows for the efficient production of beef, and a bit later in this section, we consider the consequences of their strong preference for red meat. The Italians eat more pasta—not a surprise. History is important. The product was actually invented in China, but in 1270, Marco Polo is reputed to have brought the innovation back to Italy, where it has flourished. Proximity to China also explains the high rate of Japanese noodle (but not dried pasta) consumption.

How about alcohol and tobacco? Grapes grow best in France and Italy, so a combination of climate and soil conditions explains at least part of the pattern of wine consumption seen in Exhibit 4.2. Culture also influences the laws, age limits, and such related to alcohol. The legal environment also has implications for the consumption of cigarettes. Indeed, the most striking patterns in the table are not the current consumption numbers; the interesting data are the five-year growth rates. Demand is shrinking remarkably fast almost everywhere. These dramatic declines in consumption represent a huge cultural shift that the world seldom sees.

Any discussion of tobacco consumption leads immediately to consideration of the consequences of consumption. One might expect that a high consumption of the romance products—flowers, candy, and wine—might lead to a high birthrate. Reference to Exhibit 4.3 doesn't yield any clear conclusions. The Germans have some of the highest consumption levels of the romantic three but the lowest birthrate among the eight countries.

Perhaps the Japanese diet's emphasis on fish yields them the longest life expectancy. But length of life among the eight affluent countries represented in the table shows little variation. How people die, however, does vary substantially across the countries. The influence

---

[5]See Cadbury's Web site for the history of chocolate, www.cadbury.co.uk. Chocolate is also an important product in Switzerland, where the consumption per capita is more than 12 kg. The mountain climate is cooler, and of course, Nestlé has corporate headquarters there.

Finding horse or donkey as your entrée would not be romantic or even appetizing in most places around the world. Even though horse consumption is generally declining in France, here in Paris you can still buy a steed steak at the local *bouchers chevaleries*. Escargot *oui*, Eeyore *oui*! And we note a recent article in *The Wall Street Journal* advocating the consumption of dog in the United States, including a recipe. Yikes![6]

of fish versus red meat consumption on the incidence of heart problems is easy to see. The most interesting datum in the table is the extremely high incidence of stomach cancer in Japan. The latest studies suggest two culprits: (1) salty foods such as soy sauce and (2) the bacterium *Helicobacter pylori*. The latter is associated with the unsanitary conditions prevalent in Japan immediately after World War II, and it is still hurting health in Japan today. Finally, because stomach cancer in Japan is so prevalent, the Japanese have developed the most advanced treatment of the disease, that is, both procedures and instruments. Even though the death rate is highest, the treatment success rate is likewise the highest in Japan. Whether you are in Tacoma, Toronto, or Tehran, the best medicine for stomach cancer may be a ticket to Tokyo. Indeed, this last example well demonstrates that culture not only affects consumption; it also affects production (of medical services in this case)!

The point is that culture matters.[7] It is imperative for foreign marketers to learn to appreciate the intricacies of cultures different from their own if they are to be effective in foreign markets.

---

[6]Jonathan Safran Foer, "Let Them Eat Dog," *The Wall Street Journal*, October 31, 2009, p. W10.

[7]Lawrence E. Harrison and Samuel P. Huntington (eds.), *Culture Matters* (New York: Basic Books, 2000).

Exhibit 4.3
Consequences of Consumption

Country	Birthrate (per 100,000)	Life Expectancy	Death Rate per 100,000			
			Ischemic Heart Disease	Diabetes Mellitus	Lung Cancer	Stomach Cancer
France	12.8	81.4	71.2	21.8	45.3	8.1
Germany	8.1	80.1	176.2	29.8	50.1	13.4
Italy	9.6	81.4	134.8	31.4	58.9	18.8
Netherlands	10.9	80.7	76.2	22.2	61.4	8.9
Spain	10.6	81.0	87.1	23.0	47.1	13.0
United Kingdom	13.0	79.6	162.6	10.8	54.7	9.2
Japan	8.4	82.7	55.8	10.3	46.5	38.1
United States	13.9	78.1	172.8	25.3	53.6	4.2

Source: EuroMonitor 2010.

The Floriad, the biggest exhibition of flowers on earth, happens once every decade. You can go to the next one in 2012.

Outside the Aalsmeer Flower Auction—notice the jet landing at nearby Schiphol Airport, which serves both Amsterdam and Aalsmeer.

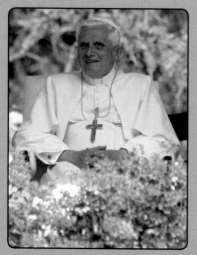

The Pope in St. Peter's Square on Easter Sunday surrounded by Dutch flowers.

We all love flowers. But for the Dutch, flowers are more important than that. For them, it's more like a national fascination, fixation, or even a fetish for flowers. **Why?**

The answer is an instructive story about culture and international markets, the broader subjects of this chapter. The story starts with geography, goes through the origins and elements of culture, and ends with the Dutch being the masters of the exhibition, consumption, and production of flowers.

Geography. The rivers and the bays make the Netherlands a great trading country. But the miserable weather, rain, and snow more than 200 days per year make it a colorless place, gray nearly year-round. The Flying Dutchmen not only went to the Spice Islands for spice for the palate; they also went to the eastern Mediterranean for spice for the eyes. The vibrant colors of the tulip first came to Europe from the Ottoman Empire on a Dutch ship in 1561.

History. The Dutch enthusiasm for the new "visual drug" was great. Its most potent form was, ironically, the black tulip. Prices exploded, and speculators bought and sold promissory notes guaranteeing the future delivery of black tulip bulbs. This derivatives market yielded prices in today's dollars of $1 million or more for a single bulb, enough to buy a 5-story house in central Amsterdam today. Not only did the tulip mania create futures markets, it also caused the first great market bust in recorded history. Prices plummeted when the government took control in 1637. Now at the Amsterdam flower market, you can buy a black tulip bulb for about a dollar!

The Amsterdam flower market—a busy place for local consumers and tourists.

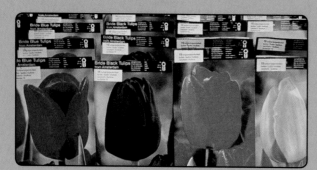

Four hundred years later, the one-dollar black tulip is available in the Amsterdam flower market.

A view of a Dutch harbor with trading ships circa 1600.

Inside Aalsmeer, 150 football fields of cut flowers, 20 million per day, are readied for auction.

The bidders in four huge auction rooms pay attention to the "clock" as high starting prices tick down. The wholesale buyer that stops the clock pays the associated price in this the archetypical "Dutch auction."

Technology and Economics.

The technology in the story comes in the name of Carolus Clusius, a botanist who developed methods for manipulating the colors of the tulips in the early 1600s. This manipulation added to their appeal and value, and the tulip trade became international for the Dutch.

Social Institutions.

Every Easter Sunday, the Pope addresses the world at St. Peter's Square in Rome reciting, "Bedankt voor bloemen." Thus, he thanks the Dutch nation for providing the flowers for this key Catholic ritual. The Dutch government, once every tenth year, sponsors the largest floriculture exhibition in the world, the Floriad. You can go next in 2012. Finally, at the Aalsmeer Flower Auction near Amsterdam, the prices are set for all flowers in all markets around the world. The Dutch remain the largest exporters of flowers (60 percent global market share), shipping them across Europe by trucks and worldwide by air freight.

Outside again at Aalsmeer, trucks are loaded for shipment by land across Europe and airfreight worldwide.

Cultural Values.

The high value the Dutch place on flowers is reflected in many ways, not the least of which is their high consumption rate, as seen in Exhibit 4.2.

Aesthetics as Symbols.

Rembrandt Van Rijn's paintings, including his most famous *Night Watch* (1642, Rijksmuseum, Amsterdam), reflect a dark palette. Artists generally paint in the colors of their surroundings. A quarter century later, his compatriot Vincent Van Gogh used a similar bleak palette when he worked in Holland. Later, when Van Gogh went to the sunny and colorful south of France, the colors begin to explode on his canvases. And, of course, there he painted flowers!

Rembrandt's *Night Watch*.

Van Gogh's *Vase with Fifteen Sunflowers*, painted in the south of France in 1889, and sold to a Japanese insurance executive for some $40 million in 1987, at the time the highest price ever paid for a single work of art. The Japanese are also big flower consumers—see Exhibit 4.2.

Van Gogh's *Potato Eaters*, painted in The Netherlands in 1885.

CROSSING BORDERS 4.1   Human Universals: The Myth of Diversity?

Yes, culture's influence is pervasive. But as anthropologist Donald E. Brown correctly points out, we are all human. And since we are all of the same species, we actually share a great deal. Here's a few of the hundreds of traits we share:

Use metaphors

Have a system of status and roles

Are ethnocentric

Create art

Conceive of success and failure

Create groups antagonistic to outsiders

Imitate outside influences

Resist outside influences

Consider aspects of sexuality private

Express emotions with face

Reciprocate

Use mood-altering drugs

Overestimate objectivity of thought

Have a fear of snakes

Recognize economic obligations in exchanges of goods and services

Trade and transport goods

Indeed, the last two suggest that we might be characterized as the "exchanging animal."

Source: Donald E. Brown, *Human Universals* (New York: McGraw-Hill, 1991).

Definitions and Origins of Culture

LO2

The origins of culture

There are many ways to think about culture. Dutch management professor Geert Hofstede refers to culture as the "software of the mind" and argues that it provides a guide for humans on how to think and behave; it is a problem-solving tool.[8] Anthropologist and business consultant Edward Hall provides a definition even more relevant to international marketing managers: "The people we were advising kept bumping their heads against an invisible barrier. . . . We knew that what they were up against was a completely different way of organizing life, of thinking, and of conceiving the underlying assumptions about the family and the state, the economic system, and even Man himself."[9] The salient points in Hall's comments are that cultural differences are often invisible and that marketers who ignore them often hurt both their companies and careers. Finally, James Day Hodgson, former U.S. ambassador to Japan, describes culture as a "thicket."[10] This last metaphor holds hope for struggling international marketers. According to the ambassador, thickets are tough to get through, but effort and patience often lead to successes.

Most traditional definitions of **culture** center around the notion that culture is the sum of the *values, rituals, symbols, beliefs,* and *thought processes* that are *learned* and *shared* by a group of people,[11] then *transmitted* from generation to generation.[12] So culture resides in the individual's mind. But the expression "a culture" recognizes that large collectives of people can, to a great degree, be like-minded.

[8]Geert Hofstede, *Culture's Consequences*, 2nd ed. (Thousand Oaks, CA: Sage, 2001); Susan P. Douglas, "Exploring New Worlds: The Challenge of Global Marketing," *Journal of Marketing*, January 2001, pp. 103–9.

[9]Edward T. Hall, *The Silent Language* (New York: Doubleday, 1959), p. 26.

[10]James D. Hodgson, Yoshihiro Sano, and John L. Graham, *Doing Business in the New Japan, Succeeding in America's Richest Foreign Market* (Latham, MD: Rowman & Littlefield, 2008).

[11]Please note that the group may be smaller than that defined by nation. See Rosalie Tung, "The Cross-Cultural Research Imperative: The Need to Balance Cross-Cultural and Intra-National Diversity," *Journal of International Business Studies* 39 (2008), pp. 41–46; Jean-Francois Ouellet, "Consumer Racism and Its Effects on Domestic Cross-Ethnic Product Purchase: An Empirical Test in the United States, Canada, and France," *Journal of Marketing* 71 (2007), pp. 113–28.

[12]Melvin Herskovitz, *Man and His Works* (New York: Alfred A. Knopf, 1952), p. 634. See also Chapter 10, "Culture," in Raymond Scupin and Christopher R. Decorse, *Anthropology: A Global Perspective*, 6th ed. (Englewood Cliffs, NJ: Prentice Hall, 2005).

Exhibit 4.4
Origins, Elements, and Consequences of Culture

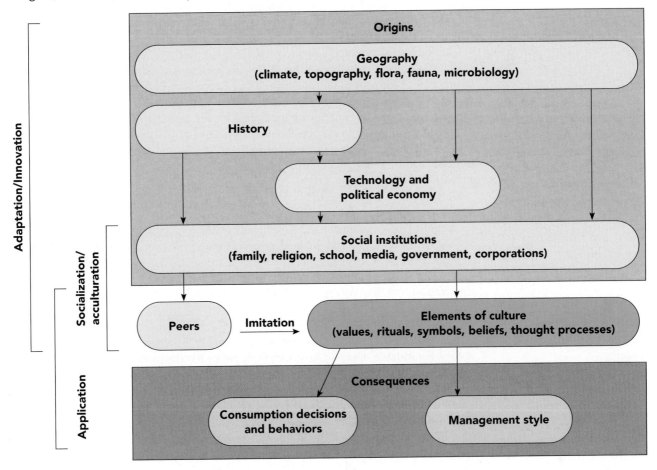

The best international marketers will not only appreciate the cultural differences pertinent to their businesses, but they will also understand the origins of these differences. Possession of the latter, deeper knowledge will help marketers notice cultural differences in new markets and foresee changes in current markets of operation. Exhibit 4.4 depicts the several causal factors and social processes that determine and form cultures and cultural differences. Simply stated, humans make *adaptations* to changing environments through *innovation*. Individuals learn culture from social institutions through *socialization* (growing up) and *acculturation* (adjusting to a new culture). Individuals also absorb culture through role modeling, or imitation of their peers. Finally, people make decisions about consumption and production through *application* of their cultural-based knowledge. More details are provided below.

Geography
In the previous chapter, we described the immediate effects of geography on consumer choice. But geography exercises a more profound influence than just affecting the sort of jacket you buy. Indeed, geography (broadly defined here to include climate, topography, flora, fauna, and microbiology) has influenced history, technology, economics, our social institutions, perhaps even the boy-to-girl birth ratio,[13] and, yes, our ways of thinking.[14] Geographical influences manifest themselves in our deepest cultural values developed

---

[13]Nicholoas Bakalar, "Why Does Latitude Affect Boy-Girl Ratios?" *International Herald Tribune*, April 23, 2009, p. 10.

[14]Richard E. Nisbett, *The Geography of Thought: How Asians and Westerners Think Differently . . . and Why* (New York: The Free Press, 2003).

through the millennia, and as geography changes, humans can adapt almost immediately. One sees the latter happening in the new interaction rituals evolving from the HIV/AIDS disaster or more recently the SARS outbreak in China. The ongoing cultural divides across the English Channel or the Taiwan Strati are also representative of geography's historical salience in human affairs.

The ideas of two researchers are particularly pertinent to any discussion of geography's influence on everything from history to present-day cultural values. First, Jared Diamond,[15] a professor of physiology, tells us that historically, innovations spread faster east to west than north to south. Before the advent of transoceanic shipping, ideas flowed over the Silk Road but not across the Sahara or the Isthmus of Panama. He uses this geographical approach to explain the dominance of Euro-Asian cultures, with their superior technology and more virulent germs, over African and American cultures. Indeed, Diamond's most important contribution is his material on the influence of microbiology on world history.

Second, Philip Parker,[16] a marketing professor, argues for geography's deep influence on history, economics, and consumer behavior. For example, he reports strong correlations between the latitude (climate) and the per capita GDP of countries. Empirical support can be found in others' reports of climate's apparent influence on workers' wages.[17] Parker, like Diamond before him, explains social phenomena using principles of physiology. The management implications of his treatise have to do with using ambient temperature as a market segmentation variable. We return to this issue in Chapter 8.

History

The impact of specific events in history can be seen reflected in technology, social institutions, cultural values, and even consumer behavior. Diamond's book is filled with examples. For instance, much of American trade policy has depended on the happenstance of tobacco (i.e., the technology of a new cash crop) being the original source of the Virginia colony's economic survival in the 1600s. In a like manner, the Declaration of Independence, and thereby Americans' values and institutions, was fundamentally influenced by the coincident 1776 publication of Adam Smith's *The Wealth of Nations*. Notice too that the military conflicts in the Middle East in 2003 bred new cola brands as alternatives to Coca-Cola—Mecca Cola, Muslim Up, Arab Cola, and ColaTurka.[18]

The Political Economy

For most of the 20th century, four approaches to governance competed for world dominance: colonialism, fascism, communism, and democracy/free enterprise. Fascism fell in 1945. Colonialism was also a casualty of World War II, though its death throes lasted well into the second half of the century. Communism crumbled in the 1990s.[19] One pundit even declared the "end of history."[20] Unfortunately, we have September 11 and the conflicts in the Middle East to keep the list of bad things growing. Much more detail is included in Chapters 6 and 7 on the influences of politics and the legal environment on the culture of commerce and consumption, so we will leave this important topic until then. The main point here is for you to appreciate the influence of the political economy on social institutions and cultural values and ways of thinking.

---

[15]Jared Diamond's *Guns, Germs and Steel: The Fates of the Human Societies* (New York: Norton, 1999) is a Pulitzer Prize winner, recipient of the Phi Beta Kappa Award in Science, and a wonderful read for anyone interested in history and/or innovation. PBS also has produced a video version of *Guns, Germs and Steel*. Also see Diamond's more recent book, *Collapse* (New York: Viking, 2005).

[16]Philip Parker's *Physioeconomics* (Cambridge, MA: MIT Press, 2000) is a data-rich discussion of global economics well worth reading.

[17]Evert Van de Vliert, "Thermoclimate, Culture, and Poverty as Country-Level Roots of Workers' Wages," *Journal of International Business Studies* 34, no. 1 (2003), pp. 40–52.

[18]See http://www.colaturka.com.tr.

[19]Some might argue that communism has survived in North Korea, Cuba, or the Peoples' Republic of China, but at least in the last case, free enterprise is on the ascendancy. The former look more like dictatorships to most.

[20]Francis Fukuyama, *The End of History and the Last Man* (New York: The Free Press, 1992).

Technology Sit back for a moment and consider what technological innovation has had the greatest impact on institutions and cultural values in the past 50 years in the United States. Seriously, stop reading, look out your window, and for a moment consider the question.

There are many good answers, but only one best one. Certainly jet aircraft, air conditioning, televisions,[21] computers, mobile phones, and the Internet all make the list. But the best answer is most likely the pill.[22] That is, the birth control pill, or more broadly birth control techniques, have had a huge effect on everyday life for most Americans and people around the world.[23] Mainly, it has freed women to have careers and freed men to spend more time with kids. Before the advent of the pill, men's and women's roles were proscribed by reproductive responsibilities and roles. Now half the marketing majors in the United States are women, and 10 percent of the crews on U.S. Navy ships are women. Before the pill, these numbers were unimaginable.

Obviously, not everyone is happy with these new "freedoms." For example, in 1968, the Roman Catholic Church forbade use of the birth control pill. But the technology of birth control undeniably has deeply affected social institutions and cultural values. Families are smaller, and government and schools are forced to address issues such as abstinence and condom distribution.

Finally, the reader will notice that technology does not solve all problems. For example, few would argue with the idea that the United States leads the world in healthcare technology, yet this technological leadership doesn't deliver the best healthcare system.[24] Other aspects of culture make a difference. Thus, citizens in many countries around the world have greater longevity (the most objective measure of the quality of healthcare delivery in a country), as mentioned earlier in this chapter. Consumer lifestyle choices and the financial structure affect the U.S. healthcare system dramatically as well. Please see Exhibit 4.5 for a quick comparison of systems across countries.

Social Institutions Social institutions including *family, religion, school, the media, government*, and *corporations* all affect the ways in which people relate to one another, organize their activities to live in harmony with one another, teach acceptable behavior to succeeding generations, and govern themselves. The positions of men and women in society, the family, social classes,[25] group behavior, age groups, and how societies define decency and civility are interpreted differently within every culture. In cultures in which the social organizations result in close-knit family units, for example, a promotion campaign aimed at the family unit is usually more effective than one aimed at individual family members. Travel advertising in culturally divided Canada has pictured a wife alone for the English-speaking market segment but a man and wife together for the French-speaking segments of the population, because the latter are traditionally more closely bound by family ties.

The roles and status positions found within a society are influenced by the dictates of social institutions. The caste system in India is one such institution. The election of a low-caste person—once called an "untouchable"—as president made international news because it was such a departure from traditional Indian culture. Decades ago, brushing against an untouchable or even glancing at one was considered enough to defile a Hindu of high status. Even though the caste system has been outlawed, it remains a part of the culture.

---

[21]Sandra K. Smith Speck and Abhijit Roy, "The Interrelationships between Television Viewing, Values, and Perceived Well-Being: A Global Perspective," *Journal of International Business Studies* 39, no. 7 (2008), pp. 1197–219.

[22]Bernard Asbell, *The Pill: A Biography of the Drug that Changed the World* (New York: Random House, 1995).

[23]"Go Forth and Multiply a Lot Less," *The Economist*, October 31, 2009, pp. 29–30.

[24]T. R. Reid, "No Country for Sick Men," *Newsweek*, September 21, 2009.

[25]Tuba Ustuner and Douglas B. Holt, "Toward a Theory of Consumption in Less Industrialized Countries," *Journal of Consumer Research* (2010), online.

Exhibit 4.5
Comparison of Healthcare Systems

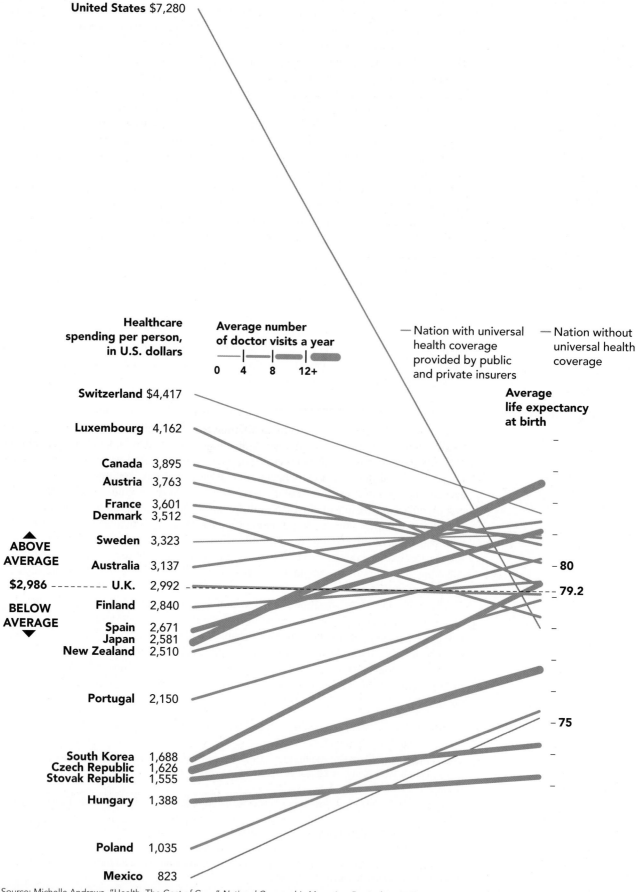

United States $7,280

Healthcare spending per person, in U.S. dollars

Average number of doctor visits a year

0   4   8   12+

— Nation with universal health coverage provided by public and private insurers

— Nation without universal health coverage

Average life expectancy at birth

Switzerland $4,417
Luxembourg 4,162
Canada 3,895
Austria 3,763
France 3,601
Denmark 3,512
Sweden 3,323
Australia 3,137

▲ ABOVE AVERAGE
$2,986 - - - - - U.K. 2,992
BELOW AVERAGE ▼
Finland 2,840
Spain 2,671
Japan 2,581
New Zealand 2,510

Portugal 2,150

South Korea 1,688
Czech Republic 1,626
Stovak Republic 1,555
Hungary 1,388

Poland 1,035

Mexico 823

— 80
— 79.2

— 75

Source: Michelle Andrews, "Health, The Cost of Care," *National Geographic Magazine*, December 2009.

Family. Family forms and functions vary substantially around the world, even around the country.[26] For example, whereas nepotism is seen as a problem in American organizations, it is more often seen as an organizing principle in Chinese and Mexican[27] firms. Or consider the Dutch executive who lives with his mother, wife, and kids in a home in Maastricht that his family has owned for the last 300 years. Then there's the common practice of the high-income folks in Cairo buying an apartment house and filling it up with the extended family—grandparents, married siblings, cousins, and kids. Or how about the Japanese mother caring for her two children pretty much by herself, often sleeping with them at night, while her husband catches up on sleep during his four hours a day commuting via train. And there's the American family in California—both parents work to support their cars, closets, and kids in college, all the while worrying about aging grandparents halfway across the country.

Even the ratio of male to female children is affected by culture (as well as latitude). In most European countries the ratio is about fifty-fifty. However, the gender percentage of boys aged one to six years is 52 in India and of those aged one to four years is 55 in China. Obviously these ratios have long-term implications for families and societies. Moreover, the favoritism for boys is deep-seated in such cultures, as demonstrated by the Chinese *Book of Songs*, circa 800 BC:

> When a son is born
> Let him sleep on the bed,
> Clothe him with fine clothes.
> And give him jade to play with. . . .
> When a daughter is born,
> Let her sleep on the ground,
> Wrap her in common wrappings,
> And give her broken tiles for playthings.

All these differences lead directly to differences in how children think and behave. For example, individualism is being taught the first night the American infant is tucked into her own separate bassinette. Values for egalitarianism are learned the first time Dad washes the dishes in front of the kids or Mom heads off to work or the toddler learns that both Grandpa and little brother are properly called "you." And there is some good news about gender equality to share: The education gap between men and women is narrowing in many places around the world—for example, the majority of university students in the United States are now women.

Religion. In most cultures, the first social institution infants are exposed to outside the home takes the form of a church, mosque, shrine, or synagogue. The impact of religion on the value systems of a society and the effect of value systems on marketing must not be underestimated. For example, Protestants believe that one's relationship with God is a personal one, and confessions are made directly through prayer. Alternatively, Roman Catholics confess to priests, setting up a hierarchy within the Church. Thus some scholars reason that Protestantism engenders egalitarian thinking. But no matter the details, religion clearly affects people's habits, their outlook on life, the products they buy, the way they buy them, and even the newspapers they read.

The influence of religion is often quite strong, so marketers with little or no understanding of a religion may readily offend deeply. One's own religion is often not a reliable guide to another's beliefs. Most people do not understand religions other than their own, and/or what is "known" about other religions is often incorrect. The Islamic religion is

---

[26]Michael Finkel's description of a hunter-gather tribe's everyday life, as observed in Tanzania, is important as a representation of family life and structure in people's primordial state. See "The Hadza," *National Geographic*, December 2009, pp. 94–118; also see John L. Graham, "Mother and Child Reunion," *Orange County Register*, January 11, 2009.

[27]Anabella Davila and Marta M. Elvira, "Culture and Human Resource Management in Latin America." In *Managing Human Resources in Latin America*, ed. Marta M. Elvira and Anabella Davila. (London: Routledge, 2005), pp. 3–24.

a good example of the need for a basic understanding of all major religions. More than one billion people in the world embrace Islam, yet major multinational companies often offend Muslims. The French fashion house of Chanel unwittingly desecrated the Koran by embroidering verses from the sacred book of Islam on several dresses shown in its summer collections. The designer said he had taken the design, which was aesthetically pleasing to him, from a book on India's Taj Mahal and that he was unaware of its meaning. To placate a Muslim group that felt the use of the verses desecrated the Koran, Chanel had to destroy the dresses with the offending designs, along with negatives of the photos taken of the garments. Chanel certainly had no intention of offending Muslims, since some of its most important customers embrace Islam. This example shows how easy it is to offend if the marketer, in this case the designer, has not familiarized him- or herself with other religions.

School.   Education, one of the most important social institutions, affects all aspects of the culture, from economic development to consumer behavior. The literacy rate of a country is a potent force in economic development. Numerous studies indicate a direct link between the literacy rate of a country and its capability for rapid economic growth. According to the World Bank, no country has been successful economically with less than 50 percent literacy, but when countries have invested in education, the economic rewards have been substantial. Literacy has a profound effect on marketing. Communicating with a literate market is much easier than communicating with one in which the marketer must depend on symbols and pictures. Increasingly, schools are seen as leading to positive cultural changes and progress across the planet.

The Media.   The four social institutions that most strongly influence values and culture are schools, churches, families, and, most recently, the media. In the United States during the past 30 years, women have joined the workforce in growing numbers, substantially reducing the influence of family on American culture. Media time (TV and increasingly the Internet and mobile phones) has replaced family time—much to the detriment of American culture, some argue. At this time, it is hard to gauge the long-term effects of the hours spent with Bart Simpson or an EverQuest cleric-class character. Indeed, the British Prime Minister's cameo on *The Simpsons* reflects its prominence around the world.

In the United States, kids attend school 180 days per year; in China, they attend 251 days—that's six days a week. There's a great thirst for the written word in China—here children read books rented from a street vendor.

American kids spend only 180 days per year in school. Contrast that with 251 days in China, 240 days in Japan, and 200 days in Germany. Indeed, Chinese officials are recognizing the national disadvantages of too much school—narrow minds. Likewise, Americans more and more complain about the detrimental effects of too much media. Many decry the declining American educational system as it produces a lower percentage of college graduates than twelve other countries, including Russia, Japan, and France.[28]

Government.   Compared with the early (during childhood) and direct influences of family, religion, school, and the media, governments hold relatively little sway. Cultural values and thought patterns are pretty much set before and during adolescence. Most often governments try to influence the thinking and behaviors of adult citizens for the citizens' "own good." For example, the French government has been urging citizens to procreate since the time of Napoleon. Now the government is

---

[28]Michael E. Porter, "Why America Needs an Economic Strategy," *BusinessWeek*, November 10, 2008, pp. 39–42; "The Underworked American [child]," *The Economist*, June 13, 2009, p. 40.

offering a new "birth bonus" of $800, given to women in their seventh month of pregnancy—despite France having one of the highest fertility rates in the European Union (see Exhibit 4.1). Likewise the Japanese government is spending $225 million to expand day-care facilities toward increasing the falling birthrate and better employing women in the workforce.[29] Or notice the most recent French and British government-allowed bans of *hijabs* (head scarves worn by Muslim schoolgirls) or the Dutch government initiative to ban *burkas* in that country (full-body coverings warn by Muslim women)[30] or the Swiss government's ban of the construction of minarets.[31] Also, major changes in governments, such as the dissolution of the Soviet Union, can have noticeable impacts on personal beliefs and other aspects of culture.

Of course, in some countries, the government owns the media and regularly uses propaganda to form "favorable" public opinions. Other countries prefer no separation of church and state—Iran is currently ruled by religious clerics, for example. Governments also affect ways of thinking indirectly, through their support of religious organizations and schools. For example, both the Japanese and Chinese governments are currently trying to promote more creative thinking among students through mandated changes in classroom activities and hours. Finally, governments influence thinking and behavior through the passage, promulgation, promotion, and enforcement of a variety of laws affecting consumption and marketing behaviors. The Irish government is newly concerned about its citizens' consumption of Guinness and other alcoholic products. Their studies suggest excessive drinking costs the country 2 percent of GDP, so to discourage underage drinking, the laws are being tightened (see the end of Chapter 16 for more details).

Corporations.   Of course, corporations get a grip on us early through the media. But more important, most innovations are introduced to societies by companies, many times multinational companies. Indeed, merchants and traders have throughout history been the primary conduit for the diffusion of innovations, whether it be over the Silk Road or via today's air freight and/or the Internet. Multinational firms have access to ideas from around the world. Through the efficient distribution of new products and services based on these new ideas, cultures are changed, and new ways of thinking are stimulated. The crucial role of companies as change agents is discussed in detail in the last section of this chapter.

Elements of Culture

LO3

The elements of culture

Previously culture was defined by listing its five elements: values, rituals, symbols, beliefs, and thought processes. International marketers must design products, distribution systems, and promotional programs with due consideration of each of the five.

Cultural Values   Underlying the cultural diversity that exists among countries are fundamental differences in cultural values, that is, the importance of things and ideas. The most useful information on how cultural values influence various types of business and market behavior comes from seminal work by Geert Hofstede.[32] Studying more than 90,000 people in 66 countries, he found that the cultures of the nations studied differed along four primary dimensions. Subsequently, he and hundreds of other researchers have determined that a wide variety of business and consumer behavior patterns are associated with three of those four dimensions.[33] The four[34] dimensions are as follows: the Individualism/Collective Index (IDV), which focuses on self-orientation; the Power Distance Index (PDI), which focuses

---

[29]Tomoko Yamazaki and Komaki Ito, "Japan: Boosting Growth with Day Care," *Bloomberg BusinessWeek*, January 4, 2010, pp. 96–97.

[30]"The War of French Dressing," *The Economist,* January 16, 2010, pp. 49–50.

[31]Deborah Ball, "Muslim Leaders Condemn Swiss Minaret Ban," *The Wall Street Journal*, November 30, 2009.

[32]Hofstede, *Culture's Consequences.*

[33]Debanjan Mitra and Peter N. Golder, "Whose Culture Matters? Near-Market Knowledge and Its Impact on Foreign Market Entry Timing," *Journal of Marketing Research* 39, no. 3 (August 2002), pp. 350–65; Boonghee Yoo and Naveen Donthu, "Culture's Consequences, a Book Review," *Journal of Marketing Research* 39, no. 3 (August 2002), pp. 388–89.

[34]In a subsequent study, a fifth dimension, Long-Term Orientation (LTO), was identified as focusing on cultures' temporal orientations. See Geert Hofstede and Michael Harris Bond, "The Confucius Connection," *Organizational Dynamics* 16, no. 4 (Spring 1988), pp. 4–21; Hofstede, *Culture's Consequences.*

Exhibit 4.6
Hofstede's Indexes,
Language, and Linguistic
Distance

Source: Geert Hofstede, *Culture's Consequences* (Thousand Oaks, CA: Sage, 2001). Used by permission of Geert Hofstede.

Country	IDV Score	PDI Score	UAI Score	Primary Language	Distance from English
Arab countries	38	80	68	Arabic	5
Australia	90	36	51	English	0
Brazil	38	69	76	Portuguese	3
Canada	80	39	48	English (French)	0, 3
Colombia	13	67	80	Spanish	3
Finland	63	33	59	Finnish	4
France	71	68	86	French	3
Germany	67	35	65	German	1
Great Britain	89	35	35	English	0
Greece	35	60	112	Greek	3
Guatemala	6	95	101	Spanish	3
India	48	77	40	Dravidian	3
Indonesia	14	78	48	Bahasa	7
Iran	41	58	59	Farsi	3
Japan	46	54	92	Japanese	4
Mexico	30	81	82	Spanish	3
Netherlands	80	38	53	Dutch	1
New Zealand	79	22	49	English	0
Pakistan	14	55	70	Urdu	3
South Korea	18	60	85	Korean	4
Taiwan	17	58	69	Taiwanese	6
Turkey	37	66	85	Turkish	4
United States	91	40	46	English	0
Uruguay	36	61	100	Spanish	3
Venezuela	12	81	76	Spanish	3

on authority orientation; the Uncertainty Avoidance Index (UAI), which focuses on risk orientation; and the Masculinity/Femininity Index (MAS), which focuses on assertiveness and achievement. The Individualism/Collectivism dimension has proven the most useful of the four dimensions, justifying entire books on the subject.[35] Because the MAS has proven least useful, we will not consider it further here. Please see Exhibit 4.6 for details.

During the 1990s, Robert House[36] and his colleagues developed a comparable set of data, more focused on values related to leadership and organizations. Their data are by themselves quite valuable, and aspects of their study nicely coincide with Hofstede's data, collected some 25 years earlier. The importance of this work has yielded important criticisms and discussion.[37]

Individualism/Collectivism Index.   The Individualism/Collective Index refers to the preference for behavior that promotes one's self-interest. Cultures that score high in IDV reflect an "I" mentality and tend to reward and accept individual initiative, whereas those low in individualism reflect a "we" mentality and generally subjugate the individual

---

[35]Harry C. Triandis, *Individualism and Collectivism* (Boulder, CO: Westview Press, 1995).

[36]Robert J. House, Paul J. Hanges, Mansour Javidan, Peter W. Dorfman, and Vipin Gupta (eds.), *Culture, Leadership, and Organizations: The Globe Study of 62 Societies* (Thousand Oaks, CA: Sage, 2004).

[37]Bradley L. Kirkman, Kevin B. Lowe, and Cristina Gibson, "A Quarter Century of Cultures' Consequences: A Review of Empirical Research Incorporating Hofstede's Cultural Values Framework," *Journal of International Business Studies* 37 (2006), pp. 285–320; Kwock Leung, "Editor's Introduction to the Exchange between Hofstede and GLOBE," *Journal of International Business Studies* 37 (2006), p. 881; Geert Hofstede, "What Did GLOBE Really Measure? Researchers' Minds versus Respondents' Minds," *Journal of International Business Studies* 37 (2006), pp. 882–96; Mansour Javidan, Robert J. House, Peter W. Dorfman, Paul J. Hanges, and Mary Sully de Luque, "Conceptualizing and Measuring Cultures and Their Consequences: A Comparative Review of GLOBE's and Hostede's Approaches," *Journal of International Business Studies* 37 (2006), pp. 897–914; Peter B. Smith, "When Elephants Fight, the Grass Gets Trampled: The GLOBE and Hofstede Projects," *Journal of International Business Studies* 37 (2006), pp. 915–21; P. Christopher Earley, "Leading Cultural Research in the Future: A Matter of Paradigms and Taste," *Journal of International Business Studies* 37 (2006), pp. 922–31.

to the group. This distinction does not mean that individuals fail to identify with groups when a culture scores high on IDV but rather that personal initiative and independence are accepted and endorsed. Individualism pertains to societies in which the ties between individuals are loose; everyone is expected to look after him- or herself and his or her immediate family. Collectivism, as its opposite, pertains to societies in which people from birth onward are integrated into strong, cohesive groups, which throughout people's lifetimes continue to protect them in exchange for unquestioning loyalty.

Power Distance Index.   The Power Distance Index measures the tolerance of social inequality, that is, power inequality between superiors and subordinates within a social system. Cultures with high PDI scores tend to be hierarchical, with members citing social roles, manipulation, and inheritance as sources of power and social status. Those with low scores, in contrast, tend to value equality and cite knowledge and respect as sources of power. Thus, people from cultures with high PDI scores are more likely to have a general distrust of others (not those in their groups) because power is seen to rest with individuals and is coercive rather than legitimate. High PDI scores tend to indicate a perception of differences between superior and subordinate and a belief that those who hold power are entitled to privileges. A low PDI score reflects more egalitarian views.

Uncertainty Avoidance Index.   The Uncertainty Avoidance Index measures the tolerance of uncertainty and ambiguity among members of a society. Cultures with high UAI scores are highly intolerant of ambiguity and as a result tend to be distrustful of new ideas or behaviors. They tend to have a high level of anxiety and stress and a concern with security and rule following. Accordingly, they dogmatically stick to historically tested patterns of behavior, which in the extreme become inviolable rules. Those with very high UAI scores thus accord a high level of authority to rules as a means of avoiding risk. Cultures scoring low in uncertainty avoidance are associated with a low level of anxiety and stress, a tolerance of deviance and dissent, and a willingness to take risks. Thus, those cultures low in UAI take a more empirical approach to understanding and knowledge, whereas those high in UAI seek absolute truth.

Cultural Values and Consumer Behavior.   A variety of studies have shown cultural values can predict such consumer behaviors as word-of-mouth communications,[38] impulsive buying,[39] responses of both surprise[40] and disgust,[41] the propensity to complain,[42] responses to service failures,[43] and even movie preferences.[44] Going back to the e-trading example that opened this chapter, we can see how Hofstede's notions of cultural values might help us predict the speed of diffusion of such new consumer services as equity investments and electronic auctions in Japan and France. As shown in Exhibit 4.6, the United States scores the highest of all countries on individualism, at 91, with Japan at 46 and France at 71. Indeed, in America, where individualism reigns supreme, we might predict that the "virtually social" activity of sitting alone at one's computer might be most acceptable. In both Japan and France, where values favor group activities, face-to-face conversations with stockbrokers and neighbors might be preferred to impersonal electronic communications.

---

[38]Desmond Lam, Alvin Lee, and Richard Mizerski, "The Effects of Cultural Values in Word-of-Mouth Communication," *Journal of International Marketing* 17, no. 3 (2009), pp. 55–70.

[39]Yinlong Zhang, Karen Page Winterich, and Vikas Mittal, "Power-Distance Belief and Impulsive Buying," *Journal of Marketing Research* 47 (2010).

[40]Ana Valenzuela, Barbar Mellers, and Judi Strebel, "Pleasurable Surprises: A Cross-Cultural Study of Consumer Responses to Unexpected Incentives," *Journal of Consumer Research* 36 (2010).

[41]Daisann McLane, "Tackling the Yuck Factor,'" *National Geographic Traveler*, January 2010, pp. 26–28.

[42]Piotr Chelminski and Robin A. Coulter, "The Effects of Cultural Individualism and Self-Confidence on Propensity to Voice: From Theory to Measurement to Practice," *Journal of International Marketing* 15 (2007), pp. 94–118.

[43]Haksin Chan, Lisa C. Wan, and Leo Y. M. Sin, "The Contrasting Effects of Culture on Consumer Tolerance: Interpersonal Face and Impersonal Fate," *Journal of Consumer Research* 36, no. 2 (2009), pp. 292–304; Haskin Chan and Lisa C. Wan, "Consumer Responses to Service Failures: A Resource Preference Model of Cultural Influences," *Journal of International Marketing* 16, no. 1 (2008), pp. 72–97.

[44]J. Samuel Craig, William H. Greene, and Susan P. Douglas, "Culture Matters: Consumer Acceptance of U.S. Films in Foreign Markets," *Journal of International Marketing* 13 (2006), pp. 80–103.

CROSSING BORDERS 4.2

It's Not the Gift That Counts, but How You Present It

Giving a gift in another country requires careful attention if it is to be done properly. Here are a few suggestions.

JAPAN

Do not open a gift in front of a Japanese counterpart unless asked, and do not expect the Japanese to open your gift.

Avoid ribbons and bows as part of the gift wrapping. Bows as we know them are considered unattractive, and ribbon colors can have different meanings.

Always offer the gift with both hands.

EUROPE

Avoid red roses and white flowers, even numbers, and the number 13. Do not wrap flowers in paper.

Do not risk the impression of bribery by spending too much on a gift.

ARAB WORLD

Do not give a gift when you first meet someone. It may be interpreted as a bribe.

Do not let it appear that you contrived to present the gift when the recipient is alone. It looks bad unless you know the person well. Give the gift in front of others in less personal relationships.

LATIN AMERICA

Do not give a gift until after a somewhat personal relationship has developed, unless it is given to express appreciation for hospitality.

Gifts should be given during social encounters, not in the course of business.

Avoid the colors black and purple; both are associated with the Roman Catholic Lenten season.

CHINA

Never make an issue of a gift presentation—publicly or privately. But always deliver gifts with two hands.

Gifts should be presented privately, with the exception of collective ceremonial gifts at banquets or after speeches.

RUSSIA

Generally speaking, Russians take pleasure in giving and receiving gifts—so take plenty. Something for the kids is a good idea.

When invited to a Russian home, bring chocolates or wine, but not vodka.

Bringing a bouquet of flowers is a good idea, but make it an odd number. Even numbers are for funerals.

UNITED STATES

Gifts that are too ostentatious can cause big problems.

Source: James Day Hodgson, Yoshiro Sano, and John L. Graham, *Doing Business in the New Japan* (Latham, MD: Rowman and Littlefield, 2008); www.executiveplanet.com, 2010.

Similarly, both Japan (92) and France (86) score quite high on Hofstede's Uncertainty Avoidance Index, and America scores low (46). Based on these scores, both Japanese and French investors might be expected to be less willing to take the risks of stock market investments—and indeed, the security of post office deposits or bank savings accounts is preferred. So in both instances, Hofstede's data on cultural values suggest that the diffusion of these innovations will be slower in Japan and France than in the United States. Such predictions are consistent with research findings that cultures scoring higher on individualism and lower on uncertainty avoidance tend to be more innovative.[45]

Perhaps the most interesting application of cultural values and consumer behavior regards a pair of experiments done with American and Chinese students.[46] Both groups were shown print ads using other-focused emotional appeals (that is, a couple pictured having fun on the beach) versus self-focused emotional appeals (an individual having fun on the beach). The researchers predicted that the individualistic Americans would respond more favorably

---

[45]Jan-Benedict E. M. Steenkamp, Frenkel ter Hofstede, and Michel Wedel, "A Cross-National Investigation into the Individual and National Cultural Antecedents of Consumer Innovativeness," *Journal of Marketing* 63 (April 1999), pp. 55–69.

[46]Jennifer L. Aaker and Patti Williams, "Empathy vs. Pride: The Influence of Emotional Appeals across Cultures," *Journal of Consumer Research* 25 (December 1998), pp. 241–61.

Every Muslim is enjoined to make the hajj, or pilgrimage to Mecca, once in his or her lifetime if physically able. Here, some 2 million faithful come from all over the world annually to participate in what is one of the largest ritual meetings on Earth.[47]

to the self-focused appeals and the collectivistic Chinese to the other-focused appeals. They found the opposite. Their second experiment helped explain these unexpected results. That is, in both cases, what the participants liked about the ads was their *novelty* vis-à-vis their own cultures. So, even in this circumstance, cultural values provide useful information for marketers. However, the complexity of human behavior, values, and culture is manifest.

Rituals

Life is filled with **rituals**, that is, patterns of behavior and interaction that are learned and repeated. The most obvious ones are associated with major events in life. Marriage ceremonies and funerals are good examples. Perhaps the one most important to most readers

---

[47]Hassan M. Fattar, "The Price of Progress: Transforming Islam's Holiest Sight," *The New York Times International*, March 8, 2007, p. A4.

Dressed in the ritual color of saffron (orange), thousands of pilgrims of the Lord Shiva descend one of the over 100 *Ghats* in Varanasi, India, to perform *puja* (ritual cleansing of the soul). Varanasi (also known as Benares or Banaris) is one of the oldest and holiest cities in India. It is believed to be the home of Lord Shiva (Hindu god) and the location of the first sermon by Buddha, so followers of numerous religions flock to Varanasi on a daily basis. Each day at sunrise and sunset, pilgrims crowd the *Ghats* (steps to the holy river/Mother Ganga/ the River Ganges) to immerse themselves in the water and perform *puja*. On the busiest day of the ritual, some 5–10 million participate (according to Professor Rika Houston). Meanwhile, televised rituals such as the Academy Awards and World Cup soccer draw billions in the form of virtual crowds.

of this book is the hopefully proximate graduation ritual—*Pomp and Circumstance*, funny hats, long speeches, and all. Very often these rituals differ across cultures. Indeed, there is an entire *genre* of foreign films about weddings.[48] Perhaps the best is *Monsoon Wedding*. Grooms on white horses and edible flowers are apparently part of the ceremony for high-income folks in New Delhi.

Life is also filled with little rituals, such as dinner at a restaurant or a visit to a department store or even grooming before heading off to work or class in the morning. In a nice restaurant in Madrid, dessert may precede the entrée, but dinner often starts at about midnight, and the entire process can be a three-hour affair. Walking into a department store in the United States often yields a search for an employee to answer questions. Not so in Japan, where the help bows at the door as you walk in. Visit a doctor in the States and a 15-minute wait in a cold exam room with nothing on but a paper gown is typical. In Spain the exams are often done in the doctor's office. There's no waiting, because you find the doctor sitting at her desk.

Rituals are important. They coordinate everyday interactions and special occasions. They let people know what to expect. In the final chapter of the text, we discuss the ritual of business negotiations, and that ritual varies across cultures as well.

Symbols

Anthropologist Edward T. Hall tells us that culture is communication. In his seminal article about cultural differences in business settings, he talks about the "languages" of time, space, things, friendships, and agreements.[49] Indeed, learning to interpret correctly the symbols that surround us is a key part of socialization. And this learning begins immediately after birth, as we begin to hear the language spoken and see the facial expressions and feel the touch and taste the milk of our mothers.[50] We begin our discussion of symbolic systems with language, the most obvious part and the part that most often involves conscious communication.

Language.

We should mention that for some around the world, language is itself thought of as a social institution, often with political importance. Certainly the French go to extreme lengths and expense to preserve the purity of their *français*. In Canada, language has been the focus of political disputes including secession, though things seem to have calmed down there most recently. Unfortunately, as the number of spoken languages continues to decline worldwide, so does the interesting cultural diversity of the planet.

The importance of understanding the language of a country cannot be overestimated, particularly if you're selling your products in France! The successful international marketer must achieve expert communication, which requires a thorough understanding of the language as well as the ability to speak it. Advertising copywriters should be concerned less with obvious differences between languages and more with the idiomatic and symbolic[51] meanings expressed. It is not sufficient to say you want to translate into Spanish, for instance, because across Spanish-speaking Latin America, the language vocabulary varies widely. *Tambo*, for example, means a roadside inn in Bolivia, Colombia, Ecuador, and Peru; a dairy farm in Argentina and Uruguay; and a brothel in Chile. If that gives you a problem, consider communicating with the people of Papua New Guinea. Some 750 languages, each distinct and mutually unintelligible, are spoken there. This crucial issue of accurate translations in marketing communications is discussed further in Chapters 8 and 16.

The relationship between language and international marketing is important in another way. Recent studies indicate that a new concept, **linguistic distance**, is proving useful to

---

[48]Other excellent films in this genre include *Cousin, Cousine* (French), *Four Weddings and a Funeral* (U.K.), *Bend It Like Beckham* (U.K., Asian immigrants), *Wedding in Galilee* (Palestine/Israel), and *The Wedding Banquet* (Taiwan). Also see Cam Simpson, "For Jordanians, Shotgun Weddings Can Be a Problem," *The Wall Street Journal*, June 5, 2007, pp. A1, A11.

[49]Edward T. Hall, "The Silent Language in Overseas Business," *Harvard Business Review*, May–June 1960, pp. 87–96. A discussion of the salience of Hall's work appears in John L. Graham, "Culture and Human Resources Management." In *The Oxford Handbook of International Business*, ed. Alan M. Rugman and Thomas L. Brewer (Oxford: Oxford University Press, 2008), pp. 503–36.

[50]The spices a nursing mother consumes actually affect the flavor of the milk she produces.

[51]Eric Yorkston and Gustavo E. De Mello, "Linguistic Gender Marking and Categorization," *Journal of Consumer Research* 32 (2005), pp. 224–34.

marketing researchers in market segmentation and strategic entry decisions. Linguistic distance has been shown to be an important factor in determining differences in values across countries and the amount of trade between countries.[52] The idea is that crossing "wider" language differences increases transaction costs.

Over the years, linguistics researchers have determined that languages around the world conform to family trees[53] based on the similarity of their forms and development. For example, Spanish, Italian, French, and Portuguese are all classified as Romance languages because of their common roots in Latin. Distances can be measured on these linguistic trees. If we assume English[54] to be the starting point, German is one branch away, Danish two, Spanish three, Japanese four, Hebrew five, Chinese six, and Thai seven. These "distance from English" scores are listed for a sampling of cultures in Exhibit 4.6.

Other work in the area is demonstrating a direct influence of language on cultural values, expectations, and even conceptions of time. For example, as linguistic distance from English increases, individualism decreases.[55] These studies are among the first in this genre, and much more work needs to be done. However, the notion of linguistic distance appears to hold promise for better understanding and predicting cultural differences in both consumer and management values, expectations, and behaviors. Another area of new research interest is the relationship between bilingualism/biculturalism and consumer behaviors and values. For example, bilingual consumers process advertisements differently if heard in their native versus second language,[56] and bicultural consumers, different from bilingual only consumers, can switch identities and perception frames.[57]

Moreover, the relationship between language spoken and cultural values holds deeper implications. That is, as English spreads around the world via school systems and the Internet, cultural values of individualism and egalitarianism will spread with it. For example, both Chinese Mandarin speakers and Spanish speakers must learn two words for "you" (*ni* and *nin* and *tu* and *usted*, respectively). The proper use of the two depends completely on knowledge of the social context of the conversation. Respect for status is communicated by the use of *nin* and *usted*. In English there is only one form for "you."[58] Speakers can ignore social context and status and still speak correctly. It's easier, and social status becomes less important. *Français* beware!

Aesthetics as Symbols. Art communicates. Indeed, Confucius is reputed to have opined, "A picture is worth a thousand words." But, of course, so can a dance or a song. As we acquire our culture, we learn the meaning of this wonderful symbolic system represented in its **aesthetics**, that is, its arts, folklore, music, drama, dance, dress, and cosmetics. Customers everywhere respond to images, myths, and metaphors that help them define their personal and national identities and relationships within a context of culture and product benefits. The uniqueness of a culture can be spotted quickly in symbols having distinct meanings. Think about the subtle earth tones of the typical Japanese restaurant compared with the bright reds and yellows in the decor of ethnic Chinese restaurants.

---

[52]Jennifer D. Chandler and John L. Graham, "Relationship-Oriented Cultures, Corruption, and International Marketing Success," *Journal of Business Ethics* 92(2) (2010), pp. 251–67.

[53]For the most comprehensive representation of global linguistic trees, see Jiangtian Chen, Robert R. Sokal, and Merrit Ruhlen, "Worldwide Analysis of Genetic and Linguistic Relationships of Human Populations," *Human Biology* 67, no. 4 (August 1995), pp. 595–612.

[54]We appreciate the ethnocentricity in using English as the starting point. However, linguistic trees can be used to measure distance from any language. For example, analyses using French or Japanese as the starting point have proven useful as well.

[55]Joel West and John L. Graham, "A Linguistics-Based Measure of Cultural Distance and Its Relationship to Managerial Values," *Management International Review* 44, no. 3 (2004), pp. 239–60.

[56]Stefano Puntoni, Bart de Langhe, and Stijn M.J. van Osselaer, "Bilingualism and the Emotional Intensity of Advertising Language," *Journal of Consumer Research* 35 (2009), pp. 1012–25.

[57]David Luna, Torsten Ringberg, and Laura A. Peracchio, "One Individual, Two Identities: Frame Switching Biculturals," *Journal of Consumer Research* 35, no. 2 (2008), pp. 279–93.

[58]In English, there was historically a second second-person form. That is, "thee" was the informal form up until the last century. Even in some Spanish-speaking countries, such as Costa Rica, the "tu" is being dropped in a similar manner.

Exhibit 4.7

Metaphorical Journeys through 23 Nations

Source: From Martin J. Gannon, *Understanding Global Cultures, Metaphorical Journeys through 23 Nations*, 2nd ed. Copyright © 2001. Reprinted by permission of Sage Publications.

The Thai Kingdom	The Traditional British House
The Japanese Garden	The Malaysian *Balik Kampung*
India: The Dance of Shiva	The Nigerian Marketplace
Bedouin Jewelry and Saudi Arabia	The Israeli Kibbutzim and Moshavim
The Turkish Coffeehouse	The Italian Opera
The Brazilian Samba	Belgian Lace
The Polish Village Church	The Mexican Fiesta
Kimchi and Korea	The Russian Ballet
The German Symphony	The Spanish Bullfight
The Swedish *Stuga*	The Portuguese Bullfight
Irish Conversations	The Chinese Family Altar
American Football	

Similarly, a long-standing rivalry between the Scottish Clan Lindsay and Clan Donald caused McDonald's Corporation some consternation when it chose the Lindsay tartan design for new uniforms for its workers. Godfrey Lord Macdonald, Chief of Clan Donald, was outraged and complained that McDonald's had a "complete lack of understanding of the name." Of course, the plaid in the uniforms is now the least of the firm's worries as British consumers are becoming more concerned about health-related matters.

Without culturally consistent interpretations and presentations[59] of countries' aesthetic values, a host of marketing problems can arise. Product styling must be aesthetically pleasing to be successful, as must advertisements and package designs. Insensitivity to aesthetic values can offend, create a negative impression, and, in general, render marketing efforts ineffective or even damaging. Strong symbolic meanings may be overlooked if one is not familiar with a culture's aesthetic values. The Japanese, for example, revere the crane as being very lucky because it is said to live a thousand years. However, the use of the number four should be avoided completely because the word for four, *shi*, is also the Japanese word for death. Thus teacups are sold in sets of five, not four, in Japan.

Finally, one author has suggested that understanding different cultures' metaphors is a key doorway to success. In Exhibit 4.7, we list the metaphors Martin Gannon[60] identified to represent cultures around the world. In the fascinating text, he compares "American Football" (with its individualism, competitive specialization, huddling, and ceremonial celebration of perfection) to the "Spanish Bullfight" (with its pompous entrance parade, audience participation, and the ritual of the fight) to the "Indian Dance of the Shiva" (with its cycles of life, family, and social interaction). Empirical evidence is beginning to accumulate supporting the notion that metaphors matter.[61] Any good international marketer would see fine fodder for advertising campaigns in the insightful descriptions depicted.

Beliefs   Of course, much of what we learn to believe comes from religious training. But to consider matters of true faith and spirituality adequately here is certainly impossible. Moreover, the relationship between superstition and religion is not at all clear. For example, one explanation of the origin about the Western aversion to the number 13 has to do with Jesus sitting with his 12 disciples at the Last Supper.

However, many of our beliefs are secular in nature. What Westerners often call superstition may play quite a large role in a society's belief system in another part of the world. For example, in parts of Asia, ghosts, fortune telling, palmistry, blood types, head-bump reading, phases of the moon, faith healers, demons, and soothsayers can all be integral elements of society. Surveys of advertisements in Greater China show a preference for an "8" as the last digit in prices listed—the number connotes "prosperity" in Chinese culture. The

---

[59]Michael W. Allen, Richa Gupta, and Arnaud Monnier, "The Interactive Effect of Cultural Symbols and Cultural Values on Taste Evaluations," *Journal of Consumer Research* 35, no. 2 (2008), pp. 294–308.

[60]Martin J. Gannon, *Understanding Global Cultures, Metaphorical Journeys through 23 Nations*, 2nd ed. (Thousand Oaks, CA: Sage, 2001).

[61]Cristina B. Gibson and Mary E. Zeller-Bruhn, "Metaphors and Meaning: An Intercultural Analysis of the Concept of Work," *Administrative Science Quarterly* 46, no. 2 (2001), pp. 274–303.

Russian Orthodox priests prepare to bless an assembly line at a Niva sport-utility plant near Moscow, part of a joint venture between General Motors and AvtoVaz. The Niva is the best-selling SUV in Russia, making a profit for GM. Comrade Lenin would have had a tough time with this one!

Beijing Olympics started on 8–8–08 for a reason! And recall the Japanese concern about Year of the Fire Horse discussed earlier.

Called art, science, philosophy, or superstition—depending on who is talking—the Chinese practice of *feng shui* is an important ancient belief held by Chinese, among others. Feng shui is the process that links humans and the universe to *ch'i*, the energy that sustains life and flows through our bodies and surroundings, in and around our homes and workplaces. The idea is to harness this ch'i to enhance good luck, prosperity, good health, and honor for the owner of a premise and to minimize the negative force, *sha ch'i*, and its effect. Feng shui requires engaging the services of a feng shui master to determine the positive orientation of a building in relation to the owner's horoscope, the date of establishment of the business, or the shape of the land and building. It is not a look or a style, and it is more than aesthetics: Feng shui is a strong belief in establishing a harmonious environment through the design and placement of furnishings and the avoidance of buildings facing northwest, the "devil's entrance," and southwest, the "devil's backdoor." Indeed, Disney has even "feng-shuied" all its new rides in Hong Kong Disneyland.

Too often, one person's beliefs are another person's funny story. To discount the importance of myths, beliefs, superstitions, or other cultural beliefs, however strange they may appear, is a mistake because they are an important part of the cultural fabric of a society and influence all manner of behavior. For the marketer to make light of superstitions in other cultures when doing business there can be an expensive mistake. Making a fuss about being born in the right year under the right phase of the moon or relying heavily on handwriting and palm-reading experts, as in Japan, can be difficult to comprehend for a Westerner who refuses to walk under a ladder, worries about the next seven years after breaking a mirror, buys a one-dollar lottery ticket, and seldom sees a 13th floor in a building.

Thought Processes

We are now learning in much more detail the degree to which ways of thinking vary across cultures. For example, new studies are demonstrating cultural differences in consumer impatience[62] and in how consumers make decisions about products—culture seems to matter more in snap judgments than in longer deliberations.[63] Richard Nisbett,

[62]Haipen (Allan) Chen, Sharon Ng, and Akshay R. Rao, "Cultural Differences in Consumer Impatience," *Journal of Marketing Research* 42 (2007), pp. 291–301.

[63]Donnel A. Briley and Jennifer L. Aaker, "When Does Culture Matter? Effects of Personal Knowledge on the Correction of Culture-Based Judgments," *Journal of Marketing Research* 43 (2008), pp. 395–408.

in his wonderful book *The Geography of Thought*,[64] broadly discusses differences in "Asian and Western" thinking. He starts with Confucius and Aristotle and develops his arguments through consideration of historical and philosophical writings and findings from more recent behavioral science research, including his own social-psychological experiments. Although he acknowledges the dangers surrounding generalizations about Japanese, Chinese, and Korean cultures, on the one hand, and European and American cultures, on the other, many of his conclusions are consistent with our own work related to international negotiations, cultural values, and linguistic distance.

A good metaphor for his views involves going back to Confucius's worthy picture. Asians tend to see the whole picture and can report details about the background and foreground. Westerners alternatively focus on the foreground and can provide great detail about central figures but see relatively little in the background. This difference in perception—focus versus big picture—is associated with a wide variety of differences in values, preferences, and expectations about future events. Nisbett's book is essential reading for anyone marketing products and services internationally. His insights are pertinent to Japanese selling in Jacksonville or Belgians selling in Beijing.

Each of the five cultural elements must be evaluated in light of how they might affect a proposed marketing program. Newer products and services and more extensive programs involving the entire cycle, from product development through promotion to final selling, require greater consideration of cultural factors. Moreover, the separate origins and elements of culture we have presented interact, often in synergistic ways. Therefore, the marketer must also take a step back and consider larger cultural consequences of marketing actions.

Cultural Sensitivity and Tolerance

Successful foreign marketing begins with **cultural sensitivity**—being attuned to the nuances of culture so that a new culture can be viewed objectively, evaluated, and appreciated. Cultural sensitivity, or cultural empathy, must be carefully cultivated. That is, for every amusing, annoying, peculiar, or repulsive cultural trait we find in a country, others see a similarly amusing, annoying, or repulsive trait in our culture. For example, we bathe, perfume, and deodorize our bodies in a daily ritual that is seen in many cultures as compulsive, while we often become annoyed with those cultures less concerned with natural body odor. Just because a culture is different does not make it wrong. Marketers must understand how their own cultures influence their assumptions about another culture. The more exotic the situation, the more sensitive, tolerant, and flexible one needs to be.[65] Being culturally sensitive will reduce conflict and improve communications and thereby increase success in collaborative relationships.

Besides knowledge of the origins and elements of cultures, the international marketer also should have an appreciation of how cultures change and accept or reject new ideas. Because the marketer usually is trying to introduce something completely new (such as e-trading) or to improve what is already in use, how cultures change and the manner in which resistance to change occurs should be thoroughly understood.

Cultural Change

Culture is dynamic in nature; it is a living process.[66] But the fact that cultural change is constant seems paradoxical, because another important attribute of culture is that it is conservative and resists change. The dynamic character of culture is significant in assessing new markets even though changes face resistance. Societies change in a variety of ways. Some have change thrust upon them by war (for example, the changes in Japan after World War II) or by natural disaster. More frequently, change is a result of a society seeking ways to solve the problems created by changes in its environment. One view is that culture is the accumulation of a series of the best solutions to problems faced in common by members of

---

[64]Nisbett, *The Geography of Thought*.

[65]Paul Vitello, "When a Kiss Is More Than a Kiss," *The New York Times*, May 6, 2007, Section 4, p. 1.

[66]Indeed, aspects of Hofstede's values scores have been shown to vary over time. See Steve Jenner, Bren MacNab, Donnel Briley, Richard Brislin, and Reg Worthley, "Culture Change and Marketing," *Journal of International Marketing* 21, no. 2 (2008), pp. 161–72.

CROSSING BORDERS 4.3   Thumbs that Rule

Ha Mok-min is feeling like a gunslinger these days. At the English-language cram school she attends during winter break, students jealous of her international bragging rights line up to duel with her. "They come with their cell phones boasting they can beat me," the 16-year-old sighs, her deadpan manner lending her the air of a champion accustomed to—even weary of—fame. "I let them try." With another young South Korean, Bae Yeong-ho, her Team Korea won an international competition held in New York to determine who could send text messages the fastest and most accurately. "When others watch me texting, they think I'm not that fast and they can do better," said Bae, a 17-year-old high school dropout who dyes his hair a light chestnut color and is studying to be an opera singer. "So far, I've never lost a match." In the New York competition, he typed six characters a second. "If I can think faster I can type faster," he said.

The inaugural Mobile World Cup, hosted by the South Korean cell phone maker LG Electronics, brought together two-person teams from 13 countries who had clinched their national titles by beating a total of six million contestants. Marching behind their national flags, they gathered for an international clash of dexterous

digits. Behind Ha and Bae were an American team, followed by the Argentine team.

Since their return home, with $50,000 prizes, Ha and Bae have become something like heroes to the "thumb tribe"—those youngsters who feel more comfortable texting than talking. Ha averages 150 to 200 messages a day—"average among my friends," she said defensively. "Some send as many as 500 a day." In 2009, Ha also won the South Korean national title, over 2.8 million competitors, by thumbing 7.25 characters a second. (The best score among participants in their 40s was 2.2 characters a second.) Bae, the previous national champion, has typed as many as 8 characters a second, but he did not compete last year.

It remains tough for even the most technologically savvy older person to keep up with this thumb tribe. On *The Daily Show* in January 2010, Bill Gates even admitted to host Jon Stewart that he had begun tweeting—for the first time just that month! Human communication systems are changing at the speed of "Mok-min."

Sources: Choe Sang-Hun, "Rule of Thumbs: Koreans Reign in Texting World," *The New York Times*, January 28, 2010, p. A12; "Le Snooze? We Lose," *Los Angeles Times*, May 8, 2009, p. A38.

a given society. In other words, culture is the means used in adjusting to the environmental and historical components of human existence.

Accidents have provided solutions to some problems; invention has solved many others. Usually, however, societies have found answers by looking to other cultures from which they can borrow ideas. Cultural borrowing is common to all cultures. Although each society has a few unique situations facing it (such as stomach cancer in Japan), most problems confronting societies are similar in nature.

Cultural Borrowing

LO4

The impact of cultural borrowing

Cultural borrowing is a responsible effort to learn from others' cultural ways in the quest for better solutions to a society's particular problems.[67] Thus cultures unique in their own right are the result, in part, of imitating a diversity of others. Some cultures grow closer together and some further apart with contact.[68] Consider, for example, American (U.S.) culture and a typical U.S. citizen, who begins breakfast with an orange from the eastern Mediterranean, a cantaloupe from Persia, or perhaps a piece of African watermelon. After her fruit and first coffee, she goes on to waffles, cakes made by a Scandinavian technique from wheat domesticated in Asia Minor. Over these she pours maple syrup, invented by the Native Americans of the eastern U.S. woodlands. As a side dish, she may have the eggs of a species of bird domesticated in Indochina or thin strips of the flesh of an animal domesticated in eastern

[67]Consider a discussion about Japanese teenagers as the leaders of cultural change on the planet: Amy Chozick, "Land of the Rising Karaoke Hot Tub," *The Wall Street Journal*, March 9, 2007, p. W1.

[68]Kwok Leung, Rabi S. Bhagat, Nancy B. Buchan, Miriam Erez, and Cristina Gibson, "Culture and International Business: Recent Advances and Their Implications for Future Research," *Journal of International Business Studies* 36 (2006), pp. 357–78.

Asia that have been salted and smoked by a process developed in northern Europe. While eating, she reads the news of the day, imprinted in characters invented by the ancient Semites upon a material invented in China by a process also invented in China. As she absorbs the accounts of foreign troubles, she will, if she is a good conservative citizen, thank a Hebrew deity in an Indo-European language that she is 100 percent American.[69]

Actually, this citizen is correct to assume that she is 100 percent American, because each of the borrowed cultural facets has been adapted to fit her needs, molded into uniquely American habits, foods, and customs. Americans behave as they do because of the dictates of their culture. Regardless of how or where solutions are found, once a particular pattern of action is judged acceptable by society, it becomes the approved way and is passed on and taught as part of the group's cultural heritage. Cultural heritage is one of the fundamental differences between humans and other animals. Culture is learned; societies pass on to succeeding generations solutions to problems, constantly building on and expanding the culture so that a wide range of behavior is possible. The point is, of course, that though many behaviors are borrowed from other cultures, they are combined in a unique manner that becomes typical for a particular society. To the foreign marketer, this similar-but-different feature of cultures has important meaning in gaining cultural empathy.

Similarities: An Illusion

For the inexperienced marketer, the similar-but-different aspect of culture creates illusions of similarity that usually do not exist. Several nationalities can speak the same language or have similar race and heritage, but it does not follow that similarities exist in other respects—that a product acceptable to one culture will be readily acceptable to the other, or that a promotional message that succeeds in one country will succeed in the other. Even though people start with a common idea or approach, as is the case among English-speaking Americans and the British, cultural borrowing and assimilation to meet individual needs translate over time into quite distinct cultures. A common language does not guarantee a similar interpretation of words or phrases. Both British and Americans speak English, but their cultures are sufficiently different that a single phrase has different meanings to each and can even be completely misunderstood. In England, one asks for a lift instead of an elevator, and an American, when speaking of a bathroom, generally refers to a toilet, whereas in England a bathroom is a place to take a tub bath. Also, the English "hoover" a carpet, whereas Americans vacuum. The movie title *The Spy Who Shagged Me* means nothing to most Americans but much to British consumers. Indeed, anthropologist Edward Hall warns that Americans and British have a harder time understanding each other because of their *apparent* and *assumed* cultural similarities.

The growing economic unification of Europe has fostered a tendency to speak of the "European consumer." Many of the obstacles to doing business in Europe have been or will be eliminated as the European Union takes shape, but marketers, eager to enter the market, must not jump to the conclusion that an economically unified Europe means a common set of consumer wants and needs. Cultural differences among the members of the European Union are the product of centuries of history that will take centuries to ameliorate.[70] The United States itself has many subcultures that even today, with mass communications and rapid travel, defy complete homogenization. To suggest that the South is in all respects culturally the same as the northeastern or midwestern parts of the United States would be folly, just as it would be folly to assume that the unification of Germany has erased cultural differences that arose from over 40 years of political and social separation.

Marketers must assess each country thoroughly in terms of the proposed products or services and never rely on an often-used axiom that if it sells in one country, it will surely sell in another. As worldwide mass communications and increased economic and social interdependence of countries grow, similarities among countries will increase, and common

---

[69]Ralph Linton, *The Study of Man* (New York: Appleton-Century-Crofts, 1936), p. 327.

[70]Tuba Ustuner and Douglas B. Holt, "Dominated Consumer Acculturation: The Social Construction of Poor Migrant Women's Consumer Identity Projects in a Turkish Squatter," *Journal of Consumer Research* 34 (2007), pp. 41–56.

market behaviors, wants, and needs will continue to develop. As this process occurs, the tendency will be to rely more on apparent similarities when they may not exist. A marketer is wise to remember that a culture borrows and then adapts and customizes to its own needs and idiosyncrasies; thus, what may appear to be the same on the surface may be different in its cultural meaning.

Resistance to Change

A characteristic of human culture is that change occurs. That people's habits, tastes, styles, behavior, and values are not constant but are continually changing can be verified by reading 20-year-old magazines. However, this gradual cultural growth does not occur without some resistance; new methods, ideas, and products are held to be suspect before they are accepted, if ever. Moreover, research shows that consumers in different cultures display differing resistance.[71]

The degree of resistance to new patterns varies. In some situations, new elements are accepted completely and rapidly; in others, resistance is so strong that acceptance is never forthcoming. Studies show that the most important factors in determining what kind and how much of an innovation will be accepted is the degree of interest in the particular subject, as well as how drastically the new will change the old—that is, how disruptive the innovation will be to presently acceptable values and behavior patterns. Observations indicate that those innovations most readily accepted are those holding the greatest interest within the society and those least disruptive. For example, rapid industrialization in parts of Europe has changed many long-honored attitudes involving time and working women. Today, there is an interest in ways to save time and make life more productive; the leisurely continental life is rapidly disappearing. With this time consciousness has come the very rapid acceptance of many innovations that might have been resisted by most just a few years ago. Instant foods, labor-saving devices, and fast-food establishments, all supportive of a changing attitude toward work and time, are rapidly gaining acceptance.

An understanding of the process of acceptance of innovations is of crucial importance to the marketer. The marketer cannot wait centuries or even decades for acceptance but must gain acceptance within the limits of financial resources and projected profitability periods. Possible methods and insights are offered by social scientists who are concerned with the concepts of planned social change. Historically, most cultural borrowing and the resulting

---

[71]Mark Cleveland, Michel Laroche, and Nicolas Papadopoulos, "Cosmopolitanism, Consumer Ethnocentrism, and Materialism: An Eight-Country Study of Antecedents and Outcomes," *Journal of International Marketing* 17, no. 1 (2009), pp. 116–46; Gerald J. Tellis, Eden Yen, and Simon Bell, "Global Consumer Innovativeness: Cross-Country Differences and Commonalities," *Journal of International Marketing* 17, no. 2 (2009), pp. 1–22.

MTV meets Mom in Mumbai (formerly Bombay), India. Culture does change—dress and even names of major cities! Even so, a local resident tells us everyone still calls it Bombay despite the official alteration.

change has occurred without a deliberate plan, but increasingly, changes are occurring in societies as a result of purposeful attempts by some acceptable institution to bring about change, that is, planned change.

Planned and Unplanned Cultural Change

LO5

The strategy of planned change and its consequences

The first step in bringing about planned change in a society is to determine which cultural factors conflict with an innovation, thus creating resistance to its acceptance. The next step is an effort to change those factors from obstacles to acceptance into stimulants for change. The same deliberate approaches used by the social planner to gain acceptance for hybrid grains, better sanitation methods, improved farming techniques, or protein-rich diets among the peoples of underdeveloped societies can be adopted by marketers to achieve marketing goals.[72]

Marketers have two options when introducing an innovation to a culture: They can wait for changes to occur, or they can spur change. The former requires hopeful waiting for eventual cultural changes that prove their innovations of value to the culture; the latter involves introducing an idea or product and deliberately setting about to overcome resistance and to cause change that accelerates the rate of acceptance. The folks at Fidelity Investments in Japan, for example, pitched a tent in front of Tokyo's Shinjuku train station and showered commuters investment brochures and demonstrations of Japanese-language WebXpress online stock trading services to encourage faster changes in Japanese investor behavior. However, as mentioned previously, the changes have not happened fast enough for most foreign firms targeting this business and similar financial services.

Obviously not all marketing efforts require change to be accepted. In fact, much successful and highly competitive marketing is accomplished by a strategy of **cultural congruence**. Essentially this strategy involves marketing products similar to ones already on the market in a manner as congruent as possible with existing cultural norms, thereby minimizing resistance. However, when marketing programs depend on cultural change to be successful, a company may decide to leave acceptance to a strategy of unplanned change—that is, introduce a product and hope for the best. Or a company may employ a strategy of **planned change**—that is, deliberately set out to change those aspects of the culture offering resistance to predetermined marketing goals.

As an example of unplanned cultural change, consider how the Japanese diet has changed since the introduction of milk and bread soon after World War II. Most Japanese, who were predominantly fish eaters, have increased their intake of animal fat and protein to the point that fat and protein now exceed vegetable intake. As many McDonald's hamburgers are likely to be eaten in Japan as the traditional rice ball wrapped in edible seaweed, and American hamburgers are replacing many traditional Japanese foods. Burger King purchased Japan's homegrown Morinaga Love restaurant chain, home of the salmon burger—a patty of salmon meat, a slice of cheese, and a layer of dried seaweed, spread with mayonnaise and stuck between two cakes of sticky Japanese rice pressed into the shape of a bun—an eggplant burger, and other treats. The chain was converted and now sells Whoppers instead of the salmon-rice burger.

The Westernized diet has caused many Japanese to become overweight. To counter this trend, the Japanese are buying low-calorie, low-fat foods to help shed excess weight and are flocking to health clubs. All this began when U.S. occupation forces introduced bread, milk, and steak to Japanese culture. The effect on the Japanese was unintentional, but nevertheless, change occurred. Had the intent been to introduce a new diet—that is, a strategy of planned change—specific steps could have been taken to identify resistance to dietary change and then to overcome these resistances, thus accelerating the process of change.

Marketing strategy is judged culturally in terms of acceptance, resistance, or rejection. How marketing efforts interact with a culture determines the degree of success or failure. All too often marketers are not aware of the scope of their impact on a host culture. If a strategy of planned change is implemented, the marketer has some responsibility to determine the consequences of such action.

---

[72]Two very important books on this topic are Everett M. Rogers, *Diffusion of Innovations*, 4th ed. (New York: The Free Press, 1995), and Gerald Zaltman and Robert Duncan, *Strategies for Planned Change* (New York: John Wiley & Sons, 1979).

Summary

A complete and thorough appreciation of the origins (geography, history, political economy, technology, and social institutions) and elements (cultural values, rituals, symbols, beliefs, and ways of thinking) of culture may well be the single most important gain for a foreign marketer in the preparation of marketing plans and strategies. Marketers can control the product offered to a market—its promotion, price, and eventual distribution methods—but they have only limited control over the cultural environment within which these plans must be implemented. Because they cannot control all the influences on their marketing plans, they must attempt to anticipate the eventual effect of the uncontrollable elements and plan in such a way that these elements do not preclude the achievement of marketing objectives. They can also set about to effect changes that lead to quicker acceptance of their products or marketing programs.

Planning marketing strategy in terms of the uncontrollable elements of a market is necessary in a domestic market as well, but when a company is operating internationally, each new environment that is influenced by elements unfamiliar and sometimes unrecognizable to the marketer complicates the task. For these reasons, special effort and study are needed to absorb enough understanding of the foreign culture to cope with the uncontrollable features. Perhaps it is safe to generalize that of all the tools the foreign marketer must have, those that help generate empathy for another culture are the most valuable. Each of the cultural elements is explored in depth in subsequent chapters. Specific attention is given to business customs, political culture, and legal culture in the following chapters.

Key Terms

Culture	Rituals	Cultural sensitivity	Cultural congruence
Social institutions	Linguistic distance	Cultural borrowing	Planned change
Cultural values	Aesthetics		

Questions

1. Define the key terms listed above.
2. What role does the marketer play as a change agent?
3. Discuss the three cultural change strategies a foreign marketer can pursue.
4. "Culture is pervasive in all marketing activities." Discuss.
5. What is the importance of cultural empathy to foreign marketers? How do they acquire cultural empathy?
6. Why should a foreign marketer be concerned with the study of culture?
7. What is the popular definition of culture? Where does culture come from?
8. "Members of a society borrow from other cultures to solve problems that they face in common." What does this mean? What is the significance to marketing?
9. "For the inexperienced marketer, the 'similar-but-different' aspect of culture creates an illusion of similarity that usually does not exist." Discuss and give examples.
10. Outline the elements of culture as seen by an anthropologist. How can a marketer use this cultural scheme?
11. Social institutions affect culture and marketing in a variety of ways. Discuss, giving examples.
12. "Markets are the result of the three-way interaction of a marketer's efforts, economic conditions, and all other elements of the culture." Comment.
13. What are some particularly troublesome problems caused by language in foreign marketing? Discuss.
14. Suppose you were asked to prepare a cultural analysis for a potential market. What would you do? Outline the steps and comment briefly on each.
15. Cultures are dynamic. How do they change? Are there cases in which changes are not resisted but actually preferred? Explain. What is the relevance to marketing?
16. How can resistance to cultural change influence product introduction? Are there any similarities in domestic marketing? Explain, giving examples.
17. Innovations are described as either functional or dysfunctional. Explain and give examples of each.
18. Defend the proposition that a multinational corporation has no responsibility for the consequences of an innovation beyond the direct effects of the innovation, such as the product's safety, performance, and so forth.
19. Find a product whose introduction into a foreign culture may cause dysfunctional consequences and describe how the consequences might be eliminated and the product still profitably introduced.

Chapter 5

Culture, Management Style, and Business Systems

CHAPTER OUTLINE

CHAPTER LEARNING OBJECTIVES

What you should learn from Chapter 5:

LO1 The necessity for adapting to cultural differences

LO2 How and why management styles vary around the world

LO3 The extent and implications of gender bias in other countries

LO4 The importance of cultural differences in business ethics

LO5 The differences between relationship-oriented and information-oriented cultures

Global Perspective

DO BLONDES HAVE MORE FUN IN JAPAN?

Recounts one American executive, "My first trip to Japan was pretty much a disaster for several reasons. The meetings didn't run smoothly because every day at least 20, if not more, people came walking in and out of the room just to look at me. It is one thing to see a woman at the negotiation table, but to see a woman who happens to be blonde, young, and very tall by Japanese standards (5'8" with no shoes) leading the discussions was more than most of the Japanese men could handle."

"Even though I was the lead negotiator for the Ford team, the Japanese would go out of their way to avoid speaking directly to me. At the negotiation table I purposely sat in the center of my team, in the spokesperson's strategic position. Their key person would not sit across from me, but rather two places down. Also, no one would address questions and/or remarks to me—to everyone (all male) on our team—but none to me. They would never say my name or acknowledge my presence. And most disconcerting of all, they appeared to be laughing at me. We would be talking about a serious topic such as product liability, I would make a point or ask a question, and after a barrage of Japanese they would all start laughing."

Another example regards toys and consumer behavior. For years, Barbie dolls sold in Japan looked different from their U.S. counterparts. They had Asian facial features, black hair, and Japanese-inspired fashions.

Then about seven years ago, Mattel Inc. conducted consumer research around the world and learned something surprising: The original Barbie, with her yellow hair and blue eyes, played as well in Hong Kong as it did in Hollywood. Girls didn't care if Barbie didn't look like them, at least if you believed their marketing research.

"It's all about fantasies and hair," said Peter Broegger, general manager of Mattel's Asian operations. "Blonde Barbie sells just as well in Asia as in the United States."

So Mattel began rethinking one of the basic tenets of its $55 billion global industry—that children in different countries want different playthings. The implications were significant for kids, parents, and particularly the company. In the past, giants such as Mattel, Hasbro Inc., and Lego Co. produced toys and gear in a variety of styles. But Mattel went the other direction, designing and marketing one version worldwide. Sales plummeted, forcing a Barbie makeover that most recently includes Hello Kitty clothes and a new video game, iDesign. Now, even at age 50, Barbie is making money again.

Sources: James D. Hodgson, Yoshihiro Sano, and John L. Graham, *Doing Business with the New Japan, Succeeding in America's Richest International Market* (Latham, MD: Rowman & Littlefield, 2008); Lisa Banon and Carlta Vitzthum, "One-Toy-Fits-All: How Industry Learned to Love the Global Kid," *The Wall Street Journal*, April 29, 2003, p. A1; Andrea Chang, "Barbie Brings in the Bucks," *Los Angeles Times*, January 30, 2010, p. B3.

Perhaps nothing causes more problems for Americans negotiating in other countries than their impatience. Everyone around the world knows that delaying tactics work well against time-conscious U.S. bargainers.

Culture, including all its elements, profoundly affects management style and overall business systems. This is not a new idea. German sociologist Max Weber made the first strong case back in 1930.[1] Culture not only establishes the criteria for day-to-day business behavior but also forms general patterns of values and motivations. Executives are largely captives of their heritages and cannot totally escape the elements of culture they learned growing up.

In the United States, for example, the historical perspective of individualism and "winning the West" seems to be manifest in individual wealth or corporate profit being dominant measures of success. Japan's lack of frontiers and natural resources and its dependence on trade have focused individual and corporate success criteria on uniformity, subordination to the group, and society's ability to maintain high levels of employment. The feudal background of southern Europe tends to emphasize maintenance of both individual and corporate power and authority while blending those feudal traits with paternalistic concern for minimal welfare for workers and other members of society. Various studies identify North Americans as individualists, Japanese as consensus oriented and committed to the group, and central and southern Europeans as elitists and rank conscious. Although these descriptions are stereotypical, they illustrate cultural differences that are often manifest in business behavior and practices. Such differences also coincide quite well with Hofstede's scores listed in Exhibit 4.5 in the last chapter.[2]

A lack of empathy for and knowledge of foreign business practices can create insurmountable barriers to successful business relations. Some businesses plot their strategies with the idea that their counterparts from other business cultures are similar to themselves and are moved by similar interests, motivations, and goals—that they are "just like us." Even though that may be true in some respects, enough differences exist to cause frustration, miscommunication, and, ultimately, failed business opportunities if these differences are not understood and responded to properly.

Knowledge of the *management style*—that is, the business culture, management values, and business methods and behaviors—existing in a country and a willingness to accommodate the differences are important to success in an international market. Unless marketers remain flexible by accepting differences in basic patterns of thinking, local business tempo, religious practices, political structure, and family loyalty, they are hampered, if not prevented, from reaching satisfactory conclusions to business transactions. In such situations, obstacles take many forms, but it is not unusual to have one negotiator's business proposition accepted over another's simply because "that one understands us."

This chapter focuses on matters specifically related to management style. Besides an analysis of the need for adaptation, it reviews differences in management styles and ethics and concludes with a discussion of culture's influence on strategic thinking.

Required Adaptation

LO1

The necessity for adapting to cultural differences

Adaptation is a key concept in international marketing, and willingness to adapt is a crucial attitude. Adaptation, or at least accommodation, is required on small matters as well as large ones.[3] In fact, small, seemingly insignificant situations are often the most crucial. More than tolerance of an alien culture is required. Affirmative acceptance, that is, open tolerance may be needed as well. Through such affirmative acceptance, adaptation becomes easier because empathy for another's point of view naturally leads to ideas for meeting cultural differences.

[1]Max Weber, *The Protestant Ethic and Spirit of Capitalism* (London: George Allen & Unwin, 1930, 1976).

[2]Geert Hofstede, *Culture's Consequences*, 2nd ed. (Thousand Oaks, CA: Sage, 2001).

[3]Emily Maltby, "Expanding Abroad? Avoid Cultural Gaffes," *The Wall Street Journal*, January 19, 2010, p. B5.

As a guide to adaptation, all who wish to deal with individuals, firms, or authorities in foreign countries should be able to meet 10 basic criteria: (1) open tolerance, (2) flexibility, (3) humility, (4) justice/fairness, (5) ability to adjust to varying tempos, (6) curiosity/interest, (7) knowledge of the country, (8) liking for others, (9) ability to command respect, and (10) ability to integrate oneself into the environment. In short, add the quality of adaptability to the qualities of a good executive for a composite of the successful international marketer. It is difficult to argue with these 10 items. As one critic commented, "They border on the 12 Boy Scout laws." However, as you read this chapter, you will see that it is the obvious that we sometimes overlook.

Degree of Adaptation

Adaptation does not require business executives to forsake their ways and change to local customs; rather, executives must be aware of local customs and be willing to accommodate those differences that can cause misunderstandings. Essential to effective adaptation is awareness of one's own culture and the recognition that differences in others can cause anxiety, frustration, and misunderstanding of the host's intentions. The self-reference criterion (SRC) is especially operative in business customs. If we do not understand our foreign counterpart's customs, we are more likely to evaluate that person's behavior in terms of what is familiar to us. For example, from an American perspective, a Brazilian executive interrupting frequently during a business meeting may seem quite rude, even though such behavior simply reflects a cultural difference in conversational coordination.

The key to adaptation is to remain American but to develop an understanding of and willingness to accommodate the differences that exist. A successful marketer knows that in China it is important to make points without winning arguments; criticism, even if asked for, can cause a host to lose face. In Germany, it is considered discourteous to use first names unless specifically invited to do so. Instead, address a person as Herr, Frau, or Fraulein with the last name. In Brazil, do not be offended by the Brazilian inclination to touch during conversation. Such a custom is not a violation of your personal space but rather the Brazilian way of greeting, emphasizing a point, or making a gesture of goodwill and friendship. A Chinese, German, or Brazilian does not expect you to act like one of them. After all, you are American, not Chinese, German, or Brazilian, and it would be foolish for an American to give up the ways that have contributed so notably to American success. It would be equally foolish for others to give up their ways. When different cultures meet, open tolerance and a willingness to accommodate each other's differences are necessary. Once a marketer is aware of cultural differences and the probable consequences of failure to adapt or accommodate, the seemingly endless variety of customs must be assessed. Where does one begin? Which customs should be absolutely adhered to? Which others can be ignored? Fortunately, among the many obvious differences that exist between cultures, only a few are troubling.

Imperatives, Electives, and Exclusives

Business customs can be grouped into *imperatives*, customs that must be recognized and accommodated; *electives*, customs to which adaptation is helpful but not necessary; and *exclusives*, customs in which an outsider must not participate. An international marketer must appreciate the nuances of cultural imperatives, cultural electives, and cultural exclusives.

Cultural Imperatives.   Cultural imperatives are the business customs and expectations that must be met and conformed to or avoided if relationships are to be successful. Successful businesspeople know the Chinese word *guanxi*,[4] the Japanese *ningen kankei*, or the Latin American *compadre*. All refer to friendship, human relations, or attaining a level of trust.[5] They also know there is no substitute for establishing friendship in some cultures before effective business negotiations can begin.

---

[4]Alaka N. Rao, Jone L. Pearce, and Katherine Xin, "Governments, Reciprocal Exchange, and Trust Among Business Associates," *Journal of International Business Studies* 36 (2005), pp. 104–18; Kam-hon Lee, Gong-ming Qian, Julie H. Yu, and Ying Ho, "Trading Favors for Marketing Advantage: Evidence from Hong Kong, China, and the United States" *Journal of International Marketing* 13 (2005), pp. 1–35.

[5]Srilata Zaheer and Akbar Zaheer, "Trust across Borders," *Journal of International Business Studies* 37 (2006), pp. 21–29.

Informal discussions, entertaining, mutual friends, contacts, and just spending time with others are ways *guanxi*, *ningen kankei*, *compadre*, and other trusting relationships are developed. In those cultures in which friendships are a key to success, the businessperson should not slight the time required for their development. Friendship motivates local agents to make more sales, and friendship helps establish the right relationship with end users, which leads to more sales over a longer period. Naturally, after-sales service, price, and the product must be competitive, but the marketer who has established *guanxi*, *ningen kankei*, or *compadre* has the edge. Establishing friendship is an imperative in many cultures. If friendship is not established, the marketer risks not earning trust and acceptance, the basic cultural prerequisites for developing and retaining effective business relationships.

The significance of establishing friendship cannot be overemphasized, especially in those countries where family relationships are close. In China, for example, the outsider is, at best, in fifth place in order of importance when deciding with whom to conduct business. The family is first, then the extended family, then neighbors from one's hometown, then former classmates, and only then, reluctantly, strangers—and the last only after a trusting relationship has been established.

In some cultures, a person's demeanor is more critical than in other cultures. For example, it is probably never acceptable to lose your patience, raise your voice, or correct someone in public, no matter how frustrating the situation. In some cultures such behavior would only cast you as boorish, but in others, it could end a business deal. In Asian cultures it is imperative to avoid causing your counterpart to lose face. In China, to raise your voice, to shout at a Chinese person in public, or to correct one in front of his or her peers will cause that person to lose face.

A complicating factor in cultural awareness is that what may be an imperative to avoid in one culture is an imperative to do in another. For example, in Japan, prolonged eye contact is considered offensive, and it is imperative that it be avoided. However, with Arab and Latin American executives, it is important to make strong eye contact, or you run the risk of being seen as evasive and untrustworthy.

BEIJING, CHINA: German Chancellor Angela Merkel and Chinese Prime Minister Wen Jiabao toast after the EU–China Business Summit at the Great Hall of the People in Beijing. The summit was boosted by the settlement of a trade row that had left 80 million Chinese-made garments piled up in European seaports, unable to be delivered to shops under a quota pact agreed to at the time. Drinking half a bottle is a cultural elective, but taking a sip is more of an imperative in this case.

Cultural Electives.   Cultural electives relate to areas of behavior or to customs that cultural aliens may wish to conform to or participate in but that are not required. In other words, following the custom in question is not particularly important but is permissible. The majority of customs fit into this category. One need not greet another man with a kiss (a custom in some countries), eat foods that disagree with the digestive system (so long as the refusal is gracious), or drink alcoholic beverages (if for health, personal, or religious reasons). However, a symbolic attempt to participate in such options is not only acceptable but also may help establish rapport. It demonstrates that the marketer has studied the culture. Japanese do not expect a Westerner to bow and to understand the ritual of bowing among Japanese, yet a symbolic bow indicates interest and some sensitivity to Japanese culture that is acknowledged as a gesture of goodwill. It may help pave the way to a strong, trusting relationship.

A cultural elective in one county may be an imperative in another. For example, in some cultures, one can accept or tactfully and politely reject an offer of a beverage, whereas in other cases, the offer of a beverage is a special ritual and to refuse it is an insult. In the Czech Republic, an aperitif or other liqueur offered at the beginning of a business meeting, even in the morning, is a way to establish goodwill and trust. It is a sign that you are being welcomed as a friend. It is imperative that you accept unless you make it clear to your Czech counterpart that the refusal is because of health or religion. Chinese business negotiations often include banquets at which large quantities of alcohol are consumed in an endless series of toasts. It is imperative that you participate in the toasts with a raised glass of the offered beverage, but to drink is optional. Your Arab business associates will offer coffee as part of the important ritual of establishing a level of friendship and trust; you should accept, even if you only take a ceremonial sip. Cultural electives are the most

CROSSING BORDERS 5.2

The American Tourist and the Mexican Fisherman

An American tourist was at the pier of a small coastal Mexican village when a small boat with just one fisherman docked. Inside the small boat were several large yellowfin tuna. The tourist complimented the Mexican on the quality of the fish and asked how long it took to catch them.

The Mexican replied, "Only a little while."

The tourist then asked, "Why didn't you stay out longer and catch more fish?"

The Mexican replied, "With this I have enough to support my family's needs."

The tourist then asked, "But what do you do with the rest of your time?"

The Mexican fisherman said, "I sleep late, fish a little, play with my children, take a siesta with my wife, Maria, stroll into the village each evening where I sip wine and play guitar with my amigos. I have a full and busy life."

The tourist scoffed, "I can help you. You should spend more time fishing and with the proceeds, buy a bigger boat. With the proceeds from the bigger boat you could buy several boats. Eventually you would have a fleet of fishing boats. Instead of selling your catch to a middleman you could sell directly to the processor, eventually opening your own cannery. You would control the product, processing, and distribution. You could leave this small village and move to Mexico City, then Los Angeles, and eventually to New York City where you could run your ever-expanding enterprise."

The Mexican fisherman asked, "But, how long will this take?"

The tourist replied, "15 to 20 years."

"But what then?" asked the Mexican.

The tourist laughed and said, "That's the best part. When the time is right you would sell your company stock to the public and become very rich, you would make millions."

"Millions?… Then what?"

The American said, "Then you would retire. Move to a small coastal fishing village where you would sleep late, fish a little, play with your grandkids, take a siesta with your wife, stroll to the village in the evenings where you could sip wine and play your guitar with your amigos."

Source: Author unknown.

equals 2,000 hours. The Americans appear to be in the middle of hours worked, far above the northern Europeans and way below the South Koreans. Most Americans are getting about two weeks of paid vacation, while in Europe they are taking between four and six weeks! In South Korea and other Asian nations, Saturday is a workday. Although we do not list the numbers for China, the new pressures of free enterprise are adding hours and stress there as well. However, the scariest datum isn't in the table. While hours worked are decreasing almost everywhere, in the States the numbers are increasing, up 36 hours from 1990. Thank you Max Weber! We wonder: How will things be in 2020?

Affiliation and Social Acceptance. In some countries, acceptance by neighbors and fellow workers appears to be a predominant goal within business. The Asian outlook is reflected in the group decision making so important in Japan, and the Japanese place high importance on fitting in with their group. Group identification is so strong in Japan that when a worker is asked what he does for a living, he generally answers by telling you he works for Sumitomo or Mitsubishi or Matsushita, rather than that he is a chauffeur, an engineer, or a chemist.

Power and Achievement. Although there is some power seeking by business managers throughout the world, power seems to be a more important motivating force in South American countries. In these countries, many business leaders are not only profit oriented but also use their business positions to become social and political leaders. Related, but different, are the motivations for achievement also identified by management researchers in the United States. One way to measure achievement is by money in the bank; another is high rank—both aspirations particularly relevant to the United States.

Communication Styles

Edward T. Hall, professor of anthropology and for decades a consultant to business and government on intercultural relations, tells us that communication involves much more than just words. His article "The Silent Language of Overseas Business," which appeared

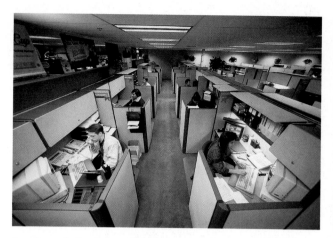

Speaking of office space: Notice the individualism reflected in the American cubicles and the collectivism demonstrated by the Japanese office organization.

in the *Harvard Business Review* in 1960,[20] remains a most worthwhile read. In it he describes the symbolic meanings (**silent languages**) of *time, space, things, friendships,* and *agreements* and how they vary across cultures. In 1960 Hall could not have anticipated the innovations brought on by the Internet. However, all of his ideas about cross-cultural communication apply to that medium as well. We begin here with a discussion of communication in the face-to-face setting and then move to the electronic media.

Face-to-Face Communication.
No language readily translates into another because the meanings of words differ widely among languages. For example, the word "marriage," even when accurately translated, can connote very different things in different languages—in one it may mean love, in another restrictions. Although language is the basic communication tool of marketers trading in foreign lands, managers, particularly from the United States, often fail to develop even a basic understanding of just one other language, much less master the linguistic nuances that reveal unspoken attitudes and information.

On the basis of decades of anthropological fieldwork, Hall[21] places 11 cultures along a high-context/low-context continuum (see Exhibit 5.2). Communication in a high-context culture depends heavily on the contextual (*who* says it, *when* it is said, *how* it is said) or nonverbal aspects of communication, whereas the low-context culture depends more on explicit, verbally expressed communications.

A brief exemplar of the high-/low-context dimension of communication style regards an international marketing executive's description of a Los Angeles business entertainment event: "I picked him [a German client] up at his hotel near LAX and asked what kind of food he wanted for dinner. He said, 'Something local.' Now in LA local food is Mexican food. I'd never met anyone that hadn't had a taco before! We went to a great Mexican place in Santa Monica and had it all, guacamole, salsa, enchiladas, burritos, a real Alka-Seltzer kind of night. When we were done I asked how he liked the food. He responded rather blandly, 'It wasn't very good.'"

The American might have been taken aback by his client's honest, and perhaps too direct, answer. However, the American knew well about German frankness[22] and just rolled with the "blow." Germans, being very low-context oriented, just deliver the information without any social padding. Most Americans would soften the blow some with an answer more like, "It was pretty good, but maybe a bit too spicy." And a high-context oriented

---

[20]*Harvard Business Review*, May–June 1960, pp. 87–96.

[21]Edward T. Hall, "Learning the Arabs' Silent Language," *Psychology Today*, August 1979, pp. 45–53. Hall has several books that should be read by everyone involved in international business, including *The Silent Language* (New York: Doubleday, 1959), *The Hidden Dimension* (New York: Doubleday, 1966), and *Beyond Culture* (New York: Anchor Press-Doubleday, 1976).

[22]Interestingly, the etymology of the term "frankness" has to do with the Franks, an ancient Germanic tribe that settled along the Rhine. This is not mere coincidence; it's history again influencing symbols (that is, language)!

Exhibit 5.2
Context, Communication, and Cultures: Edward Hall's Scale

Note: Patterned after E. T. Hall.

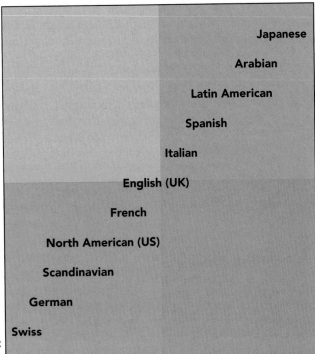

High Context
(Implicit,
Emphasis
on Context
of Communication)

Japanese

Arabian

Latin American

Spanish

Italian

English (UK)

French

North American (US)

Scandinavian

German

Swiss

Low Context
(Explicit,
Emphasis
on Content
of Communication)

Japanese would really pad the response with something like, "It was very good. Thanks." But then the Japanese would never order Mexican food again.

An American or German might view the Japanese response as less than truthful, but from the Japanese perspective, he was just preserving a harmonious relationship. Indeed, the Japanese have two words for truth, *honne* (true mind) and *tatemae* (official stance).[23] The former delivers the information, and the latter preserves the relationship. And in high-context Japan, the latter is often more important.

Internet Communications.
The message on a business-to-business Web site is an extension of the company and should be as sensitive to business customs as any other company representative would be. Once a message is posted, it can be read anywhere, at any time. As a consequence, the opportunity to convey an unintended message is infinite. Nothing about the Web will change the extent to which people identify with their own languages and cultures; thus, language should be at the top of the list when examining the viability of a company's Web site.

Estimates are that 78 percent of today's Web site content is written in English, but an English e-mail message cannot be understood by 35 percent of all Internet users. A study of businesses on the European continent highlights the need for companies to respond in the languages of their Web sites. One-third of the European senior managers surveyed said they would not tolerate English online. They do not believe that middle managers can use English well enough to transact business on the Internet.

At the extreme are the French, who even ban the use of English terms. The French Ministry of Finance issued a directive that all official French civil service correspondence must avoid common English-language business words such as *start-up* and *e-mail;* instead, *jeune pousse* (literally, "a young plant") and *courrier électronique* are recommended.

The solution to the problem is to have country-specific Web sites, like those of IBM and Marriott. Dell Computer, for example, makes its Premier Pages Web sites built for

---

[23]James D. Hodgson, Yoshihiro Sano, and John L. Graham, *Doing Business with the New Japan* (Boulder, CO: Rowman & Littlefield, 2008).

its business clients, available in 12 languages. A host of companies specialize in Web site translations; in addition, software programs are available to translate the company message into another language. However, cultural and linguistic correctness remains a problem with machine translation. If not properly done, English phrases are likely to be translated in a way that will embarrass or even damage a company. One way to avoid this issue is to prepare the original source material in easy-to-translate English, devoid of complicated phrases, idioms, or slang. Unfortunately, no machine translation is available that can manage all the nuances of language or syntax.

It would be ideal if every representative of your company spoke fluently the language of and understood the culture of your foreign customers or business associates; but that is an impossible goal for most companies. However, there is no reason why every person who accesses a company's Web site should not be able to communicate in his or her own language if a company wants to be truly global.

In addition to being language friendly, a Web site should be examined for any symbols, icons, and other nonverbal impressions that could convey an unwanted message. Icons that are frequently used on Web sites can be misunderstood. For example, an icon such as a hand making a high-five sign will be offensive in Greece; an image of a thumb-to-index finger, the A-OK gesture, will infuriate visitors in Brazil; a two-fingered peace sign when turned around has a very crude meaning to the British; and AOL's "You've Got Mail" looks a lot like a loaf of bread to a European. Colors can also pose a problem; green is a sacred color in some Middle Eastern cultures and should not be used for something frivolous like a Web background.

Finally, e-mail use and usage rates by managers are also affected by culture. That is, businesspeople in high-context cultures do not use the medium to the same extent as those in low-context cultures. Indeed, the structure of the Japanese language has at least hindered the diffusion of Internet technologies in that country.[24] Moreover, businesspeople in Hong Kong behave less cooperatively in negotiations using e-mail than in face-to-face encounters.[25] Much of the contextual information so important in high-context cultures simply cannot be signaled via the computer.

Formality and Tempo

The breezy informality and haste that seem to characterize American business relationships appear to be American exclusives that businesspeople from other countries not only fail to share but also fail to appreciate. A German executive commented that he was taken aback when employees of his Indiana client called him by his first name. He noted, "In Germany you don't do that until you know someone for 10 years—and never if you are at a lower rank." This apparent informality, however, does not indicate a lack of commitment to the job. Comparing British and American business managers, an English executive commented about the American manager's compelling involvement in business: "At a cocktail party or a dinner, the American is still on duty."

Even though Northern Europeans seem to have picked up some American attitudes in recent years, do not count on them being "Americanized." As one writer says, "While using first names in business encounters is regarded as an American vice in many countries, nowhere is it found more offensive than in France," where formality still reigns. Those who work side by side for years still address one another with formal pronouns. France is higher on Hofstede's Power Distance Index (PDI) than the United States, and such differences can lead to cultural misunderstandings. For example, the formalities of French business practices as opposed to Americans' casual manners are symbols of the French need to show rank and Americans' tendency to downplay it. Thus, the French are dubbed snobbish by Americans, while the French consider Americans crude and unsophisticated.

Haste and impatience are probably the most common mistakes of North Americans attempting to trade in the Middle East. Most Arabs do not like to embark on serious business discussions until after two or three opportunities to meet the individual they are dealing with; negotiations are likely to be prolonged. Arabs may make rapid decisions once they are prepared to do so, but they do not like to be rushed, and they do not like deadlines. The managing

[24]Ibid.

[25]Guang Yang and John L. Graham, "The Impact of Computer-Mediated Communications on the Process and Outcomes of Buyer–Seller Negotiations," working paper, University of California, Irvine, 2010.

partner of the Kuwait office of KPMG Peat Marwick says of the "fly-in visit" approach of many American businesspeople, "What in the West might be regarded as dynamic activity—the 'I've only got a day here' approach—may well be regarded here as merely rude."

Marketers who expect maximum success have to deal with foreign executives in ways that are acceptable to the foreigner. Latin Americans depend greatly on friendships but establish these friendships only in the South American way: slowly, over a considerable period of time. A typical Latin American is highly formal until a genuine relationship of respect and friendship is established. Even then, the Latin American is slow to get down to business and will not be pushed. In keeping with the culture, *mañana* (tomorrow) is good enough. How people perceive time helps explain some of the differences between U.S. managers and those from other cultures.

P-Time versus M-Time

Research has demonstrated that managers in Anglo cultures such as the United States tend to be more concerned with time management than managers from either Latin or Asian cultures.[26] Our stereotype of Latin cultures, for example, is "they are always late," and their view of us is "you are always prompt." Neither statement is completely true, though both contain some truth. What is true, however, is that the United States is a very time-oriented society—time is money to us—whereas in many other cultures, time is to be savored, not spent.

Edward T. Hall defines two time systems in the world: **monochronic** and **polychronic time**. *M-time*, or *monochronic time*, typifies most North Americans, Swiss, Germans, and Scandinavians. These Western cultures tend to concentrate on one thing at a time. They divide time into small units and are concerned with promptness. M-time is used in a linear way, and it is experienced as almost tangible, in that one saves time, wastes time, bides time, spends time, and loses time. Most low-context cultures operate on M-time. *P-time*, or *polychronic time*, is more dominant in high-context cultures, where the completion of a human transaction is emphasized more than holding to schedules. P-time is characterized by the simultaneous occurrence of many things and by "a great involvement with people." P-time allows for relationships to build and context to be absorbed as parts of high-context cultures.

One study comparing perceptions of punctuality in the United States and Brazil found that Brazilian timepieces were less reliable and public clocks less available than in the United States. Researchers also found that Brazilians more often described themselves as late arrivers, allowed greater flexibility in defining *early* and *late*, were less concerned about being late, and were more likely to blame external factors for their lateness than were Americans.[27] Please see comparisons of 31 countries in Exhibit 5.3. We note that one study has found the index useful as it well predicts the number of days necessary for obtaining a business license in the 31 countries.[28]

The American desire to get straight to the point and get down to business is a manifestation of an M-time culture, as are other indications of directness. The P-time system gives rise to looser time schedules, deeper involvement with individuals, and a wait-and-see-what-develops attitude. For example, two Latin colleagues conversing would likely opt to be late for their next appointments rather than abruptly terminate the conversation before it came to a natural conclusion. P-time is characterized by a much looser notion of being on time or late. Interruptions are routine, delays to be expected. It is not so much putting things off until *mañana* as it is the concept that human activity is not expected to proceed like clockwork.

Most cultures offer a mix of P-time and M-time behavior but have a tendency to adopt either more P-time or M-time with regard to the role time plays. Some are similar to Japan, where appointments are adhered to with the greatest M-time precision but P-time is followed once a meeting begins. The Japanese see U.S. businesspeople as too time bound and driven by schedules and deadlines that thwart the easy development of friendships.

When businesspeople from M-time and P-time meet, adjustments need to be made for a harmonious relationship. Often clarity can be gained by specifying tactfully, for example,

[26]Glen H. Brodowsky, Beverlee B. Anderson, Camille P. Schuster, Ofer Meilich, and M. Ven Venkatesan, "If Time Is Money Is It a Common Currency? Time in Anglo, Asian, and Latin Cultures," *Journal of Global Marketing* 21, no. 4 (2008), pp. 245–58.

[27]Robert Levine, *The Geography of Time* (New York: Basic Books, 1998).

[28]Runtian Jing and John L. Graham, "Regulation vs. Values: How Culture Plays Its Role," *Journal of Business Ethics* 80, no. 4 (2008), pp. 791–806.

Exhibit 5.3
Speed Is Relative

Rank of 31 countries for overall pace of life [combination of three measures: (1) minutes downtown pedestrians take to walk 60 feet, (2) minutes it takes a postal clerk to complete a stamp-purchase transaction, and (3) accuracy in minutes of public clocks].

Source: Robert Levine, "The Pace of Life in 31 Countries," *American Demographics*, November, 1997. Copyright © 2010 Crain Communication. Reprinted with permission.

Overall Pace	Country	Walking 60 Feet	Postal Service	Public Clocks
1	Switzerland	3	2	1
2	Ireland	1	3	11
3	Germany	5	1	8
4	Japan	7	4	6
5	Italy	10	12	2
6	England	4	9	13
7	Sweden	13	5	7
8	Austria	23	8	9
9	Netherlands	2	14	25
10	Hong Kong	14	6	14
11	France	8	18	10
12	Poland	12	15	8
13	Costa Rica	16	10	15
14	Taiwan	18	7	21
15	Singapore	25	11	4
16	United States	6	23	20
17	Canada	11	21	22
18	South Korea	20	20	16
19	Hungary	19	19	18
20	Czech Republic	21	17	23
21	Greece	14	13	29
22	Kenya	9	30	24
23	China	24	25	12
24	Bulgaria	27	22	17
25	Romania	30	29	5
26	Jordan	28	27	19
27	Syria	29	28	27
28	El Salvador	22	16	31
29	Brazil	31	24	28
30	Indonesia	26	26	30
31	Mexico	17	31	26

whether a meeting is to be on "Mexican time"[29] or "American time." An American who has been working successfully with the Saudis for many years says he has learned to take plenty of things to do when he travels. Others schedule appointments in their offices so they can work until their P-time friend arrives. The important thing for the U.S. manager to learn is adjustment to P-time in order to avoid the anxiety and frustration that comes from being out of synchronization with local time. As global markets expand, however, more businesspeople from P-time cultures are adapting to M-time.

Negotiations Emphasis

Business negotiations are perhaps the most fundamental commercial rituals. All the just-discussed differences in business customs and culture come into play more frequently and more obviously in the negotiating process than in any other aspect of business. The basic elements of business negotiations are the same in any country: They relate to the product, its price and terms, services associated with the product, and, finally, friendship between vendors and customers. But it is important to remember that the negotiating process is complicated, and the risk of misunderstanding increases when negotiating with someone from another culture.

Attitudes brought to the negotiating table by each individual are affected by many cultural factors and customs often unknown to the other participants and perhaps unrecognized by the individuals themselves. His or her cultural background conditions each negotiator's understanding and interpretation of what transpires in negotiating sessions. The possibility of offending one another or misinterpreting others' motives is especially high when one's self-reference criteria (SRC) is the basis for assessing a situation. One standard rule in

[29]Ken Ellingwood, "Just Late Enough to Be Early," *Los Angeles Times*, September 12, 2009, pp. A1, A25.

negotiating is "know thyself" first and "know your counterpart" second. The SRC of both parties can come into play here if care is not taken. How business customs and culture influence negotiations is the focus of Chapter 19.

Marketing Orientation

The extent of a company's *marketing orientation* has been shown to relate positively to profits. Although American companies are increasingly embracing this notion (and marketing in general),[30] firms in other countries have not been so fast to change from the more traditional *production* (consumers prefer products that are widely available), *product* (consumers favor products that offer the best quality, performance, or innovative features), and *selling* (consumers and businesses alike will not buy enough without prodding) orientations. For example, in many countries, engineers dominate corporate boards, and the focus is more toward a product orientation. However, more profitable American firms have adopted strong marketing orientations wherein everyone in the organization (from shop floor to finance) is encouraged to, and even receive rewards if, they generate, disseminate, and respond to marketing intelligence (that is, consumers' preferences, competitions' actions, and regulators' decisions). Recently researchers have empirically verified that for various complex reasons, including cultural explanations, a marketing orientation is less prevalent in a number of other countries;[31] and it can be difficult to encourage such an orientation across diverse business units in global companies.[32]

Gender Bias in International Business

LO3

The extent and implications of gender bias in other countries

The gender bias against female managers that exists in some countries, coupled with myths harbored by male managers, creates hesitancy among U.S. multinational companies to offer women international assignments. Although women now constitute more than half of the U.S. workforce,[33] they represent relatively small

Two ways to prevent the harassment of women. Mika Kondo Kunieda, a consultant at the World Bank in Tokyo explains, "I ride in a special women-only metro car that runs between 7:20 and 9:20 am. The cars were created in 2005 due to frequent complaints that women were being groped and sexually harassed. I was a victim a few times when I was younger, and it was—and still is—a humiliating experience. I had to learn how to position myself against moves even in the most overcrowded train. Now, I've seen a few men get visibly anxious when they realize they've accidentally boarded a car during women-only time!"[34] The Koran also specifies the cover-up pictured here in Riyadh, Saudi Arabia.

[30]John F. Gaski and Michael J. Etzel, "National Aggregate Consumer Sentiment toward Marketing: A Thirty-Year Retrospective and Analysis," *Journal of Consumer Research* 31 (2005), pp. 859–67.

[31]Sin et al., "Marketing Orientation"; John Kuada and Seth N. Buatsi, "Market Orientation and Management Practices in Ghanaian Firms: Revisiting the Jaworski and Kohli Framework," *Journal of International Marketing* 13 (2005), pp. 58–88; Reto Felix and Wolfgang Hinck, "Market Orientation of Mexican Companies," *Journal of International Marketing* 13 (2005), pp. 111–27.

[32]Paul D. Ellis, "Distance, Dependence and Diversity of Markets: Effects on Market Orientation," *Journal of International Business Studies* 38 (2007), pp. 374–86.

[33]"We Did It!" *The Economist*, January 2, 2010, p. 7.

[34]"Eye on the World," *Marie Claire*, April 2007, p. 134.

CROSSING BORDERS 5.3   Cultures Change, Albeit Slowly

SEOUL

In a time-honored practice in South Korea's corporate culture, the 38-year-old manager at an online game company took his 10-person team on twice-weekly after-work drinking bouts. He exhorted his subordinates to drink, including a 29-year-old graphic designer who protested that her limit was two glasses of beer. "Either you drink or you get it from me tomorrow," the boss told her one evening.

She drank, fearing that refusing to do so would hurt her career. But eventually, unable to take the drinking any longer, she quit and sued. In May, in the first ruling of its kind, the Seoul High Court said that forcing a subordinate to drink alcohol was illegal, and it pronounced the manager guilty of a "violation of human dignity." The court awarded the woman $32,000 in damages for the incidents, which occurred in 2004.

The ruling was as much a testament to women's growing presence in corporate life there as a confirmation of changes already under way. As an increasing number of women have joined companies as professionals, corporate South Korea has struggled to change the country's corporate culture, starting with its attitude toward alcohol.

TOKYO

The experience of Kayoko Mura illustrates a big shift in attitudes of Japanese companies toward female workers. When Mura quit her accounting job 16 years ago, food giant Kagome Co. did little to stop her. She was getting married and felt she could not ask for a transfer to Tokyo, where she and her husband were to live.

But last summer, Kagome's Tokyo office sought out Mura, now 44 years old, and wooed her back to the same kind of job she had had before. It also assigned a system engineer to work with her until she got up to speed with the computer system. Kagome even accepted her request to work part-time, just three days a week, six hours a day. "There are many women who quit after we had spent time and money in training," says Tomoko Sone, a Kagome spokeswoman. "For the company, [not hiring them back] is such a waste."

OSLO

Beginning in 2008, all public companies in Norway were mandated to have at least 40 percent women among their board members. Before the law passed in 2003, 7 percent of corporate board members were women. But the number has risen quickly, as suggested in Exhibit 5.4, to 36 percent in 2008, though 75 companies have yet to meet the quota. Statoil's Chairman of the Board, Grace Reksten Skaugen, explains her gender's advantages: "Women feel more compelled than men to do their homework, and we can afford to ask the hard questions, because women are not always expected to know the answers." Reksten Skaugen was voted Norway's chairperson of the year for 2007.

Sources: Norimitsu Onishi, "Corporate Korea Corks the Bottle as Women Rise," *The New York Times*, June 10, 2007, pp. 1, 4; Miho Inada, "Japanese Companies Woo Women Back to Work," *The Wall Street Journal*, July 23, 2007, pp. B1, B3; Siri Terjesen and Val Singh, "Female Presence on Corporate Boards: A Multi-Country Study," *Journal of Business Ethics* 85 (2008), pp. 55–63; "We Did It!" *The Economist*, January 2, 2010, p. 7.

percentages of the employees who are chosen for international assignments—less than 20 percent. Why? The most frequently cited reason is the inability for women to succeed abroad. As one executive was quoted as saying, "Overall, female American executives tend not to be as successful in extended foreign work assignments as are male American executives." Unfortunately, such attitudes are shared by many and probably stem from the belief that the traditional roles of women in male-dominated societies preclude women from establishing successful relationships with host-country associates. An often-asked question is whether it is appropriate to send women to conduct business with foreign customers in cultures where women are typically not in managerial positions. To some, it appears logical that if women are not accepted in managerial roles within their own cultures, a foreign woman will not be any more acceptable.

In many cultures—Asian, Middle Eastern, and Latin American—women are not typically found in upper levels of management (see Exhibit 5.4), and men and women are treated very differently. Moreover, the preferred leadership prototypes of male and female leaders varies across countries as well.[35] Indeed, the scariest newspaper headline ever written

---

[35]Lori D. Paris, Jon P. Howell, Peter W. Dorfman, and Paul J. Hanges, "Preferred Leadership Prototypes of Male and Female Leaders in 27 Countries," *Journal of International Business Studies* 40 (2009), pp. 1396–405.

Exhibit 5.4
Few and Far Between

Source: Siri Terjesen and Val Singh, "Female Presence on Corporate Boards: A Multi-Country Study," *Journal of Business Ethics* 85 (2008), pp. 55–63.

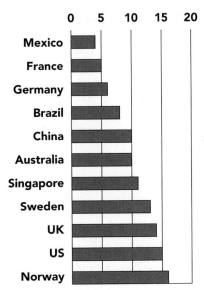

Female directors on corporate boards as a percentage of total.

may have been "Asia, Vanishing Point for as Many as 100 Million Women." The article, appearing in the *International Herald Tribune* in 1991,[36] points out that the birthrate in most countries around the world is about 105 boys for every 100 girls. However, in countries like the United States or Japan, where generally women outlive men, there are about 96 men per 100 women in the population. The current numbers of men per 100 women in other Asian countries are as follows: Korea 102, China 103, India 109, and Pakistan 106. The article describes systematic discrimination against females from birth. Now illegal everywhere, ultrasound units are still being used for making gender-specific abortion decisions, and all this prejudice against females is creating disruptive shortages of women. In some provinces in China, there are currently 120 men per 100 women.

Despite the substantial prejudices toward women in foreign countries, evidence suggests that prejudice toward foreign women executives may be exaggerated and that the treatment local women receive in their own cultures is not necessarily an indicator of how a foreign businesswoman is treated. It would be inaccurate to suggest that there is no difference in how male and female managers are perceived in different cultures. However, this difference does not mean that women cannot be successful in foreign postings.

A key to success for both men and women in international business often hinges on the strength of a firm's backing. When a female manager receives training and the strong backing of her firm, she usually receives the respect commensurate with the position she holds and the firm she represents. For success, a woman needs a title that gives immediate credibility in the culture in which she is working and a support structure and reporting relationship that will help her get the job done.[37] In short, with the power of the corporate organization behind her, resistance to her as a woman either does not materialize or is less troublesome than anticipated. Once business negotiations begin, the willingness of a business host to engage in business transactions and the respect shown to a foreign businessperson grow or diminish depending on the business skills he or she demonstrates, regardless of gender. As one executive stated, "The most difficult aspect of an international assignment is getting sent, not succeeding once sent."

The number of women in managerial positions (all levels) in most European countries, with the exception of Germany, is comparable to the United States. The International Labor Organization notes that in the United States, 43 percent of managerial positions are held by women, in Britain 33 percent, and in Switzerland 28 percent. In Germany, however, the picture is different. According to one economic source, German female executives hold just 9.2 percent of management jobs and meet stiff resistance from their male counterparts when they vie for upper-level positions. But the good news is an indication that some German businesses are attempting to remedy the situation. One step taken to help boost women up the executive ladder is a so-called cross-mentoring system organized by Lufthansa and seven other major corporations. High-ranking managers in one company offer advice to female managers in another firm in an effort to help them develop the kind of old-boy network that allows male managers to climb the corporate ladder successfully.[38]

---

[36]See January 7, 1991, p. 1.

[37]Nancy J. Adler, *International Dimensions of Organizational Behavior* (Mason, OH: Southwestern College Publishing, 2007).

[38]For broader information about global women's equality (including scores for economic participation and opportunity), go to http://www.weforum.org for the *World Economic Forum's Gender Gap Index*, 2007. On the economic opportunity scale, the United States ranks third, Norway eleventh, Germany thirty-second, Japan eighty-third, and Saudi Arabia one hundred-fifteenth, last on the list of 115 countries.

As world markets become more global and international competition intensifies, U.S. companies need to be represented by the most capable personnel available, from entry level to CEO. Research shows that global companies are requiring international experience for top executive positions. Executives who have had international experience are more likely to get promoted, have higher rewards, and have greater occupational tenure. The lack of international experience should not be a structural barrier to breaking through the glass ceiling in corporate America; to limit the talent pool simply because of gender seems shortsighted. The good news is that things are improving worldwide for women in management, and the topic of gender in multinational companies is receiving increasing research attention as well.[39]

So what about our female Ford executive mentioned at the start of the chapter? She was having no fun in Japan when we left her story. However, by all accounts (from peers, supervisors, and even Japanese counterparts) that first encounter was not representative of her continuing successes with the Japanese. She attributes her subsequent effectiveness to the strong support of her male Ford team members and her own recognition of the importance of building personal relationships with the Japanese. She explains:

> My husband, also a Ford manager working with Japanese clients, and I decided to have a few of our Mazda associates over for an "All-American" dinner during their next trip to Detroit. So, we started out inviting three people to our home. We thought this would be a nice intimate way to get to know one another and provide the Japanese with an honest-to-goodness home-made American meal. By the eve of the dinner word had gotten out and we had thirteen for dinner. They sort of invited themselves, they changed their meetings around, and some even flew in from the Chicago Auto Show. We had a wonderful time and for the first time they saw me as a person. A mom and a wife as well as a business associate. We talked about families, some business, not particulars, but world economics and the auto industry in general. The dinner party was a key turning point in my relationships with Mazda.[40]

Business Ethics

The importance of cultural differences in business ethics

The moral question of what is right or appropriate poses many dilemmas for domestic marketers. Even within a country, ethical standards are frequently not defined or always clear. The problem of business ethics is infinitely more complex in the international marketplace because value judgments differ widely among culturally diverse groups.[41] That which is commonly accepted as right in one country may be completely unacceptable in another, though at least one study has shown relative consistency across 41 countries in the ethics of persuading superiors.[42] Giving business gifts of high value, for example, is generally condemned in the United States, but in many countries of the world, gifts are not only accepted but also expected.[43]

Corruption Defined

Indeed, consistent with the discussions about language, the meaning of the word corruption varies considerably around the world. In formerly communist countries where Marxism was an important part of the educational system for many, *profits* can be seen as a kind of

---

[39]For example, see K. Praveen Parboteeah, Martin Hoegl, and John B. Cullen, "Managers' Gender Role Attitudes: A Country Institutional Profile Approach," *Journal of International Business Studies* 39, no. 5 (2008), pp. 795–813; William Newburry, Liuba Y. Belkin, and Paradis Ansari, "Perceived Career Opportunities from Globalization Capabilities and Attitudes towards Women in Iran and the U.S.," *Journal of International Business Studies* 39, no. 5 (2008), pp. 814–32.

[40]Hodgson, Sano, and Graham, *Doing Business with the New Japan.*

[41]Pallab Paul, Abhijit Roy, and Kausiki Mukjhopadhyay, "The Impact of Cultural Values on Marketing Ethical Norms: A Study in India and the United States," *Journal of International Marketing* 14 (2006), pp. 28–56; Jatinder J. Singh, Scott J. Vitell, Jamal Al-Khatif, and Irvine Clark III, "The Role of Moral Intensity and Personal Moral Philosophies in the Ethical Decision Making of Marketers: A Cross-Cultural Comparison of China and the United States," *Journal of International Marketing* 15 (2007), pp. 86–112; Srivatsa Seshadri and Greg M. Broekemier, "Ethical Decision Making: Panama-United States Differences in Consumer and Marketing Contexts," *Journal of Global Marketing* 22 (2009), pp. 299–311.

[42]David A. Ralston, Carolyn P. Egri, Maria Teresa de la Garza Carranza, and Prem Ramburuth, and 44 colleagues, "Ethical Preferences for Influencing Superiors: A 41 Society Study," *Journal of International Business Studies* 40 (2009), pp. 1022–45.

[43]See http://www.ethics.org and http://www.business-ethics.org for more pertinent information.

Pope Benedict XVI wrote that the Harry Potter books and movies can "deeply distort Christianity in the soul, before it can grow properly." Meanwhile, Antonio Banderas perhaps helped improve European acceptability for *Shrek 2* when he showed up for the Madrid premiere. In any case, products and services directed at kids get special attention from parents and regulators around the world.

corruption. What American managers view as essential, others view as a sign of exploitation. The *individualism* so important to Americans can also be seen as a kind of corruption. The Japanese have an expression: "The nail that sticks up gets hammered down." In India many attribute the decline in the society there to the *rampant consumerism*, such as that promoted on MTV. Of course, such rampant consumerism is what kept the American economy afloat right after the turn of the century. In some countries, there is no greater Satan than *R-rated American movies* with their sex and violence. In China, *missionaries* and religious movements are viewed by the government as potentially dangerous and disruptive. Many in sub-Saharan Africa view Western *intellectual property laws* as a kind of exploitation that prevents treatment of AIDS for millions. During the 1997–1998 financial crisis, many government leaders in Southeast Asia decried *currency speculation* as the worst kind of corruption.

Finally, please recall the 2003 homogenization of Barbie described at the beginning of the chapter. Here's what we predicted in a previous edition of this text: "And then there is *Barbie* having great fun in Japan these days. We hope the love affair lasts, but we are not confident it will. The article does describe the extensive marketing research Mattel did with kids. But there is no mention made about marketing research with their parents.[44] We guarantee that selling a big-busted, blonde doll to their daughters will be viewed as a kind of corruption by some Asian parents, and perhaps governmental officials as well. Particularly, if America is perceived as pursuing military and economic hegemony, a strong reaction against symbols of America will follow. Watch out Barbie, GI Joe, and your other toy store friends."

Our criticism of Mattel then was on the mark in three ways. First, sales of Barbie declined worldwide after the global standardization. Second, parents and governments did react. Most scandalous was the Saudi Arabian Barbie ban, underscored on the Web site of the Saudi Committee for the Propagation of Virtue and Prevention of Vice: "Jewish Barbie dolls, with their revealing clothes and shameful postures, accessories and tools are symbols of decadence of the perverted West. Let us beware of her dangers and be careful."[45] Third, Mattel's strategy boosted the sales of its competitors, MGA Entertainment, Inc.'s, multi-ethnic Bratz, Razanne, and, in the Arabian Gulf states, Fulla. Razanne and Fulla were both designed with Muslim girls and Muslim parents in mind. Fulla has waist-length black hair

---

[44]Lisa Bannon and Carlta Vitzthum, "One-Toy-Fits-All," *The Wall Street Journal*, April 29, 2003, p. A1.

[45]"Saudis Bust Barbie's 'Dangers,'" *CBS News*, September 10, 2003.

HOME-GROWN BUSINESS?
As the global economy slowed and China's exports slumped, Beijing cut sales taxes on car and real-estate purchases in certain situations, in hopes of revving up its own consumer engine. At right, a man and woman took a break outside a shop selling Barbie dolls in October. Apparently blonde Barbie doesn't appear to corrupt kids in China!

欢迎光临
Welcome to my dream house!

with red streaks, a round face with big brown eyes, a tan, a flatter chest than Barbie, and clothes that conceal her elbows and knees. We will again touch on this topic as it pertains to marketing research in Chapter 8. But for now, we switch from Barbie to bribery, another kind of corruption.

The Western Focus on Bribery

Before the Enron, WorldCom, and Madoff scandals, to most Americans, the word corruption meant bribery. Now in the domestic context, fraud has moved to the more prominent spot in the headlines.[46] But high-profile foreign cases of bribery, such as those involving the German giant Siemens and the execution of China's top food and drug official for accepting bribes, underscore the ethical and legal complexities of international business. During the 1970s, for U.S. companies engaged in international markets, bribery became a national issue with public disclosure of political payoffs to foreign recipients by U.S. firms. At the time, the United States had no laws against paying bribes in foreign countries. But for publicly held corporations, the Securities and Exchange Commission's (SEC) rules required accurate public reporting of all expenditures. Because the payoffs were not properly disclosed, many executives were faced with charges of violating SEC regulations.

The issue took on proportions greater than that of nondisclosure because it focused national attention on the basic question of ethics. The business community's defense was that payoffs were a way of life throughout the world: If you didn't pay bribes, you didn't do business. The decision to pay a bribe creates a major conflict between what is ethical and proper and what appears to be profitable and sometimes necessary for business. Many global competitors perceive payoffs as a necessary means to accomplish business goals. A major complaint of U.S. businesses was that other countries did not have legislation as restrictive as does the United States. The U.S. advocacy of global antibribery laws has led to a series of accords by the member nations of the Organization for Economic Cooperation and Development (OECD), the Organization of American States (OAS), and the United Nations Convention against Corruption (UNCAC). Long considered almost a way of business life, bribery and other forms of corruption are now being increasingly criminalized.

Leaders around the world realize that democracy depends on the confidence the people have in the integrity of their government and that corruption undermines economic liberalization. The actions of the OAS, OECD, and UNCAC will obligate a majority of the world's trading nations to maintain a higher standard of ethical behavior than has existed before.

[46]Robert J. Rhee, "The Madoff Scandal, Market Regulatory Failure and the Business Education of Lawyers," *Journal of Corporation Law* 35, no. 2 (2010), pp. 363–92.

Exhibit 5.5
Transparency International Corruption Perception Index

Higher numbers correspond to a lower prevalence of bribe taking. The top 25 and bottom 25 are shown; see http://www.transparency.org for the most complete and up-to-date listings.

Rank	Country	CPI Score	Rank	Country	CPI Score
1	New Zealand	9.4	154	Paraguay	2.1
2	Denmark	9.3	154	Yemen	2.1
3	Singapore	9.2	158	Cambodia	2.0
3	Sweden	9.2	158	Central African Republic	2.0
5	Switzerland	9.0	158	Laos	2.0
6	Finland	8.9	158	Tajikistan	2.0
6	Netherlands	8.9	162	Angola	1.9
8	Australia	8.7	162	Congo Brazzaville	1.9
8	Canada	8.7	162	Democratic Republic of Congo	1.9
8	Iceland	8.7	162	Guinea-Bissau	1.9
11	Norway	8.6	162	Kyrgyzstan	1.9
12	Hong Kong	8.2	168	Burundi	1.8
12	Luxembourg	8.2	168	Equatorial Guinea	1.8
14	Germany	8.0	168	Guinea	1.8
14	Ireland	8.0	168	Iran	1.8
16	Austria	7.9	168	Haiti	1.8
17	Japan	7.7	168	Turkmenistan	1.8
17	United Kingdom	7.7	174	Uzbekistan	1.7
19	USA	7.5	175	Chad	1.6
20	Barbados	7.4	176	Iraq	1.5
21	Belgium	7.1	176	Sudan	1.5
22	Qatar	7.0	178	Myanmar	1.4
22	St. Lucia	7.0	179	Afghanistan	1.3
24	France	6.9	180	Somalia	1.1
25	Chile	6.7			

Source: Corruption Perceptions Index 2009. Used by permission of Transparency International. The most recent updated Index is available at http://www.transparency.org.

An international organization called Transparency International (TI)[47] is dedicated to "curbing corruption through international and national coalitions encouraging governments to establish and implement effective laws, policies and anti-corruption programs." The brand name "Transparency International" has proven most insightful, as more scholars are finding a clear relationship between the availability of information and lower levels of corruption.[48] Among its various activities, TI conducts an international survey of businesspeople, political analysts, and the general public to determine their perceptions of corruption in 180 countries. In the Corruption Perception Index (CPI), shown in part in Exhibit 5.5, New Zealand, with scores of 9.4 out of a maximum of 10, was perceived to be the least corrupt, and Somalia, with scores of 1.1, as the most corrupt. TI also ranks 22 bribe-paying countries, and the ranking is reported in Exhibit 5.6 in its entirety. TI is very emphatic that its intent is not to expose villains and cast blame but to raise public awareness that will lead to constructive action. As one would expect, those countries receiving low scores are not pleased; however, the effect has been to raise public ire and debates in parliaments around the world—exactly the goal of TI.

The most notable datum in TI's CPI scores is Japan's speedy ascendance in the last decade from a score of 5.8 in 1998 to 7.7 in 2009. As a point of comparison, the United

---

[47]http://www.transparency.org.

[48]Cassandra E. DiRienzo, Jayoti Das, Kathryn T. Cort, and John Burbridge Jr., "Corruption and the Role of Information," *Journal of International Business Studies* 38 (2007), pp. 320–32.

Exhibit 5.6

Transparency International Bribe Payers Index*

Higher scores correspond to lower levels of bribe paying internationally.

Source: Reprinted from Bribe Payers Index. Copyright © 2009, Transparency International: the global coalition against corruption. Used with permission. For more information, visit http://www.transparency.org.

Rank	Country	2008
1	Belgium	8.8
1	Canada	8.8
3	Netherlands	8.7
3	Switzerland	8.7
5	Germany	8.6
5	Japan	8.6
5	United Kingdom	8.6
8	Australia	8.5
9	France	8.1
9	Singapore	8.1
9	USA	8.1
12	Spain	7.9
13	Hong Kong	7.6
14	South Africa	7.5
14	South Korea	7.5
14	Taiwan	7.5
17	Brazil	7.4
17	Italy	7.4
19	India	6.8
20	Mexico	6.6
21	China	6.5
22	Russia	5.9

*Based on responses to questions such as: In the business sectors with which you are most familiar, please indicate how likely companies from the following countries are to pay or offer bribes to win or retain business in this country (respondent's country of residence).

States has stayed the same in the rankings over the same time period at 7.5. No large, affluent country has moved up the rankings this fast. Now, at least according to TI, America is more corrupt than Japan! Although the difference between the two major exporters is perhaps insignificant, the numbers fly in the face of older Americans' criticisms of Japan as "corrupt."

Indeed, Japan's successes in reducing corruption in its business system are all the more remarkable because of its relationship-oriented culture, which would be predicted by many to favor bribery. Finally, the critics are strangely mute regarding the influence of outside pressure, in the form of the aforementioned OECD antibribery convention, which Japan joined in 1999 (the United States also joined the OECD convention in 1999). Long-time observers argue that major changes within Japan often result from such outside influences. Thus, the years 1999–2001 appear to represent the key turning point in Japan's fight against corruption.

Transparency International's CPI is also proving useful in academic studies of the causes and consequences of bribery. Completely consistent with our discussion of the origins and elements of culture in Chapter 4 (see Exhibit 4.4), higher levels of bribery have been found in low-income nations and nations with a communist past, both aspects of the political economy. Additionally, higher levels of bribery have been found in collectivistic (IDV) and high power distance (PDI) countries. Moreover, higher levels of bribery and legal constraints such as the Foreign Corrupt Practices Act have deterred firms' participation in such countries.[49] Firms seem generally to eschew investments in corrupt countries as well.[50]

[49]H. Rika Houston and John L. Graham, "Culture and Corruption in International Markets: Implications for Policy Makers and Managers," *Consumption, Markets, and Culture* 4, no. 3 (2000), pp. 315–40; Jennifer D. Chandler and John L. Graham, "Relationship-Oriented Cultures, Corruption, and International Marketing Success," *Journal of Business Ethics* 92(2) (2010), pp. 251–67.

[50]Utz Weitzel and Sjors Berns, "Cross-Border Takeovers, Corruption, and Related Aspects of Governance," *Journal of International Business Studies* 37 (2006), pp. 786–806; Alvaro Cuervo-Cazurra, "Who Cares about Corruption," *Journal of International Business Studies* 37 (2006), pp. 807–22.

Finally, when executives of multinational firms behave ethically in such countries, they also tend to promote more ethical business behaviors among their host country counterparts.[51]

Bribery: Variations on a Theme

Although bribery is a legal issue, it is also important to see bribery in a cultural context to understand different attitudes toward it. Culturally, attitudes about bribery are significantly different among different peoples. Some cultures seem to be more open about taking bribes, whereas others, like the United States, are publicly contemptuous of such practices. But U.S. firms are far from virtuous—we believe the TI "grade" of a C (7.2) to be about right. Regardless of where the line of acceptable conduct is drawn, there is no country where the people consider it proper for those in position of political power to enrich themselves through illicit agreements at the expense of the best interests of the nation. A first step in understanding the culture of bribery is to appreciate the limitless variations that are often grouped under the word *bribery*. The activities under this umbrella term range from extortion through subornation to lubrication.

Bribery and Extortion.

The distinction between bribery and extortion depends on whether the activity resulted from an offer or from a demand for payment. Voluntarily offered payment by someone seeking unlawful advantage is **bribery**. For example, it is bribery if an executive of a company offers a government official payment in exchange for the official incorrectly classifying imported goods so the shipment will be taxed at a lower rate than the correct classification would require. However, it is *extortion* if payments are extracted under duress by someone in authority from a person seeking only what he or she is lawfully entitled to. An example of extortion would be a finance minister of a country demanding heavy payments under the threat that a contract for millions of dollars would be voided.

On the surface, extortion may seem to be less morally wrong because the excuse can be made that "if we don't pay, we don't get the contract" or "the official (devil) made me do it." But even if it is not legally wrong, it is morally wrong—and in the United States it is legally wrong.

Lubrication and Subornation.

Another variation of bribery is the difference between lubrication and subornation. **Lubrication** involves a relatively small sum of cash, a gift, or a service given to a low-ranking official in a country where such offerings are not prohibited by law. The purpose of such a gift is to facilitate or expedite the normal, lawful performance of a duty by that official. This practice is common in many countries of the world. A small payment made to dock workers to speed up their pace so that unloading a truck takes a few hours rather than all day is an example of lubrication.

Subornation, in contrast, generally involves giving large sums of money—frequently not properly accounted for—designed to entice an official to commit an illegal act on behalf of the one offering the bribe. Lubrication payments accompany requests for a person to do a job more rapidly or more efficiently; subornation is a request for officials to turn their heads, to not do their jobs, or to break the law.

Agent's Fees.

A third type of payment that can appear to be a bribe but may not be is an agent's fee. When a businessperson is uncertain of a country's rules and regulations, an agent may be hired to represent the company in that country. For example, an attorney may be hired to file an appeal for a variance in a building code on the basis that the attorney will do a more efficient and thorough job than someone unfamiliar with such procedures. While this practice is often a legal and useful procedure, if a part of that agent's fee is used to pay bribes, the intermediary's fees are being used unlawfully. Under U.S. law, an official who knows of an agent's intention to bribe may risk prosecution and jail time. The Foreign Corrupt Practices Act (FCPA) prohibits U.S. businesses from paying bribes openly or using intermediaries as conduits for a bribe when the U.S. manager knows that part of the

---

[51]Yadong Luo, "Political Behavior, Social Responsibility, and Perceived Corruption: A Structural Perspective," *Journal of International Business Studies* 37 (2006), pp. 747–66; Chuck C. Y. Kwok and Solomon Tadesse, "The MNC as an Agent of Change for Host-Country Institutions: FDI and Corruption," *Journal of International Business Studies* 37 (2006), pp. 767–85.

intermediary's payment will be used as a bribe. Attorneys, agents, distributors, and so forth may function simply as conduits for illegal payments. The process is further complicated by legal codes that vary from country to country; what is illegal in one country may be winked at in another and be legal in a third.

The answer to the question of bribery is not an unqualified one. It is easy to generalize about the ethics of political payoffs and other types of payments; it is much more difficult to make the decision to withhold payment of money when the consequences of not making the payment may affect the company's ability to do business profitably or at all. With the variety of ethical standards and levels of morality that exist in different cultures, the dilemma of ethics and pragmatism that faces international business cannot be resolved until the anticorruption accords among the OECD, UN, and OAS members are fully implemented and multinational businesses refuse to pay extortion or offer bribes.

The Foreign Corrupt Practices Act, which prohibits American executives and firms from bribing officials of foreign governments, has had a positive effect. According to the latest Department of Commerce figures, since 1994, American businesses have bowed out of 294 major overseas commercial contracts valued at $145 billion rather than paying bribes. This information corroborates the academic evidences cited previously. Even though there are numerous reports indicating a definite reduction in U.S. firms paying bribes, the lure of contracts is too strong for some companies. Lockheed Corporation made $22 million in questionable foreign payments during the 1970s. More recently the company pled guilty to paying $1.8 million in bribes to a member of the Egyptian national parliament in exchange for lobbying for three air cargo planes worth $79 million to be sold to the military. Lockheed was caught and fined $25 million, and cargo plane exports by the company were banned for three years. Lockheed's actions during the 1970s were a major influence on the passing of the FCPA. The company now maintains one of the most comprehensive ethics and legal training programs of any major corporation in the United States.

It would be naive to assume that laws and the resulting penalties alone will put an end to corruption. Change will come only from more ethically and socially responsible decisions by both buyers and sellers and by governments willing to take a stand.

Ethical and Socially Responsible Decisions

Behaving in an ethically and socially responsible way should be the hallmark of every businessperson's behavior, domestic or international. Most of us know innately the socially responsible or ethically correct response to questions about knowingly breaking the law, harming the environment, denying someone his or her rights, taking unfair advantage, or behaving in a manner that would bring bodily harm or damage. Meanwhile, the complex relationships among politics, corruption, and corporate social responsibility are only now beginning to receive attention on the part of scholars and practitioners.[52] Unfortunately, the difficult issues are not the obvious and simple right-or-wrong ones, and differences in cultural values influence the judgment of managers.[53] In many countries, the international marketer faces the dilemma of responding to sundry situations where local law does not exist, where local practices appear to condone a certain behavior, or where a company willing to "do what is necessary" is favored over a company that refuses to engage in certain practices. In short, being socially responsible and ethically correct are not simple tasks for the international marketer.

[52]Peter Rodriguez, Donald S. Siegel, Amy Hillman, and Lorraine Eden, "Three Lenses on the Multinational Enterprise: Politics, Corruption, and Corporate Social Responsibility," *Journal of International Business Studies* 37 (2006), pp. 733–46.

[53]David A. Waldman, Mary Sully de Luque, Nathan Washburn, Robert J. House, Bolanle Adetoun, Angel Barrasa, Mariya Bobina, Muzaffer Bodur, Yi-jung Chen, Sukhendu Debbarma, Peter Dorfman, Rosemary R. Dzuvichu, Idil Evcimen, Pingping Fu, Mikhail Grachev, Roberto Gonzalez Duarte, Vipin Gupta, Deanne N. Den Hartog, Annebel H.B. de Hoogh, Jon Howell, Kuen-yung Jone, Hayat Kabasakal, Edvard Konrad, P. L. Koopman, Rainhart Lang, Cheng-chen Lin, Jun Liu, Boris Martinez, Almarie E. Munley, Nancy Papalexandris, T. K. Peng, Leonel Prieto, Narda Quigley, James Rajasekar, Francisco Gil Rodriguez, Johannes Steyrer, Betania Tanure, Henk Theirry, V. M. Thomas, Peter T. van den Berg, and Celeste P. M. Wilderom, "Cultural Leadership Predictors of Corporate Social Responsibility Values of Top Management: A GLOBE Study of 15 Countries," *Journal of International Business Studies* 37 (2006), pp. 823–37.

In normal business operations, difficulties arise in making decisions, establishing policies, and engaging in business operations in five broad areas: (1) employment practices and policies, (2) consumer protection, (3) environmental protection, (4) political payments and involvement in political affairs of the country, and (5) basic human rights and fundamental freedoms. In many countries, laws may help define the borders of minimum ethical or social responsibility, but the law is only the floor above which one's social and personal morality is tested. The statement that "there is no controlling legal authority" may mean that the behavior is not illegal, but it does not mean that the behavior is morally correct or ethical. Ethical business conduct should normally exist at a level well above the minimum required by law or the "controlling legal authority." In fact, laws are the markers of past behavior that society has deemed unethical or socially irresponsible.

Perhaps the best guides to good business ethics are the examples set by ethical business leaders. However, three ethical principles also provide a framework to help the marketer distinguish between right and wrong, determine what ought to be done, and properly justify his or her actions. Simply stated, they are as follows:

- **Utilitarian ethics.** Does the action optimize the "common good" or benefits of all constituencies? And who are the pertinent constituencies?

- **Rights of the parties.** Does the action respect the rights of the individuals involved?

- **Justice or fairness.** Does the action respect the canons of justice or fairness to all parties involved?

Answers to these questions can help the marketer ascertain the degree to which decisions are beneficial or harmful and right or wrong and whether the consequences of actions are ethical or socially responsible. Perhaps the best framework to work within is defined by asking: Is it legal? Is it right? Can it withstand disclosure to stockholders, to company officials, to the public?

Although the United States has clearly led the campaign against international bribery, European firms and institutions are apparently putting more effort and money into the promotion of what they are calling "corporate social responsibility." For example, the watchdog group CSR (Corporate Social Responsibility) Europe, in cooperation with INSEAD (the European Institute of Administrative Affairs) business school outside Paris, is studying the relationship between investment attractiveness and positive corporate behaviors on several dimensions. Their studies find a strong link between firms' social responsibility and European institutional investors' choices for equity investments.[54] All this is not to say that European firms do not still have their own corporate misbehaviors. However, we expect more efforts in the future to focus on measuring and monitoring corporate social responsibility around the world.

Finally, we mention three notable examples of corruption fighting, ranging across the levels of government, corporate, and individual initiatives. First, the government of Norway is investing its vast oil profits in only ethical companies; it recently withdrew funds from companies such as Walmart, Boeing, and Lockheed Martin, in line with its ethical criteria.[55] Second, Alan Boekmann, CEO of the global construction company Fluor Corp., is fed up with the corruption in his own business. He, along with colleagues at competitor firms, has called for a program of outside auditors to determine the effectiveness firms' antibribery programs.[56] Third, in 2001, Alexandra Wrage founded Trace International, an Annapolis, Maryland, nonprofit that provides corruption reports about potential foreign clients and training for executives involved in business in difficult areas.[57] We laud all such efforts.

---

[54]See http://www.csreurope.org.

[55]Mark Landler, "Norway Tries to Do Well by Doing Good," *The New York Times*, May 4, 2007, pp. C1, C4.

[56]Katherine Yung, "Fluor Chief in War on Bribery," *Dallas Morning News*, January 21, 2007, pp. 1D, 4D.

[57]Eamon Javers, "Steering Clear of Foreign Snafus," *BusinessWeek*, November 12, 2007, p. 76. Also see http://www.traceinternational.org.

Culture's Influence on Strategic Thinking

Perhaps Lester Thurow provided the most articulate description of how culture influences managers' thinking about business strategy.[58] Others are now examining his ideas in even deeper detail.[59] Thurow distinguished between the British–American "individualistic" kind of capitalism and the "communitarian" form of capitalism in Japan and Germany. The business systems in the latter two countries are typified by cooperation among government, management, and labor, particularly in Japan. Contrarily, adversarial relationships among labor, management, and government are more the norm in the United Kingdom, and particularly in the United States. We see these cultural differences reflected in Hofstede's results—on the IDV scale, the United States is 91, the United Kingdom is 89, Germany is 67, and Japan is 46.

We also find evidence of these differences in a comparison of the performance of American, German, and Japanese firms.[60] In the less individualistic cultures, labor and management cooperate—in Germany labor is represented on corporate boards, and in Japan, management takes responsibility for the welfare of the labor force. Because the welfare of the workforce matters more to Japanese and German firms, their sales revenues are more stable over time. American-style layoffs are eschewed. The individualistic American approach to labor–management relations is adversarial—each side takes care of itself. So we see damaging strikes and huge layoffs that result in more volatile performance for American firms. Recent studies are uncovering stability as one of global investors' key criteria.[61]

Circa 2000, the American emphasis on competition looked like the best approach, and business practices around the world appeared to be converging on the American model. But it is important to recall that key word in Adam Smith's justification for competition—"frequently." It's worth repeating here: "By pursuing his own interest he frequently promotes that of society…." Smith wrote *frequently*, not *always*. A competitive, individualistic approach works well in the context of an economic boom. During the late 1990s, American firms dominated Japanese and European ones. The latter seemed stodgy, conservative, and slow in the then-current hot global

[58]Lester Thurow, *Head to Head* (New York: William Morrow, 1992).

[59]Gordon Redding, "The Thick Description and Comparison of Societal Systems of Capitalism," *Journal of International Business Studies* 36, no. 2 (2005), pp. 123–55; Michael A. Witt and Gordon Redding, "Culture, Meaning, and Institutions: Executive Rationale in Germany and Japan," *Journal of International Business Studies* 40 (2009), pp. 859–85.

[60]Cathy Anterasian, John L. Graham, and R. Bruce Money, "Are U.S. Managers Superstitious about Market Share?" *Sloan Management Review* 37, no. 4 (1996), pp. 67–77.

[61]Vincentiu Covrig, Sie Tin Lau, and Lilian Ng, "Do Domestic and Foreign Fund Managers Have Similar Preferences for Stock Characteristics? A Cross-Country Analysis," *Journal of International Business Studies* 37 (2006), pp. 407–29; Kate Linebaugh and Jeff Bennett, "Marchionne Upends Chrysler's Ways," *The Wall Street Journal*, January 12, 2010, pp. B1, B2.

WORK WANTED: Chinese migrant workers advertise their skills while waiting for employers in the Sichuan city of Chengdu on a Monday in 2010. The government expects the total number of migrants looking for jobs this year to reach at least 25 million.

After two decades of stagnation in Japan, the social contract of lifetime employment is softening. This change is reflected in more frequent corporate layoffs, frustrating job searches, and "tent villages" in public places such as Ueno Park in Tokyo. But even at their worst point in history, Japanese jobless are just a trickle compared with the torrent of pink slips and homeless folks when the American economy heads south.

information economy. However, downturns in a competitive culture can be ugly things. For example, the instability and layoffs at Boeing during the commercial aircraft busts of the late 1990s and early 2000s have been damaging not only to employees and their local communities, but also to shareholders. And during the dramatic economic downturn in 2008–2009, Asian firms tended to eschew layoffs, compared with their American counterparts,[62] and even rejected the U.S. as the benchmark for best management practices.[63] It should also be mentioned that Thurow and others writing in this area omitted a fourth kind of capitalism—that common in Chinese cultures.[64] Its distinguishing characteristics are a more entrepreneurial approach and an emphasis on *guanxi* (one's network of personal connections)[65] as the coordinating principle among firms. This fourth kind of capitalism is also predicted by culture. Chinese cultures are high on PDI and low on IDV, and the strong reciprocity implied by the notion of *guanxi* fits the data well.

Synthesis: Relationship-Oriented vs. Information-Oriented Cultures

LO5

The differences between relationship-oriented and information-oriented cultures

With increasing frequency, studies note a strong relationship between Hall's high-/low-context and Hofstede's Individualism/Collective and Power Distance indices. For example, low-context American culture scores relatively low on power distance and high on individualism, whereas high-context Arab cultures score high on power distance and low on individualism. This result is not at all surprising, given that Hofstede[66] leans heavily on Hall's ideas in developing and labeling the dimensions of culture revealed via his huge database. Indeed, the three dimensions—high/low context, IDV, and PDI—are correlated above the $r = 0.6$ level, suggesting all three dimensions are largely measuring the same thing.[67] Likewise, when we compare linguistic distance (to English) and Transparency International's Corruption Perception Index to the other three, we see similar levels of correlations among all five dimensions. And while metrics for other dimensions of business culture do not yet exist, a pattern appears to be evident (see Exhibit 5.7).

The pattern displayed is not definitive, only suggestive. Not every culture fits every dimension of culture in a precise way. However, the synthesis is useful in many ways. Primarily, it gives us a simple yet logical way to think about many of the cultural differences described in Chapters 4 and 5. For example, American culture is low context, individualistic (IDV), low power distance (PDI), obviously close to English, monochronic time–oriented, linguistically direct, and foreground focused,[68] and it achieves efficiency through competition; therefore, it

[62]Evan Ramsatd, "Koreans Take Pay Cuts to Stop Layoffs," *The Wall Street Journal*, March 3, 2009, online.

[63]"China Rethinks the American Way," *BusinessWeek*, June 15, 2009, p. 32.

[64]Don Y. Lee and Philip L. Dawes, "Guanxi, Trust, and Long-Term Orientation in Chinese Business Markets," *Journal of International Marketing* 13, no. 2 (2005), pp. 28–56; Flora Gu, Kineta Hung, and David K. Tse, "When Does Guanxi Matter? Issues of Capitalization and Its Darkside," *Journal of Marketing* 72, no. 4 (2008), pp. 12–28; Roy Y. J. Chua, Michael W. Morris, and Paul Ingram, "Guanxi vs. Networking: Distinctive Configurations of Affect- and Cognition-Based Trust in the Networks of Chinese vs. American Managers," *Journal of International Business Studies* 40, no. 3 (2009), pp. 490–508.

[65]Mark Lam and John L. Graham, *Doing Business in the New China, The World's Most Dynamic Market* (New York: McGraw-Hill, 2007).

[66]Hofstede, *Culture's Consequences*.

[67]This continuum has also been labeled "social context salience" by H. Rika Houston and John L. Graham, "Culture and Corruption in International Markets: Implications for Policy Makers and Managers," *Consumption, Markets, and Culture* 4, no. 3 (2000), pp. 315–40.

[68]Richard E. Nisbett, *The Geography of Thought* (New York: The Free Press, 2003).

Exhibit 5.7
Dimensions of Culture: A
Synthesis

Information-Oriented (IO)	Relationship-Oriented (RO)
Low context	High context
Individualism	Collectivism
Low power distance	High power distance (including gender)
Bribery less common	Bribery more common*
Low distance from English	High distance from English
Linguistic directness	Linguistic indirectness
Monochronic time	Polychronic time
Internet	Face-to-face
Foreground	Background
Competition	Reduce transaction costs

*We note that Singapore, Hong Kong, Japan, and Chile do not fit all the rules here. Most would agree that all four are relationship-oriented cultures.

is categorized hereafter in this book as an *information-oriented culture*. Alternatively, Japanese culture is high context, collectivistic, high power distance, far from English, polychronic (in part), linguistically indirect, and background focused, and it achieves efficiency through reduction of transaction costs; therefore, it is properly categorized as a *relationship-oriented culture*. All these traits are so even though both the United States and Japan are high-income democracies. Both cultures do achieve efficiency but through different emphases. The American business system uses competition, whereas the Japanese depend more on reducing transaction costs.

The most managerially useful aspect of this synthesis of cultural differences is that it allows us to make predictions about unfamiliar cultures. Reference to the three metrics available gives us some clues about how consumers and/or business partners will behave and think. Hofstede has provided scores for 78 countries and regions, and we have included them in the appendix to this chapter. Find a country on his lists, and you have some information about that market and/or person. One might expect Trinidad to be an information-oriented culture and Russia a relationship-oriented culture, and so on. Moreover, measures of linguistic distance (any language can be used as the focal one, not just English) are available for every country and, indeed, every person. Thus, we would expect that someone who speaks Javanese as a first language to be relationship oriented.

In closing, we are quite encouraged by the publication of the important book *Culture Matters*.[69] We obviously agree with the sentiment of the title and hope that the book will help rekindle the interest in culture's pervasive influences that Max Weber and others initiated so long ago.

---

[69] Lawrence I. Harrison and Samuel P. Huntington (eds.), *Culture Matters* (New York: Basic Books, 2000).

Summary

Management styles differ around the world. Some cultures appear to emphasize the importance of information and competition, while others focus more on relationships and transaction cost reductions. However, there are no simple answers, and the only safe generalization is that businesspersons working in another country must be sensitive to the business environment and must be willing to adapt when necessary. Unfortunately, to know when such adaptation is necessary is not always easy; in some instances adaptation is optional, whereas in others, it is actually undesirable. Understanding the culture you are entering is the only sound basis for planning.

Business behavior is derived in large part from the basic cultural environment in which the business operates and, as such, is subject to the extreme diversity encountered among various cultures and subcultures. Environmental considerations significantly affect the attitudes, behavior, and outlook of foreign businesspeople. Motivational patterns of such businesspeople depend in part on their personal backgrounds, their business positions, their sources of authority, and their own personalities.

Varying motivational patterns inevitably affect methods of doing business in different countries. Marketers in some countries thrive on competition; in others, they do everything possible to eliminate it. The authoritarian, centralized decision-making orientation in some nations contrasts sharply with democratic decentralization in others. International variation characterizes contact level, ethical orientation, negotiation outlook, and nearly every part of doing business. The foreign marketer can take no aspect of business behavior for granted.

The new breed of international businessperson that has emerged in recent years appears to have a heightened sensitivity to cultural variations. Sensitivity, however, is not enough; the international trader must be constantly alert and prepared to adapt when necessary. One must always realize that, no matter how long in a country, the outsider is not a local; in many countries, that person may always be treated as an outsider. Finally, one must avoid the critical mistake of assuming that knowledge of one culture will provide acceptability in another.

Key Terms

Cultural imperative	Silent languages	Bribery	Principle of utilitarian ethics
Cultural elective	M-time	Lubrication	Principle of justice
Cultural exclusive	P-time	Subornation	or fairness

Questions

1. Define the key terms listed above.

2. "More than tolerance of an alien culture is required; there is a need for affirmative acceptance of the concept 'different but equal.'" Elaborate.

3. "We should also bear in mind that in today's business-oriented world economy, the cultures themselves are being significantly affected by business activities and business practices." Comment.

4. "In dealing with foreign businesses, the marketer must be particularly aware of the varying objectives and aspirations of management." Explain.

5. Suggest ways in which persons might prepare themselves to handle unique business customs that may be encountered in a trip abroad.

6. Business customs and national customs are closely interrelated. In which ways would one expect the two areas to coincide, and in which ways would they show differences? How could such areas of similarity and difference be identified?

7. Identify both local and foreign examples of cultural imperatives, electives, and exclusives. Be prepared to explain why each example fits into the category you have selected.

8. Contrast the authority roles of top management in different societies. How do the different views of authority affect marketing activities?

9. Do the same for aspirational patterns.

10. What effects on business customs might be anticipated from the recent rapid increases in the level of international business activity?

11. Interview some foreign students to determine the types of cultural shock they encountered when they first came to your country.

12. Differentiate between:

    Private ownership and family ownership

    Decentralized and committee decision making

13. In which ways does the size of a customer's business affect business behavior?

14. Compare three decision-making authority patterns in international business.

15. Explore the various ways in which business customs can affect the structure of competition.

16. Why is it important that the business executive be alert to the significance of differing management styles?

17. Suggest some cautions that an individual from a relationship-oriented culture should bear in mind when dealing with someone from an information-oriented culture.

18. Political payoffs are a problem. How would you react if you faced the prospect of paying a bribe? What if you knew that by not paying, you would not be able to complete a $10 million contract?

19. Differentiate among the following:

    bribery

    extortion

    lubrication

    subornation

20. Distinguish between P-time and M-time.

21. Discuss how a P-time person reacts differently from an M-time person in keeping an appointment.

22. What is meant by "laws are the markers of past behavior that society has deemed unethical or socially irresponsible"?

23. What are the three ethical principles that provide a framework to help distinguish between right and wrong? Explain.

24. Visit Transparency International's Web site and check to see how the CPI Index for countries listed in Exhibits 5.4 and 5.5 have changed. After searching TI's databank, explain why the changes have occurred. The site is found at http://www.transparency.org.

25. Discuss the pros and cons of "there is no controlling legal authority" as a basis for ethical behavior.

26. "The *company.com* page is a company's front door and that doorway should be global in scope." Discuss. Visit several Web pages of major multinational companies and evaluate their "front door" to the global world.

27. Visit the Web sites of Shell and Nike and compare their statements on corporate values. What are the major issues each addresses? Do you think their statements are useful as guides to ethical and socially responsible decision making?

28. Go to your favorite Web reference source and access some recent news articles on Nike and alleged human rights violations. Access the Nike statement on corporate values and write a brief statement on the alleged violations and Nike's statement of corporate values.

Appendix: Index Scores for Countries and Regions

Country	Power Distance	Uncertainty Avoidance	Individualism/ Collectivism	Masculinity/ Femininity	Long-Term/ Short-Term Orientation	Primary Language	Distance from English
Argentina	49	86	46	56		Spanish	3
Australia total	36	51	90	61	31	English	0
Aborigines	80	128	89	22	10	Australian	7
Austria	11	70	55	79	31	German	1
Bangladesh	80	60	20	55	40	Bengali	3
Belgium total	65	94	75	54	38	Dutch	1
Dutch speakers	61	97	78	43		Dutch	1
French speakers	67	93	72	60		French	3
Brazil	69	76	38	49	65	Portuguese	3
Bulgaria	70	85	30	40		Bulgarian	3
Canada total	39	48	80	52	23	English	0
French speakers	54	60	73	45	30	French	3
Chile	63	86	23	28		Spanish	3
China	80	30	20	66	118	Mandarin	6
Colombia	67	80	13	64		Spanish	3
Costa Rica	35	86	15	21		Spanish	3
Czech Republic	57	74	58	57	13	Czech	3
Denmark	18	23	74	16	46	Danish	1
Ecuador	78	67	8	63		Spanish	3
Estonia	40	60	60	30		Estonian	4
Finland	33	59	63	26	41	Finnish	4
France	68	86	71	43	39	French	3
Germany	35	65	67	66	31	German	1
Great Britain	35	35	89	66	25	English	0
Greece	60	112	35	57		Greek	3
Guatemala	95	101	6	37		Spanish	3
Hong Kong	68	29	25	57	96	Cantonese	6
Hungary	46	82	80	88	50	Hungarian	4
India	77	40	48	56	61	Dravidian	3
Indonesia	78	48	14	46		Bahasa	7
Iran	58	59	41	43		Farsi	3
Ireland	28	35	70	68	43	English	0
Israel	13	81	54	47		Hebrew	5
Italy	50	75	76	70	34	Italian	3
Jamaica	45	13	39	68		English	0
Japan	54	92	46	95	80	Japanese	4
Korea (South)	60	85	18	39	75	Korean	4
Luxembourg	40	70	60	50		Luxembourgish	1
Malaysia	104	36	26	50		Malay	7

Country/Region	PDI	IDV	MAS	UAI	LTO	Language	
Malta	56	59	47	96		Maltese	5
Mexico	81	30	69	82		Spanish	3
Morocco	70	46	53	68		Arabic	5
Netherlands	38	80	14	53	44	Dutch	1
New Zealand	22	79	58	49	30	English	0
Norway	31	69	8	50	44	Norwegian	1
Pakistan	55	14	50	70	0	Urdu	3
Panama	95	11	44	86		Spanish	3
Peru	64	16	42	87		Spanish	3
Philippines	94	32	64	44	19	Tagalog	7
Poland	68	60	64	93	32	Polish	3
Portugal	63	27	31	104	30	Portuguese	3
Romania	90	30	42	90		Romanian	3
Russia	93	39	36	95		Russian	3
Salvador	66	19	40	94		Spanish	3
Singapore	74	20	48	8	48	Mandarin	6
Slovakia	104	52	110	51	38	Slovak	3
South Africa	49	65	63	49		Afrikaans	1
Spain	57	51	42	86	19	Spanish	3
Surinam	85	47	37	92		Dutch	1
Sweden	31	71	5	29	33	Swedish	1
Switzerland total	34	68	70	58	40	German	1
German speakers	26	69	72	56		German	1
French speakers	70	64	58	70		French	3
Taiwan	58	17	45	69	87	Taiwanese	6
Thailand	64	20	34	64	56	Thai	7
Trinidad	47	16	58	55		English	0
Turkey	66	37	45	85		Turkish	4
United States	40	91	62	46	29	English	0
Uruguay	61	36	38	100		Spanish	3
Venezuela	81	12	73	76		Spanish	3
Vietnam	70	20	40	30	80	Vietnamese	7
Yugoslavia total	76	27	21	88		Serbo-Croatian	3
Croatia (Zagreb)	73	33	40	80		Serbo-Croatian	3
Serbia (Beograd)	86	25	43	92		Serbo-Croatian	3
Slovenia (Ljubljana)	71	27	19	88		Slovene	3
Regions							
Arab countries	80	38	53	68		Arabic	5
East Africa	64	27	41	52	25		8
West Africa	77	20	46	54	16		8

Source: Geert Hofstede, *Culture's Consequences*, 2nd ed. (Thousand Oaks, CA: Sage, 2001).

Chapter 6

The Political Environment:

A CRITICAL CONCERN

CHAPTER LEARNING OBJECTIVES

What you should learn from Chapter 6:

LO1 What the sovereignty of nations means and how it can affect the stability of government policies

LO2 How different governmental types, political parties, nationalism, targeted fear/animosity, and trade disputes can affect the environment for marketing in foreign countries

LO3 The political risks of global business and the factors that affect stability

LO4 The importance of the political system to international marketing and its effect on foreign investments

LO5 The impact of political and social activists, violence, and terrorism on international business

LO6 How to assess and reduce the effect of political vulnerability

LO7 How and why governments encourage foreign investment

Global Perspective

WORLD TRADE GOES BANANAS

Rather than bruising Chiquita Bananas, the wrath of politics instead hammered Prosciutto di Parma ham from Italy, handbags from France, and bath oils and soaps from Germany. These and a host of other imported products from Europe were all slapped with a 100 percent import tariff as retaliation by the U.S. government against EU banana-import rules that favored Caribbean bananas over Latin American bananas. Keep in mind that no bananas are exported from the United States, yet the United States has been engaged in a trade war over the past seven years that has cost numerous small businesses on both sides of the Atlantic millions of dollars. But how can this be, you ask? Politics, that's how!

One small business, Reha Enterprises, for example, sells bath oil, soaps, and other supplies imported from Germany. The tariff on its most popular product, an herbal foam bath, was raised from 5 percent to 100 percent. The customs bill for six months spiraled to $37,783 from just $1,851—a 1,941 percent tax increase. For a small business whose gross sales are less than $1 million annually, it was crippling. When Reha heard of the impending "banana war," he called everyone—his congressperson, his senator, the United States Trade Representative (USTR). When he described his plight to the USTR, an official there expressed amazement. "They were surprised I was still importing," because they thought the tariff would cut off the industry entirely. That was their intention, which of course would have meant killing Reha Enterprises as well.

In effect, he was told it was his fault that he got caught up in the trade war. He should have attended the hearings in Washington, just like Gillette and Mattel, and maybe his products would have been dropped from the targeted list, just as theirs were. Scores of European products, from clothing to stoves to glass Christmas ornaments, dolls, and ballpoint pens, that were originally targeted for the retaliatory tariffs escaped the tariff. Aggressive lobbying by large corporations, trade groups, and members of Congress got most of the threatened imported products off the list. The USTR had published a list of the targeted imports in the Federal Register, inviting affected companies to testify. Unfortunately, the Federal Register was not on Reha's reading list.

In that case, he was told, he should have hired a lobbyist in Washington to keep him briefed. Good advice—but it doesn't make much sense to a company that grosses less than $1 million a year. Other advice received from an official of the USTR included the off-the-record suggestion that he might want to change the customs number on the invoice so it would appear that he was importing goods not subject to the tariff, a decision that could, if he were caught, result in a hefty fine or jail. Smaller businesses in Europe faced similar problems as their export business dried up because of the tariffs.

How did this banana war start? The European Union imposed a quota and tariffs that favored imports from former colonies in the Caribbean and Africa, distributed by European firms, over Latin American bananas distributed by U.S. firms. Chiquita Brands International and Dole Food Company, contending that the EU's "illegal trade barriers" were costing $520 million annually in lost sales to Europe, asked the U.S. government for help. The government agreed that unfair trade barriers were damaging their business, and 100 percent tariffs on selected European imports were levied. Coincidentally, Chiquita Brands' annual political campaign contributions increased from barely over $40,000 in 1991 to $1.3 million in 1998.

A settlement was finally reached that involved high tariffs on Latin America bananas and quotas (with no tariffs) on bananas from Europe's former colonies. But the bruising over bananas continued, and not in a straightforward way! In 2007 the issue shifted to banana bending. That is, bananas from Latin America tend to be long and straight, while those from the non-tariff countries are short and bent. Because the latter are not preferred by the shippers or retailers (the bendier ones don't stack as neatly and economically), the bananas from the former colonies were still not preferred. And new regulations were adopted by the European Commission that mandated that bananas must be free from "abnormal curvature of the fingers." So the bendy banana producers threatened to renege on the whole agreement. Circa 2007 everyone involved found this prospect very unappealing.

The tale does have a happy ending though. In 2009, after marathon meetings among all parties in Geneva, the 16-year banana split was finally healed: The European Union cut import tariffs on bananas grown in Latin America by U.S. firms.

Sources: "U.S. Sets Import Tariffs in Latest Salvo in Ongoing Battle over Banana Trade," *Minneapolis Star Tribune*, March 4, 1999; Timothy Dove, "Hit by a $200,000 Bill from the Blue," *Time*, February 7, 2000, p. 54; Jeremy Smith, "EU Heading for Trade Crunch over Bananas," *Reuters*, November 14, 2007.

No company, domestic or international, large or small, can conduct business without considering the influence of the political environment within which it will operate. One of the most undeniable and crucial realities of international business is that both host and home governments are integral partners. A government reacts to its environment by initiating and pursuing policies deemed necessary to solve the problems created by its particular circumstances. Reflected in its policies and attitudes toward business are a government's ideas of how best to promote the national interest, considering its own resources and political philosophy. A government controls and restricts a company's activities by encouraging and offering support or by discouraging and banning or restricting its activities—depending on the pleasure of the government.

International law recognizes the sovereign right of a nation to grant or withhold permission to do business within its political boundaries and to control where its citizens conduct business. Thus, the political environment of countries is a critical concern for the international marketer. This chapter examines some of the more salient political considerations in assessing global markets.

The Sovereignty of Nations

LO1

What the sovereignty of nations means and how it can affect the stability of government policies

In the context of international law, a *sovereign state* is independent and free from all external control; enjoys full legal equality with other states; governs its own territory; selects its own political, economic, and social systems; and has the power to enter into agreements with other nations. **Sovereignty** refers to both the powers exercised by a state in relation to other countries and the supreme powers exercised over its own members.[1] A state sets requirements for citizenship, defines geographical boundaries, and controls trade and the movement of people and goods across its borders. Additionally, a citizen is subject to the state's laws even when beyond national borders. It is with the extension of national laws beyond a country's borders that much of the conflict in international business arises. This reasoning is especially true when another country considers its own sovereignty to be compromised

Nations can and do abridge specific aspects of their sovereign rights to coexist with other nations. The European Union, North American Free Trade Agreement (NAFTA), North Atlantic Treaty Organization (NATO), and World Trade Organization (WTO)[2] represent examples of nations voluntarily agreeing to give up some of their sovereign rights

---

[1]For those interested in learning more about the concept of sovereignty, see Stephen D. Krasner (ed.), *Problematic Sovereignty* (New York: Columbia University Press, 2001).

[2]"Global Trade Talks Founder on Farm-Subsidy Issues," *The Wall Street Journal Online*, June 21, 2007.

THUMBS-UP: U.S. President Barack Obama, Italian Prime Minister Silvio Berlusconi, and Russian President Dmitry Medvedev mugged for the camera during a group photo after an April G-20 summit in London aimed at fixing the crises-wracked global economy. All leaders of the G20 nations signed a joint communiqué promising to "resist protectionism." Their April 2009 agreement marked the nadir of the world trade bust (a decline of more than 12 percent) that marked the year. The celebration symbolizes their successful dodging of the Smoot-Hawley tariff bullet that dramatically exacerbated the Great Depression of the 1930s.

to participate with member nations for a common, mutually beneficial goal. The leaders of the G20 nations ceded some sovereignty in their hugely important April 2009 agreement to "reject protectionism" at the nadir of the 2009 crash, when world trade had declined more than 12 percent. The bad memories of the Smoot-Hawley disaster of the Great Depression apparently made the decision one to celebrate, as the accompanying picture shows.

As indicated in Exhibit 1.4 (page 24), the United States's involvement in international political affiliations is surprisingly low (i.e., it is largely sovereign). Indeed, when it comes to participation in international treaty regimes, the United States is ranked near the bottom of the 72 countries included in *Foreign Policy* magazine rankings, tied with Iran and Israel (at 68th) and ahead of only Hong Kong and Taiwan.[3] Most notably, the Kyoto Protocol on global climate change and the International Criminal Court were rejected by the Bush administration, along with lesser known treaties such as the Basel Convention on the Control of Transboundary Movement of Hazardous Wastes. This apparent lack of international political engagement is particularly hard to understand given the wide acceptance that such agreements lead to peace and mutual understanding.[4] Fortunately, President Obama has now set a more positive tone for international cooperation and agreements, one welcomed by the rest of the world.

Countries that agree to relinquish some of their sovereignty often are subject to a nagging fear that too much has been given away. For example, the WTO is considered by some as the biggest threat so far to national sovereignty. Adherence to the WTO inevitably means the loss of some degree of national sovereignty, because the member nations have pledged to abide by international covenants and arbitration procedures that can override national laws and have far-reaching ramifications for citizens. Sovereignty was one of the issues at the heart of the spat between the United States and the European Union over Europe's refusal to lower tariffs and quotas on bananas (see the Global Perspective). And critics of the free trade agreements with both South Korea and Peru claim America's sacrifice of sovereignty is too great.

Foreign investment can also be perceived as a threat to sovereignty and thus become a rallying cry by opposing factions. The Chinese national oil company's proposed purchase of Unocal was opposed on such grounds. As American banks struggled to maintain liquidity during the 2008 home mortgage debacle, huge investments from overseas were solicited and received from one class of foreign investors that U.S. politicians particularly disfavored—the so-called "sovereign wealth funds" that entail vast pools of money controlled by foreign governments from China and the Middle East.[5] At the same time, members of the U.S. Congress have demanded that China raise the value of its currency, but that would make it even easier for Chinese firms and their government to buy American assets.[6] Of course, the Chinese resist the latter political pressure as a threat to their sovereignty. Ironically, Americans have criticized Mexico for hindering similar sorts of American investments. That is, Mexico badly needs privately financed electricity generating plants to meet electrical power demands and to upgrade the country's overloaded transmission network. The Mexican government entered into an agreement with a Belgian company to build a power plant that would bypass the state electricity monopoly and sell electricity directly to large Mexican manufacturers. But the Mexican constitution limits private ownership of utilities, and any exception requires a two-thirds vote of the legislature. The Institutional Revolutionary Party (PRI) saw the attempt to open Mexico's protected energy industry as an assault on Mexican sovereignty and blocked the agreement. What all this conflict highlights is that national sovereignty is a critical issue in assessing the environment in which a firm operates.

---

[3]"Measuring Globalization," *Foreign Policy*, November/December 2007, pp. 68–77.

[4]John L. Graham, "The Big Secret of World Peace," *Journal of Commerce*, February 13, 1995, OPED page; John L. Graham, "Trade Brings Peace," in J. Runzo and N. Martin (eds.), *War and Reconciliation* (Cambridge: Cambridge University Press, 2011); Thomas L. Friedman, *The World Is Flat* (New York: Farrar, Straus, and Giroux, 2005).

[5]Peter S. Goodman and Louise Story, "Overseas Investors Buying U.S. Holdings at Record Pace," *The New York Times*, January 20, 2008, pp. 1, 14.

[6]"Lost in Translations," *The Economist*, January 19, 2008, pp. 73–75.

Stability of Government Policies

The ideal political climate for a multinational firm is a stable, friendly government. Unfortunately, governments are not always stable and friendly, nor do stable, friendly governments always remain so. Radical shifts in government philosophy when an opposing political party ascends to power,[7] pressure from nationalist and self-interest groups, weakened economic conditions, bias against foreign investment, or conflicts among governments are all issues that can affect the stability of a government. Because foreign businesses are judged by standards as variable as there are nations, the stability and friendliness of the government in each country must be assessed as an ongoing business practice.

At the top of the list of political issues concerning foreign businesses is the stability or instability of prevailing government policies. Governments might change[8] or new political parties might be elected, but the concern of the multinational corporation is the continuity of the set of rules or codes of behavior and the continuation of the rule of law—regardless of which government is in power. A change in government, whether by election or coup, does not always mean a change in the level of political risk. In Italy, for example, more than 50 different governments have been formed since the end of World War II. While the political turmoil in Italy continues, business goes on as usual. In contrast, India has had as many different governments since 1945 as Italy, with several in the past few years favorable to foreign investment and open markets. However, much government policy remains hostile to foreign investment. Senior civil servants who are not directly accountable to the electorate but who remain in place despite the change of the elected government continue with former policies. Even after elections of parties favoring economic reform, the bureaucracy continues to be staffed by old-style central planners in India.

Conversely, radical changes in policies toward foreign business can occur in the most stable governments. The same political party, the Institutional Revolutionary Party (PRI), controlled Mexico from 1929 to 2000. During that period, the political risk for foreign investors ranged from expropriation of foreign investments to Mexico's membership in NAFTA and an open door for foreign investment and trade. In recent years, the PRI created a stable political environment for foreign investment, in contrast to earlier expropriations and harassment. Beginning with the elections in 2000, however, a new era in Mexican politics emerged as a result of profound changes within the PRI brought about by then-president Ernesto Zedillo. Since 1929, the Mexican president had selected his successor, who, without effective challenge, was always elected. President Zedillo changed the process by refusing to nominate a candidate; instead he let the nomination be decided by an open primary—the first in seven decades. From a field of four candidates, the PRI selected Labastida Ochoa, and the opposing party PAN[9] selected Vicente Fox who, though considered a long shot, won the presidency. Although the PAN had gained strength for several years in the congress and among state governments, its presidential candidates never had a winning chance until the 2000 election.

Some African countries are unstable, with seemingly unending civil wars, boundary disputes, and oppressive military regimes. Even relatively stable and prosperous Kenya fell victim to political violence in 2008 that greatly disrupted growth in commerce in the entire region.[10] Sierra Leone has had three changes in government in five years; the most recent coup d'etat ended the country's brief experiment with democracy. Shortly after the coup, a civil war erupted, and UN peacekeeping forces have had to maintain the peace. Central Africa, where ethnic wars have embroiled seven nations, is one of the most politically unstable regions in the world. Thus, Africa is trapped in a vicious cycle: For its nations to prosper, they need foreign investment. But investment is leery of unstable nations, which

---

[7]Sabrina Tavernise, "Debate Intensifies in Turkey over Head Scarf Ban," *The New York Times*, January 19, 2008, p. A5.

[8]Sebastian Moffett, "Japanese Prime Minister Steps Down after Less than One Year in Office," *The Wall Street Journal Online*, September 12, 2007.

[9]PAN stands for Partido Accion National. PAN and PRI are the largest of eight political parties in Mexico.

[10]Michela Wrong, "Kenya's Turmoil Cuts off Its Neighbors," *Los Angeles Times*, January 14, 2008, p. C4.

CHAOTIC CONDITIONS: On the first Sunday after the quake, at 9:00 a.m., the streets of downtown Port-au-Prince are filled with people scavenging. Onlookers add to the crowd.

is the status of much of Africa.[11] A recent World Bank study showed that the 47 nations of sub-Saharan Africa were attracting less than \$2 billion annually in direct foreign investment—about one-tenth of what a developing nation such as Mexico attracts.

If there is potential for profit and if permitted to operate within a country, multinational companies can function under any type of government as long as there is some long-run predictability and stability. PepsiCo, for example, operated profitably in the Soviet Union when it had one of the world's most extreme political systems. Years before the disintegration of the USSR's Communist Party, PepsiCo established a very profitable countertrade business with the USSR. The company exchanged Pepsi syrup for Russian vodka, thus avoiding the legally complicated financial transactions of the time.[12]

Socioeconomic and political environments invariably change, as they have in the Soviet Union and Mexico. There are five main political causes of instability in international markets: (1) some forms of government seem to be inherently unstable, (2) changes in political parties during elections can have major effects on trade conditions, (3) nationalism, (4) animosity targeted toward specific countries, and (5) trade disputes themselves.

Forms of Government

LO2

How different governmental types, political parties, nationalism, targeted fear/animosity, and trade disputes can affect the environment for marketing in foreign countries

Circa 500 BC, the ancient Greeks conceived of and criticized three fundamental forms of government: rule by one, rule by few, and rule by many. The common terms for these forms in use today are monarchy (or dictatorship), aristocracy (or oligarchy), and democracy. About the same time in history Cyrus the Great, monarch of Persia, declared that the purpose of government was to serve the people, not vice versa. Cyrus's notion is embedded in the constitutions of most modern nations. Following the collapse of colonialism beginning with World War II and communism circa 1990, the world seemed to have agreed that free-enterprise democracy was the best solution to all the criticisms of government since the time of Aristotle, Cyrus, and the others.[13]

Thus, of the more than 200 sovereign states on the planet, almost all have at least nominally representative governments with universal suffrage for those 18 years and over. In

---

[11]Visit http://www.eiu.com for abstracts of the Economist Intelligence Unit's country reports of current political and economic data. Some information on this site is available for a fee only, but other sources are free.

[12]Visit the Pepsi Web site in Russia for a history of Pepsi in Russia, Pepsi advertising in Russia, and other information: http://www.pepsi.ru.

[13]Francis Fukuyama, *The End of History and the Last Man* (New York: The Free Press, 1992).

Exhibit 6.1
A Sampling of
Government Types

Source: http://www.cia.gov/cia/
publications/factbook/, 2008.

Country	Government Type
Afghanistan	Islamic republic
Belarus	Republic in name, though in fact a dictatorship
Bosnia and Herzegovina	Emerging federal democratic republic
Burma (Myanmar)	Military junta
Canada	Confederation with parliamentary democracy
China	Communist state
Congo, Democratic	Dictatorship, presumably undergoing a transition to representative government
Cuba	Communist state
Iran	Theocratic republic
Libya	Jamahiriya (a state of the masses) in theory, governed by the populace through local councils; in fact a military dictatorship
North Korea	Communist state, one-man dictatorship
Saudi Arabia	Monarchy
Somalia	No permanent national government; transitional, parliamentary federal government
Sudan	Authoritarian regime—ruling military junta
United Kingdom	Constitutional monarchy
United States	Constitutional federal republic
Uzbekistan	Republic; authoritarian presidential rule, with little power outside the executive branch
Vietnam	Communist state

about 10 percent of the nations voting is required; in the rest it is voluntary. A few countries have some unusual rules for suffrage: In Bolivia, you can vote at 18 if you are married and at 21 if single; in Peru, police and military personnel cannot vote; in Croatia, you can vote at 16 if employed; in Lebanon, only women with at least an elementary education can vote (though all men can vote); and Saudi Arabia precludes women from voting. The last appears to be the only state still completely in the dark ages with regards to suffrage. Exhibit 6.1 lists a sampling of the countries that are currently taking a different approach to the conventional wisdom of representational democracy. More troubling though is the apparent backsliding of some countries toward autocracy and away from democracy, such as Nigeria, Kenya, Bangladesh, Venezuela, Georgia, and Kyrgyzstan.[14] Haiti's government has been literally crushed by the great earthquake of 2010.[15] Indeed, according to the Heritage Foundation, the United States experienced its biggest drop in "economic freedom" because of the controlling impact of the economic stimuli of 2008–2009.[16] Meanwhile, we can all witness perhaps the world's greatest experiment in political and economic change: the race between Russian "big-bang" reform and Chinese gradualism as communism is left further behind in both countries.[17]

The Central Intelligence Agency[18] claims to have taken a look beyond the facade of constitutions in their descriptors. For example, Iran (modern Persia) is defined as a "theocratic republic," recognizing that the constitution codifies Islamic principles of government as interpreted from the Koran. Although political parties are allowed to function, they hold little political power. Instead, the Supreme Leader controls all-important decisions of the government, including who is allowed to run for president in Iran.

---

[14]"Crying for Freedom ," *The Economist*, January 16, 2010, pp. 58–60.

[15]Marci Lacey, "Haiti's Icon of Power, Now Palace for Ghosts," *The New York Times*, January 23, 2010.

[16]Terry Miller, "The U.S. Isn't as Free as It Used to Be," *The Wall Street Journal*, January 20, 2010, p. A17.

[17]Brian Bremmer, "The Dragon's Way or the Tiger's?" *BusinessWeek*, November 20, 2006, pp. 55–62; N. Mark Lam and John L. Graham, *Doing Business in China Now, The World's Most Dynamic Market* (New York: McGraw-Hill, 2007).

[18]http://www.cia.gov/cia/publications/factbook/, 2010.

EYES ON THE POLLS: Portraits of Ayatollah Ali Khamenei (the Supreme Leader) and the late Ayatollah Ruhollah Khomeini loom over Iranian women lined up to vote at a mosque south of Tehran. As mandated by law, women and men waited in separate lines at polling places with more than one ballot box. The current government also specifies the public dress of the women pictured.

Political Parties

For most countries around the world, it is particularly important for the marketer to know the philosophies of all major political parties within a country, because any one of them might become dominant and alter prevailing attitudes and the overall business climate.[19] In countries where two strong political parties typically succeed one another in control of the government, it is important to know the direction each party is likely to take.[20] In Great Britain, for example, the Labour Party traditionally has been more restrictive regarding foreign trade than the Conservative Party. The Labour Party, when in control, has limited imports, whereas the Conservative Party has tended to liberalize foreign trade when it is in power. A foreign firm in Britain can expect to seesaw between the liberal trade policies of the Conservatives and the restrictive ones of Labour. Of course, in the United States, the Democratic Congress was reluctant to ratify free trade pacts negotiated by George Bush's Republican administration in the White House.[21]

An astute international marketer must understand all aspects of the political landscape to be properly informed about the political environment. Unpredictable and drastic shifts in government policies deter investments, whatever the cause of the shift. In short, a current assessment of political philosophy and attitudes within a country is important in gauging the stability and attractiveness of a government in terms of market potential.

Nationalism

Economic and cultural nationalism, which exists to some degree within all countries, is another factor important in assessing business climate. Nationalism can best be described as an intense feeling of national pride and unity, an awakening of a nation's people to pride in their country. This pride can take an anti–foreign business bias, where minor harassment and controls of foreign investment are supported, if not applauded.[22] Economic nationalism has as one of its central aims the preservation of national economic autonomy, in that residents identify their interests with the preservation of the sovereignty of the state in

[19]Paul M. Vaaler, Burkhard N. Schrage, and Steven A. Block, "Counting the Investor Vote: Political Business Cycle Effects on Sovereign Bond Spreads in Developing Countries," *Journal of International Business Studies* 36, no. 1 (2005), pp. 62–88.

[20]Joy C. Shaw, "Taiwan's KMT Wins Big in Legislative Elections," *The Wall Street Journal Online*, January 12, 2008.

[21]Steven R. Weisman, "Bush in Accord with Democrats on Trade Pacts," *The New York Times*, May 11, 2007, pp. 1, C7.

[22]David Pierson, "China Pursues Oil on U.S. Turf," *Los Angeles Times*, October 22, 2009, pp. B1, B4.

CROSSING BORDERS 6.1 Coke's Back, and It Still Has the Secret

For almost 100 years, the formula for making Coca-Cola has been a closely guarded secret. Then the government of India ordered Coca-Cola to disclose it or cease operations in that country. A secret ingredient called 7-X supposedly gives Coke its distinctive flavor. The government's minister for industry told the Indian parliament that Coca-Cola's Indian branch would have to transfer 60 percent of its equity shares to Indians and hand over its know-how by April 1978 or shut down.

Indian sales accounted for less than 1 percent of Coca-Cola's worldwide sales, but the potential market in India, a country of 800 million, was tremendous. The government refused to let the branch import the necessary ingredients, and Coca-Cola—whose products were once as abundant as the bottled drinking water sold in almost every Indian town of more than 50,000—packed up its bags and left the country. The minister for industry said that Coca-Cola's activities in India "furnish a classic example of how multinational corporations operating in a low-priority, high-profit area in a developing country attain run-away growth and . . . trifle with the weaker indigenous industry."

Sixteen years later, India's attitudes toward foreign investment changed, and Coca-Cola reentered the market without having to divulge its formula. During

Coke's 16-year exile, however, Pepsi Cola came to India and captured a 26 percent market share. Not to worry; there is plenty of growth potential for both, considering that India's per capita consumption is just 3 eight-ounce bottles a year, versus about 12 for Pakistan and over 500 in Mexico. To forestall further political vulnerability, Coke sold 49 percent of its Indian bottler subsidiary to institutional investors and employees. The company hopes this move will put to rest an issue that concerned the Indian government, which wanted Indians to own part of Coke's local operation—in other words, Coke took steps to domesticate its operations.

But India is still a tough market. Most recently, a water quality dispute, domestic price competition, a pesticide scare, and cool weather have hurt Coke's sales in India, despite a general global rebound in revenues and profits. And, after Coke's failed first entry into the Indian energy drink market with a new brand called "Shocker," let's hope it doesn't get burned with its second try, "Burn!"

Sources: Craig Simons, "India Coke Plant Still Closed as Water Woes Argued," *Atlanta Journal-Constitution*, December 16, 2007, p. F1; "Coke India Chief Bullish on India Becoming Top 5 Global Market," *Asia Pulse*, January 15, 2008; "Coca-Cola: A Second Shot at Energy Drinks," *MarketWatch: Global Round-Up*, January 2010, p. 39.

which they reside. In other words, national interest and security are more important than international relations.

Feelings of nationalism are manifested in a variety of ways, including a call to "buy our country's products only" (e.g., "Buy American"), restrictions on imports, restrictive tariffs, and other barriers to trade. They may also lead to control over foreign investment, often regarded with suspicion, which then becomes the object of intensive scrutiny and control. Generally speaking, the more a country feels threatened by some outside force or the domestic economy declines, the more nationalistic it becomes in protecting itself against intrusions.

During the period after World War II, when many new countries were founded and many others were seeking economic independence, manifestations of militant nationalism were rampant. Expropriation of foreign companies, restrictive investment policies, and nationalization of industries were common practices in some parts of the world. During this period, India imposed such restrictive practices on foreign investments that companies such as Coca-Cola, IBM, and many others chose to leave rather than face the uncertainty of a hostile economic climate. In many Latin American countries, similar attitudes prevailed and led to expropriations and even confiscation of foreign investments.

By the late 1980s, militant nationalism had subsided; today, the foreign investor, once feared as a dominant tyrant that threatened economic development, is often sought as a source of needed capital investment.[23] Nationalism comes and goes as conditions and

---

[23]Muammar el Qaddafi, the leader of Libya, has changed his approach to international relations from supporting terrorism to supporting trade, for example. See "Rehabilitating Libya," *The New York Times* (editorial), January 8, 2007, p. 14.

attitudes change, and foreign companies welcomed today may be harassed tomorrow and vice versa.

Although militant economic nationalism has subsided, nationalistic feelings can be found even in the most economically prosperous countries. When U.S. negotiators pushed Japan to import more rice to help balance the trade deficit between the two countries, nationalistic feelings rose to a new high. Deeply rooted Japanese notions of self-sufficiency, self-respect, and concern for the welfare of Japanese farmers caused Japan to resist any change for several years. It was only after a shortfall in the Japanese rice harvests that restrictions on rice imports were temporarily eased. Even then, all imported foreign rice had to be mixed with Japanese rice before it could be sold.

Targeted Fear and/or Animosity

It is important for marketers not to confuse nationalism, whose animosity is directed generally toward *all* foreign countries, with a widespread fear or animosity directed at a particular country. This confusion was a mistake made by Toyota in the United States in the late 1980s and early 1990s. Sales of Japanese cars were declining in the States, and an advertising campaign was designed and delivered that assumed the problem was American nationalism. However, nationalism was clearly not the problem, because sales of German cars were not experiencing the same kinds of declines. The properly defined problem was "Americans' *fear* of Japan." Indeed, at the time, Americans considered the economic threat from Japan greater than the military threat from the Soviet Union. So when Toyota spent millions on an advertising campaign showing Camrys being made by Americans in a Toyota plant in Kentucky, it may well have exacerbated the fear that the Japanese were "colonizing" the United States.

Best-selling titles in France, including *The World Is Not Merchandise*, *Who Is Killing France? The American Strategy*, and *No Thanks Uncle Sam*, epitomize its animosity toward the United States. Although such attitudes may seem odd in a country that devours U.S. movies, eats U.S. fast foods, views U.S. soap operas, and shops at U.S. Walmart stores, national animosity—whatever the cause—is a critical part of the political environment. The United States is not immune to the same kinds of directed negativism either. The rift between France and the United States over the Iraq–U.S. war led to hard feelings on both sides and an American backlash against French wine, French cheese, and even products Americans thought were French. French's mustard felt compelled to issue a press release stating that it is an "American company founded by an American named 'French.'" Thus, it is quite clear that no nation-state, however secure, will tolerate penetration by a foreign company into its market and economy if it perceives a social, cultural, economic, or political threat to its well-being.

Trade Disputes

Finally, narrow trade disputes themselves can roil broader international markets. At the beginning of the chapter we discussed our favorite example—bananas. Among several hot issues circa 2010 were undervalued Chinese currency, the ban on beef imports into Japan, Chinese subsidies in apparent violation of WTO rules, farm subsidies in developed countries, and the long-simmering AIRBUS–Boeing battle over subsidies. Any of these disputes might boil over and affect other aspects of international trade, but at least at this writing, cooler heads seem to be prevailing—along with the WTO dispute resolution processes.

Political Risks of Global Business

LO3

The political risks of global business and the factors that affect stability

Issues of sovereignty, differing political philosophies, and nationalism are manifest in a host of governmental actions that enhance the risks of global business. Risks can range from confiscation, the harshest, to many lesser but still significant government rules and regulations, such as exchange controls, import restrictions, and price controls that directly affect the performance of business activities. Although not always officially blessed initially, social or political activist groups can provoke governments into actions that prove harmful to business. Of all the political risks, the most costly are those actions that result in a transfer of equity from the company to the government, with or without adequate compensation.

Confiscation, Expropriation, and Domestication

LO4

The importance of the political system to international marketing and its effect on foreign investments

The most severe political risk is **confiscation**, that is, the seizing of a company's assets without payment. Two notable confiscations of U.S. property occurred when Fidel Castro became the leader in Cuba and later when the Shah of Iran was overthrown. Confiscation was most prevalent in the 1950s and 1960s when many underdeveloped countries saw confiscation, albeit ineffective, as a means of economic growth.

Less drastic, but still severe, is **expropriation**, where the government seizes an investment but makes some reimbursement for the assets. For example, in 2008 the Chavez regime in Venezuela expropriated Mexico's CEMEX operations, paying a negotiated price.[24] Often the expropriated investment is nationalized; that is, it becomes a government-run entity. A third type of risk is **domestication**, which occurs when host countries gradually cause the transfer of foreign investments to national control and ownership through a series of government decrees that mandate local ownership and greater national involvement in a company's management. The ultimate goal of domestication is to force foreign investors to share more of the ownership, management, and profits with nationals than was the case before domestication.

Rather than a quick answer to economic development, expropriation and nationalization have often led to nationalized businesses that were inefficient, technologically weak, and noncompetitive in world markets. Risks of confiscation and expropriation appear to have lessened over the last two decades (with exceptions in Latin America, particularly Venezuela),[25] because experience has shown that few of the desired benefits materialize after government takeover.[26] Today, countries often require prospective investors to agree to share ownership, use local content, enter into labor and management agreements, and share participation in export sales as a condition of entry; in effect, the company has to become domesticated as a condition for investment.

Countries now view foreign investment as a means of economic growth. As the world has become more economically interdependent, it has become obvious that much of the economic success of countries such as South Korea, Singapore, and Taiwan is tied to foreign investments. Nations throughout the world that only a few years ago restricted or forbade foreign investments are now courting foreign investors as a much needed source of capital and technology. Additionally, they have begun to privatize telecommunications, broadcasting, airlines, banks, railroads, and other nationally owned companies as a means of enhancing competition and attracting foreign capital.

The benefits of privatizing are many. In Mexico, for example, privatization of the national telephone company resulted in almost immediate benefits when the government received hundreds of millions of dollars of much needed capital from the sale and immediate investment in new telecommunications systems. A similar scenario has played out in Brazil, Argentina, India, and many eastern European countries. Ironically, many of the businesses that were expropriated and nationalized in earlier periods are now being privatized.

Economic Risks

Even though expropriation and confiscation are waning as risks of doing business abroad, international companies are still confronted with a variety of economic risks that can occur with little warning. Restraints on business activity may be imposed under the banner of national security to protect an infant industry, to conserve scarce foreign exchange, to raise revenue, or to retaliate against unfair trade practices, among a score of other real or imagined reasons. These economic risks are an important and recurring part of the political environment that few international companies can avoid.

Exchange Controls.

Exchange controls stem from shortages of foreign exchange held by a country. When a nation faces shortages of foreign exchange and/or a substantial amount of capital is leaving the country, controls may be levied over all movements of capital or selectively against the most politically vulnerable companies to conserve the

---

[24]Steven Bodzin, "Cemex Handing Plants to Chavez," *The Globe and Mail*, August 28, 2008, p. B5.

[25]Simon Romero, "Chavez Takes over Foreign-Controlled Oil Projects in Venezuela," *The New York Times*, May 2, 2007, p. A3.

[26]Marla Dickerson, "Woes Mount for Mexico's State Oil Titan," *Los Angeles Times*, January 2, 2008, pp. C1, C4.

Exhibit 6.2

How Complicated Things Can Get!

Sources: "Myanmar's Crumbling Kit," *Asiaweek*, March 2, 2001, p. 8; Michael Vatikiotis, "Neighbors Lean on Myanmar," *International Herald Tribune*, February 2, 2005, p. 7; "Myanmar Military Confirms No Change in Fuel Rations," *Dow Jones International*, December 31, 2007.

Exchange controls also are extended to products by applying a system of multiple exchange rates to regulate trade in specific commodities classified as necessities or luxuries. Necessary products are placed in the most favorable (low) exchange categories, while luxuries are heavily penalized with high foreign exchange rates. Myanmar (formerly known as Burma), for example, has three exchange rates for the kyat (Kt): the official rate (Kt6:U.S.$1), the market rate (Kt100–125:U.S.$1), and an import duty rate (Kt100:U.S.$1). Because the kyat is not convertible—that is, not officially exchangeable for currencies that can be spent outside the country—investors are severely affected by tax liability, and their ability to send profits outside the country is diminished. Under such exchange rates, tax liability can be very high. For instance, a profit of Kt135,000 is worth U.S.$22,500 at the official exchange rate of Kt6 to U.S.$1, but at the market rate, the investor has earned only U.S.$1,000. The exchange rate difference means that the investor has to pay tax on U.S.$21,500 of nonexistent, unearned income. It seems not much makes sense in Myanmar these days.

supply of foreign exchange for the most essential uses. A recurrent problem for the foreign investor is getting profits in and out of the host country without loss of value, which can occur when a currency is devalued. Exhibit 6.2 illustrates how exchange controls can affect an international company's profits. Many countries maintain regulations for control of currency, and should an economy suffer a setback or foreign exchange reserves decline severely, the controls on convertibility are imposed quickly.

Local-Content Laws. In addition to restricting imports of essential supplies to force local purchase, countries often require a portion of any product sold within the country to have local content, that is, to contain locally made parts. Thailand, for example, requires that all milk products contain at least 50 percent milk from local dairy farmers. Contrary to popular belief, local-content requirements are not restricted to Third World countries. The European Union has had a local-content requirement as high as 45 percent for "screwdriver operations," a name often given to foreign-owned assemblers, and NAFTA requires 62 percent local content for all cars coming from member countries.

Import Restrictions. Selective restrictions on the import of raw materials, machines, and spare parts are fairly common strategies to force foreign industry to purchase more supplies within the host country and thereby create markets for local industry. Although this restriction is an attempt to support the development of domestic industry, the result is often to hamstring and sometimes interrupt the operations of established industries. The problem then becomes critical when there are no adequately developed sources of supply within the country.

Tax Controls. Taxes must be classified as a political risk when used as a means of controlling foreign investments. In such cases, they are raised without warning and in violation of formal agreements. India, for example, taxes PepsiCo and the Coca-Cola Company 40 percent on all soda bottled in India. And, using a different angle of attack, India is attempting to collect $40 million in taxes on travel tickets sold online from Sabre's (an airlines reservations service) data center in Tulsa, Oklahoma. The Indian government contends that Sabre has a permanent establishment in India in the form of data flows between Sabre's Tulsa processing center and the desktop computers of travel agents in India. To underdeveloped countries with economies constantly threatened with a shortage of funds, unreasonable taxation of successful foreign investments appeals to some government officials as the handiest and quickest means of finding operating funds. As the Internet grows in importance, countries will surely seize on Internet transactions as a lucrative source of revenue.

Price Controls. Essential products that command considerable public interest, such as pharmaceuticals, food, gasoline, and cars, are often subjected to price controls. Such controls applied during inflationary periods can be used to control the cost of living. They also may be used to force foreign companies to sell equity to local interests. A side effect on the local economy can be to slow or even stop capital investment.

The consequences of the U.S. embargo of Cuba: A brand new German Mercedes for a foreign diplomat (black plate), a relatively new Chinese Chery Q (red provisional plate), and one of the newest American cars you can find on the island, a 1957 Chevy (yellow citizen's plate), certainly with a refurbished engine. A variety of other European and Asian brands ply the streets of Havana, almost all recent models. No new American models are in sight.

Labor Problems.   In many countries, labor unions have strong government support that they use effectively in obtaining special concessions from business. Layoffs may be forbidden, profits may have to be shared, and an extraordinary number of services may have to be provided. In fact, in many countries, foreign firms are considered fair game for the demands of the domestic labor supply. In France, the belief in full employment is almost religious in fervor; layoffs of any size, especially by foreign-owned companies, are regarded as national crises. We should also note that some multinational companies are more powerful than local labor unions. Walmart closed a store in Quebec rather than let it be unionized.

Political Sanctions   In addition to economic risks, one or a group of nations may boycott another nation, thereby stopping all trade between the countries, or may issue sanctions against the trade of specific products. The United States has long-term boycotts of trade with Cuba and Iran and has come under some criticism for its demand for continued sanctions against Cuba and its threats of future sanctions against countries that violate human rights issues.[27]

History indicates that sanctions are almost always unsuccessful in reaching desired goals, particularly when other major nations' traders ignore them. For example, the Chinese recently signed an agreement with Iran that will bring $70 billion of natural gas to China. Please see Crossing Borders 6.2 for more on this issue. This lack of success is the case with Cuba, North Korea, and Iran, where the undesirable behavior that the sanctions were imposed to change continues, and the only ones who seem to be hurt are the people[28] and companies that get caught in the middle.

[27]Ginger Thompson, "Imposing Conditions, OAS Lifts Its Suspension of Cuba," *Washington Post*, June 4, 2009, online.

[28]Barbara Demick, "North Koreans' Misery Amplified a Hundredfold," *Los Angeles Times*, February 3, 2010, pp. A1, A7.

CROSSING BORDERS 6.2	Trade Does Not Work as a Stick, Only as a Carrot

It was 1807 when Thomas Jefferson proposed trade sanctions as an innovation in diplomacy. The donkeys he endeavored to persuade were quite big and quite stubborn—England and France. The goal was to get these warring nations to leave American ships alone on the high seas. Lacking a competitive navy, our third president dreamed up the trade embargo; rather than using trade as a carrot, he planned to withhold trade and use it as a stick. However, instead of changing French or English policies and behaviors, Jefferson's policy actually endangered New England traders. They complained:

> Our ships all in motion, once whiten'd the ocean;
> They sail'd and return'd with a Cargo;
> Now doom'd to decay, they are fallen a prey,
> To Jefferson, worms, and EMBARGO.

Jefferson's embargo fell apart in just 15 months. Only the War of 1812 settled the problems with English aggression at sea.

Consider the track record of trade sanctions in the last century. In 1940 the United States told the Japanese to get out of China, and the ensuing embargo of gasoline and scrap metal led directly to the Pearl Harbor attack. Since 1948 Arab countries have boycotted Israel. Given that countries trade most with their close neighbors, you have to wonder how much this lack of trade has promoted the continuing conflicts in the area. Israel is still there. In 1959 Fidel Castro took over Cuba, and for the next 50+ years, the United States has boycotted sugar and cigars, but Castro remained in charge. OPEC's 1973 oil flow slowdown was intended to get America to stop supporting Israel. However, the dollars still flow fast to Israel and now Egypt as well.

In 1979 the United States told the Soviets to get out of Afghanistan. They refused. America boycotted the Moscow Olympics and stopped selling the Soviets grain and technology. The Soviet response: They continued to kill Afghans (and, by the way, Soviet soldiers) for another 10 years. Moreover, in 1984 they and their allies' athletes stayed away from the Olympics in Los Angeles. And the high-tech embargo didn't work anyway. A San Diego division of Caterpillar lost millions of dollars in service contracts for Soviet natural gas pipelines in the mid-1970s. These revenues were lost permanently, because the Soviets taught themselves how to do the maintenance and overhauls. In 1989 a Moscow weapons research facility had every brand of computer then available in the West: IBMs, Apples, and the best from Taiwan and Japan as well.

Perhaps the 1980s' multilateral trade sanctions imposed on South Africa hastened apartheid's demise. But look how well the world's 10-year embargo of Iraq changed policy there. Using trade as a weapon killed kids while Saddam Hussein celebrated at $12 million birthday parties. Indeed, the best prescription for Middle East peace (and American taxpayers' wallets, by the way) is all sides dropping all embargoes.

The end of the last century witnessed great strides in the elimination of ill-conceived trade sanctions. Perhaps most important was the U.S. Senate's and President's approvals of permanently normalized trade relations (PNTR) with China. However, other important steps were the relaxation of some of the trade restrictions on Vietnam, North Korea, Iran, and Cuba. Indeed, as a result of President Clinton's diplomacy, North and South Koreans marched together at the Sydney Olympics; Americans can now buy pistachio nuts and carpets from Tehran, and U.S. firms can sell medical supplies and services in Havana. Remarkable!

These same kinds of carrots need to be thrown in the direction of the other countries on America's blacklist—Myanmar, Angola, Libya, Sudan, and Syria. Be certain that the chorus of criticism regarding human rights, freedom of the press, and democracy should continue, loud and clear. But instead of dropping bombs (or threatening to), we should be selling them computers and Internet connections. The cost of a cruise missile is about the same as 2,000 Apple computers! And at the most fundamental level, coercion does not work. Exchange does.

Source: John L. Graham, "Trade Brings Peace," in Joseph Runzo and Nancy M. Martin (eds.), *War and Reconciliation* (Cambridge, MA: Cambridge University Press, 2011).

Political and Social Activists and Nongovernmental Organizations

Although not usually officially sanctioned by the government, the impact of **political and social activists** (PSAs) can also interrupt the normal flow of trade. PSAs can range from those who seek to bring about peaceful change to those who resort to violence and terrorism to effect change. When well organized, the actions of PSAs can succeed.

The most entertaining protest technique was pioneered by French farmers. Perhaps they were inspired by that American export, *Animal House*. In any case, French farmers like to throw their food. Here they tossed tomatoes and such at McDonald's; they've also lobbed lamb chops at their own trade ministers.

THE NEW POWER OF PEACEFUL PROTESTS

I like to believe that people in the long run are going to do more to promote peace than our governments. Indeed, I think that people want peace so much that one of these days governments had better get out of the way and let them have it.

—Dwight D. Eisenhower

We believe that peace happens because people want it to, not because politicians ordain it so. Our ideas are not new. Karl Popper's *Open Society*[29] and Jonathan Schell's *Unconquerable World*[30] make the same kinds of arguments. We just think in today's world of punitive trade sanctions and military muscle, it is important to remind folks that there are more viable alternatives for international relations and global persuasion.[31]

The organizers (PSAs) of these various demonstrations understand that two things are important in protests: (1) getting large numbers of people to show up and

Apparently they pay attention in Taiwan. Most recently, fishermen pitched perch in Taipei to protest the Japanese fishing fleet's presence in their waters.

PROTESTING MILK PRICES: A farmer sprayed milk on police forces during a protest against falling milk prices outside the European Commission headquarters in Brussels. European dairy farmers are seeking more aid to cope with a sharp drop in milk prices. An udderly fantastic shot!

BARING THEIR DISMAY: Members of the Pirate Party parade through Berlin's Tegel Airport in their underwear to protest government plans to test full-body scans as an invasion of citizens' privacy.

(2) producing memorable pictures.

On these pages are some of our favorite pictures. Please note that to the extent that the Sea Shepherd Conservation Society activists used force to board the Japanese ship (below), we cannot condone their methods. Property damage and violence are never justified; and their use demonstrates a pathetic lack of creative thinking about integrated marketing communications (see Chapter 16).

Activists of the Bharatiya Janata Party wearing "evil" masks shout antigovernment slogans near the Union Carbide plant in the central Indian city of Bhopal on the eve of World Environment Day. The activists protested to draw the attention of the government to chemical waste and demanded the cleanup of hazardous waste in the area. The leak from the Union Carbide pesticide plant in 1984 was one of the world's worst industrial accidents, killing 3,000 people and leaving thousands of others with lifetime illnesses.

They were "pirates" to some, "hostages" to others. But two anti-whaling activists (an Australian and a Briton from the Sea Shepherd Conservation Society) who drew global attention by forcibly boarding a Japanese harpoon ship in Antarctic waters have demonstrated how the emotional clash over Japan's annual whale hunt can disrupt even the best international friendships.

[29]Karl R. Popper, *The Open Society and Its Enemies*, 5th ed. (Princeton, NJ: Princeton University Press, 1966).

[30]Jonathan Schell, *The Unconquerable World: Power, Nonviolence, and the Will of the People* (New York: Metropolitan Books, 2003).

[31]Taken from John L. Graham, *Trade Brings Peace*, 2011.

LO5

The impact of political
and social activists,
violence, and terrorism
on international business

In the previous pages, the protesters use creativity to make a point. We do not recommend the destructive sort of protest previously represented.

One of the most effective and best-known PSA actions was against Nestlé due to the sale of baby formula in Third World markets. The worldwide boycott of Nestlé products resulted in substantial changes in the company's marketing. More recently, activists of the Free Burma Campaign (FBC) have applied enough pressure to cause several U.S. garment companies to stop importing textiles from Myanmar. Furthermore, activists on several U.S. college campuses boycotted Pepsi Cola drinks and PepsiCo-owned Pizza Hut and Taco Bell stores, saying that the company's commercial activities contributed to the abysmal human rights in Myanmar. The results of the boycott were serious enough that PepsiCo sold its stake in its joint venture in Myanmar and withdrew from that market. The concern was that potential losses in the United States outweighed potential profits in Myanmar. Holland's Heineken and Denmark's Carlsberg beer companies withdrew from Myanmar for similar reasons.

The rather broad issue of globalization is the also the focus of many PSA groups. The demonstrations in Seattle during a 1999 WTO meeting and in Washington, DC, against the World Bank and the International Monetary Fund (IMF), along with similar demonstrations in other countries, reflect a growing concern about a global economy. Whether (or not) misguided, uninformed, or just "wackos," as they have been described, PSAs can be a potent force in rallying public opinion and are an important political force that should not be dismissed, as companies such as Nike, McDonald's, and Nestlé know.

The Internet has become an effective tool of PSAs to spread the word about whatever cause they sponsor. During protest rallies against the U.S.–Iraq war, organizers were able to coordinate protest demonstrations in 600 cities worldwide and to disseminate information easily. A Google search for "peace protest" during that time (2003) resulted in 788,000 entries (about 660,000 in 2008), including news briefs, Web sites for peace organizations, online petitions for peace, where to show up with your placard, where to send your dollars, and how to write your member of Congress.

Often associated with political activism, **nongovernmental organizations** (NGOs) are increasingly affecting policy decisions made by governments.[32] Many are involved in peaceful protests, lobbying, and even collaborations with governmental organizations.

---

[32]Hildy Teegen, Jonathan P. Doh, and Sushil Vachani, "The Importance of Non-Governmental Organizations (NGOs) in Global Governance and Value Creation: An International Business Research Agenda," *Journal of International Business Studies* 35, no. 6 (2004), pp. 463–83.

POLITICAL DISASTER STRIKES KENYA: In the Nairobi slum of Kibera, supporters of opposition leader Raila Odinga tear up a key railway that ran from the coast to Uganda. As many as 12 people were killed in the associated clashes. Of course, this destruction will do great damage to commerce and progress to all the countries in Eastern Africa. Let's hope the highway and international airport south of Nairobi stay intact, as they supply all of Europe with flowers from the burgeoning greenhouses in the area, and flower exports are a key source of revenue for the formerly thriving Kenyan economy.

Exhibit 6.3

U.S. State Department Travel Warnings (in order of date of posting, most recent first)

Source: http://travel.state.gov/travel/, 2010.

Haiti	Chad	Colombia
Pakistan	Mali	Guinea
Sudan	Sri Lanka	Lebanon
Somalia	Nepal	Cote d'Ivoire
Mauritania	Algeria	Philippines
Burundi	Indonesia	Colombia
Cote d'Ivoire	Yemen	Philippines
Somalia	Nepal	Afghanistan
Iraq	Syria	

Many also are involved in mitigating much of the human misery plaguing parts of the planet. Some NGOs have received global recognition—the Red Cross and Red Crescent, Amnesty International, Oxfam, UNICEF, Care, and Habitat for Humanity are examples—for their good works, political influence, and even their brand power.[33]

Violence, Terrorism, and War

Although not usually government initiated, violence is another related risk for multinational companies to consider in assessing the political vulnerability of their activities. The world continues to be victimized by thousands of terrorist attacks each year.[34] Terrorism has many different goals. Multinationals are targeted to embarrass a government and its relationship with firms, to generate funds by kidnapping executives to finance terrorist goals, to use as pawns in political or social disputes not specifically directed at them, and to inflict terror within a country, as did the events of September 11, 2001.

September 11 has raised the cost of doing business domestically and internationally. The dominance of the United States in world affairs exposes U.S. businesses to a multitude of uncertainties, from the growing danger of political violence to investment risks in emerging markets. In the past 30 years, 80 percent of terrorist attacks against the United States have been aimed at American businesses. Since September 11, McDonald's, KFC, and Pizza Hut combined have been bombed in more than 10 countries, including Turkey, Saudi Arabia, Russia, Lebanon, and China; most attacks have been linked with militant Islamic groups. There are reasons to expect that businesses will become increasingly attractive to terrorists, both because they are less well defended than government targets and because of what they symbolize. Based on the threats of terrorism and other violence, the U.S. State Department posts travel warnings on its Web site (see Exhibit 6.3 for a

[33]See the excellent book by John A. Quelch and Nathalie Laidler-Kylander, *The New Global Brands: Managing Non-Governmental Organizations in the 21st Century* (Mason, OH: South-Western, 2006).

[34]John M. Glionna, "Twin Hotel Blasts Kill 9 People in Indonesian Capital," *Los Angeles Times*, July 17, 2009, p. A25.

The communist government of Cuba disallows private advertising. Here at the corner of 23rd and L, the "Times Square" of Havana, the only signage you can see are the names of the movies and a political ad about the Cuban 5. Pictured are five Cuban nationals being held in American prisons, convicted of espionage against the United States. The Cuban government considers the five to be heroes that were infiltrating terrorist groups in south Florida, intent on attacking Cuba.

recent listing). However, many international travelers appear to regularly ignore those warnings.[35]

Finally, we note strong reasons to believe that international warfare is fast becoming obsolete. The number of wars has declined steadily since the end of the Cold War. Even though politicians in almost all countries use xenophobia to consolidate their own political power, the threat of one country attacking another is declining fast. Some predict a coming war in space, with satellites used as weapons, but the multinational collaboration on the International Space Station makes such a possibility seem remote.[36] In 1996, political scientist Samuel Huntington[37] notoriously predicted a clash of civilizations. In his vision, the world was already divided up into nine civilizations (or cultural groupings): Western, Latin America, African, Islamic, Sinic, Hindu, Orthodox, Buddhist, and Japanese. This prediction reminds us of several others in the early 1990s who suggested the world would soon devolve into three spheres of influence based on trade, dominated by Japan, the European Union, and the United States. There may be some sense to the latter classification; time zones exercise an important influence on trade patterns that favor north–south exchanges. However, both theories oversimplify power and trade relations as they are unfolding. Both theories also ignore the successes of the World Trade Organization and the fast multiplying bilateral trade agreements, such as that between the United States and South Korea. And certainly the facts included in Exhibit 6.4 suggest that these warnings about a new clash of civilizations are off the mark. Although three of the six wars ongoing in 2010 were international ones (in Afghanistan/Pakistan, Yemen/Saudi Arabia, and Iraq/U.S.), the other three are better examples of civil wars (in Somalia, Sudan, and the drug war in Mexico). Rather than state-to-state or civilization-to-civilization military action, the greater threats to peace and commerce for the twenty-first century remain civil strife and terrorism. Finally, we note with some hope that civil conflicts can be settled through negotiation: Consider as

---

[35]"Who Do We Trust?" *Condé Nast Traveler*, March 2005, pp. 53–62.

[36]"Disharmony in the Spheres," *The Economist*, January 19, 2008, pp. 25–28.

[37]Samuel P. Huntington, *The Clash of Civilizations and the Remaking of the World Order* (New York: Simon and Schuster, 1996); Fouad Ajami, "The Clash," *The New York Times*, January 6, 2008.

Exhibit 6.4
Armed Conflicts Around the World

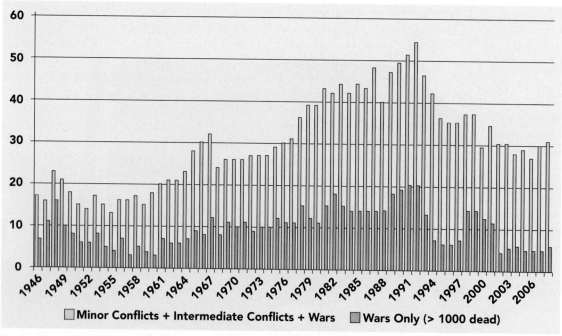

Source: The International Peace Research Institute, Oslo, http://www.prio.no 2010.

examples the recent histories of the relatively peaceful dissolution of the Soviet Union, the divorce of the Czech and Slovak Republics, the marriage of East and West Germany, the Hong Kong handover to China by the United Kingdom, the current trade overtures between China and Taiwan,[38] and the ongoing discussions between the United Kingdom and Scotland.[39]

Cyberterrorism and Cybercrime

Always on the horizon is the growing potential for cyberterrorism and cybercrime.[40] Although still in its infancy, the Internet provides a vehicle for terrorist and criminal attacks by foreign and domestic antagonists wishing to inflict damage on a company with little chance of being caught. One problem in tracing cyberterrorists and criminals is that it is hard to determine if a cyberattack has been launched by a rogue state, a terrorist, or a hacker as a prank. The "I Love You" worm, which caused an estimated $25 billion in damage, was probably just an out-of-control prank. However, the Melissa virus and the denial of service (DoS) attacks that overloaded the Web sites of CNN, ZDNet, Yahoo!, and Amazon.com with a flood of electronic messages, crippling them for hours, were considered purposeful attacks on specific targets. Most recently, the government of China has been criticized for blocking text messaging in strife-torn regions and disrupting the local operations of Google.[41]

Each wave of viruses gets more damaging and spreads so rapidly that considerable harm is done before it can be stopped. The "Slammer," for example, brought Internet service to a crawl. It doubled its numbers every 8.5 seconds during the first minute of its attack and infected more than 75,000 hosts within 10 minutes.[42] After infecting hundreds of thousands of computers in Europe and North America, the "Goner worm" traveled to Australia overnight and brought down government agencies, financial and manufacturing sites, and at least 25 MNCs. Whether perpetrated by pranksters or hackers out to do harm, these incidents show that tools for cyberterrorism can be developed to do considerable damage to a company, an entire industry, or a country's infrastructure.

Because of mounting concern over the rash of attacks, business leaders and government officials addressed a Group of 8[43] conference convened to discuss cybercrime, expressing the urgent need for cooperation among governments, industry, and users to combat the growing menace of cybercrime. As the Internet grows, "it's only a matter of time before every terrorist, anarchist, thief, and prankster with a PC and a phone line will be waging a virtual war and inflicting real harm."[44]

Assessing Political Vulnerability

LO6

How to assess and reduce the effect of political vulnerability

There are at least as many reasons for a company's political vulnerability as there are political philosophies, economic variations, and cultural differences. Some companies appear to be more politically vulnerable than others, in that they receive special government attention. Depending on the desirability of a company, this special attention may result in positive actions toward the company or in negative attention.

Unfortunately, a marketer has no absolute guidelines to follow to determine whether a company and its products will be subject to political attention. Countries seeking investments in high-priority industries may well excuse companies from taxes, customs duties, quotas, exchange controls, and other impediments to investment. In a bid to attract foreign investment and increase exports, India announced a new trade policy that eases restraints and offers tax breaks for companies developing and maintaining infrastructure. Conversely, firms either marketing products not considered high priority or that fall from favor for some other reason often face unpredictable government restrictions.

---

[38]"Reunification by Trade?" *The Economist*, August 8, 2009, pp. 37–38.

[39]"Straining at the Leash," *The Economist, The World in 2009*, November 19, 2009, p. 98.

[40]"Overseas Security Threats to U.S. Business Cited," *Los Angeles Times*, December 28, 2007, p. C2.

[41]Johanna Neuman, "Google's China Move Wakes Washington," *Los Angeles Times*, January 15, 2010.

[42]For more information, see http://www.silicondefense.com.

[43]The Group of 8 (G8) Nations consisted of government representatives from Britain, Canada, France, Germany, Italy, Japan, Russia, and the United States who convene periodically to examine issues that affect the group. Most recently the group has been expanded to the G20.

[44]Mark Mazzetti, "Senators Warned of Terror Attack by July," *The New York Times*, February 3, 2010, p. A6.

As a case in point, Continental Can Company's joint venture to manufacture cans for the Chinese market faced a barrage of restrictions when the Chinese economy weakened. China decreed that canned beverages were wasteful and must be banned from all state functions and banquets. Tariffs on aluminum and other materials imported for producing cans were doubled, and a new tax was imposed on canned-drink consumption. For Continental Can, an investment that had the potential for profit after a few years was rendered profitless by a change in the attitude of the Chinese government.

Politically Sensitive Products and Issues

Although there are no specific formulas to determine a product's vulnerability at any point, there are some generalizations that help identify the tendency for products to be politically sensitive. Products that have or are perceived to have an effect on the environment, exchange rates, national and economic security, and the welfare of people (and particularly children—recall the story of Barbie in Saudi Arabia from the previous chapter) or that are publicly visible, subject to public debate, or associated with their country of origin are more likely to be politically sensitive.

Fast-food restaurants, which are intended to be visible, have often been lightning rods for groups opposed to foreign companies. Authorities closed a KFC restaurant for health reasons (two flies were seen in the kitchen) after months of protesters arguing that foreign investment should be limited to high technology. "India does not need foreign investment in junk-food," said the leader of a protesting farmers' group. The store was later reopened by court order.

Health is often the subject of public debate, and products that affect or are affected by health issues can be sensitive to political concerns. The European Union has banned hormone-treated beef for more than a decade. There is a question about whether the ban is a valid health issue or just protection for the European beef industry. The World Trade Organization concluded in 1989 that the ban had no scientific basis; nevertheless, Europe has yet to lift the ban. Reluctance to respond to the WTO directive may have been the result of the outcry against genetically modified (GM) foods that has, for all practical purposes, caused GM foods to be banned in Europe. Public opinion against Frankenfood has been so strong that Unilever announced that it would stop using GM ingredients in all its products in Britain. Additionally, 11 leading restaurant chains, including McDonald's, Pizza Hut, Wimpy, and Burger King, have gone GM-free. The issue in the United States has not risen to the same level of concern as in Europe; to forestall such adverse public opinion, many U.S. companies are slowing the introduction of GM foods. Fearing a strong public reaction as in Europe, McDonald's has decided to stop using genetically modified potatoes for its french fries in its U.S. stores.

Forecasting Political Risk

In addition to qualitative measures of political vulnerability, a number of firms are employing systematic methods of measuring political risk.[45] Political risk assessment is an attempt to forecast political instability to help management identify and evaluate political events and their potential influence on current and future international business decisions. Perhaps the greatest risk to international marketers is the threat of the government actually failing, causing chaos in the streets and markets. *Foreign Policy* magazine uses 12 criteria to rank countries on its "Failed States Index."[46] The list of criteria includes demographic pressures, human flight, uneven development, and the like. (See Exhibit 6.5.)

---

[45]See http://www.prsgroup.com for a wealth of information on political risk assessments.
[46]"The Failed States Index," *Foreign Policy*, July/August 2007, pp. 54–65.

Exhibit 6.5

Top 20 States in Danger of Failing (ranked in order of closest to failure)

Source: From *Foreign Policy*, "Failed States Index," May/June 2009, online. Copyright 2009 by Foreign Policy. Reproduced with permission of *Foreign Policy* via Copyright Clearance Center.

Somalia	Central African Republic	Nigeria
Zimbabwe	Guinea	Ethiopia
Sudan	Pakistan	North Korea
Chad	Ivory Coast	Yemen
Dem. Rep. of Congo	Haiti	Bangladesh
Iraq	Burma	East Timor
Afghanistan	Kenya	

CROSSING BORDERS 6.3

When States Fail: Dodging the Bullet in Former Yugoslavia

One pundit suggested that nations with McDonald's don't attack one another. Perhaps Yugoslavia was the exception that proves the rule?

During most of the 78-day air war against Yugoslavia in 1999, McDonald's kept the burgers flipping while NATO kept the bombs dropping. After only one night of air strikes, mobs of youths, whipped to patriotic fervor by the state-controlled media's attacks on the "NATO criminals and aggressors," targeted six McDonald's stores, smashing windows and scribbling insults on doors and walls. McDonald's Corporation was forced to temporarily close its 15 restaurants in Yugoslavia. Weeks later, when local managers flung the doors open again, they accomplished an extraordinary comeback using an unusual marketing strategy: They put McDonald's U.S. citizenship on the back burner.

Within a week after the attacks, they had launched a campaign to identify the plight of ordinary Serbs with the Mac. "McDonald's is sharing the destiny of all people here," read a sign at one branch. A key aspect of the campaign was to present McDonald's as a Yugoslav company. Restaurants promoted the McCountry, a domestic pork burger with paprika garnish, and lowered its price. Pork is considered the most Serbian of meats.

In a national flourish to evoke Serbian identity and pride, McDonald's produced posters and lapel buttons showing the golden arches topped with a traditional Serbian cap called the *sajkaca* (pronounced shy-KACH-a). The managing director said McDonald's needed to get Serbs to view the company as their own. He

masterminded the campaign to "Serbify" McDonald's. It was in this vein that he and his team decided to redesign the logo with the Serbian cap cocked at a haughty angle over one arch. Traditional national emblems, like the *sajkaca*, a strong, unique Serbian symbol, had undergone a revival in recent years with the rise of Serbian nationalism. "By adding this symbol of our cultural heritage, we hoped to denote our pride in being a local company."

Additionally, more than 3,000 free burgers were delivered to the participants of the Belgrade marathon, which was dominated by an anti-NATO theme. At the same time, the company announced that for every burger sold, it would donate one dinar (about a nickel) to the Yugoslav Red Cross to help victims of NATO's air strikes. It also handed out free cheeseburgers at anti-NATO rallies.

Once the war was over, the company basked in its success. Cash registers were ringing at prewar levels. McDonald's restaurants around the country were thronged with Serbs hungry for Big Macs and fries. And why not, asks 16-year-old Jovan Stojanovic, munching on a burger. "I don't associate McDonald's with America," he says. "Mac is ours." This claim is music to McDonald's ears. "We managed to save our brand."

And in 2009, McDonald's began negotiations to open its first store in previously war-torn Bosnia/Herzegovina. May the peace persist.

Sources: Robert Block, "How Big Mac Kept from Becoming a Serb Archenemy," *The Wall Street Journal*, September 3, 1999; John Kozak, "McDonald's Can't Serve Up World Peace," *The Guardian*, April 26, 2005, p. 27; "McDonald's Arrives in Sarajevo, Bosnia and Herzegovina," *Property Xpress*, October 9, 2009, online.

Risk assessment is used to estimate the level of risk a company is assuming when making an investment and to help determine the amount of risk it is prepared to accept. In the former Soviet Union and in China, the risk may be too high for some companies, but stronger and better financed companies can make longer-term investments in those countries that will be profitable in the future. Additionally, one study found that compared with American and Japanese managers, French managers' market entry decisions appear to be more influenced by concerns about political risk in foreign markets.[47] Early risk is accepted in exchange for being in the country when the economy begins to grow and risk subsides.

During the chaos that arose after the political and economic changes in the Soviet Union, the newly formed republics were eager to make deals with foreign investors, yet the problems and uncertainty made many investors take a wait-and-see attitude. However, as one executive commented, "If U.S. companies wait until all the problems are solved, somebody else will get the business." Certainly the many companies that are investing in the former Soviet Union or China do not expect big returns immediately; they are betting on the future. For a marketer doing business in a foreign country, a necessary part of any market analysis

---

[47]Jennifer D. Chandler and John L. Graham, "Relationship-Oriented Cultures, Corruption, and International Marketing Success," *Journal of Business Ethics* 92, no. 2 (2010), pp. 251–67.

is an assessment of the probable political consequences of a marketing plan, since some marketing activities are more susceptible to political considerations than others.

Lessening Political Vulnerability

Although a company cannot directly control or alter the political environment of the country within which it operates, a specific business venture can take measures to lessen its degree of susceptibility to politically induced risks.

Foreign investors frequently are accused of exploiting a country's wealth at the expense of the national population and for the sole benefit of the foreign investor. This attitude is best summed up in a statement made by a recent president of Peru: "We have had massive foreign investment for decades but Peru has not achieved development. Foreign capital will now have to meet government and social goals." Such charges are not wholly unsupported by past experiences.

As long as these impressions persist, the political climate for foreign investors will continue to be hostile. Companies must manage external affairs in foreign markets to ensure that the host government and the public are aware of their contributions to the economic, social, and human development of the country. Relations between governments and MNCs are generally positive if the investment (1) improves the balance of payments by increasing exports or reducing imports through import substitution; (2) uses locally produced resources; (3) transfers capital, technology, and/or skills; (4) creates jobs; and/or (5) makes tax contributions.

In addition to the economic contributions a company makes, corporate philanthropy also helps create positive images among the general population. Many MNCs strive to benefit countries through their social programs, which polish their image as well. For example, Microsoft, recognizing that developing countries need sophisticated technical assistance, pledged more than $100 million in technology and training as part of a deal to put government services online in Mexico. Cisco Systems, the leading maker of Internet hardware, relies on nonprofit organizations to run its 10,000 networking academies, which train college and high school students to create computer networks in 150 countries. In China, Procter & Gamble is helping local schools and universities train and educate leaders. And in Malaysia, Motorola and Intel have instituted training programs to enhance the skills of local workers.

Merck, the pharmaceutical company, has developed a pill to fight river blindness in Africa and Latin America. River blindness is a parasitic disease transmitted to humans through the bite of the black fly commonly found along the riverbanks in some African countries. The parasite infiltrates, multiplies, and spreads throughout the body for as long as 15 years, causing acute skin rashes, terrible itching, and sometimes disfigurement or blindness. The pill is taken just once a year and has been proven to prevent the disease. Merck contributed millions of doses to fight the disease in developing countries.[48]

Although companies strive to become good corporate citizens in their host countries, political parties seeking publicity or scapegoats for their failures often serve their own interests by focusing public opinion on the negative aspects of MNCs, whether true or false. Companies that establish deep local roots and show by example, rather than meaningless talk, that their strategies are aligned with the long-term goals of the host country stand the best chance of overcoming a less than positive image. "In times like these," says one executive, "global citizenship is perhaps more important than ever."[49] An effective defense for the multinational company is to actively participate in improving the lives of local citizens.

In addition to corporate activities focused on the social and economic goals of the host country and good corporate citizenship, MNCs can use other strategies to minimize political vulnerability and risk.

Joint Ventures

Typically less susceptible to political harassment, joint ventures can be with locals or other third-country multinational companies; in both cases, a company's financial exposure is limited. A joint venture with locals helps minimize anti-MNC feelings, and a joint venture with another MNC adds the additional bargaining power of a third country.

---

[48]David Shook, "Merck Is Treating the Third World," *BusinessWeek Online,* October 10, 2002.

[49]Susan E. Reed, "Business; Technology Companies Take Hope in Charity," *The New York Times,* March 23, 2003, p. 17.

practices adhere to Islamic law and permit the transaction of business. Mortgages for property are difficult because payment of interest is forbidden under Islamic law. Buyers of real property have to use a financier, who buys the property and then sells it to them in return for repayments of the capital. Instead of charging interest, a financier either sells the property at a higher price or sells it at the same price and takes additional payments to cover what would have been interest. Of the other ways to comply with Islamic law in financial transactions, trade with markup or cost-plus sale (*murabaha*) and leasing (*ijara*) are the most frequently used. In both *murabaha* and *ijara,* a mutually negotiated margin is included in the sale price or leasing payment. These practices meet the requirements of *Shari'ah* by enabling borrowers and lenders to share in the rewards as well as losses in an equitable fashion. They also ensure that the process of wealth accumulation and distribution in the economy is fair and representative of true productivity. Strict fundamentalists often frown on such an arrangement, but it is practiced and is an example of the way the strictness of Islamic law can be reconciled with the laws of non-Islamic legal systems.

Because the laws are based on interpretation of the Koran, the international marketer must have knowledge of the religion's tenets and understand the way the law may be interpreted in each region. Regional courts can interpret Islamic law from the viewpoint of fundamentalists (those that adhere to a literal interpretation of the Koran), or they may use a more liberal translation. A company can find local authorities in one region willing to allow payment of interest on deferred obligations as stipulated in a contract, while in another region, all interest charges may be deleted and replaced with comparable "consulting fees." In yet another, authorities may void a contract and declare any payment of interest illegal. Marketers conducting business in Islamic-law countries must be knowledgeable about this important legal system.

Marxist–Socialist Tenets

As socialist countries become more directly involved in trade with non-Marxist countries, it has been necessary to develop a commercial legal system that permits them to engage in active international commerce. The pattern for development varies among the countries because each has a different background, and each is at a different stage in its development of a market-driven economy. For example, central European countries such as the Czech Republic and Poland had comprehensive codified legal systems before communism took over, and their pre–World War II commercial legal codes have been revised and reinstituted. Consequently, they have moved toward a legal model with greater ease than some others have. Russia and most of the republics of the former Soviet Union and China have had to build from scratch an entire commercial legal system. Under the premise that law, according to **Marxist–socialist tenets**, is strictly subordinate to prevailing economic conditions, such fundamental propositions as private ownership, contracts, due process, and other legal mechanisms have had to be developed. China and Russia differ, however, in that each has taken a different direction in its political economic growth. Russia is moving toward a democratic system. China is attempting to activate a private sector within a multicomponent, or mixed, economy in a socialist legal framework; that is, it tries to "perform its functions according to law and contribute to the development of socialist democracy and political civilization in China."

Both countries have actively passed laws, though the process has been slow and often disjointed. China has implemented hundreds of new laws and regulations governing trade, yet the process is hampered by vaguely written laws, the lack of implementation mechanisms for the new laws, and an ineffective framework for dispute resolution and enforcement. A good example is China's attempt to control what goes on in Chinese cyberspace by applying the States Secrets Law to the Internet. The definition of a state secret is so broad that it can cover any information not cleared for publication with the relevant authorities.

Russia's experience has been similar to China's, in that vaguely worded laws have been passed without mechanisms for implementation. The situation in Russia is often described as chaotic because of the laws' lack of precision. For example, to illegally receive or disseminate commercial secrets has become a crime, but the law provides no exact definition of a commercial secret. Copyright law violations that cause "great damage" are listed but with no clear definition of how much damage constitutes "great." Both China and Russia are hampered by not having the heritage of a legal commercial code to build on, as many of the Eastern-bloc European countries had.

The international marketer must be concerned with the differences among common law, code law, Islamic law, and socialist legal systems when operating between countries; the rights of the principals of a contract or some other legal document under one law may be significantly different from their rights under the other. It should be kept in mind that there could also be differences between the laws of two countries whose laws are based on the same legal system. Thus, the problem of the marketer is one of anticipating the different laws regulating business, regardless of the legal system of the country.

Jurisdiction in International Legal Disputes

LO2

The important factors in the jurisdiction of legal disputes

Determining whose legal system has jurisdiction when a commercial dispute arises is another problem of international marketing. A frequent error is to assume that disputes between citizens of different nations are adjudicated under some supranational system of laws. Unfortunately, no judicial body exists to deal with legal commercial problems arising among citizens of different countries. Confusion probably stems from the existence of international courts such as the World Court at The Hague and the International Court of Justice, the principal judicial organ of the United Nations. These courts are operative in international disputes between sovereign nations of the world rather than between private citizens and/or companies.

Legal disputes can arise in three situations: between governments, between a company and a government, and between two companies. The World Court can adjudicate disputes between governments, whereas the other two situations must be handled in the courts of the country of one of the parties involved or through arbitration. Unless a commercial dispute involves a national issue between nation states, the International Court of Justice or any similar world court does not handle it. Because there is no "international commercial law," the foreign marketer must look to the legal system of each country involved—the laws of the home country, the laws of the countries within which business is conducted, or both.[8]

When international commercial disputes must be settled under the laws of one of the countries concerned, the paramount question in a dispute is: Which law governs? Jurisdiction is generally determined in one of three ways: (1) on the basis of jurisdictional clauses included in contracts, (2) on the basis of where a contract was entered into, or (3) on the basis of where the provisions of the contract were performed.

The most clear-cut decision can be made when the contracts or legal documents supporting a business transaction include a jurisdictional clause. A clause similar to the following establishes jurisdiction in the event of disagreements:

> That the parties hereby agree that the agreement is made in Oregon, USA, and that any question regarding this agreement shall be governed by the law of the state of Oregon, USA.

This clause establishes that the laws of the state of Oregon would be invoked should a dispute arise. If the complaint were brought in the court of another country, it is probable that the same Oregon laws would govern the decision. Cooperation and a definite desire to be judicious in foreign legal problems have led to the practice of foreign courts judging disputes on the basis of the law of another country or state whenever applicable. Thus, if an injured party from Oregon brings suit in the courts of Mexico against a Mexican over a contract that included the preceding clause, it would not be unusual for the Mexican courts to decide on the basis of Oregon law. This tendency assumes, of course, it has been recognized that Oregon law prevailed in this dispute, either as a result of the prior agreement by the parties or on some other basis.

---

[8]For a legal and thorough discussion of the globalization of jurisdiction, see Paul Schiff Berman, "The Globalization of Jurisdiction," *University of Pennsylvania Law Review*, December 2002, p. 311; Yadong Luo, "Transactional Characteristics, Institutional Environment, and Joint Venture Contracts," *Journal of International Business Studies* 36, no. 2 (2005), pp. 209–30.

International Dispute Resolution

LO3

The various methods of dispute resolution

When things go wrong in a commercial transaction—the buyer refuses to pay, the product is of inferior quality, the shipment arrives late, or any one of the myriad problems that can arise—what recourse does the international marketer have? The first step in any dispute is to try to resolve the issue informally, but if that fails, the foreign marketer must resort to more resolute action. Such action can take the form of conciliation, arbitration, or, as a last resort, litigation. Most international businesspeople prefer a settlement through arbitration rather than by suing a foreign company.

Conciliation

Most disputes that arise in commercial transactions are settled informally. When resolution is not forthcoming however, conciliation can be an important first step in settling a dispute. Conciliation (also known as *mediation*) is a nonbinding agreement between parties to resolve disputes by asking a third party to mediate differences. The function of the mediator is to carefully listen to each party and to explore, clarify, and discuss the various practical options and possibilities for a solution with the intent that the parties will agree on a solution. Unlike arbitration and litigation, conciliation sessions are private, and all conferences between parties and the mediator are confidential; the statements made by the parties may not be disclosed or used as evidence in any subsequent litigation or arbitration. The track record for the conciliation process is excellent, with a majority of disputes reaching settlement and leading to the resumption of business between the disputants.

Conciliation is considered especially effective when resolving disputes with Chinese business partners, because they feel less threatened by conciliation than arbitration. The Chinese believe that when a dispute occurs, informal, friendly negotiation should be used first to solve the problem; if that fails, conciliation should be tried. In fact, some Chinese companies may avoid doing business with companies that resort first to arbitration. Conciliation can be either formal or informal. Both sides agreeing on a third party to mediate can establish informal conciliation. Formal conciliation is conducted under the auspices of some tribunal such as the Beijing Conciliation Center, which assigns one or two conciliators to mediate. If an agreement is reached, a conciliation statement based on the signed agreement is recorded. Although conciliation may be the friendly route to resolving disputes in China, it is not legally binding; thus, an arbitration clause should be included in all conciliation agreements. Experience has shown that having an arbitration clause in the conciliation agreement makes it easier to move to arbitration if necessary.

Arbitration

If conciliation is not used or an agreement cannot be reached, the next step is *arbitration*. When all else fails, arbitration rather than litigation is the preferred method for resolving international commercial disputes. The usual arbitration procedure is for the parties involved to select a disinterested and informed party or parties as referees to determine the merits of the case and make a judgment that both parties agree to honor. Although informal arbitration is workable, most arbitration is conducted under the auspices of one of the more formal domestic and international arbitration groups organized specifically to facilitate the resolution of commercial disputes. These groups have formal rules for the process and experienced arbitrators to assist. In most countries, decisions reached in formal arbitration are enforceable under the law.

The popularity of arbitration has led to a proliferation of arbitral centers established by countries, organizations, and institutions. All have adopted standardized rules and procedures to administer cases, and each has its strengths and weaknesses. Some of the more active are the following:

- The Inter-American Commercial Arbitration Commission
- The Canadian-American Commercial Arbitration Commission (for disputes between Canadian and U.S. businesses)
- The London Court of Arbitration (decisions are enforceable under English law and English courts)
- The American Arbitration Association (www.adr.org/)
- The International Chamber of Commerce (www.iccwbo.org/; select Arbitration)

CROSSING BORDERS 7.1

České Budějovice, Privatization, Trademarks, and Taste Tests—What Do They Have in Common with Anheuser-Busch? Budweiser, That's What!

Anheuser-Busch (AB) launched a massive public relations program in the small Czech town of České Budějovice, where a local brewery produces "Budweiser Budvar." Anheuser-Busch planted trees along main avenues, opened a new cultural center offering free English courses to citizens and management advice to budding entrepreneurs, and ran newspaper ads touting the possibilities of future cooperation.

Anheuser-Busch's goal was to win support for a minority stake in the Czech state-owned brewery, Budějovicky Budvar N.P., when the government privatized it. So why was AB interested in a brewery whose annual production of 500,000 barrels is the equivalent of two days' output for AB?

Part ownership is critically important to Anheuser-Busch for two reasons. It is in search of new markets in Europe, and it wants to be able to market the Budweiser brand in Europe. So what's the connection? AB doesn't have the rights to use the Budweiser brand in Europe because Budějovicky Budvar N.P. owns it. Its public relations plan didn't work because many Czechs see Budvar as the "family silver." Although the Czech prime minister asked publicly for American investors to put money into the Czech Republic, Czech Budweiser was not on the government's privatization list. "I believe in the strength of American investors, but I do not believe in the quality of American beer."

Anheuser-Busch established the name Budweiser in the United States when German immigrants founded the St. Louis family brewery and began selling under the Budweiser brand in 1876, 19 years before the Czech brewery opened. The Czechs claim they have been using the name since before Columbus discovered the New World and that Budweiser refers to Budwis, the original name of the city where Budvar is located. That is the name commonly referred to beer brewed in that area hundreds of years before AB started brewing Budweiser.

The Anheuser-Busch Company markets Budweiser brand beer in North America, but in Europe, it markets Busch brand beer, because the Czechs have the rights to the use of the name Budweiser. Diplomacy and public relations didn't work, so what next? The parties have each other tied up in legal wrangling over who has the rights to the Budweiser name and to derivations of it, such as Bud. More than 40 lawsuits and 40 administrative cases are pending across Europe. Because U.S. law protects Anheuser-Busch's rights to the Budweiser label in the United States, the Czechs sell their beer as "Czechvar."

The Czech brewery exports to 37 countries, mainly in Europe, and AB has sales in more than 70 countries around the world. Anheuser-Busch sought a court order to have the Czech company's products taken off the shelves in Hong Kong, won a ruling in Hungary, and has launched similar lawsuits in the United Kingdom and the United States. AB said the Czech brewery had imported and sold beer in the United States labeled "Budweiser Budvar" in the state of Maryland. It also says the Czech brewery is mimicking its name to confuse beer drinkers and cash in on the U.S. company's success.

The Czech government petitioned the WTO to grant beer regions the same kind of labeling protection that it gives to wine regions. Just as sparkling wines made in the Champagne region of France are the only ones legally entitled to call themselves champagne, it would mean that only beers brewed in České Budějovice could call themselves Budweiser and only those brewed in Pilzen, another Czech town, could claim to be Pilsner. It seems unlikely that this request will win approval, because Pilsner has become a generic designation for a style of beer, and unlike the grapes that come from Champagne, the malt and the hops that go into its beer do not come exclusively from České Budějovice.

The legal battle for the exclusive right to use the brand names Bud and Budweiser has spread worldwide. So far, this tactic hasn't worked too well either. Britain's high court allowed both companies to use the names Bud and Budweiser, whereas Switzerland's highest court banned Anheuser-Busch from selling beer under the Bud name.

We all know that the proof of who's best is in the tasting, right? Both lagers have legions of fans. The U.S. version lives up to its old slogan of "king of beers," at least as far as sales go: It's the top-selling beer in the world. The Czech version—nicknamed the "beer of kings" because it comes from a town that once brewed for royalty—has large followings in Germany and other parts of Europe. So the *St. Louis Post-Dispatch* hosted a blind taste test to determine which beer is better—Budvar won. And, most recently the Europeans have won another battle: In 2009, Anheuser-Busch agreed to merge with InBev, with its global headquarters now in Leuven, Belgium.

Visit the Budvar Web site (www.budvar.cz) for the history of Budvar and a tour of the plant.

Sources: A1 Stamborski, "Battle of the Buds: Taste Testers Say That Budvar Is Better," *St. Louis Post-Dispatch*, November 28, 1999, p. E1; "Prime Minister Says Budvar Will Stay Czech," *Modern Brewery*, March 2000; Gregory Cancelada, "Czech Brewery Retains Right to Use 'Budweiser' and 'Bud' Trademarks," *St. Louis Post-Dispatch*, February 17, 2003; http://www.AB-Inbev.com, 2010.

The procedures used by formal arbitration organizations are similar. Arbitration under the rules of the International Chamber of Commerce (ICC) affords an excellent example of how most organizations operate. When an initial request for arbitration is received, the chamber first attempts conciliation between the disputants. If this fails, the process of arbitration is started. The plaintiff and the defendant select one person each from among acceptable arbitrators to defend their case, and the ICC Court of Arbitration appoints a third member, generally chosen from a list of distinguished lawyers, jurists, and professors.

The history of ICC effectiveness in arbitration has been spectacular. An example of a case that involved arbitration by the ICC concerned a contract between an English business and a Japanese manufacturer. The English business agreed to buy 100,000 plastic dolls for 80 cents each. On the strength of the contract, the English business sold the entire lot at $1.40 per doll. Before the dolls were delivered, the Japanese manufacturer had a strike; the settlement of the strike increased costs, and the English business was informed that the delivery price of the dolls had increased from 80 cents to $1.50 each. The English business maintained that the Japanese firm had committed to make delivery at 80 cents and should deliver at that price. Each side was convinced that it was right.

The Japanese, accustomed to code law, felt that the strike was beyond their control (an act of God) and thus compliance with the original provisions of the contract was excused. The English, accustomed to common law, did not accept the Japanese reasons for not complying because they considered a strike part of the normal course of doing business and not an act of God. The dispute could not be settled except through arbitration or litigation; they chose arbitration. The ICC appointed an arbitrator who heard both sides and ruled that the two parties would share proportionately in the loss. Both parties were satisfied with the arbitration decision, and costly litigation was avoided. Most arbitration is successful, but success depends on the willingness of both parties to accept the arbitrator's rulings.

Contracts and other legal documents should include clauses specifying the use of arbitration to settle disputes. Unless a provision for arbitration of any dispute is incorporated as part of a contract, the likelihood of securing agreement for arbitration after a dispute arises is reduced. A typical arbitration clause is as follows:

> Any controversy or claim arising out of or relating to this contract shall be determined by arbitration in accordance with the International Arbitration Rules of the American Arbitration Association.

Including the number of arbitrators, the place of arbitration (city and/or country), and the language of the arbitration in the clause is also useful.[9]

Although an arbitration clause in a contract can avert problems, sometimes enforcing arbitration agreements can be difficult. Arbitration clauses require agreement on two counts: (1) The parties agree to arbitrate in the case of a dispute according to the rules and procedures of some arbitration tribunal and (2) they agree to abide by the awards resulting from the arbitration. Difficulty arises when the parties to a contract fail to honor the agreements. Companies may refuse to name arbitrators, refuse to arbitrate, or, after arbitration awards are made, refuse to honor the award. In most countries, arbitration clauses are recognized by the courts and are enforceable by law within those countries. More than 120 countries have ratified the Convention on the Recognition and Enforcement of Foreign Arbitral Awards, also known as the New York Convention, which binds them to uphold foreign arbitration awards. Under the New York Convention, the courts of the signatory countries automatically uphold foreign arbitral awards issued in member countries. In addition to the New York Convention, the United States is a signatory of the Inter-American Convention on International Arbitration, to which many Latin American countries are party. The United States is also party to a number of bilateral agreements containing clauses providing for enforcement of arbitral awards. When all else fails, the final step to solve a dispute is litigation.

---

[9]The American Arbitration Association, www.iccwbo.org (select Arbitration).

Litigation   Lawsuits in public courts are avoided for many reasons. Most observers of lawsuits between citizens of different countries believe that almost all victories are spurious because the cost, frustrating delays, and extended aggravation that these cases produce are more oppressive by far than any matter of comparable size. In India, for instance, there is a backlog of more than three million cases, and litigating a breach of contract between private parties can take a decade or more. The best advice is to seek a settlement, if possible, rather than sue. Other deterrents to **litigation** are the following:

- Fear of creating a poor image and damaging public relations.
- Fear of unfair treatment in a foreign court. (Fear that a lawsuit can result in unfair treatment, perhaps intentionally, is justifiable, because the decision could be made by either a jury or a judge not well versed in trade problems and the intricacies of international business transactions.)
- Difficulty in collecting a judgment that may otherwise have been collected in a mutually agreed settlement through arbitration.
- The relatively high cost and time required when bringing legal action. The Rheem Manufacturing Company, a billion-dollar manufacturer of heating and air conditioning systems, estimates that by using arbitration over litigation, it has reduced the time and cost of commercial-dispute resolution by half.
- Loss of confidentiality. Unlike arbitration and conciliation proceedings, which are confidential, litigation is public.

One authority suggests that the settlement of every dispute should follow four steps: First, try to placate the injured party; if this does not work, conciliate, arbitrate, and, finally, litigate. The final step is typically taken only when all other methods fail. Furthermore, in some cases, problem-solving approaches may be warranted within the context of even litigated disputes.[10] This approach is probably wise whether one is involved in an international dispute or a domestic one.

Protection of Intellectual Property Rights: A Special Problem

LO4

The unique problems of protecting intellectual property rights internationally

Companies spend millions of dollars establishing brand names or trademarks to symbolize quality and design a host of other product features meant to entice customers to buy their brands to the exclusion of all others. Millions more are spent on research to develop products, processes, designs, and formulas that provide companies with advantages over their competitors. Such intellectual or industrial properties are among the more valuable assets a company may possess. Brand names such as Kodak, Coca-Cola, and Gucci; processes such as xerography; and computer software are invaluable. One financial group estimated that the Marlboro brand had a value of $33 billion, Kellogg's $9 billion, Microsoft $9.8 billion, and Levi's $5 billion; all have experienced infringement of their intellectual property rights. Normally, property rights can be legally protected to prevent other companies from infringing on such assets. Companies must, however, keep a constant vigil against piracy and counterfeiting. Moreover, with increasing frequency, companies are developing new technologies to prevent piracy, but counterfeiters are relentless in their criticism of and technological attacks on even the most sophisticated security measures.[11]

Counterfeiting and Piracy   Counterfeit and pirated goods come from a wide range of industries—apparel, automotive parts, agricultural chemicals, pharmaceuticals, books (yes, even management books such as the one you are reading right now),[12] records, films, computer software, mobile

---

[10]Chang Zhang, David A. Griffith, and S. Tamer Cavusgil, "The Litigated Dissolution of International Distribution Relationships: A Process Framework and Propositions," *Journal of International Marketing* 14, no. 2 (2006), pp. 85–115.

[11]Eric Schine, "Faking out the Fakers," *BusinessWeek*, June 4, 2007, pp. 75–79; Ethan Smith, "Napster Format Shift Would Enable More Players," *The Wall Street Journal*, January 7, 2008, p. B2.

[12]Don Lee, "Ripping Off Good Reads in China," *Los Angeles Times*, April 24, 2005, pp. C1, C10.

Exhibit 7.2

Piracy Rates for
Computer Software,
Top and Bottom 20

Source: From *2010 BSA and IDC
Global Software Piracy Study,*
Business Software Alliance. Reprinted
with permission. *Seventh Annual
BSA/IDC Global Software Piracy
Study* (Washington, DC: Business
Software Alliance, 2010), www.bsa
.org/globalstudy. One hundred two
countries and regions are ranked.

Highest Piracy Rates		Lowest Piracy Rates	
Georgia	95%	United States	20%
Zimbabwe	92	Japan	21
Bangladesh	91	Luxembourg	21
Moldova	91	New Zealand	22
Armenia	90	Australia	25
Yemen	90	Austria	25
Sri Lanka	89	Belgium	25
Azerbaijan	88	Finland	25
Libya	88	Sweden	25
Belarus	87	Switzerland	25
Venezuela	87	Denmark	26
Indonesia	86	United Kingdom	27
Vietnam	85	Germany	28
Ukraine	85	Netherlands	28
Iraq	85	Canada	29
Pakistan	84	Norway	29
Algeria	84	Israel	33
Cameroon	83	Ireland	35
Nigeria	83	Singapore	35
Paraguay	82	South Africa	35

phones,[13] baby formula, auto parts, and even cars themselves.[14] Estimates are that more than 10 million fake Swiss timepieces carrying famous brand names such as Cartier and Rolex are sold every year, netting illegal profits of at least $500 million. Although difficult to pinpoint, lost sales from the unauthorized use of U.S. patents, trademarks, and copyrights amount to more than $300 billion annually. That translates into more than two million lost jobs. Software, music, and movies are especially attractive targets for pirates because they are costly to develop but cheap to reproduce and distribute over the Internet. Pirated CD music sales are estimated to exceed $5 billion annually and are growing at 6 percent per year. And unauthorized U.S. software that sells for $500 in this country can be purchased for less than $10 in East Asia. The Business Software Alliance, a trade group, estimates that software companies lost over $16.5 billion in the Asia-Pacific region, $16.4 billion in Europe, and $9.4 billion in North America in 2009. Judging from the press on the topic, one might conclude that China is the biggest piracy problem. However, China has moved fast off the list of 20 worst piracy rates, according to Exhibit 7.2. At this writing, it ranks #27 and piracy has fallen to 79 percent, down from 92 percent just a few years earlier. Moreover, the dollars lost in the Unites States because of software piracy are the most in the world at $8.4 billion, with China coming in a close second at $7.6 billion. China's progress is due primarily to education programs, enforcement, and Microsoft's historic agreement with Lenovo. We also note that other populous nations have made major progress in reducing software piracy (e.g., Russia down 11, Brazil down 10, Japan and Vietnam both down 7 percent, India down 11 percent) between 2004 and 2009.[15]

Recent research implies that for companies like Microsoft, some level of piracy actually can serve the company. It can be seen as a kind of product trial that ultimately builds commitment. As updated versions of products become available, purchases may actually follow. Particularly as countries such as China begin to enforce WTO statutes on piracy, customers conditioned on pirated goods may indeed be willing and able to pay for the new versions.

---

[13]"Talk Is Cheap," *The Economist,* November 21, 2009, p. 68.

[14]Mark Landler, "Germans See Imitation in Chinese Cars," *The New York Times*, September 12, 2007, p. B3.

[15]*Sixth Annual BSA and IDC Global Software Piracy Study* (Washington, DC: Business Software Alliance, 2009), http://www.bsa.org/globalstudy; Howard W. French, "China Media Battle Hints at Shift on Intellectual Property," *The New York Times,* January 6, 2007, p. A3; Bruce Einhorn and Steve Hamm, "A Big Windows Cleanup, China Is Discovering that It Pays to Sell PCs that Contain Legitimate Microsoft Software," *BusinessWeek,* June 4, 2007, p. 80.

Although counterfeit CDs, toys, and similar products cost companies billions of dollars in lost revenue and have the potential of damaging the product's brand image, the counterfeiting of pharmaceuticals can do serious physical harm. In Colombia, investigators found an illegal operation making more than 20,000 counterfeit tablets a day of the flu drug Dristan, a generic aspirin known as Dolex, and Ponstan 500, a popular painkiller made by Pfizer. The counterfeited pills contained boric acid, cement, floor wax, talcum powder, and yellow paint with high lead levels, all used to replicate the genuine medications' appearance.

Counterfeit drugs range from copies that have the same efficacy as the original to those with few or no active ingredients to those made of harmful substances. A pharmaceutical manufacturers' association estimates that 2 percent of the $327 billion worth of drugs sold each year are counterfeit, or about $6 billion worth. In some African and Latin American nations, as much as 60 percent are counterfeit. The World Health Organization thinks 8 percent of the bulk drugs imported into the United States are counterfeit, unapproved, or substandard.

Another problem is collusion between the contract manufacturer and illegitimate sellers. In China, exact copies of New Balance shoes were fabricated by contract manufacturers who were New Balance suppliers. They flooded the market with genuine shoes that were sold for as little as $20. Unilever discovered that one of its suppliers in Shanghai made excess cases of soap, which were sold directly to retailers. One of Procter & Gamble's Chinese suppliers sold empty P&G shampoo bottles to another company, which filled them with counterfeit shampoo. Counterfeiting and piracy of intellectual property constitute outright theft, but the possibility of legally losing the rights to intellectual property because of inadequate protection of property rights and/or a country's legal structure is another matter.

Finally, it should be mentioned that some critics argue that MNCs have pushed the current intellectual property regime too far in favor of the firms, particularly with the most recent WTO TRIPS Agreement, to be discussed in more detail subsequently.[16] The critics suggest that the so-called tight rein the firms hold on the production of intellectual property has actually served to limit creativity and the associated benefits to the people that the intellectual property (IP) laws are intended to serve. Such arguments pitch antitrust laws against IP laws. The argument goes on.

Inadequate Protection

The failure to protect intellectual property rights adequately in the world marketplace can lead to the legal loss of rights in potentially profitable markets. Because patents, processes, trademarks, and copyrights are valuable in all countries, some companies have found their assets appropriated and profitably exploited in foreign countries without license or reimbursement.[17] Furthermore, they often learn that not only are other firms producing and selling their products or using their trademarks, but the foreign companies are the rightful owners in the countries where they operate.

There have been many cases in which companies have legally lost the rights to trademarks and have had to buy back these rights or pay royalties for their use. The problems of inadequate protective measures taken by the owners of valuable assets stem from a variety of causes. One of the more frequent errors is assuming that because the company has established rights in the United States, they will be protected around the world or that rightful ownership can be established should the need arise. This assumption was the case with McDonald's in Japan, where enterprising Japanese registered its golden arches trademark. Only after a lengthy and costly legal action with a trip to the Japanese Supreme Court was McDonald's able to regain the exclusive right to use the trademark in Japan. After having to "buy" its trademark for an undisclosed amount, McDonald's maintains a very active program to protect its trademarks.

---

[16]Susan Sell, *Power and Ideas, North–South Politics of Intellectual Property and Antitrust* (Albany: State University of New York Press, 1998); Susan Sell, *Intellectual Property Rights: A Critical History* (Boulder, CO: Lynne Rienners Publishers, 2006).

[17]John Hagedoorn, Danielle Cloodt, and Hans van Kranenburg, "Intellectual Property Rights and the Governance of International R&D Partnerships," *Journal of International Business Studies* 36, no. 2 (2005), pp. 156–74.

Similarly, a South Korean company legally used the Coach brand on handbags and leather goods. The company registered the Coach trademark first and has the legal right to use that mark in Korea. The result is that a Coach-branded briefcase that is virtually identical to the U.S. product can be purchased for $135 in South Korea versus $320 in the United States. A U.S. attorney who practices with a South Korean firm noted that he has seen several instances in which a foreign company will come to Korea and naively start negotiating with a Korean company for distribution or licensing agreements, only to have the Korean company register the trademark in its own name. Later, the Korean company will use that registration as leverage in negotiations or, if the negotiations fall apart, sell the trademark back to the company. Many businesses fail to take proper steps to legally protect their intellectual property. They fail to understand that some countries do not follow the common-law principle that ownership is established by prior use or to realize that registration and legal ownership in one country does not necessarily mean ownership in another.

Prior Use versus Registration

In the United States, a common-law country, ownership of IP rights is established by **prior use**—whoever can establish first use is typically considered the rightful owner. In many code-law countries, however, ownership is established by **registration** rather than by prior use—the first to register a trademark or other property right is considered the rightful owner. For example, a trademark in Jordan belongs to whoever registers it first in Jordan. Thus you can find "McDonald's" restaurants, "Microsoft" software, and "Safeway" groceries all legally belonging to Jordanians. After a lengthy court battle that went to the Spanish Supreme Court, Nike lost its right to use the "Nike" brand name for sports apparel in Spain. Cidesport of Spain had been using Nike for sports apparel since 1932 and sued to block Nike (U.S.) sportswear sales. Because Cidesport does not sell shoes under the Nike label, Nike (U.S.) will be able to continue selling its brand of sports shoes in Spain. A company that believes it can always establish ownership in another country by proving it used the trademark or brand name first is wrong and risks the loss of these assets.

Besides the first-to-register issue, companies may encounter other problems with registering. China has improved intellectual property rights protection substantially and generally recognizes "first to invent." However, a Chinese company can capture the patent for a product invented elsewhere; it needs only to reverse-engineer or reproduce the product from published specifications and register it in China before the original inventor. Latvia and Lithuania permit duplicate registration of trademarks and brand names. A cosmetics maker registered Nivea and Niveja cosmetics brands in the former Soviet Union in 1986 and again in Latvia in 1992, but a Latvian firm had registered and had been selling a skin cream called Niveja since 1964. Neither the Soviet nor the Latvian authorities notified either firm. Applicants are responsible for informing themselves about similar trademarks that are already registered. The case is being taken to the Supreme Court of Latvia. It is best to protect IP rights through registration. Several international conventions provide for simultaneous registration in member countries.

International Conventions

Many countries participate in international conventions designed for mutual recognition and protection of intellectual property rights. There are three major international conventions:

1. The Paris Convention for the Protection of Industrial Property, commonly referred to as the Paris Convention, includes the United States and 100 other countries.

2. The Inter-American Convention includes most of the Latin American nations and the United States.

3. The Madrid Arrangement, which established the Bureau for International Registration of Trademarks, includes 26 European countries.

In addition, the World Intellectual Property Organization (WIPO) of the United Nations is responsible for the promotion of the protection of intellectual property and for the administration of the various multilateral treaties through cooperation among its member states.[18]

---

[18]Visit http://www.wipo.org, the home page of the WIPO, for detailed information on the various conventions and the activities of WIPO.

Furthermore, two multicountry patent arrangements have streamlined patent procedures in Europe. The first, the Patent Cooperation Treaty (PCT), facilitates the process for application for patents among its member countries. It provides comprehensive coverage, in that a single application filed in the United States supplies the interested party with an international search report on other patents to help evaluate whether or not to seek protection in each of the countries cooperating under the PCT. The second, the European Patent Convention (EPC), established a regional patent system allowing any nationality to file a single international application for a European patent. Companies have a choice between relying on national systems when they want to protect a trademark or patent in just a few member countries and applying for protection in all 27 member states. Trademark protection is valid for 10 years and is renewable; however, if the mark is not used within 5 years, protection is forfeited. Once the patent or trademark is approved, it has the same effect as a national patent or trademark in each individual country designated on the application.

The Trade-Related Aspects of Intellectual Property Rights (TRIPs) agreement, a major provision of the World Trade Organization, is the most comprehensive multilateral agreement on intellectual property to date. TRIPs sets standards of protection for a full range of intellectual property rights that are embodied in current international agreements. The three main provisions of the TRIPs agreement required that participating members be in compliance with minimum standards of protection by 2006, set procedures and remedies for the enforcement of IP rights, and made disputes between WTO members with respect to TRIPs obligations subject to the WTO's dispute settlement procedures.[19]

Once a trademark, patent, or other intellectual property right is registered, most countries require that these rights be used and properly policed. The United States is one of the few countries in which an individual can hold a patent without the patented entity being manufactured and sold throughout the duration of the patent period. Other countries feel that in exchange for the monopoly provided by a patent, the holder must share the product with the citizens of the country. Hence, if patents are not produced within a specified period, usually from one to five years (the average is three years), the patent reverts to public domain.

This rule is also true for trademarks; products bearing the registered mark must be sold within the country, or the company may forfeit its right to a particular trademark. McDonald's faced that problem in Venezuela. Even though the McDonald's trademark was properly registered in that code-law country, the company did not use it for more than two years. Under Venezuelan law, a trademark must be used within two years or it is lost. Thus, a Venezuelan-owned "Mr. McDonalds," with accompanying golden arches, is operating in Venezuela. The U.S. McDonald's Corporation faces a potentially costly legal battle if it decides to challenge the Venezuelan company.

Individual countries expect companies to actively police their intellectual property by bringing violators to court. Policing can be a difficult task, with success depending in large measure on the cooperation of the country within which the infringement or piracy takes place. A lack of cooperation in some countries may stem from cultural differences regarding how intellectual property is viewed. In the United States, the goal of protection of IP is to encourage invention and to protect and reward innovative businesses. In Korea, the attitude is that the thoughts of one person should benefit all. In Japan, the intent is to share technology rather than protect it; an invention should serve a larger, national goal, with the rapid spread of technology among competitors in a manner that promotes cooperation. In light of such attitudes, the lack of enthusiasm toward protecting intellectual property can be better understood. The United States is a strong advocate of protection, and at U.S. insistence, many countries are becoming more cooperative about policing cases of infringement and piracy. After decades of debate, European Union ministers agreed on a common continentwide system for patented inventions. Instead of being forced to submit an application in all EU countries' languages, inventors can submit only one, in English, French, or German. Finally, as the legal system evolves in China, authorities there have now begun enforcing local companies' patents at the expense of foreign firms.[20]

[19]For a discussion of TRIPs, visit http://www.wto.org and select Intellectual Property.

[20]"Battle of Ideas," *The Economist*, April 25, 2009, p. 68.

The three faces of piracy and/or reform, depending how you look at them. (1) American youths, particularly on college campuses, are protesting the current intellectual property laws and the associated enforcement tools. The fellow with the eyepatch was attending a seminar on the topic led by former Attorney General Alberto Gonzales.[21]

(2) Aside from the United States, the biggest piracy problem is China. Here Jackie Chan helps the Chinese government crack down, forecasting the probable path of IP piracy in China. That is, pirates have turned into policemen historically in the United States, Japan, and Taiwan as the production of intellectual property took off in each country.[22] The same will happen in China during the next decade as artists, researchers, and entrepreneurs there produce new ideas worth protecting.

(3) The HIV/AIDS epidemic is an economic and health catastrophe that many in sub-Saharan Africa and other developing countries[23] believe is exacerbated by drug companies' pricing policies and protection of intellectual property.[24] Here protestors march toward the U.S. embassy in Pretoria, South Africa.

Other Managerial Approaches to Protecting Intellectual Property

LO5

How to protect against piracy and counterfeiting

The traditional, but relatively feeble, remedies for American companies operating in countries such as China are several: (1) prevention, that is, engage local representation and diligently register IP with the appropriate agencies; (2) pursue negotiation and alternative dispute resolution; (3) complain to the Chinese authorities; and (4) complain to the U.S. government and World Trade Organization (WTO). Beyond these traditional strategies, research is now being conducted to better understand consumers' motivations with respect

---

[21]Lorenzo Munoz and Jon Healey, "Students Do Not Share Gonzales' View on Piracy," *Los Angeles Times*, April 29, 2005, pp. C1, C9.

[22]N. Mark Lam and John L. Graham, *China Now, Doing Business in the World's Most Dynamic Market* (New York: McGraw-Hill, 2007).

[23]Amelia Gentleman, "Battle Pits Patent Rights against Low-Cost Generic Drugs," *The New York Times*, January 30, 2007, p. C5; "Clinton, Drug Companies Strike Deal to Lower AIDS Drug Prices," *The Wall Street Journal*, May 8, 2007.

[24]John E. Cook and Roger Bate, "Pharmaceuticals and the Worldwide HIV Epidemic: Can a Stakeholder Model Work?" *Journal of Public Policy & Marketing* 23, no. 2 (2004), pp. 140–52.

to counterfeit brands,[25] and creative thinkers of enterprise have come up with several new ideas that we briefly describe next.[26]

Microsoft.

Bill Gates's negotiation strategy with Chinese software pirates demonstrates his guile, prescience, and patience. He accidentally revealed his strategy in 1998 in an interview at the University of Washington:

> Although about 3 million computers get sold every year in China, people don't pay for the software. Someday they will, though. And as long as they're going to steal it, we want them to steal ours. They'll get sort of addicted, and then we'll somehow figure out how to collect something in the next decade.

Well, it didn't take a decade for this marketing/product trial approach to work. On April 18, 2006, one day ahead of Chinese President Hu Jintao's arrival in Redmond, Washington, for dinner at Gates's home and on his way to a meeting with President George W. Bush, Gates inked a deal with Lenovo for $1.2 billion of software to be included in the Chinese firm's computers.

Philips.

One of the originators of "open innovation" is Philips Research in the Netherlands. Thirty years ago, it pioneered the concept of partnering[27] to develop and market new ideas. Open innovation for Philips also means that it buys ideas from R&D partners and sells ideas to marketing partners, rather than developing and marketing only its own ideas. One project exemplifies its innovative approach to developing and protecting intellectual property in China. The PHENIX Initiative was a commercial, industrial, and R&D project to develop mobile interactive digital services for the 2008 Olympics. Led by France Telecom, it involved financing and technology contributions from both European and Chinese corporations and governmental organizations.

Although many American firms have established design and R&D centers in China already, U.S. government restrictions on high-tech export and American executives' competitive angst prevent associations such as the PHENIX Initiative for U.S. firms in China. Thus, our arm's-length relationships in China limit both the amount of technology we develop and the degree of protection afforded it compared with European and Asian competitors. Moreover, our pleas for the Chinese government to "protect *our* intellectual property" sound exploitative to both the authorities and the public there.

Warner Bros.

Finally, we suggest an excellent way for IP-rich firms to make money in China currently and in the near future, using the oldest pricing strategy of all: *Charge what the market will bear*. Even with the reluctant help of the Chinese authorities in enforcing the WTO/TRIPs agreement, Chinese consumers will continue the creative copying of foreign intellectual property until they are charged what they perceive as "reasonable" prices. Indeed, we applaud the recent heroic, albeit controversial, marketing strategies of Warner Bros. in China, which nearly halved the prices of its DVDs to $1.88 and distributed the products within days of their release in theaters—earlier than anywhere else in the world.

This pricing approach is quite consistent with one we have long advocated, namely, adjusting prices on the basis of the comparative income levels in developing countries. That is, a fair price (from the Chinese point of view) would take into account the income and purchasing power differentials between consumers in the United States and China. For example, circa 2007, the ratio between U.S. and Chinese GDP per capita at purchase price parity was approximately $40,000 to $6,500. Adjusting the current U.S. price of about $10 for a DVD on Amazon.com, a "reasonable" price to charge in China would be about $1.50. And we particularly appreciate the tactical nuance of adding the $.38 to achieve the very lucky price the Warner Bros. marketers are both charging and getting in China—$1.88!

---

[25]Keith Wilcox, Hyeong Min Kim, and Sankar Sen, "Why Do Consumers Buy Counterfeit Brands?" *Journal of Marketing Research* 46, no. 2 (2009), pp. 247–59.

[26]See Lam and Graham, *China Now*, for more details.

[27]"What's Mine Is Yours," *The Economist*, May 30, 2009, p. 80.

Warner Bros. is also trying to create a market for high-quality DVD rentals in a partnership with Union Voole Technology in China. Inexpensive video-on-demand systems price the multi-view rentals at less than $1 and deliver via the Internet.[28]

Cyberlaw: Unresolved Issues

LO6

The many issues of evolving cyberlaw

The Internet is by its nature a global enterprise for which no political or national boundaries exist. Although this global reach is its strength, it also creates problems when existing laws do not clearly address the uniqueness of the Internet and its related activities. Existing law is vague or does not completely cover such issues as gambling, the protection of domain names, taxes, jurisdiction in cross-border transactions, contractual issues, piracy[29] (as discussed in the last section), and censorship. The very public dispute between Google and the government of China during 2010 is an important example of the last issue.[30] The European Union, the United States, and many other countries are drafting legislation to address the myriad legal questions not clearly addressed by current law. But until these laws apply worldwide, companies will have to rely on individual-country laws, which may or may not provide protection.[31] When you add together the unprecedented dynamism of the cyber industry to a fledgling legal system as in China, you end up with a rather wild regulatory environment. China is currently trying to monitor and censor text messaging.[32] But perhaps the most interesting battle brewing in the Chinese bureaucracy is over which ministry will regulate the online version of *World of Warcraft*, the most popular such game in the country.[33] The General Administration of Press and Publication and the Ministry of Culture are the two combatants in this interesting game, and it's a certainty that Blizzard Entertainment hopes they do not reach an agreement to share the control over the Chinese operations of the company.

Domain Names and Cybersquatters

Unfortunately, the ease with which Web names can be registered and the low cost of registering has led to thousands being registered. **Cybersquatters (CSQs)** buy and register descriptive nouns, geographic names, names of ethnic groups and pharmaceutical substances, and other similar descriptors and hold them until they can be sold at an inflated price. For example, a cybersquatter sold "www.themortgage.com" for $500,000; the record price paid so far is $7.5 million for the domain name "www.business.com." If a cybersquatter has registered a generic domain name that a company wants, the only recourse is to buy it.

Another ploy of CSQs is to register familiar names and known trademarks that divert traffic from intended destinations or to sell competing products. eBay, the world's largest online auction house, was embroiled in a dispute with an entrepreneur in Nova Scotia who registered "www.ebay.ca," thus forcing the U.S. company to use "www.ca.ebay.com" for its newly launched Canadian Web site until it was successful in regaining the use of "www.ebay.ca"; both Web addresses now go to the same site.

Cybersquatters register a well-known brand or trademark that misdirects a person to the CSQ's site or to a competing company's site. For example, an adult entertainment Web site registered "www.candyland.com." Hasbro, the toy company, markets a game for children called "Candy Land." Disturbed by the thought that customers might end up at an adult entertainment site, Hasbro wanted to have the site vacated. It had the option of suing to have it removed or buying the domain name. Hasbro elected to sue, and though the adult Web site was not directly infringing on its trademark, the courts deemed it to be damaging to the reputation of Hasbro and its children's game. The Web address now takes you directly to a Hasbro site.

[28]Dawn C. Chmielewski, "Warner Takes New Tack against Piracy," *Los Angeles Times*, November 4, 2008, pp. C1, C6.

[29]"The Spider and the Web," *The Economist*, August 29, 2009, p. 49.

[30]"Google and China, Flower for a Funeral," *The Economist*, January 16, 2010, pp. 41–42.

[31]Jefferson Graham, "File-Sharing Beat Goes On," *USA Today*, June 29, 2005, p. 3B.

[32]Sharon LaFraniere, "China to Scan Text Messages to Spot 'Unhealthy Content,'" *The New York Times*, January 20, 2010, p. A5.

[33]Michael Wines, "Online Warfare Prompts an Offline Clash in China," *The New York Times*, November 7, 2009, p. A4.

Potential customers visit a Microsoft booth in Beijing. When Chinese bloggers use Microsoft's service to post messages and type in such terms as "democracy," "capitalism," "liberty," or "human rights," they get a yellow light and a computer warning: "This message includes forbidden language. Please delete the prohibited expression." Microsoft has agreed to this sort of censorship, explaining that it is just following local laws and that the company still provides a most useful service to its Chinese clients. The critics disagree. The argument goes on.

Other cybersquatting abuses that can pose a serious threat to business include parody sites, protest sites, and hate sites. A good example is "www.walmartsucks.org," a site highly critical of Walmart. This type of Web site may be difficult to prevent because the right to free speech is protected. The only defense Walmart might have is to challenge the Web site's right to use a trade name to direct someone to the site.

It is easy to imagine many situations in which the actions of companies or information posted on a site can lead to a lawsuit when Internet content is unlawful in one country but not in the host country. For example, an American studio that makes a movie with nude scenes could be prosecuted in a country that bans nudity in movies. Not only would the movie studio be liable, but the Internet service provider could be liable for material posted on its Web site. Writers and publishers could face libel suits in countries with laws restrictive of free speech, where weak or nonexistent free speech protections are tools to intimidate and censor.[34] Internet publishers or individual Web site owners fear they can be sued for defamation from any or many jurisdictions, merely because their articles can be downloaded anywhere in the world. Lawsuits involving libel, defamation, and product liability cause companies to voluntarily restrict their Web sites to selected countries rather than leave themselves open to legal action. The Internet is not a libel-free zone.

Most country's courts are inclined to assert jurisdiction over online activity, wherever it originates, so long as harm is experienced locally and the sense is that the party responsible either knew or ought to have known that the harm was a likely consequence of its actions. Most agree, though, that laws that are expressly designed to apply not just in a single country but worldwide are necessary to untangle the legal hassles that are occurring.

Of 100 business leaders polled by the International Chamber of Commerce, more than one-third said legal uncertainty covering Internet operations affected "significant business decisions." The most immediate impact, according to the ICC, is clear: Many online merchants refuse to sell outside their home countries.

Taxes   Another thorny issue in e-commerce concerns the collection of taxes. A typical tax system relies on knowing where a particular economic activity is located. But the Internet enables individual workers to operate in many different countries while sitting at the same desk. When taxes should be collected, where they should be collected, and by whom are all issues under consideration by countries around the world. In the past, a company was deemed to have a taxable presence in a country if it had a permanent establishment there. But whether the existence of a server or a Web site qualifies as such a presence is not clear. One proposal that has enthusiastic support from tax authorities is for servers to be designated as "virtual permanent establishments" and thus subject to local taxes.

To pinpoint when and where a sale takes place in cyberspace is difficult, and unless elusive taxpayers can be pinpointed, any tax may be difficult to collect. In "brick-and-mortar" sales, the retailer collects, but when the Internet site is in one country and the customer is in another, who collects? One proposal is to have shipping companies such as FedEx or credit card companies collect—obviously, neither party is receiving this suggestion enthusiastically.

The EU Commission has announced plans for a directive to force foreign companies to levy value-added tax (VAT) on services delivered via the Internet, television, or radio to customers in the European Union. Foreign companies with sales via the Internet of over €100,000 (~$125,000) inside the European Union would have to register in at least one EU

[34]Mark Magnier and Joseph Menn, "As China Censors the Internet, Money Talks," *Los Angeles Times*, June 17, 2005, pp. A1, A14.

country and levy VAT at that country's rate, somewhere between 15 percent and 25 percent. The tax is justified on the basis of leveling the playing field. That is, EU companies have to charge their EU customers VAT, whereas foreign companies supplying the same service to the same customers are duty free. However, U.S. companies are protesting, calling the proposal "e-protectionism." Although the EU plan is only a proposal now, as the value of Internet transactions increases, the taxman will sooner or later get his share.[35] Perhaps the most egregious example of strange Internet taxing comes from France. The Ministry of Culture there proposed a tax on online advertising revenues, aimed at American firms such as Google, Microsoft, AOL, Yahoo!, and Facebook, to pay for new subsidies for the French music, movie, and publishing industries.[36]

Jurisdiction of Disputes and Validity of Contracts

As countries realize that existing laws relating to commerce do not always clearly address the uniqueness of the Internet and its related activities, a body of cyberlaw is gradually being created. Two of the most troubling areas are determining whose laws will prevail in legal disputes between parties located in different countries and establishing the contractual validity of electronic communications. The European Union is having the most difficulty in reconciling the vast differences in the laws among its member states to create a uniform law. For example, a draft regulation debated in Brussels and other European capitals would have required vendors to comply with 27 different, and sometimes bizarre, sets of national rules on consumer protection—ranging from dozens of restrictions on advertising to France's requirement that all contracts must be concluded in French, regardless of whether businesses intend to sell goods for export to France.

The EU Commission has adopted an e-commerce directive that will permit online retailers to trade by the rules of their home country unless the seller had enticed or approached the consumer by way of advertising. Then, any legal action is to take place in the consumer's country of residence. The rationale is that if a company actively seeks customers in a given country, it ought to be willing to abide by that country's consumer protection laws. Whether the directive will be accepted by all 27 member states is still problematic.

The European Commission has begun to review the entire regulatory framework for the technological infrastructure of the information society. The commission is working on various pieces of legislation intended to place electronic commerce on an equal footing with conventional commerce. One of the first steps was to introduce an EU-wide computer network dubbed EEJ net that provides an easy way to resolve small-scale disputes out of court. Problems over deliveries, defective products, or products that do not fit their description can be dealt with by a single one-stop national contact point, or clearinghouse, in each member state. The consumer will be able to find information and support in making a claim to the out-of-court dispute resolution system in the country where the product supplier is based.

Establishing the validity of contractual law for e-commerce is making substantial progress also. India, for example, recently passed a law that recognizes e-mail as a valid form of communication, electronic contracts as legal and enforceable, and digital signatures as binding. Several countries are preparing, or have passed, legislation similar to the United Kingdom's that allows digital signatures to be used in the creation of online contracts that are as legally binding as any paper-based original document.

Commercial Law within Countries

When doing business in more than one country, a marketer must remain alert to the different legal systems. This problem is especially troublesome for the marketer who formulates a common marketing plan to be implemented in several countries. Although differences in languages and customs may be accommodated, legal differences between countries may still present problems for a marketing program.

LO7

The legal differences between countries and how those differences can affect international marketing plans

---

[35]For a report on a resolution on cross-border tax issues proposed by the OECD, see "OECD Launches Project on Improving the Resolution of Cross-Border Tax Disputes," http://www.oecd.org, and select Taxation. The OECD proposes a variety of issues related to the Internet, all of which can be found at this site.

[36]"France and the Internet, Helicopters at the Ready," *The Economist*, January 16, 2010, pp. 63–64.

Marketing Laws

All countries have laws regulating marketing activities in promotion, product development, labeling, pricing, and channels of distribution. Usually the discrepancies across markets cause problems for trade negotiators, particularly for managers and their firms. For example, the United States does not allow the buying or selling of human organs,[37] and it restricts the use of human stem cells in medical research to develop treatments for a variety of diseases.[38] Other nations have different laws.[39] The ethics of both issues are quite controversial, and adding an international dimension just complicates things even more. In the case of the current international trade in human organs, Europeans can legally travel to foreign countries for transplants. However, the European Union Parliament is considering making it a criminal offense to do so. Meanwhile, the U.S. government is considering relaxing laws regulating stem cell research as scientists in other nations, unfettered by similar restrictions, are making important advances in the field.

Some countries may have only a few marketing laws with lax enforcement; others may have detailed, complicated rules to follow that are stringently enforced. For example, Sweden banned all television advertising to children in 1991. Greece, Norway, Denmark, Austria, and the Netherlands all restrict advertising directed at children. Recently, the European Commission threatened to restrict all advertising of soft drinks and snack foods to children, and PepsiCo volunteered to curb its advertising to kids in response.[40] At the same time, the American food industry is arguing against such actions in the United States. It is interesting to note that the U.S. Federal Trade Commission and the sugared food and toy manufacturers went down a similar path toward restricting advertising to children in the late 1970s. The industry made a few minor concessions at the time but began ignoring previous commitments during the 1980s. All these developments will be interesting to follow as childhood obesity continues to be a major public health issue in all affluent countries.

There often are vast differences in enforcement and interpretation among countries with laws that cover the same activities. Laws governing sales promotions in the European Union offer good examples of such diversity. In Austria, premium offers, free gifts, or coupons are considered cash discounts and are prohibited. Premium offers in Finland are allowed with considerable scope as long as the word *free* is not used and consumers are not coerced into buying products. France also regulates premium offers, which are, for all practical purposes, illegal there because selling for less than cost or offering a customer a gift or premium conditional on the purchase of another product is illegal. French law does permit sales twice a year, in January and August, which can legally last four to six weeks. This event is so popular that it is advertised on radio and TV, and special police are even required to control the crowds. One poll indicated that over 40 percent of the French set aside money during the year for sale time, and 56 percent will spend less money on essentials to buy things on sale. The good news here is that many of these restrictions on marketing activities are being softened. Most recently, holiday sales[41] and longer store hours[42] are being allowed in several European countries. China has relaxed some of its restrictions on direct marketing that particularly affected companies such as Mary Kay.[43]

The various product comparison laws, a natural and effective means of expression, are another major stumbling block. In Germany, comparisons in advertisements are always subject to the competitor's right to go to the courts and ask for proof of any implied or stated superiority. In Canada, the rulings are even more stringent: All claims and statements

---

[37]Nancy Scheper-Hughes, "Organs without Borders," *Foreign Policy*, January/February 2005, pp. 26–27.

[38]Robert L. Paarlberg, "The Great Stem Cell Race," *Foreign Policy*, May/June 2005, pp. 44–51.

[39]Amelia Gentleman, "Transplant Scheme Preys on Poor Indians," *International Herald Tribune*, January 30, 2008, p. 2.

[40]Andrew Ward and Jeremy Grant, "PepsiCo Says It Has Curbed Advertising to Children," *Financial Times,* February 28, 2005, http://www.FT.com.

[41]Cecilie Rohwedder, "Achtung Christmas Shoppers!" *The Wall Street Journal*, December 24, 2007, pp. B1, B2.

[42]Marcus Walker, "Longer Store Hours in Germany," *The Wall Street Journal*, January 8, 2007, p. A5.

[43]Katherine Yung, "Mary Kay Sales Plans Get Beijing Blessing," *Dallas Morning News*, December 5, 2006, pp. D1, D7.

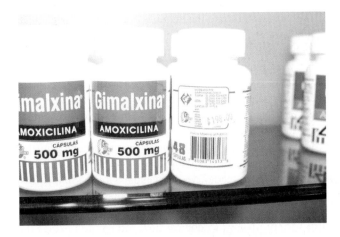

Laws regarding healthcare marketing differ substantially around the world. In Mexico, prescriptions often are not required for powerful drugs. At this farmacia in the Cancun airport, tourists can buy the pictured antibiotic over the counter at bargain prices. Quality is an issue, but availability is not. In the Philippines and other developing countries, you can buy yourself a kidney on the black market—the global price is around $2,000. However, U.S. laws prohibit the buying and selling of human organs. In South Korea, the government supports stem cell research that is restricted in the United States by federal laws.

must be examined to ensure that any representation to the public is not false or misleading. Such representation cannot be made verbally in selling or be contained in or on anything that comes to the attention of the public (such as product labels, inserts in products, or any other form of advertising, including what may be expressed in a sales letter). Courts have been directed by Canadian law to take into account, in determining whether a representation is false or misleading, the "general impression" conveyed by the representation as well as its literal meaning.[44] The courts are expected to apply the "credulous person standard," which means that if any reasonable person could possibly misunderstand the representation, the representation is misleading. In essence, puffery, an acceptable practice in the United States, could be interpreted in Canada as false and misleading advertising. Thus, a statement such as "the strongest drive shaft in Canada" would be judged misleading unless the advertiser had absolute evidence that the drive shaft was stronger than any other drive shaft for sale in Canada.

China is experimenting with a variety of laws to control how foreign companies do business, and some of those experiments have gone well, but some badly. Some regulations are being relaxed, such as those controlling foreign advertising companies. Even so, censorship of advertising and program content[45] are constant concerns. Televised ads for "offensive" products such as feminine hygiene pads, hemorrhoid medications, and even athlete's food ointment are not allowed during the three daily mealtimes.[46] The Chinese authorities banned a LeBron James Nike TV ad because it "violates regulations that mandate all advertisements in China should uphold national dignity and interest and respect the motherland's culture."[47] Apparently LeBron battling a kung fu master isn't appropriate in the land of Confucius. Also, magazines have been ordered to use a direct translation of the often-obscure name that appears on their license or use no English name at all. Thus, *Cosmopolitan* would become "Trends Lady," *Woman's Day* would become "Friends of Health," and *Esquire* would become "Trends Man." The movie *Avatar* also competed for Chinese screens with a government-sponsored film about the life of Confucius; at least temporarily, *Avatar* was allowed to show only on 3D screens, thus allowing Confucius the "appropriate" screen time.[48] A Guns N' Roses album was banned in the country for its objectionable title, *Chinese Democracy.*"[49] Such diversity of laws among countries extends to advertising, pricing, sales agreements, and other commercial activities. Indeed, studies suggest that governmental policies affect marketing success in a variety of ways[50] including actually forestalling some firms from taking a marketing orientation in their operations.[51]

There is some hope that the European Union will soon have a common commercial code. One step in that direction is the proposal to harmonize the pan-European regulation of promotions based on the conservative laws that cover promotions in Germany, Austria, and Belgium. However, this proposal is meeting with strong resistance from several groups because of its complex restrictions.[52] Meanwhile, others push for even broader-based

[44]Richard W. Pollay, "Considering the Evidence, No Wonder the Court Endorses Canada's Restrictions on Cigarette Advertising," *Journal of Public Policy & Marketing* 23, no. 1 (2004), pp. 80–88.

[45]"Bond in Beijing," *The Wall Street Journal*, January 31, 2007, p. A12; Don Lee and Jim Puzzanghera, "China Closing Curtains on U.S. Movies," *Los Angeles Times*, December 12, 2007, pp. C1, C4; Geoffrey A. Fowler, "Online-Video Firms Brace as China Tightens Rules," *The Wall Street Journal*, January 4, 2008.

[46]Geoffrey A. Fowler, "China Cracks Down on Commercials," *The Wall Street Journal*, February 19, 2004, p. B7.

[47]"China Bans Nike's LeBron Commercial," *Associated Press*, December 6, 2004.

[48]Ben Fritz and David Pierson, "Chinese Pull an 'Avatar' Switch," *Los Angeles Times*, January 19, 2010, p. B6.

[49]James T. Areddy, "Guns N' Roses New Album Is Up Against a Chinese Wall," *The Wall Street Journal*, November 22, 2008, online.

[50]Stefan Stremersch and Aurelie Lemmens, "Sales Growth of New Pharmaceuticals across the Globe: The Role of Regulatory Regimes," *Marketing Science* 28, no. 4 (2009), pp. 690–708.

[51]Rilian Qu and Christine T. Ennew, "Developing a Market Orientation in a Transitional Economy: The Role of Government Regulation and Ownership Structure," *Journal of Public Policy & Marketing* 24, no. 1 (2005), pp. 82–89.

[52]"EU Sets Cap on TV Ads and Product Placement," *International Herald Tribune*, November 14, 2006, p. 16.

A Greenpeace protester peers out from inside a plastic rubbish bin in Hong Kong, where activists were calling on the government to develop a comprehensive recycling industry that they claim will create 2,000 new jobs. A study by Greenpeace found that only 148 out of 18,200 rubbish bins in Hong Kong have waste separation compartments. It called on the government to revamp its current waste management procedures to facilitate a comprehensive system to reduce, recover, and recycle.

harmonization of marketing regulations involving the United States, United Nations, and the WTO.

Although the European Union may sometimes appear a beautiful picture of economic cooperation, there is still the reality of dealing with 27 different countries, cultures, and languages, as well as 27 different legal systems. Even though some of Germany's complicated trade laws were revoked in 2000, groups such as the Center for Combating Unfair Competition, an industry-financed organization, continue to work to maintain the status quo. Before the German law was revoked, the Center's lawyers filed 1,000 lawsuits a year, going after, for example, a grocery store that offered discount coupons or a deli that gave a free cup of coffee to a customer who had already bought 10; its efforts will surely continue.

Although the goal of full integration and a common commercial code has not been totally achieved in the European Union, decisions by the European Court continue to strike down individual-country laws that impede competition across borders. In a recent decision, the European Court ruled that a French cosmetics company could sell its wares by mail in Germany and advertise them at a markdown from their original prices, a direct contradiction of German law. As the Single European Market Act is implemented, many of the legal and trade differences that have existed for decades will vanish. Surprisingly enough, standards set by the European Union for food, software, cars, and other items affect U.S. product standards as well. In many cases, the reconciliation of so many different consumer protection standards that existed in European countries prior to the European Union resulted in rules more rigorous than those for many U.S. products. Consequently, many U.S. products have had to be redesigned to comply with European standards. For example, Carrier air conditioners have been redesigned to comply with European recycling rules; Microsoft has modified contracts with software makers; Internet service providers give consumers a wider choice of technologies; and McDonald's has ceased including soft plastic toys with its Happy Meals and has withdrawn all genetically engineered potatoes from its restaurants worldwide. All this change is because of the need to reconcile U.S. standards with those of the European Union.

Green Marketing Legislation

Multinational corporations also face a growing variety of legislation designed to address environmental issues. Global concern for the environment extends beyond industrial pollution, hazardous waste disposal, and rampant deforestation to include issues that focus directly on consumer products. Green marketing laws focus on environmentally friendly products and product packaging and its effect on solid waste management.

Germany has passed the most stringent green marketing laws that regulate the management and recycling of packaging waste. The new packaging laws were introduced in three phases. The first phase required all transport packaging, such as crates, drums, pallets, and Styrofoam containers, to be accepted back by the manufacturers and distributors for recycling. The second phase required manufacturers, distributors, and retailers to accept all returned secondary packaging, including corrugated boxes, blister packs, packaging designed to prevent theft, packaging for vending machine applications, and packaging for promotional purposes. The third phase requires all retailers, distributors, and manufacturers to accept returned sales packaging, including cans, plastic containers for dairy products, foil wrapping, Styrofoam packages, and folding cartons such as cereal boxes. The requirement for retailers to take back sales packaging has been suspended as long as the voluntary green dot program remains a viable substitute. A green dot on a package identifies manufacturers that have agreed to ensure a regular collection of used packaging materials directly from the consumer's home or from designated local collection points.

Reclaiming recyclables extends beyond packaging to automobiles. Since 2006, manufacturers based in European Union nations must take back any cars they produced that no longer have resale value and pay for proper disposal. Similarly, 85 percent of a scrapped car's material must be recovered for future use.

Many European countries also have devised schemes to identify products that comply with certain criteria that make them more environmentally friendly than similar products. Products that meet these criteria are awarded an "ecolabel" that the manufacturer can display on packaging to signal to customers that it is an environmentally friendly product. The European Union is becoming more aggressive in issuing new directives and in harmonizing ecolabeling and other environmental laws across all member states. Ecolabeling and EU packaging laws are discussed in more detail in the chapter on consumer products (Chapter 13).[53]

Foreign Countries' Antitrust Laws

With the exception of the United States, antitrust laws were either nonexistent or not enforced in most of the world's countries for the better part of the twentieth century. However, the European Union,[54] Japan, and many other countries have begun to actively enforce their antitrust laws, patterned after those in the United States. Antimonopoly, price discrimination, supply restrictions, and full-line forcing are areas in which the European Court of Justice has dealt severe penalties. For example, before Procter & Gamble was allowed to buy VP-Schickedanz AG, a German hygiene products company, it had to agree to sell off one of the German company's divisions that produced Camelia, a brand of sanitary napkins. Because P&G already marketed a brand of sanitary napkins in Europe, the commission was concerned that allowing P&G to keep Camelia would give the company a controlling 60 percent of the German sanitary products market and 81 percent of Spain's. More recently, the European Union fined Intel $1.45 billion for monopolistic abuses in its marketing in Europe. In addition, the firm must make mandated adjustments in its marketing practices and operations.[55]

The United States also intervenes when non-U.S. companies attempt to acquire American companies. Nestlé's proposed $2.8 billion acquisition of Dreyer's Grand Ice Cream hit a roadblock as U.S. antitrust officials opposed the deal on grounds that it would lead to less competition and higher prices for gourmet ice cream in the United States. At times, companies are subject to antitrust charges in more than one country. Microsoft had a partial victory against antitrust charges brought in the United States, only to face similar anticompetitive charges against Microsoft's Windows operating system in the European Union. The probe is based on possible competitive benefits to European software concerns if legal limits were placed on Microsoft. American companies have faced antitrust violations since the trust-busting days of President Theodore Roosevelt but much less so in other parts of the world. Enforcement of antitrust in Europe was almost nonexistent until the early stages of the European Union established antitrust legislation. And, now China is getting into the game. The Anti-Monopoly Bureau of the Ministry of Commerce considered its first such case and eventually approved the Anheuser-Busch/InBev merger.[56]

U.S. Laws Apply in Host Countries

All governments are concerned with protecting their political and economic interests domestically and internationally; any activity or action, wherever it occurs, that adversely threatens national interests is subject to government control. Leaving

LO8

The different ways U.S. laws can be applied to U.S. companies operating outside the United States

[53]For information on the EU's environmental directives, as well as other information about the European Union, visit http://www.europa.eu.int. This address will take you to the home page, where you can search for topics and visit various information sources about the European Union.

[54]Charles Forelle, "Microsoft Yields in EU Antitrust Battle," *The Wall Street Journal*, October 23, 2007; Charles Forelle, "EU Probes Pharmaceutical Industry on Dwindling New Patents, Drugs," *The Wall Street Journal*, January 16, 2008.

[55]Charles Forrelle and Don Clark, "Intel Fine Jolts Tech Firm," *The Wall Street Journal*, May 14, 2009, pp. A1, A14.

[56]"InBev-Anheuser-Busch: China's First Public Merger Decision Under the AML," *Venulex Legal Summaries* Q4 (2008), pp. 1–3.

the political boundaries of a home country does not exempt a business from home-country laws. Regardless of the nation where business is done, a U.S. citizen is subject to certain laws of the United States. What is illegal for an American business at home can also be illegal by U.S. law in foreign jurisdictions for the firm, its subsidiaries, and licensees of U.S. technology.

Laws that prohibit taking a bribe, trading with the enemy, participating in a commercial venture that negatively affects the U.S. economy, participating in an unauthorized boycott such as the Arab boycott, or any other activity deemed to be against the best interests of the United States apply to U.S. businesses and their subsidiaries and licensees regardless of where they operate. Thus, at any given time a U.S. citizen in a foreign country must look not only at the laws of the host country but at home law as well.

The question of jurisdiction of U.S. law over acts committed outside the territorial limits of the country has been settled by the courts through application of a long-established principle of international law, the "objective theory of jurisdiction." This concept holds that even if an act is committed outside the territorial jurisdiction of U.S. courts, those courts can nevertheless have jurisdiction if the act produces effects within the home country. The only possible exception may be when the violation is the result of enforced compliance with local law.

Foreign Corrupt Practices Act

Recall from Chapter 5 that the Foreign Corrupt Practices Act (FCPA) makes it illegal for companies to pay bribes to foreign officials, candidates, or political parties. Stiff penalties can be assessed against company officials, directors, employees, or agents found guilty of paying a bribe or of knowingly participating in or authorizing the payment of a bribe. However, also recall that bribery, which can range from lubrication to extortion, is a common business custom in many countries, even though illegal.[57]

The original FCPA lacked clarity, and early interpretations were extremely narrow and confusing. Subsequent amendments in the Omnibus Trade and Competitiveness Act clarified two of the most troubling issues. Corporate officers' liability was changed from having *reason to know* that illegal payments were made to *knowing* of or authorizing illegal payments. In addition, if it is customary in the culture, small (grease or lubrication) payments made to encourage officials to complete routine government actions such as processing papers, stamping visas, and scheduling inspections are not illegal per se.

The debate continues as to whether the FCPA puts U.S. businesses at a disadvantage. Some argue that U.S. businesses are at a disadvantage in international business transactions in those cases in which bribery payments are customary, whereas others contend that it has little effect and, indeed, that it helps companies to "just say no." The truth probably lies somewhere in between. The consensus is that most U.S. firms are operating within the law, and several studies indicate that the FCPA has not been as detrimental to MNCs' interests as originally feared, because exports to developed and developing countries continue to be favorable.

Although U.S. firms seem able to compete and survive without resorting to corruption in the most corrupt societies, it does not mean that violations do not occur or that companies are not penalized for violations. For example, a U.S. environmental engineering firm was found to have made corrupt payments to an Egyptian government official to assist the company in gaining a contract. The company agreed not to violate the FCPA in the future, to pay a civil fine of $400,000, and to reimburse the Department of Justice for the costs of the investigation. Furthermore, the company agreed to establish FCPA compliance procedures and to provide certifications of compliance annually for five years. Other firms have paid even larger fines in recent years, and the Justice Department has agreed not to prosecute firms with "excellent" training programs in place.

---

[57]For discussions of the FCPA, updates, and other information, visit the FCPA home page at http://www.usdoj.gov/criminal/fraud/fcpa.html.

CROSSING BORDERS 7.2

The Kind of Correspondence an International Marketer Doesn't Want to See

FOR IMMEDIATE RELEASE   CRM
FRIDAY, MAY 20, 2005   (202) 514-2008
WWW.USDOJ.GOV   TDD (202) 514-1888

DPC (TIANJIN) LTD. CHARGED WITH VIOLATING THE FOREIGN CORRUPT PRACTICES ACT

WASHINGTON, D.C.—Acting Assistant Attorney General John C. Richter of the Criminal Division today announced the filing of a one-count criminal information charging DPC (Tianjin) Co. Ltd.—the Chinese subsidiary of Los Angeles-based Diagnostic Products Corporation (DPC)—with violating the Foreign Corrupt Practices Act of 1977 (FCPA) in connection with the payment of approximately $1.6 million in bribes in the form of illegal "commissions" to physicians and laboratory personnel employed by government-owned hospitals in the People's Republic of China.

The company, a producer and seller of diagnostic medical equipment, has agreed to plead guilty to the charge, adopt internal compliance measures, and cooperate with ongoing criminal and SEC civil investigations. An independent compliance expert will be chosen to audit the company's compliance program and monitor its implementation of new internal policies and procedures. DPC Tianjin has also agreed to pay a criminal penalty of $2 million.

The bribes were allegedly paid from late 1991 through December 2002 for the purpose and effect of obtaining and retaining business with these hospitals. According to the criminal information and a statement of facts filed in court, DPC Tianjin made cash payments to laboratory personnel and physicians employed in certain hospitals in the People's Republic of China in exchange for agreements that the hospitals would obtain DPC Tianjin's products and services. This practice, authorized by DPC Tianjin's general manager, involved personnel who were employed by hospitals owned by the legal authorities in the People's Republic of China and, thus, "foreign officials" as defined by the FCPA.

In most cases, the bribes were paid in cash and hand-delivered by DPC Tianjin salespeople to the person who controlled purchasing decisions for the particular hospital department. DPC Tianjin recorded the payments on its books and records as "selling expenses." DPC Tianjin's general manager regularly prepared and submitted to Diagnostic Products Corporation its financial statements, which contained its sales expenses. The general manager also caused approval of the budgets for sales expenses of DPC Tianjin, including the amounts DPC Tianjin intended to pay to the officials of the hospitals in the following quarter or year.

The "commissions," typically between 3 percent and 10 percent of sales, totaled approximately $1,623,326 from late 1991 through December 2002, and allowed Depu to earn approximately $2 million in profits from the sales.

DPC Tianjin's parent company, Diagnostic Products Corporation, is the subject of an FCPA enforcement proceeding filed earlier today by the U.S. Securities and Exchange Commission. The SEC ordered the company to cease and desist from violating the FCPA and to disgorge approximately $2.8 million in ill-gotten gains, representing its net profit in the People's Republic of China for the period of its misconduct plus prejudgment interest ...

U.S. Antitrust Laws that Apply in Foreign Markets

Antitrust enforcement has two purposes in international commerce. The first is to protect American consumers by ensuring that they benefit from products and ideas produced by foreign competitors as well as by domestic competitors. Competition from foreign producers is important when imports are, or could be, a major source of a product or when a single firm dominates a domestic industry. This issue becomes relevant in many joint ventures, particularly if the joint venture creates a situation in which a U.S. firm entering a joint venture with a foreign competitor restricts competition for the U.S. parent in the U.S. market.

The second purpose of antitrust legislation is to protect American export and investment opportunities against any privately imposed restrictions. The concern is that all U.S.-based firms engaged in the export of goods, services, or capital should be allowed to compete on merit and not be shut out by restrictions imposed by bigger or less principled competitors.

of the unrestricted export of commodities in short supply, such as Western cedar. Items that do not require a license for a specific destination can be shipped with the notation "NLR" (no license required) on the Shipper's Export Declaration. Some export restrictions on high-technology products have been recently eased, which we hope marks the beginning of a new trend.[64]

National Security Laws

American firms, their foreign subsidiaries, or foreign firms that are licensees of U.S. technology cannot sell products to a country in which the sale is considered by the U.S. government to affect national security. Furthermore, responsibility extends to the final destination of the product, regardless of the number of intermediaries that may be involved in the transfer of goods.

In the last century, an extensive export control system was created to slow the spread of sensitive technologies to the former Soviet Union, China, and other communist countries that were viewed as major threats to U.S. security. The control of the sale of goods considered to have a strategic and military value was extremely strict. But with the end of the Cold War, export controls were systematically dismantled until 1999, when a congressional committee reported Chinese espionage activities and American aerospace companies transferring sensitive technology irresponsibly. Following the report, legislation was passed again restricting the export of products or technologies that might be used by other countries for defense applications.

The events of September 11, 2001, added another set of restrictions related to weapons of mass destruction (WMD). Unfortunately, many of the products used in WMD are difficult to control because they have dual purposes; that is, they have legitimate uses as well as being important in manufacturing WMD. For example, Iraq, which was allowed to import medical equipment despite a U.N. embargo, purchased, under the pretext of medical benefits, six machines that destroy kidney stones. The manufacturer accepted the claim that Saddam Hussein was concerned about kidney stones in the Iraqi population and began shipping the machines. However, integral components of these machines are high-precision electronic switches that are also used to set off the chain reaction in thermonuclear weapons. When 120 additional switches as "spare parts" were ordered, a red flag went up, and the shipments were stopped.

Countless numbers of dual-purpose technologies are exported from the United States. A sticking point with dual-purpose exports is the intent of the buyer. Silicon Graphics Inc. (SGI) sold computer equipment to a Russian nuclear laboratory that contended it was for nonmilitary use, which would have been legal. However, the Department of Justice ruled that since the sale was made to a government-operated facility involved in both civil and noncivil activities, SGI should have applied for the correct export license. Thus, SGI paid a fine of $1 million plus a $500,000 fine for each of the export violations. National security laws prohibit a U.S. company, its subsidiaries, joint ventures, or licensees from selling controlled products without special permission from the U.S. government. The consequences of violation of the Trading with the Enemy Act can be severe: fines, prison sentences, and, in the case of foreign companies, economic sanctions.

Exports are controlled for the protection and promotion of human rights, as a means of enforcing foreign policy, because of national shortages, to control technology,[65] and for a host of other reasons the U.S. government deems necessary to protect its best interests. In years past, the government restricted trade with South Africa (human rights) and restricted the sale of wheat to the Soviet Union in retaliation for its invasion of Afghanistan (foreign policy). Currently, the government restricts trade with Iran (foreign policy) and the sale of

---

[64]James Auger, "United States to Ease Technology-Export Restrictions," *Global Insight Daily Analysis*, January 23, 2008. We note that other countries also restrict exports for a variety of reasons. For example, see "Russian Government Mulls Additional Grain Export Restrictions," *Russia and CIS General Newswire, Interfax*, November 15, 2007.

[65]Deborah Zabarenko, "U.S. Policy Curbs Global Space Cooperation," *Reuters*, June 23, 2005; "U.S. in Talks with Boeing over Sensor Sales to China," *Reuters*, July 7, 2005; "Space Station, No Plan B for Outer Space," *The Economist*, March 12, 2005, pp. 75–76.

CROSSING BORDERS 7.3 | The Consequences of Mixing Politics and Security

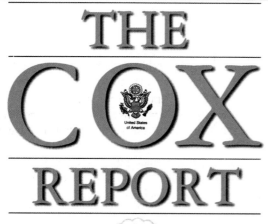

THE COX REPORT

THE UNANIMOUS *and* BIPARTISAN

REPORT *of the* HOUSE SELECT COMMITTEE

ON U.S. NATIONAL SECURITY *and*

In 1999 the Cox Report was published, making shocking claims about China's military aggressiveness toward the United States. The verbiage on the back cover delivered the gist of the argument:

China's Target: America

"The unanimous, bipartisan Cox Report is one of the most stunning documents ever to come from the U.S. Congress—a shocking account of how the People's Republic of China has targeted America for subversion, high-tech theft, and nuclear challenge.

How Communist China has replaced the former Soviet Union as America's chief military rival—and acquired the means to target nuclear missiles on American cities...."

At the time, the report was widely criticized as politically motivated and shallow in substance. Moreover, the events of September 11 rendered the argument, at best, obsolete. But the combination of the political attack on China and the associated renewed restrictions on sales of high-technology goods and expertise has had a long-term chilling effect on U.S. sales in the world's fastest growing market. During 1999, the U.S. market share of merchandise exports to China fell from 10 percent to 8 percent, and the loss of competitiveness has remained permanent.

Sources: *The Cox Report* (Washington, DC: Regency, 1999); N. Mark Lam and John L. Graham, *China Now, Doing Business in the World's Most Dynamic Market* (New York: McGraw-Hill, 2007).

leading-edge electronics (control of technology), and it prohibits the export of pesticides that have not been approved for use in the United States (to avoid the return of residue of unauthorized pesticides in imported food and protect U.S. consumers from the so-called circle of poison). In each of these cases, U.S. law binds U.S. businesses, regardless of where they operate.

Determining Export Requirements

The first step when complying with export licensing regulations is to determine the appropriate license for the product. Products exported from the United States require a general or a validated export license, depending on the product, where it is going, the end use, and the final user. The *general license* permits exportation of certain products that are not subject to EAR control with nothing more than a declaration of the type of product, its value, and its destination. The *validated license,* issued only on formal

Fortunately, there are often internal staff and research agencies that are quite experienced in these kinds of cross-cultural communication tasks.

Second, the environments within which the research tools are applied are often different in foreign markets. Rather than acquire new and exotic methods of research, the international marketing researcher must develop the capability for imaginative and deft applications of tried and tested techniques in sometimes totally strange milieus. The mechanical problems of implementing foreign marketing research often vary from country to country. Within a foreign environment, the frequently differing emphases on the kinds of information needed, the often limited variety of appropriate tools and techniques available, and the difficulty of implementing the research process constitute challenges facing most international marketing researchers.

This chapter deals with the operational problems encountered in gathering information in foreign countries for use by international marketers. The emphasis is on those elements of data generation that usually prove especially troublesome in conducting research in an environment other than the United States.

Breadth and Scope of International Marketing Research

The basic difference between domestic and foreign market research is the broader scope needed for foreign research, necessitated by higher levels of uncertainty. Research can be divided into three types on the basis of information needs: (1) general information about the country, area, and/or market; (2) information necessary to forecast future marketing requirements by anticipating social, economic, consumer, and industry trends within specific markets or countries; and (3) specific market information used to make product, promotion, distribution, and price decisions and to develop marketing plans. In domestic operations, most emphasis is placed on the third type, gathering specific market information, because the other data are often available from secondary sources.

A country's political stability, cultural attributes, and geographical characteristics are some of the kinds of information not ordinarily gathered by domestic marketing research departments, but they are required for a sound assessment of a foreign market. This broader scope of international marketing research is reflected in Unisys Corporation's planning steps, which call for collecting and assessing the following types of information:

1. **Economic and demographic.** General data on growth in the economy, inflation, business cycle trends, and the like; profitability analysis for the division's products; specific industry economic studies; analysis of overseas economies; and key economic indicators for the United States and major foreign countries, as well as population trends, such as migration, immigration, and aging.

2. **Cultural, sociological, and political climate.** A general noneconomic review of conditions affecting the division's business. In addition to the more obvious subjects, it covers ecology, safety, and leisure time and their potential impacts on the division's business.

3. **Overview of market conditions.** A detailed analysis of market conditions that the division faces, by market segment, including international.

4. **Summary of the technological environment.** A summary of the state-of-the-art technology as it relates to the division's business, carefully broken down by product segments.

5. **Competitive situation.** A review of competitors' sales revenues, methods of market segmentation, products, and apparent strategies on an international scope.[3]

---

[3]Apparently companies engage in corporate espionage. See Evan Ramstad, "Chip Executives Arrested in South Korea," *The Wall Street Journal*, February 3, 2010; John J. Fialka, "Hugger-Mugger in the Executive Suite," *The New York Times*, February 2, 2010, p. W10. Apparently governments also get into the industrial competitive intelligence game. Associated Press, "China Denies U.S. Trade Espionage," *The Wall Street Journal*, July 20, 2009.

Such in-depth information is necessary for sound marketing decisions. For the domestic marketer, most such information has been acquired after years of experience with a single market, but in foreign countries, this information must be gathered for each new market.

There is a basic difference between information ideally needed and that which is collectible and/or used. Many firms engaged in foreign marketing do not make decisions with the benefit of the information listed.[4] Cost, time, and human elements are critical variables. Some firms have neither the appreciation for information nor adequate time or money for the implementation of research. As a firm becomes more committed to foreign marketing and the cost of possible failure increases, greater emphasis is placed on research.

The Research Process

A marketing research study is always a compromise dictated by the limits of time, cost, and the present state of the art. A key to successful research is a systematic and orderly approach to the collection and analysis of data. Whether a research program is conducted in New York or New Delhi, the **research process** should follow these steps:

1. Define the research problem and establish research objectives.
2. Determine the sources of information to fulfill the research objectives.
3. Consider the costs and benefits of the research effort.
4. Gather the relevant data from secondary or primary sources, or both.
5. Analyze, interpret, and summarize the results.
6. Effectively communicate the results to decision makers.

Although the steps in a research program are similar for all countries, variations and problems in implementation occur because of differences in cultural and economic development. Whereas the problems of research in England or Canada may be similar to those in the United States, research in Germany, South Africa, or Mexico may offer a multitude of difficult distinctions. These distinctions become apparent with the first step in the research process—formulation of the problem. The subsequent text sections illustrate some frequently encountered difficulties facing the international marketing researcher.

Defining the Problem and Establishing Research Objectives

LO1

The importance of problem definition in international research

After examining internal sources of data, the research process should begin with a definition of the research problem and the establishment of specific research objectives.[5] The major difficulty here is converting a series of often ambiguous business problems into tightly drawn and achievable research objectives. In this initial stage, researchers often embark on the research process with only a vague grasp of the total problem. A good example of such a loosely defined problem is that of Russian airline Aeroflot. The company undertook a branding study to inform its marketing decisions regarding improving its long-standing reputation for poor safety standards and unreliable service. This goal is a tough challenge for international marketing researchers.

This first, most crucial step in research is more critical in foreign markets because an unfamiliar environment tends to cloud problem definition. Researchers either fail to anticipate the influence of the local culture on the problem or fail to identify the self-reference criterion (SRC) and therefore treat the problem definition as if it were in the researcher's home environment. In assessing some foreign business failures, it becomes apparent that research was conducted, but the questions asked were more appropriate for the U.S. market than for the foreign one. For example, all of Disney's years of research and experience in

---

[4]Bent Petersen, Torben Pedersen, and Marjorie A. Lyles, "Closing the Knowledge Gaps in Foreign Markets," *Journal of International Business Studies* 39, no. 7 (2008), pp. 1097–113.

[5]Scholars in the field also struggle with defining the problem. See Mike W. Peng, "Identifying the Big Question in International Business Research," *Journal of International Business Studies* 35, no. 2 (2004), pp. 99–108; Susan B. Douglas and C. Samuel Craig, "On Improving the Conceptual Foundations of International Marketing Research," *Journal of International Marketing* 14, no. 1 (2006), pp. 1–22.

keeping people happy standing in long lines could not help Disney anticipate the scope of the problems it would run into with Disneyland Paris. The firm's experience had been that the relatively homogeneous clientele at both the American parks and Tokyo Disneyland were cooperative and orderly when it came to queuing up. Actually, so are most British and Germans. But the rules about queuing in other countries such as Spain and Italy are apparently quite different, creating the potential for a new kind of intra-European "warfare" in the lines. Understanding and managing this multinational customer service problem has required new ways of thinking. Isolating the SRC and asking the right questions are crucial steps in the problem formulation stage.

Other difficulties in foreign research stem from failures to establish problem limits broad enough to include all relevant variables. Information on a far greater range of factors is necessary to offset the unfamiliar cultural background of the foreign market. Consider proposed research about consumption patterns and attitudes toward hot milk-based drinks. In the United Kingdom, hot milk-based drinks are considered to have sleep-inducing, restful, and relaxing properties and are traditionally consumed prior to bedtime. People in Thailand, however, drink the same hot milk-based drinks in the morning on the way to work and see them as invigorating, energy-giving, and stimulating. If one's only experience is the United States, the picture is further clouded, because hot milk-based drinks are frequently associated with cold weather, either in the morning or the evening, and for different reasons each time of day. The market researcher must be certain the problem definition is sufficiently broad to cover the whole range of response possibilities and not be clouded by his or her self-reference criterion.

Indeed, this clouding is a problem that Mattel Inc. ran into headlong. The company conducted a coordinated global research program using focus groups of children in several countries. Based on these findings, the firm cut back on customization and ignored local managers' advice by selling an unmodified Barbie globally. Not only was it dangerous to ignore the advice of local managers; it was also dangerous to ignore parents' opinions involving toys. Kids may like a blonde Barbie, but parents may not. Unfortunately, our predictions about Barbie in a previous edition of this book proved correct: As we mentioned in previous chapters, sales of blonde Barbie dramatically declined in several foreign markets following the marketing research error.

Once the problem is adequately defined and research objectives established, the researcher must determine the availability of the information needed. If the data are available—that is, if they have been collected already by some other agency—the researcher should then consult these **secondary data** sources.

Problems of Availability and Use of Secondary Data

LO2

The problems of availability and use of secondary data

The U.S. government provides comprehensive statistics for the United States; periodic censuses of U.S. population, housing, business, and agriculture are conducted and, in some cases, have been taken for over 100 years. Commercial sources, trade associations, management groups, and state and local governments provide the researcher with additional sources of detailed U.S. market information. Often the problem for American marketing researchers is sorting through too much data!

Availability of Data

While the quantity and quality of marketing-related data available in the United States is unmatched in other countries, things are improving.[6] The data available on and in Japan is a close second, and several European countries do a good job of collecting and reporting data. Indeed, on some dimensions, the quality of data collected in these latter countries can actually exceed that in the United States. However, in many countries, substantial data collection has been initiated only recently.[7] Through the continuing efforts of organizations

---

[6]"The Government and the Geeks," *The Economist*, February 6, 2010, pp. 65–66.

[7]See GIS analyses based on the 2000 Census in China at http://www.geodemo.com, Demographic Consulting, Inc.

CROSSING BORDERS 8.1   Headache? Take Two Aspirin and Lie Down

Such advice goes pretty far in countries such as Germany, where Bayer invented aspirin more than 100 years ago, and the United States. But people in many places around the world don't share such Western views about medicine and the causes of disease. Many Asians, including Chinese, Filipinos, Koreans, Japanese, and Southeast Asians, believe illnesses such as headaches are the result of the imbalance between *yin* and *yang*. *Yin* is the feminine, passive principle that is typified by darkness, cold, or wetness. Alternatively, *yang* is the masculine, active principle associated with light, heat, or dryness. All things result from their combination, and bad things like headaches result from too much of one or the other. Acupuncture and moxibustion (heating crushed wormwood or other herbs on the skin) are common cures. Many Laotians believe pain can be caused by one of the body's 32 souls being lost or by sorcerers' spells. The exact cause is often determined by examining the yolk of a freshly broken egg. In other parts of the world,

such as Mexico and Puerto Rico, illness is believed to be caused by an imbalance of one of the four body humors: "blood—hot and wet; yellow bile—hot and dry; phlegm—cold and wet; and black bile—cold and dry." Even in the high-tech United States, many people believe that pain is often a "reminder from God" to behave properly.

Now Bayer is marketing aspirin as a preventive drug for other ailments, such as intestinal cancer and heart attack. But in many foreign markets for companies such as Bayer, a key question to be addressed in marketing research is how and to what extent aspirin can be marketed as a supplement to the traditional remedies. That is, will little white pills mix well with phlegm and black bile?

Sources: Larry A. Samovar, Richard E. Porter, and Lisa A. Stefani, *Communication between Cultures*, 3rd ed. (Belmont, CA: Wadsworth Publishing, 1998), pp. 224–25; the direct quote is from N. Dresser, *Multicultural Manners: New Rules for Etiquette for a Changing Society* (New York: John Wiley & Sons, 1996), p. 236; see also "Aspirin Truly Merits Consideration as One of the Wonders of World," *Star-Ledger*, September 18, 2007, p. 67.

such as the United Nations and the Organization for Economic Cooperation and Development (OECD), improvements are being made worldwide.

In addition, with the emergence of eastern European countries as potentially viable markets, a number of private and public groups are funding the collection of information to offset a lack of comprehensive market data. Several Japanese consumer goods manufacturers are coordinating market research on a corporate level and have funded dozens of research centers throughout eastern Europe. As market activity continues in eastern Europe and elsewhere, market information will improve in quantity and quality. To build a database on Russian consumers, one Denver, Colorado, firm used a novel approach to conduct a survey: It ran a questionnaire in Moscow's *Komsomolskaya Pravda* newspaper asking for replies to be sent to the company. The 350,000 replies received (3,000 by registered mail) attested to the willingness of Russian consumers to respond to marketing inquiries. The problems of availability, reliability, and comparability of data and of validating secondary data are described in the following sections.

Another problem relating to the availability of data is researchers' language skills. For example, though data are often copious regarding the Japanese market, being able to read Japanese is a requisite for accessing them, either online or in text. This problem may seem rather innocuous, but only those who have tried to maneuver through foreign data can appreciate the value of having a native speaker of the appropriate language on the research team.

Reliability of Data   Available data may not have the level of reliability necessary for confident decision making for many reasons. Official statistics are sometimes too optimistic, reflecting national pride rather than practical reality, while tax structures and fear of the tax collector often adversely affect data.

Although not unique to them, less developed countries are particularly prone to being both overly optimistic and unreliable in reporting relevant economic data about their countries. China's National Statistics Enforcement Office recently acknowledged that it had uncovered about 60,000 instances of false statistical reports since beginning a crackdown on false data reporting several months earlier.[8] More recently the head of China's National Bureau of Statistics was fired for his involvement in an unfolding corruption scandal.[9] Seeking advantages or hiding failures, local officials, factory managers, rural enterprises, and others file fake numbers on everything from production levels to birthrates. For example, a petrochemical plant reported one year's output to be $20 million, 50 percent higher than its actual output of $13.4 million. Finally, if you believe the statistics, until 2000, the Chinese in Hong Kong were the world-champion consumers of fresh oranges—64 pounds per year per person, twice as much as Americans. However, apparently about half of all the oranges imported into Hong Kong, or some $30 million worth, were actually finding their way into the rest of China, where U.S. oranges were illegal.

Willful errors in the reporting of marketing data are not uncommon in the most industrialized countries either. Often print media circulation figures are purposely overestimated even in OECD countries. The European Union (EU) tax policies can affect the accuracy of reported data also. Production statistics are frequently inaccurate because these countries collect taxes on domestic sales. Thus, some companies shave their production statistics a bit to match the sales reported to tax authorities. Conversely, foreign trade statistics may be blown up slightly because each country in the European Union grants some form of export subsidy. Knowledge of such "adjusted reporting" is critical for a marketer who relies on secondary data for forecasting or estimating market demand.

Comparability of Data

LO3

Sources of secondary data

Comparability of available data is the third shortcoming faced by foreign marketers. In the United States, current sources of reliable and valid estimates of socioeconomic factors and business indicators are readily available. In other countries, especially those less developed, data can be many years out of date as well as having been collected on an infrequent and unpredictable schedule. Naturally, the rapid change in socioeconomic features being experienced in many of these countries makes the problem of currency a vital one. Furthermore, even though many countries are now gathering reliable data, there are generally no historical series with which to compare the current information. Comparability of data can even be a problem when the best commercial research firms collect data across countries, and managers are well advised to query their vendors about this problem.

A related problem is the manner in which data are collected and reported. Too frequently, data are reported in different categories or in categories much too broad to be of specific value. The term *supermarket*, for example, has a variety of meanings around the world. In Japan a supermarket is quite different from its American counterpart. Japanese supermarkets usually occupy two- or three-story structures; they sell foodstuffs, daily necessities, and clothing on respective floors. Some even sell furniture, electric home appliances, stationery, and sporting goods; some have a restaurant. General merchandise stores, shopping centers, and department stores are different from stores of the same name in the United States.

Validating Secondary Data

The shortcomings discussed here should be considered when using any source of information. Many countries have similarly high standards for the collection and preparation of data as those generally found in the United States, but secondary data from any source, including the United States, must be checked and interpreted carefully. As a practical matter, the following questions should be asked to effectively judge the reliability of secondary data sources:

1. Who collected the data? Would there be any reason for purposely misrepresenting the facts?
2. For what purposes were the data collected?
3. How (by what methodology) were the data collected?
4. Are the data internally consistent and logical in light of known data sources or market factors?

---

[8]Mark L. Clifford, "How Fast Is China Really Growing?" *BusinessWeek*, March 10, 2003, p. 65; "The Art of the Chinese Massage," *The Economist*, May 23, 2009, p. 82.

[9]"Chinese Statistics Chief Fired in Scandal Inquiry," *International Herald Tribune*, October 20, 2006, p. 3.

Checking the consistency of one set of secondary data with other data of known validity is an effective and often-used way of judging validity. For example, a researcher might check the sale of baby products with the number of women of childbearing age and birthrates, or the number of patient beds in hospitals with the sale of related hospital equipment. Such correlations can also be useful in estimating demand and forecasting sales. As is the case with many data sets, Hofstede's well-worn data sets described in Chapters 4 and 5 have proven valid vis-à-vis a variety of dependent variables, and it is still worthwhile to compare his measures of cultural values to other measures of the same variables.[10]

In general, the availability and accuracy of recorded secondary data increase as the level of economic development increases. There are exceptions; India is at a lower level of economic development than many countries but has accurate and relatively complete government-collected data.

Fortunately, interest in collecting high-quality statistical data rises as countries realize the value of extensive and accurate national statistics for orderly economic growth. This interest in improving the quality of national statistics has resulted in remarkable improvement in the availability of data over the last 25 years. However, when no data are available or the secondary data sources are inadequate, it is necessary to begin the collection of primary data.

The appendix to this chapter includes a comprehensive listing of secondary data sources, including Web sites on a variety of international marketing topics. Indeed, almost all secondary data available on international markets can now be discovered or acquired via the Internet. For example, the most comprehensive statistics regarding international finances, demographics, consumption, exports, and imports are accessible through a single source, the U.S. Department of Commerce at www.stat-usa.gov. Many other governmental, institutional, and commercial sources of data can be tapped into on the Internet as well. You can find supplementary information about this text at www.mhhe.com/cateora15e.

Gathering Primary Data: Quantitative and Qualitative Research

LO4

Quantitative and qualitative research methods

If, after seeking all reasonable secondary data sources, research questions are still not adequately answered, the market researcher must collect **primary data**—that is, data collected specifically for the particular research project at hand. The researcher may question the firm's sales representatives, distributors, middlemen, and/or customers to get appropriate market information. Marketing research methods can be grouped into two basic types: quantitative and qualitative research. In both methods, the marketer is interested in gaining knowledge about the market.

In *quantitative research*, usually a large number of respondents are asked to reply either verbally or in writing to structured questions using a specific response format (such as yes/no) or to select a response from a set of choices. Questions are designed to obtain specific responses regarding aspects of the respondents' behavior, intentions, attitudes, motives, and demographic characteristics. Quantitative research provides the marketer with responses that can be presented with precise estimations. The structured responses received in a survey can be summarized in percentages, averages, or other statistics. For example, 76 percent of the respondents prefer product A over product B, and so on. Survey research is generally associated with quantitative research, and the typical instrument used is a questionnaire administered by personal interview, mail, telephone, and, most recently, over the Internet.

Scientific studies, including tightly designed experiments, often are conducted by engineers and chemists in product-testing laboratories around the world. There, product designs and formulas are developed and tested in consumer usage situations. Often those results are integrated with consumer opinions gathered in concurrent survey studies. One of the best

---

[10]Linhui Tang and Peter E. Koveos, "A Framework to Update Hofstede's Cultural Values Indices: Economic Dynamics and Institutional Stability," *Journal of International Business Studies* 39, no. 6 (2008), pp. 1045–64; Robbert Maseland and Andre van Hoorn, "Explaining the Negative Correlation between Values and Practices: A Note on the Hofstede-GLOBE Debate," *Journal of International Business Studies* 40, no. 3 (2009), pp. 527–32.

examples of this kind of marketing research comes from Tokyo. You may not know it, but the Japanese are the world champions of bathroom and toilet technology. Japan's biggest company in that industry, Toto, has spent millions of dollars developing and testing consumer products. Thousands of people have collected data (using survey techniques) about the best features of a toilet, and at the company's "human engineering laboratory," volunteers sit in a Toto bathtub with electrodes strapped to their skulls to measure brain waves and "the effects of bathing on the human body." Toto is now introducing one of its high-tech (actually low-tech compared with what it offers in Japan) toilets in the U.S. market. It's a $600 seat, lid, and control panel that attaches to the regular American bowl. It features a heated seat and deodorizing fan.

In *qualitative research*, if questions are asked, they are almost always open-ended or in-depth, and unstructured responses that reflect the person's thoughts and feelings on the subject are sought. Consumers' first impressions about products may be useful. Direct observation of consumers in choice or product usage situations is another important qualitative approach to marketing research. One researcher spent two months observing birthing practices in American and Japanese hospitals to gain insights into the export of healthcare services. Nissan Motors sent a researcher to live with an American family (renting a room in their house for six weeks) to directly observe how Americans use their cars. Most recently the British retailer TESCO sent teams to live with American families to observe their shopping behaviors in advance of its new entry in the U.S. supermarket battleground with Walmart and others.[11] Anderson Worldwide, Nynex, and Texas Commerce Bank have all employed anthropologists who specialize in observational and in-depth interviews in their marketing research. Qualitative research seeks to interpret what the people in the sample are like—their outlooks, their feelings, the dynamic interplay of their feelings and ideas, their attitudes and opinions, and their resulting actions. The most often used form of qualitative questioning is the focus group interview. However, oftentimes, in-depth interviewing of individuals can be just as effective while consuming far fewer resources.

Qualitative research is used in international marketing research to formulate and define a problem more clearly and to determine relevant questions to be examined in subsequent research. It is also used to stimulate ad message ideas and where interest centers on gaining an understanding of a market rather than quantifying relevant aspects. For example, a small group of key executives at Solar Turbines International, a division of Caterpillar Tractor Company, called on key customers at their offices around the world. They discussed in great depth, with both financial managers and production engineers, potential applications and the demand for a new size of gas-turbine engine the company was considering developing. The data and insights gained during the interviews to a large degree confirmed the validity of the positive demand forecasts produced internally through macroeconomic modeling. The multimillion-dollar project was then implemented. During the discussions, new product features were suggested by the customer personnel that proved most useful in the development efforts.

Qualitative research is also helpful in revealing the impact of sociocultural factors on behavior patterns and in developing research hypotheses that can be tested in subsequent studies designed to quantify the concepts and relevant relationships uncovered in qualitative data collection. Procter & Gamble has been one of the pioneers of this type of research—the company has systematically gathered consumer feedback for some 70 years. It was the first company to conduct in-depth consumer research in China. In the mid-1990s, P&G began working with the Chinese Ministry of Health to develop dental hygiene programs that have now reached millions there.

Oftentimes the combination of qualitative and quantitative research proves quite useful in consumer markets and business-to-business marketing settings as well. In one study, the number of personal referrals used in buying financial services in Japan was found to be much greater than that in the United States.[12] The various comments made by the executives during interviews in both countries proved invaluable in interpreting the quantitative

[11]Cecillie Rohwedder, "Tesco Studies Hard for U.S. Debut," *The Wall Street Journal*, June 28, 2007, pp. B1, B2.

[12]R. Bruce Money, "Word-of-Mouth Referral Sources for Buyers of International Corporate Financial Services," *Journal of World Business* 35, no. 3 (Fall 2000), pp. 314–29.

results, suggesting implications for managers and providing ideas for further research. Likewise, the comments of sales managers in Tokyo during in-depth interviews helped researchers understand why individual financial incentives did not work with Japanese sales representatives.[13]

As we shall see later in this chapter, using either research method in international marketing research is subject to a number of difficulties brought about by the diversity of cultures and languages encountered.

Problems of Gathering Primary Data

The problems of collecting primary data in foreign countries are different only in degree from those encountered in the United States. Assuming the research problem is well defined and the objectives are properly formulated, the success of primary research hinges on the ability of the researcher to get correct and truthful information that addresses the research objectives. Most problems in collecting primary data in international marketing research stem from cultural differences among countries and range from the inability or unwillingness[14] of respondents to communicate their opinions to inadequacies in questionnaire translation.

Ability to Communicate Opinions

The ability to express attitudes and opinions about a product or concept depends on the respondent's ability to recognize the usefulness and value of such a product or concept. It is difficult for a person to formulate needs, attitudes, and opinions about goods whose use may not be understood, that are not in common use within the community, or that have never been available. For example, someone who has never had the benefits of an office computer will be unable to express accurate feelings or provide any reasonable information about purchase intentions, likes, or dislikes concerning a new computer software package. The more complex the concept, the more difficult it is to design research that will help the respondent communicate meaningful opinions and reactions. Under these circumstances, the creative capabilities of the international marketing researcher are challenged.

No company has had more experience in trying to understand consumers with communication limitations than Gerber. Babies may be their business, but babies often can't talk, much less fill out a questionnaire. Over the years, Gerber has found that talking to and observing both infants and their mothers are important in marketing research. In one study, Gerber found that breast-fed babies adapted to solid food more quickly than bottle-fed babies because breast milk changes flavor depending on what the mother has eaten. For example, infants were found to suck longer and harder if their mother had recently eaten garlic. In another study, weaning practices were studied around the world. Indian babies were offered lentils served on a finger. Some Nigerian children got fermented sorghum, fed by the grandmother through the funnel of her hand. In some parts of tropical Asia, mothers "food-kissed" prechewed vegetables into their babies' mouths. Hispanic mothers in the United States tend to introduce baby food much earlier than non-Hispanic mothers and continue it well beyond the first year. All this research helps the company decide which products are appropriate for which markets. For example, the Vegetable and Rabbit Meat and the Freeze-Dried Sardines and Rice flavors popular in Poland and Japan, respectively, most likely won't make it to American store shelves.

Willingness to Respond

Cultural differences offer the best explanation for the unwillingness or the inability of many to respond to research surveys. The role of the male, the suitability of personal gender-based inquiries, and other gender-related issues can affect willingness to respond.

In some countries, the husband not only earns the money but also dictates exactly how it is to be spent. Because the husband controls the spending, it is he, not the wife, who should

---

[13]R. Bruce Money and John L. Graham, "Sales Person Performance, Pay, and Job Satisfaction: Tests of a Model Using Data Collected in the U.S. and Japan," *Journal of International Business Studies* 30, no. 1 (1999), pp. 149–72.

[14]Fang Wu, Rudolf R. Sinkovics, S. Tamer Cavusgil, and Anthony S. Roath, "Overcoming Export Manufacturers' Dilemma in International Expansion," *Journal of International Business Studies* 38 (2007), pp. 283–302.

be questioned to determine preferences and demand for many consumer goods. In some countries, women would never consent to be interviewed by a man or a stranger. A French Canadian woman does not like to be questioned and is likely to be reticent in her responses. In some societies, a man would certainly consider it beneath his dignity to discuss shaving habits or brand preference in personal clothing with anyone—most emphatically not a female interviewer.

Anyone asking questions about any topic from which tax assessment could be inferred is immediately suspected of being a tax agent. Citizens of many countries do not feel the same legal and moral obligations to pay their taxes as do U.S. citizens. Tax evasion is thus an accepted practice for many and a source of pride for the more adept. Where such an attitude exists, taxes are often seemingly arbitrarily assessed by the government, which results in much incomplete or misleading information being reported. One of the problems revealed by the government of India in a recent population census was the underreporting of tenants by landlords trying to hide the actual number of people living in houses and flats. The landlords had been subletting accommodations illegally and were concealing their activities from the tax department.

In the United States, publicly held corporations are compelled by the Securities and Exchange Commission (SEC) to disclose certain operating figures on a periodic basis. In many European countries, however, such information is seldom if ever released and then most reluctantly. For example, in Germany attempts to enlist the cooperation of merchants in setting up an in-store study of shelf inventory and sales information ran into strong resistance because of suspicions and a tradition of competitive secrecy. The resistance was overcome by the researcher's willingness to approach the problem step by step. As the retailer gained confidence in the researcher and realized the value of the data gathered, more and more requested information was provided. Besides the reluctance of businesses to respond to surveys, local politicians in underdeveloped countries may interfere with studies in the belief that they could be subversive and must be stopped or hindered. A few moments with local politicians can prevent days of delay.

Although such cultural differences may make survey research more difficult to conduct, it is possible. In some communities, locally prominent people could open otherwise closed doors; in other situations, professional people and local students have been used as interviewers because of their knowledge of the market. Less direct measurement techniques and nontraditional data analysis methods may also be more appropriate. In one study, Japanese supermarket buyers rated the nationality of brands (foreign or domestic) as relatively unimportant in making stocking decisions when asked directly; however, when an indirect,

Midnight in New Delhi—both customer service and telephone survey research are being outsourced to lower-wage English-speaking countries. Cost savings of such outsourcing must be balanced with consumer reluctance in cross-cultural communication settings, particularly those involving voluntary responses to marketing research.

paired-comparison questioning technique was used, brand nationality proved to be the most important factor.[15]

Sampling in Field Surveys

LO5

Multicultural sampling and its problems in less-developed countries

The greatest problem in sampling stems from the lack of adequate demographic data and available lists from which to draw meaningful samples. If current, reliable lists are not available, sampling becomes more complex and generally less reliable. In many countries, telephone directories, cross-index street directories, census tract and block data, and detailed social and economic characteristics of the population being studied are not available on a current basis, if at all. The researcher has to estimate characteristics and population parameters, sometimes with little basic data on which to build an accurate estimate.

To add to the confusion, in some South American, Mexican, and Asian cities, street maps are unavailable, and in some Asian metropolitan areas, streets are not identified and houses are not numbered. In contrast, one of the positive aspects of research in Japan and Taiwan is the availability and accuracy of census data on individuals. In these countries, when a household moves, it is required to submit up-to-date information to a centralized government agency before it can use communal services such as water, gas, electricity, and education.

The effectiveness of various methods of communication (mail, telephone, personal interview, and Internet) in surveys is limited. In many countries, telephone ownership is extremely low, making telephone surveys virtually worthless unless the survey is intended to cover only the wealthy. In Sri Lanka, fewer than 19 percent of the residents have landline telephones and less than 7 percent Internet access—that is, only the wealthy.

The adequacy of sampling techniques is also affected by a lack of detailed social and economic information. Without an age breakdown of the total population, for example, the researcher can never be certain of a representative sample requiring an age criterion, because there is no basis of comparison for the age distribution in the sample. A lack of detailed information, however, does not prevent the use of sampling; it simply makes it more difficult. In place of probability techniques, many researchers in such situations rely on convenience samples taken in marketplaces and other public gathering places.

McDonald's got into trouble over sampling issues. The company was involved in a dispute in South Africa over the rights to its valuable brand name in that fast emerging market. Part of the company's claim revolved around the recall of the McDonald's name among South Africans. In the two surveys the company conducted and provided as proof in the proceedings, the majority of those sampled had heard the company name and could recognize the logo. However, the Supreme Court judge hearing the case took a dim view of the evidence because the surveys were conducted in "posh, white" suburbs, whereas 79 percent of the South African population is black. Based in part on these sampling errors, the judge threw out McDonald's case.

Inadequate mailing lists and poor postal service can be problems for the market researcher using mail to conduct research. For example, in Nicaragua, delays of weeks in delivery are not unusual, and expected returns are lowered considerably because a letter can be mailed only at a post office. In addition to the potentially poor mail service within countries, the extended length of time required for delivery and return when a mail survey is conducted from another country further hampers the use of mail surveys. Although airmail reduces this time drastically, it also increases costs considerably.

Language and Comprehension

The most universal survey research problem in foreign countries is the language barrier. Differences in idiom and the difficulty of exact translation create problems in eliciting the specific information desired and in interpreting the respondents' answers.[16] Types of scales appropriate in some cultures, such as reverse-worded items, are problematic in other cultures.[17] Equivalent

---

[15]Frank Alpert, Michael Kamins, Tomoaki Sakano, Naoto Onzo, and John L. Graham, "Retail Buyer Beliefs, Attitudes, and Behaviors toward Pioneer and Me-Too Follower Brands: A Comparative Study of Japan and the United States," *International Marketing Review* 18, no. 2 (2001), pp. 160–87.

[16]Shi Zhang and Bernd H. Schmitt, "Creating Local Brands in Multilingual International Markets," *Journal of Marketing Research* 38 (August 2001), pp. 313–25.

[17]Nancy Wong, Aric Rindfleisch, and James E. Burroughs, "Do Reverse-Worded Items Confound Measures in Cross-Cultural Research? The Case of the Material Values Scale," *Journal of Consumer Research* 30, no. 1 (June 2003), pp. 72–91.

CROSSING BORDERS 8.2   French Is Special

The word on the table that morning was "cloud computing."

To translate the English term for computing resources that can be accessed on demand on the Internet, a group of French experts had spent 18 months coming up with *informatique en nuage*, which literally means "computing in cloud." France's General Commission of Terminology and Neology—a 17-member group of professors, linguists, scientists, and a former ambassador—had gathered in a building overlooking the Louvre to approve the term.

Keeping the French language relevant isn't easy in the Internet age. For years, French bureaucrats have worked hard to keep French up to date by diligently coming up with equivalents for English terms. Although most French people say "le weekend" and "un surfer," the correct translations of the terms are *fin de semaine* ("end of the week") and *aquaplanchiste* ("water boarder"—which makes one wonder what term they use for that kind of torture). A start-up company is referred to as *jeune pousse*, or young shoot (the term *pousse* refers to vegetable sprouts), and the World Wide Web is translated as *toile d'araignée mondiale* (literally, global spider web).

But technological advancements mean new Anglicisms are spreading over the Internet at warp speed, leaving the French scratching their heads. Before a word such as "cloud computing" or "podcasting" (*diffusion pour baladeur*) receives a certified French equivalent, it needs to be approved by three organizations and get a government minister's seal of approval, according to rules laid out by the state's General Delegation for the French Language and the Languages of France. The process can be a linguistic odyssey taking years. "Rigor cannot be compromised," said Xavier North, the 57-year-old civil servant who heads the General Delegation.

On its Web site, the General Delegation for the French Language reminds French citizens that the terms beach volleyball, beach tennis, and beach hockey are not always correct. As these sports are becoming more popular, "they are often taking place . . . in arenas," the General Delegation states. As these sports don't necessarily take place on beaches, the word beach should be replaced with "on sand (*sur sable*). Hence, the terms hockey *sur sable*, tennis *sur sable*, and volley *sur sable* are recommended by the General Commission of Terminology and Neology.

The French have achieved some success in their efforts. A recent study of language selection policies of the International Electrotechnical Commission (IEC) members reports, "Results show that the English and French languages are moderately used for technical work while the English language is purely used for communication." Of course, we are not sure what the sentence quoted actually means, so we do not know how heartily to congratulate the French officials!

Source: Max Colchester, "The French Get Lost in the Clouds over a New Term in the Internet Age," *The Wall Street Journal*, October 14, 2009; Hans Teichmann, "Language Selection Policies in International Standardization: Perceptions of the IEC Member Countries," *International Journal of IT Standards & Standardization Research* 7, no. 2 (2009), pp. 23–42.

concepts may not exist in all languages. Family, for example, has different connotations in different countries. In the United States, it generally means only the parents and children. In Italy and many Latin countries, it could mean the parents, children, grandparents, uncles, aunts, cousins, and so forth. The meaning of names for family members can differ too, depending on the context within which they are used. In the Italian culture, the words for aunt and uncle are different for the maternal and paternal sides of the family. The concept of affection is a universal idea, but the manner in which it is manifested in each culture may differ. Kissing, an expression of affection in the West, is alien to many Eastern cultures and even taboo in some.

Literacy poses yet another problem. In some less developed countries with low literacy rates, written questionnaires are completely useless. Within countries, too, the problem of dialects and different languages can make a national questionnaire survey impractical. In India, there are 14 official languages and considerably more unofficial ones. One researcher has used pictures of products as stimuli and pictures of faces as response criteria in a study of eastern German brand preferences to avoid some of the difficulties associated with language differences and literacy in international research. Still others have used other nonverbal kinds of response elicitation techniques, such as pictures and collages.[18]

---

[18]Gerald Zaltman, "Rethinking Marketing Research: Putting the People Back In," *Journal of Marketing Research* 34 (November 1997), pp. 424–37.

Marketing researchers in India have to consider the problems of language diversity. Here the primary 13 languages (besides English) are listed on a 20-rupee note.

Furthermore, a researcher cannot assume that a translation into one language will suffice in all areas where that language is spoken. For example, a researcher in Mexico requested a translation of the word *outlet*, as in *retail outlet*, to be used in Venezuela. It was read by Venezuelans to mean an electrical outlet, an outlet of a river into an ocean, and the passageway into a patio. Of course the responses were useless—though interesting. Thus, it will always be necessary for a native speaker of the target country's language to take the "final cut" of any translated material.

In all countries all marketing communications, including research questionnaires, must be written *perfectly*. If not, consumers and customers will not respond with accuracy, or even at all. The obvious solution of having questionnaires prepared or reviewed by a native speaker of the language of the country is frequently overlooked. Even excellent companies such as American Airlines bring errors into their measurement of customer satisfaction by using the same questionnaire in Spanish for their surveys of passengers on routes to Spain and Mexico. A question regarding meal preferences, for example, may cause confusion because to a Spaniard, orange juice is *zumo de naranja*, while a Mexican would order *jugo de naranja*. These apparently subtle differences are no such things to Spanish speakers. Marketers use three different techniques, back translation, parallel translation, and decentering, to help ferret out translation errors ahead of time.

Back Translation. In back translation, the questionnaire is translated from one language to another, and then a second party translates it back into the original, and the two original language versions are compared. This process often pinpoints misinterpretations and misunderstandings before they reach the public. In one study regarding advertising themes, a soft-drink company wanted to use a very successful Australian advertising theme, "Baby, it's cold inside," in Hong Kong. It had the theme translated from English into Cantonese by one translator and then retranslated by another from Cantonese into English, in which the statement came out as "Small mosquito, on the inside it is very cold." Although "small mosquito" is the colloquial expression for "small child" in Hong Kong, the intended meaning was lost in translation.

Parallel Translation. Back translations may not always ensure an accurate translation because of commonly used idioms in both languages. Parallel translation is used to overcome this problem. In this process, more than two translators are used for the back translation; the results are compared, differences discussed, and the most appropriate translation selected. Most recently, researchers have suggested augmenting this process by integrating pretesting steps and iteratively adapting the translations.[19]

Decentering. A third alternative, known as decentering, is a hybrid of back translation. It is a successive process of translation and retranslation of a questionnaire, each time

---

[19]Susan P. Douglas and C. Samuel Craig, "Collaborative and Iterative Translation: An Alternative Approach to Back Translation," *Journal of International Marketing* 15, no. 1 (2007), pp. 30–43.

The complexities of the Japanese language confront second graders in Kyoto, where students write some of the 200-plus characters for the sound *shou*. The language commonly uses 15,000 kanji characters, which are borrowed from Chinese. The differences in the structure of the language from English make translation of questionnaires a most daunting task.

by a different translator. For example, an English version is translated into French and then translated back to English by a different translator. The two English versions are compared, and where there are differences, the original English version is modified and the process is repeated. If there are still differences between the two English versions, the original English version of the second iteration is modified, and the process of translation and back translation is repeated. The process continues to be repeated until an English version can be translated into French and back translated, by a different translator, into the same English. In this process, the wording of the original instrument undergoes a change, and the version that is finally used and its translation have equally comprehensive and equivalent terminologies in both languages.

Regardless of the procedure used, proper translation and the *perfect* use of the local language in a questionnaire are of critical importance to successful research design. Because of cultural and national differences, confusion can just as well be the problem of the researcher as of the respondent. The question itself may not be properly worded in the English version, or English slang or abbreviated words may be translated with a different or ambiguous meaning. Such was the case mentioned earlier with the word *outlet* for *retail outlet*. The problem was not with the translation as much as with the term used in the question to be translated. In writing questions for translation, it is important that precise terms, not colloquialisms or slang, be used in the original to be translated. One classic misunderstanding that occurred in a *Reader's Digest* study of consumer behavior in western Europe resulted in a report that France and Germany consumed more spaghetti than did Italy. This rather curious and erroneous finding resulted from questions that asked about purchases of "packaged and branded spaghetti." Italians buy their spaghetti in bulk; the French and Germans buy branded and packaged spaghetti. Because of this crucial difference, the results underreported spaghetti purchases by Italians. Had the goal of the research been to determine how much branded and packaged spaghetti was purchased, the results would have been correct. However, because the goal was to know about total spaghetti consumption, the data were incorrect. Researchers must always verify that they are asking the right question.

Some of the problems of cross-cultural marketing research can be addressed after data have been collected. For example, we know that consumers in some countries such as Japan tend to respond to rating scales more conservatively than Americans. That is, on a 1 to 7 scale anchored by "extremely satisfied" and "extremely dissatisfied," Japanese tend to answer more toward the middle (more 3s and 5s), whereas Americans' responses tend toward the extremes (more 1s and 7s). Such a response bias can be managed through statistical standardization procedures to maximize comparability.[20] Some translation problems can be detected and mitigated post hoc through other statistical approaches as well.[21]

[20]Hans Baumgartner and Jan-Benedict E. M. Steenkamp, "Response Styles in Marketing Research: A Cross-National Investigation," *Journal of Marketing Research* 38 (May 2001), pp. 143–56; Martijin G. De Jong, Jan-Benedict E. M. Steenkamp, Jean-Paul Fox, and Hans Baumgartner, "Using Item Response Theory to Measure Extreme Response Style in Marketing Research: A Global Investigation," *Journal of Marketing Research* 45, no. 1 (2008), pp. 260–78.

[21]S. Durvasula, R. G. Netemeyer, J. C. Andrews, and S. Lysonski, "Examining the Cross-National Applicability of Multi-Item, Multi-Dimensional Measures Using Generalizability Theory," *Journal of International Business Studies* 37 (2006), pp. 469–83; Martijin G. De Jong, Jan-Benedict E. M. Steenkamp, and Jean-Paul Fox, "Relaxing Measurement Invariance in Cross-National Consumer Research Using a Hierarchical IRT Model," *Journal of Consumer Research* 34 (2007), pp. 260–72; Yi He, Michael A. Merz, and Dana L. Alden, "Diffusion of Measurement Invariance Assessment in Cross-National Empirical Marketing Research: Perspectives from the Literature and a Survey of Researchers," *Journal of International Marketing* 16, no. 2 (2008), pp. 64–83; Martijn G. de Jong, Jan-Benedict E. M. Steenkamp, and Bernard P. Veldkamp, "A Model for the Construction of Country-Specific Yet Internationally Comparable Short-Form Marketing Scales," *Marketing Science* 29, no. 4 (2009), pp. 674–89.

Multicultural Research: A Special Problem

As companies become global marketers and seek to standardize various parts of the marketing mix across several countries, multicultural studies become more important. A company needs to determine to what extent adaptation of the marketing mix is appropriate.[22] Thus, market characteristics across diverse cultures must be compared for similarities and differences before a company proceeds with standardization on any aspect of marketing strategy. The research difficulties discussed thus far have addressed problems of conducting research within a culture. When engaging in multicultural studies, many of these same problems further complicate the difficulty of cross-cultural comparisons.[23]

Multicultural research involves countries that have different languages, economies, social structures, behavior, and attitude patterns. When designing multicultural studies, it is essential that these differences be taken into account.[24] An important point to keep in mind when designing research to be applied across cultures is to ensure comparability and equivalency of results. Different methods may have varying reliabilities in different countries. Such differences may mean that different research methods should be applied in individual countries.

In some cases, the entire research design may have to be different between countries to maximize the comparability of the results. For example, in Latin American countries, it may be difficult to attract consumers to participate in either focus groups or in-depth interviews because of different views about commercial research and the value of their time. And Japanese, compared with American businesspeople, tend not to respond to mail surveys. The latter problem was handled in two recent studies by using alternative methods of questionnaire distribution and collection in Japan. In one study, attitudes of retail buyers regarding pioneer brands were sought. In the U.S. setting, a sample was drawn from a national list of supermarket buyers, and questionnaires were distributed and collected by mail. Alternatively, in Japan, the questionnaires were distributed through contact people at 16 major supermarket chains and then returned by mail directly to the Japanese researchers. The second study sought to compare the job satisfaction of American and Japanese sales representatives. The questionnaires were delivered and collected via the company mail system for the U.S. firm. For the Japanese firm, participants in a sales training program were asked to complete the questionnaires during the program. Although the authors of both studies suggest that the use of different methods of data collection in comparative studies threatens the quality of the results, the approaches taken were the best (only) practical methods of conducting the research.

The adaptations necessary to complete these cross-national studies serve as examples of the need for resourcefulness in international marketing research. However, they also raise serious questions about the reliability of data gathered in cross-national research. Evidence suggests that often insufficient attention is given not only to nonsampling errors and other problems that can exist in improperly conducted multicultural studies but also to the appropriateness of research measures that have not been tested in multicultural contexts.

Research on the Internet: A Growing Opportunity

To keep up with the worldwide growth in Internet use is literally impossible. We know that at this writing, there are more than 1.8 billion users in more than 200 countries. About one-sixth of the users are in the United States, but more than half of the hosts are there. The fastest growing market for the Internet is now China, with 375 million users at last count.[25] International Internet use is growing almost

---

[22]Amanda J. Broderick, Gordon E. Greenley, and Rene Dentiste Mueller, "The Behavioral Homogeneity Evaluation Framework: Multi-Level Evaluations of Consumer Involvement in International Segmentation," *Journal of International Business Studies* 38 (2007), pp. 746–63.

[23]Masaski Kotabe, "Contemporary Research Trends in International Marketing," in *Oxford Handbook of International Business*, 2nd edition, ed. Alan Rugman (Oxford: Oxford University Press, 2009), Chapter 17.

[24]James Reardon, Chip Miller, Bram Foubert, Irena Vida, and Liza Rybina, "Antismoking Messages for the International Teenage Segment: The Effectiveness of Message Valence and Intensity across Different Cultures," *Journal of International Marketing* 14, no. 3 (2006), pp. 114–36.

[25]Euromonitor.com, 2010.

twice as fast as American use. Growth in countries such as Costa Rica was dramatically spurred by the local government's decision to reclassify computers as "educational tools," thus eliminating all import tariffs on the hardware. The demographics of users worldwide are as follows: 60 percent male and 40 percent female; average age about 32 years; about 60 percent college educated; median income of about $60,000; usage time about 2.5 hours per week; and main activities of e-mail and finding information. The percentage of home pages by language is as follows: English, 80 percent; Japanese, 4 percent; German, 3 percent; French, 2 percent; Spanish, 1 percent; and all others less than 1 percent each.

For many companies, the Internet provides a new and increasingly important medium for conducting a variety of international marketing research. Indeed, a survey of marketing research professionals suggests that the most important influences on the industry are the Internet and globalization. New product concepts and advertising copy can be tested over the Internet for immediate feedback. Worldwide consumer panels[26] have been created to help test marketing programs across international samples. It has been suggested that there are at least eight different uses for the Internet in international research:

1. **Online surveys and buyer panels.** These can include incentives for participation, and they have better "branching" capabilities (asking different questions based on previous answers) than more expensive mail and phone surveys.

2. **Online focus groups.** Bulletin boards can be used for this purpose.

3. **Web visitor tracking.** Servers automatically track and time visitors' travel through Web sites.

4. **Advertising measurement.** Servers track links to other sites, and their usefulness can therefore be assessed.

5. **Customer identification systems.** Many companies are installing registration procedures that allow them to track visits and purchases over time, creating a "virtual panel."

6. **E-mail marketing lists.** Customers can be asked to sign up on e-mail lists to receive future direct marketing efforts via the Internet.

7. **Embedded research.** The Internet continues to automate traditional economic roles of customers, such as searching for information about products and services, comparison shopping among alternatives, interacting with service providers, and maintaining the customer–brand relationship. More and more of these Internet processes look and feel like research processes themselves. The methods are often embedded directly into the actual purchase and use situations and therefore are more closely tied to actual economic behavior than traditional research methods. Some firms even provide the option of custom designing products online—the ultimate in applying research for product development purposes.

8. **Observational research (also known as netnography).** Chat rooms, blogs, and personal Web sites can all be systematically monitored to assess consumers' opinions about products and services.

Clearly, as the Internet continues to grow, even more types of research will become feasible, and the extent to which new translation software has an impact on marketing communications and research over the Internet will be quite interesting to watch. Some companies now provide translation services for questionnaires, including commonly used phrases such as "rate your satisfaction level."[27] Surveys in multiple languages can be produced quickly, given the translation libraries now available from some application service providers. Finally, as is the case in so many international marketing contexts, privacy is and will continue to be a matter of personal and legal considerations. A vexing challenge facing international marketers will be the cross-cultural concerns about privacy and the enlistment of cooperative consumer and customer groups.

---

[26]Information regarding worldwide Internet panels is available at http://www.decisionanalyst.com.

[27]See, for example, http://www.markettools.com.

The ability to conduct primary research is one of the exciting aspects about the Internet. However, the potential bias of a sample universe composed solely of Internet respondents presents some severe limitations, and firms vary substantially in their abilities to turn data collected into competitive advantages.[28] Nevertheless, as more of the general population in countries gain access to the Internet, this tool will be all the more powerful and accurate for conducting primary research. Also, the Internet can be used as one of several methods of collecting data, offering more flexibility across countries.

Today the real power of the Internet for international marketing research is the ability to easily access volumes of secondary data. These data have been available in print form for years, but now they are much easier to access and, in many cases, are more current. Instead of leafing through reference books to find two- or three-year-old data, as is the case with most printed sources, you can often find up-to-date data on the Internet. Such Internet sites as www.stat-usa.gov provide almost all data that are published by the U.S. government. If you want to know the quantity of a specific product being shipped to a country, the import duties on a product, and whether an export license is required, it's all there, via your computer. A variety of private firms also provide international marketing information online. See the Appendix of this chapter for more detail.

Estimating Market Demand

The unprecedented events of the crash in world trade during 2009 have yielded a scary variety of headlines facing international forecasters—"What Went Wrong with Economics?" "Managing in the Fog," and "Strategic Plans Lose Favor" to name just a few.[29] In assessing current product demand and forecasting future demand, reliable historical data are required.[30] As previously noted, the quality and availability of secondary data frequently are inadequate; nevertheless, estimates of market size must be attempted to plan effectively. Despite limitations, some approaches to demand estimation are usable with minimum information. The success of these approaches relies on the ability of the researcher to find meaningful substitutes or approximations for the needed economic, geographic, and demographic relationships.

When the desired statistics are not available, a close approximation can be made using local production figures plus imports, with adjustments for exports and current inventory levels. These data are more readily available because they are commonly reported by the United Nations and other international agencies. Once approximations for sales trends are established, historical series can be used as the basis for projections of growth. In any straight extrapolation however, the estimator assumes that the trends of the immediate past will continue into the future. This assumption can be problematic when the pertinent past has included a major unique event, positive or negative, such as the 2009 crash in world trade.[31] In a rapidly developing economy, extrapolated figures may not reflect rapid growth and must be adjusted accordingly. Given the greater uncertainties and data limitations associated with foreign markets, two methods of forecasting demand are particularly suitable for international marketers: expert opinion and analogy.

Expert Opinion

For many market estimation problems, particularly in foreign countries that are new to the marketer, **expert opinion** is advisable. In this method, experts are polled for their opinions about market size and growth rates. Such experts may be the companies' own sales managers or outside consultants and government officials. The key in using expert opinion to

---

[28]Tho D. Nguyen and Nigel J. Barrett, "The Knowledge-Creating Role of the Internet in International Business: Evidence from Vietnam," *Journal of International Marketing* 14, no. 2 (2006), pp. 116–47.

[29]"What Went Wrong with Economics?" *The Economist*, July 18, 2009, pp. 11–12; "Managing in the Fog," *The Economist*, February 28, 2009, pp. 67–68; Joann S. Lublin and Dana Mattioli, "Strategic Plans Lose Favor," *The New York Times*, January 25, 2010, p. B7.

[30]Although more than 20 years old, still the best summary of forecasting methods and their advantages, disadvantages, and appropriate applications is David M. Georgoff and Robert G. Murdick, "Manager's Guide to Forecasting," *Harvard Business Review*, January–February 1986, pp. 110–20.

[31]Don E. Schultz, "Is This the Death of Data," *Marketing News*, September 15, 2009, p. 19.

help forecast demand is **triangulation**, that is, comparing estimates produced by different sources. One of the tricky parts is how best to combine the different opinions.

Developing scenarios is useful in the most ambiguous forecasting situations, such as predicting demand for accounting services in emerging markets such as China and Russia or trying to predict the impact of SARS on tourism to Hong Kong. Moreover, statistical analyses of past data are fundamentally weak, because they cannot capture the potential impacts of extreme events[32] such as SARS. Experts with broad perspectives and long experience in markets will be better able to anticipate such major threats to stability and/or growth of market demand.

Analogy   Another technique is to estimate by **analogy**. This method assumes that demand for a product develops in much the same way in all countries, as comparable economic development occurs in each country.[33] First, a relationship must be established between the item to be estimated and a measurable variable[34] in a country that is to serve as the basis for the analogy. Once a known relationship is established, the estimator attempts to draw an analogy between the known situation and the country in question. For example, suppose a company wanted to estimate the market growth potential for a beverage in country X, for which it had inadequate sales figures, but the company had excellent beverage data for neighboring country Y. In country Y, per capita consumption is known to increase at a predictable ratio as per capita gross domestic product (GDP) increases. If per capita GDP is known for country X, per capita consumption for the beverage can be estimated using the relationships established in country Y.

Caution must be used with analogy though because the method assumes that factors other than the variable used (in the preceding example, GDP) are similar in both countries, such as the same tastes, taxes, prices, selling methods, availability of products, consumption patterns,[35] and so forth. For example, the 13 million WAP (Wireless Access Protocol) users in Japan led to a serious overestimation of WAP adoptions in Europe—the actual figure of 2 million was less than the 10 million forecasted. Or consider the relevance of the adoption rate of personal computers or cell phones in the Unites States as they help predict adoption rates in the other four countries listed in Exhibit 8.1. How might Apple Computer use the American data to help predict demand in Japan? Despite the apparent drawbacks to analogy, it can be useful when data are limited.

All the methods for market demand estimation described in this section are no substitute for original market research when it is economically feasible and time permits. Indeed, the best approach to forecasting is almost always a *combination* of macroeconomic database approaches and interviews with potential and current customers. Triangulation of alternative approaches is always best, and the discussion of discrepancies across sources and methods can raise important questions about current and future forecasting efforts.[36] As adequate data sources become available, as would be the situation in most of the economically

---

[32]Pierpaolo Andriani and Bill McKelvey, "Beyond Gaussian Averages: Redirecting International Business and Management Research toward Extreme Events and Power Laws," *Journal of International Business Studies* 38 (2007), pp. 1212–30.

[33]Such an approach is now being used to predict the depth of the housing market decline in the United States and other markets by making comparisons to the housing boom–bust cycle experienced by Japan in the 1980s and 1990s. See Robert J. Shiller, "Things that Go Boom," *The Wall Street Journal*, February 8, 2007, p. A15.

[34]These variables may include population and other demographics or usage rates or estimates, and so forth. Using combinations of such variables is also referred to as a *chain-ratio* approach to forecasting.

[35]Gerard J. Tellis, Stefan Stremerch, and Eden Yin, "The International Takeoff of New Products: The Role of Economics, Culture, and Country Innovativeness," *Marketing Science* 22, no. 2 (2003), pp. 188–208; Sean Dwyer, Hani Mesak, and Maxwell Hsu, "An Exploratory Examination of the Influence of National Culture on Cross-National Product Diffusion," *Journal of International Marketing* 13, no. 2 (2005), pp. 1–27; Roger J. Calantone, David A. Griffith, and Goksel Yalcinkaya, "An Empirical Examination of a Technology Adoption Model for the Context of China," *Journal of International Marketing* 14, no. 4 (2006), pp. 1–27.

[36]A.N.M. Waheeduzzaman, "Market Potential Estimation in International Markets: A Comparison of Methods," *Journal of Global Marketing* 21, no. 4 (2008), pp. 307–20.

Exhibit 8.1

(a) Personal Computer and (b) Mobile Phone Diffusion Rate (per 1,000 people)

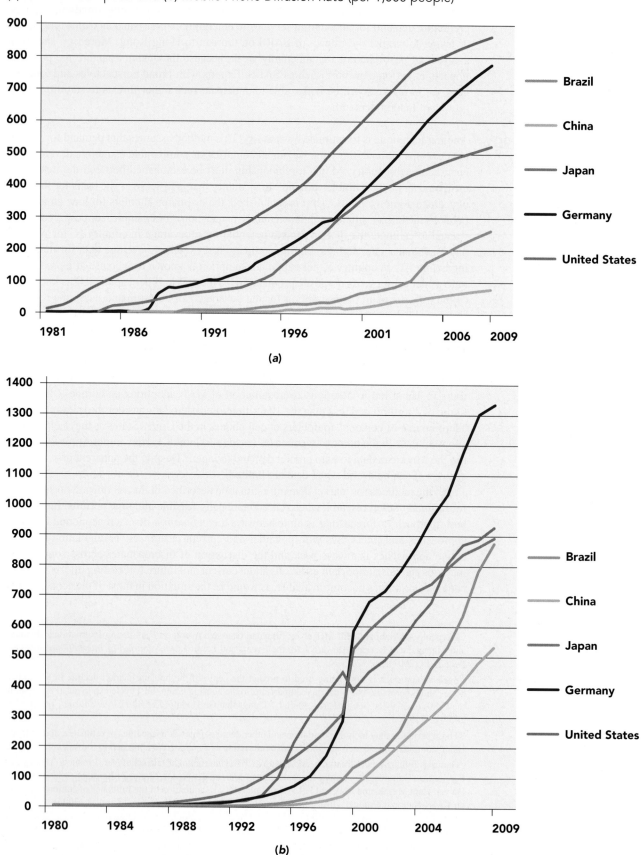

(a)

(b)

Source: World Bank, *World Development Indicators 2010* (Washington, DC: World Bank, 2010); Euromonitor.com, 2010.

CROSSING BORDERS 8.3   Forecasting the Global Healthcare Market

In 2000, Johns Hopkins Hospital in Baltimore treated more than 7,500 patients from foreign countries. That's up from just 600 in 1994. And there were no hassles with insurance companies and HMOs. In fact, many of these patients paid cash—even for $30,000 surgical procedures! The Mayo Clinic in Rochester, Minnesota, has been serving foreigners for decades. The number there has jumped by about 15 percent in five years to more than 1,000 per year. Similar growth is happening in places such as Mount Sinai Hospital in Miami, the University of Texas Cancer Center, and the UCLA Medical Center. The Mayo Clinic has even set up a Muslim prayer room to make patients and their families feel more comfortable. Fast growth, yes (some say exponential), but will it continue? Forecasting this demand so that decisions can be made about staffing and numbers of beds is a daunting project indeed.

Demand in Mexico and Latin America seems to be coming primarily for treatment of infectious and digestive diseases and cancer. Demand from the Middle East stems more from genetic diseases, heart diseases, cancer, and asthma. From Asia, wealthy patients are coming mainly to California for treatment of cancer and coronary diseases. Europeans travel to the United States

for mental illness services, cancer and heart disease, and AIDS treatments. Given that Japan has the world's best success rate for treating stomach cancer, one would forecast that to be a growth sector in the future.

But perhaps the strangest market to forecast is that for prostheses for the global war wounded. Johns Hopkins contracted to replace limbs for soldiers involved in a border clash between Ecuador and Peru at $35,000 per patient. The description in *The Wall Street Journal* article might have been a bit overzealous: "There are wars all over the world, bombs all over the world. Casualty patients are a new and enriching market niche." Forecasting demand for prostheses is in some ways easy—all researchers have to do is track the data on wars worldwide, as listed in Exhibit 6.4 in Chapter 6. Fortunately the demand was falling before 2010. However, the sad reality of the Haitian earthquake means an estimate of over 40,000 prostheses needed for the survivors of that tragedy.

Sources: "U.S. Hospitals Attracting Patients from Abroad," *USA Today*, July 22, 1997, p. 1A; Ron Hammerle, "Healthcare Becoming a Lot Less Local," *Modern Healthcare*, March 20, 2000, p. 40; Tom Philips, "Haiti Earthquake Creating a Generation of Amputees, Doctors Warn," *Manchester Guardian*, January 21, 2010.

developed countries, more technically advanced techniques such as multiple regression analysis or input–output analysis can be used.

Finally, it should go without saying that forecasting demand is one of the most difficult and important business activities. All business plans depend entirely on forecasts of a future that no one can see. Even the best companies make big mistakes.

Problems in Analyzing and Interpreting Research Information

Once data have been collected, the final steps in the research process are the analysis and interpretation of findings in light of the stated marketing problem. Both secondary and primary data collected by the market researcher are subject to the many limitations just discussed. In any final analysis, the researcher must take into consideration these factors and, despite their limitations, produce meaningful guides for management decisions.

Accepting information at face value in foreign markets is imprudent. The meanings of words, the consumer's attitude toward a product, the interviewer's attitude, or the interview situation can distort research findings. Just as culture and tradition influence the willingness to give information, so they influence the information given. Newspaper circulation figures, readership and listenership studies, retail outlet figures, and sales volume can all be distorted through local business practices. To cope with such disparities, the foreign market researcher must possess three talents to generate meaningful marketing information.

First, the researcher must possess a high degree of cultural understanding of the market in which research is being conducted. To analyze research findings, the social customs, semantics, current attitudes, and business customs of a society or a subsegment of a society must be clearly understood. At some level, it will be absolutely necessary to have a native of the target country involved in the interpretation of the results of any research conducted in a foreign market.

Second, a creative talent for adapting research methods is necessary. A researcher in foreign markets often is called on to produce results under the most difficult circumstances and short deadlines. Ingenuity and resourcefulness, willingness to use "catch as catch can" methods to get facts, patience (even a sense of humor about the work), and a willingness to be guided by original research findings even when they conflict with popular opinion or prior assumptions are all considered prime assets in foreign marketing research.

Third, a skeptical attitude in handling both primary and secondary data is helpful. For example, it might be necessary to check a newspaper pressrun over a period of time to get accurate circulation figures or to deflate or inflate reported consumer income in some areas by 25 to 50 percent on the basis of observable socioeconomic characteristics. Indeed, where data are suspect, such triangulation through the use of multiple research methods will be crucial.

These essential traits suggest that a foreign marketing researcher should be a foreign national or should be advised by a foreign national who can accurately appraise the data collected in light of the local environment, thus validating secondary as well as primary data. Moreover, regardless of the sophistication of a research technique or analysis, there is no substitute for decision makers themselves getting into the field for personal observation.

Responsibility for Conducting Marketing Research
Depending on the size and degree of involvement in foreign marketing, a company in need of foreign market research can rely on an outside, foreign-based agency or on a domestic company with a branch within the country in question. It can conduct research using its own facilities or employ a combination of its own research force with the assistance of an outside agency.

A trend toward decentralization of the research function is apparent. In terms of efficiency, local analysts appear able to provide information more rapidly and accurately than a staff research department. The obvious advantage to decentralization of the research function is that control rests in hands closer to the market. Field personnel, resident managers, and customers generally have more intimate knowledge of the subtleties of the market and an appreciation of the diversity that characterizes most foreign markets. One disadvantage of decentralized research management is possible ineffective communications with home-office executives. Another is the potential unwarranted dominance of large-market studies in decisions about global standardization. That is to say, larger markets, particularly the United States, justify more sophisticated research procedures and larger sample sizes, and

Both Ford and Philips keep track of European technology and consumers and develop products for global markets at their research centers in Aachen, Germany. Some of the best technical universities are close by in Belgium, the Netherlands, and Germany.

results derived via simpler approaches that are appropriate in smaller countries are often erroneously discounted.

A comprehensive review of the different approaches to multicountry research suggests that the ideal approach is to have local researchers in each country, with close coordination between the client company and the local research companies. This cooperation is important at all stages of the research project, from research design to data collection to final analysis. Furthermore, two stages of analysis are necessary. At the individual-country level, all issues involved in each country must be identified, and at the multicountry level, the information must be distilled into a format that addresses the client's objectives. Such recommendations are supported on the grounds that two heads are better than one and that multicultural input is essential to any understanding of multicultural data. With just one interpreter of multicultural data, there is the danger of one's self-reference criterion resulting in data being interpreted in terms of one's own cultural biases. Self-reference bias can affect the research design, questionnaire design, and interpretation of the data.

If a company wants to use a professional marketing research firm, many are available. Most major advertising agencies and many research firms have established branch offices worldwide. Moreover, foreign-based research and consulting firms have seen healthy growth. Of the 10 largest marketing research firms in the world (based on revenues), 4 are based in the United States, including the largest; 3 are in the United Kingdom; 1 is in France; 1 is in Germany; and 1 is in the Netherlands. The latest count of marketing research firms in China is more than 400 and growing fast. In Japan, where understanding the unique culture is essential, the quality of professional marketing research firms is among the best. A recent study reports that research methods applied by Japanese firms and American firms are generally similar, but with notable differences in the greater emphasis of the Japanese on forecasting, distribution channels, and sales research. A listing of international marketing research firms is printed annually in April as an advertising supplement in *Marketing News.*

An increasingly important issue related to international marketing research is the growing potential for governmental controls on the activity. In many countries, consumer privacy issues are being given new scrutiny as the Internet expands companies' capabilities to gather data on consumers' behaviors.

Communicating with Decision Makers

LO6

Using international marketing research

Most of the discussion in this chapter has pertained to getting information from or about consumers, customers, and competitors. It should be clearly recognized, however, that getting the information is only half the job. Analyses and interpretation of that information must also be provided to decision makers in a timely manner.[37] High-quality international information systems design will be an increasingly important competitive tool as commerce continues to globalize, and resources must be invested accordingly.[38]

Decision makers, often top executives, should be directly involved not only in problem definition and question formulation but also in the fieldwork of seeing the market and hearing the voice of the customers in the most direct ways when the occasion warrants (as in new foreign markets). Top managers should have a "feel" for their markets that even the best marketing reports cannot provide.

Finally, international marketers face an additional obstacle to obtaining the best information about customers. At the most basic level, marketing research is mostly a matter of interaction with customers. Marketing decision makers have questions about how best to serve

---

[37]Anne L. Souchon, Adamantios Diamantopoulos, Hartmut H. Holzmuller, Catherine N. Axxin, James M. Sinkula, Heike Simmet, and Geoffrey R. Durden, "Export Information Use: A Five-Country Investigation of Key Determinants," *Journal of International Marketing* 11, no. 3 (2003), pp. 106–27.

[38]Nicoli Juul Foss and Torben Pedersen, "Organizing Knowledge Processes in the Multinational Corporation: An Introduction," *Journal of International Business Studies* 35, no. 5 (2004), pp. 340–49; Ram Mudambi and Pietro Navarra, "Is Knowledge Power? Knowledge Flows, Subsidiary Power and Rent-Seeking within MNCs," *Journal of International Business Studies* 35, no. 5 (2004), pp. 385–406.

customers, and those questions are posed and answered often through the media of questionnaires and research agencies. Even when both managers and customers speak the same language and are from the same culture, communication can become garbled in either direction. That is, customers misunderstand the questions and/or managers misunderstand the answers. Throw in a language/cultural barrier, and the chances of misinformation expand dramatically.

There is no better (or worse) case of such communication problems than the Toyota accelerator problems of 2010. Even great companies can make big mistakes. By not correcting flaws in Toyota product accelerators in the United States soon enough, the world's best automaker did billions of dollars of damage to its annual performance and perhaps its brand equity in the United States. The fundamental communication problem within Toyota was well described at the time:

> There is a cultural element to this penchant for mismanaging crisis. The shame and embarrassment of owning up to product defects in a nation obsessed with craftsmanship and quality raises the bar on disclosure and assuming responsibility. And a high-status company like Toyota has much to lose since its corporate face is at stake. The shame of producing defective cars is supposed to be other firms' problems, not Toyota's, and the ongoing PR disaster reveals just how unprepared the company is for crisis management and how embarrassed it is. In addition, employees' identities are closely tied to their company's image, and loyalty to the firm overrides concerns about consumers.
>
> There is also a culture of deference inside corporations that makes it hard for those lower in the hierarchy to question their superiors or inform them about problems. The focus on consensus and group is an asset in building teamwork, but also can make it hard to challenge what has been decided or designed. Such cultural inclinations are not unknown elsewhere around the world, but they are exceptionally powerful within Japanese corporate culture and constitute significant impediments to averting and responding to a crisis.[39]

We would add an additional culture-based explanation: the Japanese penchant for avoiding bad news. Indeed, the Japanese have two words for truth, *tatemae* and *honne*. *Tatemae* is the public, face-saving truth, whereas *honne* is the factual truth, irrespective of the damage it might do to the all-important social relationships within and between Japanese companies.[40] Such internal communication problems have also manifested themselves in other hierarchical, relationship-based cultures such as South Korea and Vietnam.[41] Researchers have identified a number of factors that are associated with better communication within such multinational companies, including frequency of communication instances, face-to-face communication opportunities,[42] employee incentives for sharing information,[43] and cultural similarities.[44] Another study offered "global environmental turbulence"[45] as a communication-inhibiting factor as well, and certainly Toyota was facing the extreme version of this problem: the precipitous decline in world trade and its own sales contemporaneously with its product quality problems.

---

[39]See the excellent article by Jeff Kinston, "A Crisis Made in Japan," *The Wall Street Journal*, February 6–7, 2010, pp. W1–2.

[40]James Day Hodgson, Yoshihiro Sano, John L. Graham, *Doing Business in the New Japan* (Boulder, CO: Rowman & Littlfield, 2008).

[41]Malcolm Gladwell, *Outliers* (New York: Little Brown, 2008); John U. Farley, Scott Hoenig, Donald R. Lehmann, and Hoang Thuy Nguyen, "Marketing Metrics Use in a Transitional Economy: The Case of Vietnam," *Journal of Global Marketing* 21, no. 3 (2008), pp. 179–90.

[42]Niels Noorderhaven and Anne-Wil Harzing, "Knowledge-Sharing and Social Interaction within MNEs," *Journal of International Business Studies* 40, no. 5 (2009), pp. 719–41.

[43]Gary Oddou, Joyce S. Osland, and Roger N. Blakeney, "Repatriating Knowledge: Variables Influencing the 'Transfer' Process," *Journal of International Business Studies* 40, no. 2 (2009), pp. 181–99.

[44]Martin S. Roth, Satish Jayachandran, Mourad Dakhli, and Deborah A. Colton, "Subsidiary Use of Foreign Marketing Knowledge," *Journal of International Marketing* 17, no. 1 (2009), pp. 1–29.

[45]Ruby P. Lee, Qimei Chen, Daikwan Kim, and Jean L. Johnson, "Knowledge Transfer between MNCs' Headquarters and Their Subsidiaries: Influences on and Implications for New Product Outcomes," *Journal of International Marketing* 16, no. 2 (2008), pp. 1–31.

Exhibit 8.2
Managing the Cultural Barrier in International Marketing Research

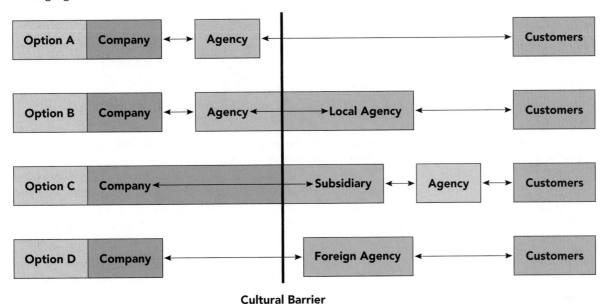

Cultural Barrier

Such problems can be exacerbated when research agencies are also involved. The four kinds of company–agency–customer relationships possible are presented in Exhibit 8.2. Options B and C are better suited for managing the cultural barrier across the chain of communication. That is, in both cases, the cultural barrier is bridged *within* a company wherein people that have a common corporate culture and work together on an everyday basis. In B the translation (in the broadest sense of the term—that is, of both questionnaires and reports) is worked out between employees of the international marketing research agency. In C the translation is managed within the company itself. In cases A and D, both cultural and organizational barriers are being crossed simultaneously, thus maximizing the chances for miscommunication. Indeed, these same company–agency–customer considerations are pertinent to other kinds of communications between companies and customers, such as advertising and distribution channel control, and this unique international topic will be addressed again in subsequent chapters.

Summary

The basic objective of the market research function is providing management with information for more accurate decision making. This objective is the same for domestic and international marketing. In foreign marketing research, however, achieving that objective presents some problems not encountered on the domestic front.

Customer attitudes about providing information to a researcher are culturally conditioned. Foreign market information surveys must be carefully designed to elicit the desired data and at the same time not offend the respondent's sense of privacy. Besides the cultural and managerial constraints involved in gathering information for primary data, many foreign markets have inadequate or unreliable bases of secondary information. Such challenges suggest three keys to successful international marketing research: (1) the inclusion of natives of the foreign culture on research teams; (2) the use of multiple methods and triangulation; and (3) the inclusion of decision makers, even top executives, who must on occasion talk directly to or directly observe customers in foreign markets.

Key Terms

Marketing research
International marketing research
Research process

Secondary data
Primary data
Back translation

Parallel translation
Decentering
Multicultural research

Expert opinion
Triangulation
Analogy

Questions

1. Define the key terms listed on the previous page.

2. Discuss how the shift from making "market entry" decisions to "continuous operations" decisions creates a need for different types of information and data.

3. Discuss the breadth and scope of international marketing research. Why is international marketing research generally broader in scope than domestic marketing research?

4. The measure of a competent researcher is the ability to utilize the most sophisticated and adequate techniques and methods available within the limits of time, cost, and the present state of the art. Comment.

5. What is the task of the international marketing researcher? How is it complicated by the foreign environment?

6. Discuss the stages of the research process in relation to the problems encountered. Give examples.

7. Why is the formulation of the research problem difficult in foreign market research?

8. Discuss the problems of gathering secondary data in foreign markets.

9. "In many cultures, personal information is inviolably private and absolutely not to be discussed with strangers." Discuss.

10. What are some problems created by language and the ability to comprehend the questions in collecting primary data? How can a foreign market researcher overcome these difficulties?

11. Discuss how decentering is used to get an accurate translation of a questionnaire.

12. Discuss when qualitative research may be more effective than quantitative research.

13. Sampling presents some major problems in market research. Discuss.

14. Select a country. From secondary sources found on the Internet, compile the following information for at least a five-year period prior to the present:

principal imports	principal exports
gross national product	chief of state
major cities and population	principal agricultural crop

15. "The foreign market researcher must possess three essential capabilities to generate meaningful marketing information." What are they? Discuss.

Appendix: Sources of Secondary Data

For almost any marketing research project, an analysis of available secondary information is a useful and inexpensive first step. Although there are information gaps, particularly for detailed market information, the situation on data availability and reliability is improving. The principal agencies that collect and publish information useful in international business are presented here, with some notations regarding selected publications.

A. Web Sites for International Marketing

1. www.stat-usa.gov STAT-USA/Internet is clearly the single most important source of data on the Internet. STAT-USA, a part of the U.S. Department of Commerce's Economics and Statistics Administration, produces and distributes at a nominal subscription fee the most extensive government-sponsored business, economic, and trade information databases in the world today, including the National Trade Data Bank, Economic Bulletin Board, and Global Business Procurement Opportunities.

2. www.trade.gov/index.asp The Web site of the Commerce Department's International Trade Administration provides export assistance, including information about trade events, trade statistics, tariffs and taxes, marketing research, and so forth.

3. www.usatradeonline.gov Provides import and export information on more than 18,000 commodities, but the user must subscribe.

4. www.census.gov/foreign-trade/www/ The U.S. Census Bureau provides a variety of international trade statistics.

5. www.cia.gov/library/publications/the-world-factbook/ Find the CIA *World Factbook* here, as well as other pertinent trade information.

6. www.customs.ustreas.gov The U.S. Customs Service provides information regarding customs procedures and regulations.

7. www.opic.gov The Overseas Private Investment Corporation (OPIC) provides information regarding its services.

8. www.exim.gov The Export-Import Bank of the United States (Ex-Im Bank) provides information related to trade financing services provided by the U.S. government.

9. www.imf.org The International Monetary Fund (IMF) provides information about the IMF and international banking and finance.

10. www.wto.org The World Trade Organization (WTO) provides information regarding its operations.

11. www.oecd.org The Organization of Economic Cooperation and Development (OECD) provides information regarding OECD policies and associated data for 29 member countries.

12. www.jetro.go.jp The Japan External Trade Organization (JETRO) is the best source for data on the Japanese market.

13. www.euromonitor.com Euromonitor is a company providing a variety of data and reports on international trade and marketing.

14. publications.worldbank.org *World Development Indicators (WDI) Online* offers the World Bank's comprehensive database on development data, covering more than 600 indicators, 208 economies, and 18 regional income groups.

15. University-based Web sites. The best such site is Michigan State University's Center for International Business Education and Research (http://globaledge.msu.edu/resourceDesk/).

16. www.worldchambers.com The World Network of Chambers of Commerce and Industry provides data and addresses regarding chambers of commerce around the world.

17. http://world.wtca.org The World Trade Centers Association provides information about services provided by the World Trade Centers in the United States, including export assistance, trade leads, training programs, and trade missions.

18. www.worldtrademag.com *World Trade* magazine provides its annual Resource Guide to products, goods, and services for international trade.

19. www.mhhe.com/gilly15e The online learning center that accompanies this text provides supplementary support materials for both instructors and students.

B. U.S. Government Sources

The U.S. government actively promotes the expansion of U.S. business into international trade. In the process of keeping U.S. businesses informed of foreign opportunities, the U.S. government generates a considerable amount of general and specific market data for use by international market analysts. The principal source of information from the U.S. government is the Department of Commerce, which makes its services available to U.S. businesses in a variety of ways. First, information and assistance are available either through personal consultation in Washington, DC, or through any of the US&FCS (U.S. and Foreign Commercial Service) district offices of the International Trade Administration of the Department of Commerce located in key cities in the United States. Second, the Department of Commerce works closely with trade associations, chambers of commerce, and other interested associations in providing information, consultation, and assistance in developing international commerce. Third, the department publishes a wide range of information available to interested persons at nominal cost.

1. National Trade Data Bank (NTDB). The Commerce Department provides a number of the data sources mentioned previously, plus others in its computerized information system in the National Trade Data Bank. The NTDB is a one-step source for export promotion and international trade data collected by 17 U.S. government agencies. Updated each month and released on the Internet, the NTDB enables the reader to access more than 100,000 trade-related documents. The NTDB contains the latest census data on U.S. imports and exports by commodity and country; the complete CIA (Central Intelligence Agency) *World Factbook*; current market research reports compiled by the U.S. and Foreign Commercial Service; the complete *Foreign Traders Index*, which contains over 55,000 names and addresses of individuals and firms abroad that are interested in importing U.S. products; State Department country reports on economic policy and trade practices; the publications *Export Yellow Pages, A Basic Guide to Exporting* and the *National Trade Estimates Report on Foreign Trade Barriers*; the *Export Promotion Calendar*; and many other data series. The NTDB is also available at over 900 federal depository libraries nationwide.

In addition, the Department of Commerce provides a host of other information services. Beyond the material available through the Department of Commerce, consultation and information are available from a variety of other U.S. agencies. For example, the Department of State, Bureau of the Census, and Department of Agriculture can provide valuable assistance in the form of services and information for an American business interested in international operations.

2. www.export.gov/tradeleads/index.asp This Web site connects you to the Export.gov Trade Leads Database, which contains prescreened, time-sensitive leads and Government Tenders gathered through U.S. Commercial Service offices around the world. You can search leads and receive notification when new leads are posted.

3. buyusa.gov Provides details about the services offered by the U.S. Commercial Service.

C. Other Sources

1. Directories

a. Directory of American Firms Operating in Foreign Countries. New York: World Trade Academy Press. Alphabetically lists U.S. firms with foreign subsidiaries and affiliates operating in over 125 countries; also lists the foreign operations grouped by countries.

b. Directory of United States Importers and United States Exporters. New York: Journal of Commerce. Annual. (Also on CD-ROM.) Contain verified business profiles on a total of 60,000 active trading companies. These annual guides also include a product index with the Harmonized Commodity Code numbers, customs information, foreign consulates, embassies, and international banks.

c. Encyclopedia of Global Industries. Detroit: Gale. Alphabetically covers 125 vital international industries, providing in-depth information including statistics, graphs, tables, charts, and market share.

d. Export Yellow Pages. Washington, DC: Venture Publishing–North America; produced in cooperation with the Office of Export Trading Company Affairs and International Trade Administration. Annual. Provides detailed information on over 12,000 export service providers and trading companies, agents, distributors, and companies outside the United States; also includes a product/service index and an alphabetical index.

e. World Directory of Trade and Business Associations. London: Euromonitor, 1995. (Also on CD-ROM.) Contains entries from a broad range of sectors, giving details of publications produced, aims and objectives of the association, and whether they provide assistance in further research.

2. Marketing Guides

a. Exporters Encyclopaedia. Wilton, CT: Dun & Bradstreet. Annual. Comprehensive world marketing guide, in five sections; section two, "Export Markets," gives important market information on 220 countries (import and exchange regulations, shipping services, communications data, postal information, currency, banks, and embassies); other sections contain general export information. Also available are regional guides for Asia-Pacific, Europe, and Latin America and export guides for single countries.

b. U.S. Custom House Guide. Hightstown, NJ: K-III Directory Co. Annual. Provides a comprehensive guide to importing, including seven main sections: import how-to, ports sections, directory of services, tariff schedules (Harmonized Tariff Schedules of the United States), special and administrative provisions, custom regulations, and samples of import documents.

3. General sources of international business and economic data and customized reports. These exemplary Web sites are generally accessible for corporations with substantial research needs and budgets:

a. Economist Intelligence Unit www.eiu.com The Economist Intelligence Unit (EIU) describes itself as providing "a constant flow of analysis and forecasts on more than 200 countries and eight key industries." It helps "executives make informed business decisions through dependable intelligence delivered online, in print, in customized research as well as through conferences and peer interchange." The EIU represents a very high level of analysis. Its products are for sale (an annual subscription runs in the four figures), it facilitates the initial aggregation of information, and it undertakes preliminary analyses. At an intermediate level, within the industries it targets, we have found EIU to be very helpful.

b.   Oxford Analytica www.oxan.org Oxford Analytica is self-described as "an international, independent consulting firm drawing on a network of over 1,000 senior faculty members at Oxford and other major universities and research institutions around the world." If the CIA Factbook is a Chevy sort of resource and the EIU is a Cadillac, then Oxan is a Lamborghini. Fees run to the five figures, depending on what you order. Among the publicly accessible sources, Oxford Analytica is one of the very best. Its reputation rests "on its ability to harness the expertise of pre-eminent scholar experts to provide business and government leaders with timely and authoritative analysis of world events. It is a unique bridge between the world of ideas and the world of enterprise." A review of its clients clearly indicates the level of professionalism the firm strives for and apparently attains.

Chapter 9

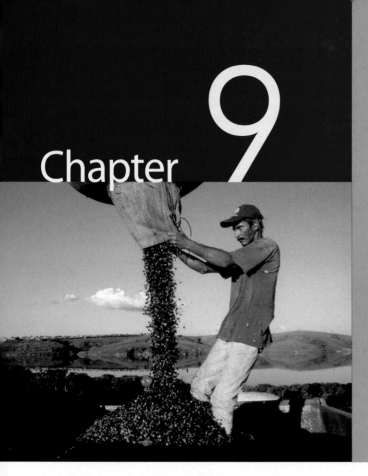

Economic Development and the Americas

CHAPTER OUTLINE

CHAPTER LEARNING OBJECTIVES

What you should learn from Chapter 9:

LO1 The importance of time zones for trade relationships and marketing operations

LO2 The political and economic changes affecting global marketing

LO3 The connection between the economic level of a country and the marketing task

LO4 The variety of stages of economic development among American nations

LO5 Growth factors and their role in economic development

LO6 Marketing's contribution to the growth and development of a country's economy

LO7 The foundational market metrics of American nations

LO8 The growing importance of trading associations among American nations

Global Perspective

DESYNCHRONOSIS? SOMETHING GEORGE CLOONEY CAUGHT *UP IN THE AIR?*

The medical term sounds much more ominous than mere jet lag. But whatever you call it, it's still a powerful force. The *Encyclopedia Britannica* tells us:

> Physiological desynchronization is caused by transmeridian (east-west) travel between different time zones. The severity and extent of jet lag vary according to the number of time zones crossed as well as the direction of travel—most people find it difficult to travel eastward (i.e., to adapt a shorter day as opposed to a longer one). The resulting symptoms include extreme fatigue, sleep disturbances, loss of concentration, disorientation, malaise, sluggishness, gastrointestinal upset, and loss of appetite.[1]

Some international executives seem to handle it well though.

Raj Subramaniam, the Senior Vice President of International Marketing at FedEx has spent almost as much time overseas as he has at the company's Memphis headquarters in the 18 years he has worked there. True, that includes two long-term postings in Hong Kong and Toronto. But even since Subramaniam returned to Tennessee in 2006, he has been logging major miles, visiting FedEx's far-flung offices to oversee global marketing plans and customer service. It's a schedule that suits him, and he takes the opportunity to drop in on old haunts and discover new cities. "The worst thing you can possibly do is stay in the hotel, drink the bottled water, and just look out the window," says the seasoned traveler, who offers a few of his secrets for travelling successfully.

1. Days on the road? I'd say 125 or so, out of which about 100 are outside the U.S.

2. Way to fly? Typically I fly on Cathay Pacific, Emirates, and British Airways. They offer direct flights, and the service is excellent. I'm looking for a reasonable meal and then to read a book and go to sleep. These airlines do a great job of allowing those simple pleasures to happen.

3. Airtime? It's the best time to unplug your electronic leash and read. Right now I'm catching up on a few issues of *Foreign Affairs* magazine.

4. Trip tip? Pack light, and pack running shoes. Travel equals jet lag, so when I get to my destination, I try to hit the gym as quickly as I possibly can.

5. Favorite hotel? The Conrad in Hong Kong. Typically the flight from L.A. lands by 5:30 a.m. I'm at the hotel by 6:30, and I head to the gym. By 7:30, I'm having breakfast on the 59th floor overlooking Victoria Harbor, and by 9:00 I'm in the office. It works beautifully.

Some have a tougher time. Benjamin Southan, correspondent for Businesstraveller.com recounts his story:

> In Sydney . . . I'd woken at four in the morning with extreme jet lag and figured I may as well run it off, but I'd packed in a daze—no socks, and no shorts. Well, I could do without socks, I thought, and I had a pair of normal shorts. I could run in those. Big mistake. The loose fit I preferred when lounging around worked less well when running around; my sockless feet rubbed, particularly once I'd warmed up; and it was very warm, even at five in the morning. And because it was going to be a short run, I hadn't bothered to grab a map, or work out where I was going. I kept the harbour to one side, and turned around after 15 minutes or so, taking what I thought was a shortcut as my feet were beginning to hurt. Second big mistake.
>
> An hour later, exhausted, I half-jogged, half-shuffled through the less than salubrious Kings Cross area. No socks, sweat-stained through T-shirt, one hand holding up my shorts, and wondering why no one would meet my eye so I could ask them the way back to the harbour.... When I finally found my way back to the hotel, the receptionist alternated between professional concern and person disgust, with the latter claiming victory. I fell into the lift as the first businessmen were coming down for breakfast, and once in my room pressed the "do not disturb" button and collapsed into bed. I'd allowed myself a day to acclimatize in Sydney before my appointments started, and it was the last trouble I had with jet lag that trip, sleeping for 20 hours and waking only to empty the minibar of chocolate and soft drinks. So much for the weight management.

Sources: Benjamin Southan, "Fit to Drop," *Business Traveller* (UK/ Europe Edition), October 2009, p. 82; Eugenia Levenson, "Road Warrior," *Fortune*, April 27, 2009, p. 24.

Exhibit 9.1
Three Regional Trading Areas Roughly Defined by Time Zones

Source: World Bank, 2010.

Region	Population	GDP
The Americas	.91 billion	$19.1 trillion
Europe, Africa, Middle East	1.9 billion	$19.6 trillion
Asia Pacific	3.5 billion	$12.5 trillion

LO1

The importance of time zones for trade relationships and marketing operations

Time zones make a difference. Jet lag is an important problem. Virtual meetings across time zones are more than just inconvenient; they can disrupt sleep and family life. Indeed, our own studies have demonstrated that among three kinds of distances that international marketers must traverse—miles, time zones, and cultural distances—time zones have the greatest influence on the success of their commercial efforts abroad.[2] Moreover, most countries also maintain good trade relationships with contiguous countries. Thus, we can also see an associated pattern of economic growth and global trade that will extend well into the 21st century. It consists of three multinational market regions that comprise major trading blocs: the Americas, Europe, and Asia. Further, the common time zones give the Europeans advantages in both Africa and the Middle East. Within each trading bloc are fully industrialized countries, as typified by the United States, Germany, and Japan; rapidly industrializing countries such as Brazil, Russia, and China that are close on the heels of the fully industrialized; and other countries that are achieving economic development but at more modest rates. See Exhibit 9.1 for the grossest metrics for each trading bloc.

Many American companies have organized their international operations according to these geographic or temporal, if you like, constraints. For example, Quiksilver manages its global operations from three bases: Huntington Beach, California, for the Americas (and corporate headquarters); St. Jean De Luz, France, for Europe; and Avalon, New South Wales, Australia, for the Asia/Pacific region. Among its $2 billion in global revenues in 2009, approximately 47 percent came from the Americas, 40 percent from Europe, and 13 percent from the Asia/Pacific.

Our presentation of regional market metrics is likewise organized in Chapters 9–11. In this chapter, we first discuss economic development and marketing, then focus on the character of and opportunities for commerce in the Americas. While the United States and Canada are affluent, industrialized countries, most of the countries in the American region better fit the descriptor "developing," and some are doing so very fast indeed. In Chapter 10, we focus on the European Union, as it represents the benchmark for regional commercial and political cooperation, and then we turn to the broader opportunities among its time zone neighbors—the rest of Europe, Africa, and the Middle East. In Chapter 11 we characterize the opportunities in the bustling Asia/Pacific region that includes the majority of people on the planet.

Marketing and Economic Development

LO2

The political and economic changes affecting global marketing

Not many years ago, large parts of the developing world were hostile to foreign investment and imposed severe regulatory barriers to foreign trade.[3] But few nations are content with the economic status quo; now, more than ever, they seek economic growth, improved standards of living, and an opportunity for the good life as part of the global consumer world.[4] Latin American and other emerging markets throughout the world will account for 75 percent of the world's total growth in the next two decades and beyond, according to U.S. Department of Commerce estimates. The transition from socialist to market-driven economies, the liberalization of trade and investment policies in developing countries, the transfer of public-sector enterprises to the private sector,

---

[2] Jennifer D. Chandler and John L. Graham, "Relationship-Oriented Cultures, Corruption, and International Marketing Success," *Journal of Business Ethics* 92(2) (2010), pp. 251–67.

[3] James C. McKinley Jr., "For U.S. Exporters in Cuba, Business Trumps Politics," *The New York Times*, November 12, 2007, p. A3.

[4] Stephen Kotkin, "First World, Third World (Maybe Not in That Order)," *The New York Times*, May 6, 2007, p. 7.

and the rapid development of regional market alliances are changing the way countries will trade and prosper in the 21st century.

Argentina, Brazil, Mexico, China, South Korea, Poland, Turkey, India, and Vietnam[5] are some of the countries undergoing impressive changes in their economies and are emerging as vast markets. These and other countries have an ever-expanding and changing demand for goods and services. As countries prosper and their people are exposed to new ideas and behavior patterns via global communications networks, old stereotypes, traditions, and habits are cast aside or tempered, and new patterns of consumer behavior emerge. Luxury cars in China;[6] Avon cosmetics in South Korea; Walmart discount stores in Argentina, Brazil, Mexico, China, and Thailand; McDonald's beefless Big Macs in India; Whirlpool washers and refrigerators in eastern Europe; Sara Lee food products in Indonesia; and Amway products in the Czech Republic represent opportunities in emerging markets.

LO3

The connection between the economic level of a country and the marketing task

The economic level of a country is the single most important environmental element to which the foreign marketer must adjust the marketing task. The stage of economic growth within a country affects the attitudes toward foreign business activity,[7] the demand for goods, the distribution systems found within a country, and the entire marketing process.[8] In static economies, consumption patterns become rigid, and marketing is typically nothing more than a supply effort. In a dynamic economy, consumption patterns change rapidly.[9] Marketing constantly faces the challenge of detecting and providing for new levels of consumption, and marketing efforts must be matched with ever-changing market needs and wants. The current level of economic development dictates the kind and degree of market potential that exists, while knowledge of the dynamism of the economy allows the marketer to prepare for economic shifts and emerging markets.[10]

Economic development is generally understood to mean an increase in national production reflected by an increase in the average per capita gross domestic product (GDP) or gross national income (GNI).[11] Besides an increase in average per capita GNI or GDP, most interpretations of the concept also imply a widespread distribution of the increased income. Economic development, as commonly defined today, tends to mean rapid economic growth and increases in consumer demand—improvements achieved "in decades rather than centuries."

Stages of Economic Development

The United Nations classifies a country's stage of economic development on the basis of its level of industrialization. It groups countries into three categories:

MDCs (more-developed countries). Industrialized countries with high per capita incomes, such as Canada, England, France, Germany, Japan, and the United States. Exhibit 9.2 summarizes data regarding the standards of living in the most populous American countries that evince a spectrum of development despite their similar sizes. The reader will notice that those at the lowest levels of development often do not

---

[5]"WTO—Landmark of Vietnam's 20-Year Renewal Process," *Asia Pulse*, January 2, 2008.

[6]Jason Leow and Gordon Fairclough, "Rich Chinese Fancy Luxury Cars," *The Wall Street Journal*, April 12, 2007, pp. B1, B6.

[7]Terrance H. Witkowski, "Antiglobal Challenges to Marketing in Developing Countries: Exploring the Ideological Divide," *Journal of Public Policy & Marketing* 24, no. 1 (2005), pp. 7–23.

[8]Ramarao Desiraju, Harikesh Nair, and Pradeep Chintagunta, "Diffusion of New Pharmaceutical Drugs in Developing and Developed Nations," *International Journal of Research in Marketing* 21, no. 4 (2004), pp. 341–57.

[9]Seung Ho Park, Shaomin Li, and David K. Tse, "Market Liberalization and Firm Performance During China's Economic Transition," *Journal of International Business Studies* 37 (2006), pp. 127–47.

[10]Kevin Zheng Zhou, David K. Tse, and Julie Juan Li, "Organizational Changes in Emerging Economies: Drivers and Consequences," *Journal of International Business Studies* 37 (2006), pp. 248–63.

[11]Gross domestic product (GDP) and gross national income (GNI) are two measures of a country's economic activity. GDP is a measure of the market value of all goods and services produced within the boundaries of a nation, regardless of asset ownership. Unlike GNI, GDP excludes receipts from that nation's business operations in foreign countries, as well as the share of reinvested earnings in foreign affiliates of domestic corporations. In most cases and for most applications, the differences between the two are insubstantial. For example, the World Bank reports GDP for China in 2008 as $4.33 trillion and GNI as $4.37 trillion.

Exhibit 9.2
Standards of Living in the Eight Most Populous American Countries

| Country | Population (millions) | GDI/Capita | Medical Resources per 1000 Persons | | Household Ownership % | | |
			Doctors	Hospital Beds	Color TV	Refrigerator	Shower
United States	307	$46662	2.4	3.1	99	100	99
Brazil	194	$ 7627	2.0	—	96	93	81
Mexico	109	$ 9805	2.0	1.6	95	85	81
Colombia	46	$ 4063	1.5	1.3	81	71	99
Argentina	41	$ 7492	3.2	2.0	96	92	96
Canada	34	$39401	2.2	3.3	99	100	99
Peru	29	$ 4120	1.3	1.4	56	39	70
Venezuela	29	$12438	1.3	—	92	97	74

Source: Euromonitor International 2010.

collect or report data suitable for international resources such as Euromonitor International or the World Bank.

LDCs (less-developed countries). Industrially developing countries just entering world trade, many of which are in Asia and Latin America, with relatively low per capita incomes.

LLDCs (least-developed countries). Industrially underdeveloped, agrarian, subsistence societies with rural populations, extremely low per capita income levels, and little world trade involvement. Such LLDCs are found in Central Africa and parts of Asia. Violence and the potential for violence are often associated with LLDCs.

The UN classification has been criticized because it no longer seems relevant in the rapidly industrializing world. In addition, many countries that are classified as LDCs are industrializing at a very rapid rate, whereas others are advancing at more traditional rates of economic development. It is interesting to note in Exhibit 9.2 the differences in income and consumer possessions across the eight most populous American nations.

Countries that are experiencing rapid economic expansion and industrialization and do not exactly fit as LDCs or MDCs are more typically referred to as **newly industrialized countries (NICs).** These countries have shown rapid industrialization of targeted industries and have per capita incomes that exceed other developing countries. They have moved away from restrictive trade practices and instituted significant free market reforms; as a result, they attract both trade and foreign direct investment. Chile, Brazil, Mexico, South Korea, Singapore, and Taiwan are some of the countries that fit this description. These NICs have become formidable exporters of many products, including steel, automobiles, machine tools, clothing, and electronics, as well as vast markets for imported products.

LO4

The variety of stages of economic development among American nations

Brazil provides an example of the growing importance of NICs in world trade, exporting everything from alcohol-based fuels to carbon steel. Brazilian orange juice, poultry, soybeans, and weapons (Brazil is the world's sixth-largest weapons exporter) compete with U.S. products for foreign markets. Embraer, a Brazilian aircraft manufacturer, has sold planes to more than 60 countries and provides a substantial portion of the commuter aircraft used in the United States and elsewhere. Even in automobile production, Brazil is a world player; it ships more than 200,000 cars, trucks, and buses to Third World countries annually. Volkswagen has produced more than 3 million VW Beetles in Brazil and has invested more than $500 million in a project to produce the Golf and Passat automobiles. The firm also recently announced a deal to sell $500 million worth of auto parts to a Chinese partner. General Motors invested $600 million to create what it calls "an industrial complex"—a collection of 17 plants occupied by suppliers such as Delphi, Lear, and Goodyear to deliver preassembled modules to GM's line workers. All in all, auto and auto parts makers are

Brazilian production of coffee (on left) has almost always determined world prices for the brew. Now this commercial dominance is being challenged in two ways. First, Vietnam's burgeoning new production (on right) caused world coffee prices to crash in recent years, from a high of $1.85 per pound in 1997 to about $.50 in 2001. And Starbuck's is changing the global game in retail coffee distribution—including in its store in the heart of São Paulo, the historical center of coffee production in Brazil and the world.

investing more than $2.8 billion aimed at the 200 million people in the Mercosur market, the free trade group formed by Argentina, Brazil, Paraguay, and Uruguay.

Economic Growth Factors

LO5

Growth factors and their role in economic development

Why have some countries grown so rapidly and successfully while others with similar or more plentiful resources languished? Some analysts attribute the faster growth of some to cultural values, others to cheap labor, and still others to an educated and literate population. Certainly all of these factors have contributed to growth, but other important factors are present in all the rapidly growing economies, many of which seem to be absent in those nations that have not enjoyed comparable economic growth.

The factors that existed to some extent during the economic growth of NICs were as follows:

- Political stability in policies affecting their development.
- Economic and legal reforms. Poorly defined and/or weakly enforced contract and property rights are features the poorest countries have in common.
- Entrepreneurship. In all of these nations, free enterprise in the hands of the self-employed was the seed of the new economic growth.
- Planning. A central plan with observable and measurable development goals linked to specific policies was in place.
- Outward orientation. Production for the domestic market and export markets with increases in efficiencies and continual differentiation of exports from competition was the focus.

- Factors of production. If deficient in the factors of production—land (raw materials), labor, capital, management, and technology—an environment existed where these factors could easily come from outside the country and be directed to development objectives.

- Industries targeted for growth. Strategically directed industrial and international trade policies were created to identify those sectors where opportunity existed. Key industries were encouraged to achieve better positions in world markets by directing resources into promising target sectors.

- Incentives to force a high domestic rate of savings and direct capital to update the infrastructure, transportation, housing, education, and training.

- Privatization of state-owned enterprises (SOEs) that had placed a drain on national budgets. Privatization released immediate capital to invest in strategic areas and gave relief from a continuing drain on future national resources. Often when industries are privatized, the new investors modernize, thus creating new economic growth.

The final factors that have been present are large, accessible markets with low tariffs. During the early growth of many countries, the first large open market was the United States, later joined by Europe and now, as the fundamental principles of the World Trade Organization (WTO) are put into place, by much of the rest of the world.

Although it is customary to think such growth factors as applying only to industrial growth, the example of Chile shows that economic growth can occur with agricultural development as its economic engine. Chile's economy has expanded at an average rate of 7.2 percent since 1987 and is considered one of the least risky Latin American economies for foreign investment. However, since 1976 when Chile opened up trade, the relative size of its manufacturing sector declined from 27.3 percent of GDP in 1973 to less than half that in 2010.[12] Agriculture, in contrast, has not declined. Exports of agricultural products have been the star performers. Chile went from being a small player in the global fruit market, exporting only apples in the 1960s, to one of the world's largest fruit exporters by 2000. Sophisticated production technology and management methods were applied to the production of table grapes, wine, salmon from fish farms, and a variety of other processed and semiprocessed agricultural products. Salmon farming, begun in the early 1980s, has made salmon a major export item. Salmon exports to the United States are 40,000 tons annually, whereas U.S. annual production of farm-raised salmon is only 31,000 tons. Chile is also a major exporter of the fishmeal that is fed to hatchery-raised salmon.

Chile's production technology has resulted in productivity increases and higher incomes. Its experience indicates that manufacturing is not the only way for countries to grow economically. The process is to continually adapt to changing tastes, constantly improve technology, and find new ways to prosper from natural resources. Contrast Chile today with the traditional agriculturally based economies that are dependent on one crop (e.g., bananas) today and will still be dependent on that same crop 20 years from now. This type of economic narrowness was the case with Chile a few decades ago when it depended heavily on copper. To expand its economy beyond dependency on copper, Chile began with what it did best—exporting apples. As the economy grew, the country invested in better education and infrastructure and improved technology to provide the bases to develop other economic sectors, such as grapes, wine, salmon, and tomato paste.

Regional cooperation and open markets are also crucial for economic growth. As will be discussed in detail in Chapter 10, being a member of a multinational market region is essential if a country is to have preferential access to regional trade groups. As steps in that direction, in 2003 Chile and in 2005 Central American countries (including banana producers) signed free trade agreements with the United States.[13]

---

[12]World Bank, "World Development Indicators," 2010.

[13]"Chile and U.S. Sign Accord on Free Trade," *The New York Times*, June 7, 2003, p. 3; David Armstrong, "CAFTA Signed into Law," *San Francisco Chronicle*, August 3, 2005, p. C1.

Information Technology, the Internet, and Economic Development

In addition to the growth factors previously discussed, a country's investment in information technology (IT) is an important key to economic growth. The cellular phone,[14] the Internet, and other advances in IT open opportunities for emerging economies to catch up with richer ones.[15] New, innovative electronic technologies can be the key to a sustainable future for developed and developing nations alike.

Because the Internet cuts transaction costs and reduces economies of scale from vertical integration, some argue that it reduces the economically optimal size for firms. Lower transaction costs enable small firms in Asia or Latin America to work together to develop a global reach. Smaller firms in emerging economies can now sell into a global market. It is now easier, for instance, for a tailor in Hong Kong to make a suit by hand for an executive in Memphis. One of the big advantages that rich economies have is their closeness to wealthy consumers, and this advantage will erode as transaction costs fall.

The Internet accelerates the process of economic growth by speeding up the diffusion of new technologies to emerging economies. Unlike the decades required for many developing countries to benefit from railways, telephones, or electricity, the Internet is spreading rapidly throughout Latin America and the rest of the world. Information technology can jump-start national economies and allow them to leapfrog from high levels of illiteracy to computer literacy.

Mobile phones and other wireless technologies greatly reduce the need to lay a costly telecom infrastructure to bring telephone service to areas not served.[16] In Caracas, Venezuela, for example, where half of the city's 5 million people lives in nonwired slums, cell phones with pay-as-you-go cards have provided service to many residents for the first time. The Internet allows for innovative services at a relatively inexpensive cost. Telecenters in many developing countries provide public telephone, fax, computer, and Internet services where students can read online books and local entrepreneurs can seek potential business partners. Medical specialists from Belgium help train local doctors and surgeons in Senegal via video linkups between classrooms and operating centers and provide them with Internet access to medical journals and databases. Traveling there to teach would be prohibitively expensive; via Internet technology, it costs practically nothing.

Objectives of Developing Countries

A thorough assessment of economic development and marketing should begin with a brief review of the basic facts and objectives of economic development.

Industrialization is the fundamental objective of most developing countries.[17] Most countries see in economic growth the achievement of social as well as economic goals. Better education, better and more effective government, the elimination of many social inequities, and improvements in moral and ethical responsibilities are some of the expectations of developing countries. Thus, economic growth is measured not solely in economic goals but also in social achievements. Regarding the last, consider for a moment the tremendous efforts Brazil has undertaken in preparing for the 2012 Olympics.

Because foreign businesses are outsiders, they often are feared as having goals in conflict with those of the host country. Considered exploiters of resources, many multinational firms were expropriated in the 1950s and 1960s. Others faced excessively high tariffs and quotas, and foreign investment was forbidden or discouraged. Today, foreign investors are seen as vital partners in economic development. Experience with state-owned businesses proved to be a disappointment to most governments. Instead of being engines for accelerated economic growth, state-owned enterprises were mismanaged, inefficient drains on state treasuries. Many countries have deregulated industry, opened their doors to foreign investment, lowered trade barriers, and begun privatizing SOEs. The trend toward privatization is currently a major economic phenomenon in industrialized as well as in developing countries.

---

[14]Nandini Lakshman, "Nokia: Lessons Learned, Reward Reaped," *BusinessWeek*, July 30, 2007, p. 32.

[15]Simon Cox, "High-Tech Hopefuls, A Special Report on Technology in India and China," *The Economist*, November 10, 2007, pp. 1–25.

[16]Jack Ewing and Edel Rodriguez, "Upwardly Mobile in Africa," *BusinessWeek*, September 4, 2007, pp. 64–71.

[17]"Chocolate, Thinking out of the Box," *The Economist*, April 7, 2007, p. 65.

Exhibit 9.3
Infrastructure of Most Populous American Countries

Country	Travel by Rail (passenger-km per capita)	Passenger Cars/1000 People	Energy Consumption (tonnes oil equivalent per capita)	Computers in Use per 1000	Mobile Phones in Use per 1000	Literacy Rate (%)	University Students (per 1000)
United States	27	430	7.5	867	929	100	47
Brazil	93	105	1.2	260	876	92	29
Mexico	—	147	1.6	163	767	93	23
Colombia	0.2	42	0.7	111	1005	94	25
Argentina	198	138	1.9	105	1217	98	38
Canada	43	555	9.9	1085	673	100	34
Peru	5.3	24	0.6	154	809	93	22
Venezuela	—	78	2.9	130	1053	95	40

Source: Euromonitor International, 2010.

Infrastructure and Development

One indicator of economic development is the extent of social overhead capital, or infrastructure, within the economy. **Infrastructure** represents those types of capital goods that serve the activities of many industries. Included in a country's infrastructure are paved roads, railroads, seaports, communication networks, financial networks, and energy supplies[18] and distribution[19]—all necessary to support production and marketing. The quality of an infrastructure directly affects a country's economic growth potential and the ability of an enterprise to engage effectively in business. See Exhibit 9.3 for some comparisons of infrastructure among the eight largest American countries.

Infrastructure is a crucial component of the uncontrollable elements facing marketers. Without adequate transportation facilities, for example, distribution costs can increase substantially, and the ability to reach certain segments of the market is impaired. The lack of readily available educational assets hampers not only the ability to communicate to residents (literacy) but also firms' ability to find qualified local marketing managers. To a marketer, the key issue is the impact of a country's infrastructure on a firm's ability to market effectively. Business efficiency is affected by the presence or absence of financial and commercial service infrastructure found within a country—such as advertising agencies, warehousing storage facilities, credit and banking facilities, marketing research agencies, and satisfactory specialized middlemen. Generally speaking, the less developed a country is, the less adequate the infrastructure is for conducting business. Companies do market in less-developed countries, but often they must modify their offerings and augment existing levels of infrastructure.

Countries begin to lose economic development ground when their infrastructure cannot support an expanding population and economy. A country that has the ability to produce commodities for export may be unable to export them because of an inadequate infrastructure. For example, Mexico's economy has been throttled by its archaic transport system. Roads and seaports are inadequate, and the railroad system has seen little modernization since the 1910 Revolution. Please see Exhibit 9.3 for some of the numbers associated with this problem. If it were not for Mexico's highway system (though it, too, is in poor condition), the economy would have come to a halt; Mexico's highways have consistently carried more freight than its railroads. Conditions in other Latin American countries are no better. Shallow harbors and inadequate port equipment in part make a container filled with computers about $1,000 more expensive to ship from Miami to San Antonio, Chile (about 3,900 miles), than the same container shipped from Yokohama, Japan, to Miami (8,900 miles).

---

[18]"Chavez Declares an 'Electricity Emergency' in Venezuela," *Reuters*, February 9, 2010, online.

[19]Chris Kraul and Marcelo Soares, "Brazil's Frayed Wires Finally Short Out," *Los Angeles Times*, November 12, 2009, p. A22.

Marketing's Contributions

LO6 ▰▰

Marketing's contribution to the growth and development of a country's economy

How important is marketing to the achievement of a nation's goals? Unfortunately, marketing (or distribution) is not always considered meaningful to those responsible for planning. Economic planners frequently are more production oriented than marketing oriented and tend to ignore or regard distribution as an inferior economic activity. Given such attitudes, economic planners generally are more concerned with the problems of production, investment, and finance than the problems of efficiency of distribution.

Marketing is an economy's arbitrator between productive capacity and consumer demand. The marketing process is the critical element in effectively utilizing production resulting from economic growth; it can create a balance between higher production and higher consumption. An efficient distribution and channel system and all the attendant liaisons match production capacity and resources with consumer needs, wants, and purchasing power.

Marketing in a Developing Country

A marketer cannot superimpose a sophisticated marketing strategy on an underdeveloped economy.[20] Marketing efforts must be keyed to each situation, custom tailored for each set of circumstances. A promotional program for a population that is 50 percent illiterate is vastly different from a program for a population that is 95 percent literate. Pricing in a subsistence market poses different problems from pricing in an affluent society. In evaluating the potential in a developing country, the marketer must make an assessment of the existing level of market development and receptiveness within the country, as well as the firm's own capabilities and circumstances.[21]

Level of Market Development

The level of market development roughly parallels the stages of economic development. Exhibit 9.4 illustrates various stages of the marketing process as it evolves in a growing economy. The table is a static model representing an idealized evolutionary process. As discussed previously, economic cooperation and assistance, technological change, and political, social, and cultural factors can and do cause significant deviations in this evolutionary process. However, the table focuses on the logic and interdependence of marketing and economic development. The more developed an economy, the greater the variety of marketing functions demanded, and the more sophisticated and specialized the institutions become to perform marketing functions.

As countries develop, the distribution channel systems develop. In the retail sector, specialty stores, supermarkets, and hypermarkets emerge, and mom-and-pop stores and local brands often give way to larger establishments. In short, the number of retail stores declines, and the volume of sales per store increases. Additionally, a defined channel structure from manufacturer to wholesaler to retailer develops and replaces the import agent that traditionally assumed all the functions between importing and retailing.

Advertising agencies, facilities for marketing research, repair services,[22] specialized consumer-financing agencies,[23] and storage and warehousing facilities are facilitating agencies created to serve the particular needs of expanded markets and economies. These institutions do not come about automatically, and the necessary marketing structure does not simply appear. Part of the marketer's task when studying an economy is to determine what in the foreign environment will be useful and how much adjustment will be necessary to carry out stated objectives. In some developing countries, it may be up to the marketer to institute the foundations of a modern market system.

[20]Y. Luo, "Market-Seeking MNEs in an Emerging Market: How Parent–Subsidiary Links Shape Overseas Success," *Journal of International Business Studies* 35, no. 4 (2003), pp. 290–309.

[21]Donna L. Paul and Rossitza B. Wooster, "Strategic Investments by US Firms in Transition Economies," *Journal of International Business Studies* 39 (March 2008), pp. 249–66; "Indian Retailing, Getting Cheaper and Better," *The Economist*, February 3, 2007, pp. 64–65.

[22]Ian Alum, "New Service Development Process: Emerging versus Developed Markets," *Journal of Global Marketing* 20, no. 2/3 (2007), pp. 43–56.

[23]Katrijn Gielens and Marnik G. Dekimpe, "The Entry Strategy of Retail Firms into Transition Economies," *Journal of Marketing* 71 (2007), pp. 196–212.

Exhibit 9.4
Evolution of the Marketing Process

Stage	Substage	Example	Marketing Functions	Marketing Institutions	Channel Control	Primary Orientation	Resources Employed	Comments
Agricultural and raw materials	Self-sufficient	Nomadic or hunting tribes	None	None	Traditional authority	Subsistence	Labor Land	Labor intensive No organized markets
	Surplus commodity product	Agricultural economy, such as coffee, bananas	Exchange	Small-scale merchants, traders, fairs, export-import	Traditional authority	Entrepreneurial Commercial	Labor Land	Labor and land intensive Product specialization Local markets Import oriented
Manufacturing	Small scale	Cottage industry	Exchange Physical distribution	Merchants, wholesalers, export-import	Middlemen	Entrepreneurial Financial	Labor Land Technology Transportation	Labor intensive Product standardization and grading Regional and export markets Import oriented
	Mass production	U.S. economy, 1885–1914	Demand creation Physical distribution	Merchants, wholesalers, traders, and specialized institutions	Producer	Production and finance	Labor Land Technology Transportation Capital	Capital intensive Product differentiation National, regional, and export markets
Marketing	Commercial-transition	U.S. economy, 1915–1929	Demand creation Physical distribution Market information	Large-scale and chain retailers	Producer	Entrepreneurial Commercial	Labor Land Technology Transportation Capital Communication	Capital intensive Changes in structure of distribution National, regional, and export markets
	Mass distribution	U.S. economy, 1950 to present	Demand creation Physical distribution Market information Market and product planning, development	Integrated channels of distribution Increase in specialized middlemen	Producer Retailer	Marketing	Labor Land Technology Transportation Capital Communication	Capital and land intensive Rapid product innovation National, regional, and export markets

CROSSING BORDERS 9.1

Marketing in the Third World: Teaching, Pricing, and Community Usage

Much of the marketing challenge in the developing world, which is not accustomed to consumer products, is to get consumers to use the product and to offer it in the right sizes. For example, because many Latin American consumers can't afford a seven-ounce bottle of shampoo, Gillette sells it in half-ounce plastic bottles. And in Brazil, the company sells Right Guard in plastic squeeze bottles instead of metal cans.

But the toughest task for Gillette is convincing Third World men to shave. Portable theaters called mobile propaganda units are sent into villages to show movies and commercials that tout daily shaving. In South African and Indonesian versions, a bewildered bearded man enters a locker room where clean-shaven friends show him how to shave. In the Mexican film, a handsome sheriff is tracking bandits who have kidnapped a woman. He pauses on the trail, snaps a double-edged blade into his razor, and lathers his face to shave. In the end, of course, the smooth-faced sheriff gets the

woman. From packaging blades so that they can be sold one at a time to educating the unshaven about the joys of a smooth face, Gillette is pursuing a growth strategy in the developing world.

What Gillette does for shaving, Colgate-Palmolive does for oral hygiene. Video vans sent into rural India show an infomercial designed to teach the benefits of toothpaste and the proper method of brushing one's teeth. "If they saw the toothpaste tube, they wouldn't know what to do with it," says the company's Indian marketing manager. The people need to be educated about the need for toothpaste and then how to use the product. Toothpaste consumption has doubled in rural Brazil in a six-year period.

Sources: David Wessel, "Gillette Keys Sales to Third World Taste," *The Wall Street Journal*, January 23, 1986, p. 30; "Selling to India," *The Economist*, May 1, 2000; Raja Ramachandran, "Understanding the Market Environment of India," *Business Horizons*, January/February 2000, p. 44; Euromonitor International, 2010.

The limitation of Exhibit 9.4 in evaluating the market system of a particular country is that the system is in a constant state of flux. To expect a neat, precise progression through each successive growth stage, as in the geological sciences, is to oversimplify the dynamic nature of marketing development. So some ventures will not succeed no matter how well planned. A significant factor in the acceleration of market development is that countries or areas of countries have been propelled from the 18th to the 21st century in the span of two decades via borrowed technology.

Marketing structures of many developing countries are simultaneously at many stages. It is not unusual to find traditional small retail outlets functioning side by side with advanced, modern markets. This situation is especially true in food retailing, where a large segment of the population buys food from small produce stalls, while the same economy supports modern supermarkets equal to any found in the United States.

Demand in Developing Countries

The data in Exhibit 9.5 represent the diversity of consumption patterns across types of countries. Notice the higher percentages of expenditures for food in developing countries, whereas the costs of housing are more important in affluent countries. Also note the high costs of health goods and medical services associated with the mostly private-sector health-care system of the United States. You may recall from Chapter 4 that the government-based, tax-dollar supported systems in many other affluent countries deliver equal or better longevity to their citizens, particularly in Japan. Affluence also allows higher proportions to be spent on leisure activities than is the case in developing countries.

Estimating market potential in less-developed countries involves additional challenges. Most of the difficulty arises from the coexistence of three distinct kinds markets in each country: (1) the traditional rural/agricultural sector, (2) the modern urban/high-income sector, and (3) the often very large transitional sector usually represented by low-income urban slums. The modern sector is centered in the capital city and has jet airports, international hotels, new factories, and an expanding Westernized middle class. The traditional rural sector tends to work in the countryside, as it has for centuries. Directly juxtaposed to the modern sector, the transitional sector contains those moving from the country to the large cities. Production and consumption patterns vary across the three sectors. Latin America

Exhibit 9.5

Consumption Patterns in Most Populous American Countries

Country	Occupants per household	Food	Alcohol, Tobacco	Clothing	Housing	Health Goods, Medical Services	Transportation	Communications	Leisure	Education
United States	2.6	2174	618	1159	5998	5956	3332	720	2959	701
Brazil	3.6	1257	96	168	758	224	226	279	173	365
Mexico	3.9	1277	130	154	726	260	939	95	136	212
Colombia	3.8	871	150	130	447	376	318	109	161	154
Argentina	3.7	820	135	292	621	153	517	149	356	47
Canada	2.6	2082	890	937	5064	1343	3287	500	2173	372
Peru	4.1	809	55	159	274	170	255	85	66	207
Venezuela	4.5	2206	228	310	913	363	719	383	293	475

Household Expenditures ($/capita)

Source: Euromonitor International, 2010.

The irony of Parker Brothers' introduction of Monopoly to Ecuador in 2009 is rather amusing, given President Rafael Correa's announcement of new *anti-monopoly* laws just the year before. He was reacting to Carlos Slim's giant Mexican Telmex takeover of Ecuador Telecom.

currently has a population of about 600 million, about two-thirds of which would be classified as middle class by one definition—that is, within the income per capita band of $5,000 to $20,000 at purchase price parity.[24] The modern sector demands products and services similar to those available in any industrialized country; the remaining 200 million in the transitional and rural sectors, however, demand items more indigenous and basic to subsistence. As one authority on developing markets observed, "A rural consumer can live a sound life without many products. Toothpaste, sugar, coffee, washing soap, bathing soap, kerosene are all bare necessities of life to those who live in semi-urban and urban areas." One of the greatest challenges of the 21st century is to manage and market to the transitional sector in developing countries. The large-city slums perhaps present the greatest problems for smooth economic development.

Increasingly marketing research efforts are being focused on the lowest income segments in Latin America. For example, McCann Worldgroup's office in Bogota, Colombia (owned by the global advertising conglomerate Interpublic Group), developed a new division called "Barrio." The launch of the new division is based on a two-year, $2.5 million research project in which McCann sent employees across Latin America to live for a week with families earning between $350 to $700 per month. The agency amassed 700 hours of video recordings and thousands of questionnaires to develop a clearer picture of how consumers behave in the region's poorer districts. A problem discovered for one of their major clients was a misperception that Nido Rindes Diario, a powdered milk product of Nestle SA, was viewed narrowly as formula appropriate for babies only. A new product positioning was developed, based on the finding that for the poorest families in Latin America, food means survival. One executive explained, "The study found that the meaning of food is energy and strength to work, to carry through the day, to not get sick." To communicate the product's usefulness for the whole family, a radio advertisement was designed using a trumpet and bongo-drum jingle whose verses are a play on the Spanish word *rinde*, which means both long-lasting and productiveness. The jingle suggested that both the consumers of the product and their money would "produce more."[25]

The companies that will benefit in the future from emerging markets in Latin America and elsewhere are the ones that invest when it is difficult and initially unprofitable. In some

---

[24]There are many ways to define "middle class." See "Who's in the Middle," *The Economist Special Report on the New Middle Class,* February 14, 2009, p. 4.

[25]Antonio Regalado, "McCann Offers Peek at Latin America's Poor," *The Wall Street Journal,* December 8. 2008, p. B6.

of the less-developed countries, the marketer will institute the very foundations of a modern market system, thereby gaining a foothold in an economy that will someday be highly profitable. The price paid for entering in the early stages of development may be a lower initial return on investment, but the price paid for waiting until the market becomes profitable may be a blocked market with no opportunity for entry.

Big Emerging Markets (BEMs)

As mentioned previously, the U.S. Department of Commerce estimates that over 75 percent of the expected growth in world trade over the next two decades will come from the more than 130 developing countries; a small core of these countries will account for more than half of that growth.[26] Commerce researchers also predict that imports to the countries identified as **big emerging markets (BEMs)**, with half the world's population and accounting for 25 percent of the industrialized world's GDP today, will by 2010 be 50 percent of that of the industrialized world. With a combined GDP of over $2 trillion, BEMs already account for as large a share of world output as Germany and the United Kingdom combined, and exports to the BEMs exceed exports to Europe and Japan combined.[27]

Big emerging markets share a number of important traits. They

- Are all geographically large.
- Have significant populations.
- Represent sizable markets for a wide range of products.
- Have strong rates of growth or the potential for significant growth.
- Have undertaken significant programs of economic reform.
- Are of major political importance within their regions.
- Are "regional economic drivers."
- Will engender further expansion in neighboring markets as they grow.

Although these criteria are general and each country does not meet all of them, India, China, Brazil, Mexico, Poland, Turkey, and South Africa are prominent examples of countries the Department of Commerce has identified as BEMs.[28] Other countries such as Egypt, Venezuela, and Colombia may warrant inclusion in the near future. The list is fluid, because some countries will drop off while others will be added as economic conditions change. Inducements for those doing business in BEMs include export–import bank loans and political risk insurance channeled into these areas.

The BEMs differ from other developing countries in that they import more than smaller markets and more than economies of similar size. As they embark on economic development, demand increases for capital goods to build their manufacturing base and develop infrastructure. Increased economic activity means more jobs and more income to spend on products not yet produced locally. Thus, as their economies expand, there is accelerated growth in demand for goods and services, much of which must be imported. Thus, BEM merchandise imports are expected to be nearly $1 trillion higher than they were in 1990; if services are added, the amount jumps beyond the trillion-dollar mark.

Because many of these countries lack modern infrastructure, much of the expected growth will be in industrial sectors such as information technology, environmental technology, transportation, energy technology, healthcare technology, and financial services. What is occurring in the BEMs is analogous to the situation after World War II when tremendous demand was created during the reconstruction of Europe. As Europe rebuilt

---

[26]Debabrata Talukdar, Sumila Gulyani, and Lawrence F. Salmen, "Customer-Orientation in the Context of Development Projects: Insights from the World Bank," *Journal of Public Policy & Marketing* 24, no. 1 (2005), pp. 100–11.

[27]C. K. Prahalad and Allen Hammond, "Serving the World's Poor, Profitably," *Harvard Business Review* 80, no. 9 (September 2002), pp. 24–32.

[28]William J. Holstein, "Emerging Markets, Emerging Giants," *The New York Times,* April 22, 2007, p. 4.

its infrastructure and industrial base, demand for capital goods exploded; as more money was infused into its economies, consumer demand also increased rapidly. For more than a decade, Europe could not supply its increasing demand for industrial and consumer goods. During that period, the United States was the principal supplier because most of the rest of the world was rebuilding or had underdeveloped economies. Meeting this demand produced one of the largest economic booms the United States had ever experienced. As we shall see later in the chapter, consumer markets and market segments in the BEMs are already booming. Unlike the situation after World War II, however, the competition will be fierce as Japan, China, Europe, the NICs, and the United States vie for these big emerging markets.

The Americas[29]

Within the Americas, the United States, Canada, Central America, and South America have been natural if sometimes contentious trading partners. As in Europe, the Americas are engaged in all sorts of economic cooperative agreements, with NAFTA being the most significant and Mercosur and DR-CAFTA gaining in importance.

North American Free Trade Agreement (NAFTA)

Preceding the creation of the North American Free Trade Agreement (NAFTA), the United States and Canada had the world's largest bilateral trade agreement; each was the other's largest trading partner. Despite this unique commercial relationship, tariff and other trade barriers hindered even greater commercial activity. To further support trade activity, the two countries established the United States–Canada Free Trade Area (CFTA), designed to eliminate all trade barriers between the two countries. The CFTA created a single, continental commercial market for all goods and most services. The agreement between the United States and Canada was not a customs union like the European Community; no economic or political union of any kind was involved. It provided only for the elimination of tariffs and other trade barriers.

Shortly after both countries had ratified the CFTA, Mexico announced that it would seek free trade with the United States. Mexico's overtures were answered positively by the United States, and talks on a U.S.–Mexico free trade area began. Mexico and the United States had been strong trading partners for decades, but Mexico had never officially expressed an interest in a free trade agreement until the president of Mexico, Carlos Salinas de Gortari, announced that Mexico would seek such an agreement with the United States and Canada.

---

[29]For a comprehensive list of all trade agreements in the Americas, with links to specific documents, visit http://www.sice.oas.org and select Trade Agreements.

Geographic proximity allows Mexicans from Baja, California, to attend Padres baseball games in close-by San Diego. The team maintains this successful store just across the border in Plaza Rio shopping center in Tijuana. And of course, historically, Padre Junipero Serra had visited both places in the late 1700s while establishing the chain of missions in old Spanish California. NAFTA also has given Taco Bell a second shot at making it in Mexico; this store is in Monterrey. The company's 1992, pre-NAFTA incursion failed.

CROSSING BORDERS 9.2   Taco Bell Tries Again

It sounds like a fast-food grudge match: Taco Bell is taking on the homeland of its namesake by reopening for the first time in 15 years in Mexico. Defenders of Mexican culture see the chain's reentry as a crowning insult to a society already overrun by U.S. chains, from Starbucks and Subway to KFC. "It's like bringing ice to the Arctic," complained pop culture historian Carlos Monsiváis.

In Mexico, the company is projecting a more "American" fast-food image by adding French fries—some topped with cheese, sour cream, ground meat, and tomatoes—to the menu of its first store, which opened in late September 2007 in the northern city of Monterrey. Other than the fries and sales of soft-serve ice cream, "our menu comes almost directly from the U.S. menu," said Managing Director Steven Pepper.

Some of the names have been changed to protect the sacred: The hard-shelled items sold as "tacos" in the United States have been renamed "tacostadas." This made-up word is a play on "tostada," which for Mexicans is a hard, fried disk of cornmeal that is always served flat, with toppings. But while Mexicans eagerly buy many American brands, the taco holds a place of honor in the national cuisine. Mexicans eat them everywhere, any time of day, buying them from basket-toting street vendors in the morning or slathering them in salsa at brightly lit taquerias to wrap up a night on the town.

Taco Bell has taken pains to say that it's not trying to masquerade as a Mexican tradition. "One look alone is enough to tell that Taco Bell is not a 'taqueria,'" the

company said in a half-page newspaper ad. "It is a new fast-food alternative that does not pretend to be Mexican food." It's still a mixed message for Mexicans like Marco Fragoso, a 39-year-old office worker sitting down for lunch at a traditional taqueria in Mexico City, because the U.S. chain uses traditional Mexican names for its burritos, gorditas, and chalupas. "They're not tacos," Fragoso said. "They're folded tostadas. They're very ugly."

Taco Bell failed with an earlier, highly publicized launch in Mexico City in 1992, when it opened a few outlets next to KFC restaurants. Now Taco Bell, KFC, and Pizza Hut are owned by Yum! Brands. But Mexicans were less familiar with foreign chains back then, the economy was on the verge of a crisis, and NAFTA had yet to be signed. The restaurants didn't even last two years. Since then, free trade and growing migration have made U.S. brands ubiquitous in Mexico, influencing everything from how people dress to how they talk.

Graham Allan, president of Yum! Brands, says two years of market research have convinced him that the firm will succeed this time. The company is building its second store in another Monterrey suburb and is opening between 8 and 10 more locations in its first year, with plans to eventually reach 300 stores. The first stores will be company-owned, and franchise opportunities will open up in later years.

Sources: Michael Arndt, "Tacos without Borders," *BusinessWeek*, September 3, 2007, p. 12; Mark Stevenson, "Another Run for the Border," *Los Angeles Times*, October 15, 2007, p. C4.

Despite the disparity between Mexico's economy and the economies of the other two countries, there were sound reasons for such an alliance. Canada is a sophisticated industrial economy, resource rich, but with a small population and domestic market. Mexico desperately needs investment, technology, exports, and other economic reinforcement to spur its economy. Even though Mexico has an abundance of oil and a rapidly growing population, the number of new workers is increasing faster than its economy can create new jobs. The United States needs resources (especially oil) and, of course, markets. The three need one another to compete more effectively in world markets, and they need mutual assurances that their already dominant trading positions in the others' markets are safe from protection pressures. When NAFTA was ratified and became effective in 1994, a single market of 360 million people with a $6 trillion GNP emerged.

NAFTA required the three countries to remove all tariffs and barriers to trade over 15 years, and beginning in 2008, all tariff barriers were officially dropped.[30] Some nagging disagreements still persist, such as allowing Mexican trucks and truckers free access to U.S. roads. But for the most part, NAFTA is a comprehensive trade agreement that

[30]Jenalia Moreno, "Trade Tariffs End, Marking a NAFTA Milestone: U.S., Mexico Tout New Growth, but Some Farmers Feel Squeezed Out," *Houston Chronicle*, January 2, 2008.

Exhibit 9.6
Key Provisions of NAFTA

Market access

Within 10 years of implementation, all tariffs will be eliminated on North American industrial products traded among Canada, Mexico, and the United States. All trade between Canada and the United States not already duty free will be duty free as provided for in CFTA. Mexico will immediately eliminate tariffs on nearly 50 percent of all industrial goods imported from the United States, and remaining tariffs will be phased out entirely within 15 years.

Nontariff barriers

In addition to the elimination of tariffs, Mexico will eliminate nontariff barriers and other trade-distorting restrictions. The U.S. exporters will benefit immediately from the removal of most import licenses that have acted as quotas, essentially limiting the importation of products into the Mexican market. NAFTA also eliminates a host of other Mexican barriers, such as local-content, local-production, and export-performance requirements that have limited U.S. exports.

Rules of origin

NAFTA reduces tariffs only for goods made in North America. Tough rules of origin will determine whether goods qualify for preferential tariff treatment under NAFTA. Rules of origin are designed to prevent free riders from benefiting through minor processing or transshipment of non-NAFTA goods. For example, Japan could not assemble autos in Mexico and avoid U.S. or Canadian tariffs and quotas unless the auto had a specific percentage of Mexican (i.e., North American) content. For goods to be traded duty free, they must contain substantial (62.5 percent) North American content. Because NAFTA rules of origin have been strengthened, clarified, and simplified over those contained in the U.S.–Canada Free Trade Agreement, they supersede the CFTA rules.

Customs administration

Under NAFTA, Canada, Mexico, and the United States have agreed to implement uniform customs procedures and regulations. Uniform procedures ensure that exporters who market their products in more than one NAFTA country will not have to adapt to multiple customs procedures. Most procedures governing rules-of-origin documentation, record keeping, and verification will be the same for all three NAFTA countries. In addition, the three will issue advanced rulings, on request, about whether or not a product qualifies for tariff preference under the NAFTA rules of origin.

Investment

NAFTA will eliminate investment conditions that restrict the trade of goods and services to Mexico. Among the conditions eliminated are the requirements that foreign investors export a given level or percentage of goods or services, use domestic goods or services, transfer technology to competitors, or limit imports to a certain percentage of exports.

Services

NAFTA establishes the first comprehensive set of principles governing services trade. Both U.S. and Canadian financial institutions are permitted to open wholly owned subsidiaries in Mexico, and all restrictions on the services they offer will be lifted. NAFTA opens Mexico's market for international truck, bus, and rail transport and eliminates the requirement to hand off cargo to a Mexican vehicle upon entry into Mexico, saving U.S. industry both time and money. Also, U.S. truck and bus companies will have the right to use their own drivers and equipment for cross-border cargo shipment and passenger service with Mexico.

Intellectual property

NAFTA will provide the highest standards of protection of intellectual property available in any bilateral or international agreement. The agreement covers patents, trademarks, copyrights, trade secrets, semiconductor integrated circuits, and copyrights for North American movies, computer software, and records.

Government procurement

NAFTA guarantees businesses fair and open competition for procurement in North America through transparent and predictable procurement procedures. In Mexico, PEMEX (the national oil company), CFE (the national electric company), and other government-owned enterprises will be open to U.S. and Canadian suppliers.

Standards

NAFTA prohibits the use of standards and technical regulations used as obstacles to trade. However, NAFTA provisions do not require the United States or Canada to lower existing health, environmental, or safety regulations, nor does NAFTA require the importation of products that fail to meet each country's health and safety standards.

addresses, and in most cases improves, all aspects of doing business within North America. See Exhibit 9.6 for some of the key provisions of the trade agreement. The elimination of trade and investment barriers among Canada, Mexico, and the United States creates one of the largest and richest markets in the world. Cross-border cooperation seems to ameliorate other long-standing areas of conflict such as legal and illegal immigration. NAFTA also has paved the way for Walmart to move into Mexico and the Mexican supermarket giant Gigante to move into the United States. Other cross-border services are also thriving, including entertainment and healthcare.

CROSSING BORDERS 9.3   In Quebec, They Prefer Pepsi

Up until the 1980s, Coke was king in Quebec. Then the local advertising executives at J. Walter Thompson took a risk. Standard practice for both Coke and Pepsi had been to simply translate U.S. campaigns into French. But being second in the market forced creativity, and based on qualitative research, the ad execs recommended a new selling point: comedy.

It was risky, because while Pepsi had been adopted as a self-effacing term by some Quebecers, it was also a derogatory slur used by non-francophones to describe them. If the marketing plan was seen as offensive, Pepsi could become a pariah.

"Young Quebecers in the 1980s . . . were crowning their own celebrities and creating their own made-in-Quebec lifestyle," wrote the J. Walter Thompson company in a submission to the Cassies, the Canadian Advertising Awards. "Research revealed an inner confidence among Quebec target groups. . . . Since Quebec was culturally unique, it had developed its own entertainment system complete with its own stars," especially in the comedy milieu. "It was a style of comedy that used typical Quebecois stereotypes to redefine the emerging new 'street-smart' culture of young, urban Quebecers."

Claude Meunier, famous for his absurdist humor on *Ding et Dong* television skits, was chosen. The theme of Meunier's ads remained an intractable *joie de vivre* and an undying love of Pepsi. His brief, 30-second spots debuted in 1985 and featured a variety of characters and a humor only Quebecers could appreciate; they became an instant hit.

Pepsi came almost neck-and-neck with Coke the same year. By 1986, David had surpassed Goliath and continued to thrive, even though Coke fought back, outspending Pepsi two-to-one on six media campaigns between 1985 and 1993.

"Quebecers had the sentiment that a multinational corporation finally took the trouble to try and understand them, using the same language, with the same accents," says Luc Dupont, a Canadian marketing professor. A nation moored in a sea of English could empathize with company fighting for purchase in an ocean of Coke. "Subconsciously, Quebecers identify with products that are No. 2," Dupont said. "In addition to the absurd humour and joy of life, they like to say, 'We're different here. We changed things.'"

The Meunier campaign would last 18 years, aided by the fact Meunier became the star of *La Petite Vie*, an early 1990s Quebec sitcom watched by 4 million out of a possible 6 million viewers every Monday night. The Meunier Pepsi campaign won the 1993 CASSIE Best of Show advertising award.

Today, Coke dominates the global market with 51 percent of total sales, compared with Pepsi's 22 percent. But in Quebec, the Pepsi stable of soft drinks owns 61 percent of the market against Coke's 20. It is a dominance unseen anywhere else in North America. "Pepsi's ad campaign allowed us to feed that image of ourselves as different," Dupont said. "Even though in fact, we are not so different." The Pepsi Meunier campaign is taught in textbooks now, Dupont said, as a lesson in how to adapt to your market and change with the times.

The latest TV spot may be the best yet: A Scandinavian-sounding tourist, with the insouciance of Mr. Bean, walks into a *casse-croute* somewhere in Quebec's hinterland and makes the mistake of ordering a Coke. The snack bar falls silent. Wildlife stops in the forest. Traffic grinds to a halt in Old Quebec. People stick their heads out of windows. When the waiter finally pops open a can of the blue and red in front of him, the tourist clues in: "*Ah! Ici, c'est Pepsi.*"

Pepsi is celebrating its 75th anniversary in Quebec this year, honoring the opening of the Montreal plant in 1934 (its first outside the United States). It's rolling out a new logo and ad campaign. It's also putting $40 million into its Montreal bottling facilities, one of several plants in the province employing a total of 1,200 people. That investment, along with large amounts of money spent sponsoring sports and culture (among them the Colisée Pepsi arena in Quebec City and the Pepsi Forum in Montreal) is another key to its success.

We also note that the Quebec province flag is blue and white. while the Canadian flag is red and white. As we will see in Chapter 16, colors often make such a difference.

Sources: Konrad Yakabuski, "How Pepsi Won Quebec," *The Globe and Mail*, August 28, 2008, p. B1-2; Rene Bremmer, *The Gazette*, July 11, 2009, online.

Furthermore, U.S. and foreign investors with apparel and footwear factories in Asia have been encouraged to relocate their production operations to Mexico. For example, Victoria's Secret lingerie chain opened a new manufacturing plant near Mexico City. The company previously had used contractors in Asia for its lingerie line. Even with wages in Mexico three times the monthly wages in Sri Lanka, the company will still come out ahead because moving goods from Mexico City to the United States is cheaper and faster than moving them from Colombo—the time needed to make a sample can be cut from weeks to days. Mexican goods have no tariffs, whereas Sri Lankan goods carry a 19 percent duty.

Total foreign direct investment in Mexico has averaged $11 billion a year since 1995 as companies from all over the world poured money into auto and electronics plants, telecommunications, petrochemicals, and a host of other areas. A large chunk of investment is earmarked for factories that will use Mexico as an export platform for the rest of North America, and increasingly the rest of Latin America.

Job losses have not been as drastic as once feared, in part because companies such as Lucent Technologies have established *maquiladora* plants in anticipation of the benefits from NAFTA. The plants have been buying more components from U.S. suppliers, while cutting back on Asian sources. Miles Press, a $2 million maker of directory cards, saw orders from Lucent grow 20 percent in just a few months. Berg Electronics, a $700 million component maker, expects to triple sales to Lucent's Guadalajara plant next year. This ripple effect has generated U.S. service-sector jobs as well. Fisher-Price shifted toy production for the U.S. market from Hong Kong to a plant in Monterrey. Celadon Trucking Services, which moves goods produced for Fisher-Price from Mexico to the United States, has added 800 new U.S. drivers to the payroll.

During the protracted economic slump following the dot-com bust in the United States, *maquiladora* plants were closing at an uncomfortable rate. Manufacturing migrated to other low-paying countries such as China, Guatemala, and Vietnam. Most recently, in the depths of the unemployment environment in all three countries, new immigration rules have limited Mexican farm workers from coming north.[31] Even so, the bleak predictions by the critics of NAFTA[32] have not been borne out. By the broadest measure of consumer benefits, the per capita income levels at purchase price parity have steadily increased in all three countries: from $7,110 in 1994 to $14,270 in 2008 in Mexico; $21,050 to $36,220 in Canada; and $26,230 to $46,970 in the United States during the same time period.[33]

NAFTA is a work in progress. It is still too early to pass judgment; after all, the European Union has been in existence for more than 50 years and has had its ups and downs. NAFTA is a mere babe in arms in comparison. What is happening is that economic relationships among the three countries are becoming more intense each day, for the most part quietly and profitably. In short, at least 20 years are needed for an objective evaluation of NAFTA to be possible.

United States–Central American Free Trade Agreement–Dominican Republic Free Trade Agreement (DR-CAFTA)

In August 2005, President George Bush signed into law a comprehensive free trade agreement among Costa Rica, the Dominican Republic, El Salvador, Guatemala, Honduras, Nicaragua, and the United States.[34] The agreement includes a wide array of tariff reductions aimed at increasing trade and employment among the seven signatories. Thus, DR-CAFTA represents another important step toward the ultimate goal of a free trade agreement encompassing all the Americas. See Exhibit 9.7 for a listing of American countries involved in trade associations. The statistics included there reflect fundamental measures of their attractiveness to international marketers. Perhaps most useful will be the data reported in

LO7

The foundational market metrics of American nations

[31]P. J. Huffstutter, "Hiring Foreign Farmworkers Gets Tougher under New Rule," *Los Angeles Times*, February 12, 2010, p. B2.

[32]Eduardo Porter, "NAFTA Is a Sweet Deal, So Why Are They So Sour?" *The New York Times*, February 11, 2008, p. A24.

[33]World Bank, 2010.

[34]Beyond NAFTA and DR-CAFTA, the United States has free trade agreements approved for 10 other countries: Australia, Bahrain, Chile, Israel, Jordan, Morocco, Oman, Peru, and Singapore. Agreements with Colombia, South Korea, and Panama await Congressional approval.

Exhibit 9.7
American Market Regions Fundamental Market Metrics

(in parentheses) = average annual growth rate, 2004–2009 as a percentage

Association Country	Population (millions)	GNI* (billions $)	Exports* of Goods (billions $)	Imports* of Goods (billions $)	Ease of Doing Business Index	GNI/ capita* ($)	Internet Users (per 1000 people)
North American Free Trade Agreement (NAFTA)							
United States	306.6 (0.9)	14306.6 (4.0)	1068.3 (5.6)	1566.1 (1.3)	3	46662 (3.1)	741 (2.3)
Mexico	108.6 (1.1)	1068.8	299.3 (4.1)	233.9 (3.5)	55	9805	230 (6.5)
Canada	33.7 (1.0)	1325.9 (6.3)	313.3 (−0.4)	319.6 (3.1)	8	39401 (5.2)	769 (3.1)
Dominican Republic–Central American Free Trade Agreement (DR-CAFTA)							
Guatemala	14.0 (2.5)	37.6 (9.7)	2.4 (−4.2)	10.7 (6.4)	117	2678 (7.0)	184 (24.6)
Costa Rica	4.6 (1.5)	28.3 (9.7)	8.7 (6.6)	11.3 (6.4)	120	6172 (8.1)	398 (13.8)
El Salvador	6.6 (0.4)	21.5 (7.0)	3.8 (3.6)	6.9 (1.7)	81	3489 (6.6)	175 (12.5)
Nicaragua	5.7 (1.3)	5.8 (6.3)	1.4 (13.6)	3.5 (9.4)	113	1008 (4.9)	48 (15.7)
Honduras	7.5 (2.0)	14.5 (11.6)	2.7 (10.2)	6.3 (8.5)	136	1948 (9.4)	112 (27.7)
Dominican Republic	10.1 (1.4)	43.5 (17.1)	6.6 (2.2)	18.1 (15.9)	102	4309 (15.4)	296 (27.3)
United States	as above						
Caribbean Community and Common Market (CARICOM)							
Antigua and Barbuda	.09 (1.2)	(7.4)	.08 (7.4)	.8 (12.1)	44	12595 (6.1)	811 (27.2)
Bahamas	.34 (1.2)	7.4 (3.8)	.54 (2.6)	2.3 (4.0)	59	21503 (2.5)	462 (9.8)
Barbados	.26 (0.3)	2.9	.3 (3.8)	1.5 (1.2)	—	11154	801 (6.2)
Belize	.31 (2.1)	1.3 (6.1)	.3 (9.0)	.9 (11.0)	75	4091 (3.9)	151 (21.2)
Dominica	.07 (−0.3)	.4 (6.9)	.04 (0.1)	.2 (10.0)	76	5254 (7.2)	829 (22.4)
Grenada	.10 (0.3)	.6 (8.3)	.06 (9.5)	.4 (8.6)	88	5926 (8.0)	240 (4.2)
Guyana	.76 (0.0)	1.1	.8 (7.2)	1.4 (16.2)	98	1447	293 (9.1)
Haiti	10.0 (1.6)	7.0	.6 (10.6)	1.7 (5.9)	154	700	112 (25.0)
Jamaica	2.7 (0.5)	11.3 (3.3)	1.4 (−0.4)	4.5 (3.5)	67	4143 (2.8)	663 (10.5)
St. Kitts-Nevis	.05 (1.3)	.5 (7.6)	.04 (−3.2)	.3 (9.7)	70	10062 (6.2)	327 (5.7)
St. Lucia	.17 (1.0)	1.0 (5.5)	.1 (11.8)	.7 (9.7)	34	5530 (4.5)	618 (23.6)
St. Vincent and the Grenadines	.11 (0.1)	.6 (8.6)	.05 (5.5)	.4 (10.6)	62	5423 (8.5)	663 (55.2)
Surinam	.52 (1.0)	2.7	1.9 (16.0)	1.4 (13.2)	148	5192	112 (12.9)
Trinidad-Tobago	1.3 (0.4)	20.6 (9.9)	18.1 (23.2)	7.7 (9.8)	78	15404 (9.4)	183 (8.4)
Latin American Integration Association (LAIA, aka ALADI)							
Argentina	40.3 (1.0)	302.2 (15.9)	55.7 (10.0)	38.9 (11.6)	112	7492 (14.8)	811 (14.0)
Bolivia	9.8 (1.8)	15.6 (13.2)	4.7 (17.2)	4.2 (18.2)	158	1582 (11.2)	143 (26.3)
Brazil	193.7 (1.1)	1477 (18.1)	151.1 (9.3)	127.5 (15.2)	127	7627 (16.9)	452 (18.8)
Chile	17.0 (1.0)	138.0 (9.5)	51.9 (9.8)	41.1 (10.6)	40	8129 (8.3)	342 (12.1)
Colombia	45.7 (1.5)	185.5 (14.6)	33.3 (15.4)	35.6 (16.3)	49	4063 (12.9)	475 (39.1)
Cuba	11.2 (0.0)	—	3.3 (9.1)	13.4 (22.8)	—	—	143 (11.2)
Ecuador	13.6 (1.1)	38.5 (10.4)	13.3 (11.4)	14.7 (12.4)	133	2824 (9.2)	109 (17.6)
Mexico	as above						
Paraguay	6.3 (1.8)	16.3	3.4 (15.7)	8.7 (23.0)	122	2587	112 (26.5)
Peru	29.0 (1.4)	119.5	25.1 (14.4)	20.2 (11.4)	65	4120	269 (17.7)
Uruguay	3.4 (0.2)	30.5 (19.3)	5.8 (14.5)	7.4 (18.8)	109	9079 (19.1)	448 (21.3)
Venezuela	28.6 (1.7)	355.5 (26.7)	95.4 (22.9)	38.6 (18.3)	178	12438 (24.5)	313 (30.0)

*Current U.S. dollars

Sources: Euromonitor International, 2010; World Bank, 2010

the last four columns: the size of the import market, the ease of doing business, and the resources available to consumers, including both money and communication infrastructure. The Ease of Doing Business Index[35] is a ranking based on a combination of 10 different measures, such as ease of . . . "starting a business," "registering property," and "enforcing a contract." For details, see www.doingbusiness.org.

Southern Cone Free Trade Area (Mercosur)[36]

LO8

The growing importance of trading associations among American nations

Mercosur (including Argentina, Bolivia, Brazil, Chile, Paraguay, and Uruguay) is the second-largest common-market agreement in the Americas after NAFTA. The Treaty of Asunción, which provided the legal basis for Mercosur, was signed in 1991 and formally inaugurated in 1995. The treaty calls for a common market that would eventually allow for the free movement of goods, capital, labor, and services among the member countries, with a uniform external tariff. Because Mercosur members were concerned about sacrificing sovereign control over taxes and other policy matters, the agreement envisioned no central institutions similar to those of the European Union institutions.

Since its inception, Mercosur has become the most influential and successful free trade area in South America. With the addition of Bolivia and Chile in 1996, Mercosur became a market of 220 million people with a combined GDP of nearly $1 trillion and the third largest free trade area in the world. More recently Colombia and Ecuador have become associate members, with Venezuela to follow shortly; Mexico has observer status as well. Mercosur has demonstrated greater success than many observers expected. The success can be attributed to the willingness of the region's governments to confront some very tough issues caused by dissimilar economic policies related to the automobile and textile trade and to modify antiquated border customs procedures that initially created a bottleneck to smooth border crossings. The lack of surface and transportation infrastructure to facilitate trade and communications is a lingering problem that is being addressed at the highest levels.

Mercosur has pursued agreements aggressively with other countries and trading groups. For example, there are concrete negotiations under way to create a free trade program with Mexico, talks with Canada regarding a free trade agreement, and talks between Chile and Mercosur aimed at gradual and reciprocal trade liberalization.

In addition, negotiations have been under way since 1999 for a free trade agreement between the European Union and Mercosur, the first region-to-region free trade accord. A framework agreement was signed in 1995, and the long-term objective is to reach convergence in all areas—cooperation, trade, market access, intellectual property, and political dialogue. The two blocs propose the largest free trade area in the world. The advantages of the accord to Mercosur will mainly come from lifting trade barriers on agricultural and agro-industrial products, which account for the lion's share of Mercosur exports to Europe. However, that point will also be a major stumbling block if the European Union is unwilling to open its highly protected agricultural sector to Brazilian and Argentine imports. Nevertheless, one official of the European Union indicated that the European Union was already in the process of reforming its Common Agricultural Policy. Although negotiations will not be easy, Mercosur and the European Union should be able to reach an accord. As we shall see in the next section, Mercosur has assumed the leadership in setting the agenda for the creation of a free trade area of the Americas or, more likely, a South American Free Trade Area (SAFTA).

Latin American Progress

A political and economic revolution has been taking place in Latin America over the past three decades. Most of the countries have moved from military dictatorships to democratically elected governments, and sweeping economic and trade liberalization is replacing the economic model most Latin American countries followed for decades. We make this claim despite the recent backsliding of a few countries in the region, such as Venezuela. Privatization of state-owned enterprises and other economic, monetary, and trade policy reforms show a broad shift away from the inward-looking policies of import substitution

---

[35]Euromonitor International, 2010.

[36]See http://www.mercosur.org.uy/.

(that is, manufacturing products at home rather than importing them) and protectionism so prevalent in the past. The trend toward privatization of SOEs in the Americas followed a period in which governments dominated economic life for most of the 20th century. State ownership was once considered the ideal engine for economic growth. Instead of economic growth, however, they ended up with inflated public-sector bureaucracies, complicated and unpredictable regulatory environments, the outright exclusion of foreign and domestic private ownership, and inefficient public companies. Fresh hope for trade and political reforms is now being directed even to communist Cuba.[37]

Today many Latin American countries are at roughly the same stage of liberalization that launched the dynamic growth in Asia during the 1980s and 1990s. In a positive response to these reforms, investors have invested billions of dollars in manufacturing plants, airlines, banks, public works, and telecommunications systems. Because of its size and resource base, the Latin American market has always been considered to have great economic and market possibilities. The population of nearly 600 million is nearly twice that of the United States and 100 million more than the European Community.

The strength of these reforms was tested during the last two decades, a turbulent period both economically and politically for some countries. Argentina, Brazil, and Mexico were affected by the economic meltdown in Asia in 1997 and the continuing financial crisis in Russia. The Russian devaluation and debt default caused a rapid deterioration in Brazil's financial situation; capital began to flee the country, and Brazil devalued its currency. Economic recession in Brazil—coupled with the sharp devaluation of the real— reduced Argentine exports, and Argentina's economic growth slowed. Mexico was able to weather the Russian debt default partly because of debt restructuring and other changes after the major devaluation and recession in the early 1990s. However, competition with Chinese manufacturing has yielded slower growth than predicted at the time of passage of the North American Free Trade Agreement (NAFTA). Other Latin American countries suffered economic downturns that led to devaluations and, in some cases, political instability. Nevertheless, Latin America is still working toward economic reform. Finally, not reflected in the data in Exhibit 9.7 is the surprising resilience in the developing countries vis-à-vis the United States and Canada to the lingering economic malaise following the recession of 2008–2009.[38]

Latin American Economic Cooperation

Besides the better-known NAFTA and Mercosur, other Latin American market groups (Exhibit 9.7) have had varying degrees of success. Plagued with tremendous foreign debt, protectionist economic systems, triple-digit inflation, state ownership of basic industries, and overregulation of industry, most Latin American countries were in a perpetual state of economic chaos. In such conditions, trade or integration among member countries stagnated. But as discussed previously, sparked by the success of Mercosur and NAFTA, Latin America has seen a wave of genuine optimism about the economic miracle under way, spurred by political and economic reforms from the tip of Argentina to the Rio Grande. Coupled with these market-oriented reforms is a desire to improve trade among neighboring countries by reviving older agreements or forming new ones. Many of the trade groups are seeking ties to Mercosur, the European Union, or both.

Latin American Integration Association.

The long-term goal of the LAIA, better known by its Spanish acronym, ALADI,[39] is a gradual and progressive establishment of a Latin American common market. One of the more important aspects of LAIA that differs from LAFTA, its predecessor, is the differential treatment of member countries according to their level of economic development. Over the years, negotiations among member countries have lowered duties on selected products and eased trade tensions over quotas, local-content requirements, import licenses, and other trade barriers. An important

---

[37]Katherine Yung, "When Cuba Opens Up . . . " *Dallas Morning News*, March 11, 2007, pp. D1, D6.

[38]"Counting Their Blessings," *The Economist*, January 2, 2010, pp. 25–28; Jack Ewing, Vikas Bajaj, and Keith Bradsher, "An Uneven World of Debt," *The New York Times*, February 8, 2010, pp. B1, B3, B6.

[39]http://www.aladi.org, 2008.

People queued for a Chinese-made bus at city center in Havana. China is making major sales and investments in the infrastructures of the developing world, including in Cuba, a member country of LAIA and a fellow "communist" country.

feature of LAIA is the provision that permits members to establish bilateral trade agreements among member countries. It is under this proviso that trade agreements have been developed among LAIA members.

Caribbean Community and Common Market (CARICOM).[40]   The success of the Caribbean Free Trade Association led to the creation of the Caribbean Community and Common Market. CARICOM member countries continue in their efforts to achieve true regional integration. The group has worked toward a single-market economy and in 2000 established the CSME (CARICOM Single Market and Economy) with the goal of a common currency for all members. The introduction of a common external tariff structure was a major step toward that goal. CARICOM continues to seek stronger ties with other groups in Latin America and has signed a trade agreement with Cuba.

NAFTA to FTAA or SAFTA?   Initially NAFTA was envisioned as the blueprint for a free trade area extending from Alaska to Argentina. The first new country to enter the NAFTA fold was to be Chile, then membership was to extend south until there was a Free Trade Area of the Americas (FTAA) by 2005. The question now is whether there will be an FTAA or whether there will be a tri-country NAFTA in the north and a South American Free Trade Area (SAFTA) led by Brazil and the other member states of Mercosur in the south. The answer to this question rests in part with the issue of fast-track legislation and the policies of President Obama.

Strategic Implications for Marketing

Surfacing in the emerging markets in the Americas and around the world is a vast population whose expanding incomes are propelling them beyond a subsistence level to being viable consumers. As a country develops, incomes change, population concentrations shift, expectations for a better life adjust to higher standards, new infrastructures evolve, and social capital investments are made. Market behavior changes, and eventually groups of consumers with common tastes and needs (i.e., market segments) arise.[41]

When incomes rise, new demand is generated at all income levels for everything from soap to automobiles. Furthermore, large households can translate into higher disposable incomes. Young working people in Latin America and Asia usually live at home until they marry. With no rent to pay, they have more discretionary income and can contribute to

[40]http://www.caricom.org, 2008.

[41]Peter G. P. Walters and Saeed Samiee, "Marketing Strategy in Emerging Markets: The Case of China," *Journal of International Marketing* 11, no. 1 (2003), pp. 97–106.

household purchasing power. Countries with low per capita incomes are potential markets for a large variety of goods; consumers show remarkable resourcefulness in finding ways to buy what really matters to them. In the United States, the first satellite dishes sprang up in the poorest parts of Appalachia. Similarly, in Mexico, homes with color televisions outnumber those with showers.

As incomes rise to middle-class range, demand for more costly goods increases for everything from disposable diapers to automobiles. Incomes for the middle class in emerging markets are less than those in the United States, but spending patterns are different, so the middle class has more to spend than comparable income levels in the United States would indicate. For example, members of the middle class in emerging markets do not own two automobiles and suburban homes, and healthcare and housing in some cases are subsidized, freeing income to spend on refrigerators, TVs, radios, better clothing, and special treats. Exhibit 9.5 illustrates the percentage of household income spent on various classes of goods and services. More household money goes for food in emerging markets than in developed markets, but the next category of high expenditures for emerging and developed countries alike is appliances and other durable goods. Spending by the new rich, however, is a different story. The new rich want to display their wealth; they want to display status symbols such as Rolex watches, Louis Vuitton purses, and Mercedes-Benz automobiles.

One analyst suggests that as a country passes the $5,000 per capita GNP level, people become more brand conscious and forgo many local brands to seek out foreign brands they recognize. At $10,000, they join those with similar incomes who are exposed to the same global information sources. They join the "$10,000 Club" of consumers with homogeneous demands who share a common knowledge of products and brands. They become global consumers. If a company fails to appreciate the strategic implications of the $10,000 Club, it will miss the opportunity to participate in the world's fastest growing global consumer segment. More than 1 billion people in the world now have incomes of $10,000 or better. Companies that look for commonalties among these 1 billion consumers will find growing markets for global brands.

Markets are changing rapidly, and identifiable market segments with similar consumption patterns are found across many countries. Emerging markets will be the growth areas of the 21st century.

Summary

The ever-expanding involvement in world trade of more and more people with varying needs and wants will test old trading patterns and alliances. The global marketer of today and tomorrow must be able to react to market changes rapidly and to anticipate new trends within constantly evolving market segments that may not have existed as recently as last year. Many of today's market facts will likely be tomorrow's historical myths.

Along with dramatic shifts in global politics, the increasing scope and level of technical and economic growth have enabled many nations to advance their standards of living by as much as two centuries in a matter of decades. As nations develop their productive capacity, all segments of their economies will feel the pressure to improve. The impact of these political, social, and economic trends will continue to be felt throughout the world, resulting in significant changes in marketing practices. Furthermore, the impact of information technology will speed up the economic growth in every country. Marketers must focus on devising marketing plans designed to respond fully to each level of economic development.

Brazil and the rest of Latin America continue to undergo rapid political and economic changes that have brought about the opening of most countries in the region to foreign direct investments and international trade. And though emerging markets present special problems, they are promising markets for a broad range of products now and in the future. Emerging markets create new marketing opportunities for MNCs as new market segments evolve. The economic advantages of geography and trade continue to favor market integration and cooperation among American countries on both continents.

Key Terms

Economic development	Newly industrialized countries (NICs)	Infrastructure	Big emerging markets (BEMs)

Questions

1. Define the key terms listed on the previous page.

2. Is it possible for an economy to experience economic growth as measured by total GNP without a commensurate rise in the standard of living? Discuss fully.

3. Why do technical assistance programs by more affluent nations typically ignore the distribution problem or relegate it to a minor role in development planning? Explain.

4. Discuss each of the stages of evolution in the marketing process. Illustrate each stage with a particular country.

5. As a country progresses from one economic stage to another, what in general are the marketing effects?

6. Select a country in the agricultural and raw materials stage of economic development and discuss what changes will occur in marketing when it passes to a manufacturing stage.

7. What are the consequences of each stage of marketing development on the potential for industrial goods within a country? For consumer goods?

8. Discuss the significance of economic development to international marketing. Why is the knowledge of economic development of importance in assessing the world marketing environment? Discuss.

9. The Internet accelerates the process of economic growth. Discuss.

10. Discuss the impact of the IT revolution on the poorest countries.

11. Select one country in each of the three stages of economic development. For each country, outline the basic existing marketing institutions and show how their stages of development differ. Explain why.

12. Why should a foreign marketer study economic development? Discuss.

13. The infrastructure is important to the economic growth of an economy. Comment.

14. What are the objectives of economically developing countries? How do these objectives relate to marketing? Comment.

15. Using the list growth factors, evaluate Mexico and Brazil as to their prospects for rapid growth. Which factors will be problems for Mexico or Brazil?

16. What is marketing's role in economic development? Discuss marketing's contributions to economic development.

17. Discuss the economic and trade importance of the big emerging markets.

18. One of the ramifications of emerging markets is the creation of a middle class. Discuss.

19. The needs and wants of a market and the ability to satisfy them are the result of the three-way interaction of the economy, culture, and the marketing efforts of businesses. Comment.

20. Discuss the strategic implications of marketing in Mexico.

21. Discuss the consequences to the United States of not being a part of SAFTA.

22. Discuss the strategic marketing implications of NAFTA.

23. Visit the Web pages for NAFTA and Mercosur and locate each group's rules of origin. Which group has the most liberal rules of origin? Why is there a difference?

24. NAFTA has been in existence for several years—how has it done? Review Exhibit 9.6, which discusses the initial provisions of the agreement, and, using the Internet, evaluate how well the provisions have been met.

Chapter 10

Europe, Africa, and the Middle East

CHAPTER OUTLINE

Global Perspective: Might Free Trade Bring Peace to the Middle East?

La Raison d'Etre
    Economic Factors
    Political Factors
    Geographic and Temporal Proximity
    Cultural Factors

Patterns of Multinational Cooperation

Global Markets and Multinational Market Groups

Europe
    European Integration
    European Union
    Eastern Europe and the Baltic States
    The Commonwealth of Independent States

Africa

Middle East

Implications of Market Integration
    Strategic Implications
    Market Metrics
    Marketing Mix Implications

CHAPTER LEARNING OBJECTIVES

What you should learn from Chapter 10:

LO1 The reasons for economic union

LO2 Patterns of international cooperation

LO3 The evolution of the European Union

LO4 Evolving patterns of trade as eastern Europe and the former Soviet states embrace free-market systems

LO5 Strategic implications for marketing in the region

LO6 The size and nature of marketing opportunities in the European/African/Middle East regions

Global Perspective

MIGHT FREE TRADE BRING PEACE TO THE MIDDLE EAST?

The nearly complete destruction of the continental European economies by World War II seriously endangered the stability of Europe's social and political institutions. Europe's leaders knew that to rebuild from the ruins, it was essential to form new kinds of international institutions to ensure prosperity, stability, and peace in the region. The first of these institutions was the European Coal and Steel Community, established in 1952 to integrate the coal and steel industries of France, West Germany, Italy, Belgium, the Netherlands, and Luxembourg. Fifty years later, based on the success of this first small experiment in economic interdependence, we now see the European Union with 27 member nations and 3 candidate countries set to join during the next few years. The economies have burgeoned, but more important, peace has persisted.

Might such an approach work in the war-torn Middle East? Let's consider the possibilities and potential of a Middle Eastern Union. The crux of the problem is Jerusalem. The holy Old City is a matter of faith to so many. For Christians it is sacred because of its associations with Christ. For Jews it has served as the center for their people—not only in a national way but, more important, in a religious sense. For Muslims only Mecca and Medina are more important spiritual places. And the fighting over the real estate that represents its spiritual events appears perpetual.

Jerusalem can be a primary part of the solution. But we must look beyond the rockets and bombs of the day. We must imagine a safe, prosperous, and peaceful place. Imagine an international shrine. Perhaps the Old City would be administered by Buddhists or Norwegians or the United Nations. Israel would have its grand capital to the west, in the New City, and the Palestinians to the east a bit.

Religious tourism would feed the economies in both countries, as well as the surrounding area. Imagine the possibilities! In 2000, before the most recent insanity of violence, tourism brought in $3.2 billion in revenues for Israel. Compare that with Disneyland in Orange County, California. That park's yearly 10 million visitors spend about $100 each on tickets, food, and souvenirs. Add in the transportation, hotel, and restaurant revenues appreciated in the neighborhood, and that's more than a couple of billion dollars a year coming to the Anaheim environs.

The Church of the Holy Sepulcher (built over the tomb of Jesus) would draw Christians. The Wailing Wall is the most holy place for Jews. Muslims would flock to the Dome of the Rock (Mohammed was carried by the angel Gabriel for a visit to Heaven after praying at the Rock). The most enlightened tourists would visit all three. Disney might consult on the queuing problems. Staying open 24/7 would expand capacity by allowing jet-lagged pilgrims access to the more popular places. And outside the Old City are Bethlehem, Hebron, Nazareth, Jericho, the Sea of Galilee, the Dead Sea, and the Red Sea, to name only the more obvious attractions. We're talking $10 billion to $20 billion in annual revenues if things are done right—that's about 10 to 15 percent of the current GDP of Israel.

To the east, the new Hijaz Railway Corp. is already working on a line connecting Iran and Jordan via Syria and is talking about lines connecting Iraq, Turkey, and Europe as well—all for the sake of religious tourism. Indeed, the line's original purpose was taking pilgrims to Medina from Damascus—that was, before Lawrence of Arabia severed it for carrying arms and troops during World War I. The current company executives reckon the two-day trip from Tehran to Amman will cost only about $100 and the Shiite Muslims of Iran will flock to their holy sites in the area. Why not run the line all the way to east Jerusalem?

How about Jerusalem as the site for the 2020 Olympic games? That's another $5 billion in revenues. And ignoring the dollars for a moment, please consider the sentiments associated with "the 2020 Jerusalem Games" juxtaposed with the disaster of Munich in 1972. And ignoring the dollars for another moment, imagine the spiritual splendor for so many millions visiting the sources of their faith, treading some of the original paths of David, Jesus, and Mohammed.

This little fantasy presumes a peaceful political division of Israel and Palestine along the lines reaffirmed in the Oslo Accords. It presumes a dropping of all commercial boycotts in the region. It presumes that Palestinians won't have to risk being shot while "hopping the fence" to work in Israel. It presumes that companies like Nestlé will be able to integrate the operations of their complementary plants in the area. It presumes that the United States and other countries will send to the region legions of tourists rather than boatloads of weapons. It presumes an open, international, and, most important, a whole Old City of Jerusalem. And it presumes free trade and travel among all nations in the region allowing all to prosper in new ways.

Finally, as Pulitzer Prize–winner Jared Diamond points out, the Middle East, historically referred to as the

Within a short walk of one another in the Old City of Jerusalem are three of the most important holy sites for Muslims (the Dome of the Rock), Jews (the Wailing Wall), and Christians (the Church of the Holy Sepulchre). Peace in the region would yield a bonanza of religious tourism.

Fertile Crescent, was the cradle of civilization. It became so long ago because of innovation and trade in the region. One can only imagine what free trade in the area would produce now.

Sources: John L. Graham, "Trade Brings Peace," paper delivered at the Global Ethics and Religion Forum; Clare Hall, Cambridge University conference, *War and Reconciliation: Perspectives of the World Religions,* May 26, 2003, Cambridge, England; Jared Diamond, *Collapse: How Societies Choose to Fail or Succeed* (New York: Viking, 2005).

Following the success of aforementioned European Steel and Coal Community, a global economic revolution began in 1958 when the European Economic Community was ratified and Europe took the step that would ultimately lead to the present-day European Union (EU). Until then, skeptics predicted that the experiment would never work and that the alliance would fall apart quickly. It was not until the single market was established that the United States, Japan, and other countries gave serious thought to creating other alliances. The establishment of common markets, coupled with the trend away from planned economies to the free market system in Latin America, Asia, and eventually the former Soviet Union, created fertile ground that sparked the drive to form trade alliances and free markets the world over. Nation after nation embraced the free market system, implementing reforms in their economic and political systems with the desire to be part of a multinational market region in the evolving global marketplace. Traditions that are centuries old are being altered, issues that cannot be resolved by decree are being negotiated to acceptable solutions, governments and financial systems are restructuring, and companies are being reshaped to meet new competition and trade patterns.

The evolution and growth of **multinational market regions**—those groups of countries that seek mutual economic benefit from reducing interregional trade and tariff barriers— are the most important global trends today. Organizational form varies widely among market regions, but the universal goals of multinational cooperation are economic benefits for the participants and the associated peace between[1] and within countries.[2] The world

[1]By far the strongest evidence for the "trade causes peace" notion is that provided by Solomon W. Polachek, "Why Democracies Cooperate More and Fight Less: The Relationship between International Trade and Cooperation," *Review of International Economics* 5, no. 3 (1997), pp. 295–309; additional evidence is supplied at http://www.cpbp.org, click on Peace Monitor, then Countries; Jonathan Schell, *The Unconquerable World* (New York: Metropolitan Books, 2003); Thomas Friedman, *The World Is Flat* (New York: Farrar, Straus, and Giroux, 2005).

[2]Studies of the causes of civil wars supports their belief; see Paul Collier, "The Market for Civil War," *Foreign Policy,* May/June 2003, pp. 38–45.

is awash in economic cooperative agreements as countries look for economic alliances to expand access to free markets. Indeed, part of the efforts of the 192 member countries in the United Nations include mutual economic development; the World Trade Organization, with its 153 members and 30 observers, is wholly dedicated to making trade among nations more efficient.

Regional economic cooperative agreements have been around since the end of World War II. The most successful one is the European Union (EU), the world's largest multinational market region and foremost example of economic cooperation. Multinational market groups form large markets that provide potentially significant opportunities for international business. As it became apparent in the late 1980s that the European Union was to achieve its long-term goal of a single European market, a renewed interest in economic cooperation followed, with the creation of several new alliances. The North American Free Trade Agreement (NAFTA) and the Latin American Integration Association (LAIA) in the Americas and the Association of Southeast Asian Nations (ASEAN) and Asia-Pacific Economic Cooperation (APEC) in the Asian-Pacific Rim are all relatively new or reenergized associations that are gaining strength and importance as multinational market regions.

Along with the growing trend of economic cooperation, concerns about the effect of such cooperation on global competition are emerging. Governments and businesses worry that the European Union, NAFTA, and other cooperative trade groups will become regional trading blocs without trade restrictions internally but with borders protected from outsiders. But as each of these trade groups continues to create new agreements with other countries and groups, the networked global economy and free trade are clearly on the ascendance. The benefits are clear for consumers; however, global companies face richer and more intense competitive environments.

La Raison d'Etre

LO1

The reasons for economic union

Successful economic union requires favorable economic, political, cultural, and geographic factors as a basis for success. Major flaws in any one factor can destroy a union unless the other factors provide sufficient strength to overcome the weaknesses. In general, the advantages of economic union must be clear-cut and significant, and the benefits must greatly outweigh the disadvantages before nations forgo any part of their sovereignty. Many of the associations formed in Africa and Latin America have had little impact because perceived benefits were not sufficient to offset the partial loss of sovereignty.

Economic Factors

Every type of economic union shares the development and enlargement of market opportunities as a basic orientation; usually, markets are enlarged through preferential tariff treatment for participating members, common tariff barriers against outsiders, or both. Enlarged, protected markets stimulate internal economic development by providing assured outlets and preferential treatment for goods produced within the customs union, and consumers benefit from lower internal tariff barriers among the participating countries. In many, but not all cases, external and internal barriers are reduced because of the greater economic security afforded domestic producers by the enlarged market.[3]

Nations with complementary economic bases are least likely to encounter frictions in the development and operation of a common market unit. However, for an economic union to survive, it must have agreements and mechanisms in place to settle economic disputes. In addition, the total benefit of economic integration must outweigh individual differences that are sure to arise as member countries adjust to new trade relationships. The European Union includes countries with diverse economies, distinctive monetary systems, developed agricultural bases, and different natural resources. It is significant that most of the problems encountered by the European Union have arisen over agriculture

[3]Michele Fratianni and Chan Hoon Oh, "Expanding RTAs, Trade Flows, and the Multinational Enterprise," *Journal of International Business Studies* 40, no. 7 (2009), pp. 1206–27.

and monetary policy. In the early days of the European Community (now the European Union), agricultural disputes were common. The British attempted to keep French poultry out of the British market, France banned Italian wine, and the Irish banned eggs and poultry from other member countries. In all cases, the reason given was health and safety, but the stronger motives were the continuation of the age-old policies of market protection. Such skirmishes are not unusual, but they do test the strength of the economic union. In the case of the European Union, the European Commission was the agency used to settle disputes and charge the countries that violated EU regulations.

Political Factors

Political amenability among countries is another basic requisite for the development of a supranational market arrangement. Participating countries must have comparable aspirations and general compatibility before surrendering any part of their national sovereignty. State sovereignty is one of the most cherished possessions of any nation and is relinquished only for a promise of significant improvement of the national position through cooperation.

Economic considerations are the basic catalyst for the formation of a customs union group, but political elements are equally important. The uniting of the original European Union countries was partially a response to the outside threat of the Soviet Union's great political and economic power; the countries of western Europe were willing to settle their "family squabbles" to present a unified front to the Russian bear. The communist threat no longer exists, but the importance of political unity to fully achieve all the benefits of economic integration has driven European countries to form the Union (EU).

Geographic and Temporal Proximity

Although geographic and temporal proximity are not absolutely imperative for cooperating members of a customs union, such closeness does facilitate the functioning of a common market. Indeed, the most recent research demonstrates that more important than physical distance are differences across time zones.[4] That is, trade tends to travel more easily in north–south directions than it did in ancient times. However, transportation networks (basic to any marketing system) are likely to be interrelated and well developed when countries are close together. Issues of immigration, legal and illegal, also promote closer economic integration between close neighbors. One of the first major strengths of the European Union was its transportation network; the opening of the tunnel between England and France further bound this common market. Countries that are widely separated geographically have major barriers to overcome in attempting economic fusion. However, with increasing efficiencies in communication and transportation, the importance of such factors appears to be waning.

Cultural Factors

As mentioned in the last chapter, the United States has bilateral free trade agreements in progress and approved with several nations in addition to multilateral agreements such as NAFTA and DR-CAFTA (Dominican Republic, Central American Countries, and the U.S.). But generally, cultural similarity eases the shock of economic cooperation with other countries. The more similar the culture, the more likely an agreement is to succeed, because members understand the outlook and viewpoints of their colleagues. Although there is great cultural diversity in the European Union, key members share a long-established Christian heritage and are commonly aware of being European. However, even this aspect of diversity may be unimportant as negotiations proceed with Turkey about EU membership. Language, as a part of culture, has not created as much a barrier for EU countries as was expected. Nearly every educated European can do business in at least two or three languages, so the linguistic diversity of several major languages did not much impede trade.

---

[4]Contrast Jared Diamond's *Guns, Germs, and Steel* (New York: W. W. Norton, 1999) and Jennifer Chandler and John L. Graham, "Relationship-Oriented Cultures, Corruption, and International Marketing Success," *Journal of Business Ethics*, 92 (2010), pp. 251–67.

Patterns of Multinational Cooperation

LO2
Patterns of international cooperation

Of course, at the most general level, the World Trade Organization represents the most important and comprehensive trade agreement in history. At this writing, it appears that Russia will soon be invited to join the WTO.[5] However, beyond the WTO, multinational market groups take several other forms, varying significantly in the degree of cooperation, dependence, and interrelationship among participating nations. There are five fundamental groupings for regional economic integration, ranging from regional cooperation for development, which requires the least amount of integration, to the ultimate integration of political union.

Regional Cooperation Groups.
The most basic economic integration and cooperation is the *regional cooperation for development (RCD)*. In the RCD arrangement, governments agree to participate jointly to develop basic industries beneficial to each economy. Each country makes an advance commitment to participate in the financing of a new joint venture and to purchase a specified share of the output of the venture. An example is the project between Colombia and Venezuela to build a hydroelectric generating plant on the Orinoco River. They shared jointly in construction costs, and they share the electricity produced.

Free Trade Area.
A free trade area (FTA) requires more cooperation and integration than the RCD. It is an agreement between two or more countries to reduce or eliminate customs duties and nontariff trade barriers among partner countries while members maintain individual tariff schedules for external countries. Essentially, an FTA provides its members with a mass market without barriers to impede the flow of goods and services.[6]

Customs Union.
A customs union represents the next stage in economic cooperation. It enjoys the free trade area's reduced or eliminated internal tariffs and adds a common external tariff on products imported from countries outside the union. The customs union is a logical stage of cooperation in the transition from an FTA to a common market. The European Union was a customs union before becoming a common market. Customs unions exist between France and Monaco, Italy and San Marino, and Switzerland and Liechtenstein, to name some examples.

Common Market.
A common market agreement eliminates all tariffs and other restrictions on internal trade, adopts a set of common external tariffs, and removes all restrictions on the free flow of capital and labor among member nations. Thus, a common market is a common marketplace for goods as well as for services (including labor) and for capital. It is a unified economy and lacks only political unity to become a political union. The Treaty of Rome, which established the European Economic Community (EEC) in 1957, called for common external tariffs and the gradual elimination of intramarket tariffs, quotas, and other trade barriers. The treaty also called for the elimination of restrictions on the movement of services, labor, and capital; prohibition of cartels; coordinated monetary and fiscal policies; common agricultural policies; use of common investment funds for regional industrial development; and similar rules for wage and welfare payments. The EEC existed until the Maastricht Treaty created the European Union, an extension of the EEC into a political union.

Political Union.
Political union is the most fully integrated form of regional cooperation. It involves complete political and economic integration, either voluntary or enforced. The most notable enforced political union was the Council for Mutual Economic Assistance (COMECON), a centrally controlled group of countries organized by the Soviet Union. With the dissolution of the Soviet Union and the independence of the Eastern European bloc, COMECON was disbanded.

---

[5]Stephen Castle, "EU to Fast-Track Russia on WTO," *International Herald Tribune*, January 26–27, 2008, p. 13.

[6]The European Free Trade Area is a good example. See http://www.efta.int/, 2010.

A *commonwealth* of nations is a voluntary organization providing for the loosest possible relationship that can be classified as economic integration. The British Commonwealth includes Britain and countries formerly part of the British Empire. Some of its members still recognize the British monarch as their symbolic head, though Britain has no political authority over any commonwealth country. Its member states had received preferential tariffs when trading with Great Britain, but when Britain joined the European Community, all preferential tariffs were abandoned. A commonwealth can best be described as the weakest of political unions and is mostly based on economic history and a sense of tradition. Heads of state meet every three years to discuss trade and political issues they jointly face, and compliance with any decisions or directives issued is voluntary.

Two new political unions came into existence in the 1990s: the Commonwealth of Independent States (CIS), made up of the republics of the former Soviet Union, and the European Union (EU). The European Union was created when the 12 nations of the European Community ratified the **Maastricht Treaty**. The members committed themselves to economic and political integration. The treaty allows for the free movement of goods, persons, services, and capital throughout the member states; a common currency; common foreign and security policies, including defense; a common justice system; and cooperation between police and other authorities on crime, terrorism, and immigration issues. Although not all the provisions of the treaty have been universally accepted, each year the EU members become more closely tied economically and politically. Now that the Economic and Monetary Union is put in place and all participating members share a common currency, the European Union is headed toward political union as well.

Global Markets and Multinational Market Groups
The globalization of markets, the restructuring of the eastern European bloc into independent market-driven economies, the dissolution of the Soviet Union into independent states, the worldwide trend toward economic cooperation, and enhanced global competition make it important that market potential be viewed in the context of regions of the world rather than country by country.

This section presents basic information and data on markets and market groups in Europe, Africa, and the Middle East. Existing economic cooperation agreements within each of these regions are reviewed. The reader must appreciate that the status of cooperative agreements and alliances among nations has been extremely fluid in some parts of the world. Many are fragile and may cease to exist or may restructure into a totally different form. Several decades will probably be needed for many of the new trading alliances that are now forming to stabilize into semipermanent groups.

Europe
Within Europe, every type of multinational market grouping exists. The European Union, European Economic Area, and the European Free Trade Area are the most established cooperative groups (see Exhibits 10.1 and 10.2). Of escalating economic importance are the fledgling capitalist economies of eastern Europe and the three Baltic states that gained independence from the Soviet Union just prior to its breakup. Key issues center on their economic development and economic alliance with the European Union. Also within the European region is the Commonwealth of Independent States. New and untested, this coalition of 12 former USSR republics may or may not survive in its present form to take its place among the other multinational market groups.

European Integration
Of all the multinational market groups, none is more secure in its cooperation or more important economically than the European Union (Exhibit 10.3). From its beginning, it has made progress toward achieving the goal of complete economic integration and, ultimately, political union. However, many people, including Europeans, had little hope for the success of the European Economic Community, or the European Common Market as it is often called, because of the problems created by integration and the level of national sovereignty that would have to be conceded to the community. After all, 1,000 years of

LO3 ▮▮▮▮

The evolution of the European Union

Exhibit 10.1
European Market Regions Fundamental Market Metrics

(in parentheses) = average annual growth rate 2004–2009 as a percentage

Association	Country (year entered union)	Population (millions)	GNI* (billions $)	Exports* of Goods (billions $)	Imports* of Goods (billions $)	Ease of Doing Business Index	GNI/ capita* ($)	Internet Users (per 1000 people)
European Union (EU)								
	Belgium (founder)[e]	10.6 (0.5)	469.8 (5.3)	381.5 (4.5)	356.9 (4.6)	20	44068 (4.8)	735 (6.5)
	Denmark (1973)	5.5 (0.4)	319.5 (5.4)	93.3 (4.3)	84.1 (4.7)	5	57968 (4.9)	868 (2.6)
	Germany (founder)[e]	82.0 (−0.1)	3322.8 (3.7)	1137.8 (4.6)	950.5 (5.8)	27	40521 (3.8)	785 (5.2)
	Greece (1981)[e]	11.3 (0.4)	326.4 (7.3)	20.2 (5.8)	60.0 (2.7)	100	29010 (6.9)	359 (12.3)
	Spain (1986)[e]	45.5 (1.5)	1368.9 (6.9)	217.2 (3.8)	295.8 (2.8)	51	30072 (5.4)	627 (9.3)
	France (founder)[e]	62.4 (1.6)	2691.4 (5.3)	474.9 (2.4)	534.3 (4.6)	31	43089 (4.6)	591 (8.5)
	Ireland (1973)[e]	4.4 (2.0)	197.2 (4.5)	116.6 (2.1)	61.2 (−0.8)	7	44327 (2.4)	703 (15.3)
	Italy (founder)[e]	60.1 (1.7)	2085.4 (3.9)	408.2 (3.0)	415.7 (4.0)	74	34726 (3.2)	518 (2.0)
	Luxembourg (founder)[e]	0.5 (1.2)	43.2 (7.7)	12.5 (0.5)	15.3 (−1.9)	53	99970 (6.4)	844 (5.3)
	Netherlands (founder)[e]	16.4 (0.2)	799.2 (5.0)	435.2 (6.5)	383.5 (6.2)	28	48700 (4.8)	530 (4.5)
	Austria (1995)[e]	8.4 (0.6)	374.6 (5.5)	132.2 (3.4)	138.8 (4.1)	26	44682 (4.8)	633 (3.4)
	Portugal (1986)[e]	10.7 (0.4)	232.3	44.0 (5.9)	69.8 (7.2)	48	21682	444 (8.9)
	Finland (1995)[e]	5.4 (0.4)	245.8 (5.2)	60.4 (−0.2)	61.3 (3.9)	14	46167 (4.8)	847 (3.8)
	Sweden (1995)	9.2 (0.5)	413.5 (3.0)	131.6 (1.3)	148.6 (3.6)	17	44939 (2.5)	839 (0.4)
	United Kingdom (1973)	6.16 (0.6)	2231.3 (0.0)	358.0 (0.5)	485.6 (1.0)	6	36215 (−0.7)	836 (5.9)
	Czech Republic (2004)	10.3 (0.2)	44.7 (11.5)	114.7 (11.3)	105.5 (9.1)	66	17269 (11.2)	578 (12.5)
	Estonia (2004)	1.3 (−0.3)	17.7 (9.2)	9.0 (8.8)	10,2 (4.1)	22	13317 (9.5)	724 (7.9)
	Cyprus (2004)[e]	0.9 (1.1)	22.4	1.5 (6.0)	10.0 (12.2)	36	25732 (7.0)	434 (6.3)
	Latvia (2004)	2.6 (−0.6)	25.2 (13.4)	7.2 (12.6)	9.1 (5.3)	29	11194 (14.0)	641 (14.2)
	Lithuania (2004)	3.3 (−0.6)	35.4 (9.9)	16.5 (12.1)	18.4 (8.3)	25	10582 (10.6)	569 (14.4)
	Hungary (2004)	10.0 (−0.2)	142.3	84.6 (9.0)	77.9 (5.5)	41	14230	592 (16.1)
	Malta (2004)[e]	0.4 (0.4)	2.3 (6.2)	2.6 (−0.3)	4.2 (2.0)	—	5741 (5.8)	530 (8.9)
	Poland (2004)	38.0 (−0.1)	517.4	140.0 (1.13)	146.5 (10.9)	72	13605	550 (13.4)
	Slovenia (2004)[e]	2.0 (0.3)	45.8 (7.3)	22.9 (7.6)	23.7 (6.1)	57	22635 (7.0)	524 (7.5)
	Slovak Republic (2004)	5.4 (0.1)	91.6	56.2 (8.9)	54.0 (6.8)	35	16963	559 (15.7)
	Bulgaria (2007)	7.5 (−0.7)	44.7 (12.4)	17.1 (21.3)	23.8 (10.5)	42	5950 (13.1)	337 (16.1)
	Romania (2007)	21.4 (−0.3)	192.0	41.2 (11.9)	54.6 (10.8)	45	8971	312 (21.0)
EU Candidate Countries								
	Croatia	4.4 (−0.1)	66.9	9.7 (3.9)	21.3 (5.1)	110	15636	557 (12.5)
	Macedonia, FYR	2.0 (0.1)	9.4	2.8 (11.1)	5.1 (11.6)	69	4673	452 (16.4)
	Turkey	71.5 (1.3)	785.5	103.9 (10.5)	138.2 (7.2)	63	10910	388 (22.7)
European Free Trade Area (EFTA)								
	Iceland	0.3 (2.0)	11.4 (−2.1)	3.8 (5.8)	3.3 (−2.8)	11	35386 (−4.1)	675 (3.2)
	Liechtenstein	.04 (0.9)	—	—	—	—	—	662 (0.6)
	Norway	4.8 (1.0)	382.5 (8.1)	120.6 (7.9)	69.8 (7.4)	10	79709 (7.1)	869 (2.9)
	Switzerland	7.6 (0.5)	533.5	169.1 (7.5)	148.6 (6.1)	19	64015	796 (3.5)

*Current U.S. $.

[e]Eurozone.

Source: Euromonitor International, 2010; World Bank, 2010.

Some in Warsaw suggest the picture includes two icons of imperialism. Soviet dictator Joseph Stalin "gave" the people of Poland his 1950s version of great architecture. The Poles have now turned his infamous Palace of Culture and Science into a movie theater (Kinoteka) and office tower. Others see Coca-Cola and its ever-present, powerful advertising as a new kind of control. The argument about globalization goes on.

economic separatism had to be overcome, and the European Common Market is quite heterogeneous. There are language and cultural differences, individual national interests, political differences, and centuries-old restrictions designed to protect local national markets.

Historically, standards have been used to effectively limit market access. Germany protected its beer market from the rest of Europe with a purity law requiring beer sold in Germany to be brewed only from water, hops, malt, and yeast. Italy protected its pasta market by requiring that pasta be made only from durum wheat. Incidentally, the European Court of Justice has struck down both the beer and pasta regulations as trade violations. Such restrictive standards kept competing products, whether from other European countries or elsewhere, out of their respective markets. Skeptics, doubtful that such cultural, legal, and social differences could ever be overcome, held little hope for a unified Europe. Their skepticism has proved wrong. Today, many marvel at how far the European Union has come. Although complete integration has not been fully achieved, a review of the structure of the European Union, its authority over member states, the Single European Act, the European Economic Area, the Maastricht Treaty, and the Amsterdam Treaty will show why the final outcome of full economic and political integration now seems more certain.

Exhibit 10.2
The European Economic Area: EU, EFTA, and Associates

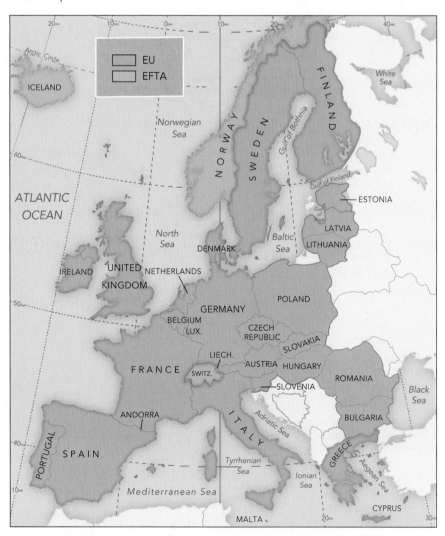

Exhibit 10.3

From the European Coal and Steel Community to Monetary Union

Source: "Chronology of the EU," http://www.europa.eu.int/ (select Abc). Reprinted with permission from the European Communities.

1951	Treaty of Paris	European Coal and Steel Community (ECSC) (founding members are Belgium, France, Germany, Italy, Luxembourg, and the Netherlands).
1957	Treaty of Rome	Blueprint, European Economic Community (EEC).
1958	European Economic Community	Ratified by ECSC founding members. Common market is established.
1960	European Free Trade Association	Established by Austria, Denmark, Norway, Portugal, Sweden, Switzerland, and United Kingdom.
1973	Expansion	Denmark, Ireland, and United Kingdom join EEC.
1979	European monetary system	The European Currency Unit (ECU) is created. All members except the UK agree to maintain their exchange rates within specific margins.
1981	Expansion	Greece joins EEC.
1985	1992 Single Market Program	White paper for action introduced to European Parliament.
1986	Expansion	Spain and Portugal join EEC.
1987	**Single European Act**	Ratified, with full implementation by 1992.
1992	Treaty on European Union	Also known as **Maastricht Treaty**. Blueprint for Economic and Monetary Union (EMU).
1993	Europe 1992	Single European Act in force (January 1, 1992).
1993	European Union	Treaty on European Union (Maastricht Treaty) in force, with monetary union by 1999.
1994	European Economic Area	The EEA was formed with EU members and Norway and Iceland.
1995	Expansion	Austria, Finland, and Sweden join EU. Established procedures for expansion to Central and Eastern Europe.
1997	**Amsterdam Treaty**	
1999	Monetary union	Conversion rates are fixed, and euro used by banking and finance industry. Consumer prices are quoted in local currency and in euros.
2002	Banknotes and coins	Circulation of euro banknotes and coins begins January 1, and legal status of national banknotes and coins canceled July 1, 2002.
2004	Expansion	Ten new countries join EU.
2007	Expansion	Bulgaria and Romania join.

Even though several member states are not fully implementing all the measures, they are making progress. The proportion of directives not yet implemented in all 27 member states has fallen dramatically. Taxation has been one of the areas where implementation lags and reform continues to be necessary. Value-added and registration taxes for automobiles, for example, at one time ranged from 15 percent in Luxembourg to 218 percent in Denmark. Then a midsized Mercedes in Haderslev, Denmark, cost $90,000, nearly triple the amount you would have paid in Flensburg, Germany, just 30 miles south. A Honda Civic cost the British consumer 89 percent more than it cost continental customers. Scotch in Sweden had an $18 tax, nine times the amount levied in Italy. The EU finance ministers have addressed these issues and made some progress, even though tax-raising ability is a sacred power of the nation-state. The full implementation of the legislation is expected to

Each month the European Parliament meets for three weeks here in Brussels, Belgium, and then moves for one week to meet in Strasbourg, France. The inconvenience of the fourth week move was a concession to French pride—or perhaps the cheese is better there?

take several years. Although all proposals have not been met, the program for unification has built up a pace that cannot be reversed.

European Union[7]

EU Institutions. The European Union's institutions form a federal pattern with executive, parliamentary, and judicial branches: the European Commission, the Council of Ministers, the European Parliament, and the Court of Justice, respectively. Their decision-making processes have legal status and extensive powers in fields covered by common policies. The European Union uses three legal instruments: (1) regulations binding the member states directly and having the same strength as national laws; (2) directives also binding the member states but allowing them to choose the means of execution; and (3) decisions addressed to a government, an enterprise, or an individual, binding the parties named. Over the years, the Union has gained an increasing amount of authority over its member states.

The European Commission initiates policy and supervises its observance by member states, and it proposes and supervises execution of laws and policies. Commission members act only in the interest of the European Union, and their responsibilities are to ensure that the EU rules and the principles of the common market are respected. For example, in separate actions, the Commission recently approved the sale of Sun Microsystems to Oracle,[8] but it has pushed Google and others to shorten the time they store consumer data.[9]

The Council of Ministers is the decision-making body of the European Union; it is the Council's responsibility to debate and decide which proposals of the **Single European Act** to accept as binding on EU members. The Council can enact into law all proposals by majority vote except for changes in tax rates on products and services, which require unanimous vote. The Council, for example, drafted the Maastricht Treaty, which was presented to member states for ratification.

The **European Parliament** originally had only a consultative role that passed on most Union legislation. It can now amend and adopt legislation, though it does not have the

[7]http://europa.eu.int, 2008.

[8]Matthew Saltmarsh, "Sale of Sun Micro to Oracle Wins Approval of Europeans," *The New York Times,* January 22, 2010, p. B2.

[9]Eric Pfanner, "In Europe, Challenges for Google," *The New York Times*, February 2, 2010, pp. B1, B5.

CROSSING BORDERS 10.1   Lost in Translation

There are any number of things that Europeans don't like about the European Union—including its very declaration. Sharp-eyed professors have spotted what they say is evidence of the "political translation" of the EU's Berlin Declaration. Specifically, both the Danish and English versions downplay the emotional language of the original German, they claim. Instead of stating that the EU member states are united in "happiness," the translation notes they have united "for the better" or "for the common good."

An EU spokesman argues the texts had been agreed by the national governments. The German-language version of the declaration reads: "We, the citizens in the European Union, are united *zu unserem Gluck*." The controversy stems from that final phrase, which might be rendered in English as "united in our fortune/happiness." Instead, the English-language version reads: "We, the citizens of the European Union, have united for the better."

In the Danish version, the word "*Gluck*" has been replaced with "*vor faelles bedste*," meaning "for the common good." Professor Henning Koch from Copenhagen University told the Danish paper *Politiken* that the low-key translation could be no coincidence. "It would come as a big surprise to me if the translators are bad at German. So then it's a political translation," he said. Gushing added that emotional terms were something Danes feared.

Professor Rudinger Gorner, head of the German department at University of London, echoed Koch's point, looking at the English version of the Declaration. He told the BBC that the German phrase used in the declaration implies that it is "really a fortunate thing we have united." Instead, he said, "The English rendering certainly downplays the meaning. There's no doubt that if one wanted to express the German sentiment, one could do so." He also noted a subtle difference, in that the English version "suggests something happening in the future."

Mats Persson of the Eurosceptic thinktank Open Europe, which focuses on EU reform, concedes the clear struggle over the translation of the declaration: "It is quite common that people use the maximum room available to accommodate shades of meaning." He also noted, "The Swedish version . . . reads quite awkwardly. The Berlin Declaration is a reflection of a political compromise, and this is reflected in the translations."

Finally, a spokesman for the EU Council said all the translations of the declaration were "official" and had been agreed to by the national delegations of the member states.

Sources: "EU Effusion 'Lost in Translation,'" *BBC News*, March 27, 2007; D. Cooper, "Berlin Declaration Bypasses EU's Citizens," *Financial Times*, June 23, 2007, p. 8.

---

power to initiate legislation. It also has extensive budgetary powers that allow it to be involved in major EU expenditures.

The European Court of Justice (ECJ) is the European Union's Supreme Court. It is responsible for challenging any measures incompatible with the Treaty of Rome and for passing judgment, at the request of a national court, on the interpretation or validity of points of EU law. The court's decisions are final and cannot be appealed in national courts. For example, Estée Lauder Companies appealed to the ECJ to overrule a German court's decision to prohibit it from selling its Clinique product. The German court had ruled that the name could mislead German consumers by implying medical treatment. The ECJ pointed out that Clinique is sold in other member states without confusing the consumer and ruled in favor of Estée Lauder. This decision marked a landmark case, because many member countries had similar laws that were in essence nontariff trade barriers designed to protect their individual markets. If the German court ruling against Estée Lauder had been upheld, it would have made it difficult for companies to market their products across borders in an identical manner. This case is but one example of the ECJ's power in the European Union and its role in eliminating nontariff trade barriers.

Economic and Monetary Union (EMU).
The EMU, a provision of the Maastricht Treaty, established the parameters of the creation of a common currency for the European Union, the *euro*, and established a timetable for its implementation. In 2002, a central bank was established, conversion rates were fixed, circulation of euro banknotes and

Exhibit 10.4
The Euro

Source: Euro, http://www.europa.eu
.int/euro. Reprinted with permission
from the European Communities.

Notes. There are seven euro notes in different colors and sizes, denominated in 500, 200, 100, 50, 20, 10 and 5 euros. The designs symbolize Europe's architectural heritage, with windows and gateways on the front side as symbols of the spirit of openness and cooperation in the European Union. The reverse side features a bridge from a particular age, a metaphor for communication among the people of Europe and the rest of the world.

Coins. There are eight euro coins, denominated in 2 and 1 euros, then 50, 20, 10, 5, 2, and 1 cent. Every coin will carry a common European face—a map of the European Union against a background of transverse lines to which are attached the stars of the European flag. On the obverse, each member state will decorate the coins with their own motifs, for example, the King of Spain or some national hero. Regardless of the motif, every coin can be used and will have the same value in all the member states.

Sign. The graphic symbol for the euro was inspired by the Greek letter epsilon, in reference to the cradle of European civilization and to the first letter of the word *Europe*. It looks like an *E* with two clearly marked, horizontal parallel lines across it. The parallel lines are meant to symbolize the stability of the euro. The official abbreviation is "EUR."

It took some selling for the Greeks to adopt the euro instead of the 2,500-year-old drachma. The truck seen here in Athens's Syntagma Square was equipped with video projectors and euro information stands and traveled to 40 Greek towns, informing folks about the new currency.

coins was completed (see Exhibit 10.4), and the legal tender status of participating members' banknotes and coins was canceled. To participate, members must meet strict limits on several financial and economic criteria, including national deficit, debt, and inflation. The 12 member states employing the euro beginning in January 1, 2001, were Austria, Belgium, Finland, France, Germany, Greece, Ireland, Italy, Luxembourg, the Netherlands, Portugal, and Spain. Denmark voted in 2000 not to join the monetary union, leaving Britain and Sweden still undecided. Denmark's rejection of the euro caused a broader debate about the EU's future. Anti-euro advocates exploited fears of a "European superstate" and local interference from Brussels rather than relying on economic arguments when pushing for rejection. However, in 2007 Slovenia and in 2008 both Malta and Cyprus switched their currencies to the euro. Others may choose to follow[10] or not[11] depending, it seems, on the relative strength of the euro versus the U.S. dollar.

The original 40-year-old operating rules of the EC were proving to be inadequate in dealing with the problems that confront the European Union today. Expansion beyond its present 27 members (see Exhibit 10.1), managing the conversion to the euro and EMU, and speaking with one voice on foreign policy that directly affects the European continent are all issues that require greater agreement among members and thus more responsibility and authority for the institutions of the European Union. The **Amsterdam Treaty** increases the authority of the institutions of the European Union and is designed to accommodate the changes brought about by the monetary union and the admission of new members.

Expansion of the European Union. The process of enlargement has been the most important item on the EU's agenda. Ten new countries were added in 2004, some ahead of schedule. Bulgaria and Romania entered as planned in 2007, and talks with Turkey, Macedonia, and Croatia are continuing. Negotiations with Turkey have had their

---

[10]"Cyprus, Malta Change to the Euro," *The Wall Street Journal* (online), January 2, 2008.

[11]Andrew E. Kramer, "Seeing Trouble in Greece, Baltic States Rethink Euro Plans," *The New York Times*, February 12, 2010, pp. B1, B6.

CROSSING BORDERS 10.2   The Death of the Drachma

Having officially joined the European Union on January 1, 2001, Greece began phasing out the -drachma, Europe's oldest currency and the survivor of some 2,500 years of war and economic turmoil. Below, highlights from its storied history.   —MEGAN JOHNSTON

Source: March 2001 *Money*. Used by permission of *Money* magazine.

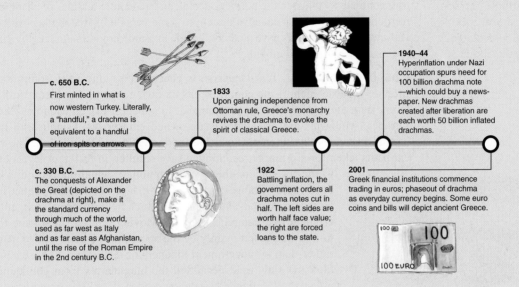

c. 650 B.C.
First minted in what is now western Turkey. Literally, a "handful," a drachma is equivalent to a handful of iron spits or arrows.

c. 330 B.C.
The conquests of Alexander the Great (depicted on the drachma at right), make it the standard currency through much of the world, used as far west as Italy and as far east as Afghanistan, until the rise of the Roman Empire in the 2nd century B.C.

1833
Upon gaining independence from Ottoman rule, Greece's monarchy revives the drachma to evoke the spirit of classical Greece.

1922
Battling inflation, the government orders all drachma notes cut in half. The left sides are worth half face value; the right are forced loans to the state.

1940–44
Hyperinflation under Nazi occupation spurs need for 100 billion drachma note —which could buy a newspaper. New drachmas created after liberation are each worth 50 billion inflated drachmas.

2001
Greek financial institutions commence trading in euros; phaseout of drachma as everyday currency begins. Some euro coins and bills will depict ancient Greece.

ups and downs, but the Muslim majority nation has economically benefited from its new openness.[12] A broader preoccupation for the European Union is the prospect of illegal immigrants from former Soviet states surging across poorly guarded borders of the newer and/ or candidate states and making their way farther west within the EU. The European Union is demanding that borders be sealed, but the new and candidate states are reluctant to jeopardize relations with neighboring communities. Furthermore, the European Union fears a flood of cheap labor even if the borders are closed; it wants a long transition period before freedom of movement of labor, whereas the applicants say their citizens should be allowed to work anywhere in the EU once they are members.

In 2007 the European Union celebrated its golden anniversary. Most would agree that it has been a tremendous success, delivering peace and prosperity to hundreds of millions of people that previously had lived with frequent wars and accompanying economic and social hardships. The 2008–2009 global recession has posed daunting short-term challenges to the integrity of the Union though; an early recovery[13] stalled in late 2009,[14] and Ireland, Portugal, Spain, and particularly Greece[15] are experiencing continuing problems. The long-term challenges facing the Union in the next 50 years appear to fall into three categories: (1) improving the Union's economic performance, (2) deciding how to limit the political aspects of union, and (3) deciding about further enlargement. The last

[12]Stanley Reed, "Turkey Turns Outward," *BusinessWeek*, October 12, 2009, pp. 40–41.

[13]Marcus Walker and David Gauthier-Villars, "Europe Recovers as U.S. Lags," *The Wall Street Journal*, August 14, 2009, pp. A1–2.

[14]Paul Hannon, "Euro-Zone Economy Stumbles," *The Wall Street Journal*, February 12, 2010, online.

[15]Nicholas Kulish, "Germany, Forced to Buoy Greece, Rues Euro Shift," *The Wall Street Journal*, February 11, 2010, pp. A1, A3.

problem may well disappear as both multilateral and bilateral agreements continue to multiply around the world and as the WTO continues to gain influence and traction in trade barrier reduction.

Eastern Europe and the Baltic States

LO4

Evolving patterns of trade as eastern Europe and the former Soviet states embrace free-market systems

Eastern Europe and the Baltic states, satellite nations of the former Soviet Union, have moved steadily toward establishing postcommunist market reforms. New business opportunities are emerging almost daily, and the region is described as anywhere from chaotic with big risks to an exciting place with untold opportunities. Both descriptions fit as countries continue to adjust to the political, social, and economic realities of changing from the restrictions of a Marxist–socialist system to some version of free markets and capitalism. However, these countries have neither all made the same progress nor had the same success in economic reform and growth.[16]

Eastern Europe. It is dangerous to generalize beyond a few points about eastern Europe, because each of the countries has its own economic problems and is at a different stage in its evolution from a socialist to a market-driven economy. Most eastern European countries are privatizing state-owned enterprises, establishing free market pricing systems, relaxing import controls, and wrestling with inflation. The very different paths taken toward market economies have resulted in different levels of progress.

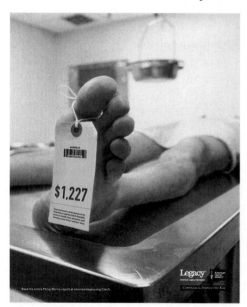

Countries such as the Czech Republic,[17] which moved quickly to introduce major changes, seem to have fared better than countries such as Hungary, Poland, and Romania, which held off privatizing until the government restructured internally. Moving quickly allows the transformation to be guided mainly by the spontaneity of innovative market forces rather than by government planners or technocrats. Those countries that took the slow road permitted the bureaucrats from communist days to organize effectively to delay and even derail the transition to a market economy.

Yugoslavia has been plagued with internal strife over ethnic divisions, and four of its republics (Croatia, Slovenia, Macedonia, and Bosnia/Herzegovina) seceded from the federation, leaving Serbia and Montenegro in the reduced Federal Republic of Yugoslavia. Soon after seceding, a devastating ethnic war broke out in Croatia and Bosnia/Herzegovina that decimated their economies. A tentative peace maintained by United Nations peacekeepers now exists, but for all practical purposes, the economies of Croatia and Bosnia are worse now than ever before. Most recently, the Kosovo region of Serbia also declared its independence, and political tension remains.[18]

As demand for tobacco declines in more-developed countries, manufacturers direct more marketing efforts in the direction of emerging economies. Indeed, recently Philip Morris published a report estimating the cost savings for the Czech government at $1,227 every time a smoker dies. Apparently, the company did not think through the public relations implications of this grisly bit of research.

Nevertheless, most countries in the region continue to make progress in building market-oriented institutions and adopting legislation that conforms to that of advanced market economies. The Czech Republic, Hungary, the Slovak Republic, and Poland have become members of the OECD.[19] Joining the OECD means they accept the obligations of the OECD to modernize their economies and to maintain sound macroeconomic policies and market-oriented structural reforms. The four also became members of the European Union in 2004, along with Bulgaria and Romania in 2007. And they are eager to stabilize their developing democracies and their westward tilt in foreign and security policies.

---

[16]Clifford J. Schultz II, Timothy J. Burkink, Bruno Grbac, and Natasa Renko, "When Policies and Marketing Systems Explode: An Assessment of Food Marketing in the War-Ravaged Balkans and Implications for Recovery, Sustainable Peace, and Prosperity," *Journal of Public Policy & Marketing* 24, no. 1 (2005), pp. 24–37.

[17]Judy Dempsey, "In a Car, a Lesson in Russian-European Trade," *The New York Times*, January 1, 2008.

[18]Tracy Wilkinson, "Kosovo Takes a Big Leap of Faith," *Los Angeles Times*, February 18, 2008, pp. A1, A6.

[19]http://www.oecd.org.

group are often more sophisticated than those of the individual countries.[37] Despite the problems and complexities of dealing with the new markets, the overriding message to the astute international marketer continues to be opportunity and profit potential.

Opportunities.   Economic integration creates large mass markets. Many national markets, too small to bother with individually, take on new dimensions and significance when combined with markets from cooperating countries. Large markets are particularly important to businesses accustomed to mass production and mass distribution because of the economies of scale and marketing efficiencies that can be achieved. In highly competitive markets, the benefits derived from enhanced efficiencies are often passed along as lower prices that lead to increased purchasing power.

Most multinational groups have coordinated programs to foster economic growth as part of their cooperative efforts. Such programs work to the advantage of marketers by increasing purchasing power, improving regional infrastructure, and fostering economic development. Despite the problems that are sure to occur because of integration, the economic benefits from free trade can be enormous.

Major savings will result from the billions of dollars now spent in developing different versions of products to meet a hodgepodge of national standards.[38] Philips and other European companies invested a total of $20 billion to develop a common switching system for Europe's several different telephone networks. This figure compares with the $3 billion spent in the United States for a common system and $1.5 billion in Japan for a single system.

Market Barriers.   The initial aim of a multinational market is to protect businesses that operate within its borders. An expressed goal is to give an advantage to the companies within the market in their dealings with other countries of the market group. Analysis of the interregional and international trade patterns of the market groups indicates that such goals have been achieved.

Companies willing to invest in production facilities in multinational markets may benefit from protectionist measures because these companies become a part of the market. Exporters, however, are in a considerably weaker position. This prospect confronts many U.S. exporters who face the possible need to invest in Europe to protect their export markets in the European Union. The major problem for small companies may be adjusting to the EU standards. A company selling in one or two EU member countries and meeting standards there may find itself in a situation of having to change standards or be closed out when an EU-wide standard is adopted.

A manufacturer of the hoses used to hook up deep-fat fryers and other gas appliances to gas outlets faced such a problem when one of its largest customers informed the company that McDonald's was told it could no longer use that manufacturer's hoses in its British restaurants. The same thing happened at EuroDisney. Unfortunately, when the common standards were written, only large MNCs and European firms participated, so they had the advantage of setting standards to their benefit. The small company had only two choices: Change or leave. In this particular case, it appears that competitors were working to keep the company out of the market. There are, however, enough questions about threaded fittings and compatibility that the company worked with individual countries to gain entrance to their markets—just as it had before a single market existed.

| Market Metrics | In this section, we present three tables with fundamental metrics reflecting the size and character of markets in the eight most populous countries in the greater region. Looking across these tables, we see the widest disparity in standards of living, infrastructures, and consumer purchases. As in the Americas, the disparity appears to correlate with latitude, |

LO6

The size and nature of marketing opportunities in the European/African/ Middle East regions

---

[37]Kevin J. O'Brien, "EU Considers a Telecommunications 'Superregulator,'" *International Herald Tribune*, August 13, 2007, p. 10.

[38]John W. Miller, "EU Food-Safety Agency Backs Products from Cloned Animals," *The Wall Street Journal*, January 12, 2008, online.

Exhibit 10.7
Standard of Living in the Eight Most Populous Countries in the Europe/Africa/Middle East Region

Country	Population (millions)	GNI per Capita	Medical Resources Per 1000 persons		Household Ownership %		
			Doctors	Hospital Beds	Color TV	Refrigerator	Shower
Nigeria	155	$ 1,273	0.4	—	34	23	63
Russia	142	10,966	4.4	9.6	97	97	63
Ethiopia	83	320	—	—	—	—	—
Germany	82	40,521	3.6	8.2	98	99	99
Egypt	77	2,133	0.6	2.4	87	93	78
Iran	74	4,540	0.9	—	—	—	—
Turkey	72	10,910	1.6	2.9	93	98	80
Congo, DR	66	154	—	—	—	—	—

Source: Euromonitor International, 2010.

with greater economic development associated with distance from the equator. We also see the lack of data for the least developed countries in Africa and the Middle East. And we have not included in these data direct measures of political instability and other risks—those can be found in other chapters, such as Chapters 5 and 17.

Exhibit 10.7 presents standards of living across the eight countries. The range of GNI per capita is astonishing, with Germany at more than $40,000 and the Democratic Republic of Congo at less than $200. Russia, Turkey, and Iran (as best as we can tell) are moving up the development ladder relatively fast.

Exhibit 10.8 compares the infrastructures of the countries. Again we see the wide disparities north to south. Perhaps the most interesting data involve the relative strength of Iran, particularly with regard to the numbers of university students. It is these university students that have been the catalyst for political protests in the country of late. But when it comes to opportunities for development and hiring good marketers in the future, these last numbers provide some hope.

Exhibit 10.9 briefly enumerates consumption patterns. For Ethiopia and the Democratic Republic of Congo, we can only guess, and it is quite difficult to imagine conducting systematic primary consumer research in either country. The dollars spent on education in Turkey are promising. Of course, the German statistics jump off the page across the columns. Indeed, perhaps the most shocking datum in this book is the German

Exhibit 10.8
Infrastructures of the Eight Most Populous Countries of the Europe/Africa/Middle East Region

Country	Travel by Rail (passenger-km per capita)	Passenger Cars/1000	Energy Consumption (tones oil equivalent)	Computers in Use per 1000 people	Mobile Phones in Use per 1000 people	Literacy Rate %	University Students per 1000 people
Nigeria	1	12	—	16	500	74%	5
Russia	1262	194	4.9	166	1434	100	56
Ethiopia	0.4	1	—	9	50	41	3
Germany	944	491	3.8	779	1336	100	28
Egypt	768	30	1.0	60	649	73	34
Iran	200	24	2.7	111	753	87	27
Turkey	75	93	1.5	76	983	90	26
Congo, DR	—	2	—	—	184	79	1

Source: Euromonitor International, 2010.

Exhibit 10.9

Consumption Patterns in the Eight Most Populous Countries in Europe/Africa/Middle East Region

Country	People per Household	Household Expenditures ($/capita)								
		Food	Alcohol, Tobacco	Clothing	Housing	Health Goods, Services	Transportation	Communication	Leisure	Education
Nigeria	4.9	1779	15	43	113	28	45	13	13	24
Russia	2.7	1068	87	431	489	142	999	161	327	75
Ethiopia	5.3	—	—	—	—	—	—	—	—	—
Germany	2.8	2628	819	1153	5757	1117	3074	703	2165	159
Egypt	4.1	716	42	120	391	85	62	43	47	72
Iran	3.8	656	13	125	761	180	129	88	106	44
Turkey	3.9	1466	242	347	1630	130	838	262	129	116
Congo, DR	3.6	—	—	—	—	—	—	—	—	—

Source: Euromonitor International, 2010

per capita expenditure on alcohol and tobacco, at some $819/year, more than double the entire annual per capita income in Ethiopia and more than four times that in the Democratic Republic of Congo! Of course, we do not blame the Germans, and recall that Canadians spend even more on the psychoactive substances (see Exhibit 9.5 in the previous chapter). Such contrasts in standards of living among human beings are simply incomprehensible.

Marketing Mix Implications

Companies are adjusting their marketing mix strategies to reflect anticipated market changes in the single European market. In the past, companies often charged different prices in different European markets. Nontariff barriers between member states supported price differentials and kept lower-priced products from entering those markets where higher prices were charged. For example, Colgate-Palmolive Company adapted its Colgate toothpaste into a single formula for sale across Europe at one price. Before changing its pricing practices, Colgate sold its toothpaste at different prices in different markets.

Beddedas Shower Gel is priced in the middle of the market in Germany and as a high-priced product in the United Kingdom. As long as products from lower-priced markets could not move to higher-priced markets, such differential price schemes worked. Now, however, under the EU rules, companies cannot prevent the free movement of goods, and parallel imports from lower-priced markets to higher-priced markets are more likely to occur. Price standardization among country markets will be one of the necessary changes to avoid the problem of parallel imports. With the adoption of the euro, price differentials are much easier to spot, and the consumer can search for the best bargains in brand-name products more easily. Furthermore, the euro is making marketing on the Internet a much simpler task for European firms. On balance, a single currency will make competition in Europe a lot fairer and also a lot tougher.

In addition to initiating uniform pricing policies, companies are reducing the number of brands they produce to focus on advertising and promotion efforts. For example, Nestlé's several brands of yogurt in the European Union were reduced to a single brand. Unilever winnowed its 1,600 brands down to focus on 400 core brands. It plans to develop master brands in certain markets such as the European Union and to market others globally. A major benefit from an integrated Europe is competition at the retail level. Europe lacks an integrated and competitive distribution system that would support small and midsized outlets. The elimination of borders could result in increased competition among retailers and the creation of Europewide distribution channels.

Finally, all international marketers should see market integration around the world in a positive light. Trade among close neighbors will always be important—distance does make a difference. But overall, local integration ultimately serves globalization and harmonization of the world trading system, thus reducing the costs of business and delivering greater choice to consumers and greater opportunities to marketers.

Summary

The experiences of the multinational market groups developed since World War II point up both the successes and the hazards such groups encounter. The various attempts at economic cooperation represent varying degrees of success and failure, but almost without regard to their degree of success, the economic market groups have created great excitement among marketers. In the near future, these regional groupings will continue to form trade agreement ties with other nations and regions, thus paving the way for truly globalized markets where consumers dominate.

For companies, the economic benefits possible through cooperation relate to more efficient marketing and production. Marketing efficiency is effected through the development of mass markets, encouragement of competition, improvement of personal income, and various psychological market factors. Production efficiency derives from specialization, mass production for mass markets, and the free movement of the factors of production. Economic integration also tends to foster political harmony among the countries involved; such harmony leads to stability and peace, which are beneficial to the marketer as well as the countries' citizens.

The marketing implications of multinational market groups may be studied from the viewpoint of firms located inside the market or of firms located outside, which wish to sell to the markets. For each viewpoint the problems and opportunities are somewhat different; regardless of the location of the marketer, however, multinational market groups provide great opportunity for the creative marketer who wishes to expand volume. Market groupings make it economically feasible to enter new markets and to employ new marketing strategies that could not be applied to the smaller markets represented by individual countries. At the same time, market groupings intensify competition by protectionism within a market group but may foster greater protectionism between regional markets. Mercosur and ASEAN+3 (to be discussed in the next chapter), for example, suggest the growing importance of economic cooperation and integration. Such developments will continue to confront the international marketer by providing continually growing market opportunities and challenges.

Finally, the European/African/Middle East regions include perhaps the greatest diversity in income levels and cultures possible, providing daunting challenges for international marketing managers with responsibilities in the area.

Key Terms

Multinational market regions	Common market	Maastricht Treaty	European Parliament
Free trade area (FTA)	Political union	Single European Act	Amsterdam Treaty
Customs union			

Questions

1. Define the key terms listed above.
2. Elaborate on the problems and benefits that multinational market groups represent for international marketers.
3. Explain the political role of multinational market groups.
4. Identify the factors on which one may judge the potential success or failure of a multinational market group.
5. Explain the marketing implications of the factors contributing to the successful development of a multinational market group.
6. Imagine that the United States was composed of many separate countries with individual trade barriers. What marketing effects might be visualized?
7. Discuss the possible types of arrangements for regional economic integration.
8. Differentiate between a free trade area and a common market. Explain the marketing implications of the differences.
9. It seems obvious that the founders of the European Union intended it to be a truly common market, so much so that economic integration must be supplemented by political integration to accomplish these objectives. Discuss.
10. The European Commission, the Council of Ministers, and the Court of Justice of the European Union have gained power in the last decade. Comment.

11. Select any three countries that might have some logical basis for establishing a multinational market organization and illustrate their compatibility as a regional trade group. Identify the various problems that would be encountered in forming multinational market groups of such countries.

12. U.S. exports to the European Union are expected by some to decline in future years. What marketing actions might a company take to counteract such changes?

13. "Because they are dynamic and because they have great growth possibilities, the multinational markets are likely to be especially rough-and-tumble for the external business." Discuss.

14. Differentiate between a customs union and a political union.

15. Why have African nations had such difficulty in forming effective economic unions?

16. Discuss the implications of the European Union's decision to admit eastern European nations to the group.

Chapter 11

The Asia Pacific Region

CHAPTER OUTLINE

CHAPTER LEARNING OBJECTIVES

What you should learn about in Chapter 11:

LO1 The dynamic growth in the region

LO2 The importance and slow growth of Japan

LO3 The importance of the Bottom-of-the-Pyramid Markets

LO4 The diversity across the region

LO5 The interrelationships among countries in the region

LO6 The diversity within China

The Hong Kong dollar continues to be freely convertible, and foreign exchange, gold, and securities markets continue to operate as before. Hong Kong is a free society with legally protected rights. The Hong Kong SAR government continues to pursue a generally noninterventionist approach to economic policy that stresses the predominant role of the private sector. The first test came when the Hong Kong financial markets had a meltdown in 1997 that reverberated around the financial world and directly threatened the mainland's interests. Beijing's officials kept silent; when they said anything, they expressed confidence in the ability of Hong Kong authorities to solve their own problems.

The decision to let Hong Kong handle the crisis on its own is considered strong evidence that the relationship is working for the best for both sides, considering that China has so much riding on Hong Kong. Among other things, Hong Kong is the largest investor in the mainland, investing more than $100 billion over the last few years for factories and infrastructure. The Hong Kong stock market is the primary source of capital for some of China's largest state-owned enterprises. China Telcom, for example, raised $4 billion in an initial public offering there.

Most business problems that have arisen stem from fundamental concepts such as clear rules and transparent dealings that are not understood the same way on the mainland as they are in Hong Kong. Many thought the territory's laissez-faire ways, exuberant capitalism, and gung-ho spirit would prove unbearable for Beijing's heavy-handed communist leaders. But except for changes in tone and emphasis, even opponents of communist rule concede that Beijing is honoring the "one country, two systems" arrangement.

Taiwan, The Republic of China (ROC).

Mainland–Taiwanese economic relations continue to improve as both have entered the World Trade Organization. As both sides implement WTO provisions, they are ending many restrictions and now implement direct trade—not that they have not been trading. Taiwanese companies have invested over $50 billion in China, and about 250,000 Taiwanese-run factories are responsible for about 12 percent of China's exports. Estimates of real trade are even higher if activities conducted through Hong Kong front companies are taken into consideration.

It is best to wrap future talks on the One China debate inside a bundle of more concrete issues, such as establishing the "three direct links"—transportation, trade, and communications. The three direct links issue must be faced because each country has joined the WTO, and the rules insist that members communicate about trade disputes and other issues. Trade

Two giant pandas, four-year-old male Le Le and two-year-old female Ya Ye, are being loaded onto the Panda Express, a FedEx plane, that is airlifting them from China to the Memphis, Tennessee, zoo for a ten-year visit. Whether it is pandas, time-sensitive deliveries, or cost-saving solutions, FedEx delivers high-value shipments door-to-door to as many as 210 countries. Also, notice the white arrow embedded in the FedEx logo (between the E and the x) that connotes motion. Not only does China use pandas as rewards for trade, it also uses them as enticements. Indeed, it has used "Panda Diplomacy" for some 1400 years! Two Pandas were offered to Taiwan in 2006, but were rejected—at the time they were called the "Trojan Pandas" by those arguing for refusal. A new government on the island accepted the pair in 2008, and they now reside in the Taipei Zoo.

fits well with both countries' needs. Taiwanese companies face rising costs at home; China offers a nearly limitless pool of cheap labor and engineering talent. Taiwan's tech powerhouses also crave access to China's market.

For Beijing, the Taiwanese companies provide plentiful jobs at a time when bloated SOEs are laying off millions. They also bring the latest technology and management systems, which China needs as a member of the WTO. In any case, Taiwan continues to stand tall in the East Asian economy.[14]

Japan

LO2

The importance and slow growth of Japan

Japan's fast growth in the 1970s and 1980s amazed the world. Then came the early 1990s, and Japan's economy produced a stunning surprise. Almost abruptly, it slowed, sputtered, and stalled. Stagnation set in and tenaciously persisted. Four explanatory themes have emerged, each with a basis in observable fact, namely, Japan's (1) faulty economic policies, (2) inept political apparatus, (3) disadvantages due to global circumstances, and (4) cultural inhibitions.

Each of these four has their proponents, each their own rationale. So let's examine each separately.

Faulty Economic Policies.

A wealth of facts describe Japan's economic pain during the 1990s, but none more so than its stock market collapse. In the early 1990s, its Nikkei index level plummeted from over 35,000 to under 13,000. At this writing, it hovers at about 10,000. Japan's woefully inflated real estate values similarly hit the skids. Its once huge (and to some Americans, alarming) flow of investment into this country simply dried up. The end result found Japan with an economy once accustomed to nearly double-digit annual growth rates struggling, at first just to stay above no-growth levels, and then crashing to "minus growth," that is, a recession, in 1998.

Economic recessions are not, of course, unknown. But the peculiar feature of Japan's 1990's version was its decade-long persistence. Unsurprisingly, most economists sought to convince us that faulty economic policies both triggered the onset and the persistence of Japan's troubles. They explained with commendable brevity: "The bubble burst." But why the bubble, and why did it burst? The most common answer went somewhat as follows: Decades of galloping economic recovery success had bred a prideful national overconfidence. Growing willingness to take exaggerated risks followed. Heavy borrowing soon drove up levels of marginal investment. Eventually, lending agencies began to edge away from confidence toward caution. With the caution flag up, almost suddenly the whole inflated structure collapsed. Caution also filtered down to consumer levels. Spending habits were curtailed. With a fall in product demand, industry was forced to cut back both output and hiring. Unemployment soared to unheard of levels for that nation. The main casualty, however, was the widespread deterioration of national confidence.

No sector was hit harder than Japan's lending institutions, especially its huge, world-class banks. With the crash, the banks looked at loan portfolios splashed with red ink. Lending had to be restricted, a practice that dried up sources of capital needed for financing economic recovery. And so it went, one discouraging development following another, until a verifiable national crisis existed.

Seeing all this, American authorities and economists could not resist the temptation to offer remedies. "Draconian measures are needed," they chanted from across the Pacific. Understandable advice from on high, no doubt, but it reflected ignorance of the Japanese society's cultural prejudice against any action that might call for bold or rapid change. Always remember, Japan values stability above all else. Part of the problem is that most economists focused on overall economic performance and the dramatic slowdown in Japan's growth, tax revenues, and the potential disaster of deflation. And therefore, most economists have missed the real miracle of Japan's economic prowess. Please see Exhibit 11.1.

---

[14]Alex Frangos, "Thailand, Taiwan Post Strong GDP Growth," *The Wall Street Journal*, February 22, 2010, online.

Exhibit 11.1
Japan's GNI per Capita
(current international $)

Source: World Bank, 2010.

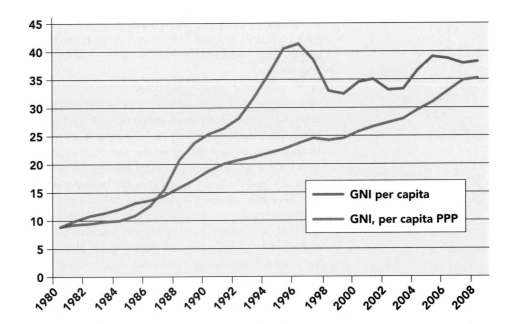

If we control for **purchase price parity (PPP)** in the per capita GDP calculations, Japanese growth simply wavered during the 1990s. That is, the PPP calculation takes into account deflation and best reflects the average well-being of the Japanese people. Per capita income fell, but so did prices. You can see that Japan pretty much avoided the Asian financial crisis that resulted in a precipitous economic decline in neighboring South Korea. Indeed, using this metric, the stability of the Japanese economy is miraculous, particularly given the troubles its close neighbors experienced in 1997 and the dimensions of both its stock and property market declines in the early 1990s. It is hard to imagine how the United States's economic performance might respond to simultaneous 60 percent declines in both the NYSE and the housing markets.

The Political Explanation.
Views of economists on Japan's crisis have not been the only ones heard. Political pundits also rose to the challenge. They found two major villains:

Villain #1: The Country's Long Entrenched Liberal Democratic Political Party.

Villain #2: The Hidebound Japanese Bureaucracy.

Back in the 1970s, an authority on just about everything Japanese, one Frank Gibney, had written a seminal book on the nation. He called it *The Fragile Superpower.* His insight into the possible future of Japan's then surging economy was confirmed when the 1990s brought on crisis conditions. "Fragile" proved to be an apt tag.

In a new appraisal, Gibney has written that Japan became the victim of "one-party sickness," an ailment brought on by a 40-year hardening of political arteries. Meanwhile, many observers thought politicians had to share blame with Japan's powerful bureaucracy. Many observers, both inside and outside Japan, had long since come to believe that the bureaucracy actually controlled its elected politicians. Of course, in a consensus-type society, it is not easy, particularly for outsiders, to tell where one institution's power leaves off and another's begins. In any event, to those who championed a political explanation of Japan's woes, these two national institutions were viewed as joint culprits. Meanwhile, other observers, particularly within Japan, were dissatisfied with either the economic or political explanations they were hearing. They felt compelled to look for deeper roots.

Global Circumstances Have Hurt.
The third explanation for Japan's end-of-the-century economic problems has more to do with three circumstances beyond their control.

First, the Japanese population, like the western European population, is shrinking faster than the American. While American baby-boomers circa 2005 were at their peak of productivity, both the Japanese and Europeans were about 10 years ahead in adjusting their economic, political, and cultural systems and institutions to population declines and graying hair. And this adjustment is costly—just wait until 2015 in the United States to see how costly.

Second, Japan has a serious disadvantage in the information age: its complex language. Not only did its three alphabet systems hinder software innovations appropriate for world markets, but the fundamental indirectness of the Japanese linguistic system hinders electronic information flows in general. So Japan has been late to participate in the information technology explosion that drove the American economy to precarious heights in the late 1990s. We would be the first to argue that Japan is now catching up, particularly as software advances have made the structure of the Japanese language less a hindrance in the digital age. Also, 9/11 caused a slowdown in international travel that pushed Japanese business-people to become more adept with e-mail and other electronic communication media.

Third, with American baby boomer households operating at peak consumption levels and oil at historically low real prices, sports utility vehicles (SUVs) became the rage in the United States during 1990–2007. Japanese auto firms, which drove the 1980s boom in Japan, came quite late to the American SUV market. Honda was the last entrant, which in the short run was a huge national economic disadvantage for Japan. But the reluctance to bet so much on big car designs has proven much to the advantage of Japanese car makers. A good argument can be made that they are leading Japan toward a new resurgence; that is, assuming Toyota can regain its former prowess.

The Cultural Explanation.   In the mid-nineties, we became aware of what might be called "The Cultural Causation" theory. This theory went something as follows: Immediately after World War II, a shattered Japanese nation arrived at a consensus goal for national recovery. That consensual goal provided the incentive for its spectacular progress, decade after decade. Then during the late 1980s, the Japanese people stepped back and looked around at their manifest achievement. It was easy to conclude they had reached their coveted goal. So the question for them became, "all right, what's next?"

Perhaps more than any other society, the Japanese have an affinity for united effort. They seem inspired by common striving toward a common goal. Lack of one can present a problem.

Others who champion a cultural explanation of Japan's 1990s woes did not limit their reasoning to an absence of a national goal. During most of the 20th century, building a strong enterprise structure provided the key to continuing success. Then with the advent of globalized competition, this inflexible structure became a hindrance. Agility, not structure, became the prime need. As has been pointed out, American corporate enterprise has met this need through wholesale restructuring and a blizzard of mergers, acquisitions, and consolidations. Standard Japanese practices, such as lifetime employment, job promotion based not on merit but on length of service, reciprocal contractor/subcontractor loyalties, and dozens of others have inhibited adaptive corporate measures. To put it simply, the U.S. enterprise scene handled its adjustment to the new economic era better than did the Japanese.

Japan is expected to continue its slow-growth economy during the second decade of the 21st century. Even as large companies have ambitious new growth plans,[15] economic cross-currents continue to roil with unemployment,[16] and Toyota's 2010 quality problems have disrupted that crucial company's contributions to the economy. However, economists and governments all over the world are using Japan as a model for policymaking, as Japan was the first to manage a big recession and its fast-graying population by strategically growing its government debt.[17]

---

[15]Mariko Sanchanta, "High-Speed Rail Approaches Station," *The Wall Street Journal*, January 26, 2010, online.

[16]David McNeill, "In Bleak Economy, Japanese Students Grow Frustrated with Endless Job Hunt," *Chronicle of Higher Education*, February 7, 2010, online.

[17]Tomoyuki Tachikawa, "Exports Boost Japan's GDP Growth," *The Wall Street Journal*, February 15, 2010, online.

India

The wave of change that has been washing away restricted trade, controlled economies, closed markets, and hostility to foreign investment in most developing countries has finally reached India. Since its independence in 1950, the world's largest democracy had set a poor example as a model for economic growth for other developing countries and was among the last of the economically important developing nations to throw off traditional insular policies. As a consequence, India's growth had been constrained and shaped by policies of import substitution and an aversion to free markets. While other Asian countries were wooing foreign capital, India was doing its best to keep it out. Multinationals, seen as vanguards of a new colonialism, were shunned. Aside from textiles, Indian industrial products found few markets abroad other than in the former Soviet Union and eastern Europe.

Despite world-class scientists, the Indian pharmaceutical industry (with its ownership restrictions, price controls, and weak intellectual property restrictions) does not benefit from innovations and international investments compared with more open emerging economies such as China.

Now however, times have changed, and India has embarked on the most profound transformation since it won political independence from Britain. A five-point agenda that includes improving the investment climate; developing a comprehensive WTO strategy; reforming agriculture, food processing, and small-scale industry; eliminating red tape; and instituting better corporate governance has been announced. Steps already taken include the following:

- Privatizing state-owned companies as opposed to merely selling shares in them. The government is now willing to reduce its take below 51 percent and to give management control to so-called strategic investors.
- Recasting the telecom sector's regulatory authority and demolishing the monopolies enjoyed by SOEs.
- Signing a trade agreement with the United States to lift all quantitative restrictions on imports.
- Maintaining momentum in the reform of the petroleum sector.
- Planning the opening of domestic long-distance phone services, housing, and real estate and retail trading sectors to foreign direct investment.

Leaders have quietly distanced themselves from campaign rhetoric that advocated "computer chips and not potato chips" in foreign investment and a *swadeshi* (made-in-India) economy. The new direction promises to adjust the philosophy of self-sufficiency that had been taken to extremes and to open India to world markets. India now has the look and feel of the next China or Latin America.

Foreign investors[18] and Indian reformers still face problems, however. Although India has overthrown the restrictions of earlier governments, reforms meet resistance from bureaucrats, union members, and farmers, as well as from some industrialists who have lived comfortably behind protective tariff walls that excluded competition. Socialism is not dead in the minds of many in India, and religious, ethnic, and other political passions flare easily.

For a number of reasons, India still presents a difficult business environment.[19] Tariffs are well above those of developing world norms, though they have been slashed to a maximum of 65 percent from 400 percent. Inadequate protection of intellectual property rights remains a serious concern. The anti-business attitudes of India's federal and state bureaucracies continue to hinder potential investors and plague their routine operations. Policymakers have dragged their feet on selling money-losing SOEs, making labor laws flexible, and deregulating banking.

---

[18]Matthew Dolan and Eric Bellman, "Ford Makes Push to Boost Asian Presence," *The Wall Street Journal*, September 23, 2009, pp. A1–2.

[19]Mehul Srivastava, "What's Holding India Back," *BusinessWeek*, October 19, 2009, pp. 38–44.

CROSSING BORDERS 11.1   Infrastructure: India

Animals in India provide 30,000 megawatts (MW) of power, more than the 29,000 MW provided by electricity.

Because of the religious ban on the slaughter of cattle in almost all states in the country, India has the highest cattle population in the world—perhaps as many as 360 million head. Bullocks are used for plowing fields, turning waterwheels, working crushers and threshers, and above all for hauling carts. The number of bullock carts has doubled to 15 million since India's independence in 1947. Bullocks haul more tonnage than the entire railway system (though over a much shorter distance); in many parts of rural India, they are the only practical means of moving things about.

As a bonus, India's cattle produce enormous quantities of dung, which is used both as farmyard manure

and, when dried in cakes, as household fuel. Each animal produces an estimated average of 3 kilograms of dung per day. Some studies suggest that these forms of energy are the equivalent of another 10,000 MW.

Although Indian farmers prefer machines for plowing and hauling carts, bullocks and other draft animals are still in demand. Because it will take a long time for farmers to replace these draft animals with machines and there is concern that the better breeds may degenerate or become extinct, the government has developed an artificial insemination program to preserve the best breeds.

Sources: "Bullock Manure," *The Economist*, October 17, 1981, p. 88; S. Rajendran, "India: Scheme to Preserve Local Cattle Breed on Anvil," *The Hindu*, August 9, 1997; "Not Enough Bulls to Till the Land," *Times of India*, May 9, 2000; Randeep Ramesh, "India's Drivers Feel the Need for Speed," *The Guardian*, December 6, 2007, p. 29.

In addition, widespread corruption and a deeply ingrained system of bribery make every transaction complicated and expensive. One noted authority on India declared that corrupt practices are not the quaint custom of *baksheesh* but pervasive, systematic, structured, and degraded corruption running from the bottom to the top of the political order. Nevertheless, a survey of U.S. manufacturers shows that 95 percent of respondents with Indian operations plan on expanding, and none say they are leaving. They are hooked on the country's cheap, qualified labor and the potential of a massive market.

With a population now over 1 billion, India is second in size only to China, and both contain enormous low-cost labor pools. India has a middle class numbering some 250 million, about the population of the United States. Among its middle class are large numbers of college graduates, 40 percent of whom have degrees in science and engineering. India has a diverse industrial base and has become a center for computer software. India is now enjoying an information technology boom. After establishing a reputation among foreign corporations by debugging computer networks in time for Y2K, Indian companies now supply everything from animation work to the browsers used on new-generation wireless phones to e-commerce Web sites. As discussed previously, India has been an exporter of technical talent to the U.S. Silicon Valley,[20] and now many of these individuals are returning to establish IT companies of their own. Finally, there is a competitive advantage to being on the other side of the world: Wide-awake English speakers are available for 24/7 services for the United States, while their American counterparts sleep.

India not only stands firmly at the center of many success stories in California's Silicon Valley (Indian engineers provide some 30 percent of the workforce there) but is also seeing Internet enthusiasm build to a frenzy on its own shores. Indian entrepreneurs and capital are creating an Indian Silicon Valley, dubbed "Cyberabad," in Bangalore. Exports there are growing 50 percent annually, and each worker adds $27,000 of value per year, an extraordinary figure in a country where per capita GDP is about $1,000. After a little more than a decade of growth, the Indian industry has an estimated 280,000 software engineers in about 1,000 companies. Moreover, large Indian companies are now expanding their own operations abroad.[21]

---

[20]William M. Bulkeley, "IBM to Cut U.S. Jobs, Expand in India," *The Wall Street Journal*, March 26, 2009, p. B1.

[21]Mehul Srivastava and Moira Herbst, "The Return of the Outsourced Job," *Bloomberg BusinessWeek*, January 11, 2010, pp. 16–17.

The Four "Asian Tigers"

The most rapidly growing economies in this region during the 1980s and 1990s were the group sometimes referred to as the **Four Asian Tigers** (or Four Dragons): Hong Kong, South Korea, Singapore, and Taiwan. Often described as the "East Asian miracle," they were the first countries in Asia, after Japan, to move from a status of developing countries to newly industrialized countries. In addition, each has become a major influence in trade and development in the economies of the other countries within their spheres of influence. The rapid economic growth and regional influence of the member countries of the Association of Southeast Nations (ASEAN) over the last decade has prompted the U.S. Trade Representative to pursue free-trade agreements—Singapore has already signed up. They are vast markets for industrial goods and, as will be discussed later, important emerging consumer markets.

The Four Tigers are rapidly industrializing and extending their trading activity to other parts of Asia. Japan was once the dominant investment leader in the area and was a key player in the economic development of China, Taiwan, Hong Kong, South Korea, and other countries of the region. But as the economies of other Asian countries have strengthened and industrialized, they are becoming more important as economic leaders. For example, South Korea is the center of trade links with north China and the Asian republics of the former Soviet Union. South Korea's sphere of influence and trade extends to Guangdong and Fujian, two of the most productive Chinese Special Economic Zones, and is becoming more important in interregional investment as well.

South Korea exports such high-tech goods as petrochemicals, electronics, machinery, and steel, all of which are in direct competition with Japanese and U.S.-made products. In consumer products, Hyundai, Kia, Samsung, and Lucky-Goldstar (LG) are among the familiar Korean-made brand names in automobiles, microwaves, and televisions sold in the United States. Korea is also making sizable investments outside its borders. A Korean company purchased 58 percent of Zenith, the last remaining TV manufacturer in the United States. At the same time, Korea is dependent on Japan and the United States for much of the capital equipment and components needed to run its factories.

Vietnam

Vietnam's economy and infrastructure were in shambles after 20 years of socialism and war, but this country of more than 88 million is poised for significant growth. A bilateral trade agreement between the United States and Vietnam led to NTR status for Vietnam and will lower tariffs on Vietnamese exports to the United States from an average of 40 percent to less than 3 percent. For example, Vietnamese coffee is now in almost every pantry in

Vietnam has almost no cars; motorbikes deliver almost everything, including moon cakes, in Hanoi.

CROSSING BORDERS 11.2	The Benefits of Information Technology in Village Life

Delora Begum's home office is a corrugated metal and straw hut in Bangladesh with a mud floor, no toilet, and no running water. Yet in this humble setting, she reigns as the "phone lady," a successful entrepreneur and a person of standing in her community. It's all due to a sleek Nokia cell phone. Begum acquired the handset in 1999. Her telephone "booth" is mobile: During the day, it's the stall on the village's main dirt road; at night, callers drop by her family hut to use the cell phone.

Once the phone hookup was made, incomes and quality of life improved almost immediately for many villagers. For as long as he can remember, a brick factory manager had to take a two-and-a half-hour bus ride to Dhaka to order furnace oil and coal for the brick factory. Now, he avoids the biweekly trip: "I can just call if I need anything, or if I have any problems." The local carpenter uses the cell phone to check the current market price of wood, so he ensures a higher profit for the furniture he makes.

The only public telecom link to the outside world, this unit allows villagers to learn the fair value of their rice and vegetables, cutting out middlemen notorious for exploiting them. They can arrange bank transfers or consult doctors in distant cities and, in a nation where only 45 percent of the population can read and write, the cell phone allows people to dispense with a scribe to compose a letter. It also earns some $1,100 a year for its owner—twice the annual per capita income in Bangladesh.

When members of the Grand Coast Fishing Operators cooperative salt and smoke the day's catch to prepare it for market, it may seem light years away from cyberspace, but for these women, the Internet is a boon. The cooperative has set up a Web site that enables its 7,350 members to promote their produce, monitor export markets, and negotiate prices with overseas buyers before they arrive at markets in Senegal. Information technology has thus improved their economic position.

Sources: Miriam Jordan, "It Takes a Cell Phone," *The Wall Street Journal*, June 25, 1999, pp. B1; 7; World Bank, "World Development Indicators," 2010.

America, and the new competitiveness has caused prices to sharply decline on the world market. If Vietnam follows the same pattern of development as other Southeast Asian countries, it could become another Asian Tiger. Many of the ingredients are there: The population is educated and highly motivated, and the government is committed to economic growth. Some factors are a drag on development, however, including poor infrastructure, often onerous government restrictions, minimal industrial base, competition for resources with China,[22] and a lack of capital and technology, which must come primarily from outside the country. Most of the capital and technology are being supplied by three of the Asian Tigers—Taiwan, Hong Kong, and South Korea. American companies such as Intel are also beginning to make huge investments now that the embargo has been lifted.

Bottom-of-the-Pyramid Markets (BOPMs)

LO3

The importance of the Bottom-of-the-Pyramid Markets

C. K. Prahalad and his associates introduced a new concept into the discussion of developing countries and markets—**bottom-of-the-pyramid markets (BOPMs)**[23]—consisting of the 4 billion people across the globe with annual incomes of less than $1,200. These markets are not necessarily defined by national borders but rather by the pockets of poverty across countries. These 4 billion consumers are, of course, concentrated in the LDCs and LLDCs, as defined in the aforementioned U.N. classification scheme, particularly in South Asia and sub-Sahara Africa.

Prahalad's basic point is that these consumers have been relatively ignored by international marketers because of misconceptions about their lack of resources (both money and technology) and the lack of appropriateness of products and services usually developed

---

[22]Edward Wong, "Vietnam Enlists Allies to Stave Off China's Reach," *The New York Times*, February 5, 2010, p. A9.

[23]C. K. Prahalad, *The Fortune at the Bottom of the Pyramid* (Philadelphia: Wharton School Publishing, 2005).

Here we see the start of economic development. As rough as conditions are in this rural school in Lahtora, India, they're even more difficult in Tanzania. But in both places, students are eager to learn.

for more affluent consumers. Three cases demonstrate the commercial viability of such markets and their long-term potential. CEMEX, a Mexican cement company with global operations, pioneered an often[24] profitable program to build better housing for the poor that includes innovative design, financing, and distribution systems. Similarly, Aravind Eye Care System in India began with the problem of blindness among the poor and developed an innovative organization of workflow—from patient identification to postoperative care—that has yielded better vision for consumers and profits for the company. Finally, in her wonderful book about the global economy, Pietra Rivoli[25] tells the story of how small entrepreneurs clothe East Africa with old American t-shirts. All three operations include combinations of products, services, research, and promotions that are appropriate for the lowest-income neighborhoods in the world.

A comprehensive study of the development of the leather-working industry in West Africa presents a new model for creating industries and markets in BOPMs.[26] The authors describe how industry clusters evolve and can be supported by outside investments from commercial and governmental concerns. Exhibit 11.2 represents the ingredients and processes involved in establishing a viable industry cluster in a LLDC. Craftspeople must network and collaborate with one another, vendors, customers, and family[27] to attain efficiencies in production, domestic and international distribution,[28] and other marketing activities. Key to the vibrancy of the industry cluster will be a series of cluster characteristics, external inputs, and macroenvironment factors. The scheme presented might serve as a checklist for stimulating economic development through marketing in BOPMs. Entrepreneurial activities that are networked appear to be perhaps the best way to stimulate economic development and growth from within developing countries. And marketing is key.

[24]Geri Smith, "Hard Times Ease for a Cement King," *BusinessWeek*, November 9, 2009, p. 28.

[25]Pietra Rivoli, *The Travels of a T-Shirt in the Global Economy* (New York: Wiley, 2005).

[26]Eric Arnould and Jakki J. Mohr, "Dynamic Transformation for Base-of-the-Pyramid Market Clusters," *Journal of the Academy of Marketing Science* 33, no. 3 (July 2005), pp. 254–74.

[27]Madhu Viswanathan, "Exchanges in Marketing Systems: The Cases of Subsistence Consumer-Merchants in Chennai, India," *Journal of Marketing* (2010), online.

[28]Jagdish Bhagwati, *In Defense of Globalization* (Oxford: Oxford University Press, 2004).

Exhibit 11.2
Dynamic Transformation of BOPM Clusters

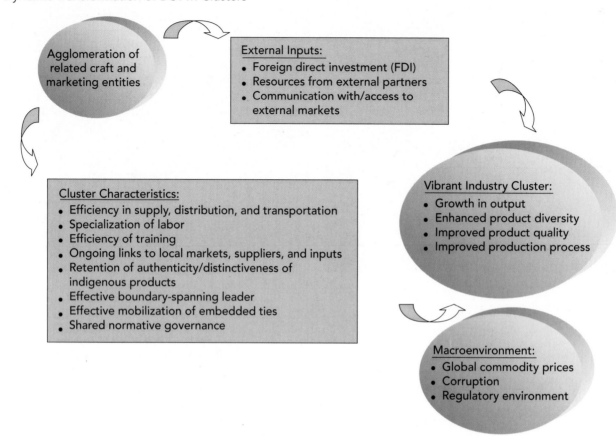

Source: Eric Arnould and Jakki J. Mohr, "Dynamic Transformation for Base-of-the-Pyramid Market Clusters," *Journal of the Academy of Marketing Science* 33, no. 3 (July 2005). Reprinted by permission of Springer.

Note: BOPM = bottom-of-the-pyramid market.

Finally, Grameen Bank, a private commercial enterprise in Bangladesh, developed a program to supply phones to 300 villages. There are only eight land phone lines for every 1,000 people in Bangladesh, one of the lowest phone-penetration rates in the world. The new network is nationwide, endeavoring to put every villager within two kilometers of a cellular phone. Already cell phone penetration has exploded, growing from 4 per 1,000 to 63.5 per 1,000 during the last four years.[29]

Market Metrics

LO4 ▦

The diversity across the region

Exhibits 11.3–11.5 display the fundamental market metrics for the eight most populous countries of the Asia Pacific region. Notice the great diversity in the way people live across the countries, and once again the north-south disparity is clear as well. The income of the Japanese dominates the first chart, along with the dearth of data for Bangladesh. The general excellence of the Japanese healthcare system that produces the longest lifespans in the world is represented, and the emphasis communism places on health is also shown for China and Vietnam.

Exhibit 11.4 compares the infrastructures of the countries. The Japanese rail system is the best in the world, while in the Philippines, people travel by boat and bus. The Vietnamese have few cars, so most travel by motorbike. It is amazing to see families of five traveling on single motorbikes in the hectic streets of Ho Chi Minh City (Saigon). The emphases put on university training in both the Philippines and Vietnam bode well for their future growth.

---

[29]World Bank, "World Development Indicators," 2008.

Exhibit 11.3
Standard of Living in the Eight Most Populous Countries in the Asia Pacific Region

| Country | Population (millions) | GNI per Capita* | Medical Resources per 1000 persons | | Household Ownership % | | |
			Doctors	Hospital Beds	Color TV	Refrigerator	Shower
China	1328	3324	1.5	2.9	97	60	45
India	1169	1016	0.6	—	34	18	46
Indonesia	230	2197	0.2	—	87	25	52
Pakistan	181	925	0.8	0.6	37	39	74
Bangladesh	162	576	0.3	—	—	—	—
Japan	128	41500	2.2	13.8	99	99	100
Philippines	92	1919	0.01	1.0	90	48	87
Vietnam	88	1056	0.7	2.6	86	30	40

*Current US $.

Source: Euromonitor International, 2009.

Exhibit 11.4
Infrastructures of the Eight Most Populous Countries of the Asia/Pacific Region

Country	Travel by Rail (passenger-km per capita)	Passenger Cars/1000	Energy Consumption (tonnes oil equivalent)	Computers in Use per 1000 People	Mobile Phones in Use per 1000 People	Literacy Rate (%)	University Students per 1000 People
China	525	20	1.6	77	532	95%	17
India	613	15	0.4	41	386	67	12
Indonesia	98	17	0.6	34	788	92	14
Pakistan	163	6	0.4	6	588	58	2
Bangladesh	25	1	0.1	37	352	55	6
Japan	3115	446	3.9	524	894	100	23
Philippines	1	8	0.3	121	831	94	29
Vietnam	48	2	—	157	1020	92	27

Source: Euromonitor International, 2009.

Seeing the rough weave of traffic on the streets of old Delhi, India, you likely can understand the need for the elevated expressways. The introduction of Tata Motor's new $2,500 car, the Nano, will only make congestion worse. The country just raised the national speed limit from 80 kph to 100 kph, spurred by a roads revolution, the centerpiece of which is the 3,650-mile golden Quadrilateral highway linking Delhi, Mumbai (Bombay), Chennai (Madras), and Kolkata (Calcutta), the most expensive public works project in the nation's history. However, we wonder: How will the traffic police keep the ubiquitous sacred cows off expressway on-ramps?

Exhibit 11.5
Consumption Patterns in the Eight Most Populous Countries in the Asia/Pacific Region

		Household Expenditures ($/capita)								
Country	People per Household	Food	Alcohol, Tobacco	Clothing	Housing	Health Goods, Services	Transportation	Communication	Leisure	Education
China	3.4	430	34	112	157	114	46	147	37	82
India	5.3	212	18	25	73	24	90	20	12	16
Indonesia	3.4	588	75	52	230	34	48	23	28	91
Pakistan	7.2	291	16	35	133	47	32	4	1	18
Bangladesh	6.0	—	—	—	—	—	—	—	—	—
Japan	2.5	3303	743	658	5916	1034	2423	910	2694	507
Philippines	4.8	456	19	29	270	42	103	8	6	58
Vietnam	4.4	285	19	29	30	54	103	10	10	51

Source: Euromonitor International, 2009.

Exhibit 11.5 briefly enumerates consumption patterns. Of course, Japan stands out. Also, notice the difference between the Chinese and Indian emphases on education.

Asia Pacific Trade Associations

LO5

The interrelationships among countries in the region

After decades of dependence on the United States and Europe for technology and markets, countries in the Asia Pacific region are preparing for the next economic leap driven by trade, investment, and technology, aided by others in the region. Though few in number, trade agreements among some of the Asian newly industrialized countries are seen as movement toward a regionwide, intra-Asian trade area, with Japan and China[30] at the center of this activity.

In years past, the United States was Japan's single largest trading partner. However, now markets in China and Southeast Asia are increasingly more important in Japanese corporate strategy for trade and direct investment. Once a source of inexpensive labor for products shipped to Japan or to third markets, these countries are now seen as viable markets. Furthermore, Japanese investment across a number of manufacturing industries is geared toward serving local customers and building sophisticated local production and supplier networks.

Present trade agreements include one multinational trade group, the Association of Southeast Asian Nations (ASEAN), which is evolving into the ASEAN Free Trade Area (AFTA); ASEAN+3, a forum for ASEAN ministers plus ministers from China, Japan, and South Korea; and the Asia-Pacific Economic Cooperation (APEC), a forum that meets annually to discuss regional economic development and cooperation.

Association of Southeast Asian Nations (ASEAN) and ASEAN+3

The primary multinational trade group in Asia is **ASEAN**.[31] Like all multinational market groups, ASEAN has experienced problems and false starts in attempting to unify the combined economies of its member nations. Most of the early economic growth came from trade outside the ASEAN group. Similarities in the kinds of products they had to export, in their natural resources, and other national assets hampered earlier attempts at intra-ASEAN trade. The steps that the countries took to expand and diversify their industrial base to foster intraregional trade when ASEAN was first created have resulted in the fastest growing economies in the region and an increase in trade among members (see Exhibit 11.6).

Four major events account for the vigorous economic growth of the ASEAN countries and their transformation from cheap-labor havens to industrialized nations: (1) the ASEAN governments' commitment to deregulation, liberalization, and privatization of their economies; (2) the decision to shift their economies from commodity based to manufacturing based; (3) the decision to specialize in manufacturing components in which they have a

[30]Carlos H. Conde, "China and ASEAN in Services Pact," *The New York Times*, January 15, 2007, p. C2.

[31]See http://www.aseansec.org; "Ajar for Business," *The Economist*, January 9, 2010, p. 44.

regarding media-based segmentation: "With media splintering into smaller and smaller communities of interest, it will become more and more important to reach those audiences wherever [whichever country] they may be. Today, media companies are increasingly delivering their content over a variety of platforms: broadcast—both TV and radio—and cable, online and print, big screen video, and the newest portable digital media including 3-D. And advertisers are using the same variety of platforms to reach their desired audience." Finally, perhaps a few famous Italian brands are the best examples: Salvatore Ferragamo shoes, Gucci leather goods, and Ferrari cars sell to the highest-income segments globally. Indeed, for all three companies, their U.S. sales are greater than their Italian sales.

In the 21st century, standardization versus adaptation is simply not the right question to ask.[12] Rather, the crucial question facing international marketers is what are the most efficient ways to segment markets.[13] Country has been the most obvious segmentation variable, particularly for Americans. But as better communication systems continue to dissolve national borders, other dimensions of global markets are growing in salience.

The Nestlé Way: Evolution Not Revolution

Nestlé certainly hasn't been bothered by the debate on standardization versus adaptation. Nestlé has been international almost from its start in 1866 as a maker of infant formula. By 1920, the company was producing in Brazil, Australia, and the United States and exporting to Hong Kong. Today, it sells more than 8,500 products produced in 489 factories in 193 countries. Nestlé is the world's biggest marketer of infant formula, powdered milk, instant coffee, chocolate, soups, and mineral water. It ranks second in ice cream, and in cereals, it ties Ralston Purina and trails only Kellogg Company. Its products are sold in the most upscale supermarkets in Beverly Hills, California, and in huts in Nigeria, where women sell Nestlé bouillon cubes alongside homegrown tomatoes and onions. Although the company has no sales agents in North Korea, its products somehow find their way into stores there, too.

The "Nestlé way" is to dominate its markets. Its overall strategy can be summarized in four points: (1) think and plan long term, (2) decentralize, (3) stick to what you know, and (4) adapt to local tastes. To see how Nestlé operates, take a look at its approach to Poland, one of the largest markets of the former Soviet bloc. Company executives decided at the outset that it would take too long to build plants and create brand awareness. Instead, the company pursued acquisitions and followed a strategy of "evolution not revolution." It purchased Goplana, Poland's second-best-selling chocolate maker (it bid for the No. 1 company but lost out) and carefully adjusted the end product via small changes every two months over a two-year period until it measured up to Nestlé's standards and was a recognizable Nestlé brand. These efforts, along with all-out marketing, put the company within striking distance of the market leader, Wedel. Nestlé also purchased a milk operation and, as it did in Mexico, India, and elsewhere, sent technicians into the field to help Polish farmers improve the quality and quantity of the milk it buys through better feeds and improved sanitation.

Nestlé's efforts in the Middle East are much longer term. The area currently represents only about 2 percent of the company's worldwide sales, and the markets, individually, are relatively small. Furthermore, regional conflicts preclude most trade among the countries. Nevertheless, Nestlé anticipates that hostility will someday subside, and when that happens, the company will be ready to sell throughout the entire region. Nestlé has set up a network of factories in five countries that can someday supply the entire region with different products. The company makes ice cream in Dubai and soups and cereals in Saudi Arabia. The Egyptian factory makes yogurt and bouillon, while Turkey produces chocolate. And a factory in Syria makes ketchup, a malted-chocolate energy food, instant noodles, and other

[12]Aviv Shoham, Maja Makovec Brencic, Vesna Virant, and Ayalla Ruvio, "International Standardization of Channel Management and Its Behavioral and Performance Outcomes," *Journal of International Marketing*, 16, no. 2 (2008), pp. 120–51.

[13]Amanda J. Broderick, Gordon E. Greenley, and Rene Dentiste Mueller, "The Behavioral Homogeneity Evaluation Framework: Multi-Level Evaluations of Consumer Involvement in International Segmentation," *Journal of International Business Studies* 38 (2007), pp. 746–63.

products. If the obstacles between the countries come down, Nestlé will have a network of plants ready to provide a complete line to market in all the countries. In the meantime, factories produce and sell mostly in the countries in which they are located.

For many companies, such a long-term strategy would not be profitable, but it works for Nestlé because the company relies on local ingredients and markets products that consumers can afford. The tomatoes and wheat used in the Syrian factory, for example, are major local agricultural products. Even if Syrian restrictions on trade remain, there are 14 million people to buy ketchup, noodles, and other products the company produces there. In all five countries, the Nestlé name and the bird-in-a-nest trademark appear on every product.

Nestlé bills itself as "the only company that is truly dedicated to providing a complete range of food products to meet the needs and tastes of people from around the world, each hour of their day, throughout their entire lives."

Benefits of Global Marketing

Few firms have truly global operations balanced across major regional markets. However, when large international market segments can be identified, economies of scale in production and marketing can be important competitive advantages for multinational companies.[14] As a case in point, Black & Decker Manufacturing Company—makers of electrical hand tools, appliances, and other consumer products—realized significant production cost savings when it adopted a pan-European strategy. It was able to reduce not only the number of motor sizes for the European market from 260 to 8 but also 15 different models to 8. Similarly, Ford estimates that by unifying product development, purchasing, and supply activities across several countries, it saves more than $3 billion a year. Finally, while Japanese firms initially dominated the mobile phone business in their home market, international competitors now pose growing challenges via better technologies developed through greater global penetration.

Transfer of experience and know-how across countries through improved coordination and integration of marketing activities is also cited as a benefit of global operations.[15] Global diversity in marketing talent leads to new approaches across markets.[16] Unilever successfully introduced two global brands originally developed by two subsidiaries. Its South African subsidiary developed Impulse body spray, and a European branch developed a detergent that cleaned effectively in European hard water. Aluminum Company of America's (Alcoa) joint venture partner in Japan produced aluminum sheets so perfect that U.S. workers, when shown samples, accused the company of hand-selecting the samples. Line workers were sent to the Japanese plant to learn the techniques, which were then transferred to the U.S. operations. Because of the benefits of such transfers of knowledge, Alcoa has changed its practice of sending managers overseas to "keep an eye on things" to sending line workers and managers to foreign locations to seek out new techniques and processes.

Marketing globally also ensures that marketers have access to the toughest customers. For example, in many product and service categories, the Japanese consumer has been the hardest to please; the demanding customers are the reason that the highest-quality products and services often emanate from that country. Competing for Japanese customers provides firms with the best testing ground for high-quality products and services.

---

[14]Natalia Vila and Ines Kuster, "Success and Internationalization: Analysis of the Textile Sector," *Journal of Global Marketing* 21, no. 2 (2008), pp. 109–26; Amar Gande, Christopher Schenzler, and Lemma W. Senbet, "Valuation Effects of Global Diversification," *Journal of International Business Studies* 40, no. 9 (2009), pp. 1515–32.

[15]Nigel Driffield, James H. Love, and Stefan Menghinello, "The Multinational Enterprise as a Source of International Knowledge Flows: Direct Evidence from Italy," *Journal of International Business Studies* 41, no. 2 (2010), pp. 350–59.

[16]Janet Y. Murray and Mike C. H. Chao, "A Cross-Team Framework on International Knowledge Acquisition on New Product Development Capabilities and New Product Market Performance," *Journal of International Marketing* 13 (2005), pp. 54–78; John Cantwell, "Location and the Multinational Enterprise," *Journal of International Business Studies* 40, no. 1 (2009), pp. 35–41; Peter J. Buckley and Niron Hashai, "Formalizing Internationalization in the Eclectic Paradigm," *Journal of International Business Studies* 40, no. 1 (2009), pp. 58–70.

CROSSING BORDERS 12.1 Swedish Takeout

Fifty years ago in the woods of southern Sweden, a minor revolution took place that has since changed the concept of retailing and created a mass market in a category where none previously existed. The catalyst of the change was and is IKEA, the Swedish furniture retailer and distributor that virtually invented the idea of self-service, takeout furniture. IKEA sells reasonably priced and innovatively designed furniture and home furnishings for a global marketplace.

The name was registered in Agunnaryd, Sweden, in 1943 by Ingvar Kamprad—the IK in the company's name. He entered the furniture market in 1950, and the first catalog was published in 1951. The first store didn't open until 1958 in Almhult. It became so incredibly popular that a year later the store had to add a restaurant for people who were traveling long distances to get there.

IKEA entered the United States in 1985. Although IKEA is global, most of the action takes place in Europe, with about 85 percent of the firm's $7 billion in sales. Nearly one-fourth of that comes from stores in Germany. This level compares with only about $1 billion in NAFTA countries.

One reason for the relatively slow growth in the United States is that its stores are franchised by Netherlands-based Inter IKEA Systems, which carefully scrutinizes potential franchisees—individuals or companies—for strong financial backing and a proven record in retailing. The IKEA Group, based in Denmark, is a group of private companies owned by a charitable foundation in the Netherlands; it operates more than 100 stores. The Group also develops, purchases, distributes, and sells IKEA products, which are available only in company stores. The items are purchased from more than 2,400 suppliers in 65 countries and shipped through 14 distribution centers. The goal of sourcing 30 percent of timber in both China and Russia has not yet been reached, but the efforts continue.

Low price is built into the company's lines. Even catalog prices are guaranteed not to increase for one year. The drive to produce affordable products inadvertently put IKEA at the forefront of the environmental movement several decades ago. In addition to lowering costs, minimization of materials and packing addressed natural resource issues. Environmentalism remains an integral operational issue at IKEA. Even the company's catalog is completely recyclable and produced digitally rather than on film.

On the day that Russia's first IKEA store opened in 2000, the wait to get in was an hour. Highway traffic backed up for miles. More than 40,000 people crammed into the place, picking clean sections of the warehouse. The store still pulls in more than 100,000 customers per week. IKEA has big plans for Russia. Company officials are placing IKEA's simple shelves, kitchens, bathrooms, and bedrooms in millions of Russian apartments that haven't been remodeled since the Soviet days. And now IKEA has opened five new stores in China's biggest cities.

Sources: Colin McMahon, "Russians Flock to IKEA as Store Battles Moscow," *Chicago Tribune*, May 17, 2000; "IKEA to March into China's Second-tier Cities [Next]," *SinoCast China Business Daily News*, August 6, 2007, p. 1; "IKEA Struggles to Source Sustainable Timber," *Environmental Data Services*, July 2009, p. 22.

Diversity of markets served carries with it additional financial benefits.[17] Spreading the portfolio of markets served brings important stability of revenues and operations to many global companies.[18] Companies with global marketing operations suffered less during the Asian market downturn of the late 1990s than did firms specializing in the area. Firms that market globally are able to take advantage of changing financial circumstances in other ways as well. For example, as tax and tariff rates ebb and flow around the world, the most global companies are able to leverage the associated complexity to their advantage.

---

[17]N. Capar and M. Kotabe have noted that for services firms, the relationship between international diversification and firm performance can be curvilinear (that is, both not enough and too much are bad); see "The Relationship between International Diversification and Performance in Service Firms," *Journal of International Business Studies* 34, no. 4 (2003), pp. 345–55; Protiti Dastidar, "International Corporate Diversification and Performance: Does Firm Self-Selection Matter?" *Journal of International Business Studies* 40, no. 1 (2009), pp. 71–85.

[18]Lee Li, Gongming Qian, and Zhengming Qian, "Product Diversification, Multinationality, and Country Involvement: What Is the Optimal Combination?" *Journal of Global Marketing* 20 (2007), pp. 5–25; Tess Stynes and Paul Ziobro, "McDonald's Sales Rise Despite U.S. Weakness," *The Wall Street Journal*, February 9, 2010, online.

CROSSING BORDERS 12.2   Apple Shops for Partners around the World

Apple has moved fast since its introduction of the iPhone, making distribution deals with U.S. and European operators. Now Steve Jobs is turning east, making plans to enter Japan, one of the biggest and most sophisticated mobile phone markets in the world.

People familiar with the situation say Jobs recently met with NTT DoCoMo Inc.'s president, Masao Nakamura, to discuss a deal to offer the iPhone in Japan through the nation's dominant mobile operator. These informants said Apple also has been talking to the No. 3 operator, Softbank Corp., and that executives from both companies have made multiple trips to Apple's Cupertino, California, headquarters. For Apple, finding a wireless partner soon in Japan is an important step in the company's oft-stated goal of gaining a 1 percent share of the global cell phone business by shipping about 10 million iPhones between the product's launch in late June 2007 and the end of 2008.

The world's second-largest economy, after the United States, is an attractive market because it not only has a strong base of iPod fans, but its nearly 100 million mobile phone users buy new phones every two years on average. Japanese consumers also are accustomed to shelling out hundreds of dollars for expensive phones with advanced capabilities, such as digital television, cameras, and music.

Yet Japan could be a difficult market to crack for Apple. More than 10 domestic mobile phone makers work closely with the three major operators to develop phones tailored to Japanese consumers' tastes. In the past, foreign mobile phone makers have not been willing to go to such lengths and generally have met with little success in selling their phones, especially when those phones do not contain essential Japanese features, such as the operators' proprietary mobile Internet technology or e-mail software that Japanese consumers are used to having.

The iPhone has been successful thus far in countries where it has been launched. Apple sold a total of 1.4 million iPhones by late September 2007. And though sales of the product did not quite meet some of the most bullish Wall Street forecasts, the iPhone has been one of the top-selling smart phones in the United States, where it is sold only through AT&T Inc., the nation's largest carrier by subscribers.

In the end, Apple has partnered with Softbank in Japan and China Unicom and is expecting the momentum to continue well into the future.

Sources: John Markoff, "A Personal Computer to Carry in a Pocket," *The New York Times*, January 8, 2007, pp. C1, C3; Yukari Iwatani and Nick Wingfield, "Apple Meets with DoCoMo, Softbank on Launching iPhone in Japan," *The Wall Street Journal* (online), December 18, 2007; Philip Michaels, "Apple: What Recession?" *Macworld*, January 2010, p. 16.

Planning for Global Markets

Planning is a systematized way of relating to the future. It is an attempt to manage the effects of external, uncontrollable factors on the firm's strengths, weaknesses, objectives, and goals to attain a desired end. Furthermore, it is a commitment of resources to a country market to achieve specific goals. In other words, planning is the job of making things happen that might not otherwise occur.

Planning allows for rapid growth of the international function, changing markets, increasing competition, and the turbulent challenges of different national markets. The plan must blend the changing parameters of external country environments with corporate objectives and capabilities to develop a sound, workable marketing program.[19] A strategic plan commits corporate resources to products and markets to increase competitiveness and profits.

Planning relates to the formulation of goals and methods of accomplishing them, so it is both a process and a philosophy. Structurally, planning may be viewed as corporate, strategic, or tactical. International **corporate planning** is essentially long term, incorporating generalized goals for the enterprise as a whole. **Strategic planning** is conducted at the highest levels of management and deals with products, capital, research, and the long- and short-term goals of the company. **Tactical planning**, or market planning, pertains to specific actions and to the allocation of resources used to implement strategic planning goals

---

[19]Wade M. Danis, Dan S. Chiaburu, and Majorie A. Lyles, "The Impact of Managerial Networking Intensity and Market-Based Strategies on Firm Growth during Institutional Upheaval: A Study of Small and Medium-Sized Enterprises in a Transition Economy," *Journal of International Business Studies* 41, no. 2 (2010), pp. 287–307.

400 inquiries. Pleased with the response, the company set up an international franchise operation based on royalties and franchise fees. Now a network of international franchised distributors markets the machines and ingredients to potential vendors. The distributors pay Lil'Orbits a franchise fee and buy machines and ingredients directly from Lil'Orbits or from one of the licensed vendors worldwide, from which Lil'Orbits receives a royalty. This entry strategy has enabled the company to enter foreign markets with minimum capital investment outside the home country. The company has over 20,000 franchised dealers in 85 countries. About 60 percent of the company's business is international.

Although franchising enables a company to expand quickly with minimum capital, there are costs associated with servicing franchisees. For example, to accommodate different tastes around the world, Lil'Orbits had to develop a more pastrylike, less sweet mix than that used in the United States. Other cultural differences have had to be met as well. For example, customers in France and Belgium could not pronounce the trade name Lil'Orbits, so Orbie is used instead. Toppings also had to be adjusted to accommodate different tastes. Cinnamon sugar is the most widely accepted topping, but in China, cinnamon is considered a medicine, so only sugar is used. In the Mediterranean region, the Greeks like honey, and chocolate sauce is popular in Spain. Powdered sugar is more popular than granulated sugar in France, where the donuts are eaten in cornucopia cups instead of on plates.

Strategic International Alliances

LO4

The increasing importance of international strategic alliances

A **strategic international alliance (SIA)** is a business relationship established by two or more companies to cooperate out of mutual need and to share risk in achieving a common objective. Strategic alliances have grown in importance over the last few decades as a competitive strategy in global marketing management. Strategic international alliances are sought as a way to shore up weaknesses and increase competitive strengths—that is, complementarity is key.[46] Firms enter into SIAs for several reasons: opportunities for rapid expansion into new markets, access to new technology,[47] more efficient production and innovation, reduced marketing costs, strategic competitive moves, and access to additional sources of products[48] and capital. Finally, evidence suggests that SIAs often contribute nicely to profits.[49]

Perhaps the most visible SIAs are now in the airline industry. American Airlines, Cathay Pacific, British Airways, Japan Airlines, Finnair, Mexicana, Malev, Iberia, LAN, Royal Jordanian, and Quantas are partners in the Oneworld Alliance, which integrates schedules and mileage programs. Competing with Oneworld are the Star Alliance (led by United, Continental, and Lufthansa) and SkyTeam (led by Air France, Delta, and KLM). These kinds of strategic international alliances imply that there is a common objective; that one partner's weakness is offset by the other's strength; that reaching the objective alone would be too costly, take too much time, or be too risky; and that together their respective strengths make possible what otherwise would be unattainable. For example, during the recent turmoil in the global airline industry, Star Alliance began moving in the direction of buying aircraft, a new strategic innovation. Relationships appear particularly strong in times of troubles—Japan Airlines leans heavily in the direction of American Airlines (both Oneworld members) rather than "outsider" Delta in its current merger/acquisition/investment talks.[50]

---

[46]Eric Fang and Shaoming Zou, "Antecedents and Consequences of Marketing Dynamic Capabilities in International Joint Ventures," *Journal of International Business Studies* 39, no. 1 (2008), pp. 1–27.

[47]http://www.lilorbits.com, 2005.

[48]John Hagedoorn, Danielle Cloodt, and Hans van Kraneburg, "Intellectual Property Rights and the Governance of International R&D Partnerships," *Journal of International Business Studies* 36 (2005), pp. 175–86; Marjorie A. Lyles and Jane E. Salk, "Knowledge Acquisition from Foreign Parents in International Joint Ventures: An Empirical Examination of the Hungarian Context," *Journal of International Business Studies* 38 (2007), pp. 3–18; Masaaki Kotabe, Denise Dunlap-Hinkler, Ronaldo Parente, and Harsh A. Mishra, "Determination of Cross-National Knowledge Transfer and Its Effect on Innovation," *Journal of International Business Studies* 38 (2007), pp. 259–82.

[49]Janet Y. Murray, Masaaki Kotabe, and Joe Nan Zhou, "Strategic Alliance–Based Sourcing and Market Performance: Evidence from Foreign Firms Operating in China," *Journal of International Business Studies* 36, no. 2 (2005), pp. 187–208.

[50]Mariko Sanchanta and Mike Esterl, "JAL Stays in AMR Alliance, Delta Out," *The Wall Street Journal*, February 7, 2010, online.

In the SkyTeam strategic alliance, U.S.-based Northwest Airlines and Dutch KLM shared several aspects of their operations, including ticketing and reservations, catering, cargo, and airport slots. As the global airline industry continues to consolidate, more strategic partnerships are being formed and disappearing. Indeed, Delta Airlines has now acquired Northwest, and soon, Delta jets will be sharing the tarmac with KLM at Schiphol Airport in Amsterdam.

An SIA with multiple objectives involves C-Itoh (Japan), Tyson Foods (United States), and Provemex (Mexico). It is an alliance that processes Japanese-style yakitori (bits of marinated and grilled chicken on a bamboo stick) for export to Japan and other Asian countries. Each company had a goal and made a contribution to the alliance. C-Itoh's goal was to find a lower-cost supply of yakitori; because it is so labor intensive, it was becoming increasingly costly and noncompetitive to produce in Japan. C-Itoh's contribution was access to its distribution system and markets throughout Japan and Asia. Tyson's goal was new markets for its dark chicken meat, a byproduct of demand for mostly white meat in the U.S. market. Tyson exported some of its excess dark meat to Asia and knew that C-Itoh wanted to expand its supplier base. But Tyson faced the same high labor costs as C-Itoh. Provemex, the link that made it all work, had as its goal expansion beyond raising and slaughtering chickens into higher value-added products for international markets. Provemex's contribution was to provide highly cost-competitive labor.

Through the alliance, they all benefited. Provemex acquired the know-how to bone the dark meat used in yakitori and was able to vertically integrate its operations and secure a foothold in a lucrative export market. Tyson earned more from the sale of surplus chicken legs than was previously possible and gained an increased share of the Asian market. C-Itoh had a steady supply of competitively priced yakitori for its vast distribution and marketing network. Thus, three companies with individual strengths created a successful alliance in which each contributes and each benefits.

Many companies also are entering SIAs to be in a strategic position to be competitive and to benefit from the expected growth in the single European market. As a case in point, when General Mills wanted a share of the rapidly growing breakfast-cereal market in Europe, it joined with Nestlé to create Cereal Partners Worldwide. The European cereal market was projected to be worth hundreds of millions of dollars as health-conscious Europeans changed their breakfast diet from eggs and bacon to dry cereal. General Mills's main U.S. competitor, Kellogg, had been in Europe since 1920 and controlled about half of the market.

For General Mills to enter the market from scratch would have been extremely costly. Although the cereal business uses cheap commodities as its raw materials, it is both capital and marketing intensive; sales volume must be high before profits begin to develop. Only recently has Kellogg earned significant profits in Europe. For General Mills to reach its goal alone would have required a manufacturing base and a massive sales force. Furthermore, Kellogg's stranglehold on supermarkets would have been difficult for an unknown to breach easily. The solution was a joint venture with Nestlé. Nestlé had everything General Mills lacked—a well-known brand name, a network of plants, and a powerful distribution system—except for the one thing that General Mills could provide: strong cereal brands.

The deal was mutually beneficial. General Mills provided the knowledge in cereal technology, including some of its proprietary manufacturing equipment, its stable of proven brands, and its knack for pitching these products to consumers. Nestlé provided its name on the box, access to retailers, and production capacity that could be converted to making General Mills's cereals. In time, Cereal Partners Worldwide intends to extend its marketing effort beyond Europe. In Asia, Africa, and Latin America, Cereal Partners Worldwide will have an important advantage over the competition because Nestlé is a dominant food producer.

As international strategic alliances have grown in importance, more emphasis has been placed on a systematic approach to forming them. Most experts in the field agree that the steps outlined in Exhibit 12.3 will lead to successful and high-performance strategic alliances. In particular, we note the wide agreement regarding the importance of building trust in the interpersonal and institutional relationships as a prerequisite of success.[51] Of course,

---

[51]Robert E. Spekman, Lynn A. Isabella, with Thomas C. MacAvoy, *Alliance Competence* (New York: Wiley, 2000).

Exhibit 12.3
Building Strategic Alliances

Primary Relationship Activity	Typical Actions, Interactions, Activities	Key Relationship Skill
Dating	Senior executives leveraging personal networks Wondering how to respond to inquiries Wondering how to seek out possibilities	Good radar; good relationship self-awareness
Imaging	Seeing the reality in possibilities Creating a shared vision from being together Involving trusted senior managers	Creating intimacy
Initiating	Bringing key executives into action Creating trust through face-to-face time	Trust building
Interfacing	Facilitating the creating of personal relationships at many levels Traveling to partner facilities and engaging in technical conversations Blending social and business time	Partnering
Committing	Demonstrating that managers are fully committed to the alliance and each other Managing the conflict inherent in making hard choices Accepting the reality of the alliance and its relationships	Commitment
Fine-tuning	Relying on mature and established relationships Facilitating interaction and relationships with future successors	Growing *with* another

Source: Adapted from Robert E. Spekman, Lynn A. Isabella, with Thomas C. MacAvoy, *Alliance Competence* (New York: Wiley, 2000), p. 81. Reproduced with permission of John Wiley & Sons, Inc.

in international business there are no guarantees; the interface between differing ethical and legal systems often makes matters more difficult.[52] And a key activity in all the steps outlined in the exhibit is international negotiation, the subject of Chapter 19.[53]

International Joint Ventures. International joint ventures (IJVs) as a means of foreign market entry have accelerated sharply during the last 30 years. Besides serving as a means of lessening political and economic risks by the amount of the partner's contribution to the venture, IJVs provide a way to enter markets that pose legal and cultural barriers that is less risky than acquisition of an existing company.

A **joint venture** is different from other types of strategic alliances or collaborative relationships in that a joint venture is a partnership of two or more participating companies that have joined forces to create a separate legal entity. Joint ventures are different from minority holdings by an MNC in a local firm.

Four characteristics define joint ventures: (1) JVs are established, separate, legal entities; (2) they acknowledge intent by the partners to share in the management of the JV;

---

[52]Alaka N. Rao, Jone L. Pearce, and Katherine Xin, "Governments, Reciprocal Exchange and Trust among Business Associates," *Journal of International Business Studies* 36 (2005), pp. 104–18; David A. Griffith, Matthew B. Myers, and Michael G. Harvey, "An Investigation of National Culture's Influence on Relationship and Knowledge Resources in Interorganizational Relationships between Japan and the United States," *Journal of International Marketing* 14 (2006), pp. 1–36; Srilata Zaheer and Akbar Zaheer, "Trust across Borders," *Journal of International Business Studies* 37 (2006), pp. 21–29.

[53]Kam-hon Lee, Gong-ming Qian, Julie H. Yu, and Ying Ho, "Trading Favors for Marketing Advantage: Evidence from Hong Kong, China, and the United States," *Journal of International Marketing* 13 (2005), pp. 1–35.

(3) they are partnerships between legally incorporated entities, such as companies, chartered organizations, or governments, and not between individuals; and (4) equity positions are held by each of the partners.

However, IJVs can be hard to manage. The choice of partners and the qualities of the relationships between the executives are important factors leading to success. Several other factors contribute to their success or failure as well: how control is shared,[54] relations with parents,[55] institutional (legal) environments,[56] marketing capabilities,[57] experience,[58] and the extent to which knowledge is shared across partners.[59] Despite this complexity, nearly all companies active in world trade participate in at least one international joint venture somewhere; many companies have dozens of joint ventures. A recent Conference Board study indicated that 40 percent of *Fortune* 500 companies were engaged in one or more IJVs. Particularly in telecommunications and Internet markets, joint ventures are increasingly favored.

Around the Asia Pacific Rim, where U.S. companies face unfamiliar legal and cultural barriers, joint ventures are preferred to buying existing businesses. Local partners can often lead the way through legal mazes and provide the outsider with help in understanding cultural nuances. A JV can be attractive to an international marketer when it enables a company to utilize the specialized skills of a local partner, when it allows the marketer to gain access to a partner's local distribution system, when a company seeks to enter a market where wholly owned activities are prohibited, when it provides access to markets protected by tariffs or quotas, and when the firm lacks the capital or personnel capabilities to expand its international activities.

In China, a country considered to be among the most challenging in Asia,[60] more than 50,000 joint ventures have been established in the 30 years since the government began allowing IJVs there. Among the many reasons IJVs are so popular is that they offer a way of getting around high Chinese tariffs, allowing a company to gain a competitive price advantage over imports. Manufacturing locally with a Chinese partner rather than importing achieves additional savings as a result of low-cost Chinese labor. Many Western brands are manufactured and marketed in China at prices that would not be possible if the products were imported.

Consortia.   Consortia are similar to joint ventures and could be classified as such except for two unique characteristics: (1) They typically involve a large number of participants and (2) they frequently operate in a country or market in which none of the participants is

---

[54]Chris Styles and Lis Hersch, "Relationship Formation in International Joint Ventures: Insights from Australian-Malaysian International Joint Ventures," *Journal of International Marketing* 13 (2005), pp. 105–34.

[55]Jeffrey Q. Bardon, H. Kevin Steensma, and Marjorie A. Lyles, "The Influence of Parent Control Structure on Parent Conflict in Vietnamese IJVs: An Organizational Justice–Based Contingency Approach," *Journal of International Business Studies* 36, no. 2 (2005), pp. 156–74.

[56]Barden, Steensma, and Lyles, "The Influence of Parent Control Structure on Parent Conflict"; Yaping Gong, Oded Shenkar, Yadong Luo, and Mee-Kau Nyaw, "Human Resources and International Joint Venture Performance: A System Perspective," *Journal of International Business Studies* 36 (2005), pp. 505–18; Rene Belderbos and Jianglei Zou, "On the Growth of Foreign Affiliates: Multinational Plant Networks, Joint Ventures, and Flexibility," *Journal of International Business Studies* 38 (2007), pp. 1095–112.

[57]Eric (Er) Fang and Shaoming Zou, "Antecedents and Consequences of Marketing Dynamic Capabilities in International Joint Ventures," *Journal of International Business Studies* 40, no. 5 (2009), pp. 742–61.

[58]Sengun Yeniyurt, Janell D. Townsend, S. Tamer Cavusgil, and Pervez Ghauri, "Mimetic and Experiential Effects in International Marketing Alliance Formations of U.S. Pharmaceuticals Firms: An Event History Analysis," *Journal of International Business Studies* 40, no. 2 (2009), pp. 301–20.

[59]Yadong Luo, "Transactional Characteristics, Institutional Environment, and Joint Venture Contracts," *Journal of International Business Studies* 36, no. 2 (2005), pp. 209–30; Changhui Zhou and Jing Li, "Product Innovation in Emerging Market-Based International Joint Ventures: An Organizational Ecology Perspective," *Journal of International Business Studies* 39, no. 7 (2008), pp. 1114–32; Jean-Paul Roy and Christine Oliver, "International Joint Venture Partner Selection: The Role of the Host-Country Legal Environment," *Journal of International Business Studies* 40, no. 5 (2009), pp. 779–802.

[60]Timothy J. Wilkinson, Andrew R. Thomas, and Jon M. Hawes, "Managing Relationships with Chinese Joint Venture Partners," *Journal of Global Marketing* 22, no. 2 (2009), pp. 109–20.

currently active. Consortia are developed to pool financial and managerial resources and to lessen risks. Often, huge construction projects are built under a consortium arrangement in which major contractors with different specialties form a separate company specifically to negotiate for and produce one job. One firm usually acts as the lead firm, or the newly formed corporation may exist independently of its originators.

Without a doubt, the most prominent international consortium has been Airbus, Boeing's European competitor in the global commercial aircraft market. Airbus Industrie was originally formed when four major European aerospace firms agreed to work together to build commercial airliners. In 2000, the four agreed to transform the consortium into a global company to achieve operations efficiencies that would allow it to compete better against Boeing. Meanwhile, Boeing is joining together with its own consortium to develop new 787 Dreamliner aircraft.[61]

Sematech, the other candidate for most prominent consortium, was originally an exclusively American operation. Sematech is an R&D consortium formed in Austin, Texas, during the 1980s to regain America's lead in semiconductor development and sales from Japan. Members included firms such as IBM, Intel, Texas Instruments, Motorola, and Hewlett-Packard. However, at the turn of the millennium even Sematech went international. Several of the founding American companies left and were replaced by firms from Taiwan, Korea, Germany, and the Netherlands (still none from Japan). The firm is also broadening its own investment portfolio to include a greater variety of international companies.

All strategic international alliances are susceptible to problems of coordination. For example, some analysts blamed the international breadth of Boeing's 787 Dreamliner consortium for the costly delays in manufacturing the new jet. Further, circumstances and/or partners can change in ways that render agreements untenable, and often such corporate relationships are short lived. Ford and Nissan launched a joint venture minivan in 1992 called the Mercury Villager/Nissan Quest. The car was mildly successful in the U.S. market, but in 2002 the joint venture stopped producing the cars—that's two years earlier than the original contract called for. Now that Nissan is controlled by French automaker Renault, it began producing its own minivan in 2003 for sale in the United States. When General Motors formed a joint venture with Daewoo, its purpose was to achieve a significant position in the Asian car market. Instead, Daewoo used the alliance to enhance its own automobile technology, and by the time the partnership was terminated, GM had created a new global competitor for itself.

Nestlé has been involved in a particularly ugly dissolution dispute with Dabur India. The Swiss firm owned 60 percent and the Indian firm 40 percent of a joint venture biscuit company, Excelcia Foods. Following months of acrimony, Dabur filed a petition with the Indian government accusing Nestlé of indulging in oppression of the minority shareholder and of mismanaging the JV company. In particular, Dabur alleged that Nestlé was purposefully running Excelcia into bankruptcy so that Nestlé could wriggle out of its "non-compete obligations and go after the India-biscuit market using another brand." Nestlé countered that the problem had more to do with the partners' inability to agree on a mutually acceptable business plan. The dispute was eventually settled out of court by Nestlé buying Dabur's 40 percent interest, shortly after which Excelcia was closed in lieu of restructuring.

Direct Foreign Investment   A fourth means of foreign market development and entry is *direct foreign investment*, that is, investment within a foreign country. Companies may invest locally to capitalize on low-cost labor, to avoid high import taxes, to reduce the high costs of transportation to market, to gain access to raw materials and technology, or as a means of gaining market entry.[62]

[61]Yan Zhang, Haiyang Li, Michael A. Hitt, and Geng Cui, "R&D Intensity and International Joint Venture Performance in an Emerging Market: Moderating Effects of Market Focus and Ownership Structure," *Journal of International Business Studies* 38 (2007), pp. 944–60.

[62]Sunil Venaik, David F. Midgley, and Timothy M. Devinney, "Dual Paths to Performance: The Impact of Global Pressures on MNC Subsidiary Conduct and Performance," *Journal of International Business Studies* 36 (2005), pp. 655–75; Tony S. Frost and Changhui Zhou, "R&D Co-Practice and 'Reverse' Knowledge Integration in Multinational Firms," *Journal of International Business Studies* 36 (2005), pp. 676–87.

Firms may either invest in or buy local companies or establish new operations facilities. The local firms enjoy important benefits aside from the investments themselves, such as substantial technology transfers[63] and the capability to export to a more diversified customer base.[64] As with the other modes of market entry, several factors have been found to influence the structure and performance of direct investments: (1) timing—first movers have advantages but are more risky; (2) the growing complexity and contingencies of contracts; (3) transaction cost structures; (4) technology and knowledge transfer;[65] (5) degree of product differentiation; (6) the previous experiences and cultural diversity of acquired firms;[66] and (7) advertising and reputation barriers. This mix of considerations and risks makes for increasingly difficult decisions about such foreign investments. But as off-putting legal restrictions[67] continue to ease with WTO and other international agreements, more and more large firms are choosing to enter markets via direct investment.

The growth of free trade areas that are tariff-free among members but have a common tariff for nonmembers creates an opportunity that can be capitalized on by direct investment. Similar to its Japanese competitors, Korea's Samsung has invested some $500 million to build television tube plants in Tijuana, Mexico, to feed the already huge NAFTA television industry centered there. Kyocera Corporation, a Japanese high-tech company, bought Qualcomm's wireless consumer phone business as a means of fast entry into the American market. Yahoo! paid $1 billion for a 40 percent stake in Chinese competitor Alibaba. Finally, Nestlé is building a new milk factory in Thailand to serve the ASEAN Free Trade Area.

A hallmark of global companies today is the establishment of manufacturing operations throughout the world.[68] This trend will increase as barriers to free trade are eliminated and companies can locate manufacturing wherever it is most cost effective. The selection of an entry mode and partners are critical decisions, because the nature of the firm's operations in the country market is affected by and depends on the choices made. The entry mode affects the future decisions because each mode entails an accompanying level of resource commitment, and changing from one entry mode to another without considerable loss of time and money is difficult.

---

[63]Donna L. Paul and Rossitza B. Wooster, "Strategic Investments by US Firms in Transition Economies," *Journal of International Business Studies* 39 (2008), pp. 249–66.

[64]Jasjit Singh, "Asymmetry of Knowledge Spillovers between MNCs and Host Country Firms," *Journal of International Business Studies* 38 (2007), pp. 764–86.

[65]Hongxin Zhao, Yadong Luo, and Taewon Suh, "Transaction Cost Determinants and Ownership-Based Entry Mode Choice: A Meta-Analytic Review," *Journal of International Business Studies* 35, no. 6 (2004), pp. 524–44; Henrik Bresman, Julian Birkinshaw, and Robert Nobel, "Knowledge Transfer in International Acquisitions," *Journal of International Business Studies* 41, no. 1 (2010), pp. 5–20; Julian Birkinshaw, Henrik Bressman, and Robert Nobel, "Knowledge Transfer in International Acquisitions: A Retrospective," *Journal of International Business Studies* 41, no. 1 (2010), pp. 21–26.

[66]Lilach Nachum and Cliff Wymbs, "Product Differentiation, External Economies, and MNE Location Choices: M&A Global Cities," *Journal of International Business Studies* 36 (2005), pp. 415–34; Rajesh Chakrabarti, Swasti Gupta-Mukherjee, and Narayanan Jayaraman, "Mars-Venus Marriages: Culture and Cross-Border M&A," *Journal of International Business Studies* 40, no. 2 (2009), pp. 216–36; Jonas F. Puck, Dirk Holtbrugge, and Alexander T. Mohr, "Beyond Entry Mode Choice: Explaining the Conversion of Joint Ventures into Wholly Owned Subsidiaries in the People's Republic of China," *Journal of International Business Studies* 40, no. 3 (2009), pp. 388–404; Mary Yoko Brannen and Mark F. Peterson, "Merging without Alienating: Interventions Promoting Cross-Cultural Organizational Integration and Their Limitations," *Journal of International Business Studies* 40, no. 3 (2009), pp. 468–89; Taco H. Reus and Bruce T. Lamont, "The Double-Edged Sword of Cultural Distance in International Acquisitions," *Journal of International Business Studies* 40, no. 8 (2009), pp. 128–36; Bulent Aybar and Aysun Ficici, "Cross-Border Acquisitions and Firm Value: An Analysis of Emerging-Market Multinationals," *Journal of International Business Studies* 40, no. 8 (2009), pp. 1317–38; Udo Zander and Lena Zander, "Opening the Grey Box: Social Communities, Knowledge, and Culture in Acquisitions," *Journal of International Business Studies* 41, no. 1 (2010), pp. 27–37.

[67]Desislava Dikova, Padma Roa Sahib, and Arjen van Witteloostuijn, "Cross-Border Acquisition Abandonment and Completion: The Effect of Institutional Differences and Organizational Learning in the International Business Service Industry, 1981-2001," *Journal of International Business Studies* 41, no. 2 (2010), pp. 223–45.

[68]Jason Dean and Jonathan Cheng, "Meet Jack Ma, Who Will Guide Yahoo in China," *The Wall Street Journal*, August 12, 2005, pp. B1, B3.

Organizing for Global Competition

An international marketing plan should optimize the resources committed to company objectives. The organizational plan includes the type of organizational arrangements and management process to be used and the scope and location of responsibility. Because organizations need to reflect a wide range of company-specific characteristics—such as size, level of policy decisions, length of chain of command, staff support, source of natural, personnel, and vendor resources,[69] degree of control, cultural differences in decision-making styles,[70] centralization, and type or level of marketing involvement—devising a standard organizational structure is difficult.[71] Many ambitious multinational plans meet with less than full success because of confused lines of authority, poor communications, and lack of cooperation between headquarters and subsidiary organizations.[72]

A single organizational structure that effectively integrates domestic and international marketing activities has yet to be devised.[73] Companies face the need to maximize the international potential of their products and services without diluting their domestic marketing efforts. Companies are usually structured around one of three alternatives: (1) global product divisions responsible for product sales throughout the world; (2) geographical divisions responsible for all products and functions within a given geographical area; or (3) a matrix organization consisting of either of these arrangements with centralized sales and marketing run by a centralized functional staff, or a combination of area operations and global product management.

Companies that adopt the global product division structure are generally experiencing rapid growth and have broad, diverse product lines. General Electric is a good example, having reorganized its global operations into six product divisions—infrastructure, industrial, commercial financial services, NBC Universal, healthcare, and consumer finance.[74] Geographic structures work best when a close relationship with national and local governments is important.

The matrix form—the most extensive of the three organizational structures—is popular with companies as they reorganize for global competition. A matrix structure permits management to respond to the conflicts that arise among functional activity, product, and geography. It is designed to encourage sharing of experience, resources, expertise, technology, and information among global business units. At its core is better decision making, in which multiple points of view affecting functional activity, product, and geography are examined and shared. A matrix organization can also better accommodate customers who themselves have global operations and global requirements.

A company may be organized by product lines but have geographical subdivisions under the product categories. Both may be supplemented by functional staff support. Exhibit 12.4 shows such a combination. Modifications of this basic arrangement are used by a majority of large companies doing business internationally.

The turbulence of global markets requires flexible organizational structures though. Forty-three large U.S. companies studied indicated that they planned a total of 137

---

[69]Zuohao Chun Zhang and Flora F. Gu, "Intra- and Interfirm Coordination of Export Manufacturers: A Cluster Analysis of Indigenous Chinese Exporters," *Journal of International Marketing* 16, no. 3 (2008), pp. 108–35.

[70]Shichun Xu, S. Tamer Cavusgil, and J. Chris White, "The Impact of Strategic Fit among Strategy, Structure, and Processes on Multinational Corporation Performance: A Multi-Method Assessment," *Journal of International Marketing* 14 (2006), pp. 1–31.

[71]Gerald Albaum, Joel Herche, Julie Yu, Felicitas Evangelista, Brian Murphy, and Patrick Poon, "Differences in Marketing Managers' Decision Making Styles within the Asia-Pacific Region: Implications for Strategic Alliances," *Journal of Global Marketing* 21 (2007), pp. 63–72; Alain Verbke and Thomas P. Kenworthy, "Multidivisional vs. Metanational Governance of the Multinational Enterprise," *Journal of International Business Studies* 39, no. 6 (2008), pp. 940–56; Beibei Dong, Shaoming Zou, and Charles R. Taylor, "Factors that Influence Multinational Corporations' Control of Their Operations in Foreign Markets: An Empirical Investigation," *Journal of International Marketing* 16, no. 1 (2008), pp. 98–119.

[72]Ingmar Bjorkman, Carl F. Fey, and Hyeon Jeong Park, "Institutional Theory and MNC Subsidiary HRM Practices: Evidence from a Three-Country Study," *Journal of International Business Studies* 38 (2007), pp. 430–46.

[73]Claude Obadia and Irena Vida, "Endogenous Opportunism in Small and Medium-Sized Enterprises' Foreign Subsidiaries: Classification and Research Propositions," *Journal of International Marketing* 14 (2006), pp. 57–86.

[74]Kelly Hewett and William O. Bearden, "Dependence, Trust, and Relational Behavior on the Part of Foreign Subsidiary Marketing Operations: Implications for Managing Global Marketing Operations," *Journal of Marketing* 65, no. 4 (October 2001), pp. 51–66.

Exhibit 12.4
Schematic Marketing Organization Plan Combining Product, Geographic, and Functional Approaches

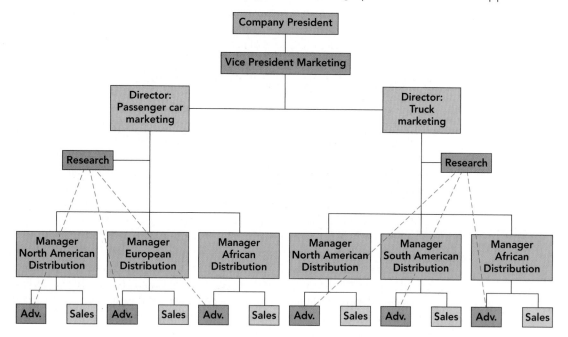

organizational changes for their international operations over a five-year period. Included were such changes as centralizing international decision making, creating global divisions, forming centers of excellence, and establishing international business units. Bausch & Lomb, one of the companies in the study, revamped its international organizational structure by collapsing its international division into a worldwide system of three regions and setting up business management committees to oversee global marketing and manufacturing strategies for four major product lines. Bausch & Lomb's goal was to better coordinate central activities without losing touch at the local level.

To the extent that there is a trend, two factors seem to be sought, regardless of the organizational structure: a single locus for direction and control and the creation of a simple line organization that is based on a more decentralized network of local companies.

Locus of Decision

Considerations of where decisions will be made, by whom, and by which method constitute a major element of organizational strategy. Management policy must be explicit about which decisions are to be made at corporate headquarters, which at international headquarters, which at regional levels, and which at national or even local levels. Most companies also limit the amount of money to be spent at each level. Decision levels for determination of policy, strategy, and tactical decisions must be established. Tactical decisions normally should be made at the lowest possible level, without country-by-country duplication. This guideline requires American headquarters' managers to trust the expertise of their local managers.

Centralized versus Decentralized Organizations

An infinite number of organizational patterns for the headquarters' activities of multinational firms exist, but most fit into one of three categories: centralized,[75] regionalized,[76] or decentralized organizations. The fact that all of the systems are used indicates that each has certain advantages and disadvantages. The chief advantages of centralization are the availability of

---

[75]Rajdeep Grewal, Murali Chandrashekaran, and Robert F. Dwyer, "Navigating Local Environments with Global Strategies: A Contingency Model of Multinational Subsidiary Performance," *Marketing Science* 27, no. 5 (2008), pp. 886–902.

[76]Jean-Luc Arregle, Paul W. Beamish, and Louis Hebert, "The Regional Dimension of MNE's Foreign Subsidiary Localization," *Journal of International Business Studies* 40, no. 1 (2009), pp. 86–107.

experts at one location, the ability to exercise a high degree of control on both the planning and implementation phases, and the centralization of all records and information.

Some companies effect extreme decentralization by selecting competent local managers and giving them full responsibility for national or regional operations. These executives are in direct day-to-day contact with the market but lack a broad company view, which can mean partial loss of control for the parent company.

In many cases, whether a company's formal organizational structure is centralized or decentralized, the informal organization reflects some aspect of all organizational systems. This reflection is especially true relative to the locus of decision making. Studies show that even though product decisions may be highly centralized, subsidiaries may have a substantial amount of local influence in pricing, advertising, and distribution decisions. If a product is culturally sensitive, the decisions are more likely to be decentralized.

Summary

Expanding markets around the world have increased competition for all levels of international marketing. To keep abreast of the competition and maintain a viable position for increasingly competitive markets, a global perspective is necessary. Global competition also requires quality products designed to meet ever-changing customer needs and rapidly advancing technology. Cost containment, customer satisfaction, and a greater number of players mean that every opportunity to refine international business practices must be examined in light of company goals. Collaborative relationships, strategic international alliances, strategic planning, and alternative market-entry strategies are important avenues to global marketing that must be implemented in the planning and organization of global marketing management.

Key Terms

Corporate planning
Strategic planning
Tactical planning

Direct exporting
Indirect exporting
Licensing

Franchising
Strategic international
  alliance (SIA)

Joint venture

Questions

1. Define the key terms listed above.

2. Define strategic planning. How does strategic planning for international marketing differ from that for domestic marketing?

3. Discuss the benefits to an MNC of accepting the global market concept. Explain the three points that define a global approach to international marketing.

4. Discuss the effect of shorter product life cycles on a company's planning process.

5. What is the importance of collaborative relationships to competition?

6. In Phases 1 and 2 of the international planning process, countries may be dropped from further consideration as potential markets. Discuss some of the conditions that may exist in a country that would lead a marketer to exclude a country in each phase.

7. Assume that you are the director of international marketing for a company producing refrigerators. Select one country in Latin America and one in Europe and develop screening criteria to use in evaluating the two countries. Make any additional assumptions that are necessary about your company.

8. "The dichotomy typically drawn between export marketing and overseas marketing is partly fictional; from a marketing standpoint, they are but alternative methods of capitalizing on foreign market opportunities." Discuss.

9. How will entry into a developed foreign market differ from entry into a relatively untapped market?

10. Why do companies change their organizations when they go from being an international to a global company?

11. Formulate a general rule for deciding where international business decisions should be made.

12. Explain the popularity of joint ventures.

13. Compare the organizational implications of joint ventures versus licensing.

14. Visit the Web sites of General Motors and Ford, both car manufacturers in the United States. Search their sites and compare their international involvement. How would you classify each—as exporter, international, or global?

15. Using the sources in Question 14, list the different entry modes each company uses.

16. Visit the Nestlé Corporation Web site (www.nestle.com/) and the Unilever Web site (www.unilever.com/). Compare their strategies toward international markets. In what ways (other than product categories) do they differ in their international marketing?

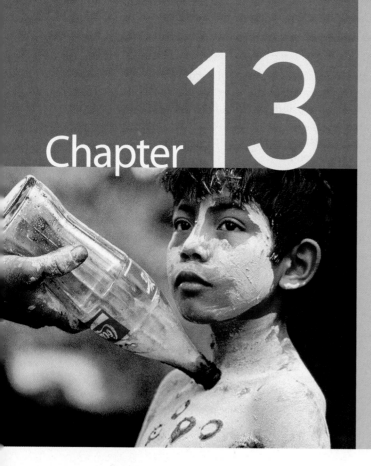

Chapter 13

Products and Services for Consumers

CHAPTER OUTLINE

CHAPTER LEARNING OBJECTIVES

What you should learn from Chapter 13:

LO1 The importance of offering a product suitable for the intended market

LO2 The importance of quality and how quality is defined

LO3 Physical, mandatory, and cultural requirements for product adaptation

LO4 The need to view all attributes of a product to overcome resistance to acceptance

LO5 Country-of-origin effects on product image

Global Perspective

CHINA—DISNEY ROLLS THE DICE AGAIN

With the opening of Disneyland in Anaheim in 1955, the notion of the modern theme park was born. The combination of the rides, various other attractions, and the Disney characters has remained irresistible. Tokyo Disneyland has also proved to be a success, making modest money for Disney through licensing and major money for its Japanese partners. Three-fourths of the visitors at the Tokyo park are repeat visitors, the best kind.

Then came EuroDisney. Dissatisfied with the ownership arrangements at the Tokyo park, the EuroDisney deal was structured very differently. Disney negotiated a much greater ownership stake in the park and adjacent hotel and restaurant facilities. Along with the greater control and potential profits came a higher level of risk.

Even before the park's grand opening ceremony in 1992, protestors decried Disney's "assault" on the French culture. The location was also a mistake—the Mediterranean climate of the alternative Barcelona site seemed much more attractive on chilly winter days in France. Managing both a multicultural workforce and clientele proved daunting. For example, what language was most appropriate for the Pirates of the Caribbean attraction—French or English? Neither attendance nor consumer purchases targets were achieved during the early years: Both were off by about 10 percent. By the summer of 1994, EuroDisney had lost some $900 million. Real consideration was given to closing the park.

A Saudi prince provided a crucial cash injection that allowed for a temporary financial restructuring and a general reorganization, including a new French CEO and a new name, Paris Disneyland. The Paris park returned to profitability, and attendance increased. However, the temporary holiday on royalties, management fees, and leases is now expired, and profits are dipping again. Disney's response was to expand with a second "Disney Studios" theme park and an adjacent retail and office complex at the Paris location. Again in 2005, the Saudi prince injected another $33 million into the park.

In 2006 Hong Kong Disneyland opened for business. The Hong Kong government provided the bulk of the investment for the project (almost 80 percent of the $3 billion needed). As in Europe, the clientele is culturally diverse, though primarily Chinese. Performances are done in Cantonese (the local dialect), Mandarin (the national language), and English. The park drew 5.2 million visitors in 2006, but attendance fell sharply to about 4 million in 2007. Disney has had to renegotiate its financial structure and schedule as a consequence. On the positive side of the ledger, the firm and the Hong Kong government are still talking about expanding the park, and Disney inked a new joint venture agreement for the online delivery of entertainment services to customers in China. In 2009 the Chinese government approved a new park in Shanghai to be managed by the Hong Kong groups with a price tag of some $4 billion. Indeed, it continues to be quite interesting to follow Mickey's international adventures; you might say it's been a rollercoaster ride.

Sources: http://www.disney.go.com; "Disney to Build Hong Kong Theme Park; Euro Disney's Profit Slumped," *Dow Jones News Service*, November 2, 1999; Richard Verrier, "Saudi Prince Helps Out EuroDisney," *Los Angeles Times*, January 12, 2005, p. C2; "Hong Kong Disney Crowds Disappoint for Second Year," *Reuters News*, December 12, 2007; Ethan Smith and James T. Areddy, "China Backs Disney Shanghai," *The Wall Street Journal*, November 11, 2009, online.

The opportunities and challenges for international marketers of consumer goods and services today have never been greater or more diverse. New consumers are springing up in emerging markets in eastern Europe, the Commonwealth of Independent States, China and other Asian countries, India, Latin America—in short, globally. Although some of these emerging markets have little purchasing power today, they promise to be huge markets in the future. In the more mature markets of the industrialized world, opportunity and challenge also abound as consumers' tastes become more sophisticated and complex, and as increases in purchasing power provide them with the means of satisfying new demands.

As described in the Global Perspective, Disney is the archetypal American exporter for global consumer markets. The distinction between products and services for such companies means little. Their DVDs are *products*, whereas cinema performances of the same movies are *services*. Consumers at the theme parks (including foreign tourists at domestic sites) pay around $100 to get in the gate, but they also spend about the same amount on hats, T-shirts, and meals while there. And the movies, of course, help sell the park tickets and the associated toys and clothing. Indeed, this lack of distinction between products and services has led to the invention of new terms encompassing both products and services, such as *market offerings*[1] and *business-to-consumer (B2C) marketing*. However, the governmental agencies that keep track of international trade still maintain the questionable product–service distinction, and thus so do we in this chapter and the next.[2] The reader should also note that when it comes to U.S. exports targeting consumers, the totals are about evenly split among the three major categories of durable goods (such as cars and computers), nondurable goods (mainly food, drugs, toys), and services (for example, tourism and telecommunications).

The trend for larger firms is toward becoming global in orientation and strategy. However, product adaptation is as important a task in a smaller firm's marketing effort as it is for global companies. As competition for world markets intensifies and as market preferences become more global, selling what is produced for the domestic market in the same manner as it is sold at home proves to be increasingly less effective. Some products cannot be sold at all in foreign markets without modification; others may be sold as is, but their acceptance is greatly enhanced when tailored specifically to market needs. In a competitive struggle, quality products and services that meet the needs and wants of consumers at an affordable price should be the goal of any marketing firm.

Quality

LO1

The importance of offering a product suitable for the intended market

Global competition is placing new emphasis on some basic tenets of business. It is shortening product life cycles and focusing on the importance of quality, competitive prices, and innovative products. The power in the marketplace is shifting from a sellers' to a customers' market, and the latter have more choices because more companies are competing for their attention. More competition and more choices put more power in the hands of the customer, and that of course drives the need for quality. Gone are the days when the customer's knowledge was limited to one or at best just a few different products. Today the customer knows what is best, cheapest, and highest quality, largely due to the Internet. It is the customer who defines quality in terms of his or her needs and resources. For example, cell phones that don't roam don't sell in Japan at any price, but in China they do very well indeed. Just ask the folks at UTStarcom, a California firm that has sold low-cost, nonroaming mobile phones in India and Vietnam, as well as China.

American products have always been among the world's best, but competition is challenging us to make even better products. In most global markets, the cost and quality of a product are among the most important criteria by which purchases are made. For consumer

---

[1] For example, see Philip Kotler and Kevin Lane Keller, *Marketing Management*, 13th ed. (Upper Saddle River, NJ: Prentice Hall, 2008).

[2] We hope that it is obvious that many of the points we make regarding the development of consumer products are pertinent to consumer services as well, and vice versa. Of course, some distinctions are still substantive. These are focused on in the section entitled "Marketing Consumer Services Globally" later in this chapter.

and industrial products alike, the reason often given for preferring one brand over another is better quality at a competitive price. Quality, as a competitive tool, is not new to the business world, but many believe that it is the deciding factor in world markets. However, we must be clear about what we mean by quality.

Quality Defined

LO2

The importance of quality and how quality is defined

Quality can be defined on two dimensions: market-perceived quality and performance quality. Both are important concepts, but consumer perceptions of a quality product often have more to do with market-perceived quality than performance quality. The relationship of quality (of course, relative to price) conformance to customer satisfaction is analogous to an airline's delivery of quality. If viewed internally from the firm's perspective (performance quality), an airline has achieved quality conformance with a safe flight and landing. But because the consumer expects performance quality to be a given, quality to the consumer is more than compliance (a safe flight and landing). Rather, cost, timely service, frequency of flights, comfortable seating, and performance of airline personnel from check-in to baggage claim are all part of the customer's experience that is perceived as being of good or poor quality. Considering the number of air miles flown daily, the airline industry is approaching zero defects in quality conformance, yet who will say that customer satisfaction is anywhere near perfection? These market-perceived quality attributes are embedded in the total product, that is, the physical or core product and all the additional features the consumer expects.

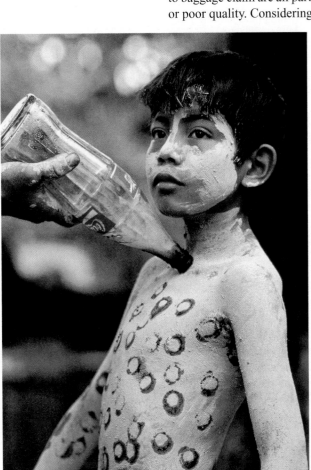

In a competitive marketplace in which the market provides choices, most consumers expect performance quality to be a given. Naturally, if the product does not perform up to their standards, it will be rejected. Compare hybrid gas-electric systems for example—Toyota's is designed to save fuel in city driving; General Motors's performs best on the highway during long trips. Which drive system offers higher quality depends on the consumer's needs. Japanese consumers find themselves stuck in traffic more frequently, whereas Americans tend toward road trip types of activities.[3] When there are alternative products, all of which meet performance quality standards, the product chosen is the one that meets market-perceived quality attributes. Interestingly, China's leading refrigerator maker recognized the importance of these market-perceived quality attributes when it adopted a technology that enabled consumers to choose from 20 different colors and textures for door handles and moldings. For example, a consumer can design an off-white refrigerator with green marble handles and moldings. Why is this important? Because it lets consumers "update their living rooms," where most Chinese refrigerators are parked. The company's motive was simple: It positioned its product for competition with multinational brands by giving the consumer another expression of quality.

Quality is also measured in many industries by objective third parties. In the United States, J.D. Power and Associates has expanded its auto quality ratings, which are based on consumer surveys, to other areas, such as computers. Customer satisfaction indexes developed first in Sweden are now being used to measure customer satisfaction across a wide variety of consumer products and services.[4] Finally, the U.S.

Products are not used in the same ways in all markets. Here, a boy in an eastern Mexican village is prepared for a "Jaguar dance" to bring rain. Clay, ashes, and the globally ubiquitous Coke bottle make for the best cat costumes. Perhaps our favorite example comes from India; in the Punjab region, *lassi* bars, a popular yoghurt drink, are often prepared in top-load washing machines!

[3]Joseph B. White, "One System, Two Visions," *The Wall Street Journal* (online), May 7, 2007.

[4]Claes Fornell, Michael D. Johnson, Eugene W. Anderson, Jaesung Cha, and Barbara Everitt Bryant, "The American Consumer Satisfaction Index: Nature, Purpose, and Findings," *Journal of Marketing* 60, no. 4 (October 1996), pp. 35–46; http://www.cfigroup.com, 2008.

CROSSING BORDERS 13.1 | The Quality of Food Is a Matter of Taste

Food preferences vary not only across countries but within them as well. For example, many Vietnamese still have to eat whatever they can lay their hands on. Pet birds and dogs are kept indoors to save them from the cooking pot. In 1998, the government tried to reduce the consumption of snakes and cats by banning their sale because the exploding rat population was damaging crops. Instead, peasants simply took to eating rats as well. The dwindling number of rats, in turn, has caused an explosion in the numbers of another tasty treat: snails.

Meanwhile, in nearby Ho Chi Minh City, the country's commercial capital, a recent survey found that 13.5 percent of children were obese—and the figure is rising. Local restaurants vie with one another in expense and luxury. Hoang Khai, a local businessman, recalls how his family always celebrated at home when he was young, because there was nowhere to go out. He decided to change all that by plowing the returns from his textile business into a restaurant lavish enough to suit the

city's business elite. The result is *Au Manoir de Khai*, a colonial villa smothered in gilt and silk where a meal with imported wine can set you back more than most Vietnamese earn in a year.

One has to wonder how ice cream from Fugetsudo, a small confectionary shop in northern Japan, would sell in either neighborhood in Vietnam. You can get fish, sea slug, whale meat, turtle, or cedar chip–flavored ice cream there. Fugetsudo's competition sells pickled-orchid, chicken-wing, shrimp, eel, and short-necked clam flavors. Mmmm! Baskin Robbins competes with its 31 flavors in Japan, but among its 32 countries served around the world, Vietnam is not among them. The average American consumes over 12 liters of ice cream per year and the Japanese less than half that. Vietnamese? Only half a liter.

Sources: "Eating Out in Vietnam," *The Economist*, December 21, 2002, pp. 49–50; Phred Dvorak, "Something Fishy Is Going On in Japan in the Ice-Cream Biz," *The Wall Street Journal*, September 4, 2002, p. 1; Eric Johnston, "Savour the Whale," *The Guardian*, July 4, 2005, p. 6; Euromonitor International, 2010; http://www.baskinrobbins.com, 2010.

Department of Commerce annually recognizes American firms for the quality of their international offerings—the Ritz Carlton Hotel chain has won the prestigious award twice.

Maintaining Quality

Maintaining performance quality is critical,[5] but frequently a product that leaves the factory with performance quality is damaged as it passes through the distribution chain. This damage is a special problem for many global brands for which production is distant from the market and/or control of the product is lost because of the distribution system within the market. When Mars Company's Snickers and other Western confectioneries were introduced to Russia, they were a big hit. Foreign brands such as Mars, Toblerone, Waldbaur, and Cadbury were the top brands—indeed, only one Russian brand placed in the top ten. But within five years, the Russian brands had retaken eight of the top spots, and only one U.S. brand, Mars's Dove bars, was in the top ten.

Red October brand chocolate (on the left) still competes well against foreign rivals Nestlé and Mars on Moscow store shelves. One advertising executive in Moscow reports that Russians are experiencing a renewed nationalism in product preferences as their economy continues to surge along with world oil prices. We have no idea what the "for Men" appeal is all about, but it apparently works in Moscow.

What happened? A combination of factors caused the decline. Russia's Red October Chocolate Factory got its act together; modernized its packaging, product mix, and equipment; and set out to capture the market. Performance quality was also an issue. When the Russian market opened to outside trade, foreign companies eager to get into the market dumped surplus out-of-date and poor-quality products. In other cases, chocolates were smuggled in and sold on street corners and were often mishandled in the process. By the time they made it to consumers, the chocolates were likely to be misshapen or discolored—poor quality compared with Russia's Red October chocolate.

---

[5]Duncan I. Simester, John R. Hauser, Birger Wernerfelt, and Roland T. Rust, "Implementing Quality Improvement Programs Designed to Enhance Customer Satisfaction: Quasi-Experiments in the United States and Spain," *Journal of Marketing Research* 37 (February 2000), pp. 102–12; Mark Landler, "Missteps Haunt Smart Car," *International Herald Tribune*, April 2–3, 2005, pp. 1, 4.

CROSSING BORDERS 13.4   Selling Coffee in Tea-Drinking Japan

My first meeting with Nestlé executives and their Japanese advertising agency was very instructive. Their strategy, which today seems absurdly wrong, but wasn't as obviously so in the 1970s, was to try to convince Japanese consumers to switch from tea to coffee. Having spent some time in Japan, I knew that tea meant a great deal to this culture, but I had no sense of what emotions they attached to coffee. I decided to gather several groups of people together to discover how they imprinted the beverage. I believed there was a message there that could open a door for Nestlé.

I structured a three-hour session with each of the groups. In the first hour, I took on the persona of a visitor from another planet, someone who had never seen coffee before and had no idea how one "used" it. I asked for help understanding the product, believing their descriptions would give me insight into what they thought of it.

In the next hour, I had them sit on the floor like elementary school children and use scissors and a pile of magazines to make a collage of words about coffee. The goal here was to get them to tell me stories with these words that would offer further clues.

In the third hour, I had participants lie on the floor with pillows. There was some hesitation among members of every group, but I convinced them I wasn't entirely out of my mind. I put on soothing music and asked the participants to relax. What I was doing was calming their active brainwaves, getting them to that tranquil point just before sleep. When they reached this state, I took them on a journey back from their adulthood, past their teenage years, to a time when they were very young. Once they arrived, I asked them to think again about coffee and to recall their earliest memory of it, the first time they consciously experienced it, and their most significant memory of it (if that memory was a different one).

I designed this process to bring participants back to their first imprint of coffee and the emotion attached to it. In most cases, though, the journey led nowhere. What this signified for Nestlé was very clear. While the Japanese had an extremely strong emotional connection to tea (something I learned without asking in the first hour of the sessions), they had, at most, a very superficial imprint of coffee. Most, in fact, had no imprint of coffee at all.

Under these circumstances, Nestlé's strategy of getting these consumers to switch from tea to coffee could only fail. Coffee could not compete with tea in the Japanese culture if it had such weak emotional resonance. Instead, if Nestlé was going to have any success in the market at all, they needed to start at the beginning. They needed to give the product meaning in this culture. They needed to create an imprint for coffee for the Japanese.

Armed with this information, Nestlé devised a new strategy. Rather than selling instant coffee to a country dedicated to tea, they created desserts for children infused with the flavor of coffee but without the caffeine. The younger generation embraced these desserts. Their first imprint of coffee was a very positive one, one they would carry throughout their lives. Through this, Nestlé gained a meaningful foothold in the Japanese market.

Coffee consumption initially burgeoned, and Starbucks might have thanked Nestlé for the help! But since 2005 per capita coffee consumption has leveled off in both Japan and the U.S. while tea drinking has inched upward. Indeed, you might say the demand for hot drinks is "fluid."

Source: Clotaire Rapaille, *The Culture Code* (New York: Broadway Books, 2006); Euromonitor International, 2010.

the older, gasoline-fueled options.[22] Additionally, the perception of innovation can often be changed if the marketer understands the perceptual framework of the consumer, as has certainly proved to be the case with the fast global diffusion of Internet use, e-tailing, and health- and beauty-related products and services.

Analyzing the five characteristics of an innovation can assist in determining the rate of acceptance or resistance of the market to a product. A product's (1) *relative advantage* (the perceived marginal value of the new product relative to the old), (2) *compatibility* (its compatibility with acceptable behavior, norms, values, and so forth), (3) *complexity* (the degree of complexity associated with product use), (4) *trialability* (the degree of economic and/or social risk associated with product use), and (5) *observability* (the ease with which the product benefits can be communicated) affect the degree of its acceptance or resistance. In general, the rate of diffusion can be postulated as positively related to relative advantage, compatibility, trialability, and observability but negatively related to complexity.

---

[22]Jane Lanhee Lee, "The Leapfrog Strategy: Fuel-Cell Advocates Say China Is Uniquely Positioned to Jump Past Petroleum," *The Wall Street Journal*, July 25, 2005, p. R6.

The evaluator must remember that it is the perception of product characteristics by the potential adopter, not the marketer, that is crucial to the evaluation. A market analyst's self-reference criterion (SRC) may cause a perceptual bias when interpreting the characteristics of a product. Thus, instead of evaluating product characteristics from the foreign user's frame of reference, the marketer might analyze them from his or her frame of reference, leading to a misinterpretation of the product's cultural importance.

Once the analysis has been made, some of the perceived newness or causes for resistance can be minimized through adroit marketing. The more congruent product perceptions are with current cultural values, the less resistance there will be and the more rapid product diffusion or acceptance will be. Finally, we should point out that the newness of the product or brand introduced can be an important competitive advantage; the pioneer brand advantage often delivers long-term competitive advantages in both domestic and foreign markets.[23]

Production of Innovations

Some consideration must be given to the inventiveness of companies[24] and countries.[25] For example, it is no surprise that most of the new ideas associated with the Internet are being produced in the United States.[26] The 227 million American users of the Internet far outnumber the 92 million Japanese users.[27] Similarly, America wins the overall R&D expenditure contest. Expenditures are about the same across member countries of the Organization for Economic Cooperation and Development, at about 2 to 3 percent of GDP, so America's large economy supports twice the R&D spending as does Japan, for example. This spending yields about three times the number of U.S. patents granted to American firms versus Japanese firms. One study suggests that national culture influences innovativeness (individualism enhances creativity[28]), but another argues that corporate culture, not national culture, is key.[29] The Japanese government diagnosed the problem as a lack of business training. Japanese engineers are not versed in marketing and entrepreneurship, and American-style educational programs are being created at a record pace to fill the gap. However, we do note a disturbing trend: The growth of American R&D spending is slower than most other competitive countries. Russia, India, and China are experiencing double-digit growth compared with America's four percent annual growth rate over the last five years.[30] Moreover, in 2009, for the first time in history, more patents were registered by foreign residents in the United States than by U.S. residents.[31]

Many Japanese firms also take advantage of American innovativeness by establishing design centers in the United States—most notable are the plethora of foreign auto design centers in Southern California. At the same time, American automobile firms have established design centers in Europe. Recent studies have shown that innovativeness varies across cultures, and companies are placing design centers worldwide. Indeed, the Ford Taurus, the car that saved Ford in the 1980s, was a European design.

Research is also now focusing on the related issue of "conversion-ability" or the success firms have when they take inventions to market. Three main factors seem to favor

---

[23]Gerald Young Gao, Yigang Pan, David K. Tse, and Chi Kin (Bennett) Yim, "Market Share Performance of Foreign and Domestic Brands in China," *Journal of International Marketing* 14 (2006), pp. 32–51.

[24]Rohit Deshpandé and John U. Farley, "Organizational Culture, Innovativeness, and Market Orientation in Hong Kong Five Years after Handover: What Has Changed?" *Journal of Global Marketing* 17, no. 4 (2004), pp. 53–75.

[25]Anyone interested in a wonderful book on this topic should read the Pulitzer Prize–winning *Guns, Germs, and Steel: The Fates of Human Societies* by Jared Diamond (New York: Norton, 1999); also see Subin Im, Cheryl Nakata, Heungsooa Park, and Young-Won Ha, "Determinants of Korean and Japanese New Product Performance: An Interrelational and Process View," *Journal of International Marketing* 11, no. 4 (2003), pp. 81–113. Also, one approach to innovation is copying—see Dexter Roberts, "Did Spark Spark a Copycat?" *BusinessWeek*, February 7, 2005, p. 64.

[26]Thomas L. Friedman, *The World Is Flat* (New York: Farrar, Straus, and Giroux, 2005).

[27]Euromonitor International, 2010.

[28]Jack A. Goncalo and Barry M. Staw, "Individualism—Collectivism and Group Creativity," *Organizational Behavior and Human Decision Processes* 100 (2006), pp. 96–109.

[29]Gerard J. Tellis, Jaideep C. Prabhu, and Rajesh K. Chandy, "Radical Innovation across Nations: The Preeminence of Corporate Culture," *Journal of Marketing* 73, no. 1 (2009), pp. 3–23.

[30]Euromonitor International, 2010.

[31]Michael Arndt, "Ben Franklin, Where Are You?" Bloomberg *BusinessWeek*, January 4, 2010, p. 29.

conversion, at least in the global pharmaceutical industry: patience (nine years seems optimal for taking a newly patented drug to approval), focus on a few important innovations, and experience.[32] Another study demonstrates that strengthening patent protections tends to favor firms in developed countries differentially more than firms in developing countries.[33] If evidence continues to accumulate in this vein, policy makers will have to reconsider the current global application of a "one-size-fits-all" intellectual property system.

Analyzing Product Components for Adaptation

A product is multidimensional, and the sum of all its features determines the bundle of satisfactions (utilities) received by the consumer. To identify all the possible ways a product may be adapted to a new market, it helps to separate its many dimensions into three distinct components, as illustrated by the **Product Component Model** in Exhibit 13.1. By using this model, the impact of the cultural, physical, and mandatory factors (discussed previously) that affect a market's acceptance of a product can be focused on the core component, packaging component, and support services component. These components include all a product's tangible and intangible elements and provide the bundle of utilities the market receives from use of the product.

LO4

The need to view all attributes of a product to overcome resistance to acceptance

Core Component

The *core component* consists of the physical product—the platform that contains the essential technology—and all its design and functional features. It is on the product platform that product variations can be added or deleted to satisfy local differences. Major adjustments in the platform aspect of the core component may be costly, because a change

Exhibit 13.1
Product Component Model

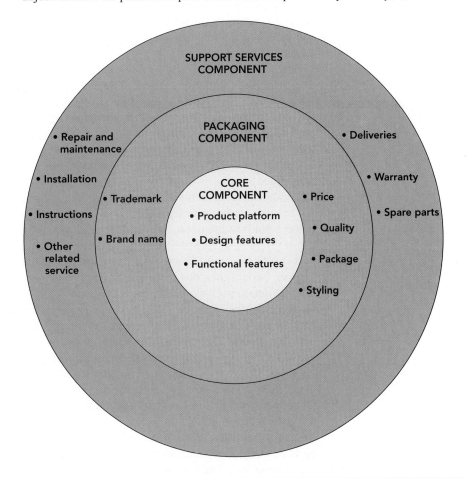

[32]Rajesh Chandy, Brigitee Hpostaken, Om Narasimhan, and Jaideep Prabhu, "From Invention to Innovation: Conversion Ability in Product Development," *Journal of Marketing Research* 43 (2006), pp. 494–508.

[33]Brent B. Allred and Walter G. Park, "Patent Rights and Innovative Activity: Evidence from National and Firm-Level Data," *Journal of International Business Studies* 38 (2007), pp. 878–900.

in the platform can affect product processes and thus require additional capital investment. However, alterations in design, functional features, flavors, color, and other aspects can be made to adapt the product to cultural variations. In Japan, Nestlé originally sold the same kind of corn flakes it sells in the United States, but Japanese children ate them mostly as snacks instead of for breakfast. To move the product into the larger breakfast market, Nestlé reformulated its cereals to more closely fit Japanese taste. The Japanese traditionally eat fish and rice for breakfast, so Nestlé developed cereals with familiar tastes—seaweed, carrots and zucchini, and coconut and papaya. The result was a 12 percent share of the growing breakfast cereal market.

For the Brazilian market, where fresh orange juice is plentiful, General Foods changed the flavor of its presweetened powdered juice substitute, Tang, from the traditional orange to passion fruit and other flavors. Changing flavor or fragrance is often necessary to bring a product in line with what is expected in a culture. Household cleansers with the traditional pine odor and hints of ammonia or chlorine popular in U.S. markets were not successful when introduced in Japan. Many Japanese sleep on the floor on futons with their heads close to the surface they have cleaned, so a citrus fragrance is more pleasing. Rubbermaid could have avoided missteps in introducing its line of baby furniture in Europe with modest changes in the core component. Its colors were not tailored to European tastes, but worst of all, its child's bed didn't fit European-made mattresses!

Functional features can be added or eliminated depending on the market. In markets where hot water is not commonly available, washing machines have heaters as a functional feature. In other markets, automatic soap and bleach dispensers may be eliminated to cut costs or to minimize repair problems. Additional changes may be necessary to meet safety and electrical standards or other mandatory (homologation) requirements. The physical product and all its functional features should be examined as potential candidates for adaptation.

Packaging Component

The *packaging component* includes style features, packaging, labeling, trademarks, brand name, quality, price, and all other aspects of a product's package. Apple Computer found out the hard way how important this component can be when it first entered the Japanese market. Some of its Macintosh computers were returned unused after customers found the wrapping on the instruction manual damaged! As with the core component, the importance of each of the elements in the eyes of the consumer depends on the need that the product is designed to serve.

Packaging components frequently require both discretionary and mandatory changes. For example, some countries require labels to be printed in more than one language, while others forbid the use of any foreign language. Meanwhile, one study has found that consumers in the United States respond negatively to bilingual packaging.[34] At Hong Kong Disneyland, the jungle cruise ride commentary is delivered in Cantonese, Mandarin, and English. Several countries are now requiring country-of-origin labeling for food products. Elements in the packaging component may incorporate symbols that convey an unintended meaning and thus must be changed. One company's red-circle trademark was popular in some countries but was rejected in parts of Asia, where it conjured up images of the Japanese flag. Yellow flowers used in another company trademark were rejected in Mexico, where a yellow flower symbolizes death or disrespect.

A well-known baby-food producer that introduced small jars of baby food in Africa, complete with labels featuring a picture of a baby, experienced the classic example of misinterpreted symbols: The company was absolutely horrified to find that consumers thought the jars contained ground-up babies. In China, though not a problem of literacy per se, Brugel, a German children's cereal brand that features cartoon drawings of dogs, cats, birds, monkeys, and other animals on the package, was located in the pet foods section of a supermarket. The label had no Chinese, and store personnel were unfamiliar with the

---

[34]Mahesh Gopinath and Myron Glassman, "The Effect of Multiple Language Product Descriptions on Product Evaluations," *Psychology & Marketing* 25, no. 3 (2008), pp. 233–61.

CROSSING BORDERS 13.5   D'oh! Or Just Dough in Dubai?

When the Dubai-based Arab satellite TV network MBC decided to introduce Fox's *The Simpsons* to the Middle East, it knew the Simpson family would have to make some fundamental lifestyle changes.

"Omar Shamshoon," as he is called on the show, looks like the same Homer Simpson, but he has given up beer and bacon, which are both against Islam, and he no longer hangs out at "seedy bars with bums and lowlifes." In Arabia, Homer's beer is soda, and his hot dogs are barbequed Egyptian beef sausages. And the donut-shaped snacks he gobbles are the traditional Arab cookies called *kahk*.

An Arabized Simpsons—called *Al Shamshoon*—made its debut in the Arab world just in time for Ramadan, a time of high TV viewership. It uses the original Simpsons animation, but the voices are dubbed into Arabic, and the scripts have been adapted to make the show more accessible, and acceptable, to Arab audiences.

The family remains, as the producers describe them, "dysfunctional." They still live in Springfield, and "Omar" is still lazy and works at the local nuclear power plant. Bart (now called "Badr") is constantly cheeky to his parents and teachers and is always in trouble. Providing the characters' voices are several popular Egyptian actors, including Mohamed Heneidy, considered the Robert DeNiro of the Middle East.

Al Shamshoon is currently broadcast daily during an early-evening prime-time slot, starting with the show's first season. If it is a hit, MBC envisions Arabizing the other 16 seasons. But there's no guarantee of success. Many Arab blogs and Internet chat sessions have become consumed with how unfunny Al Shamshoon is: "They've ruined it! Oh yes they have, *sob*.... Why?

Why, why oh why?!!!!" wrote a blogger, "Noors," from Oman.

Few shows have more obsessed fans than *The Simpsons*, and the vast online community is worried about whether classic Simpsons' dialogue can even be translated. One blogger wrote, "'Hi-diddly-ho, neighbors!' How the h— are they going to translate that? Or this great quote: Mr. Burns: 'Oooh, so Mother Nature needs a favor?! Well maybe she should have thought of that when she was besetting us with droughts and floods and poison monkeys! Nature started the fight for survival, and now she wants to quit because she's losing. Well I say, hard cheese'."

A blogger, who uses the name "Nibaq," wrote, "I am sure the effort [of] the people who made this show to translate it to Arabic could have made a good original show about an Egyptian family living in Egypt, dealing with religion, life and work and trying to keep a family together. That way they can proudly say Made in Egypt, instead of Made in USA Assembled in Egypt."

The Simpson's movie broke records worldwide in 2007. And Spanish retailer Bershka is now offering upscale Simpsons T-shirts across Latin America, Europe, and the Middle East. Indeed, it will be interesting to keep watching "D'oh!" being converted into dough in Dubai.

Sources: Yasmine El-Rashidi, "D'oh! Arabized Simpsons Aren't Getting Many Laughs," *The Wall Street Journal,* October 14, 2005, pp. B1, B2; "Microsoft Launches New Arabized Solutions and Localized Windows XP Theme Packs at Gitex 2005," *AME Info/Middle East Company News,* September 27, 2005; Frank Segers, "'Simpsons Movie' Reigns at Overseas Boxoffice," *Hollywood Reporter,* August 6, 2007; "Twentieth Century Fox L&M Launches The Simpsons with Bershka," *License Magazine ,* March 2009, p. 15.

product. It is easy to forget that in low-literacy countries, pictures and symbols are taken literally as instructions and information.

Care must be taken to ensure that corporate trademarks and other parts of the packaging component do not have unacceptable symbolic meanings. Particular attention should be given to translations of brand names and colors used in packaging. When Ford tried to sell its Pinto automobile in Brazil, it quickly found out that the car model's name translated to "tiny male genitals." White, the color symbolizing purity in Western countries, is the color for mourning in others. In China, P&G packaged diapers in a pink wrapper. Consumers shunned the pink package—pink symbolized a girl, and in a country with a one-child-per-family rule where boys are preferred, you do not want anyone to think you have a girl, even if you do.

Reasons a company might have to adapt a product's package are countless. In some countries, laws stipulate specific bottle, can, and package sizes and measurement units. If a country uses the metric system, it will probably require that weights and measurements conform to the metric system. Such descriptive words as "giant" or "jumbo" on a package or label may be illegal. High humidity or the need for long shelf life because of extended distribution systems may dictate extra-heavy packaging for some products. As is frequently mentioned, Japanese attitudes about quality include the packaging of a product. A poorly packaged product conveys an impression of poor quality to the Japanese. It is also important to determine if the packaging has other uses in the market. Lever Brothers sells Lux soap in stylish boxes in Japan because more than half of all soap cakes there are purchased during the two gift-giving seasons. Size of the package is also a factor that may make a difference to success in Japan. Soft drinks are sold in smaller-size cans than in the United States to accommodate the smaller Japanese hand. In Japan, most food is sold fresh or in clear packaging, while cans are considered dirty. So when Campbell introduced soups to the Japanese market, it decided to go with a cleaner, more expensive pop-top opener.

Labeling laws vary from country to country and do not seem to follow any predictable pattern. In Saudi Arabia, for example, product names must be specific. "Hot Chili" will not do; it must be "Spiced Hot Chili." Prices are required to be printed on the labels in Venezuela, but in Chile putting prices on labels or in any way suggesting retail prices is illegal. Coca-Cola ran into a legal problem in Brazil with its Diet Coke. Brazilian law interprets *diet* to have medicinal qualities. Under the law, producers must give the daily recommended consumption on the labels of all medicines. Coca-Cola had to get special approval to get around this restriction. Until recently in China, Western products could be labeled in a foreign language with only a small temporary Chinese label affixed somewhere on the package. Under the new Chinese labeling law, however, food products must have their name, contents, and other specifics listed clearly in Chinese printed directly on the package—no temporary labels are allowed.

Labeling laws create a special problem for companies selling products in various markets with different labeling laws and small initial demand in each. In China, for example, there is demand for American- and European-style snack foods even though that demand is not well developed at this time. The expense of labeling specially to meet Chinese law often makes market entry costs prohibitive. Forward-thinking manufacturers with wide distribution in Asia are adopting packaging standards comparable to those required in the European Union by providing standard information in several different languages on the same package. A template is designed with space on the label reserved for locally required content, which can be inserted depending on the destination of a given production batch.

Support Services Component

The *support services* component includes repair and maintenance, instructions, installation, warranties, deliveries, and the availability of spare parts. Many otherwise successful marketing programs have ultimately failed because little attention was given to this product component. Repair and maintenance are especially difficult problems in developing countries. In the United States, a consumer has the option of obtaining service from the company or from scores of competitive service retailers ready to repair and maintain anything from automobiles to lawn mowers. Equally available are repair parts from company-owned or licensed outlets or the local hardware store. Consumers in a developing country and in many developed countries may not have even one of the possibilities for repair and maintenance available in the United States, and independent service providers can be used to enhance brand and product quality.[35]

In some countries, the concept of routine maintenance or preventive maintenance is not a part of the culture. As a result, products may have to be adjusted to require less frequent maintenance, and special attention must be given to features that may be taken for granted in the United States.

The literacy rates and educational levels of a country may require a firm to change a product's instructions. A simple term in one country may be incomprehensible in another. In rural Africa, for example, consumers had trouble understanding that Vaseline Intensive Care lotion is absorbed into the skin. *Absorbed* was changed to *soaks into*, and the confusion was eliminated. The Brazilians have successfully overcome the low literacy and technical skills of users of the sophisticated military tanks it sells to Third World countries. The manufacturers include videocassette players and videotapes with detailed repair

---

[35]Ikechi Ekeledo and Nadeem M. Firoz, "Independent Service Providers as a Competitive Advantage in Developing Economies," *Journal of Global Marketing* 20 (2007), pp. 39–54.

CROSSING BORDERS 13.6   So, Your Computer Isn't Working?

Most people have two options when the desk beast starts acting up: Call the service center or read the manual. Both are becoming cross-cultural activities. With increasing frequency, service call centers are being staffed by folks in the Philippines, India, the Caribbean, and other developing countries where English is commonly spoken. The savings for the companies can be in the 90 percent range. But for consumers, it was tough enough bridging the technician–layperson gap. Now a cross-cultural layer is being added to the interaction.

At least many manufacturers are getting more adept at adapting user manuals. In some countries, the manuals are treasured for their entertainment value. Mike Adams of the translation and marketing firm Arial Global Reach explains, "Japanese people really enjoy reading documentation, but that's because Japanese documentation is actually fun to look at." Japanese manuals are often jazzed up with creative cartoons. Even program interfaces are animated. Microsoft's much-maligned Clippy the Paperclip was replaced in Japan with an animated dolphin, "And even highly technical Japanese engineers don't feel at all childish when they view or interact with these animations."

Put those cute characters in manuals in other countries and the customer will doubt the seriousness of the firm. Mark Katib, general manager of Middle East Translation Services, says most customers in that part of the world, as do Americans, prefer uncluttered, nontechnical explanations. He spends most of his time making sure that information is presented in an acceptable manner, not impinging on people's beliefs.

Apparently you cannot give an Italian a command such as "never do this." The consequences for that kind of language are calls from Italians who have broken their machines by doing exactly "this." Instead, Italian manuals must use less demanding language, like "you might consider . . . ."

The Germans will reject manuals with embedded humor. Hungarians like to fix things themselves, so their manuals are more like machine shop guides. Finally, one software maker that developed a WAN (wide-area network) used a flowing stream of text, "WAN WAN WAN WAN" on the package. To a Japanese that's the sound a dog makes, and in Japan no one would buy a product advertising itself by a barking dog.

The main point here is that "technobabble" is hard to translate in any language.

Sources: Michelle Delio, "Read the F***ing Story, then RTFM," *Wired News* , http://www.wired.com, June 4, 2002; Pete Engardio, Aaron Bernstein, and Manjeet Kripalani, "Is Your Job Next?" *BusinessWeek*, February 3, 2003, pp. 50–60; Alli McConnon, "India's Competition in the Caribbean," *BusinessWeek*, December 24, 2007, p. 75; Rudy Hirschheim, "Offshoring and the New World Order," *Communications of the ACM* 12, no. 11 (2009), pp. 132–35.

---

instructions as part of the standard instruction package. They also minimize spare parts problems by using standardized, off-the-shelf parts available throughout the world. And, of course, other kinds of cultural preferences come into play even in service manuals.

Complementary products must be considered increasingly in the marketing of a variety of high-tech products. Perhaps the best example is Microsoft's Xbox and its competitors. Sales of the Xbox had lagged those of Sony's and Nintendo's game consoles in Japan. Microsoft diagnosed the problem as a lack of games that particularly attract Japanese gamers and therefore developed a series of games to fill that gap. An early offering, a role-playing game called *Lost Odyssey*, was developed by an all-Japanese team.[36]

The Product Component Model can be a useful guide for examining the adaptation requirements of products destined for foreign markets. A product should be carefully evaluated on each of the three components to determine any mandatory and discretionary changes that may be needed.

Marketing Consumer Services Globally

As mentioned at the beginning of the chapter, much of the advice regarding adapting products for international consumer markets also applies to adapting services. Moreover, some services are closely associated with products. Good examples are the support services just described or the customer services associated with the delivery of a Big Mac to a consumer in Moscow. However, services are distinguished by

---

[36]Yukari Iwatani Kane, "Microsoft Makes Big Push to Woo Japanese with New Xbox Games," *The Wall Street Journal* (online), September 12, 2007.

four unique characteristics—intangibility, inseparability, heterogeneity, and perishability—and thus require special consideration.

Products are often classified as tangible, whereas services are *intangible*. Automobiles, computers, and furniture are examples of products that have a physical presence; they are things or objects that can be stored and possessed, and their intrinsic value is embedded within their physical presence. Insurance, dry cleaning, hotel accommodations, and airline passenger or freight service, in contrast, are intangible and have intrinsic value resulting from a process, a performance, or an occurrence that exists only while it is being created.

The intangibility of services results in characteristics unique to a service: It is *inseparable* in that its creation cannot be separated from its consumption;[37] it is *heterogeneous* in that it is individually produced and is thus unique; and it is *perishable* in that once created it cannot be stored but must be consumed simultaneously with its creation. Contrast these characteristics with a tangible product that can be produced in one location and consumed elsewhere, that can be standardized, whose quality assurance can be determined and maintained over time, and that can be produced and stored in anticipation of fluctuations in demand.

As is true for many tangible products, a service can be marketed as both an industrial (business-to-business) and a consumer service, depending on the motive of, and use by, the purchaser. For example, travel agents and airlines sell industrial or business services to a business traveler and a consumer service to a tourist. Financial services, hotels, insurance, legal services, and others may each be classified as either a business or a consumer service. As one might expect, the unique characteristics of services result in differences in the marketing of services and the marketing of consumer products.

Services Opportunities in Global Markets

International tourism is by far the largest services export of the United States, ranking behind only capital goods and industrial supplies when all exports are counted. Spending by foreign tourists visiting American destinations such as Orlando or Anaheim is roughly double that spent by foreign airlines on Boeing's commercial jets. Worldwide, tourists spent some $3.5 trillion last year, and an agency of the United Nations projects that number will grow by four times by 2020. The industry employs some 200 million people all around the world. Furthermore, the same U.N. agency predicts that China will be followed by the United States, France, Spain, Hong Kong, Italy, Britain, Mexico, Russia, and the Czech Republic as the most popular destinations in the next century. Currently, France, Spain, the United States, Italy, and China are numbers one through five. Most tourists will be, as they are today, Germans, Japanese, and Americans; Chinese will be the fourth largest group. Australians, Belgians, Austrians, Japanese, and Hong Kong residents spend the most (in that order) per capita on package holidays.[38] Currently, Japanese tourists contribute the most to U.S. tourism income, at more than $15 billion annually. Overall, the tourism business declined more than 10% during the 2008–2009 recession, and like the economy in general, no quick recovery is expected. The good news is that you may soon be able to actually leave the planet and return on Richard Branson's commercial passenger spaceship—the price for a brief visit to space, a mere $280,000.[39] That's far less than the $20 million required for a longer ride and a short stay at the International Space Station on a Russian rocket.

The dramatic growth in tourism, especially before the recession, prompted U.S. firms and institutions to respond by developing new travel services to attract both domestic and foreign customers. For example, the Four Seasons Hotel in Philadelphia created a two-day package that included local concerts and museum visits. In addition to its attractions for kids, Orlando, Florida, has an opera company with performances by world-class singers. The cities of Phoenix, Las Vegas, and San Diego formed a consortium and put together a $500,000 marketing budget specifically appealing to foreign visitors to stop at all three destinations in one trip. Even the smallest hotels are finding a global clientele on the Internet.

---

[37]Bruce D. Keillor, G. Tomas M. Hult, and Destan Kandemir, "A Study of the Service Encounter in Eight Countries," *Journal of International Marketing* 12, no. 1 (2004), pp. 9–35.

[38]Euromonitor International, 2010.

[39]John Johnson Jr., "A Giant Step for Space Tourism," *Los Angeles* Times, December 8, 2009, p. A22.

Rank 2009/2008	2009 Brand Value (millions)	2008 Brand Value (millions)	Percent Change	Country of Ownership	Description
4/4 GE	47,777	53,086	−10	U.S.	GE painted itself green with its "Ecomagination" crusade. Now it aims to color itself healthy by pushing healthcare solutions in an underserved market.
5/5 Nokia	34,864	35,942	−3	Finland	Nokia continues to lag in smart phones, but its reputation for robust construction, ease of use, and low-key style has helped it dominate mass-market handsets.
6/8 McDonald's	32,275	31,049	4	U.S.	The downturn heightened the appeal of Mickey D's low-priced fare, particularly in Britain and France, while new McCafe coffee drinks perked up sales.
7/10 Google	31,980	25,590	25	U.S.	Its new free services are pushing it beyond search. But with trustbusters on the prowl, Google faces a challenge in maintaining a cuddly brand image.
8/6 Toyota	31,330	34,050	−8	Japan	It lost money in 2008 and will likely again in '09. But deep pockets and newly focused management meant this titan should revive when the economy does.
9/7 Intel	30,636	31,261	−2	U.S.	Intel paid a $1.45 billion anti-trust fine in Europe, but that hasn't slowed the chipmaker's push into new markets, including smartphones and home electronics.
10/9 Disney	28,447	29,251	−3	U.S.	Falling attendance at its parks and sliding DVD sales are hurting. But the Mouse House continues it invest in its future, including adding Marvel for $4 billion.
11/12 Hewlett-Packard	24,096	23,509	2	U.S.	HP extended its lead over Dell and weathered the economic downturn better than most tech companies, thanks to its acquisition of services provider EDS.
12/11 Mercedes-Benz	23,867	25,577	−7	Germany	Although sales have plunged, the engineering icon has maintained its premium image with new fuel-efficient models. It needs to add small cars to its lineup.
13/14 Gillette	22,841	22,069	4	U.S.	Brisk-selling high-end razors have boosted sales. But to extend its reach to more buyers, Gillette will have to innovate at the lower end of the market, too.
14/17 Cisco	22,030	21,306	3	U.S.	The battle to rebrand itself as more than a maker of Web plumbing continues. By acquiring the Flip video camera, Cisco aims to be more consumer-focused.
15/13 BMW	21,671	23,298	−7	Germany	It has demonstrated that buyers will pay a premium for a chic, sporty compact. BMW is also benefiting from an early investment in more efficient engines.
16/16 Louis Vuitton	21,120	21,602	−2	France	The world's preeminent luxury brand has enjoyed a sales rebound in Europe this year, while continuing to tap new wealth in Asia and the Middle East.
17/18 Marlboro	19,010	21,300	−11	U.S.	As marketing restrictions tighten at home, the cigarette giant continues to push hard in emerging markets from Asia to Russia and win over millions of smokers.
18/20 Honda	17,803	19,079	−7	Japan	Despite slumping global sales, Honda's lineup of gas sippers and a profitable motorbike business has helped the automaker navigate the recession.
19/21 Samsung	16,796	17,518	−1	S. Korea	It has taken over Sony as the top TV brand and emerged as the only credible challenger to Nokia in mobile phones. To expand its appeal, it is opening an app store.
20/24 Apple	15,443	13,724	12	U.S.	Mac sales have slowed, but Apple continues to prosper thanks to the iPhone, now in its third generation, and an app store that rivals are rushing to copy.

Source: Burt Helm, "100 Best Global Brands," *BusinessWeek*, September 28, 2009, pp. 44–61.

A successful brand is the most valuable resource a company has. The brand name[46] encompasses the years of advertising, goodwill, quality evaluations, product experience, and other beneficial attributes the market associates with the product. Brand image is at the very core of business identity and strategy. Western researchers have personified brands, imbuing them with personalities and images. In a sense, the consumer–brand interaction becomes much like an interpersonal interaction, wherein cultural differences hold heavy sway. This comparison also implies that even global brands must be positioned locally, as a Japanese consumer will see and interact with the Coke brand differently than a French consumer, for example. Research shows that the importance and impact of brands vary with cultural values around the world. Thus, customers everywhere respond to images,[47] myths, and metaphors that help them define their personal and national identities within a global context of world culture and product benefits.[48]

Global brands play an important role in that process. The value of Sony, Coca-Cola, McDonald's, Toyota, and Marlboro is indisputable. One estimate of the value of Coca-Cola, the world's most valuable brand, places it at over $65 billion. In fact, one authority speculates that brands are so valuable that companies will soon include a "statement of value" addendum to their balance sheets to include intangibles such as the value of their brands. Please see Exhibit 13.2 for details. One researcher has noted that in the short run, brand

---

[46]Yih Hwai Lee and Kim Soon Ang, "Brand Name Suggestiveness: A Chinese Language Perspective," *International Journal of Research in Marketing* 20, no. 4 (2003), pp. 323–35.

[47]Tulin Erdem, Joffre Swait, and Ana Valenzuela, "Brands as Signals: A Cross-Country Validation Study," *Marketing Science* 26 (2006), pp. 679–97; Aysegul Ozsomer and Selin Altaras, "Global Brand Purchase Likelihood: A Critical Synthesis and an Integrated Conceptual Framework," *Journal of International Marketing* 16, no. 4 (2008), pp. 1–28; Donald R. Lehman, Kevin A. Keller, and John U. Farley, "The Structure of Survey-Based Brand Metrics," *Journal of International Marketing* 16, no. 4 (2008), pp. 29–56; Julien Cayla and Eric J. Arnould, "A Cultural Approach to Branding in the Global Marketplace," *Journal of International Marketing* 16, no. 4 (2008), pp. 86–112; Xuehua Wang, Zhilin Yang, and Ning Rong Liu, "The Impacts of Brand Personality and Congruity on Purchase Intention: Evidence from the Chinese Mainland's Automobile Market," *Journal of Global Marketing* 22 (2009), pp. 199–215; Francisco Guzman and Audhesh K. Paswan, "Cultural Brands from Emerging Markets: Brand Image across Host and Home Countries," *Journal of International Marketing* 17, no. 3 (2009), pp. 71–86; Ralf van der Lans and 12 coauthors, "Cross-National Logo Evaluation Analysis: An Individual-Level Approach," *Marketing Science* 28, no. 5 (2009), pp. 968–85; Yinlong Zhang and Adwait Khare, "The Impact of Accessible Identities on the Evaluation of Global vs. Local Products," *Journal of Consumer Research* 36 (2009), pp. 525–37.

[48]Douglas B. Holt, "What Becomes an Icon Most?" *Harvard Business Review*, March 2003, pp. 43–49; Yuliya Strizhakova, Robin L. Coulter, and Linda A. Price, "Branded Products as a Passport to Global Citizenship: Perspectives from Developed and Developing Countries," *Journal of International Marketing* 16, no. 4 (2008), pp. 57–85; Lily Dong and Kelly Tian, "The Use of Western Brands in Asserting Chinese National Identity," *Journal of Consumer Research* 36 (2009), pp. 504–22.

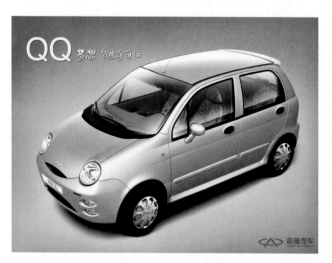

Copying is the highest form of flattery? Not so in the car business. The new QQ model from Chinese company Chery (left) resembles the Matiz or Spark from GM's Daewoo (right)—perhaps a bit too much.

Solar Turbines Inc.
A Global Industrial Marketer

With more than 80 percent of its sales outside the United States, Solar Turbines Inc. is the most global subsidiary of one of America's most global companies. More than half of Caterpillar's 2009 sales of over $32 billion were to customers outside the United States, making the parent corporation one of the country's leading exporters. Pictured here is work on the road leading to the airport at Serengeti National Park in Tanzania.

Solar industrial gas turbines are used by customers in 86 countries worldwide, in the oil and gas industries, electrical power generation, and marine propulsion. Solar promotes its products on the Internet (see www.solarturbines .com) and in brochures and print media around the world, as represented below:

Produisez l'énergie dont vous avez besoin tout en préservant l'air que vous respirez.

Les turbines à gaz n'ont pas seulement acquis la réputation de produire de l'énergie de façon super-efficace, elles la font même sans contaminer l'environnement.

La propreté du carburant (gaz naturel) et le procédé de combustion intégral dans les turbines à gaz en sont les raisons inhérentes.

Solar Turbines Incorporated a affiné cette technologie en créant des systèmes de cogénération à turbines à gaz qui répondent aux exigences actuelles du coût-efficacité et de la lutte contre la pollution atmosphérique. Nous l'avons déjà démontré avec des systèmes de cogénération de turbines à gaz d'une puissance s'échelonnant entre 1 et 10 MW, et des centrales électriques fournissant jusqu'à 50 MW, satisfaisant les besoins en énergie et en air propre d'un éventail important d'entreprises dans de nombreux pays.

Une conversation avec nous et vous saurez pourquoi, dans le monde de la production d'énergie, les turbines Solar sont un bol d'air bien frais.

Pour des renseignements supplémentaires, appelez Solar Turbines Europe SA au 00.32.(0)71.253000 ou contactez-nous au fax 00.32.(0)71.544739.

Solar Turbines
A Caterpillar Company

SOLAR CUBRE DOS TERCIOS DE LA TIERRA.

Solar tiene tantas instalaciones confiabera como Solar. Desde las heladas aguas del Mar del Norte hasta las húmedas costas tropicales de Malasia, las turbinas Solar han demostrado su seguridad de servicio bajo las peores condiciones.

El compromiso de Solar con la confiabilidad le ha ganado una y otra vez la lealtad de sus clientes en todo el mundo. Con más de 1,000 unidades instaladas, Solar tiene más del doble de instalaciones confiables que el competidor más cercano. Las instalaciones de Solar han ido y tienen como el mar sumar más 9,500 unidades con cerca de 500 millones de horas de operación.

Para que la turbo-maquinaria siga funcionando en sus plataformas confiabera. Llame a Solar Turbines Incorporated. 1601 KR 46th Street, Joplin 309, Miami, FL, E.U.A. 33870; teléfono (305) 229-6276. Fax (305) 355-6555. Porque, cuando de instalaciones confiabera de turbinas de gas se trata, nadie la cubre tan bien como Solar Turbines.

Solar Turbines
A Caterpillar Company

Caterpillar y Solar son marcas registradas de Caterpillar Inc. Solar Turbines Incorporated es una empresa subsidiaria de Caterpillar Inc.

Продукция фирмы Solar Turbines Incorporated (Солар Турбинз Инкорпорейтед)

Фирма Solar («Солар») является ведущим в мире изготовителем промышленных газовых турбин в диапазоне мощностей от 1 до 11 МВт. Компания проектирует и производит газотурбинные и турбоагрегатные установки в соответствии со стандартами качества ISO 9001.

За последние 35 лет было выпущено более 9500 турбоагрегатных установок Solar («Солар») которые отработали в совокупности свыше 500 млн. часов в 80 странах мира. Турбины Solar («Солар») с неизменным успехом работают в самых сложных климатических условиях, включая отдаленные арктические, пустынные, тропические регионы, а также морские платформы.

Долговечные и высоконадежные турбины фирмы Solar («Солар») имеют минимальный уровень выбросов, соответствующего класса, в агрегатах, входящих в семейства газовых турбин Centaur («Центавр»), Taurus («Таурус») и Mars («Марс»), могут усовершенствоваться двигателями SoLoNOx («Солоноокс»). В турбинах используются переходные технологии сгорания топлива с предварительным обеднением горючей смеси, которая позволяет снизить уровень выбросов оксидов азота до 77 130 азотс и1 при 15% содержании О2 что соответствует действующим европейским стандартам.

К началу 1996 года фирмы Solar («Солар») выполнила или выполняет заказы на установку более 270 газовых турбин с компенсаторами систем SoLoNOx для заказчиков во всем мире, включая 10 установок в Европе. Эти турбины отработали в совокупности более 1,1 млн. часов бесперебойной по продолжительности опыт

использования технологии сухого сгорания с предварительным обеднением горючей смеси.

Гатурбинные нагнетательные установки фирмы Solar («Солар»)

Фирма Solar Turbines («Солар Турбинз») выпускает нагнетательные установки с приводом от газовых турбин мощностью 1 080, 1 185, 1 506, 4 335, 5 190, 6 635, 9 695 и 11 185 кВт. Эти нагнетатели поставляются в полностью собранном и испытанном виде, что обеспечивает их установку в кратчайшие сроки. Высокая надежность, компактные размеры, небольшой вес и простое обслуживание обеспечили широкое распространение этих агрегатов для использования в отдаленных объектах и на морских платформах.

Характеристики нагнетательных установок

ГАЗОВАЯ ТУРБИНА	НОМ. ВЫХ. МОЩН., кВт	ТЕПЛОВОЙ КПД, %	ГАБАРИТНЫЕ РАЗМЕРЫ			ВЕС, кг
			Длина, м	Ширина, м	Высота, м	
Saturn 10 («Сатурн 10»)	1 080	23,7	6,2	1,8	1,9	16 532
Saturn 20 («Сатурн 20»)	1 185	24,5	6,2	1,8	1,9	16 532
Centaur 40 («Центавр 40»)	3 505	28,0	8,5	2,4	2,7	16 300
Centaur 50 («Центавр 50»)	4 335	29,6	8,5	2,4	2,7	16 300
Taurus 60 («Таурус 60»)	5 190	32,0	8,5	2,4	2,7	16 300
Taurus 70 («Таурус 70»)	6 635	33,0	9,8	2,9	3,3	30 845
Mars 90 («Марс 90»)	9 695	33,1	13,5	2,9	3,4	35 685
Mars 100 («Марс 100»)	11 185	34,0	13,5	2,7	3,4	35 685

При нормальных условиях по ISO (15oC, относительная влажность 60%, нулевые потери на входе и выхлопе). Топливо II природный газ.

An ad appearing in a French trade publication. It emphasizes the energy-saving and low-pollution attributes of the products. Notice the Caterpillar yellow in the logo and the phone number for the European subsidiary offices.

The compact size makes Solar gas turbines ideally suited for offshore oil applications in places like the North Sea, the Gulf of Mexico, and offshore Malaysia and Latin America.

A Russian-language brochure. The former Soviet Union and now the Russian oil and gas industry has remained an important customer for Solar for more than 40 years.

The Project Team

The Customer is involved as a vital member of the Project Team from the initial inquiry to final acceptance. The Customer works with and issues project specifications to our ...

Sales Engineer, who maintains initial Customer contact, prompts analysis of Customer needs, submits a comprehensive proposal to the Customer, monitors execution of the order, and submits the order to the assigned ...

Application Engineer, who is responsible for determining the best product match for Customer requirements and recommending alternative approaches as appropriate. The Application Engineer works closely with ...

Engineering and Control Systems, where gas turbines, gas compressors, and controls are designed and gas turbine packages are customized for the customers based on proven designs.

Solar Turbines sells its products and services through project teams that include both customer personnel and vendors. Solar has followed its American customers around the world, supplying equipment and services for their global ventures. Of course, the firm sells directly to a wide variety of foreign firms as well.

Personal selling is the most important aspect of the promotions mix for industrial companies like Solar. In addition to calling on clients directly, sales engineers attend key trade shows around the world, such as this one in Amsterdam.

Project Manager handles all aspects of the order, maintains liaison with the Customer, controls documentation, arranges quality audits, and is responsible for on-time shipment and scheduling equipment commissioning at the Customer site.

Manufacturing Technicians produce, assemble, and test industrial gas turbines and turbomachinery packages designed to meet specific Customer needs. Manufacturing also arranges shipment of equipment to the Customer site where …

Customer Services handles installation and start-up of the turbo-machinery, trains personnel, and provides a wide range of vital services to support Customer and operating requirements.

Suppliers are a critical element of all project teams; they provide materials and components that must meet Solar's demanding Quality Standards.

The Venezuelan offshore oil and gas platform pictured here is about a $40 million project for Solar; it includes four sets of turbomachinery. Close coordination among customer, subcontractors, and Solar is required from initial designs through powering up the facility.

Courtesy of Solar Turbines, Inc.

Solar's sales and services efforts don't stop when the machine has been turned on. After-sales services (maintenance contracts, overhaul, and spare parts) often account for one-third of some industrial manufacturers' revenues, and Solar is no exception to that rule. Pictured are company overhaul operations in Indonesia.

Solar's Marketing Affiliates

Solar sells and distributes its products through a variety of kinds of affiliates around the world. Most firms would prefer to keep things simple—direct sales worldwide. However, Solar has learned to be flexible and makes distribution decisions based on the level of business and local regulations.

Solar has packaging agreements with three Japanese companies, Mitsui Zosen, Niigata, and Yanmar. The one pictured, Yanmar, buys the turbine engines from Solar, then packages them with generators to suit Japanese regulations and customer specifications.

Delcom is Solar's distributor in Malaysia. Almost all the manufacturing is done in the United States, and Delcom's principal role is marketing in Southeast Asia. Pictured is Delcom's booth at a Malay trade show.

Solar has a variety of sales and manufacturing operations and affiliations in Mexico, including a maquiladora plant in Tijuana, offices in Mexico City, and a technology-sharing agreement with Turbinas Solar. The last facility is located in Veracruz and is pictured above.

Solar has also signed long-term alliance agreements with some of its major customers like Shell Oil. Pictured here are the Solar and Shell executives who worked on the agreement and then signed it at Solar's San Diego headquarters.

Courtesy of Solar Turbines, Inc.

Summary

Industrial (business-to-business) marketing requires close attention to the exact needs of customers. Basic differences across various markets are less than those for consumer goods, but the motives behind purchases differ enough to require a special approach. Global competition has risen to the point that industrial goods marketers must pay close attention to the level of economic and technological development of each market to determine the buyer's assessment of quality. Companies that adapt their products to these needs are the ones that should be most effective in the marketplace.

The demand for products and services in business-to-business markets is by nature more volatile than in most consumer markets.

The demand also varies by level of economic development and the quality of educational systems across countries. Ultimately, product or service quality is defined by customers, but global quality standards such as ISO 9000 are being developed that provide information about companies' attention to matters of quality. After-sale services are a hugely important aspect of industrial sales. The demand for other kinds of business services (e.g., banking, legal services, advertising) is burgeoning around the world. Trade shows are an especially important promotional medium in business-to-business marketing.

Key Terms

Derived demand	ISO 9000s	Client followers	Relationship marketing
Price–quality relationship			

Questions

1. Define the key terms listed above.
2. What are the differences between consumer and industrial goods, and what are the implications for international marketing?
3. Discuss how the various stages of economic development affect the demand for industrial goods.
4. "Industrialization is typically a national issue, and industrial goods are the fodder for industrial growth." Comment.
5. "The adequacy of a product must be considered in relation to the general environment within which it will be operated rather than solely on the basis of technical efficiency." Discuss the implications of this statement.
6. Why hasn't the United States been more helpful in setting universal standards for industrial equipment? Do you feel that the argument is economically sound? Discuss.
7. What roles do service, replacement parts, and standards play in competition in foreign marketing? Illustrate.
8. Discuss the role industrial trade fairs play in international marketing of industrial goods.
9. Describe the reasons an MNC might seek an ISO 9000 certification.
10. What ISO 9000 legal requirements are imposed on products sold in the European Union? Discuss.
11. Discuss the competitive consequences of being ISO 9000 certified.
12. Discuss how the characteristics that define the uniqueness of industrial products lead naturally to relationship marketing. Give some examples.
13. Discuss some of the more pertinent problems in pricing industrial goods.
14. What is the price–quality relationship? How does this relationship affect a U.S. firm's comparative position in world markets?
15. Select several countries, each at a different stage of economic development, and illustrate how the stage affects demand for industrial goods.
16. England has almost completed the process of shifting from the inch–pound system to the metric system. What effect do you think this will have on the traditional U.S. reluctance to make such a change? Discuss the economic implications of such a move.
17. Discuss the importance of international business services to total U.S. export trade. How do most U.S. service companies become international?
18. Discuss the international market environment for business services.

Chapter 15

International Marketing Channels

CHAPTER LEARNING OBJECTIVES

What you should learn from Chapter 15:

LO1 The variety of distribution channels and how they affect cost and efficiency in marketing

LO2 The Japanese distribution structure and what it means to Japanese customers and to competing importers of goods

LO3 How distribution patterns affect the various aspects of international marketing

LO4 The functions, advantages, and disadvantages of various kinds of middlemen

LO5 The importance of selecting and maintaining middlemen

LO6 The growing importance of e-commerce as a distribution alternative

LO7 The interdependence of physical distribution activities

Global Perspective

CENTRAL PERK IN BEIJING

All 4Ps of marketing—product, price, promotion, and place—are important for retailers, particularly the last. No one has made more profit by creating a "third place" for consumers than Starbucks. As on the TV show *Friends*, friends have a sofa to sit on, talk, and, the retailer hopes, consume. But it doesn't always work out to the retailer's advantage in Beijing:

One first-time Starbucks visitor reported, "The thing I like most is the comfortable sofa, and I think when I first saw the Starbucks I entered it and sat in the sofa. But, the servant came and told me if you don't consume coffee you can't be here. So I left because at the time I think for students like me, the price of coffee was a little bit high."

Another customer reported not knowing the rules of the game: "I remember when I first went to Starbucks I wanted an ice coffee…. But, after finishing the coffee the sugar stayed in the bottom of the cup. I don't know because there are many kinds of sugar…. I don't know what kind of sugar is right for me, for my coffee. So I want in the future … some service and lessons about what kind of sugar is added to what kind of coffee."

IKEA in Beijing has a larger store and a larger problem of this sort:

> With no plans one Saturday, Zhang Xin told his wife, son, and mother to wear something smart and hop into the family sedan. He could have taken them to the Forbidden City or the Great Wall, but he decided on another popular destination—IKEA.

Riding an escalator past a man lying on a display bed with a book opened on his belly, the clan sauntered into the crush of visitors squeezing onto the showroom path, bumping elbows and nicking ankles with their yellow shopping trolleys. Zhang said the family needed a respite from the smog and a reliable lunch. "We just came here for fun," said the 34-year-old office manager. "I suppose we could have gone somewhere else, but it wouldn't have been a complete experience."

Welcome to IKEA Beijing, where the atmosphere is more theme park than store. When the Swedish furniture giant first opened here in 1999, it hoped locals would embrace its European brand of minimalism. A decade later, Beijingers have done just that. Perhaps too much.

Every weekend, thousands of looky-loos pour into the massive showroom to use the displays. Some hop into bed, slide under the covers and sneak a nap; others bring cameras and pose with the decor. Families while away the afternoon in the store for no other reason than to enjoy the air conditioning. Visitors can't seem to resist novelties most Americans take for granted, such as free soda refills and ample seating. They also like the laid-back staffers who don't mind when a child jumps on a couch.

Purchasing anything at *Yi Jia*, as the store is called here, can seem like an afterthought. "It's the only big store in Beijing where a security guard doesn't stop you from taking a picture," said Jing Bo, 30, who was looking for promising backdrops for a photograph of his girlfriend.

The store's success can be traced, in part, to how grounded it is in the capital's zeitgeist. At a time when home ownership is more within reach and incomes are rising, IKEA offers affordable, modern furniture to an emerging middle class clamoring to be *bai ling*, or white collar. It doesn't hurt either that the understated style is a satisfying departure from, say, the faux French imperial designs favored by the older nouveaux riches and gaudy hotels.

"Our values are changing," said Lizzy Hou, a university graduate who moved to Beijing in May from neighboring Hebei province for a teaching job. "We want to be modern. I think IKEA stands for a kind of lifestyle. People don't necessarily want to buy it, but they want to at least experience it."

Imagining the possibilities here is one of the reasons Bai Yalin drove an hour and a half from her apartment to spend a day at the store with her 7-year-old son and two teenage nieces. There are few other indoor spaces, she said, where she can entertain the children free on an oppressive summer afternoon. Bai mapped out a five-hour outing. First, they had hot dogs and soft ice cream cones at noon. Then they enjoyed a long rest lounging on the beds. Bai kicked off her sandals and sprawled out on a Tromso bunk bed. The 36-year-old homemaker made herself comfortable and even answered passing shoppers' questions about the quality of the mattress. "It's soft and a great buy at this price," she told a young woman, pointing to a dangling price tag. After that, Bai and her family took group pictures. By 5:00 p.m., it was time for another meal, so they headed to the cafeteria and ate braised mushrooms with rice.

Bai and her husband, a clerk at a heating company, have bought plates and cups at IKEA, but what they'd really like one day is to rid themselves of their clunky old Chinese furniture and bring on the do-it-yourself particleboard. "Today we didn't plan to buy anything, just eat and rest," Bai said.

Though frustrated, IKEA executives hope browsers like Luo will eventually turn into buyers. That's why they don't shoo anyone away for sleeping. It's the promise of China's middle class that has girded their investment here. The privately owned company operates seven stores in China, though there have been indications that profit remains elusive.

"The brand awareness is great, but the question is, how do we get people to open up their wallets and spend money?" said Linda Xu, a company spokeswoman who rolled her eyes when she came upon a trio of slumbering customers. When Walmart and the French supermarket chain Carrefour entered China in the 1990s, many flocked to the new stores just to look and touch. Now millions of Chinese shop there every day.

IKEA has the added challenge of copycats. Brazen customers are known to come in with carpenters armed with measuring tapes to make replicas. Zhang, the office manager visiting with his family, said he bought a TV table and a couch elsewhere that looked just like IKEA furniture. "Why spend so much money when you can have the same thing cheaper?" he said.

Sources: Meera Venkatraman and Teresa Nelson, "From Servicescape to Consumptionscape: A Photo-Elicitation Study of Starbucks in the New China," *Journal of International Business Studies* 39, no. 6 (2008), pp. 1010–26; David Pierson, "Beijing Loves IKEA—But Not for Shopping," *Los Angeles Times*, August 25, 2009, online. For more on this topic, see also Edwin J. Nijssen and Susan P. Douglas, "Consumer World-Mindedness, Social-Mindedness, and Store Image," *Journal of International Marketing* 16, no. 3 (2008), pp. 84–107.

Two visitors to Beijing's IKEA enjoy a nap on a display sofa.

If marketing goals are to be achieved, a product must be made accessible to the target market at an affordable price. Getting the product to the target market can be a costly process if inadequacies within the distribution structure cannot be overcome. Forging an aggressive and reliable channel of distribution may be the most critical and challenging task facing the international marketer. Moreover, some argue that meeting such challenges is a key catalyst to economic development.

Each market contains a distribution network with many channel choices whose structures are unique and, in the short run, fixed. In some markets, the distribution structure is multilayered, complex, inefficient, even strange, and often difficult for new marketers to penetrate; in others, there are few specialized middlemen except in major urban areas; and in yet others, there is a dynamic mixture of traditional and new, evolving distribution systems available on a global scale. Regardless of the predominating distribution structure, competitive advantage will reside with the marketer best able to build the most efficient channels from among the alternatives available. And as global trade continues to burgeon and physical distribution infrastructures lag, the challenges will be even greater in the 21st century.

This chapter discusses the basic points involved in making channel decisions: channel structures; distribution patterns; available alternative middlemen; factors affecting choice of channels; and locating, selecting, motivating, and terminating middlemen.

changing.[6] Pressures for change in a country come from within and without. Multinational marketers are seeking ways to profitably tap market segments that currently are served by costly, traditional distribution systems. In India, the familiar clutter of traditional retailers is fast giving way to the wide aisles of new local and foreign supermarkets. In the United Kingdom Tesco is moving into retail banking in its stores,[7] and Anthropologie is testing the waters there as well.[8] As Carrefour's profits dip in Europe, it is importing new concepts from its hypermarkets in Brazil, such as a reduced number of SKUs.[9] Direct marketing, door-to-door selling, hypermarkets, discount houses, shopping malls, catalog selling, the Internet, and other distribution methods are being introduced in an attempt to provide efficient distribution channels. Importers and retailers also are becoming more involved in new product development;[10] for example, the Mexican appliance and electronics giant Grupo Elektra has formed an alliance with Beijing Automobile Works Group to develop and build low-cost cars for Mexico and export markets.

Some important trends in distribution will eventually lead to greater commonality than disparity among middlemen in different countries. Walmart, for example, is expanding all over the world—from Mexico to Brazil and from Europe to Asia.[11] The only major disappointment for the American juggernaut has been its lack of scale and profits in South Korea; in 2006 the firm sold its five stores there.[12] Avon is expanding into eastern Europe; Mary Kay Cosmetics and Amway into China; and L.L. Bean and Lands' End have successfully entered the Japanese market. The effect of all these intrusions into the traditional distribution systems is change that will make discounting, self-service, supermarkets, mass merchandising, and e-commerce concepts common all over the world, elevating the competitive climate to a level not known before.

As U.S. retailers have invaded Europe, staid, nationally based retailers have been merging with former competitors and companies from other countries to form Europewide enterprises.[13] Carrefour, a French global marketer, merged with Promodes, one of its fierce French competitors, to create, in the words of its CEO, "a worldwide retail leader." The U.K. supermarket giant Sainsbury has entered an alliance with Esselunga of Italy (supermarkets), Docks de France (hypermarkets, supermarkets, and discount stores), and Belgium's Delhaize (supermarkets). The alliance provides the four companies the opportunity to pool their experience and buying power to better face growing competition and opportunity afforded by the single European market and the euro.

While European retailers see a unified Europe as an opportunity for pan-European expansion, foreign retailers are attracted by the high margins and prices. Costco, the U.S.-based warehouse retailer, saw the high gross margins that British supermarkets command (7 to 8 percent compared with 2.5 to 3 percent in the United States) as an opportunity. Costco prices will initially be 10 to 20 percent cheaper than rival local retailers.

Expansion outside the home country, as well as new types of retailing, is occurring throughout Europe. El Corte Inglés, Spain's largest department store chain, not only is

---

[6]Suk-Ching Ho, "Evolution versus Tradition in Marketing Systems: The Hong Kong Food Retailing Experience," *Journal of Public Policy & Marketing* 24, no. 1 (2005), pp. 90–99; Ellyn Byron, "P&G's Global Target: Shelves of Tiny Stores," *The Wall Street Journal*, July 16, 2007, pp. A1, A10; Bruce Einhorn and Wing-Gar Cheng, "China: Where Retail Dinosaurs Are Thriving, *Bloomberg BusinessWeek*, February 1 & 8, 2010, p. 64.

[7]Kerry Capell, "Eggs, Bread, Milk—and a Mortgage," *Bloomberg BusinessWeek*, March 1, 2010, p. 20.

[8]Michael Arndt, "Urban Outfitters' Grow-Slow Strategy," *Bloomberg BusinessWeek*, March 1, 2010, p. 56.

[9]Christina Passariello, "Carrefour Net Drops Amid Overhaul Effort," *The Wall Street* Journal, February 19, 2010, online.

[10]Goksel Yalcinkaya, Roger J. Calantone, and David A. Griffith, "An Examination of Exploration Capabilities: Implications for Product Innovation and Market Performance," *Journal of International Marketing* 15 (2007), pp. 63–93.

[11]Anand Giridharadas, "Megastores Gaze Longingly at India," *International Herald Tribune*, April 2–3, 2005, pp. 13, 15.

[12]"Wal-Mart Exits Korean Market," *Los Angeles Times*, May 23, 2006, p. C3.

[13]John Dawson, "New Cultures, New Strategies, New Formats, and New Relationships in European Retailing: Some Implications for Asia," *Journal of Global Marketing* 18, no. 1/2 (2004), pp. 73–98.

moving into Portugal and other European countries but also was one of the first retailers to offer a virtual supermarket on the Internet (www.elcorteingles.es) and to sponsor two 24-hour home shopping channels in Spain. Increasingly smaller retailers are also expanding overseas.[14] Another Spanish retailer, Mango, opened a store in New York City and, along with other European competitors, was taking advantage of low costs of operation in the United States at the time associated with the sinking dollar.[15]

One of Walmart's strengths is its internal Internet-based system, which makes its transactions with suppliers highly efficient and lowers its cost of operations. Indeed, it is buying ailing retailers around the world with the intention of "saving them" with its distribution technologies. This same type of system is available on the Internet for both business-to-business and business-to-consumer transactions. For example, General Motors, Ford Motor Company, and DaimlerChrysler have created a single online site called Covisint (www.covisint.com) for purchasing automotive parts from suppliers, which is expected to save the companies millions of dollars. A typical purchase order costs Ford $150, whereas a real-time order via Covisint will cost about $15. Sears Roebuck and Carrefour of France have created GlobalNetXchange (www.gnx.com), a retail exchange that allows retailers and their suppliers to conduct transactions online. Any company with a Web browser can access the exchange to buy, sell, trade, or auction goods and services. Described as "one of the most dramatic changes in consumer-products distribution of the decade," the exchange is expected to lower costs for both buyer and supplier. As more such exchanges evolve, one can only speculate about the impact on traditional channel middlemen.

We have already seen the impact on traditional retailing within the last few years caused by e-commerce retailers such as Amazon.com, Dell Computer, eBay, and others—all of which are expanding globally. Most brick-and-mortar retailers are experimenting with or have fully developed Web sites, some of which are merely extensions of their regular stores, allowing them to extend their reach globally. L.L. Bean, Eddie Bauer, and Lands' End are examples.

One of the most challenging aspects of Web sales is delivery of goods. One of the innovative features of the 7dream program at 7-Eleven stores in Japan is the use of convenience stores for pick-up points for Web orders. It has worked so well in Japan that Ito-Yokado Corporation, owner of 7-Eleven Japan and 72 percent of the U.S. chain, is exporting the idea to U.S. stores. In the Dallas–Fort Worth area, 250 stores have installed ATM-like machines tied into a delivery and payment system that promises to make 7-Eleven stores a

[14]Karise Hutchinson, Nicholas Alexander, Barry Quinn, and Anne Marie Doherty, "Internationalization Motives and Facilitating Factors: Qualitative Evidence from Smaller Specialists Retailers," *Journal of International Marketing* 15 (2007), pp. 96–122.

[15]J. Alex Tarquinio, "Foreign Shops Invade New York," *International Herald Tribune*, January 30, 2008, pp. 9, 10.

Now that Russians can own their homes, they're spending fast in home improvement stores like this one in St. Petersburg. In English it would be called "Super Home."

depot for e-commerce. FedEx, UPS, and other package delivery services that have been the backbone of e-commerce delivery in the United States are offering similar services for foreign customers of U.S. e-commerce companies, as well as for foreign-based ones. When goods cross borders, UPS and others offer seamless shipments, including customs and brokerage. Most of these service companies are established in Europe and Japan and are building networks in Latin America and China.

The impact of these and other trends will change traditional distribution and marketing systems. While this latest retailing revolution remains in flux, new retailing and middlemen systems will be invented, and established companies will experiment, seeking ways to maintain their competitive edge. Moreover, it is becoming more dangerous to think of competitors in terms of individual companies—in international business generally, and distribution systems particularly, a networks perspective is increasingly required. That is, firms must be understood in the context of the commercial networks of which they are a part.[16] These changes will resonate throughout the distribution chain before new concepts are established and the system stabilizes. Not since the upheaval that occurred in U.S. distribution after World War II that ultimately led to the Big-Box type of retailer has there been such potential for change in distribution systems. This time, however, such change will not be limited mostly to the United States—it will be worldwide.

Distribution Patterns

LO3

How distribution patterns affect the various aspects of international marketing

Even though patterns of distribution are in a state of change and new patterns are developing, international marketers need a general awareness of the traditional distribution base. The "traditional" system will not change overnight, and vestiges of it will remain for years to come. Nearly every international firm is forced by the structure of the market to use at least some middlemen in the distribution arrangement. It is all too easy to conclude that, because the structural arrangements of foreign and domestic distribution seem alike, foreign channels are the same as or similar to domestic channels of the same name. Only when the varied intricacies of actual distribution patterns are understood can the complexity of the distribution task be appreciated. The following description of differences in retailing should convey a sense of the variety of distribution patterns in general, including wholesalers.

---

[16]Mats Forsgren, Ulf Holm, and Jan Johanson, *Managing the Embedded Multinational: A Business Network View* (Northampton, MA: Edward Elgar, 2005); see also the associated book review by Charles Dhanarah, *Journal of International Business Studies* 38 (2007), pp. 1231–33.

PEMEX (Petróleos Mexicanos), the Mexican national oil company, will not let foreign firms distribute there. However, in Malaysia, a Mobil station sits right across the boulevard from a government-owned PETRONAS (Petroliam Nasional) station.

Retail Patterns   Retailing shows even greater diversity in its structure than does wholesaling. In Italy and Morocco, retailing is composed largely of specialty houses that carry narrow lines, whereas in Finland, most retailers carry a more general line of merchandise. Retail size is represented at one end by Japan's giant department store Mitsukoshi, which reportedly enjoys the patronage of more than 100,000 customers every day, and at the other extreme by the market of Ibadan, Nigeria, where some 3,000 one- or two-person stalls serve not many more customers. Some manufacturers sell directly to consumers through company-owned stores such as Cartier and Disney, and some sell through a half-dozen layers of middlemen.

Size Patterns.

The extremes in size in retailing are similar to those that predominate in wholesaling. Exhibit 15.2 dramatically illustrates some of the variations in size and number of retailers per person that exist in some countries. The retail structure and the problems it engenders cause real difficulties for the international marketing firm selling consumer goods. Large dominant retailers can be sold to directly, but there is no adequate way to reach small retailers who, in the aggregate, handle a great volume of sales.[17] In Italy, official figures show there are 931,000 retail stores, or one store for every 63 Italians. Of the 269,000 food stores, fewer than 10,000 can be classified as large. Thus, retailers are a critical factor in adequate distribution in Italy.

Underdeveloped countries present similar problems. Among the large supermarket chains in South Africa, there is considerable concentration. Of the country's 31,000 stores, 1,000 control 60 percent of all grocery sales, leaving the remaining 40 percent of sales to be spread among 30,000 stores. To reach the 40 percent of the market served by those 30,000 stores may be difficult. In black communities in particular, retailing is on a small scale—cigarettes are often sold singly, and the entire fruit inventory may consist of four apples in a bowl.

Retailing around the world has been in a state of active ferment for several years. The rate of change appears to be directly related to the stage and speed of economic development, and even the least developed countries are experiencing dramatic changes. Supermarkets of one variety or another are blossoming in developed and underdeveloped countries alike. Discount houses that sell everything from powdered milk and canned chili to Korean TVs and DVD players are thriving and expanding worldwide.

Direct Marketing.

Selling directly to the consumer through mail, by telephone, or door-to-door is often the approach of choice in markets with insufficient or underdeveloped distribution systems. The approach, of course, also works well in the most affluent markets. Amway, operating in 42 foreign countries, has successfully expanded into Latin America and Asia with its method of direct marketing. Companies that enlist individuals to sell their products are proving to be especially popular in eastern Europe and other countries where many people are looking for ways to become entrepreneurs. In the Czech Republic, for example, Amway Corporation signed up 25,000 Czechs as distributors and sold 40,000 starter kits at $83 each in its first two weeks of business. Avon is another American company that is expanding dramatically overseas.

---

[17]Tomasz Lenartowicz and Sridhar Balasubramanian, "Practices and Performance of Small Retail Stores in Developing Economies," *Journal of International Marketing* 17 (2009), pp. 59–90.

Exhibit 15.2
Retail Structure in Selected Countries

Source: Euromonitor International, 2009.

Country	All Retailers (000)	People Served per Retailer	Internet Users (per 1,000)
United States	921	333	741
Canada	161	208	769
Argentina	429	94	309
Germany	300	270	785
Russia	470	303	285
Israel	48	154	306
South Africa	117	417	88
China	4,817	278	283
Japan	849	149	724
Australia	84	256	734

CROSSING BORDERS 15.2   It Depends on What "Not Satisfied" Means

Amway's policy is that dissatisfied customers can get a full refund at any time, no questions asked—even if the returned bottles are empty. This refund policy is a courtesy to customers and a testament that the company stands behind its products, and it is the same all over the world. But such capitalistic concepts are somewhat unfamiliar in China.

The best game in town for months among the rising ranks of Shanghai's entrepreneurs was an $84 investment for a box of soaps and cosmetics that they could sell as Amway distributors. Word of this no-lose proposition quickly spread, with some people repackaging the soap, selling it, and then turning in the containers for a refund. Others dispensed with selling altogether and scoured garbage bins instead, showing up at Amway's Shanghai offices with bags full of bottles to be redeemed.

One salesman got nearly $10,000 for eight sacks full of all kinds of empty Amway containers. And at least one barbershop started using Amway shampoos for free and returning each empty bottle for a full refund. In a few weeks, refunds were totaling more than $100,000 a day. "Perhaps we were too lenient," said Amway's Shanghai chief. Amway changed the policy, only to have hundreds of angry Amway distributors descend

on the company's offices to complain that they were cheated out of their money. Amway had to call a press conference to explain that it wasn't changing its refund policy, simply raising the standard for what is deemed dissatisfaction. If someone returns half a bottle, fine, but for empties, Amway announced it would check records to see if the person had a pattern of return.

But the company did not anticipate the unusual sense of entitlement it had engendered in China. The satisfaction-guaranteed policy did not spell out specifically what dissatisfaction meant, something people in the Western world understood. "We thought that it would be understood here, too." The change in policy left some dissatisfied. One distributor protested, "Don't open a company if you can't afford losses." Despite these initial problems, Amway apparently is learning the market—the company doubled its sales last year in China to $2 billion. And other direct marketers are also finding similar success in China.

Sources: Craig S. Smith, "Distribution Remains the Key Problem for Market Makers," *Business China*, May 13, 1996, p. 4; "In China, Some Distributors Have Really Cleaned Up with Amway," *The Wall Street Journal*, August 4, 1997, p. B1; "Avon Forays into Healthcare Sector via Direct Sales," *SinoCast China Business Daily News*, January 14, 2008, p. 1; David Barboza, "Direct Selling Flourishes in China, Providing Jobs and Igniting Criticism," *The New York Times*, December 26, 2009, pp. B1, B5.

Direct sales through catalogs have proved to be a successful way to enter foreign markets. In Japan, it has been an important way to break the trade barrier imposed by the Japanese distribution system. For example, a U.S. mail-order company, Shop America, teamed up with 7-Eleven Japan to distribute catalogs in its 4,000 stores. Shop America sells items such as compact discs, Canon cameras, and Rolex watches for 30 to 50 percent less than Tokyo stores; a Canon Autoboy camera sells for $260 in Tokyo and $180 in the Shop America catalog.

Many catalog companies are finding they need to open telephone service centers in a country to accommodate customers who have questions or problems. Hanna Andersson (the children's clothing manufacturer), for example, received complaints that it was too difficult to get questions answered and to place orders by telephone, so it opened a service center with 24 telephone operators to assist customers who generate over $5 million in sales annually. Many catalog companies also have active Web sites that augment their catalog sales.

Resistance to Change.   Efforts to improve the efficiency of the distribution system, new types of middlemen, and other attempts to change traditional ways are typically viewed as threatening and are thus resisted. A classic example is the restructuring of the film distribution business being caused by the fast changing technologies of digitization and piracy. Laws abound that protect the entrenched in their positions. In Italy, a new retail outlet must obtain a license from a municipal board composed of local tradespeople. In a two-year period, some 200 applications were made and only 10 new licenses granted. Opposition to retail innovation is everywhere, yet in the face of all the restrictions and hindrances, self-service, discount merchandising, liberal store hours, and large-scale merchandising continue to grow because they offer the consumer convenience and a broad range of quality product brands at advantageous prices. Ultimately the consumer does prevail.

Alternative Middleman Choices

A marketer's options range from assuming the entire distribution activity (by establishing its own subsidiaries and marketing directly to the end user) to depending on intermediaries for distribution of the product. Channel selection must be given considerable thought, because once initiated, it is difficult to change, and if it proves inappropriate, future growth of market share may be affected.

The channel process includes all activities, beginning with the manufacturer and ending with the final consumer. This inclusion means the seller must exert influence over two sets of channels: one in the home country and one in the foreign-market country. Exhibit 15.3 shows some of the possible channel-of-distribution alternatives. The arrows show those to whom the producer and each of the middlemen might sell. In the home country, the seller must have an organization (generally the international marketing division of a company) to deal with channel members needed to move goods between countries. In the foreign market, the seller must supervise the channels that supply the product to the end user. Ideally, the company wants to control or be directly involved in the process through the various channel members to the final user. To do less may result in unsatisfactory distribution and the failure of marketing objectives. In practice, however, such involvement throughout the channel process is not always practical or cost effective. Consequently, selection of channel members and effective controls are high priorities in establishing the distribution process.

Once the marketer has clarified company objectives and policies, the next step is the selection of specific intermediaries needed to develop a channel. External middlemen are differentiated according to whether or not they take title to the goods: **Agent middlemen** work on commission and arrange for sales in the foreign country but do not take title to the merchandise. By using agents, the manufacturer assumes trading risk but maintains the right to establish policy guidelines and prices and to require its agents to provide sales records and customer information. **Merchant middlemen** actually take title to manufacturers' goods and assume the trading risks, so they tend to be less controllable than agent middlemen. Merchant middlemen provide a variety of import and export wholesaling functions involved in purchasing for their own account and selling in other countries. Because merchant middlemen primarily are concerned with sales and profit margins on their merchandise, they are frequently criticized for not representing the best interests of a manufacturer. Unless they have a franchise or a strong and profitable brand, merchant middlemen seek goods from any source and are likely to have low brand loyalty. Ease of contact, minimized credit risk, and elimination

Exhibit 15.3
International Channel-of-Distribution Alternatives

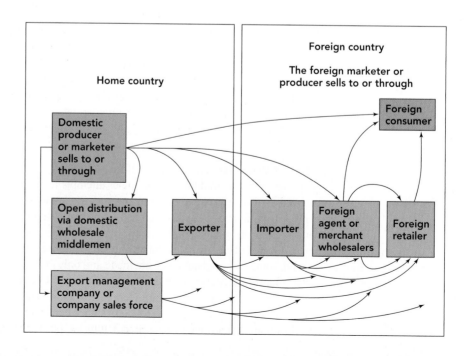

state's purchasing office deals with more than 10,000 suppliers in 20 countries. About one-third of the products purchased by that agency are produced outside the Netherlands. Finally, regarding the efficiency of the public sector versus the private sector, an important lesson was learned during the 2005 Hurricane Katrina disaster—Walmart planned for and delivered aid better than FEMA (the U.S Federal Emergency Management Agency).

Factors Affecting Choice of Channels

The international marketer needs a clear understanding of market characteristics and must have established operating policies before beginning the selection of channel middlemen. The following points should be addressed prior to the selection process:

1. Identify specific target markets within and across countries.
2. Specify marketing goals in terms of volume, market share, and profit margin requirements.
3. Specify financial and personnel commitments to the development of international distribution.
4. Identify control, length of channels, terms of sale, and channel ownership.

Once these points are established, selecting among alternative middlemen choices to forge the best channel can begin. Marketers must get their goods into the hands of consumers and must choose between handling all distribution or turning part or all of it over to various middlemen. Distribution channels vary depending on target market size, competition, and available distribution intermediaries.

Key elements in distribution decisions include the functions performed by middlemen (and the effectiveness with which each is performed), the cost of their services, their availability, and the extent of control that the manufacturer can exert over middlemen activities.

Although the overall marketing strategy of the firm must embody the company's profit goals in the short and long run, channel strategy itself is considered to have six specific strategic goals. These goals can be characterized as the six Cs of channel strategy: cost, capital, control, coverage, character, and continuity. In forging the overall channel-of-distribution strategy, each of the six Cs must be considered in building an economical, effective distribution organization within the long-range channel policies of the company. It should also be noted that many firms use multiple or hybrid channels of distribution because of the trade-offs associated with any one option. Indeed, both Dell selling computers at kiosks inside Japan's Jusco supermarkets and Toys "R" Us selling toys in food stores are good examples.

Cost

The two kinds of channel cost are (1) the capital or investment cost of developing the channel and (2) the continuing cost of maintaining it. The latter can be in the form of direct expenditure for the maintenance of the company's selling force or in the form of margins, markup, or commissions of various middlemen handling the goods. Marketing costs (a substantial part of which is channel cost) must be considered as the entire difference between the factory price of the goods and the price the customer ultimately pays for the merchandise. The costs of middlemen include transporting and storing the goods, breaking bulk, providing credit, local advertising, sales representation, and negotiations.

Despite the old truism that you can eliminate middlemen but you cannot eliminate their functions or cost, creative, efficient marketing does permit channel cost savings in many circumstances. Some marketers have found, in fact, that they can reduce cost by eliminating inefficient middlemen and thus shortening the channel. Mexico's largest producer of radio and television sets has built annual sales of $36 million on its ability to sell goods at a low price because it eliminated middlemen, established its own wholesalers, and kept margins low. Conversely, many firms accustomed to using their own sales forces in large-volume domestic markets have found they must lengthen channels of distribution to keep costs in line with foreign markets.

Capital Requirements

The financial ramifications of a distribution policy are often overlooked. Critical elements are capital requirement and cash-flow patterns associated with using a particular type of middleman. Maximum investment is usually required when a company establishes its own internal channels, that is, its own sales force. Use of distributors or dealers may lessen the capital investment, but manufacturers often have to provide initial inventories on consignment, loans, floor plans, or other arrangements. Coca-Cola initially invested in China with majority partners that met most of the capital requirements. However, Coca-Cola soon realized that it could not depend on its local majority partners to distribute its product aggressively in the highly competitive, market-share–driven business of carbonated beverages. To assume more control of distribution, it had to assume management control, and that meant greater capital investment from Coca-Cola. One of the highest costs of doing business in China is the capital required to maintain effective distribution.

Control

The more involved a company is with the distribution, the more control it exerts. A company's own sales force affords the most control but often at a cost that is not practical. Each type of channel arrangement provides a different level of control; as channels grow longer, the ability to control price,[19] volume, promotion, and type of outlets diminishes. If a company cannot sell directly to the end user or final retailer, an important selection criterion for middlemen should be the amount of control the marketer can maintain. Of course, there are risks in international distribution relationships as well—opportunism and exploitation are two. Finally, one of the most alarming examples of distribution channels out of control regards the current worldwide shortage of fish; retailers and distributors in affluent countries literally feed the demands of their voracious customers and kill the fisheries along the way.[20]

Coverage

Another major goal is full-market coverage to gain the optimum volume of sales obtainable in each market, secure a reasonable market share, and attain satisfactory market penetration. Coverage may be assessed by geographic segments, market segments, or both. Adequate market coverage may require changes in distribution systems from country to country or time to time. Coverage is difficult to extend both in highly developed areas and in sparse markets—the former because of heavy competition and the latter because of inadequate channels.

Many companies do not attempt full-market coverage but seek significant penetration in major population centers. In some countries, two or three cities constitute the majority of the national buying power. For instance, 60 percent of the Japanese population lives in the Tokyo–Nagoya–Osaka market area, which essentially functions as one massive city.

At the other extreme are many developing countries with a paucity of specialized middlemen except in major urban areas. Those that do exist are often small, with traditionally high margins. In China, for example, the often-cited billion-person market is, in reality, confined to fewer than 25 to 30 percent of the population of the most affluent cities. Even as personal income increases in China, distribution inadequacies limit marketers in reaching all those who have adequate incomes. In both extremes, the difficulty of developing an efficient channel from existing middlemen plus the high cost of distribution may nullify efficiencies achieved in other parts of the marketing mix.

To achieve coverage, a company may have to use many different channels—its own sales force in one country, manufacturers' agents in another, and merchant wholesalers in still another.

Character

The channel-of-distribution system selected must fit the character of the company and the markets in which it is doing business. Some obvious product requirements, often the first considered, relate to the perishability or bulk of the product, complexity of sale, sales service required, and value of the product.

---

[19]Ting-Jui Chou and Fu-Tang Chen, "Retail Pricing Strategies in Recession Economies: The Case of Taiwan," *Journal of International Marketing* 12, no. 1 (2004), pp. 82–102.

[20]"Japan's Tuna Crisis," *The New York Times*, June 27, 2007, p. A22; Elisabeth Rosenthal, "In Europe, the Catch of the Day is Often Illegal," *The New York Times*, January 15, 2008, pp. A1, A6.

You can buy just about anything at Stockmann's Department Store in Helsinki—men's and women's fashions, hardware (hammers, etc.) and software, bakery goods and garden supplies, fillet of reindeer and furniture, televisions—yes, everything from Audi A3s to zuccini. It even has cold storage services for your mink. But Stockmann's doesn't stock Samsung cell phones. The Korean company hasn't yet penetrated Nokia's home market. Of course, the product line is thin but rich at Cartier's in Paris. And you can find the Samsung at the Grand Bazaar (Kapali Carsi) in Istanbul, billed as the oldest and largest covered marketplace in the world. The 15th-century mall competes for customers with its 20th-century cousin, Akmerkez Etiler, in a high-income neighborhood about 10 miles away. Finally, Louis meets Lenin here on Red Square in Moscow. Russians now go for the luxury brands at the old government department store (still with the unattractive name, Gum), recently transformed into a 800,000 square foot in-door, high-end shopping mall. You can see St. Basil's Cathedral in the background, and just 200 meters across the square, Comrade Vladimir Lenin's embalmed body is entombed in a chilly mausoleum. While the old communist isn't too happy about free enterprise disturbing his view, he certainly must be pleased about the 2008 resumption of the annual Red Square May Day military parade after its seventeen-year hiatus.

Channel captains must be aware that channel patterns change; they cannot assume that once a channel has been developed to fit the character of both company and market, no more need be done. Great Britain, for example, has epitomized distribution through specialty-type middlemen, distributors, wholesalers, and retailers; in fact, all middlemen have traditionally worked within narrow product specialty areas. In recent years, however, there has been a trend toward broader lines, conglomerate merchandising, and mass marketing. The firm that neglects the growth of self-service, scrambled merchandising, or discounting may find it has lost large segments of its market because its channels no longer reflect the character of the market.

Continuity   Channels of distribution often pose longevity problems. Most agent middlemen firms tend to be small institutions. When one individual retires or moves out of a line of business, the company may find it has lost its distribution in that area. Wholesalers and especially retailers are not noted for their continuity in business either. Most middlemen have little loyalty to their vendors. They handle brands in good times when the line is making money but quickly reject such products within a season or a year if they fail to produce during that period. Distributors and dealers are probably the most loyal middlemen, but even with them, manufacturers must attempt to build brand loyalty downstream in a channel lest middlemen shift allegiance to other companies or other inducements.

Channel Management

The actual process of building channels for international distribution is seldom easy, and many companies have been stopped in their efforts to develop international markets by their inability to construct a satisfactory system of channels.

Construction of the middleman network includes seeking out potential middlemen, selecting those who fit the company's requirements, and establishing working relationships with them. In international marketing, the channel-building process is hardly routine. The closer the company wants to get to the consumer in its channel contact, the larger the sales force required. If a company is content with finding an exclusive importer or selling agent for a given country, channel building may not be too difficult; however, if it goes down to the level of subwholesaler or retailer, it is taking on a tremendous task and must have an internal staff capable of supporting such an effort.

Locating Middlemen

The search for prospective middlemen should begin with study of the market and determination of criteria for evaluating middlemen servicing that market. The checklist of criteria differs according to the type of middlemen being used and the nature of their relationship with the company. Basically, such lists are built around four subject areas: productivity or volume, financial strength, managerial stability and capability, and the nature and reputation of the business. Emphasis is usually placed on either the actual or potential productivity of the middleman.

The major problems are locating information to aid in the selection and choice of specific middlemen and discovering middlemen available to handle one's merchandise. Firms seeking overseas representation should compile a list of middlemen from such sources as the following: the U.S. Department of Commerce; commercially published directories; foreign consulates; chamber-of-commerce groups located abroad; other manufacturers producing similar but noncompetitive goods; middlemen associations; business publications; management consultants; carriers—particularly airlines; and Internet-based services such as Unibex, a global technology services provider. Unibex provides a platform for small- to medium-sized companies and larger enterprises to collaborate in business-to-business commerce.

Selecting Middlemen

LO5

The importance of selecting and maintaining middlemen

Finding prospective middlemen is less a problem than determining which of them can perform satisfactorily. Low volume or low potential volume hampers most prospects, many are underfinanced, and some simply cannot be trusted. In many cases, when a manufacturer is not well known abroad, the reputation of the middleman becomes the reputation of the manufacturer, so a poor choice at this point can be devastating.

Screening.   The screening and selection process itself should include the following actions: an exploratory letter or e-mail including product information and distributor requirements in the native language sent to each prospective middleman; a follow-up with the best respondents for specific information concerning lines handled, territory covered, size of firm, number of salespeople, and other background information; check of credit and references from other clients and customers of the prospective middleman; and, if possible, a personal check of the most promising firms. Obtaining financial information on prospective middlemen has become easier via such Internet companies as Unibex, which provides access to Dun & Bradstreet and other client information resources.

Experienced exporters suggest that the only way to select a middleman is to go personally to the country and talk to ultimate users of your product to find whom they consider to be the best distributors. Visit each possible middleman once before selecting the one to represent you; look for one with a key person who will take the new product to his or her heart and make it a personal objective to make the sale of that line a success. Furthermore, exporters stress that if you cannot sign one of the two or three customer-recommended distributors, you might be better off having no distributor in that country, because having a worthless one costs you time and money every year and may cut you out when you finally find a good one.

The Agreement.   Once a potential middleman has been found and evaluated, the task of detailing the arrangements with that middleman begins. So far the company has been in a buying position; now it must shift into a selling and negotiating position to convince the middleman to handle the goods and accept a distribution agreement that is workable for the company. Agreements must spell out specific responsibilities of the manufacturer and the middleman, including an annual sales minimum. The sales minimum serves as a basis for evaluation of the distributor; failure to meet sales minimums may give the exporter the right of termination.

Some experienced exporters recommend that initial contracts be signed for one year only. If the first year's performance is satisfactory, they should be reviewed for renewal for a longer period. This time limit permits easier termination, and more important, after a year of working together in the market, a more suitable arrangement generally can be reached.

Motivating Middlemen

The level of distribution and the importance of the individual middleman to the company determine the activities undertaken to keep the middleman motivated. On all levels, the middleman's motivation is clearly correlated with sales volume. Motivational techniques that can be employed to maintain middleman interest and support for the product may be grouped into five categories: financial rewards, psychological rewards, communications, company support, and corporate rapport.

Obviously, financial rewards must be adequate for any middleman to carry and promote a company's products. Margins or commissions must be set to meet the needs of the middleman and may vary according to the volume of sales and the level of services offered. Without a combination of adequate margin and adequate volume, a middleman cannot afford to give much attention to a product.

Being human, middlemen and their salespeople respond to psychological rewards and recognition of their efforts. A trip to the United States or to the parent company's home or regional office is a great honor. Publicity in company media and local newspapers also builds esteem and involvement among foreign middlemen.

In all instances, but particularly when cultural distances are great,[21] the company should maintain a continuing flow of communication in the form of letters, newsletters, and periodicals to all its middlemen. The more personal these are, the better. One study of exporters indicated that the more intense the contact between the manufacturer and the distributor, the better the performance by the distributor. More and better contact naturally leads to less conflict and a smoother working relationship, and relationships are key, particularly in relationship-oriented cultures in emerging markets.[22]

Finally, considerable attention must be paid to the establishment of close rapport between the company and its middlemen. In addition to methods noted, a company should be certain that the conflicts that arise are handled skillfully and diplomatically. Bear in mind that all over the world, business is a personal and vital thing to the people involved.

Terminating Middlemen

When middlemen do not perform up to standards or when market situations change, requiring a company to restructure its distribution, it may be necessary to terminate relationships. In the United States, this termination is usually a simple action regardless of the type of middlemen; they are simply dismissed. However, in other parts of the world, the middleman often has some legal protection that makes termination difficult. In Colombia, for example,

---

[21]Carl Arthur Solberg, "Product Complexity and Cultural Distance Effects on Managing International Distributor Relationships: A Contingency Approach," *Journal of International Marketing* 16, no. 3 (2008), pp. 57–83; Chenting Su, Zhilin Yang, Guijun Zhuang, Nan Zhou, and Wenyu Dou, "Interpersonal Influence as an Alternative Channel Communication Behavior in Emerging Markets: The Case of China," *Journal of International Business Studies* 40, no. 4 (2009), pp. 668–89.

[22]Gerald A. McDermott and Rafael A. Corredoira, "Network Composition, Collaborative Ties, and Upgrading In Emerging Market Firms: Lessons from the Argentine Autoparts Sector," *Journal of International Business Studies* 41, no. 2 (2010), pp. 308–29.

CROSSING BORDERS 15.3 | Managing the Humps in the Camel Market

BIRQASH, EGYPT—The sun is high and it's a slow day for selling and there's not much for a camel trader to do except scatter hay and greens and listen to the big beasts munch. Sounds like shoes walking through gravel.

Essam Ammar lifts a cell phone from his tunic. "Hi, Ahmed. No, I won't lower the price." Eyes roll. Ammar pulls the phone from his ear and looks at it; Ahmed's words crackle in the air. Click. It's not even noon. The day seems in retreat.

"I've been doing this for 29 years," says Ammar, who wears a white-lace cap and an even snowier pinstriped vest, a risky choice amid blowing dust and rubbish fires. "You have to know your camels, setting price to age. The best come from Sudan. The ones from Somalia don't adapt so well. I can tell if a camel will bite me or just run away. It is essential to know such things." The traders around him, some with blood splotches on their tunics, nod.

The Birqash camel market about 20 miles northwest of downtown Cairo is an unfortunate place to end up if you have four legs and a long neck. It's not so great these days for camel traders either. Herdsmen in Sudan and Somalia are pushing up prices but the traders—the middlemen—often can't pass the increases on to hard-pressed butchers in Cairo and across the Nile Delta. Egypt's inflation is keeping many families from buying camel, the traditional meat they ate when beef and mutton grew too expensive. It's the cruel global economic ripple that finds even the battered crossroads of places like Birqash.

"I'm making about 5,000 pounds [$915] less each year because camel prices are rising and butchers can't afford to buy and people can't afford the price of meat," says trader Ali Hamed, who hasn't seen his wife in months. "I'm married, with two children. I used to send home 350 pounds [$65] a week but now can only manage 150 pounds [$28]. My wife does the best she can. I'd like to go home more, but for the price of a train ticket I can buy two bags of wheat to feed my family."

Hamed lives in southern Egypt. His father traded camels and Hamed, who never went to school, figured that's what village boys grew up to do. Instead of a book bag, he picked up a herding stick and started

learning about camels traveling north from Sudan along the Nile or arriving in freighters from Somalia at the port of Suez. They are white, beige, the color of sand and gray. A camel can be healthy one day and die the next; it is a mystery of the trade.

Boys with bottles and brushes mark camels for sale with purple and green letters. They dart around legs, beneath tails, careful not to be kicked, and some of them will inherit a stall on market row when they become men. A trader doesn't just appear here; he is raised on stories of uncles and cousins who shoveled dung and tended wounds and cursed sick camels long before he was born.

"This market is controlled by 10 to 15 families," says Abdel Wahab Wagih, the market historian and man who keeps an eye on what enters and leaves through the gate. "The traders inherited the businesses from their fathers and grandfathers. The younger generations got educated and many of them have university degrees, but they still come here to run the family trade."

The price of camel meat has been expanding too. In the last year camel has risen from $1.80 a pound to as much as $2.90 a pound, still cheaper than beef and mutton, but costly enough that many Egyptians have crossed it off their shopping lists.

It used to be easier, though…. Taxes are higher and the Egyptian government has new health regulations and stricter inspections for camels entering the country. Some wait for days and weeks at the borders, where healthy camels are exposed to sick ones. One trader had 30 camels die before they reached the market. It all means money. Lost money.

"It's strange, you know, Egypt is a poor country but there are still a lot of rich people and they keep getting richer," Ammar says. "I guess that's how it's supposed to be."

His cell phone rings. "Hi, Ahmed." Ammar inspects his fingernails, yawns. "No, Ahmed, I'm not lowering the price." Click.

Source: Jefrey Fleishman, "Camel Trade Runs into Sand," *Los Angeles Times*, October 23, 2009, pp. A1, A29. Copyright © 2009. Reprinted with permission.

if you terminate an agent, you are required to pay 10 percent of the agent's average annual compensation, multiplied by the number of years the agent served, as a final settlement.

Competent legal advice is vital when entering distribution contracts with middlemen. But as many experienced international marketers know, the best rule is to avoid the need to terminate distributors by screening all prospective middlemen carefully. A poorly chosen distributor may not only fail to live up to expectations but may also adversely affect future business and prospects in the country.

Controlling Middlemen

The extreme length of channels typically used in international distribution makes control of middlemen especially important. Marketing objectives must be spelled out both internally and to middlemen as explicitly as possible. Standards of performance should include the sales volume objective, inventory turnover ratio, number of accounts per area, growth objective, price stability objective, and quality of publicity. Cultural differences enter into all these areas of management.[23]

Control over the system and control over middlemen are necessary in international business. The first relates to control over the distribution network, which implies overall controls for the entire system to be certain the product is flowing through desired middlemen. Some manufacturers have lost control through "secondary wholesaling" or parallel imports.[24] A company's goods intended for one country are sometimes diverted through distributors to another country, where they compete with existing retail or wholesale organizations.

The second type of control is at the middleman level. When possible, the parent company should know (and to a certain degree control) the activities of middlemen with respect to their volume of sales, market coverage, services offered, prices, advertising, payment of bills, and even profit. Quotas, reports, and personal visits by company representatives can be effective in managing middleman activities at any level of the channel.

The Internet

LO6

The growing importance of e-commerce as a distribution alternative

The Internet is an important distribution method for multinational companies and a source of products for businesses and consumers.[25] Indeed, a good argument can be made that the Internet has finally put the consumer in control of marketing and distribution globally.[26] Computer hardware and software companies and book and music retailers were the earliest e-marketers to use this method of distribution and marketing.[27] More recently there has been an expansion of other types of retailing and business-to-business (B2B) services into e-commerce.[28] Technically, e-commerce is a form of direct selling; however, because of its newness and the unique issues associated with this form of distribution, it is important to differentiate it from other types of direct marketing.

E-commerce is used to market B2B services, consumer services, and consumer and industrial products via the World Wide Web. It involves the direct marketing from a manufacturer, retailer, service provider, or some other intermediary to a final user. Some examples of e-marketers that have an international presence are Dell Computer Corporation[29] (www.dell.com), which generates nearly 50 percent of its total sales, an average of about $69 million a day, online; and Cisco Systems (www.cisco.com), which generates more than $1 billion in sales annually. Cisco's Web site appears in 14 languages and has country-specific content for 49 nations. Gateway has global sites in Japan, France, the Netherlands, Germany, Sweden, Australia, the United Kingdom, and the United States, to name a few (www.gateway.com). Sun Microsystems and its after-marketing company, SunExpress, have local-language information about more than 3,500 aftermarket products. SunPlaza enables visitors in North America, Europe, and Japan to get information online about products and services and to place orders directly in their native languages.

[23]Jody Evans and Felix T. Mavondo, "Psychic Distance and Organizational Performance: An Empirical Examination of International Retailing Operations," *Journal of International Business Studies* 33, no. 3 (2002), pp. 515–32; David A. Griffith and Matthew B. Myers, "The Performance Implications of Strategic Fit of Relational Norm Governance Strategies in Global Supply Chain Relationships," *Journal of International Business Studies* 36, no. 3 (2005), pp. 254–69.

[24]See the discussion of parallel imports in Chapter 18.

[25]Vinh Nhat Lu and Craig C. Julian, "The Internet, Strategy and Performance: A Study of Australian Export Market Ventures," *Journal of Global Marketing* 21, no. 3 (2008), pp. 231–40.

[26]"Crowned at Last, A Survey of Consumer Power," *The Economist*, April 2, 2005, insert pp. 1–16.

[27]"A Giant Sucking Sound," *The Economist,* November 7, 2009, p. 62.

[28]Carlyle Farrell, "The Role of the Internet in the Delivery of Export Promotion Services: A Web Site Content Analysis," *Journal of Global Marketing* 21, no. 4 (2008), pp. 259–70.

[29]Evan Ramstad and Gary McWilliams, "For Dell, Success in China Tells a Tale of Maturing Market," *The Wall Street Journal*, July 5, 2005, pp. A1, A8.

Besides consumer goods companies such as Lands' End, Levi, and Nike, many smaller[30] and less well-known companies have established a presence on the Internet beyond their traditional markets. An Internet customer from the Netherlands can purchase a pair of brake levers for his mountain bike from California-based Price Point. He pays $130 instead of the $190 that the same items would cost in a local bike store.

For a Spanish shopper in Pamplona, buying sheet music used to mean a 400-kilometer trip to Madrid. Now he crosses the Atlantic to shop—and the journey takes less time than a trip to the corner store. Via the Internet, he can buy directly from specialized stores and high-volume discounters in New York, London, and almost anywhere else.

E-commerce is more developed in the United States than the rest of the world, partly because of the vast number of people who own personal computers and partly because of the much lower cost of access to the Internet than found elsewhere. In addition to language, legal, and cultural differences, the cost of local phone calls (which are charged by the minute in most European countries) initially discouraged extensive use and contributed to slower Internet adoption in Europe.

Services, the third engine for growth, are ideally suited for international sales via the Internet. All types of services—banking, education, consulting, retailing, hotels, gambling—can be marketed through a Web site that is globally accessible. As outsourcing of traditional in-house tasks such as inventory management, quality control, and accounting, secretarial, translation, and legal services has become more popular among companies, the Internet providers of these services have grown both in the United States and internationally.

Moreover, online B2B enables companies to cut costs in three ways. First, it reduces procurement costs by making it easier to find the cheapest supplier, and it cuts the cost of processing the transactions. Estimates suggest that a firm's possible savings from purchasing over the Internet vary from 2 percent in the coal industry to up to 40 percent in electronic components. British Telecom claims that procuring goods and services online will reduce the average cost of processing a transaction by 90 percent and reduce the direct costs of goods and services it purchases by 11 percent. The Ford, GM, and DaimlerChrysler exchange network for buying components from suppliers could reduce the cost of making a car by as much as 14 percent.

Second, it allows better supply-chain management. For example, more than 75 percent of all Cisco orders now occur online, up from 4 percent in 1996. This connection to the supply chain allowed Cisco to reduce order cycle time from six to eight weeks to one to three weeks and to increase customer satisfaction as well.

Third, it makes possible tighter inventory control. With Walmart's direct Internet links between its inventory control system and its suppliers, each sale automatically triggers a replenishment request. Fewer out-of-stock situations, the ability to make rapid inventory adjustments, and reduced ordering and processing costs have made Walmart one of the industry's most efficient companies.

The worldwide potential for firms operating on the Internet is extraordinary, but only if they are positioned properly[31] and well supported by management.[32] The World Wide Web, as a market, is rapidly moving through the stage where the novelty of buying on the Web is giving way to a more sophisticated customer who has more and constantly improving Web sites from which to choose. In short, Web merchants are facing more competition, and Web customers have more choice. This situation means that if a company is going to be successful in this new era of marketing, the basics of good marketing cannot be overlooked. For example, Forrester Research has discovered that nearly half the international orders received by U.S. companies go unfilled, even though a typical U.S. company can expect 30 percent of its Web traffic to come from foreign countries and 10 percent of its orders to come from abroad.

---

[30]Oystein Moen, Iver Endresen, and Morten Gavlen, "Use of the Internet in International Marketing: A Case Study of Small Computer Software Firms," *Journal of International Marketing* 11, no. 4 (2003), pp. 129–49.

[31]Byeong-Joon Moon and Subash C. Jain, "Determinants of Outcomes of Internet Marketing Activities of Exporting Firms," *Journal of Global Marketing* 20 (2007), pp. 55–72.

[32]Gary Gregory, Munib Karavdic, and Shoaming Zou, "The Effects of E-Commerce on Export Marketing Strategy," *Journal of International Marketing* 15 (2007), pp. 30–57.

CROSSING BORDERS 15.4

One of the Many Dark Sides of the Internet:
Growing Organ-Supply Shortfall Creates
Windfall for Online Brokers

Growing demand for organ transplants worldwide is bringing new clout to online middlemen who charge ailing customers enormous fees to match them with scarce body parts.

These brokers have stepped in to fill a breach created by steep shortfall in supply. In rich nations, people are living longer at the same time that a drop in deaths from automobile accidents has shrunk a key source of donated organs. Because buying and selling organs is illegal almost everywhere, brokers say they match prospective patients with sources outside their own country's health system. *Forbes* located offers of transplants online priced at anywhere from 60 to 400 percent more than their typical costs. One California broker arranges kidney transplants for $140,000 and hearts, livers and lungs for $290,000. Most of these transplants are being carried

out in hospitals in developing countries, where medical and ethical standards "don't rise to Western levels."

More alarmingly, the Web sites that shill transplant deals might just be camouflaging a more nefarious business: underground organ trading. Desperate "transplant tourists" generally cannot determine whether an organ was harvested legally or if the kidney they are receiving was sold by a destitute Nepali or Brazilian, often for as little as $800. In China, authorities admitted two years ago that they have been harvesting organs from executed prisoners. Recently Beijing has agree to stop this controversial practice.

Sources: "Growing Organ-Supply Shortfall," *The Wall Street Journal*, January 12, 2007, p. B4 (from *Forbes*, January 29); "Challenge Now Is To Find Other Sources of Organs," *South China Morning Post*, October 2, 2007, p. 15.

By its very nature, e-commerce has some unique issues that must be addressed if a domestic e-vendor expects to be a viable player in the international cybermarketplace. International legal issues were discussed in Chapter 7. Particularly, high-flying Google is under censorship attack and other kinds of controls[33] in both China[34] and Italy.[35] Many other issues arise because the host-country intermediary who would ordinarily be involved in international marketing is eliminated. An important advantage of selling direct is that total costs can be lowered so that the final price overseas is considerably less than it would have been through a local-country middleman. However, such activities as translating prospective customer inquiries and orders into English and replying in the customer's language, traditionally done by a local distributor, have to be done by someone. When intermediaries are eliminated, someone, either the seller or the buyer, must assume the functions they performed. Consequently, an e-vendor must be concerned with the following issues.

1. **Culture.** The preceding chapters on culture should not be overlooked when doing business over the Web. The Web site and the product must be culturally neutral or adapted to fit the uniqueness of a market, because culture does matter.[36] In Japan, the pickiness of Japanese consumers about what they buy and their reluctance to deal with merchants at a distance must be addressed when marketing on the Web. Even a Japanese-language site can offend Japanese sensibilities. As one e-commerce consultant warns: in a product description, you wouldn't say "Don't turn the knob left," because that's too direct. Instead, you would say something like: "It would be much better to turn the knob to the right." To many Europeans, American sites come off as having too many bells and whistles because European sites are more consumer oriented. The different cultural reactions to color can be a potential problem for Web

---

[33]"Google Offers Free Web Music in China," *Los Angeles Times*, March 31, 2009, p. B3.

[34]Juliet Ye, "Chinese Video Takes Aim at Online Censorship," *The Wall Street Journal*, February 11, 2010, online.

[35]Adam Liptak, "When Free Worlds Collide," *The New York Times*, February 28, 2010, p. Opinion 1.

[36]Kai H. Lim, Kwok Leung, Choon Ling Sia, and Matthew K. Lee, "Is eCommerce Boundary-less? Effects of Individualism-Collectivism and Uncertainty Avoidance on Internet Shopping," *Journal of International Business Studies* 35, no. 6 (2004), pp. 545–59; Jan-Benedict E. M. Steenkamp and Inge Geyskens, "How Country Characteristics Affect the Perceived Value of Web Sites," *Journal of Marketing* 70 (2006), pp. 136–50.

Global Marketing on the Web at Marriott

The Internet today is the most global of any media invented so far, having leapfrogged television and radio—which may yet become global some day but are far from doing so. It is the only medium that approaches true global reach. The power of the Internet results from its many unique attributes. It is unique in its ability to:

- Encompass text, audio and video in one platform.
- Operate in a dialogue versus monologue mode.
- Operate simultaneously as mass media *and* personalized media.
- Build global "communities," unconfined by national borders.

These attributes make it the most powerful medium on earth, unparalleled in its ability to communicate, especially to a global world. It is an international marketer's dream.

However, leveraging these characteristics in an effective manner requires dealing with various substantive issues. These issues include:

- Major differences in Internet adoption rates across the globe ranging from greater than 70 percent adoption in North America to less than 2 percent for the continent of Africa. This difference greatly influences the role of the Web as part of the marketing mix in international markets. Even for advanced EU economies, the variability of adoption is great, ranging from 88 percent in the Netherlands to 49 percent in Belgium. The average for the entire continent of Africa is around 1 percent (see www.internetworldstats.com).

- Unique issues caused by technology including broadband versus narrow-band, which drive what products and services can be marketed and how. In the narrow-band world, highly graphic and video-based Web sites are not viable. An example is the elaborate photo tours of hotels on www.Marriott.com, which download quickly on broadband connections but take inordinately long on narrow band. Therefore, a site designed for one market can be ineffective in another.

Renaissance is a Marriott-owned hotel brand. It uses various media to lead customers to its all-important Web sites, including print, television, Internet, and outdoor. Three 2-page print ads are directed toward U.K., Middle Eastern, and Chinese customers, and each of them lists the Web site addresses—the first two citing www.renaissancehotels. co.uk, and the last noting www. renaissancehotels.com.cn. Even though the same Web site ultimately serves customers in both the United Kingdom and the Middle East, the ad presentation is adapted to the more conservative dress appropriate in the latter region. Finally, you can see how the campaign is also used on the streets of Shanghai. Ask your classmates what "Be fashionable" translates into on the latter two ads.

- Costs to globalize can be enormous if multiple language sites need to be built. For example, translating the 110,000-page Marriott.com Web site is a very costly undertaking, both on a one-time and ongoing basis. Add to that the costs of translating the back-end systems that feed the site, and the costs rise exponentially. For sites with a lot of constantly changing content and heavy dependence on back-end systems, maintaining foreign language sites can be prohibitively expensive.

- Implications of differing labor costs that affect return on investment (ROI). For example, in the United States, the cost of an online booking for Marriott is less than half that of a phone booking. That differential may not apply in many Third World countries, where labor costs are often very low, making it difficult to justify a Web site investment.

- Different approaches to privacy, access, and infrastructure investment also require changes to strategy by market.

  - On privacy. For example, EU laws are much more stringent than U.S. laws; as a result, the e-mail marketing strategy in the European Union is much more cautious than in the United States.

  - On access. Some countries regulate access to the Internet. For example, China only allows access to approved sites, whereas the United States does not limit Internet access.

  - On infrastructure investment. Some countries have private investment fueling the development of the telecom technology systems required to enable Internet access (e.g., the United States), whereas in other countries, state-owned phone companies have this responsibility. In general, markets that have depended state investment have been laggards in the Internet space.

Apart from all of these issues, one of the most important challenges for companies contemplating a global Internet presence is determining whether they should build "foreign market sites" or "foreign language sites." In an ideal world, with infinite resources, the answer could be to build both. However, that option is rarely possible given resource constraints. This challenge has been a key issue for Marriott International, which has responded in different ways, depending on market situations. In some cases, the hotel company tried one approach before moving to the other. In fact, Marriott's experience in this area is an excellent illustration of the issue. To clarify the issue using France or French as an example, the question was:

Should we have a global site in French that caters to ALL French-speaking customers, no matter which country they live in

OR

Should we have a site in the French language, which addresses the needs of the LOCAL French market?

Having a French language site for a global French-speaking market had significant benefits, because there is a sizable French-speaking population in the world, which includes major parts of North and Central Africa and the Caribbean islands. However, in this case, Marriot decided in favor of a local site for France. In summary, the company found that

- The needs of French customers living in France were very different from the needs of customers in French-speaking Africa or Haiti. Customers living in France prefer different destinations than those living in other French-speaking areas, such as the Caribbean.

- Promotional approaches were also different for France than for other French-speaking countries. Using a U.S. example to illustrate, sweepstakes are far more popular and accepted in the United States than in Europe.

- Finally, the French market dwarfed all other French-speaking markets combined. Therefore, if Marriott could only afford to maintain one French site, it was more cost effective to address the largest French market, namely, France.

In 2009 and 2010 Marriott International faced increased pressure from the Province of Quebec authorities in that their French language site did not meet the needs of their local population and thus, was not compliant with their local laws. In the face of fines and other business actions by the Quebec authorities, Marriott International revised their strategy concerning a French language site and decided for a change of strategy in order to be compliant with local Canada laws while at the same time continue to serve the greater France area – France, Belgium, Switzerland, the Levant and the Maghreb. It is now working to turn its France site into a French language portal, which will be released this summer, following its very successful strategy in the Latin America market; i.e. one portal for the entire region that can serve many customers across the different Francophone markets in the world where it operates.

The second series of banner ads might flash across a computer screen in China; the last panel asks visitors to click to go to the Marriott Web site there. Marriott maintains 11 Web sites to attract its global clientele to its 2,800 hotels around the world. The sites appeal to consumers in the following countries: the United States, the United Kingdom, Ireland, Australia and New Zealand, France, Germany, China, Japan, South Korea, Latin America (Spanish/Espanol), and Brazil.

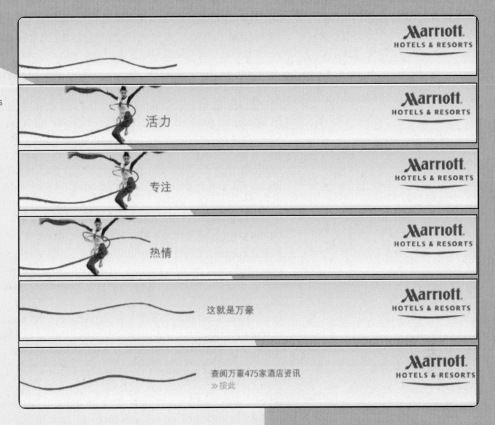

Thus, as Marriott's globalization program evolves, we see a combination of market and language approaches, deploying them across diverse markets in varied combinations as it makes the most sense for its business needs.

Paradoxically, when faced with the same question for Spanish—a Spanish-language site or a site for Spain/individual Spanish-speaking countries—Marriott decided to go for a Spanish-language site for several key reasons:

- None of the Spanish-speaking markets was very large for Marriott. Although Spain is the largest economy in the Spanish-speaking world, as of now, the company does not have enough hotels there or enough traffic from Spain to cost effectively build a site uniquely for Spain. That applies to all other Spanish-speaking countries.

- There was greater commonality of destinations among many Spanish-speaking countries—especially the Latin American countries—than among French-speaking countries. For example, the United States is an equally popular destination for almost all Latin American countries.

Ironically, Marriott initially took the opposite approach to the same question, resulting in eight Spanish sites for various Latin American countries. However, it quickly found that it was impractical to build, manage, and maintain so many sites and get the returns on investment it desired. Although this scenario may and should change as the individual markets mature and gain critical mass, it appears that it will take some years. Until then, Marriott will maintain one Spanish-language site.

In summary, the international online marketplace is highly complex and continues to evolve. There is no single approach that fits every situation; even when that appears the case, it may not be for long, as is clear from the experience described. A key focus therefore should be on making good trade-off decisions and maintaining flexibility in strategy.

Source: Shafiq Khan, Senior Vice President eCommerce with Luis Babicek, Marriott International, 2010. (Photos Courtesy of Marriott.)

sites designed for global markets. While red may be highly regarded in China or associated with love in the United States, in Spain it is associated with socialism. The point is that when designing a Web site, culture cannot be forgotten.

2. **Adaptation.** Ideally, a Web site should be translated into the languages of the target markets.[37] This translation may not be financially feasible for some companies, but at least the most important pages of the site should be translated. Simple translation of important pages is only a stopgap measure however. If companies are making a long-term commitment to sales in another country, Web pages should be designed (in all senses of the term—color, use features, etc.) for that market. One researcher suggests that if a Web site does not have at least multiple languages, a company is losing sales. It is the company's responsibility to bridge the language and cultural gap; the customer will not bother—he or she will simply go to a site that speaks his or her language. As discussed, culture does count, and as competition increases, a country-specific Web site may make the difference between success and failure.[38]

3. **Local contact.** Companies fully committed to foreign markets are creating virtual offices abroad; they buy server space and create mirror sites, whereby a company has a voice mail or fax contact point in key markets. Foreign customers are more likely to visit sites in their own country and in the local language. In Japan, where consumers seem particularly concerned about the ability to return goods easily, companies may have outlets where merchandise can be returned and picked up. These so-called click-and-mortar models have gained a large following.

4. **Payment.** The consumer should be able to use a credit card number—by e-mail (from a secure page on the Web site), by fax, or over the phone. Although this accessibility had been an important problem in burgeoning markets like China, customers and banking systems there are now beginning to catch on fast.[39]

5. **Delivery.** For companies operating in the United States, surface postal delivery of small parcels is the most cost effective but takes the longest time. For more rapid but more expensive deliveries, FedEx, UPS, and other private delivery services provide delivery worldwide. For example, Tom Clancy's bestseller *Executive Orders,* shipped express to Paris from Seattle-based Amazon.com, would cost a reader $55.52. The same book delivered in 4 to 10 weeks via surface mail costs $25.52, which is a substantial savings over the cost of the book in a Paris bookstore, where it sells for $35.38.

6. **Promotion.** Although the Web is a means of promotion, if you are engaging in e-commerce, you also need to advertise your presence and the products or services offered. The old adage "Build a better mouse trap and the world will beat a path to your door" does not work for e-commerce, just as it does not work with other products unless you tell your target market about the availability of the "better mouse trap." How do you attract visitors from other countries to your Web site? The same way you would at home—except in the local language. Search engine registration, press releases, local newsgroups and forums, mutual links, and banner advertising are the traditional methods. A Web site should be seen as a retail store, with the only difference between it and a physical store being that the customer arrives over the Internet instead of on foot.

When discussing the Internet and international channels of distribution, the question of how traditional channels will be changed by the Internet must be considered. Already, comparison shopping across the Continent via the Internet is wrenching apart commercial

---

[37]Barbar De Lollis, "Travel Firms Aim To Speak Customers' Language," *USA Today,* February 12, 2007, p. B1.

[38]Patrick Y. K. Chau, Melissa Cole, Anne P. Massey, Mitzi Montoya-Weiss, and Robert O'Keefe, "Cultural Differences in the On-Line Behavior of Consumers," *Communications of the ACM* 45, no. 10 (2002), pp. 138–43.

[39]Bruce Einhorn and Chi-Chu Tschang, "China's E-Tail Awakening," *BusinessWeek,* November 19, 2007, p. 44.

Production and Cost Limitations

Creativity is especially important when a budget is small or where there are severe production limitations, such as poor-quality printing and a lack of high-grade paper. For example, the poor quality of high-circulation glossy magazines and other quality publications in eastern Europe has caused Colgate-Palmolive to depart from its customary heavy use of print media in the West for other media. Newsprint is of such low quality in China that a color ad used by Kodak in the West is not an option. Kodak's solution has been to print a single-sheet color insert as a newspaper supplement.

The necessity for low-cost reproduction in small markets poses another problem in many countries. For example, hand-painted billboards must be used instead of printed sheets because the limited number of billboards does not warrant the production of printed sheets. In Egypt, static-filled television and poor-quality billboards have led companies such as Coca-Cola and Nestlé to place their advertisements on the sails of feluccas, boats that sail along the Nile. Feluccas, with their triangle sails, have been used to transport goods since the time of the pharaohs and serve as an effective alternative to attract attention to company names and logos.

Media Planning and Analysis

LO6

The effect of limited media, excessive media, and government regulations on advertising and promotion budgets

Few doubt that a revolution in communications is under way. Your authors notice it because the changes that occur between the two-year revisions of this textbook are the greatest when it comes to media. Yes, political events and natural disasters can dramatically impact many millions of people overnight, but the network effects of the burgeoning electronic communication media—in the form of PCs, the Internet, and mobile phones—influence not only political events and responses to national disasters but also everyday life for everyone on the planet, from camel markets in Egypt to the international space stations where humans are living off the planet! Perhaps the most eloquent description of the communications revolution comes from Bob Garfield's new book, *The Chaos Scenario*:

> … let me just share the 2007 comments of Sir Martin Sorrell, chairman of the WPP Group, the world's largest advertising agency holding company:
>
> "Slowly, the new media will cease to be thought of as new media; they will simply be additional channels of communication. And like all media that were once new but are now just media, they'll earn a well-deserved place in the media repertoire, perhaps through reverse takeovers—*but will almost certainly displace none.*"
>
> The italics are mine. The absurdity was Sir Martin's. Does he not see that the internet is not just some newfangled medium—like TV displacing radio? No, it is a revolutionary advance, along the lines of fire, agriculture, the wheel, the printing press, gunpowder, electricity, radio, manned flight, antibiotics, atomic energy…. The digital revolution is already having far-ranging effects on every aspect of our lives, from socialization to communication to information to entertainment to democracy, and these Brave New World effects will only be magnified as the Cowardly Old World collapses before our eyes. Not that this *will* happen.
>
> This *is* happening. Right now.[31]

Strong words from Mr. Garfield, but we agree with his principle point. The changes in media in the 21st century are proceeding at a blinding speed. Next we try to capture them, with due respect to the disrupted world of Sir Sorrell.

Tactical Considerations

Although nearly every sizable nation essentially has the same kinds of media, a number of specific considerations, problems, and differences are encountered from one nation to another. In international advertising, an advertiser must consider the availability, cost, coverage, and appropriateness of the media. And the constant competitive churn among these media makes for a tricky and dynamic landscape for decisions. For example, billboard ads next to highways cannot include paragraphs of text. Moreover, recent research has demonstrated that media effectiveness varies across cultures and product types; Chinese

---

[31]Bob Garfield, *The Chaos Scenario* (Nashville, TN: Stielstra Publishing, 2009), p. 11.

consumers in both Taiwan and China view print ads more positively than Americans, for example.[32] Local variations and lack of market data require added attention. Major multinationals are beginning to recognize the importance of planning communications channels as media companies continue to rationalize and evolve. Indeed, media giants such as Disney and Time Warner cover an increasingly broad spectrum of the electronic media, necessitating that MNCs rethink their relationships with media service providers.

Imagine the ingenuity required of advertisers confronted with these situations:

- In Brazil, TV commercials are sandwiched together in a string of 10 to 50 commercials within one station break.

- National coverage in many countries means using as many as 40 to 50 different media.

- Specialized media reach small segments of the market only. In the Netherlands, there are Catholic, Protestant, socialist, neutral, and other specialized broadcasting systems.

- In Germany, TV scheduling for an entire year must be arranged by August 30 of the preceding year, with no guarantee that commercials intended for summer viewing will not be run in the middle of winter.

- In Vietnam, advertising in newspapers and magazines is limited to 10 percent of space and to 5 percent of time, or three minutes an hour, on radio and TV.

Availability.   One of the contrasts of international advertising is that some countries have too few advertising media and others have too many. In some countries, certain advertising media are forbidden by government edict to accept some advertising materials. Such restrictions are most prevalent in radio and television broadcasting. In many countries, there are too few magazines and newspapers to run all the advertising offered to them. Conversely, some nations segment the market with so many newspapers that the advertiser cannot gain effective coverage at a reasonable cost. One head of an Italian advertising agency commented about his country: "One fundamental rule. You cannot buy what you want."

In China the only national TV station, CCTV, has one channel that must be aired by the country's 27 provincial/municipal stations. Recently CCTV auctioned off the most popular break between the early evening news and weather; a secured year-long, daily five-second billboard ad in this break went for $38.5 million. For this price, advertisers are assured of good coverage—more than 70 percent of households have TV sets. One of the other options for advertisers is with the 2,828 TV stations that provide only local coverage.

Cost.   Media prices are susceptible to negotiation in most countries. Agency space discounts are often split with the client to bring down the cost of media. The advertiser may find that the cost of reaching a prospect through advertising depends on the agent's bargaining ability. The per contract cost varies widely from country to country. One study showed that the cost of reaching 1,000 readers in 11 different European countries ranged from $1.58 in Belgium to $5.91 in Italy; in women's service magazines, the page cost per 1,000 circulation ranged from $2.51 in Denmark to $10.87 in Germany. Shortages of advertising time on commercial television in some markets have caused substantial price increases. In Britain, prices escalate on a bidding system. They do not have fixed rate cards; instead, there is a preempt system in which advertisers willing to pay a higher rate can bump already-scheduled spots.

Coverage.   Closely akin to the cost dilemma is the problem of coverage. Two points are particularly important: One relates to the difficulty of reaching certain sectors of the population with advertising and the other to the lack of information about coverage. In many world marketplaces, a wide variety of media must be used to reach the majority of

---

[32]Carrie La Ferle, Steven M. Edwards, and Wei-Na Lee, "Culture, Attitudes, and Media Patterns in China, Taiwan, and the U.S.: Balancing Standardization and Localization Decisions, *Journal of Global Marketing* 21, no. 3 (2008), pp. 191–206.

the markets. In some countries, large numbers of separate media have divided markets into uneconomical advertising segments. With some exceptions, a majority of the population of less developed countries cannot be reached readily through the traditional mass medium of advertising. In India, video vans are used to reach India's rural population with 30-minute infomercials extolling the virtues of a product. Consumer goods companies deploy vans year-round except in the monsoon season. Colgate hires 85 vans at a time and sends them to villages that research has shown to be promising.

Because of the lack of adequate coverage by any single medium in eastern European countries, companies must resort to a multimedia approach. In the Czech Republic, for example, TV advertising rates are high, and the lack of available prime-time spots has forced companies to use billboard advertising. In Slovenia the availability of adequate media is such a problem that companies resort to some unusual approaches to get their messages out. For example, in the summer, lasers are used to project images onto clouds above major cities. Vehicle advertising includes cement-mixers, where Kodak ads have appeared. On the positive side, crime is so low that products can be displayed in freestanding glass cabinets on sidewalks; Bosch Siemens (Germany) and Kodak have both used this method.

Lack of Market Data.   Verification of circulation or coverage figures is a difficult task. Even though many countries have organizations similar to the Audit Bureau of Circulation in the United States, accurate circulation and audience data are not assured. For example, the president of the Mexican National Advertisers Association charged that newspaper circulation figures are grossly exaggerated. He suggested that as a rule, agencies should divide these figures in two and take the result with a grain of salt. The situation in China is no better; surveys of habits and market penetration are available only for the cities of Beijing, Shanghai, and Guangzhou. Radio and television audiences are always difficult to measure, but at least in most countries, geographic coverage is known. Research data are becoming more reliable as advertisers and agencies demand better quality data.

Even where advertising coverage can be measured with some accuracy, there are questions about the composition of the market reached. Lack of available market data seems to characterize most international markets; advertisers need information on income, age, and geographic distribution, but such basic data seem chronically elusive except in the largest markets. Even the attractiveness of global television (satellite broadcasts) is diminished somewhat because of the lack of media research available.

An attempt to evaluate specific characteristics of each medium is beyond the scope of this discussion. Furthermore, such information would quickly become outdated because of the rapid changes in the international advertising media field. It may be interesting, however, to examine some of the unique international characteristics of various advertising media. In most instances, the major implications of each variation may be discerned from the data presented.

Newspapers.   The newspaper industry is suffering from lack of competition in some countries and choking because of it in others. Most U.S. cities have just one or two major daily newspapers, but in many countries, there are so many newspapers that an advertiser has trouble achieving even partial market coverage. Uruguay, population 3 million, has 21 daily newspapers with a combined circulation of 553,000. Turkey has 380 newspapers, and an advertiser must consider the political position of each newspaper so that the product's reputation is not harmed through affiliation with unpopular positions. Japan has only five national daily newspapers, and the complications of producing a Japanese-language newspaper are such that they each contain just 16 to 20 pages. But the circulation numbers are unusually large (see Exhibit 16.5). Connections are necessary to buy advertising space; *Asahi,* Japan's largest newspaper, has been known to turn down over a million dollars a month in advertising revenue. And even the Japanese giants face a graying population whose younger members are increasingly choosing the electronic media. Circulation rates have been steadily declining there.[33]

---

[33]"The Teetering Giants," *The Economist,* February 10, 2010, pp. 72–73.

CROSSING BORDERS 16.4   Advertising Themes that Work in Japan, Including a Polite Duck

Respect for tradition: Mercedes ads stress that it was the first to manufacture passenger cars.

Mutual dependence: Shiseido ads emphasize the partnership (with beauty consultants) involved in achieving beauty.

Harmony with nature: Toyotas are shown in front of Mt. Fuji.

Use of seasons: Commercials are often set in and products are often used in specific seasons only.

Newness and evolution: Products are shown to evolve from the current environment slowly.

Distinctive use of celebrities, including gaijin (foreigners): A recent study showed that 63 percent of all Japanese commercials featured hired celebrities.

Aging of society: Seniors are featured often.

Changing families: The changing role of fathers—more time spent at home—is a common theme.

Generation gaps and individualism: Younger characters are shown as more individualistic.

Self-effacing humor: A dented Pepsi can was used in an ad to demonstrate its deference to the more popular Coke.

Polite ducks: The AFLAC duck is going to Japan but with a softer quack. Instead of the American version's abrasive quack, the Japanese actor portrays the duck with a more soothing tone. "The Japanese culture does not like being yelled at," says an AFLAC spokesperson. About 70 percent of the firm's international revenues come from Japan, or some $8 billion. Although this campaign is the first to be shot specifically for Japan, the Japanese have met the duck before. The company, now Japan's largest insurer in terms of individual policies, has also used dubbed voices for American ads, including the loud "quacker." The latest version of the duck ad has been so popular that the jingle associated with it became the most downloaded ringtone in Japan!

Sources: George Fields, Hotaka Katahira, and Jerry Wind, *Leveraging Japan, Marketing to the New Asia* (San Francisco: Jossey-Bass, 2000); "ALFAC Tames Its Duck for Japanese Market," *Los Angeles Times*, May 13, 2003, p. C7; Lavonne Kuykendall, "Aflac CEO: The Duck Helps Drive Sales in Japan, *Dow Jones Newswire*, February 24, 2010, online.

In many countries, there is a long time lag before an advertisement can be run in a newspaper. In India and Indonesia, paper shortages delay publication of ads for up to six months. Furthermore, because of equipment limitations, most newspapers cannot be made larger to accommodate the increase in advertising demand.

Separation between editorial and advertising content in newspapers provides another basis for contrast on the international scene. In some countries, it is possible to buy editorial space for advertising and promotional purposes; the news columns are for sale to

Exhibit 16.5
Media Penetration in Selected Countries (% of households)

Country	Color TV	Cable TV	Satellite TV	Telephone Lines	Internet Users*	Daily Newspapers*
United States	99.0	55.1	30.8	93.5	741	161
Canada	98.9	64.3	25.7	99.1	769	172
Argentina	99.2	57.7	13.9	73.3	309	37
Germany	98.1	51.5	41.8	90.9	785	240
Russia	96.8	41.7	7.4	59.6	285	—
Israel	95.3	83.9	40.1	83.1	306	182
South Africa	67.7	0.0	6.3	17.2	88	37
China	96.5	49.3	0.0	81.2	283	83
Japan	99.0	62.4	39.9	95.2	724	518
Australia	99.2	24.3	13.9	97.0	734	129

*Per 1000 persons, not a percentage of households.

Source: Euromonitor International, 2009.

anyone who has the price. Because there is no indication that the space is paid for, it is impossible to tell exactly how much advertising appears in a given newspaper.

Magazines.   The use of foreign national consumer magazines by international advertisers has been notably low for many reasons. Few magazines have a large circulation or provide dependable circulation figures. Technical magazines are used rather extensively to promote export goods, but as with newspapers, paper shortages cause placement problems. Media planners are often faced with the largest magazines accepting up to twice as many advertisements as they have space to run them in—then the magazines decide what advertisements will go in just before going to press by means of a raffle.

Such local practices may be key factors favoring the growth of so-called international media that attempt to serve many nations. Increasingly, U.S. publications are publishing overseas editions. *Reader's Digest International* has added a new Russian-language edition to its more than 20 other language editions. Other American print media available in international editions range from *Playboy* to *Scientific American* and even include the *National Enquirer*, recently introduced to the United Kingdom. Advertisers have three new magazines through which to reach women in China: Hachette Filipachi Presse, the French publisher, is expanding Chinese-language editions of *Elle*, a fashion magazine; *Woman's Day* is aimed at China's "busy modern" woman; and *L'Evénement Sportif* is a sports magazine. These media offer alternatives for multinationals as well as for local advertisers.

Radio and Television.   Possibly because of their inherent entertainment value, radio and television have become major communications media in almost all nations. Now high-definition television (HDTV) appears to be starting to take off worldwide as well. In China, virtually all homes in major cities have a television, and most adults view television and listen to radio daily. Radio has been relegated to a subordinate position in the media race in countries where television facilities are well developed. In many countries, however, radio is a particularly important and vital advertising medium when it is the only one reaching large segments of the population.

Television and radio advertising availability varies between countries. Some countries do not permit any commercial radio or television, but several of the traditional noncommercial countries have changed their policies in recent years because television production is so expensive. Until recently, France limited commercials to a daily total of 18 minutes but now has extended the time limit to 12 minutes per hour per TV channel. South Korea has two television companies, both government owned, which broadcast only a few hours a day. They do not broadcast from midnight to 6:00 a.m., and they usually cannot broadcast between 10:00 a.m. and 5:30 p.m. on weekdays. Commercials are limited to 8 percent of airtime and shown in clusters at the beginning and end of programs. One advertiser remarked, "We are forced to buy what we don't want to buy just to get on."

Satellite and Cable TV.   Of increasing importance in TV advertising is the growth and development of satellite TV broadcasting. Sky Channel, a United Kingdom–based commercial satellite television station, beams its programs and advertising into most of Europe to cable TV subscribers. The technology that permits households to receive broadcasts directly from the satellite via a dish the size of a dinner plate costing about $350 is adding greater coverage and the ability to reach all of Europe with a single message. The expansion of TV coverage will challenge the creativity of advertisers and put greater emphasis on global standardized messages. For a comparison of penetration rates by cable TV, computers, and the Internet in the several countries, see Exhibit 16.5.

Advertisers and governments are both concerned about the impact of satellite TV. Governments are concerned because they fear further loss of control over their airwaves and the spread of "American cultural imperialism." Notice China does not allow the medium. European television programming includes such U.S. shows as *Laguna Beach: the Real Orange County*. *Wheel of Fortune* is the most popular foreign show in the United Kingdom and France, where both the U.S. and French versions are shown. American imports are so popular in France and Germany that officials fear lowbrow U.S. game shows, sitcoms, and soap operas will crush domestic producers. This battle has even reached political levels associated with differences in worldviews represented in the news. The government of France invested in developing, not surprisingly, a French-language "CNN" called *France 24* but has stopped subsidizing an English-language version.[34] *Al-Jazeera*, initially subsidized by Qatar government loans, is currently struggling to break even. Nevertheless, it is the now widely recognized Arabic "CNN" and is commensurately influential in the Middle East.

Parts of Asia and Latin America receive TV broadcasts from satellite television networks. Univision and Televisa are two Latin American satellite television networks broadcasting via a series of affiliate stations in each country to most of the Spanish-speaking world, as well as the United States. *Sabado Gigante,* a popular Spanish-language program broadcast by Univision, is seen by tens of millions of viewers in 16 countries. Star TV, a new pan-Asian satellite television network, has a potential audience of 2.7 billion people living in 38 countries from Egypt through India to Japan, and from Russia to Indonesia. Star TV was the first to broadcast across Asia but was quickly joined by ESPN and CNN. The first Asian 24-hour all-sports channel was followed by MTV Asia and a Mandarin Chinese–language channel that delivers dramas, comedies, movies, and financial news aimed at the millions of overseas Chinese living throughout Asia. Programs are delivered through cable networks but can be received through private satellite dishes.

One of the drawbacks of satellites is also their strength, that is, their ability to span a wide geographical region covering many different country markets. That means a single message is broadcast throughout a wide area. This span may not be desirable for some products; with cultural differences in language, preferences, and so on, a single

---

[34]"Sarkozy to Scrap English-Language France 24 Television–AFP," *Dow Jones International News,* January 8, 2008.

Given the ubiquitous Guinness advertising in Dublin, it's not surprising that Irish livers need assurance. Ireland is behind only the Czech Republic when it comes to per capita consumption of beer. Actually, Royal Liver Assurance is a British pension/insurance company with offices in Dublin (it was established in the 1850s as the Liverpool Liver Burial Society). "Hurling" is a rather brutal form of field hockey popular in Ireland. The Irish government recognizes the causal effects of advertising on consumption—beer ads are not allowed on radio or TV before sports programs and may not be shown more than once per night on any one channel. See http://www.eurocare.org for more on the consumption of alcohol in Ireland and other European countries.

message may not be as effective. PVI (Princeton Video Imaging) is an innovation that will make regional advertising in diverse cultures easier than it presently is when using cable or satellite television. PVI allows ESPN, which offers this service, to fill visual real estate—blank walls, streets, stadium sidings—with computer-generated visuals that look like they belong in the scene. For instance, if you are watching the "street luge" during ESPN's X-Games, you will see the racers appear to pass a billboard advertising Adidas shoes that really is not there. That billboard can say one thing in Holland and quite another in Cameroon. And if you are watching in Portland, Oregon, where Adidas might not advertise, you will see the scene as it really appears—without the billboard. These commercials can play in different languages, in different countries, and even under different brand names.

Most satellite technology involves some government regulation. Singapore, Taiwan, and Malaysia prohibit selling satellite dishes, and the Japanese government prevents domestic cable companies from rebroadcasting from foreign satellites. Such restrictions seldom work for long, however. In Taiwan, an estimated 1.5 million dishes are in use, and numerous illicit cable operators are in business. Through one technology or another, Asian households will be open to the same kind of viewing choice Americans have grown accustomed to and the advertising that it brings with it.

Direct Mail.   Direct mail is a viable medium in an increasing number of countries. It is especially important when other media are not available. As is often the case in international marketing, even such a fundamental medium is subject to some odd and novel quirks. For example, in Chile, direct mail is virtually eliminated as an effective medium because the sender pays only part of the mailing fee; the letter carrier must collect additional postage for every item delivered. Obviously, advertisers cannot afford to alienate customers by forcing them to pay for unsolicited advertisements. Despite some limitations with direct mail, many companies have found it a meaningful way to reach their markets. The Reader's Digest Association has used direct mail advertising in Mexico to successfully market its magazines.

In Southeast Asian markets, where print media are scarce, direct mail is considered one of the most effective ways to reach those responsible for making industrial goods purchases, even though accurate mailing lists are a problem in Asia as well as in other parts of the world. In fact, some companies build their own databases for direct mail. Industrial advertisers are heavy mail users and rely on catalogs and sales sheets to generate large volumes of international business. Even in Japan, where media availability is not a problem, direct mail is successfully used by marketers such as Nestlé Japan and Dell Computer. To promote its Buitoni fresh-chilled pasta, Nestlé is using a 12-page color direct mail booklet of recipes, including Japanese-style versions of Italian favorites.

In Russia, the volume of direct mail has gone from just over 150,000 letters per month to over 500,000 per month in one year. The response rate to direct mailings is as high as 10 to 20 percent in Russia, compared with only 3 to 4 percent or less in the United States. One suggestion as to why it works so well is that Russians are flattered by the attention—needless to say, that will probably change as use of the medium grows.

The Internet.   Although still evolving, the Internet has emerged as a viable medium for advertising and should be included in a company's possible media mix. Its use in business-to-business communications and promotion via catalogs and product descriptions is rapidly gaining in popularity. Because a large number of businesses have access to the Internet, the Internet can reach a large portion of the business-to-business market.

Although limited in its penetration of households globally, the Internet is being used by a growing number of companies as an advertising medium for consumer goods. Many consumer goods companies have e-stores, and others use the Internet as an advertising medium to stimulate sales in retail outlets. Waterford Crystal of Ireland set up its Web site specifically to drive store traffic. The aim is to promote its products and attract people into stores that sell Waterford crystal. Sites list and display almost the entire catalog of the Waterford collection, while stores like Bloomingdale's that stock Waterford support the promotional effort by also advertising on their Web sites.

Exhibit 16.6

Top Ten Web Sites in Three Countries (visitors per month)

Rank	France 26.1 million visitors		Germany 32.6 million visitors		Japan 53.8 million visitors	
1	Google sites	18.2	Google sites	23.0	Yahoo! sites	40.7
2	Microsoft sites	16.4	Microsoft sites	17.7	Google sites	32.0
3	France Telecom	14.0	eBay	17.4	Microsoft sites	30.0
4	Illiad/Free.fr	12.9	United-Internet sites	16.2	Rakuten Inc.	28.5
5	Grope Pages Jaunes	11.4	Time Warner Network	14.6	NTT Group	24.6
6	eBay	11.4	Wikipedia sites	12.6	FC2 Inc.	24.1
7	Yahoo! Sites	10.9	T-Online sites	12.1	Nifty Corp.	22.0
8	Skyrock Network	9.5	Yahoo! sites	11.2	Wikipedia sites	20.6
9	Groupe PPR	8.9	Otto Grupe	11.1	Livedoor	19.7
10	Wikipedia sites	8.5	Karstadt-Quelle	10.1	Amazon sites	18.4

Source: comScore Media Metrix, 2010, online.

For consumer products, the major limitation of the Internet is coverage (see Exhibit 16.5). In the United States, growing numbers of households have access to a computer, but there are fewer in other countries. However, the growing number of Internet households accessible outside the United States generally constitutes a younger, better-educated market segment with higher-than-average incomes. For many companies, this group is an important market niche. Furthermore, this limitation is only temporary as new technology allows access to the Internet via television and as lower prices for personal computers expand the household base. Exhibit 16.6 gives you some idea of the distribution of Web site visitors in three major markets. Notice the American brand names included in the lists: 5 for France, 6 for Germany, and 5 for Japan; and the dominance of Google and Microsoft. The great majority of visitors are viewing the local versions of these Web sites—that is, .fr, .de, and .jp. The most visited Web sites in the United States during the same period were Yahoo!, Time Warner, Microsoft, Google, eBay, MySpace, Ask Network, Amazon, New York Times, and Weather Channel, in that order. For China the top three were Baidu.com, QQ.com, and Google China.

As the Internet continues to grow and countries begin to assert control over what is now a medium with few restrictions, increasing limitations will be set. Beyond the control of undesirable information, issues such as pay-per-view, taxes, unfair competition, import duties, and privacy are being addressed all over the world. In Australia, local retailers are calling for changes in laws because of the loss of trade to the Internet; under current law, Internet purchases do not carry regular import duties. The Internet industry is lobbying for a global understanding on regulation to avoid a crazy quilt of confusing and contradictory rules.

Another limitation that needs to be addressed soon is the competition for Web Internet users. The sheer proliferation of the number of Web sites makes it increasingly difficult for a customer to stumble across a particular page. Search engines have now become crucial directors of Web Internet users' attention. Also, serious Internet advertisers or e-marketers will have to be more effective in communicating the existence of their Internet sites via other advertising media. Some companies are coupling their traditional television spots with a Web site; IBM, Swatch watches, AT&T, and Samsung electronics are among those going for a one-two punch of on-air and online presences. Television spots raise brand awareness of a product regionally and promote the company's Web site. In addition, a company can buy ad banners on the Web that will lead enthusiastic consumers to the company's site, which also promotes the product.

Social Media.[35] Word-of-mouth (WOM) advertising and peer recommendations have always been key influencers of brand choice, but the power of the Internet has changed the pace and reach of WOM. Social media (such as social networking, blogs,

---

[35]For an excellent summary of the exploding influence of social media circa 2010 see "A World of Connections," Special Report, *The Economist*, January 30, 2010, pp. 1–12.

Exhibit 16.7
Social Networking Goes
Mobile (% of respondents)

Source: Ipsos Insight,
November 2007.

	American Users	International Users
Sent/received SMS text	60%	25%
Sent/received e-mail	59	42
Browsed Web for news/information	59	39
Sent/received digital pictures	54	29
Played video games	42	17

virtual worlds, and video sharing) can be powerful marketing tools, but marketers are just beginning to loosen control and let consumers interact with brands on their own terms. Consumer-generated content is having an impact on brands (both positive and negative), and new media are on the agendas of marketers of all products, not just those targeted at young people. Consumers will create content about brands whether the marketers of those brands like it or not. Thus, it is vital that marketers follow, and participate in, the conversations consumers are having online.

The Internet is not delineated by national boundaries, though we note that word-of-mouth seems to work better in more information-oriented cultures.[36] In any case, consumers from many different countries and cultures can and do interact online. We are just beginning to understand the potential uses and pitfalls of this medium and the characteristics of its users. One recent study[37] distinguishes social network uses in the United States and those for a sample from abroad (that is, an aggregate of 11 countries: Brazil, Canada, China, France, Germany, India, Japan, Mexico, Russia, South Korea, and the United Kingdom). For the purposes of the study, the users consisted of consumers who had visited at least one social networking site, such as MySpace, Cyworld, Mixi, and/or Facebook. By the way, at more than 400 million per month, Facebook receives nearly three times the number of unique visitors of its closest rival, Windows Live. Facebook has more than 350 million users, of whom only 100 million are in the United States.

More than half the Americans in the sample had watched TV shows or video streams online. In addition, the Americans were significantly more likely to download TV programs, burn or copy a movie or TV show, and download a feature-length film. The Americans also owned significantly more technology than their international counterparts, and both samples owned more technology than those who had never visited a social networking site. More than half of the Americans had used their mobile devices to send or receive SMS (short message service) text and e-mails, browse the Internet for news and information, and receive digital images (see Exhibit 16.7). Although the international users exhibited similar behaviors, their mobile devices were richer with features. For example, international users are significantly more likely to have MP3s on their mobile devices than those in the United States. Also, see in Exhibit 16.8 that Australians spend more time on social media sites than any users in any other country.

Mobile Phone Applications.
As the numbers of mobile phones continues to explode around the world, so do the number of applications available to users. As one expert has most eloquently put it, "There is a big shift from holding a phone to your ear to holding it in your hand. It opens the door of information services. It's not the web, but it's a web of services that can be offered on mobile devices. It allows consumers to ask questions and marketers to deliver answers in new ways. Around the world creative people are finding ways to use mobile phones in new ways."[38]

---

[36]Desmond Lam, Alvin Lee, and Richard Mizerski, "The Effects of Cultural Values in Word-of-Mouth Communication," *Journal of International Marketing* 17, no. 3 (2009), pp. 55–70.

[37]"Social Networkers Are Also Heavy Technology Users," *Research Brief from the Center for Media Research*, November 14, 2007, http://www.centerformediaresearch.com.

[38]Rajeesh Veeraraghavan, Naga Yasodhar, and Kentaro Toyama, "Warana Unwired: Replacing PCs with Mobile Phones in a Rural Sugar Cane Cooperative," *Information Technology & International Development* 5, no. 1 (2009), pp. 81–95.

Procter & Gamble Experiments with Social Media

P&G was one of the first companies to have its virtual world headquarters on an island in Second Life, the Web-based virtual world where users interact via avatars. Sergio dos Santos, Global Hair Care—Digital Marketing Manager, and Gerry Tseng, Digital Marketing Innovation, were involved in P&G's Second Life marketing effort. They explain:

The corporate team sponsored a contest to find the right brand interested in co-creating a Second Life experiment. An open-invite P&G event was hosted in the form of a 2-hour "Second Life University" event to learn about the medium's capabilities, followed by a call-to-action for interested brands to participate in a contest to win co-sponsorship funding. It received seventy-one event attendees, ten contest entries, four close-scoring finalists, and the selection of one winner: Wella Shockwaves brand in Europe.

Shockwaves, with their tag line of "Style—Attract—Play" targets both young men and women with hair styling products such as gel, spray, mousse, and wax. They tested their hypothesis that branded functionality, which brought their "play" equity to life, would be receptive to and used by avatars. As an extension to their TV campaign, the brand created a virtual waterfight utility that allowed avatars to throw water balloons at each other. As incentive, a 3-wave contest was held to give fans the opportunity to team up and compete to win L$1 million (Linden dollars, the basic currency of Second Life) in each round. Each wave involved points for thrown water balloons and accumulated medallions from scavenger hunts, and allowed some time for Shockwaves to learn and adjust accordingly for the next wave.

This image was posted within the Second Life world to enroll participants in the Water Fight contest. It was not posted on other Web sites or used to advertise the contest to anyone outside of Second Life.

While Shockwaves products were only sold in Western and Eastern Europe at the time, P&G found that people from the United States and elsewhere wanted to participate in the "Shockwaves Water Fight" with their avatars. Initially, P&G thought about excluding non-Europeans, but ultimately decided to allow all avatars to participate. While these consumers would be unable to purchase Shockwaves products, the brand elected to study the global nature and behaviors of Second Life.

P&G learned the following from the Second Life (SL) execution:

- Second Life is not a reach mechanism: Second Life is a small pond versus today's traditional Internet channels, best suited for experimentation, research, and press release in the areas of community and socialization. If a brand is simply interested in reaching as many eyeballs as possible, perhaps a well-designed flash site with provocative content on an Internet site would better suffice as reach in SL is more difficult to do. Due to today's Second Life learning curve for average users, one can expect avatars there to be generally more creative and competitive, perhaps ideal for a brand looking for co-contributors and creative partners. SL proves to be a thriving world for a specific consumer segment, the "critics" and "creators," who are producers themselves. In the end, match your needs to each platform's focus/strength. Perhaps the use of a more globally recognized brand with increased consumer awareness may have also further driven adoption/trial in this experiment.

- Fun, simple & socialization is more important: While a contest was employed as an incentive to trial, we now hypothesize that fun, simple & socialization are more important to SL avatars than prizes & complexity. Celebrity status of their avatars may also be more important than monetary gain as well. This is also supported by other learning from the development agency's SL experiments to date. We learned that in making the game more complex, we risk lower adoption/trial of the execution as avatars may have been intimidated by the process (i.e., game rules and prize money distribution across countries and winning team avatars, interpretation of traditional contest-required legal guidelines into virtual worlds).

- Community managers and media support are key: The experiment did not receive media support; however, we utilized a community manager from the development agency who brought the contest to life via ongoing communications and in-world activities throughout all 3 waves. Word of Mouth was the primary driver to promote the contest, which would have been enhanced with media support if taken beyond experimental expectations. Word of Mouth works in SL but not as well as traditional Internet mechanisms. Should Second Life be used in a future brand execution for its unique strengths, the use of appropriate media support should compensate and increase its trial.

- Keep experiment budgets low: Keeping the experiment costs low through simple design executions allows ongoing tests in new digital channels with less ROI risk and more learning opportunities. We learned that most of our experiment's cost went to making the game's complex elements but perhaps may have been better saved in creating a fun and simple build for avatars to play with each other. This particular experiment realized more accountability to ROI than learning as it approached spending levels close to other digital tools such as online advertising and sampling.

The Shockwaves products shown are available in 15 European countries: Austria, Belgium, Denmark, Finland, Germany, Greece, Hungary, the Netherlands, Norway, Poland, Portugal, Romania, Spain, Sweden, and the United Kingdom. See www.shockwaves.com for more details.

- Maintain appropriate guidelines and principles: Expect that consumers will find loopholes and plan to embrace/adjust for them. Our experiment's game rule complexity within each wave's contest resulted in unexpected cheating allegations within waves 2 & 3. It was interesting to see how competitively close wave 3 became as we apologized for a discovered loophole in wave 2, held to the principle that we'd stay within our predefined game rules, and encouraged players to be more competitive for wave 3. This loophole could have been better prevented through the use of agency experts proficient in traditional contest rules and regulations. However, for this purpose, the Shockwaves brand authorized its bypass due to our need to learn/experiment the application of traditional rules into virtual worlds. Eliminating the contest component would have also avoided this scenario.

- Passionate consumers may not be vocal outside SL: While we received many messages in-world, not everyone wanted to be heard publicly via our external non-SL blogs as we encouraged them to do. This may have been due to the barrier of having them leave SL to perform an action elsewhere despite our promise to act on it in future potential executions if they did.

- Online conversations assisted in trial: The experiment generated over 400 blog posts around the world, most of them linked or driving traffic to Shockwaves Second Life's Web site, which represented over 104,000 unique visitors in our Web site during the period of the experiment (September through November '07) without having any additional on-line advertising. This "popularity" positioned our Web site into 1st place on Google's results page when searching for "shockwaves water fight."

Source: Gerry Tseng, Digital Marketing Innovation for P&G, and Sergio dos Santos, Global Hair Care—Digital Marketing Manager.

Exhibit 16.8
Social Media Users:
Average Time Spent on
Social Networking Sites,
October 2009 (hours per
user)

Source: Neilsen

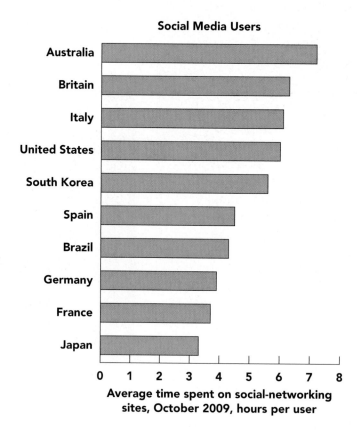

Social Media Users

Average time spent on social-networking sites, October 2009, hours per user

In Uganda, rice farmers who had trouble with aphids texted Farmer's Friend for advice and received a message telling them how to make a pesticide using soap and paraffin. A farmer with blighted tomato plants learned how to control the problem by spraying the plants with a milk-based mixture. Farmer's Friend is one of a range of phone-based services launched in 2009 by MTN, Google, and the Grameen Foundation's "Application Laboratory," or App Lab.[39]

Google Trader is another text-based system that matches buyers and sellers of agricultural produce and commodities. Sellers send a message to say where they are and what they have to offer, which will be available to potential buyers within 30 km for seven days. The user is charged about ten cents per posting. In its first five weeks of operation, the service received one million queries.

Perhaps the best measure of the importance of this creative medium was the incredible response to the Haiti earthquake of 2010. Texting the phrase "Haiti" to the number 90999 automatically donates $10 to the Red Cross. The relief agency received more than $2 million dollars within 24 hours of the earthquake. Twitter also was used as an essential communication medium during the relief efforts and another medium for soliciting and accepting donations.[40]

Other Media.   Restrictions on traditional media or their availability cause advertisers to call on lesser media to solve particular local-country problems. The cinema is an important medium in many countries, as are billboards and other forms of outside advertising. Billboards are especially useful in countries with high illiteracy rates. Hong Kong is clearly the neon capital of the world, with Tokyo's Ginza and New York's Times Square running close seconds. Indeed, perhaps the most interesting "billboard" was the Pizza Hut logo that

---

[39]For much more information on this topic see *The Economist's* "Mobile Marvels," A Special Report, September 26, 2009, pp. 1–19.

[40]Jenna Wortham, "$2 Million in Donations for Haiti, via Text Message," *The New York Times*, January 13, 2010, online.

Two novel media are shown here: (1) Not only do the Russians sell space for space tourists on their rockets; they also sell advertising space! (2) The Japanese beverage company Suntory promotes its products with "Monitor Man" during a football match at National Stadium. "Monitor Man" puts on an LCD display, showing ads for Pepsi and other products, and walks around the stadium. The job requires some muscle, as the equipment weighs about 15 pounds. All this effort is perhaps purposely reminiscent of the Simpson's "Duff Man." Ohhh yaaaa!

appeared on the side of a Russian Proton rocket launched to carry parts of the international space station into orbit. Can extraterrestrials read? Do they like pizza?

In Haiti, sound trucks equipped with powerful loudspeakers provide an effective and widespread advertising medium. Private contractors own the equipment and sell advertising space, much as a radio station would. This medium overcomes the problems of illiteracy, lack of radio and television set ownership, and limited print media circulation. In Ukraine, where the postal service is unreliable, businesses have found that the most effective form of direct business-to-business advertising is direct faxing.

In Spain, a new medium includes private cars that are painted with advertisements for products and serve as moving billboards as they travel around. This system, called *Publicoche* (derived from the words *publicidad*, meaning advertising, and *coche*, meaning car), has 75 cars in Madrid. Car owners are paid $230 a month and must submit their profession and "normal" weekly driving patterns. Advertisers pay a basic cost of $29,000 per car per month and can select the type and color of car they are interested in and which owners are most suited to the campaign, based on their driving patterns.

Campaign Execution and Advertising Agencies

The development of advertising campaigns and their execution are managed by advertising agencies. Just as manufacturing firms have become international, so too have U.S., Japanese, and European advertising agencies expanded internationally to provide sophisticated agency assistance worldwide. Local agencies also have expanded as the demand for advertising services by MNCs has developed. Thus, the international marketer has a variety of alternatives available. In most commercially significant countries, an advertiser has the opportunity to employ a local domestic agency, its company-owned agency, or one of the multinational advertising agencies with local branches. There are strengths and weaknesses associated with each. The discussion regarding firm and agency relations in Chapter 8 on pages 241–243 and Exhibit 8.2 are quite pertinent here. Moreover, the agency-company relationships can be complicated and fragile in the international context—Ford and Disneyland Paris recently changed agencies, for example.

Exhibit 16.9

World's Top Ten Advertising Agencies

2008	Agency (parent)	Headquarters	Global Revenues ($ million) 2008	Percent Change from 2007
1	BBDO Worldwide (Omnicom)	New York	635.8	1.2
2	McCann Erickson Worldwide (Interpublic)	New York	530.0	8.2
3	DraftFCB (Interpublic)	Chicago/New York	510.0	5.2
4	Epsilon/Purple@Epsilon (Alliance Data Systems)	Irving, TX	460.5	4.7
5	Digitas (Publicis)	Boston	377.0	9.3
6	Rapp (Omnicom)	New York	364.5	12.2
7	Euro RSCG Worldwide (Havas)	New York	342.7	5.5
8	Y&R (WPP)	New York	340.0	10.7
9	JWT (WPP)	New York	331.6	9.8
10	Razorfish (Microsoft)	Seattle	317	6.0

Source: From Special Report Global Marketing, *Advertising Age*, November 19, 2007. Copyright © 2010 Crain Communication. Reprinted with permission.

A local domestic agency may provide a company with the best cultural interpretation in situations in which local modification is sought,[41] but the level of sophistication can be weak. Moreover, the cross-cultural communication between the foreign client and the local agency can be problematic. However, the local agency may have the best feel for the market, especially if the multinational agency has little experience in the market. Eastern Europe has been a problem for multinational agencies that are not completely attuned to the market. In Hungary, a U.S. baby care company's advertisement of bath soap, showing a woman holding her baby, hardly seemed risqué. But where Westerners saw a young mother, scandalized Hungarians saw an unwed mother. The model was wearing a ring on her left hand; Hungarians wear wedding bands on the right hand. It was obvious to viewers that this woman wearing a ring on her left hand was telling everybody in Hungary she wasn't married. A local agency would not have made such a mistake. Finally, in some emerging markets like Vietnam, local laws require a local advertising partner.

The best compromise is a multinational agency with local branches, because it has the sophistication of a major agency with local representation. Furthermore, a multinational agency with local branches is better able to provide a coordinated worldwide advertising campaign.[42] This ability has become especially important for firms doing business in Europe. With the interest in global or standardized advertising, many agencies have expanded to provide worldwide representation. Many companies with a global orientation employ one, or perhaps two, agencies to represent them worldwide.

Compensation arrangements for advertising agencies throughout the world are based on the U.S. system of 15 percent commissions. However, agency commission patterns throughout the world are not as consistent as they are in the United States; in some countries, agency commissions vary from medium to medium. Companies are moving from the commission system to a reward-by-results system, which details remuneration terms at the outset. If sales rise, the agency should be rewarded accordingly. This method of sharing in the gains or losses of profits generated by the advertising is gaining in popularity and may become the standard. Services provided by advertising agencies also vary greatly, but few foreign agencies offer the full services found in U.S. agencies. (See Exhibit 16.9 for the largest.)

---

[41]Morris Kalliny and Salma Ghanem, "The Role of the Advertising Agency in the Cultural Message Content of Advertisements: A Comparison of the Middle East and the United States," *Journal of Global Marketing* 22, no. 4 (2009), pp. 313–28.

[42]Among multinational advertising agencies, there appears to be an advantage to early arrival in new markets. See Peter Manusson, Stanford A Westjohn, and David J. Boggs, "Order-of-Entry Effects for Service Firms in Developing Markets: An Examination of Multinational Advertising Agencies," *Journal of International Marketing* 17, no. 2 (2009), pp. 23–41.

International Control of Advertising: Broader Issues

In a previous section, specific legal restrictions on advertising were presented. Here broader issues related to the past, present, and future of the international regulation of advertising are considered.

Consumer criticisms of advertising are not a phenomenon of the U.S. market only. Consumer concern with the standards and believability of advertising may have spread around the world more swiftly than have many marketing techniques. A study of a representative sample of European consumers indicated that only half of them believed advertisements gave consumers any useful information. Six of ten believed that advertising meant higher prices (if a product is heavily advertised, it often sells for more than brands that are seldom or never advertised); nearly eight of ten believed advertising often made them buy things they did not really need and that ads often were deceptive about product quality. In Hong Kong, Colombia, and Brazil, advertising fared much better than in Europe. The non-Europeans praised advertising as a way to obtain valuable information about products; most Brazilians consider ads entertaining and enjoyable.

European Commission officials are establishing directives to provide controls on advertising as cable and satellite broadcasting expands. Deception in advertising is a thorny issue, because most member countries have different interpretations of what constitutes a misleading advertisement. Demands for regulation of advertising aimed at children is a trend appearing in both industrialized and developing countries.

Decency and the blatant use of sex in advertisements also are receiving public attention. One of the problems in controlling decency and sex in ads is the cultural variations found around the world. An ad perfectly acceptable to a Westerner may be very offensive to someone from the Middle East, or, for that matter, another Westerner. Standards for appropriate behavior as depicted in advertisements vary from culture to culture. Regardless of these variations, concern about decency, sex, and ads that demean women and men is growing. International advertising associations are striving to forestall laws by imposing self-regulation, but it may be too late; some countries are passing laws that will define acceptable standards.

The difficulty that business has with self-regulation and restrictive laws is that sex can be powerful in some types of advertisements. European advertisements for Häagen-Dazs, a premium U.S. ice cream maker, and LapPower, a Swedish laptop computer company, received criticism for being too sexy. Häagen-Dazs's ad showed a couple in various stages of undress, in an embrace, feeding ice cream to each other. Some British editorial writers and radio commentators were outraged. One commented that "the ad was the most blatant and inappropriate use of sex as a sales aid." The ad for LapPower personal computers that the Stockholm Business Council on Ethics condemned featured the co-owner of the company with an "inviting smile and provocative demeanor displayed." (Wearing a low-cut dress, she was bending over a LapPower computer.) The bottom line for both these companies was increased sales. In Britain, ice cream sales soared after the "Dedicated to Pleasure" ads appeared, and in Sweden, the co-owner stated, "Sales are increasing daily." Whether laws are passed or the industry polices itself, advertising and its effect on people's behavior have engendered international concern.

Advertising regulations are not limited to Europe; there is an enhanced awareness of the expansion of mass communications and the perceived need to effect greater control in developing countries as well. Malaysia consistently regulates TV advertising to control the effect of the "excesses of Western ways." The government has become so concerned that it will not allow "Western cultural images" to appear in TV commercials. No bare shoulders or exposed armpits are allowed, nor are touching or kissing, sexy clothing, or blue jeans. These are just a few of the prohibitions spelled out in a 41-page advertising code that the Malaysian government has been compiling for more than 10 years.

The assault on advertising and promotion of tobacco products is escalating. In the United States, tobacco firms have agreed to curtail promotion as part of government-supported class-action lawsuits. The European Union Parliament approved larger health warnings on cigarette packs. Most significantly, the World Health Organization (WHO) has launched a global campaign against the tobacco industry.[43] Dr. Gro Harlem Brundtland, director-general

---

[43]"Russian Government Approves Accession to WHO Tobacco Control Convention," *Interfax*, January 10, 2008.

of the WHO, explains, "Tobacco is a communicable disease—it's communicated through advertising, marketing and making smoking appear admirable and glamorous." A worldwide ban of tobacco advertising is just one of the stated goals of the new WHO action.

Product placement within TV programming is another area of advertising receiving the attention of regulators. In the United States, complaints have been aired regarding cigarette smoking in movies and on TV. Product placements avoid some of the regulations in markets like China, where ad time is limited. Because these practices are new to China, the growth rate has been initially dramatic. It will be interesting to follow how product placement will be regulated as the practice proliferates.

The advertising industry is sufficiently concerned with the negative attitudes and skepticism of consumers and governments and with the poor practices of some advertisers that the International Advertising Association and other national and international industry groups have developed a variety of self-regulating codes. Sponsors of these codes feel that unless the advertisers themselves come up with an effective framework for control, governments will intervene. This threat of government intervention has spurred interest groups in Europe to develop codes to ensure that the majority of ads conform to standards set for "honesty, truth, and decency." In those countries where the credibility of advertising is questioned and in those where the consumerism movement exists, the creativity of the advertiser is challenged. The most egregious control, however, may be in Myanmar (formerly Burma), where each medium has its own censorship board that passes judgment on any advertising even before it is submitted for approval by the Ministry of Information. There is even a censorship board for calendars. Content restrictions are centered on any references to the government or military, other political matters, religious themes, or images deemed degrading to traditional culture. In many countries, there is a feeling that advertising, and especially TV advertising, is too powerful and persuades consumers to buy what they do not need, an issue that has been debated in the United States for many years.

Summary

An integrated marketing communications (IMC) program includes coordination among advertising, sales management, public relations, sales promotions, and direct marketing. Global marketers face unique legal, language, media, and production limitations in every market. These must be considered when designing an IMC program. During the late 1990s, many large firms moved toward an advertising strategy of standardization. However, more recently even the most multinational companies have changed emphasis to strategies based on national, subcultural, demographic, or other market segments.

The major problem facing international advertisers is designing the best messages for each market served. The potential for cross-cultural misunderstandings is great in both public relations and the various advertising media. The availability and quality of advertising media also vary substantially around the world. Marketers may be unable to enter markets profitably for the lack of appropriate advertising media—for example, some products require the availability of TV.

Advances in communication technologies (particularly the Internet) are causing dramatic changes in the structure of the international advertising and communications industries. New problems are being posed for government regulators as well. Despite these challenges, the industry is experiencing dramatic growth as new media are developed and as new markets open to commercial advertising.

Key Terms

Integrated marketing communications (IMC)	Sales promotions	Public relations (PR)	Noise

Questions

1. Define the key terms listed above.
2. "Perhaps advertising is the side of international marketing with the greatest similarities from country to country throughout the world. Paradoxically, despite its many similarities, it may also be credited with the greatest number of unique problems in international marketing." Discuss.

3. Someone once commented that advertising is America's greatest export. Discuss.

4. With satellite TV able to reach many countries, discuss how a company can use satellite TV and deal effectively with different languages, different cultures, and different legal systems.

5. Outline some of the major problems confronting an international advertiser.

6. Defend either side of the proposition that advertising can be standardized for all countries.

7. Review the basic areas of advertising regulation. Are such regulations purely foreign phenomena?

8. How can advertisers overcome the problems of low literacy in their markets?

9. What special media problems confront the international advertiser?

10. After reading the section in this chapter on direct mail, develop guidelines to be used by a company when creating a direct mail program.

11. Will the ability to broadcast advertisements over TV satellites increase or decrease the need for standardization of advertisements? What are the problems associated with satellite broadcasting? Comment.

12. In many of the world's marketplaces, a broad variety of media must be utilized to reach the majority of the market. Explain.

13. Cinema advertising is unimportant in the United States but a major media in such countries as Austria. Why?

14. "Foreign newspapers obviously cannot be considered as homogeneous advertising entities." Explain.

15. Borrow a foreign magazine from the library. Compare the foreign advertising to that in an American magazine.

16. What is sales promotion and how is it used in international marketing?

17. Show how the communications process can help an international marketer avoid problems in international advertising.

18. Take each of the steps in the communications process and give an example of how culture differences can affect the final message received.

19. Discuss the problems created because the communications process is initiated in one cultural context and ends in another.

20. What is the importance of feedback in the communications process? Of noise?

1. (From page 470) Why would Coke and McDonald's shed the red in their logos?

For the blue and yellow uniformed Maradona and his team *Boca Junior*, Coke's red and white are also the hated colors of their main *futbol* competitor in Buenos Aires, *River Plate*. The negotiations between Coco-Cola and the *Boca Junior* club executives must have been fascinating with millions of dollars on the table, but many thousands of raucous fans as a very much involved, and potential riotous audience. So, a black and white Coke logo was the creative solution. We note that Sinteplast, a large paint company and local sponsor was able to include its red, white, and blue logo on the stadium—the colors of passion!

The red and gold of McDonald's was traded for black in Cuzco because the area is an official UNESCO World Heritage Site, and the money that supports this designation includes rules that preclude "intrusive" advertising.

Chapter 17

Personal Selling and Sales Management

CHAPTER OUTLINE

CHAPTER LEARNING OBJECTIVES

What you should learn from Chapter 17:

LO1 The role of interpersonal selling in international marketing

LO2 The considerations in designing an international sales force

LO3 The steps to recruiting three types of international salespeople

LO4 Selection criteria for international sales and marketing positions

LO5 The special training needs of international personnel

LO6 Motivation techniques for international sales representatives

LO7 How to design compensation systems for an international sales force

LO8 How to prepare Americans for foreign assignments

LO9 The changing profile of the global sales and marketing manager

Global Perspective

INTERNATIONAL ASSIGNMENTS ARE GLAMOROUS, RIGHT?

"Glamorous" is probably not the adjective the following executives would use:

> The problem as I see it with the company's talk about international managers is that they were just paying lip service to it. When I applied for the posting to Malaysia they gave me all this stuff about the assignment being a really good career move and how I'd gain this valuable international experience and so on. And don't get me wrong, we really enjoyed the posting. We loved the people and the culture and the lifestyle and when it came back to returning home, we weren't really all that keen . . . . The problem was that while I had been away, the company had undergone a wholesale restructuring . . . . This meant that when I got back, my job had been effectively eliminated.

> We have been in the United States for eleven months and I reckon it will be another six to twelve months before my wife and the kids are really settled here. I'm still learning new stuff every day at work and it has taken a long time to get used to American ways of doing things . . . . I mean if the company said, "Oh, we want you to move to South Africa in a year's time," I would really dig my heels in because it was initially very disruptive for my wife when she first came here.

And "glamorous" would not be on the tip of these expatriate spouses' tongues either:

> I found I haven't adapted to Spanish hours. I find it a continual problem because the 2–5 p.m. siesta closure is really awkward. I always find myself where I have to remind myself that from 2–5 I have a blank period that I can't do anything . . . . We started adjusting to the eating schedule. Whether we like it or not, we eat a lot later.

> We've been really fortunate we haven't had to use healthcare services here . . . . The thought of going to, needing to go to a doctor is scary because for me it would have to be someone English speaking or I wouldn't, you know, feel comfortable.

Given these kinds of problems, is that international sales position being offered to you as attractive as it looks? Will it really help your career?

Sources: Nick Forster, "The Myth of the 'International Manager,'" *International Journal of Resource Management* 11, no. 1 (February 2000), pp. 126–42; Mary C. Gilly, Lisa Peñaloza, and Kenneth M. Kambara, "The Role of Consumption in Expatriate Adjustment and Satisfaction," working paper, Paul Merage School of Business, University of California, Irvine, 2010.

LO1 ▓▓▓▓

The role of interpersonal selling in international marketing

The salesperson is a company's most direct tie to the customer; in the eyes of most customers, the salesperson is the company. As presenter of company offerings and gatherer of customer information, the sales representative is the final link in the culmination of a company's marketing and sales efforts.

Growing global competition, coupled with the dynamic and complex nature of international business, increases both the need and the means for closer ties with both customers and suppliers. Particularly in relationship-based cultures such as China, relationship marketing, built on effective communications between the seller and buyer, focuses on building long-term alliances rather than treating each sale as a one-time event.[1] Advances in information technology are allowing for increasingly higher levels of coordination across advertising, marketing research, and personal selling efforts, yielding new roles and functions in customer relationship management (CRM).[2] Similarly, such advances are changing the nature of personal selling and sales management, leading some to forecast substantial reductions in field sales efforts.

In this ever-changing environment of international business, the tasks of designing, building, training, motivating, and compensating an international sales group generate unique problems at every stage of management and development. This chapter discusses the alternatives and problems of managing sales and marketing personnel in foreign countries. Indeed, these problems are among the most difficult facing international marketers. In one survey of CEOs and other top executives, the respondents identified "establishing sales and distribution networks" and "cultural differences" as major difficulties in international operations.

Designing the Sales Force

LO2 ▓▓▓▓

The considerations in designing an international sales force

The first step in managing a sales force is its design. Based on analyses of current and potential customers, the selling environment, competition, and the firm's resources and capabilities, decisions must be made regarding the numbers, characteristics, and assignments of sales personnel. All these design decisions are made more challenging by the wide variety of pertinent conditions and circumstances in international markets. Moreover, the globalization of markets and customers, as illustrated by the IBM–Ford story in Crossing Borders 17.1, makes the job of international sales manager quite interesting.

As described in previous chapters, distribution strategies will often vary from country to country. Some markets may require a direct sales force, whereas others may not. How customers are approached can differ as well. The hard sell that may work in some countries can be inappropriate in others. Automobiles have been sold door to door in Japan for years, and only recently have stocks been sold over the Internet in Europe. More than 100,000 of Singapore's 6 million inhabitants are involved in home product sales and other forms of multilevel marketing. The size of accounts certainly makes a difference as well—notice in Crossing Borders 17.1 that an IBM sales representative works inside Ford. Selling high-technology products may allow for the greater use of American expatriates, whereas selling consulting services will tend to require more participation by native sales representatives. Selling in information-oriented cultures such as Germany may also allow for greater use of expatriates. However, relationship-oriented countries such as Japan will require the most complete local knowledge possessed only by natives. Writing about

[1]Xueming Luo, David A. Griffith, Sandra S. Liu, and Yi-Zheng Shi, "The Effects of Customer Relationships and Social Capital on Firm Performance: A Chinese Business Approach," *Journal of International Marketing* 12, no. 4 (2004), pp. 25–47; Roy Y.J. Chua, Michael W. Norris, and Paul Ingram, "*Guanxi* vs. Networking: Distinctive Configurations of Affect- and Cognition-Based Trust in the Networks of Chinese and American Managers," *Journal of International Business Studies* 40, no. 3 (2009), pp. 490–508; Nikala Lane and Nigel Peircy, "Strategizing the Sales Organization," *Journal of Strategic Marketing* 17, 3-4 (2009), pp. 307–322; Luis Filipe Lages. Garcia Silva, and Chris Styles, "Relationship Capabilities, Quality, and Innovation as Determinants of Export Performance," *Journal of International Marketing* 17, no. 4 (2009), pp. 47–70.

[2]Linda H. Shi, Shaoming Zou, J. Chris White, Regina C. McNally, and S. Tamer Cavusgil, "Global Account Management Capability: Insights from Leading Suppliers," *Journal of International Marketing* 13, no. 2 (2005), pp. 93–113.

CROSSING BORDERS 17.1   Sales Force Management and Global Customers

Did IBM really need a major overhaul to its sales compensation plan? For proof, just ask Kevin Tucker. Tucker, an IBM global account manager dedicated to Ford Motor Company, closed a $7 million sale with the automotive giant's European operations. Ford wanted Tucker and his team of IBM representatives to install networking systems in its engineering facilities. The systems would run the applications that design the company's automobiles.

Ford's installation required help from an IBM sales executive in Germany, the project's headquarters. So Tucker, whose office sits in Ford's Dearborn, Michigan, headquarters, sent an e-mail requesting the executive's assistance. And that's when things turned ugly. Although the rep in Germany did not turn his back on the project, his initial reaction was less than enthusiastic. Ford wanted the systems installed throughout Europe, yet the compensation plan for IBM's Germany-based reps rewarded only the systems that were installed in that country. With 80 percent of the work scheduled outside of Germany, the executive was left wondering: Where's the payoff? Tucker and other IBM sales incentive managers wasted three weeks discussing ways to maximize the rep's incentive. Energy that could have been focused on the customer was wasted on a pay plan. "Ford was world-centric, we were country-centric," Tucker says. "The team in Germany was asking, 'Kevin, how can you make us whole?'"

They were not the only salespeople asking that question at IBM. Tucker's predicament represents just one of many problems that were rooted in IBM's "$72 billion" sales incentive plan—a plan that had been obviously put on the back burner as the company giant tinkered with its vision.

Bob Wylie, manager of incentive strategies for IBM Canada, says, "There was the attitude that if it's outside my territory and outside my measurements, I don't get paid for it, and I don't get involved. What's in my pay plan defines what I do." Not the best setup for a company that operates in 165 countries.

Apparently, IBM has solved many of these problems. Ford signed contracts for more than $300 million with IBM to create almost all of the car company's software, including Internet and e-commerce applications in Europe and North America. Details about IBM's global sales compensation program are provided later in this chapter. And IBM continues its impressive sales force coverage in burgeoning new markets like India, where it now employs more than 50,000 professionals who are generating almost $1 billion in revenues.

Sources: Michele Marchetti, "Gamble: IBM Replaced Its Outdated Compensation Plan with a Worldwide Framework. Is It Paying Off?" *Sales & Marketing Management*, July 1996, pp. 65–69; "Ford Motor and IBM," *The Wall Street Journal Europe*, January 13, 1999, p. UK5A; "IBM Aims at $1-b India Revenue by Year-End," *Business Line (The Hindu)*, December 9, 2007.

Japan, two international marketing experts agree: "Personal selling as a rule has to be localized for even the most global of corporations and industries."[3]

Once decisions have been made about how many expatriates, local nationals, or third-country nationals a particular market requires, the more intricate aspects of design can be undertaken, such as territory allocation and customer call plans. Many of the most advanced operations research tools developed in the United States can be applied in foreign markets, with appropriate adaptation of inputs, of course.[4] For example, one company has provided tools to help international firms create balanced territories and find optimal locations for sales offices in Canada, Mexico, and Australia.[5] However, the use of such high-tech resource allocation tools requires intricate knowledge of not only geographical details but also appropriate call routines. Many things can differ across cultures—the length of sales cycles, the kinds of customer relationships, and the types of interactions with customers. Indeed, more than one study has identified substantial differences in the importance

---

[3]Johny K. Johansson and Ikujiro Nonaka, *Relentless: The Japanese Way of Marketing* (New York: Harper Business, 1997), p. 97.

[4]Laia Ferrer, Rafael Pastor, and Alberto Garcia-Villoria, "Designing Salespeople's Routes with Multiple Visits of Customers: A Case Study," *International Journal of Production Economics* 19, no. 1 (2009), pp. 46–54.

[5]See the Web site for The TerrAlign Group, http://www.terralign.com, for more detailed information.

of referrals in the sales of industrial services in Japan vis-à-vis the United States.[6] The implications are that in Japan, sales calls must be made not only on customers but also on the key people, such as bankers, in the all-important referral networks.

Recruiting Marketing and Sales Personnel

The number of marketing management personnel from the home country assigned to foreign countries varies according to the size of the operation, the availability of qualified locals, and other firm characteristics.[7] Increasingly, the number of U.S. home-country nationals (expatriates) assigned to foreign posts is smaller as the pool of trained, experienced locals grows.

The largest personnel requirement abroad for most companies is the sales force, recruited from three sources: expatriates, local nationals, and third-country nationals. A company's staffing pattern may include all three types in any single foreign operation, depending on qualifications, availability, and company needs. Sales and marketing executives can be recruited via the traditional media of advertising (including newspapers, magazines, job fairs, and the Internet), employment agencies or executive search firms,[8] and the all-important personal referrals. The last source will be crucial in many foreign countries, particularly the relationship-oriented ones.

Expatriates

The number of companies relying on **expatriate** personnel is declining as the volume of world trade increases and as more companies use locals to fill marketing positions. However, when products are highly technical, or when selling requires an extensive background of information and applications, an expatriate sales force remains the best choice. The expatriate salesperson may have the advantages of greater technical training, better knowledge of the company and its product line, and proven dependability. Because they are not locals, expatriates sometimes add to the prestige of the product line in the eyes of foreign customers. And perhaps most important, expatriates usually are able to effectively communicate with and influence headquarters' personnel.

The chief disadvantages of an expatriate sales force are the high cost, cultural and legal[9] barriers, and the limited number of high-caliber personnel willing to live abroad for extended periods. Employees are reluctant to go abroad for many reasons: Some find it difficult to uproot families for a two- or three-year assignment, increasing numbers of dual-career couples often require finding suitable jobs for spouses, and many executives believe such assignments impede their subsequent promotions at home. Recall the comments of the executives in the Global Perspective. The loss of visibility at corporate headquarters plus the belief that "out of sight is out of mind" are major reasons for the reluctance to accept a foreign assignment. Companies with well-planned career development programs have the least difficulty. Indeed, the best international companies make it crystal clear that a ticket to top management is an overseas stint. Korn/Ferry International reports in a survey of 75 senior executives from around the world that "international experience" is the attribute identified as second most important for CEOs—experience in marketing and finance positions were first and third, respectively.[10]

Expatriates commit to foreign assignments for varying lengths of time, from a few weeks or months to a lifetime. Some expatriates have one-time assignments (which may last for years), after which they return to the parent company; others are essentially professional expatriates, working abroad in country after country. Still another expatriate assignment

---

[6]R. Bruce Money, Mary C. Gilly, and John L. Graham, "National Culture and Referral Behavior in the Purchase of Industrial Services in the United States and Japan," *Journal of Marketing* 62, no. 4 (October 1998), pp. 76–87.

[7]Rene A. Belderbos and Marielle G. Heijltjes, "The Determinants of Expatriate Staffing by Japanese Multinationals in Asia: Control, Learning, and Vertical Business Groups," *Journal of International Business Studies* 36, no. 3 (2005), pp. 341–54.

[8]The largest international executive search firm is Korn/Ferry International (http://www.kornferry.com).

[9]Even if job permits are obtained, other legal problems can also crop up. See James T. Areddy, "China Charges Rio Tinto Employees," *The Wall Street Journal*, February 10, 2010, online.

[10]See "Marketing Is Fastest Route to the Executive Suite," Korn/Ferry International (http://www.kornferry.com).

are reducing payments and other benefits[48] on the premise that the assignment abroad is an integral requirement for growth, development, and advancement within the firm.

Family dissatisfaction, which causes stress within the family on returning home, is not as severe a problem as career-related complaints. A returning expatriate's dissatisfaction with the perceived future is usually the reason many resign their positions after returning to the United States. The problem is not unique to U.S. citizens; Japanese companies have similar difficulties with their personnel. The most frequently heard complaint involves the lack of a detailed plan for the expatriate's career when returning home. New home-country assignments are frequently mundane and do not reflect the experience gained or the challenges met during foreign assignment. Some feel their time out of the mainstream of corporate affairs has made them technically obsolete and thus ineffective in competing immediately on return. Finally, there is some loss of status, requiring an ego adjustment when an executive returns home.

Companies with the least amount of returnee attrition differ from those with the highest attrition in one significant way: personal career planning for the expatriate. This planning begins with the decision to send the person abroad. The initial transfer abroad should be made in the context of a long-term company career plan. Under these circumstances, the individual knows not only the importance of the foreign assignment but also when to expect to return and at what level. Near the end of the foreign assignment, the process for repatriation begins. The critical aspect of the return home is to keep the executive completely informed regarding such matters as the proposed return time, new assignment and an indication of whether it is interim or permanent, new responsibilities, and future prospects. In short, returnees should know where they are going and what they will be doing next month and several years ahead.

A report on what MNCs are doing to improve the reentry process suggests five steps:

1. Commit to reassigning expatriates to meaningful positions.

2. Create a mentor program.[49] Mentors are typically senior executives who monitor company activities, keep the expatriate informed on company activities, and act as a liaison between the expatriate and various headquarters departments.

3. Offer a written job guarantee stating what the company is obligated to do for the expatriate on return.

4. Keep the expatriate in touch with headquarters through periodic briefings and headquarters visits.

5. Prepare the expatriate and family for repatriation once a return date is set.[50]

Some believe the importance of preparing the employee and family for culture shock upon return is on a par with preparation for going abroad.

Developing Cultural Awareness

Many businesses focus on the functional skills needed in international marketing, overlooking the importance of cultural intelligence.[51] Just as the idea that "if a product sells well in Dallas, it will sell well in Hong Kong" is risky,

---

[48]Katherine Rosman, "Expat Life Gets Less Cushy," *The Wall Street Journal*, October 26, 2007, pp. W1, W10.

[49]John M. Mezias and Terri A. Scandura, "A Needs-Driven Approach to Expatriate Adjustment and Career Development: A Multiple Mentoring Perspective," *Journal of International Business Studies* 36 (2005), pp. 519–38.

[50]Mila B. Lazarova and Jean-Luc Cerdin, "Revisiting Repatriation Concerns: Organizational Support versus Career and Contextual Influences," *Journal of International Business Studies* 38 (2007), pp. 404–29.

[51]This is a topic of much discussion; see P. Christopher Earley and Elaine Mosakowski, "Cultural Intelligence," *Harvard Business Review*, October 2004, pp. 139–46; James P. Johnson, Tomasz Lenartowicz, and Salvador Apud, "Cross-Cultural Competence in International Business: Toward a Definition and Model," *Journal of International Business Studies* 37 (2006), pp. 231–58; Orly Levy, Schon Beechler, Sully Taylor, and Nakiye A. Boyacigiller, "What We Talk about When We Talk about 'Global Mindset': Managerial Cognition in Multinational Corporations," *Journal of International Business Studies* 38 (2007), pp. 231–58; William Neburry, Liuba Y. Belkin, and Paradis Ansari, "Perceived Career Opportunities from Globalization: Globalization Capabilities and Attitudes toward Women in Iran and the U.S.," *Journal of International Business Studies* 39 (2008), pp. 814–32; Gary Knight and Daekwan Kim, "International Business Competence and the Contemporary Firm," *Journal of International Business Studies* 40, no. 2 (2009), pp. 255–73.

so is the idea that "a manager who excels in Dallas will excel in Hong Kong." Most expatriate failures are not caused by lack of management or technical skills but rather by lack of an understanding of cultural differences and their effect on management skills. As the world becomes more interdependent and as companies depend more on foreign earnings, there is a growing need for companies to develop cultural awareness among those posted abroad.

Just as we might remark that someone has learned good social skills (i.e., an ability to remain poised and be in control under all social situations), so too good cultural skills can be developed.[52] These skills serve a similar function in varying cultural situations; they provide the individual with the ability to relate to a different culture even when the individual is unfamiliar with the details of that particular culture. Cultural skills can be learned just as social skills can be learned. People with cultural skills can:

- Communicate respect and convey verbally and nonverbally a positive regard and sincere interest in people and their culture.

- Tolerate ambiguity and cope with cultural differences and the frustration that frequently develops when things are different and circumstances change.

- Display empathy by understanding other people's needs and differences from their point of view.

- Remain nonjudgmental about the behavior of others, particularly with reference to their own value standards.

- Recognize and control the SRC, that is, recognize their own culture and values as an influence on their perceptions, evaluations, and judgment in a situation.

- Laugh things off—a good sense of humor helps when frustration levels rise and things do not work as planned.

The Changing Profile of the Global Manager

LO9

The changing profile of the global sales and marketing manager

Until recently the road to the top was well marked. Surveys of chief executives consistently reported that more than three-quarters had finance, manufacturing, or marketing backgrounds. As the post–World War II period of growing markets and domestic-only competition has faded, however, so too has the narrow one-company, one-industry chief executive. In the new millennium, increasing international competition, the globalization of companies, technology, demographic shifts, and the speed of overall change will govern the choice of company leaders. It will be difficult for a single-discipline individual to reach the top in the future.

The executive recently picked to head Procter & Gamble's U.S. operations is a good example of the effect globalization is having on businesses and the importance of experience, whether in Japan, Europe, or elsewhere. The head of all P&G's U.S. business was born in the Netherlands, received an MBA[53] from Rotterdam's Eramus University, then rose through P&G's marketing ranks in Holland, the United States, and Austria. After proving his mettle in Japan, he moved to P&G's Cincinnati, Ohio, headquarters to direct its push into East Asia, and then to his new position. Speculation suggests that if he succeeds in the United States, as he did in Japan, he will be a major contender for the top position at P&G.

Fewer companies today limit their search for senior-level executive talent to their home countries. Coca-Cola's former CEO, who began his ascent to the top in his native Cuba, and the former IBM vice chairman, a Swiss national who rose through the ranks in Europe, are two prominent examples of individuals who achieved the top positions of firms outside their home countries. Indeed, 14 *Fortune* 100 companies were headed by immigrant CEOs

---

[52]Jon M. Shapiro, Julie L. Ozanne, and Bige Saatcioglu, "An Interpretive Examination of the Development of Cultural Sensitivity in International Business," *Journal of International Business Studies* 39 (2008), pp. 71–87.

[53]Laurie Goering, "Foreign Business Schools Fill a Huge Gap," *Los Angeles Times*, January 14, 2008, p. C4.

CROSSING BORDERS 17.4

A school supported by the European Union teaches Britons, French, Germans, Dutch, and others to be future Europeans. The European School in a suburb of Brussels has students from 12 nations who come to be educated for life and work, not as products of motherland or fatherland but as Europeans. The European Union runs 10 European Schools in western Europe, enrolling 17,000 students from kindergarten to twelfth grade. Graduates emerge superbly educated, usually trilingual, and very, very European.

The schools are a linguistic and cultural melange. Native speakers of 36 different languages are represented in one school alone. Each year students take fewer and fewer classes in their native tongue. Early on, usually in first grade, they begin a second language, known as the "working language," which must be English, French, or German. A third language is introduced in the seventh year, and a fourth may be started in the ninth.

By the time students reach their eleventh year, they are taking history, geography, economics, advanced math, music, art, and gym in the working language. When the students are in groups talking, they are constantly switching languages to "whatever works."

Besides language, students learn history, politics, literature, and music from the perspective of all the European countries—in short, European cultures. The curriculum is designed to teach the French, German, Briton, and those of other nationalities to be future Europeans.

This same approach is being taken at the MBA level as well. The well-respected European School of Management has campuses in several cities—Berlin, Paris, Oxford, and Madrid. Students spend part of their time at each of the campuses. American MBA programs are beginning to imitate such programs. The University of Chicago School of Business now has campuses in Barcelona and Singapore. The Fuqua School at Duke offers a unique executive MBA program involving travel to several foreign countries and a substantial percentage of teaching delivered interactively over the Internet. This last program attracts students from all over the world who are willing to pay a six-figure tuition.

Sources: Glynn Mapes, "Polyglot Students Are Weaned Early Off Mother Tongue," *The Wall Street Journal,* March 6, 1990, p. A1. Reprinted by permission of *The Wall Street Journal,* © 1990 Dow Jones & Company, Inc. All Rights Reserved Worldwide. See also Kevin Cape, "Tips on Choosing the Right One, International Schools," *International Herald Tribune,* January 25, 2003, p. 7; http://fuqua.duke.edu/mba/executive/global/, 2010.

in one study. Alternatively, American-style diversity[54] is not shared by companies in competitive countries in Asia, for example.[55].

Some companies, such as Colgate-Palmolive, believe that it is important to have international assignments early in a person's career, and international training is an integral part of its entry-level development programs. Colgate recruits its future managers from the world's best colleges and business schools. Acceptance is highly competitive, and successful applicants have a BA or MBA with proven leadership skills, fluency in at least one language besides English, and some experience living abroad. A typical recruit might be a U.S. citizen who has spent a year studying in another country or a national of another country who was educated in the United States.[56]

Trainees begin their careers in a two-year, entry-level, total-immersion program that consists of stints in various Colgate departments. A typical rotation includes time in the finance, manufacturing, and marketing departments and an in-depth exposure to the company's marketing system. During that phase, trainees are rotated through the firm's ad agency, marketing research, and product management departments and then work seven months as field salespeople. At least once during the two years, trainees accompany their mentors on business trips to a foreign subsidiary. The company's goal is to develop in their trainees the skills they need to become effective marketing managers, domestically or globally.

[54]David Wassel, "U.S. Keeps Foreign PhDs," *The Wall Street Journal,* January 26, 2010, online.

[55]Joel Kotkin, "The Kids Will Be Alright," *The Wall Street Journal,* January 23–24, 2010, p. W9.

[56]Mary Beth Marklein, "Record Number of U.S. Students Study Abroad," *USA Today,* November 17, 2008, online.

On the completion of the program, trainees can expect a foreign posting, either immediately after graduation or soon after an assignment in the United States. The first positions are not in London or Paris, as many might hope, but in developing countries such as Brazil, the Philippines, or maybe Zambia. Because international sales are so important to Colgate (60 percent of its total revenues are generated abroad), a manager might not return to the United States after the first foreign assignment but rather move from one overseas post to another, developing into a career internationalist, which could lead to a CEO position.

Companies whose foreign receipts make up a substantial portion of their earnings and that see themselves as global companies rather than as domestic companies doing business in foreign markets are the most active in making the foreign experience an integrated part of a successful corporate career. Indeed for many companies, a key threshold seems to be that when overseas revenues surpass domestic revenues, then the best people in the company want to work on international accounts. Such a global orientation then begins to permeate the entire organization—from personnel policies to marketing and business strategies. This shift was the case with Gillette, which in the 1990s made a significant recruitment and management-development decision when it decided to develop managers internally. Gillette's international human resources department implemented its international-trainee program, designed to supply a steady stream of managerial talent from within its own ranks. Trainees are recruited from all over the world, and when their training is complete, they return to their home countries to become part of Gillette's global management team.

Foreign-Language Skills

Opinions are mixed on the importance of a second language for a career in international business. There are those whose attitude about another language is summed up in the statement that "the language of international business is English." Indeed, one journalist quipped, "Modern English is the Wal-Mart of languages: convenient, huge, hard to avoid, superficially friendly, and devouring all rivals in its eagerness to expand."[57]

Proponents of language skills argue that learning a language improves cultural understanding and business relationships.[58] Others point out that to be taken seriously in the business community, the expatriate must be at least conversational in the host language. Particularly when it comes to selling in foreign countries, languages are important. Says a Dutch sales training expert, "People expect to buy from sales reps they can relate to, and who understand their language and culture. They're often cold towards Americans trying to sell them products."

Some recruiters want candidates who speak at least one foreign language, even if the language will not be needed in a particular job. Having learned a second language is a strong signal to the recruiter that the candidate is willing to get involved in someone else's culture.

Although most companies offer short, intensive language-training courses for managers being sent abroad, many are making stronger efforts to recruit people who are bilingual or multilingual. According to the director of personnel at Coca-Cola, when his department searches its database for people to fill overseas posts, the first choice is often someone who speaks more than one language. We note that Chinese has now become a popular language in America's schools[59] and English in Chinese schools. Indeed, Disney is opening English languages schools in China with Mickey as part of the faculty![60]

---

[57]Mark Abley, journalist.

[58]Ellen Gamerman, "Just One Word: (That's Chinese for 'Plastics')," *The Wall Street Journal*, March 17–18, 2007, pp. P1, P5.

[59]Sam Dillon, "Foreign Languages Fade in Class—Except Chinese," *The New York Times*, January 10, 2010, online.

[60]James T. Areddy and Peter Sanders, "Chinese Learn English the Disney Way," *The Wall Street Journal*, April 20, 2009, pp. B1, B5.

We the authors feel strongly that language skills are of great importance; if you want to be a major player in international business in the future, learn to speak other languages, or you might not make it—your competition will be those European students described in Crossing Borders 17.4. A joke that foreigners tell about language skills goes something like this: What do you call a person who speaks three or more languages? Multilingual. What do you call a person who speaks two languages? Bilingual. What do you call a person who speaks only one language? An American! Maybe the rest of the world knows something we don't.

Summary

An effective international sales force constitutes one of the international marketer's greatest concerns. The company's sales force represents the major alternative method of organizing a company for foreign distribution and, as such, is on the front line of a marketing organization.

The role of marketers in both domestic and foreign markets is rapidly changing, along with the composition of international managerial and sales forces. Such forces have many unique requirements that are being filled by expatriates, locals, third-country nationals, or a combination of the three. In recent years, the pattern of development has been to place more emphasis on local personnel operating in their own lands. This emphasis, in turn, has highlighted the importance of adapting U.S. managerial techniques to local needs.

The development of an effective marketing organization calls for careful recruiting, selecting, training, motivating, and compensating of expatriate personnel and their families to ensure the maximization of a company's return on its personnel expenditures. The most practical method of maintaining an efficient international sales and marketing force is careful, concerted planning at all stages of career development.

Key Terms

Expatriate	Third-country nationals	Separation allowances	Repatriation
Local nationals	(TCNs)	Work councils	

Questions

1. Define the key terms listed above.
2. Why may it be difficult to adhere to set job criteria in selecting foreign personnel? What compensating actions might be necessary?
3. Why does a global sales force cause special compensation problems? Suggest some alternative solutions.
4. Under which circumstances should expatriate salespeople be utilized?
5. Discuss the problems that might be encountered in having an expatriate sales manager supervising foreign salespeople.
6. "To some extent, the exigencies of the personnel situation will dictate the approach to the overseas sales organization." Discuss.
7. How do legal factors affect international sales management?
8. How does the sales force relate to company organization? To channels of distribution?
9. "It is costly to maintain an international sales force." Comment.
10. Adaptability and maturity are traits needed by all salespeople. Why should they be singled out as especially important for international salespeople?
11. Can a person develop good cultural skills? Discuss.
12. Describe the attributes of a person with good cultural skills.
13. Interview a local company that has a foreign sales operation. Draw an organizational chart for the sales function and explain why that particular structure was used by that company.
14. Evaluate the three major sources of multinational personnel.
15. Which factors complicate the task of motivating the foreign sales force?
16. Why do companies include an evaluation of an employee's family among selection criteria for an expatriate assignment?
17. "Concerns for career and family are the most frequently mentioned reasons for a manager to refuse a foreign assignment." Why?
18. Discuss and give examples of why returning U.S. expatriates are often dissatisfied. How can these problems be overcome?
19. If "the language of international business is English," why is it important to develop a skill in a foreign language? Discuss.
20. The global manager of 2020 will have to meet many new challenges. Draw up a sample résumé for someone who could be considered for a top-level executive position in a global firm.

Chapter 18

Pricing for International Markets

CHAPTER OUTLINE

CHAPTER LEARNING OBJECTIVES

What you should learn from Chapter 18:

LO1 Components of pricing as competitive tools in international marketing

LO2 How to control pricing in parallel import or gray markets

LO3 Price escalation and how to minimize its effect

LO4 Countertrading and its place in international marketing practices

LO5 The mechanics of price quotations

LO6 The mechanics of getting paid

Global Perspective

THE PRICE WAR

The battle between Procter & Gamble and Kimberly-Clark brought Pampers and Huggies, respectively, to places they have never been, forcing down diaper prices worldwide, and expanding the global market for disposable diapers. A battle in Brazil between the two giants gives an interesting glimpse of the global markets of tomorrow. Disposable diapers are still considered a luxury by the vast majority of Brazil's 194 million people, whose average annual income is under $8,000. Before P&G and Kimberly arrived, rich and poor alike generally made do with cloth or nothing at all. The disposables that were available were expensive, bulky, and leaky.

When less than 5 percent of the Brazilian mass market used disposable diapers, P&G launched Pampers Uni, a no-frills, unisex diaper. Before Uni, it cost more to pay for disposable diapers than to pay for a maid to wash the cloth ones. The introduction of the relatively cheap, high-quality Uni fundamentally changed the economics of the diaper market for most middle-class Brazilians.

The plan was to put such nonessentials as disposable diapers within the reach of millions of Brazilians for the first time. At the same time, the Brazilian economy was on the upswing—inflation had subsided, and overnight, the purchasing power of the poor increased by 20 percent. Low-priced products flew off the shelves. P&G had to truck in diapers from Argentina as it struggled to open new production lines.

But the good days did not last. Kimberly-Clark entered the market and began importing Huggies from Argentina. With the help of a Unilever unit as its Brazilian distributor, Kimberly-Clark gained immediate distribution across the country and quickly made deep inroads into the market. Unilever agreed to work with Kimberly-Clark because its archrival in soap was P&G, and Kimberly-Clark's archrival in diapers was P&G. The two companies previously had entered into a global alliance to look for win–win situations when it was in both their best interests to partner and help each other, from a competitive standpoint, against the dominant P&G. The Brazilian market was the perfect case for cooperation.

With Unilever's help, Kimberly-Clark "push girls" invaded markets to demonstrate the diaper's absorption. Sales rose rapidly and began to exceed production. To increase market share, Kimberly-Clark formed an alliance with Kenko do Brazil, P&G's largest home-grown rival, and created the "Monica" brand. "Monica's Gang," a comic strip similar to "Peanuts" in the United States, sells widely in Brazil. São Paulo malls were crowded with thousands of kids waiting to get an Easter photo taken with actors in Monica suits, an honor that required the purchase of three packs of diapers. Monica diapers were a big hit, and Kimberly-Clark became number one in the Brazilian market.

It was a tough blow to P&G. The company had devoted an entire page of its annual report to how Pampers Uni had tripled its market share in Brazil, helping P&G "retain the number one position in a market that has grown fivefold." Now it suddenly found itself on the defensive. First it cut prices, a step P&G loathes. "Price cutting is like violence: No one wins," said the head of its Brazilian operation. Then it broadened its product range, rolling out an up-market diaper called Super-Seca, priced 25 percent higher than Pampers Uni. Later, in a flanking move, it also unveiled Confort-Seca, a bikini-style diaper originally developed for Thailand and priced 10 to 15 percent lower than the already-inexpensive Uni.

Kimberly-Clark fired back, matching the price cut and then introducing a cheaper version of Monica called Tippy Basic. Four weeks later, P&G cut prices another 10 percent on Super-Seca and Confort-Seca. Despite the price cuts, the two brands were still relatively expensive; then a wave of really cheap diapers arrived. Carrefour, a French retailer that is now Brazil's biggest supermarket chain, sells crudely made Bye-Bye Pipi diapers from Mexico. Despite their inferior quality, the cheap imports pulled down diaper prices across the board.

The real war started when lower prices became so attractive that consumers who otherwise could not afford diapers came into the market. As prices continued to drop, the market grew; that attracted more producers, which were mostly small, local Brazilian companies that offered even lower-priced competitive diapers. One such company, Mili, saw its market share increase from 4.8 percent to 16.2 percent over a three-year period. What accounts for growth of these smaller companies? One analyst suggests that the multinationals are too sophisticated and, thus, too expensive for the Brazilian market: "Smaller companies are just supplying what consumers need at a price they can afford." But it also can be said that as prices drop, products become more attractive to a larger segment of the total market.

Sources: Raju Narisetti and Jonathan Friedland, "Disposable Income: Diaper Wars of P&G and Kimberly-Clark Now Heat Up in Brazil," *The Wall Street Journal,* June 4, 1997, p. A1; "Brazil: Procter & Gamble Increased Market Share," *SABI* (South American Business Information), May 31, 2000; Jonathan Birchall, "New Tactics in the Battle for Babies' Bottoms," *Financial Times,* http://www.FT.com, August 24, 2006. For more information, see Kimberly-Clark's Web site at http://www.kimberly-clark.com, and Procter & Gamble's at http://www.pg.com; also see Matthew Bird and Rosabeth Moss Kanter, "Procter & Gamble Brazil (A): 2 ½ Turnarounds," *Harvard Business School Cases,* January 1, 2008, for details about the firms' decision-making approaches.

Setting and changing prices are key strategic marketing decisions. Prices both set values and communicate in international markets.[1] For example, Hong Kong Disneyland's early attendance was lower than expected, in part driven by what some called an unaffordable opening-day price of $32 a ticket.[2] Setting the right price for a product or service can be the key to success or failure. Even when the international marketer produces the right product, promotes it correctly, and initiates the proper channel of distribution, the effort fails if the product is not properly priced. Although the quality of U.S. products is widely recognized in global markets, foreign buyers, like domestic buyers, balance quality and price in their purchase decisions. An offering's price must reflect the quality and value the consumer perceives in the product. Of all the tasks facing the international marketer, determining what price to charge is one of the most difficult. It is further complicated when the company sells its product to customers in multiple country's markets.

As globalization continues, competition intensifies among multinational and home-based companies. All are seeking a solid competitive position so they can prosper as markets reach full potential. The competition for the diaper market among Kimberly-Clark, P&G, and the smaller companies illustrates how price becomes increasingly important as a competitive tool and how price competition changes the structure of a market. Whether exporting or managing overseas operations, the manager's responsibility is to set and control the price of goods in multiple markets in which different sets of variables are to be found: different tariffs, costs, attitudes, competition, currency fluctuations, and methods of price quotation.

This chapter focuses on the basic pricing policy questions that arise from the special cost, market, and competitive factors found in foreign markets. A discussion of price escalation and its control and factors associated with price setting and leasing is followed by a discussion of the use of countertrade as a pricing tool and a review of the mechanics of international price quotation. We close the chapter with a brief discussion about the mechanics of getting paid the prices charged—letters of credit and such.

LO1

Components of pricing as competitive tools in international marketing

Pricing Policy

Active marketing in several countries compounds the number of pricing problems and variables relating to price policy. Unless a firm has a clearly thought-out, explicitly defined price policy, expediency rather than design establishes prices. The country in which business is being conducted, the type of product, variations in competitive conditions, and other strategic factors affect pricing activity. Price and terms of sale cannot be based on domestic criteria alone.

Pricing Objectives

In general, price decisions are viewed two ways: pricing as an active instrument of accomplishing marketing objectives, or pricing as a static element in a business decision. If prices are viewed as an active instrument, the company *sets* prices (rather than *following* market prices)[3] to achieve specific objectives,[4] whether targeted returns on profit, targeted sales volumes, or some other specific goals.[5] The company that follows the second approach, pricing as a static element, probably exports only excess inventory, places a low priority on foreign business, and views its export sales as passive contributions to sales volume. When U.S. and Canadian international businesses were asked to rate, on a scale of 1 to 5, several factors important in price setting, total profits received an average rating of 4.70, followed by

[1] Lorraine Eden and Peter Rodriguez, "How Weak Are the Signals? International Price Indices and Multinational Enterprises," *Journal of International Business Studies* 36, no. 1 (2004), pp. 61–74.

[2] Don Lee, "Disneyland's Cost a Hurdle for Chinese," *Los Angeles Times*, September 10, 2005, pp. C1, C3.

[3] Carl Arthur Solberg, Barbara Stottinger, and Attila Yaprak, "A Taxonomy of the Pricing Practices of Exporting Firms: Evidence from Austria, Norway, and the United States," *Journal of International Marketing* 14 (2006), pp. 23–48.

[4] Andrew LaVallee, "Unilever to Test Mobile Coupons," *The Wall Street Journal*, May 29, 2009, p. B8.

[5] S. Tamer Cavusgil, Kwog Chan, and Chun Zhang, "Strategic Orientations in Export Pricing: A Clustering Approach to Create Firm Taxonomies," *Journal of International Marketing* 11, no. 1 (2003), p. 47; Christopher K. Hsee, Jean-Pierre Dube, and Yan Zhang, "The Prominence Effect in Shanghai Apartment Prices," *Journal of Marketing Research* 45, no. 2 (2008), pp. 133–44.

CROSSING BORDERS 18.2

Don't Squeeze the Charmin, Mr. Whipple—Or Change the Color

The British pay twice the price as the Germans and the French, and nearly two-and-a-half times as much as Americans, for a standard four-roll pack of toilet paper. Why? Is it price gouging, the impact of the euro, the relative value of the English pound, or just culture?

The answer is rather simple: British consumers insist on a softer, more luxurious texture than their less discriminating continental and American cousins. British toilet paper is four grams heavier per square meter because it contains more fiber than European tissues. Extensive consumer testing has established that British consumers are not willing to be fobbed off with anything less.

Another factor distinguishes the British preference for a special toilet paper roll. Go to any supermarket, and you will be confronted by an extraordinary choice of more than 50 colors, sizes, and brands. Honeysuckle, warm pink, summer peach, pearl white, meadow green, breeze blue, and magnolia are just some of the shades on offer. The reason for this variety apparently is that the British shopper insists that toilet paper match the color scheme of the bathroom. On the continent, consumers settle happily for white, with pink thrown in as a wild alternative.

Procter & Gamble captured 10 percent of the market in less than five months after offering a stronger Charmin, but it may have gone too far. There were complaints that the "wet strength" of Charmin was unsuitable for U.K. toilets. The U.K. sewage system could handle Charmin alone, but the issue was whether the system would get clogged if several rival tissues adopted the stronger tissue. Procter & Gamble agreed to halve the strength of its Charmin toilet tissue, but will the price come down? And most recently, the P&G product has also been rated worst on a forest-friendly scale by Greenpeace. Complying with this latest criticism will surely raise costs.

Sources: "Going Soft," *The Economist*, March 4, 2000; "P&G Unblocks Sewage Row with Toilet Paper Revamp," *Reuters*, May 10, 2000; Timothy Kenny, "Eurasia: Of Toilet Paper, Escalators and Hope," *The Wall Street Journal Europe*, September 16, 2005, p. A9; "Skip it, Eco-Worrier," *The Times (London)*, December 1, 2007, p. 11.

product, a skimming price may be used to maximize profits until competition forces a lower price.[12] Skimming often is used in markets with only two income levels: the wealthy and the poor. Costs prohibit setting a price that will be attractive to the lower-income market, so the marketer charges a premium price and directs the product to the high-income, relatively price-insensitive segment. Apparently this was the policy of Johnson & Johnson's pricing of diapers in Brazil before the arrival of P&G. Today such opportunities are fading away as the disparity in income levels is giving way to growing middle-income market segments. The existence of larger markets attracts competition and, as is often the case, the emergence of multiple product lines, thus leading to price competition.

A **penetration pricing policy** is used to stimulate market and sales growth by deliberately offering products at low prices. Penetration pricing most often is used to acquire and hold share of market as a competitive maneuver. However, in country markets experiencing rapid and sustained economic growth, and where large shares of the population are moving into middle-income classes, penetration pricing may be used to stimulate market growth even with minimum competition. Penetration pricing may be a more profitable strategy than skimming if it maximizes revenues as a base for fighting the competition that is sure to come.

Regardless of the formal pricing policies and strategies a company uses, the market sets the effective price for a product. Said another way, the price has to be set at a point at which the consumer will perceive value received, and the price must be within reach of the target market. As a consequence, many products are sold in very small units in some markets to bring the unit price within reach of the target market. Warner-Lambert's launch of its five-unit pack of Bubbaloo bubble gum in Brazil failed—even though bubble gum represents over 72 percent of the overall gum sector—because it was priced too high for the target market. A relaunch of a single-unit "pillow" pack brought the price within range and enabled the brand to quickly gain a respectable level of sales.

---

[12]Caroline Bingxin Li and Julie Juan Li, "Achieving Superior Financial Performance in China: Differentiation, Cost Leadership, or Both?" *Journal of International Marketing* 16, no. 3 (2008), pp. 1–22.

Chinese wait to enter Beijing's first Walmart outlet. Thousands crowded the Sam's Club store on the far western edge of Beijing as the world's biggest retailer made its first foray into a major Chinese city. Walmart now has more than 200 stores elsewhere in China; the first opened in 1996. The low-price-for-good-quality strategy of Walmart and other mass retailers such as Costco and Carrefour, the French supermarket chain, have resulted in lower retail prices in China, Japan, and other Asian countries they have entered.

As a country's economy grows and the distribution of wealth becomes more equitable, multiple income levels develop, distinct market segments emerge, and multiple price levels and price/quality perceptions increase in importance. As an example, the market for electronic consumer goods in China changed in just a few years. Instead of a market for imported high-priced and high-quality electronic goods aimed at the new rich versus cheaper, poorer quality, Chinese-made goods for the rest of the market, a multitiered market reflecting the growth of personal income has emerged.

Sony of Japan, the leading foreign seller of high-priced consumer electronic goods, was upstaged in the Chinese market when Aiwa, a competitor, recognized the emergence of a new middle-tier market for good-quality, modestly priced electronic goods. As part of a global strategy focused on slim margins and high turnover, Aiwa of Korea began selling stereo systems at prices closer to Chinese brands than to Sony's. Aiwa's product quality was not far behind that of Sony and was better than top Chinese brands, and the product resembled Sony's high-end systems. Aiwa's recognition of a new market segment and its ability to tap into it resulted in a huge increase in overall demand for Aiwa products.

Pricing decisions that were appropriate when companies directed their marketing efforts toward single market segments will give way to more sophisticated practices. As incomes rise in many foreign markets, the pricing environment a company encounters will be similar to that in the United States. As countries prosper and incomes become more equitably distributed, multiple market segments develop. As these segments emerge, Walmart, Carrefour, and other mass retailers enter the market to offer price-conscious customers good value at affordable prices. This scenario seems to repeat itself in country after country. Within these markets, an effective pricing strategy becomes crucial.

Price Escalation

LO3

Price escalation and how to minimize its effect

People traveling abroad often are surprised to find goods that are relatively inexpensive in their home country priced outrageously high in other countries. Because of the natural tendency to assume that such prices are a result of profiteering, manufacturers often resolve to begin exporting to crack these new, profitable foreign markets only to find that, in most cases, the higher prices reflect the higher costs of exporting. A case in point is a pacemaker for heart patients that sells for $2,100 in the United States. Tariffs and the Japanese distribution system add substantially to the final price in Japan. Beginning with the import tariff, each time the pacemaker changes hands, an additional cost is incurred. The product passes first through the hands of an importer, then to the company with primary responsibility for sales and service, then to a secondary or even a tertiary local distributor, and finally to the hospital. Markups at each level result in the $2,100 pacemaker selling for over $4,000 in Japan. Inflation results in price escalation, one of the major pricing obstacles facing the MNC marketer. This escalation is true not only for technical products like the pacemaker but for such products as crude oil, soft drinks, and beer. Estimates indicate that if tariffs and trade barriers on these products were abolished, the consumer would enjoy savings of 6.57 trillion yen.

Costs of Exporting

Excess profits exist in some international markets, but generally the cause of the disproportionate difference in price between the exporting country and the importing country, here termed **price escalation**, is the added costs incurred as a result of exporting products from one country to another. Specifically, the term relates to situations in which ultimate prices are raised by shipping costs, insurance, packing, tariffs, longer channels of distribution, larger middlemen margins, special taxes, administrative costs, and exchange rate fluctuations. The majority of these costs arise as a direct result of moving goods across borders from one country to another and often combine to escalate the final price to a level considerably higher than in the domestic market.

Taxes, Tariffs, and Administrative Costs

A Japanese wholesale store manager of a meat market in Tokyo arranges packs of beef imported from Australia. Earlier in the day, the government had announced Japan plans to raise its tariff on refrigerated beef imports to 50 percent from 38.5 percent, following a spike in imports. The price tag reads: "Premium beef, sirloin steak from Australia @ 258 yen per 100 grams." Tariffs are one of the main causes of price escalation for imported products.

A tariff, or duty, is a special form of taxation. Like other forms of taxes, a tariff may be levied for the purpose of protecting a market or for increasing government revenue. A tariff is a fee charged when goods are brought into a country from another country. The level of tariff is typically expressed as the rate of duty and may be levied as specific, ad valorem, or compound. A specific duty is a flat charge per physical unit imported, such as 15 cents per bushel of rye. Ad valorem duties are levied as a percentage of the value of the goods imported, such as 20 percent of the value of imported watches. Compound duties include both a specific and an ad valorem charge, such as $1 per camera plus 10 percent of its value. Tariffs and other forms of import taxes serve to discriminate against all foreign goods.

Fees for import certificates or for other administrative processing can assume such levels that they are, in fact, import taxes. Many countries have purchase or excise taxes that apply to various categories of goods; value-added or turnover taxes, which apply as the product goes through a channel of distribution; and retail sales taxes. Such taxes increase the end price of goods but in general do not discriminate against foreign goods. Tariffs are the primary discriminatory tax that must be taken into account in reckoning with foreign competition.

In addition to taxes and tariffs, a variety of administrative costs are directly associated with exporting and importing a product. Export and import licenses, other documents, and the physical arrangements for getting the product from port of entry to the buyer's location mean additional costs. Although such costs are relatively small, they add to the overall cost of exporting.

Inflation

In countries with rapid inflation or exchange variation, the selling price must be related to the cost of goods sold and the cost of replacing the items. Goods often are sold below their cost of replacement plus overhead, and sometimes are sold below replacement cost. In these instances, the company would be better off not to sell the products at all. When payment is likely to be delayed for several months or is worked out on a long-term contract, inflationary factors must be figured into the price. Inflation and lack of control over price were instrumental in an unsuccessful new-product launch in Brazil by the H. J. Heinz Company; after only two years, Heinz withdrew from the market. Misunderstandings with the local partner resulted in a new fruit-based drink being

Shoppers look at stacks of discount clothing jutting out on a sidewalk to attract potential buyers at Tokyo's Sugamo shopping district. With the stock market plunging to 16-year lows, talk of deflationary dangers, and a morass of confusion in its political leadership, Japan appeared to be headed toward a serious economic crisis. The central bank played down the possibility of deflation, saying that falling prices show the market is finally opening up to competition.

sold to retailers on consignment; that is, they did not pay until the product was sold. Faced with a rate of inflation of over 300 percent at the time, just a week's delay in payment eroded profit margins substantially. Soaring inflation in many developing countries has made widespread price controls a constant threat in many countries.

Because inflation and price controls imposed by a country and/or the global marketplace[13] are beyond the control of companies, they use a variety of techniques to inflate the selling price to compensate for inflation pressure and price controls. They may charge for extra services, inflate costs in transfer pricing, or break up products into components and price each component separately.

Inflation causes consumer prices to escalate, and consumers face ever-rising prices that eventually exclude many of them from the market. In contrast, deflation results in ever-decreasing prices, creating a positive result for consumers, but both put pressure to lower costs on everyone in the supply chain.

Deflation

The Japanese economy was in a deflationary spiral for a number of years. In a country better known for $10 melons and $100 steaks, McDonald's now sells hamburgers for 52 cents, down from $1.09; a flat screen 32-inch color television is down from $4,000 to $2,400; and clothing stores compete to sell fleece jackets for $8, down from $25 two years earlier. Consumer prices have dropped to a point that they are similar to those Japanese once found only on overseas shopping trips. The high prices prevalent in Japan before deflation allowed substantial margins for everyone in the distribution chain. As prices continued to drop over several years, those less able to adjust costs to allow some margin with deflated prices fell by the wayside. Entirely new retail categories—100-yen discount shops, clothing chains selling low-cost imported products from China, and warehouse-style department stores—have become the norm. Sales at discount stores grew by 78 percent in the late 1990s. Discounting is the way to prosper in Japan, which again helps fuel deflation. While those in the distribution chain adjusted to a different competitive environment or gave up, Japanese consumers were reveling in their newfound spending power. Japanese tourists used to travel to the United States to buy things at much cheaper prices, but as one consumer commented, "Nowadays, I feel prices in Japan are going down and America is no longer cheaper." Although she was accustomed to returning from trips to the United States carrying suitcases of bargains, she returned from her last two-week vacation with purchases that fit in one fanny pack.

In a deflationary market, it is essential for a company to keep prices low and raise brand value to win the trust of consumers. Whether experiencing deflation or inflation, an exporter has to place emphasis on controlling price escalation.

Exchange Rate Fluctuations

At one time, world trade contracts could be easily written because payment was specified in a relatively stable currency. The American dollar was the standard, and all transactions could be related to the dollar. Now that all major currencies are floating freely relative to one another, no one is quite sure of the future value of any currency. Increasingly, companies are insisting that transactions be written in terms of the vendor company's national currency, and forward hedging is becoming more common. If exchange rates are not carefully considered in long-term contracts, companies find themselves unwittingly giving 15 to 20 percent discounts. The added cost incurred by exchange rate fluctuations on a day-to-day basis must be taken into account, especially where there is a significant time lapse between signing the order and delivery of the goods. Exchange rate differentials mount. Whereas Hewlett-Packard gained nearly half a million dollars additional profit through

---

[13]Neil Shah, "Fears Rise of Euro Government Default," *The Wall Street Journal*, February 4, 2010, online.

During the mid-1990s, Mexico knocked three zeroes off the peso in response to a major devaluation. Venezuela did the same in 2008.[14] In 2005 Turkey knocked six zeroes off its lira toward its potential alignment with the European Union. Both actions affected perceptions of key constituencies. Both bills are worth about 75¢.

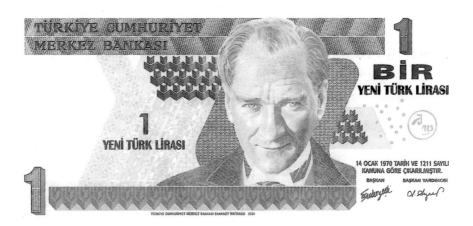

exchange rate fluctuations in one year, Nestlé lost a million dollars in six months. Other companies have lost or gained even larger amounts.

Varying Currency Values

In addition to risks from exchange rate variations, other risks result from the changing values of a country's currency relative to other currencies,[15] such as consumers' perceptions of value.[16] Consider the situation in Germany for a purchaser of U.S. manufactured goods from mid-2001 to mid-2003. During this period, the value of the U.S. dollar relative to the euro went from a strong position (U.S.$1 to € 1.8315) in mid-2001 to a weaker position in mid-2003 (U.S.$1 to €0.8499). A strong dollar produces price resistance because a larger quantity of local currency is needed to buy a U.S. dollar. Conversely, when the U.S. dollar is weak, demand for U.S. goods increases because fewer units of local currency are needed to buy a U.S. dollar. The weaker U.S. dollar, compared with most of the world's stronger currencies, that existed in mid-2003 stimulated exports from the United States. Consequently, when the dollar strengthens, U.S. exports will soften.

When the value of the dollar is weak relative to the buyer's currency (i.e., it takes fewer units of the foreign currency to buy a dollar), companies generally employ cost-plus pricing. To remain price competitive when the dollar is strong (i.e., when it takes more units of the foreign currency to buy a dollar), companies must find ways to offset the higher price caused by currency values. When the rupee in India depreciated significantly against the

[14]Annually *The Economist* publishes its Big Mac index, which predicts currency fluctuations. See "Cheesed Off," July 8, 2009, p. 74.

[15]Klaus Wertenbrouch, Dilip Soman, and Amitava Chattopadhyay, "On the Perceived Value of Money: The Reference Dependence of Currency Numerosity Effects," *Journal of Consumer Research* 34 (2007), pp. 1–10.

[16]"Venezuela: Chavez's New Currency Targets Inflation," *Tulsa World*, January 1, 2008, p. A6.

A woman looks at a poster offering a half-priced bacon and lettuce hamburger, reduced from U.S.$3.20 to $1.60 during a monthly discount at a McDonald's restaurant in downtown Tokyo. McDonald's Japan announced that it would reduce the price of hamburgers by 30 percent for a month to return to customers the profit the company made by the strong yen against U.S. dollars in importing the raw materials from abroad. McDonald's move created goodwill among its customers at a time when it is forced to lower prices to "hike" sales in an economy that is suffering a major downturn. This move is a good example of how differences in the value of currencies can be positive for a company, as in this case, or negative when the value of the dollar is much stronger than the local currency.

U.S. dollar, PC manufacturers faced a serious pricing problem. Because the manufacturers were dependent on imported components, their options were to absorb the increased cost or raise the price of PCs.

Currency exchange rate swings are considered by many global companies to be a major pricing problem. Because the benefits of a weaker dollar are generally transitory, firms need to take a proactive stance one way or the other. For a company with long-range plans calling for continued operation in foreign markets that wants to remain price competitive, price strategies need to reflect variations in currency values.

Innumerable cost variables can be identified depending on the market, the product, and the situation. The cost, for example, of reaching a market with relatively small potential may be high. High operating costs of small specialty stores like those in Mexico and Thailand lead to high retail prices. Intense competition in certain world markets raises the cost or lowers the margins available to world business. Only experience in a given marketplace provides the basis for compensating for cost differences in different markets. With experience, a firm that prices on a cost basis operates in a realm of reasonably measurable factors.

Middleman and Transportation Costs

Channel length and marketing patterns vary widely, but in most countries, channels are longer and middleman margins higher than is customary in the United States. The diversity of channels used to reach markets and the lack of standardized middleman markups leave many producers unaware of the ultimate price of a product.

Besides channel diversity, the fully integrated marketer operating abroad faces various unanticipated costs because marketing and distribution channel infrastructures are underdeveloped in many countries. The marketer can also incur added expenses for warehousing and handling of small shipments and may have to bear increased financing costs when dealing with underfinanced middlemen.

Because no convenient source of data on middleman costs is available, the international marketer must rely on experience and marketing research to ascertain middleman costs. The Campbell Soup Company found its middleman and physical distribution costs in the United Kingdom to be 30 percent higher than in the United States. Extra costs were incurred because soup was purchased in small quantities—small English grocers typically purchase 24-can cases of assorted soups (each case being hand-packed for shipment). In the United States, typical purchase units are 48-can cases of one soup purchased by the dozens, hundreds, or carloads. The purchase habits in Europe forced the company into an extra wholesale level in its channel to facilitate handling small orders.

Exporting also incurs increased transportation costs when moving goods from one country to another. If the goods go over water, insurance, packing, and handling are additional costs not generally added to locally produced goods. Such costs add yet another burden because import tariffs in many countries are based on the landed cost, which includes transportation, insurance, and shipping charges. These costs add to the inflation of the final price. The next section details how a price in the home market may more than double in the foreign market.

Sample Effects of Price Escalation

Exhibit 18.2 illustrates some of the effects the factors discussed previously may have on the end price of a consumer item. Because costs and tariffs vary so widely from country to country, a hypothetical but realistic example is used.

Exhibit 18.2
Sample Causes and Effects of Price Escalation

	Domestic Example	Foreign Example 1: Assuming the Same Channels with Wholesaler Importing Directly	Foreign Example 2: Importer and Same Margins and Channels	Foreign Example 3: Same as 2 but with 10 Percent Cumulative Turnover Tax
Manufacturing net	$ 5.00	$ 5.00	$ 5.00	$5.00
Transport, CIF	n.a.	6.10	6.10	6.10
Tariff (20 percent CIF value)	n.a.	1.22	1.22	1.22
Importer pays	n.a.	n.a.	7.32	7.32
Importer margin when sold to wholesaler (25 percent on cost)	n.a.	n.a.	1.83	1.83 +0.73
Wholesaler pays landed cost	5.00	7.32	9.15	9.88
Wholesaler margin (33⅓ percent on cost)	1.67	2.44	3.05	3.29 +0.99
Retailer pays	6.67	9.76	12.20	14.16
Retail margin (50 percent on cost)	3.34	4.88	6.10	7.08 +1.42
Retail price	$10.01	$14.64	$18.30	$22.66

Notes: All figures in U.S. dollars; CIF = cost, insurance, and freight; n.a. = not applicable. The exhibit assumes that all domestic transportation costs are absorbed by the middleman. Transportation, tariffs, and middleman margins vary from country to country, but for the purposes of comparison, only a few of the possible variations are shown.

It assumes that a constant net price is received by the manufacturer, that all domestic transportation costs are absorbed by the various middleman and reflected in their margins, and that the foreign middlemen have the same margins as the domestic middlemen. In some instances, foreign middleman margins are lower, but it is equally probable that these margins could be greater. In fact, in many instances, middlemen use higher wholesale and retail margins for foreign goods than for similar domestic goods.

Notice that the retail prices in Exhibit 18.2 range widely, illustrating the difficulty of price control by manufacturers in overseas retail markets. No matter how much the manufacturer may wish to market a product in a foreign country for a price equivalent to US$10, there is little opportunity for such control. Even assuming the most optimistic conditions for Foreign Example 1, the producer would need to cut its net by more than one-third to absorb freight and tariff costs if the goods are to be priced the same in both foreign and domestic markets. Price escalation is everywhere: A man's dress shirt that sells for $40 in the United States retails for $80 in Caracas. A $20 U.S. electric can opener is priced in Milan at $70; a $35 U.S.-made automatic toaster is priced at $80 in France.

Unless some of the costs that create price escalation can be reduced, the marketer is faced with a price that may confine sales to a limited segment of wealthy, price-insensitive customers. In many markets, buyers have less purchasing power than in the United States and can be easily priced out of the market. Furthermore, once price escalation is set in motion, it can spiral upward quickly. When the price to middlemen is high and turnover is low, they may insist on higher margins to defray their costs, which, of course, raises the price even higher. Unless price escalation can be reduced, marketers find that the only buyers left are the wealthier ones. If marketers are to compete successfully in the growth of markets around the world, cost containment must be among their highest priorities. If costs can be reduced anywhere along the chain, from manufacturer's cost to retailer markups, price escalation will be reduced. A discussion of some of the approaches to reducing price escalation follows.

Approaches to Reducing Price Escalation
Three methods used to reduce costs and lower price escalation are lowering the cost of goods, lowering tariffs, and lowering distribution costs.

Lowering Cost of Goods

If the manufacturer's price can be lowered, the effect is felt throughout the chain. One of the important reasons for manufacturing in a third country is an attempt to reduce manufacturing costs and thus price escalation. The impact can be profound if you consider that the hourly cost of skilled labor in a Mexican maquiladora is less than $3 an hour including benefits, compared with more than $10 in the United States.

In comparing the costs of manufacturing microwave ovens in the United States and in Korea, the General Electric Company found substantial differences. A typical microwave oven cost GE $218 to manufacture compared with $155 for Samsung, a Korean manufacturer. A breakdown of costs revealed that assembly labor cost GE $8 per oven and Samsung only 63 cents. Perhaps the most disturbing finding for GE was that Korean laborers delivered more for less cost: GE produced four units per person, whereas the Korean company produced nine.

Although Korea remains an important offshore manufacturing location, China has emerged as a global manufacturing powerhouse backed by an inexpensive labor force, rapidly improving production quality, new sources of capital, a more dynamic private sector, and a deliberately undervalued currency. China supplies a growing range of products to the global marketplace. Japan, the land of zero-defect quality control, is increasingly happy with the competence of Chinese workers. Star Manufacturing, a Japanese precision machine tool manufacturing company, moved 30 percent of its production to China because China's cheap labor and cheap resources reduced its production costs by 20 percent.

Eliminating costly functional features or even lowering overall product quality is another method of minimizing price escalation. For U.S.-manufactured products, the quality and additional features required for the more developed home market may not be necessary in countries that have not attained the same level of development or consumer demand. In the price war between P&G and Kimberly-Clark in Brazil, the quality of the product was decreased to lower the price. Remember that the grandmother in the grocery store chose the poorest quality and lowest priced brand of diaper. Similarly, functional features on washing machines made for the United States, such as automatic bleach and soap dispensers, thermostats to provide four different levels of water temperature, controls to vary water volume, and bells to ring at appropriate times, may be unnecessary for many foreign markets. Eliminating them means lower manufacturing costs and thus a corresponding reduction in price escalation. Lowering manufacturing costs can often have a double benefit: The lower price to the buyer may also mean lower tariffs, because most tariffs are levied on an ad valorem basis.

Lowering Tariffs

When tariffs account for a large part of price escalation, as they often do, companies seek ways to lower the rate. Some products can be reclassified into a different, and lower, customs classification.[17] An American company selling data communications equipment in Australia faced a 25 percent tariff, which affected the price competitiveness of its products. It persuaded the Australian government to change the classification for the type of products the company sells from "computer equipment" (25 percent tariff) to "telecommunication equipment" (3 percent tariff). Like many products, this company's products could be legally classified under either category. One complaint against customs agents in Russia is the arbitrary way in which they often classify products. Russian customs, for instance, insists on classifying Johnson & Johnson's 2-in-1 Shower Gel as a cosmetic with a 20 percent tariff rather than as a soap substitute, which the company considers it, at a 15 percent tariff.

How a product is classified is often a judgment call. The difference between an item being classified as jewelry or art means paying no tariff for art or a 26 percent tariff for jewelry. For example, a U.S. customs inspector could not decide whether to classify a $2.7 million Fabergé egg as art or jewelry. The difference was $0 tariff versus $700,000. An experienced freight forwarder/customs broker saved the day by persuading the customs agent that the

---

[17]Matthew Dolan, "To Outfox the Chicken Tax, Ford Strips Its Own Vans," *The Wall Street Journal*, September 22, 2009, pp. A1, A14.

CROSSING BORDERS 18.3   What Does It Mean To Be Human? 5.2 Percent, That's What

"What does it mean to be human?" asked Judge Barzilay in her chambers at the U.S. Court of International Trade. At the heart of the problem were some 60 little plastic figures of Marvel Enterprises' X-Men and other comic figures.

Marvel subsidiary Toy Biz Inc. sought to have its heroes from a range of comic characters declared nonhuman. At the time, tariffs were higher on dolls (12 percent) than toys (6.8 percent). According to the U.S. tariff code, human figures are dolls, whereas figures representing animals or "creatures," such as monsters and robots, are deemed toys.

Thus began the great debate over the figures' true being. Barbie is a doll. Pooh Bear's a toy. That much is easy. But what about Wolverine, the muscular X-Man with the metal claws that jut out from his fists? Wolverine has known many forms in his more than 40 years as a Marvel character. But is he human? Or consider Kraven, a famed hunter, who once vanquished Spiderman, thanks in part to the strength he gained from drinking secret jungle elixirs.

Toy Biz argued that the figures "stand as potent witnesses for their status as nonhuman creatures." How could they be humans if they possessed "tentacles, claws, wings or robotic limbs"? The U.S. Customs Service argued that each figure had a "distinctive individual personality." Some were Russians, Japanese, black, white, women, even handicapped. Wolverine, the government insisted, was simply "a man with prosthetic hands."

To weigh the question, Judge Barzilay sat down with a sheaf of opposing legal briefs and more than 60 action figures, including Wolverine, Storm, Rogue, Kraven, and Bonebreaker. Judge Barzilay described in her ruling how she subjected many of the figures to "comprehensive examinations." At times, that included "the need to remove the clothes of the figure." The X-Men, oddly, gave her the least trouble. They are

mutants, she declared, who "use their extraordinary and unnatural powers on the side of good or evil." Thus, the X-Men are "something other than human." Tougher for the judge were figures from the Fantastic Four and Spiderman series. After careful examination and thought, the judge found Kraven exhibited "highly exaggerated muscle tone in arms and legs." He wore a "lion's mane-like vest." Both features helped relegate him to the netherworld of robots, monsters, and devils. Case closed.

Toy Biz Inc. was elated, but fans were incensed—no way are X-Men mere creatures. "Marvel's superheroes are supposed to be as human as you or I. They live in New York. They have families and go to work. And now they're no longer human?" The current author of Marvel's *Uncanny X-Men* comic book series is also incredulous. He worked hard for a year, he says, to emphasize the X-Men's humanity, to show "that they're just another strand in the evolutionary chain." But "Don't fret, Marvel fans, a decision that the X-Men figures indeed do have 'nonhuman' characteristics further proves our characters have special, out-of-this world powers."

Although this scenario may seem trivial, it highlights just how arbitrary tariff classification can be. It pays to argue your case if you believe a product can be classified at a lower rate. For every $100,000 of plastic figures Toy Biz imports, the reclassification saves it $5,200. Not a bad day's work, considering the hundreds of thousands of dollars worth of figures the company imports annually—not to mention the undisclosed sum Toy Biz can recoup from years of overpaid tariffs.

Sources: Niel King Jr., "Is Wolverine Human? A Judge Answers No; Fans Howl in Protest," *The Wall Street Journal*, January 20, 2003; Marie Beerens, "Marvel's Two Movies Should Fuel Demand," *Investor's Business Daily*, February 19, 2008; Paul Bond, "Hasbro, Marvel Will Play Together through '17," *Hollywood Reporter*, February 18, 2009, p. 8.

Fabergé egg was a piece of art. Because the classification of products varies among countries, a thorough investigation of tariff schedules and classification criteria can result in a lower tariff.

Besides having a product reclassified into a lower tariff category, it may be possible to modify a product to qualify for a lower tariff rate within a tariff classification. In the footwear industry, the difference between "foxing" and "foxlike" on athletic shoes makes a substantial difference in the tariff levied. To protect the domestic footwear industry from an onslaught of cheap sneakers from the Far East, the tariff schedules state that any canvas or vinyl shoe with a foxing band (a tape band attached at the sole and overlapping the shoe's upper by more than one-quarter inch) be assessed at a higher duty

Hugh Jackman portraying Wolverine, an X-Men fictional character from Marvel Enterprises. A tariff classification issue arose when the company declared the imported toy characters as nonhuman toys and U.S. Customs said that they were human figure dolls—tariffs on dolls at that time were 12 percent versus 6.8 percent for toys. U.S. Customs alleged that the X-Men figures were human figures and thus should be classified as dolls, not figures featuring animals or creatures, which would mean that they could be classified as toys. Product classifications are critical when tariffs are determined. See Crossing Borders 18.3 for more details on this case.

rate. As a result, manufacturers design shoes so that the sole does not overlap the upper by more than one-quarter inch. If the overlap exceeds one-quarter inch, the shoe is classified as having a foxing band; less than one-quarter inch, a foxlike band. A shoe with a foxing band is taxed at 48 percent and one with a foxlike band (one-quarter inch or less overlap) is taxed a mere 6 percent.

There are often differential rates between fully assembled, ready-to-use products and those requiring some assembly, further processing, the addition of locally manufactured component parts, or other processing that adds value to the product and can be performed within the foreign country. For example, a ready-to-operate piece of machinery with a 20 percent tariff may be subject to only a 12 percent tariff when imported unassembled. An even lower tariff may apply when the product is assembled in the country and some local content is added.

Repackaging also may help to lower tariffs. Tequila entering the United States in containers of one gallon or less carries a duty of $2.27 per proof gallon; larger containers are assessed at only $1.25. If the cost of rebottling is less than $1.02 per proof gallon, and it probably would be, considerable savings could result. As will be discussed shortly, one of the more important activities in foreign trade zones is the assembly of imported goods, using local and frequently lower cost labor.

Lowering Distribution Costs

Shorter channels can help keep prices under control. Designing a channel that has fewer middlemen may lower distribution costs by reducing or eliminating middleman markups. Besides eliminating markups, fewer middlemen may mean lower overall taxes. Some countries levy a value-added tax on goods as they pass through channels. Goods are taxed each time they change hands. The tax may be cumulative or noncumulative. A cumulative value-added tax is based on total selling price and is assessed every time the goods change hands. Obviously, in countries where value-added tax is cumulative, tax alone provides a special incentive for developing short distribution channels. Where that is achieved, tax is paid only on the difference between the middleman's cost and the selling price. While many manufacturers had to cut prices in wake of Japan's deflation, Louis Vuitton, a maker of branded boutique goods, was able to increase prices instead. A solid brand name and direct distribution have permitted Vuitton's price strategy. Vuitton's leather monogrammed bags have become a Japanese buyer's "daily necessity," and Vuitton distributes directly and sets its own prices.

Using Foreign Trade Zones to Lessen Price Escalation

Some countries have established foreign or free trade zones (FTZs) or free ports to facilitate international trade.[18] More than 300 of these facilities operate throughout the world, storing or processing imported goods. As free trade policies in Africa, Latin America, eastern Europe, and other developing regions expand, an equally rapid expansion has taken place in the creation and use of foreign trade zones. In a free port or FTZ, payment of import duties is postponed until the product leaves the FTZ area and enters the country. An FTZ is, in essence, a tax-free enclave and not considered part of the country as far as import regulations are concerned. When an item leaves an FTZ and is imported officially into the host country of the FTZ, all duties and regulations are imposed.

Utilizing FTZs can to some extent control price escalation resulting from the layers of taxes, duties, surcharges, freight charges, and so forth. Foreign trade zones permit many of

[18]Liu Li, "Free Trade Zone in Pipeline in Xinjiang," *China Daily*, September 20, 2005.

Exhibit 18.3
How Are Foreign Trade Zones Used?

There are more than 100 foreign trade zones (FTZs) in the United States, and FTZs exist in many other countries as well. Companies use them to postpone the payment of tariffs on products while they are in the FTZ. Here are some examples of how FTZs in the United States are used.

- A Japanese firm assembles motorcycles, jet skis, and three-wheel all-terrain vehicles for import as well as for export to Canada, Latin America, and Europe.

- A U.S. manufacturer of window shades and miniblinds imports and stores fabric from Holland in an FTZ, thereby postponing a 17 percent tariff until the fabric leaves the FTZ.

- A manufacturer of hair dryers stores its product in an FTZ, which it uses as its main distribution center for products manufactured in Asia.

- A European-based medical supply company manufactures kidney dialysis machines and sterile tubing using raw materials from Germany and U.S. labor. It then exports 30 percent of its products to Scandinavian countries.

- A Canadian company assembles electronic teaching machines using cabinets from Italy; electronics from Taiwan, Korea, and Japan; and labor from the United States, for export to Colombia and Peru.

In all these examples, tariffs are postponed until the products leave the FTZ and enter the United States. Furthermore, in most situations the tariff is at the lower rate for component parts and raw materials versus the higher rate that would be charged if products were imported directly as finished goods. If the finished products are not imported into the United States from the FTZ but are shipped to another country, no U.S. tariffs apply.

Sources: Lewis E. Leibowitz, "An Overview of Foreign Trade Zones," *Europe*, Winter–Spring 1987, p. 12; "Cheap Imports," *International Business*, March 1993, pp. 98–100; "Free-Trade Zones: Global Overview and Future Prospects," http://www.stat-usa.gov, 2010.

these added charges to be avoided, reduced, or deferred so that the final price is more competitive. One of the more important benefits of the FTZ in controlling prices is the exemption from duties on labor and overhead costs incurred in the FTZ in assessing the value of goods.

By shipping unassembled goods to an FTZ in an importing country, a marketer can lower costs in a variety of ways:

- Tariffs may be lower because duties are typically assessed at a lower rate for unassembled versus assembled goods.
- If labor costs are lower in the importing country, substantial savings may be realized in the final product cost.
- Ocean transportation rates are affected by weight and volume; thus unassembled goods may qualify for lower freight rates.
- If local content, such as packaging or component parts, can be used in the final assembly, tariffs may be further reduced.

All in all, a foreign or free trade zone is an important method for controlling price escalation. Incidentally, all the advantages offered by an FTZ for an exporter are also advantages for an importer. U.S. importers use over 100 FTZs in the United States to help lower their costs of imported goods. See Exhibit 18.3 for illustrations of how FTZs are used.

Dumping   A logical outgrowth of a market policy in international business is goods priced competitively at widely differing prices in various markets. Marginal (variable) cost pricing, as discussed previously, is a way prices can be reduced to stay within a competitive price range. The market and economic logic of such pricing policies can hardly be disputed, but the practices often are classified as dumping and are subject to severe penalties and fines. Various economists define **dumping** differently. One approach classifies international shipments as dumped if the products are sold below their cost of production. Another approach characterizes dumping as selling goods in a foreign market below the price of the same goods in the home market.

World Trade Organization (WTO) rules allow for the imposition of a dumping duty when goods are sold at a price lower than the normal export price or less than the cost in the country of origin, increased by a reasonable amount for the cost of sales and profits, when this price is likely to be prejudicial to the economic activity of the importing country. A **countervailing duty** or *minimum access volume (MAV)*, which restricts the amount a country will import, may be imposed on foreign goods benefiting from subsidies, whether in production, export, or transportation.

For countervailing duties to be invoked, it must be shown that prices are lower in the importing country than in the exporting country and that producers in the importing country are being directly harmed by the dumping. A report by the U.S. Department of Agriculture indicated that levels of dumping by the United States hover around 40 percent for wheat and between 25 and 30 percent for corn, and levels for soybeans have risen steadily over the past four years to nearly 30 percent. These percentages, for example, mean that wheat is selling up to 40 percent below the cost of production. For cotton, the level of dumping for one year rose to a remarkable 57 percent, and for rice, it then stabilized at around 20 percent. The study indicated that these commodities are being dumped onto international markets by the United States in violation of WTO rules. The report found that after many years of accepting agricultural dumping, a few countries have begun to respond by investigating whether some U.S. agricultural exports are dumped. Brazil is considering a case against U.S. cotton before the WTO. Canada briefly imposed both countervailing and antidumping duties on U.S. corn imports; the United States did the same for Chinese apple juice concentrate.

Dumping is rarely an issue when world markets are strong. In the 1980s and 1990s, dumping became a major issue for a large number of industries when excess production capacity relative to home-country demand caused many companies to price their goods on a marginal-cost basis. In a classic case of dumping, prices are maintained in the home-country market and reduced in foreign markets.

Today, tighter government enforcement of dumping legislation is causing international marketers to seek new routes around such legislation. Assembly in the importing country is a way companies attempt to lower prices and avoid dumping charges. However, these *screw-driver plants,* as they are often called, are subject to dumping charges if the price differentials reflect more than the cost savings that result from assembly in the importing country. Another subterfuge is to alter the product so that the technical description will fit a lower duty category. To circumvent a 16.9 percent countervailing duty imposed on Chinese gas-filled, nonrefillable pocket flint lighters, the manufacturer attached a useless valve to the lighters so that they fell under the "nondisposable" category, thus avoiding the duty. Countries see through many such subterfuges and impose taxes. For example, the European Union imposed a $27 to $58 dumping duty per unit on a Japanese firm that assembled and sold office machines in the European Union. The firm was charged with valuing imported parts for assembly below cost.

The U.S. market is currently more sensitive to dumping than in the recent past. In fact, the Uruguay Round of the GATT included a section on antidumping that grew out of U.S. insistence on stricter controls on dumping of foreign goods in the United States at prices below those charged at home. Changes in U.S. law have enhanced the authority of the Commerce Department to prevent circumvention of antidumping duties and countervailing duties that have been imposed on a country for dumping. The United States and European Union have been the most ardent users of antidumping duties. A question asked by many though: Are dumping charges just a cover for protectionism? Previously, when an order was issued to apply antidumping and countervailing duties on products, companies charged with the violation would get around the order by slightly altering the product or by doing minor assembly in the United States or a third country. This effort created the illusion of a different product not subject to the antidumping order. The new authority of the Department of Commerce closes many such loopholes.

Leasing in International Markets

An important selling technique to alleviate high prices and capital shortages for capital equipment or high-priced durable goods[19] is the leasing system. The concept of equipment leasing has become increasingly important as a means of selling capital equipment in overseas markets. In fact, an estimated $50 billion worth (original cost) of U.S.-made and foreign-made equipment is on lease in western Europe.

The system of leasing used by industrial exporters is similar to the typical lease contracts used in the United States. Terms of the leases usually run one to five years, with

---

[19]Edward Taylor, "BMW to Cut Production, Raise Prices World-Wide," *The Wall Street Journal*, August 2–3, 2008, online.

payments made monthly or annually; included in the rental fee are servicing, repairs, and spare parts. Just as contracts for domestic and overseas leasing arrangements are similar, so are the basic motivations and the shortcomings. For example:

- Leasing opens the door to a large segment of nominally financed foreign firms that can be sold on a lease option but might be unable to buy for cash.
- Leasing can ease the problems of selling new, experimental equipment, because less risk is involved for the users.
- Leasing helps guarantee better maintenance and service on overseas equipment.
- Equipment leased and in use helps sell other companies in that country.
- Lease revenue tends to be more stable over a period of time than direct sales would be.

The disadvantages or shortcomings take on an international flavor. Besides the inherent disadvantages of leasing, some problems are compounded by international relationships. In a country beset with inflation, lease contracts that include maintenance and supply parts (as most do) can lead to heavy losses toward the end of the contract period. Furthermore, countries where leasing is most attractive are those where spiraling inflation is most likely to occur. The added problems of currency devaluation, expropriation, or other political risks are operative longer than if the sale of the same equipment were made outright. In light of these perils, leasing incurs greater risk than does outright sale; however, there is a definite trend toward increased use of this method of selling internationally, so the benefits must exceed the risk.

Countertrade as a Pricing Tool

LO4

Countertrading and its place in international marketing practices

Countertrade is a pricing tool that every international marketer must be ready to employ, and the willingness to accept a countertrade will often give the company a competitive advantage. The challenges of countertrade must be viewed from the same perspective as all other variations in international trade. Marketers must be aware of which markets will likely require countertrades, just as they must be aware of social customs and legal requirements. Assessing this factor along with all other market factors will enhance a marketer's competitive position.

One of the earliest barter arrangements occurred between the Soviet Union and PepsiCo before the ruble was convertible and before most companies were trading with the USSR. PepsiCo wanted to beat Coca-Cola into the Russian market. The only way possible was for PepsiCo to be willing to accept vodka (sold under the brand name Stolichnaya) from Russia and bottled wines (sold under the brand name of Premiat) from Romania to finance Pepsi bottling plants in those countries. From all indications, this arrangement was very profitable for Russia, Romania, and PepsiCo. Pepsi continues to use countertrade to expand its bottling plants. In a recent agreement between PepsiCo and Ukraine, Pepsi agreed to market $1 billion worth of Ukrainian-made commercial ships over an eight-year period. Some of the proceeds from the ship sales will be reinvested in the shipbuilding venture, and some will be used to buy soft-drink equipment and build five Pepsi bottling plants in the Ukraine. PepsiCo dominates the cola market in Russia and all the former Soviet republics in part because of its exclusive countertrade agreement with Russia, which locked Coca-Cola out of the Russian cola market for more than 12 years. After the Soviet Union was dismembered, the Russian economy crashed, and most of the Russian payment system broke down into barter operations. Truckloads of aspirin were swapped by one company, then traded for poultry, which in turn was bartered for lumber, in turn to be exchanged for X-ray equipment from Kazakhstan—all to settle debts. Many of these transactions involved regional electricity companies that were owed money by virtually everyone.

Although cash may be the preferred method of payment, countertrades have been an important part of trade with eastern Europe, the newly independent states, China,[20] and, to a varying degree, some Latin American and African nations. Barter, or countertrades, still constitute between 20 and 40 percent of all transactions in the economies of the former

---

[20]"Trade Financing and Insurance: Countertrade," *Economist Intelligence Unit–Country Finance*, January 22, 2008, p. 101.

Soviet bloc. Corporate debts to suppliers, payments and services, even taxes—all have a noncash component or are entirely bartered. Many of these countries constantly face a shortage of hard currencies with which to trade and thus resort to countertrades when possible. A recent purchase of 48 F-16 Falcons from Lockheed Martin was pegged at $3.5 billion. The financial package included soft loans and a massive offset program—purchases from Polish manufacturers that more than erased the costs of the deal in foreign exchange. With an economy once short of hard currency, Russia has offered a wide range of products in barter for commodities it needed. For example, Russian expertise in space technology was offered for Malaysian palm oil and rubber, and military equipment was exchanged for crude palm oil or rice from Indonesia.[21] Today, an international company must include in its market-pricing toolkit some understanding of countertrading.

Problems of Countertrading

The crucial problem confronting a seller in a countertrade negotiation is determining the value of and potential demand for the goods offered as payment. Frequently there is inadequate time to conduct a market analysis; in fact, it is not unusual to have sales negotiations almost completed before countertrade is introduced as a requirement in the transaction.

Although such problems are difficult to deal with, they can be minimized with proper preparation. In most cases where losses have occurred in countertrades, the seller has been unprepared to negotiate in anything other than cash. Some preliminary research should be done in anticipation of being confronted with a countertrade proposal. Countries with a history of countertrading are identified easily, and the products most likely to be offered in a countertrade often can be ascertained. For a company trading with developing countries, these facts and some background on handling countertrades should be a part of every pricing toolkit. Once goods are acquired, they can be passed along to institutions that assist companies in selling bartered goods.

Barter houses specialize in trading goods acquired through barter arrangements and are the primary outside source of aid for companies beset by the uncertainty of a countertrade. Although barter houses, most of which are found in Europe, can find a market for bartered goods, this effort requires time, which puts a financial strain on a company because capital is tied up longer than in normal transactions.

In the United States, there are companies that assist with bartered goods and their financing. Citibank has created a countertrade department to allow the bank to act as a consultant as well as to provide financing for countertrades. It is estimated that there are now about 500 barter exchange houses in the United States, many of which are accessible on the Internet. Some companies with a high volume of barter have their own in-house trading groups to manage countertrades. The 3M Company (Minnesota Mining and Manufacturing), for example, has a wholly owned division, 3M Global Trading (www.3m.com/globaltrading), which offers its services to smaller companies.

The Internet and Countertrading

The Internet may become the most important venue for countertrade activities. Finding markets for bartered merchandise and determining market price are two of the major problems with countertrades. Several barter houses have Internet auction sites, and a number of Internet exchanges are expanding to include global barter.

Some speculate that the Internet may become the vehicle for an immense online electronic barter economy, to complement and expand the offline barter exchanges that take place now. In short, some type of electronic trade dollar would replace national currencies in international trade transactions. This e-dollar would make international business considerably easier for many countries, because it would lessen the need to acquire sufficient U.S. or other hard currency to complete a sale or purchase.

TradeBanc, a market-making service, has introduced a computerized technology that will enable members of trade exchanges to trade directly, online, with members of other trade exchanges anywhere in the world, as long as their barter company is a TradeBanc affiliate (www.tradebanc.com). The medium of exchange could be the Universal Currency proposed by the International Reciprocal Trade Association (IRTA; www.irta.com), an association of

---

[21]Zakki P. Hakim, "Ministry Eyes Rice-for-Planes Trade Deal," *Jakarta Post*, September 20, 2005, p. 13.

trade exchanges with members including Russia, Iceland, Germany, Chile, Turkey, Australia, and the United States. The IRTA has proposed to establish and operate a Universal Currency Clearinghouse, which would enable trade exchange members to easily trade with one another using this special currency. When the system is in full swing, all goods and services from all the participating affiliates would be housed in a single database. The transactions would be cleared by the local exchanges, and settlement would be made using IRTA's Universal Currency, which could be used to purchase anything from airline tickets to potatoes.[22]

Price Quotations

LO5

The mechanics of price quotations

In quoting the price of goods for international sale, a contract may include specific elements affecting the price, such as credit, sales terms, and transportation. Parties to the transaction must be certain that the quotation settled on appropriately locates responsibility for the goods during transportation and spells out who pays transportation charges and from what point. Price quotations must also specify the currency to be used, credit terms, and the type of documentation required. Finally, the price quotation and contract should define quantity and quality. A quantity definition might be necessary because different countries use different units of measurement. In specifying a ton, for example, the contract should identify it as a metric or an English ton and as a long or short ton. Quality specifications can also be misunderstood if not completely spelled out. Furthermore, there should be complete agreement on quality standards to be used in evaluating the product. For example, "customary merchantable quality" may be clearly understood among U.S. customers but have a completely different interpretation in another country. The international trader must review all terms of the contract; failure to do so may have the effect of modifying prices even though such a change was not intended.

---

[22]You may want to visit the American Countertrade Association, http://www.countertrade.org, for a detailed discussion of the services offered by a countertrader.

CROSSING BORDERS 18.4   Psychological Pricing in China, the Lucky 8

Retailers in the United States often use prices ending in 99, and this tactic has been shown to be effective in a number of consumer studies. One explanation has to do with consumers' tendency to ignore the digits after the first rather than bothering to round to the closest number. Thus, $2.99 seems more like $2 than $3. Another explanation suggests the prices ending in 99 signal a sale price, and are therefore more attractive to consumers interested in sale prices.

A psychological pricing tactic in Chinese cultures is to include eights in the prices. Eight is attractive to Chinese consumers because it is the luckiest number among all, and the more eights the better. The number eight (八, ba) said in Chinese Mandarin sounds like the word for "prosperity" (发, fa), and it works similarly in Cantonese as well.

Thus, the 88th floor is a lucky and more valuable one in high-rise buildings in the region – in Hong Kong buildings that have far fewer floors can still get premium prices of the penthouse on the 88th floor by simply skipping "unlucky" floors omitting intermediate floors, particularly the unlucky numbers such as four. And automobile license plates and phone numbers with consecutive 8s can be worth hundreds of thousands of dollars. Finally, the opening ceremonies for the Olympic Games in Beijing began at 8 seconds, 8 minutes after 8pm (local time) on 8/8/08, thus guaranteeing the success of the Games.

Research has also shown a systematic bias in both advertised prices and stock prices for the number eight in Chinese markets. For example, among 499 prices for a variety of products listed in newspapers in Shanghai, Hong Kong, and Taiwan, 39.9% ended in 8, and the next most common ending number was 14.7% for 5. The unlucky number 4 (related to death) appeared at the end of only 1.4% of the prices. A similar study was conducted on Shanghai and Shenzen stock exchange data, and found a strong preference for share prices ending in 8, and an aversion to prices ending in the number 4.

Sources: See C. Simmons and Robert M. Schindler, "Cultural Superstitions and the Price Endings Used in Chinese Advertising," *Journal of International Marketing*, 11(2), 2003, pp. 101-111; N. Mark Lam and John L. Graham, *China Now: Doing Business in the World's Most Dynamic Market* (New York: McGraw-Hill, 2007); Philip Brown and Jason Mitchell, "Culture and Stock Price Clustering: Evidence for the Peoples' Republic of China," *Pacific-Basin Finance Journal*, 16(1/2), 2008, pp. 95–120.

Administered Pricing

Administered pricing is an attempt to establish prices for an entire market. Such prices may be arranged through the cooperation of competitors; through national, state, or local governments; or by international agreement. The legality of administered pricing arrangements of various kinds differs from country to country and from time to time. A country may condone price fixing for foreign markets but condemn it for the domestic market, for instance.

In general, the end goal of all administered pricing activities is to reduce the impact of price competition or eliminate it. Price fixing by business is not viewed as an acceptable practice (at least in the domestic market), but when governments enter the field of price administration, they presume to do it for the general welfare to lessen the effects of "destructive" competition.

The point at which competition becomes destructive depends largely on the country in question. To the Japanese, excessive competition is any competition in the home market that disturbs the existing balance of trade or gives rise to market disruptions. Few countries apply more rigorous standards in judging competition as excessive than Japan, but no country favors or permits totally free competition. Economists, the traditional champions of pure competition, acknowledge that perfect competition is unlikely and agree that some form of workable competition must be developed.

The pervasiveness of price-fixing attempts in business is reflected by the diversity of the language of administered prices; pricing arrangements are known as agreements, arrangements, combines, conspiracies, cartels, communities of profit, profit pools, licensing, trade associations, price leadership, customary pricing, or informal interfirm agreements.[23] The arrangements themselves vary from the completely informal, with no spoken or acknowledged agreement, to highly formalized and structured arrangements. Any type of price-fixing arrangement can be adapted to international business, but of all the forms mentioned, cartels are the most directly associated with international marketing.

Cartels

A **cartel** exists when various companies producing similar products or services work together to control markets for the types of goods and services they produce. The cartel association may use formal agreements to set prices, establish levels of production and sales for the participating companies, allocate market territories, and even redistribute profits. In some instances, the cartel organization itself takes over the entire selling function, sells the goods of all the producers, and distributes the profits.

Oil prices quadrupled in the mid-1970s because of OPEC's control of supplies. The $100+ per barrel oil you see in this picture was caused by burgeoning demand in China and around the world in 2008. Pertamina is the Indonesian national oil company.

The economic role of cartels is highly debatable, but their proponents argue that they eliminate cutthroat competition and rationalize business, permitting greater technical progress and lower prices to consumers. However, most experts doubt that the consumer benefits very often from cartels.

The Organization of Petroleum Exporting Countries (OPEC) is probably the best known international cartel. Its power in controlling the price of oil has resulted from the percentage of oil production it controls. In the early 1970s, when OPEC members provided the industrial world with 67 percent of its oil, OPEC was able to quadruple the price of oil. The sudden rise in price from $3 a barrel to $11 or more a barrel was a primary factor in throwing the world into a major recession. In 2000, OPEC members lowered production, and the oil price rose from $10 to over $30, creating a dramatic increase in U.S. gasoline prices. Non-OPEC oil-exporting countries benefit from the price increases, while net importers of foreign oil face economic repercussions.

One important aspect of cartels is their inability to maintain control for indefinite periods. Greed by cartel members and other problems generally weaken the control of the

---

[23]Dana Nunn and Miklos Sarvary, "Pricing Practices and Firms' Market Power in International Cellular Markets: An Empirical Study," *International Journal of Research in Marketing* 21, no. 4 (2004), pp. 377–95.

cartel. OPEC members tend to maintain a solid front until one decides to increase supply, and then others rapidly follow suit. In the short run, however, OPEC can affect global prices. Indeed, at this writing, world oil prices are above $100 a barrel, but most analysts attribute this increase more to burgeoning demand[24] than OPEC's ability to control supply.[25]

A lesser-known cartel, but one that has a direct impact on international trade, is the cartel that exists among the world's shipping companies. Every two weeks about 20 shipping-line managers gather for their usual meeting to set rates on tens of billions of dollars of cargo. They do not refer to themselves as a cartel but rather operate under such innocuous names as "The Trans-Atlantic Conference Agreement" (www.tacaconf.com). Regardless of the name, they set the rates on about 70 percent of the cargo shipped between the United States and northern Europe. Shipping between the United States and Latin American ports and between the United States and Asian ports also is affected by shipping cartels. Not all shipping lines are members of cartels, but a large number are; thus they have a definite impact on shipping. Although legal, shipping cartels are coming under scrutiny by the U.S. Congress, and new regulations may soon be passed.

Another cartel is the diamond cartel controlled by De Beers. For more than a century, De Beers has smoothly manipulated the diamond market by keeping a tight control over world supply.[26] The company mines about half the world's diamonds and takes in another 25 percent through contracts with other mining companies. In an attempt to control the other 25 percent, De Beers runs an "outside buying office" where it spends millions buying up diamonds to protect prices. The company controls most of the world's trade in rough gems and uses its market power to keep prices high.

The legality of cartels at present is not clearly defined. Domestic cartelization is illegal in the United States, and the European Union also has provisions for controlling cartels. The United States does permit firms to take cartel-like actions in foreign markets, though it does not allow foreign-market cartels if the results have an adverse impact on the U.S. economy. Archer Daniels Midland Company, the U.S. agribusiness giant, was fined

---

[24]"CPC to Continue Freeze on Oil Prices," *China Post*, March 2, 2008; Neil King Jr., Chip Cummins, and Russell Gold, "Oil Hits $100, Jolting Markets," *The Wall Street Journal*, January 3, 2008, p. A1.

[25]Robert J. Samuelson, "The Triumph of OPEC," *Newsweek*, March 17, 2008, p. 45.

[26]Eric Onstad, "De Beers May Spurn Low-Margin Russian Supply," *Reuters News*, July 20, 2007.

The De Beers company is one of the world's largest cartels, and for all practical purposes, it controls most of the world's diamonds and thus is able to maintain artificially high prices for diamonds. One of the ways in which it maintains control is illustrated by a recent agreement with Russia's diamond monopoly, in which De Beers will buy at least $550 million in rough gem diamonds from Russia, or about half of the country's annual output. By controlling supply from Russia, the second largest producer of diamonds, the South African cartel can keep prices high.

$205 million for its role in fixing prices for two food additives, lysine and citric acid. German, Japanese, Swiss, and Korean firms were also involved in that cartel. The group agreed on prices to charge and then allocated the share of the world market each company would get—down to the tenth of a decimal point. At the end of the year, any company that sold more than its allotted share was required to purchase in the following year the excess from a co-conspirator that had not reached its volume allocation target.

Although EU member countries have had a long history of tolerating price fixing, the European Union is beginning to crack down on cartels in the shipping, automobile, and cement industries, among others. The unified market and single currency have prompted this move. As countries open to free trade, powerful cartels that artificially raise prices and limit consumer choice are coming under closer scrutiny. However, the EU trustbusters are fighting tradition—since the trade guilds of the Middle Ages, cozy cooperation has been the norm. In each European country, companies banded together to control prices within the country and to keep competition out.

Government-Influenced Pricing

Companies doing business in foreign countries encounter a number of different types of government price setting. To control prices, governments may establish margins, set prices and floors or ceilings, restrict price changes, compete in the market, grant subsidies, and act as a purchasing monopsony or selling monopoly.[27] The government may also influence prices by permitting, or even encouraging, businesses to collude in setting manipulative prices. As an aside, of course, some companies need no help in price fixing—which often is illegal.[28]

The Japanese government traditionally has encouraged a variety of government-influenced price-setting schemes, However, in a spirit of deregulation that is gradually moving through Japan, Japan's Ministry of Health and Welfare will soon abolish regulation of business hours and price setting for such businesses as barbershops, beauty parlors, and laundries. Under the current practice, 17 sanitation-related businesses can establish such price-setting schemes, which are exempt from the Japanese Anti-Trust Law.

Governments of producing and consuming countries seem to play an ever-increasing role in the establishment of international prices for certain basic commodities. There is, for example, an international coffee agreement, an international cocoa agreement, and an international sugar agreement. And the world price of wheat has long been at least partially determined by negotiations between national governments.

Despite the pressures of business, government, and international price agreements, most marketers still have wide latitude in their pricing decisions for most products and markets.

Getting Paid: Foreign Commercial Payments

LO6

The mechanics of getting paid

The sale of goods in other countries is further complicated by additional risks encountered when dealing with foreign customers. Risks from inadequate credit reports on customers, problems of currency exchange controls, distance, and different legal systems, as well as the cost and difficulty of collecting delinquent accounts, require a different emphasis on payment systems. In U.S. domestic trade, the typical payment procedure for established customers is an *open account*—that is, the goods are delivered, and the customer is billed on an end-of-the-month basis. However, the most frequently used term of payment in foreign commercial transactions for both export and import sales is a letter of credit, followed closely in importance by commercial dollar drafts or bills of exchange drawn by the seller on the buyer. Internationally, open accounts are reserved for well-established customers, and cash in advance is required of only the poorest credit risks or when the character of the merchandise is such that not fulfilling the terms of

---

[27]"Apple, EU Reach iTunes Pricing Deal," *The Wall Street Journal*, January 9, 2008, online.

[28]"Canada Probes Allegations of Chocolate Price-Fixing," *The Wall Street Journal*, November 28, 2007, online; John R. Wilke, "Two U.K. Airlines Settle Price-Fixing Claims," *The Wall Street Journal*, February 15, 2008, p. A4.

"That's as worthless as a three-dollar bill"—so the old saying goes. Cuba actually has two currencies, the Cuban peso and the Cuban convertible peso. The latter is what you see above and you can exchange it for euros or Canadian dollars, but not U.S. dollars. The non-convertible Cuban peso's current value is about U.S.$1.08. The Cuban peso can be used only for domestic transactions and is worth about one-sixth of its convertible brother.

the contract may result in heavy loss. Because of the time required for shipment of goods from one country to another, advance payment of cash is an unusually costly burden for a potential customer and places the seller at a definite competitive disadvantage.

Terms of sales are typically arranged between the buyer and seller at the time of the sale. The type of merchandise, amount of money involved, business custom, credit rating of the buyer, country of the buyer, and whether the buyer is a new or old customer must be considered in establishing the terms of sale. The five basic payment arrangements—letters of credit, bills of exchange, cash in advance, open accounts, and forfaiting—are discussed in this section.

Letters of Credit

Export **letters of credit** opened in favor of the seller by the buyer handle most American exports. Letters of credit shift the buyer's credit risk to the bank issuing the letter of credit. When a letter of credit is employed, the seller ordinarily can draw a draft against the bank issuing the credit and receive dollars by presenting proper shipping documents.[29] Except for cash in advance, letters of credit afford the greatest degree of protection for the seller.

The procedure for a letter of credit begins with completion of the contract. (See Exhibit 18.4 for the steps in a letter-of-credit transaction.) Letters of credit can be revocable or irrevocable. An *irrevocable letter of credit* means that once the seller has accepted the credit, the buyer cannot alter it in any way without permission of the seller. Added protection is gained if the buyer is required to confirm the letter of credit through a U.S. bank. This irrevocable, confirmed letter of credit means that a U.S. bank accepts responsibility to pay regardless of the financial situation of the buyer or foreign bank. From the seller's viewpoint, this step eliminates the foreign political risk and replaces the commercial risk of the buyer's bank with that of the confirming bank. The confirming bank ensures payment against a confirmed letter of credit. As soon as the documents are presented to the bank, the seller receives payment.

The international department of a major U.S. bank cautions that a letter of credit is not a guarantee of payment to the seller. Rather, payment is tendered only if the seller complies exactly with the terms of the letter of credit. Because all letters of credit must be exact in their terms and considerations, it is important for the exporter to check the terms of the letter carefully to be certain that all necessary documents have been acquired and properly completed.

The process of getting a letter of credit can take days, if not weeks. Fortunately, this process is being shortened considerably as financial institutions provide letters of credit on

---

[29]Unless, of course, the letter of credit is revoked: "Neuocrine Biosciences: $5M Letter of Credit Cancelled," *Dow Jones Corporate Filings Alert*, January 14, 2008.

Exhibit 18.4
A Letter-of-Credit Transaction

Here is what typically happens when payment is made by an irrevocable letter of credit confirmed by a U.S. bank. Follow the steps in the illustration below.

1. Exporter and customer agree on terms of sale.
2. Buyer requests its foreign bank to open a letter of credit.
3. The buyer's bank prepares an irrevocable letter of credit (LC), including all instructions, and sends the irrevocable letter of credit to a U.S. bank.
4. The U.S. bank prepares a letter of confirmation and letter of credit and sends to seller.
5. Seller reviews LC. If acceptable, arranges with freight forwarder to deliver goods to designated port of entry.
6. The goods are loaded and shipped.

7. At the same time, the forwarder completes the necessary documents and sends documents to the seller.
8. Seller presents documents, indicating full compliance, to the U.S. bank.
9. The U.S. bank reviews the documents. If they are in order, issues seller a check for amount of sale.
10. The documents are airmailed to the buyer's bank for review.
11. If documents are in compliance, the bank sends documents to buyer.
12. To claim goods, buyer presents documents to customs broker.
13. Goods are released to buyer.

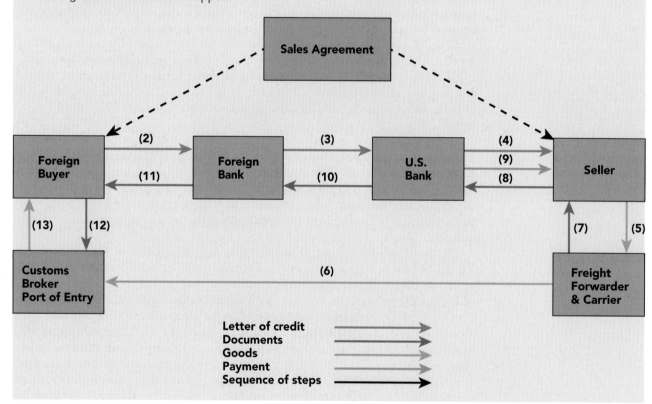

Source: Based on "A Basic Guide to Exporting," U.S. Department of Commerce, International Trade Administration, Washington, DC.

the Internet. As one example, AVG Letter of Credit Management LLC uses eTrade Finance Platform (ETFP), an e-commerce trade transaction system that enables exporters, importers, freight forwarders, carriers, and trade banks to initiate and complete trade transactions over the Internet. The company advertises that the efficiencies afforded by the Internet make it possible to lower the cost of an export letter of credit from $500-plus to $25.[30]

Bills of Exchange

Another important form of international commercial payment is **bills of exchange** drawn by sellers on foreign buyers. In letters of credit, the credit of one or more banks is involved,

---

[30]"QuestaWeb Offers Totally Automated Letter of Credit Feature," *Business Wire*, March 3, 2008.

but with bills of exchange (also known as *dollar drafts*), the seller assumes all risk until the actual dollars are received. The typical procedure is for the seller to draw a draft on the buyer and present it with the necessary documents to the seller's bank for collection. The documents required are principally the same as for letters of credit. On receipt of the draft, the U.S. bank forwards it with the necessary documents to a correspondent bank in the buyer's country; the buyer is then presented with the draft for acceptance and immediate or later payment. With acceptance of the draft, the buyer receives the properly endorsed bill of lading that is used to acquire the goods from the carrier.

Dollar drafts have advantages for the seller because an accepted draft frequently can be discounted at a bank for immediate payment. Banks, however, usually discount drafts only with recourse; that is, if the buyer does not honor the draft, the bank returns it to the seller for payment. An accepted draft is firmer evidence in the case of default and subsequent litigation than an open account would be.

Cash in Advance

The portion of international business handled on a cash-in-advance basis is not large. Cash places unpopular burdens on the customer and typically is used when credit is doubtful, when exchange restrictions within the country of destination are such that the return of funds from abroad may be delayed for an unreasonable period, or when the American exporter for any reason is unwilling to sell on credit terms. Although full payment in advance is employed infrequently, partial payment (from 25 to 50 percent) in advance is not unusual when the character of the merchandise is such that an incomplete contract can result in heavy loss. For example, complicated machinery or equipment manufactured to specification or special design would necessitate advance payment, which would be, in fact, a nonrefundable deposit.

Open Accounts

Sales on open accounts are not generally made in foreign trade except to customers of long standing with excellent credit reputations or to a subsidiary or branch of the exporter. Open accounts obviously leave sellers in a position where most of the problems of international commercial finance work to their disadvantage. Sales on open accounts are generally not recommended when the practice of the trade is to use some other method, when special merchandise is ordered, when shipping is hazardous, when the country of the importer imposes difficult exchange restrictions, or when political unrest requires additional caution.

Forfaiting

Inconvertible currencies and cash-short customers can kill an international sale if the seller cannot offer long-term financing. Unless the company has large cash reserves to finance its customers, a deal may be lost. **Forfaiting** is a financing technique for such a situation.

The basic idea of a forfaiting transaction is fairly simple: The seller makes a one-time arrangement with a bank or other financial institution to take over responsibility for collecting the account receivable. The exporter offers a long financing term to its buyer but intends to sell its account receivable, at a discount, for immediate cash. The forfaiter buys the debt, typically a promissory note or bill of exchange, on a nonrecourse basis. Once the exporter sells the paper, the forfaiter assumes the risk of collecting the importer's payments. The forfaiting institution also assumes any political risk present in the importer's country.[31]

Forfaiting is similar to factoring, but it is not the same. In *factoring,* a company has an ongoing relationship with a bank that routinely buys its short-term accounts receivable at a discount—in other words, the bank acts as a collections department for its client. In forfaiting, however, the seller makes a one-time arrangement with a bank to buy a specific account receivable.

All these ways of payment and the associated fees and, of course, the prices to be paid are most often negotiated between buyers and sellers. This leads us to the topic of the next chapter, international negotiations.

---

[31]For more information about forfaiting, visit http://www.afia-forfaiting.org.

Summary

Pricing is one of the most complicated decision areas encountered by international marketers. Rather than deal with one set of market conditions, one group of competitors, one set of cost factors, and one set of government regulations, international marketers must take all these factors into account, not only for each country in which they are operating but often for each market within a country. Market prices at the consumer level are much more difficult to control in international than in domestic marketing, but the international marketer must still approach the pricing task on a basis of established objectives and policy, leaving enough flexibility for tactical price movements. Controlling costs that lead to price escalation when exporting products from one country to another is one of the most challenging pricing tasks facing the exporter. Some of the flexibility in pricing is reduced by the growth of the Internet, which has a tendency to equalize price differentials between country markets.

The continuing growth of Third World markets coupled with their lack of investment capital has increased the importance of countertrades for most marketers, making countertrading an important tool to include in pricing policy. The Internet is evolving to include countertrades, which will help eliminate some of the problems associated with this practice.

Pricing in the international marketplace requires a combination of intimate knowledge of market costs and regulations, an awareness of possible countertrade deals, infinite patience for detail, and a shrewd sense of market strategy. Finally, letters of credit and other issues related to getting paid are discussed.

Key Terms

Parallel market	Skimming	Countervailing duty	Cartel
Gray market	Penetration pricing policy	Countertrade	Letters of credit
Exclusive distribution	Price escalation	Barter	Bills of exchange
Variable-cost pricing	Dumping	Administered pricing	Forfaiting
Full-cost pricing			

Questions

1. Define the key terms listed above.

2. Discuss the causes of and solutions for parallel imports and their effect on price.

3. Why is it so difficult to control consumer prices when selling overseas?

4. Explain the concept of price escalation and why it can mislead an international marketer.

5. What are the causes of price escalation? Do they differ for exports and goods produced and sold in a foreign country?

6. Why is it seldom feasible for a company to absorb the high cost of international transportation and reduce the net price received?

7. Price escalation is a major pricing problem for the international marketer. How can this problem be counteracted? Discuss.

8. Changing currency values have an impact on export strategies. Discuss.

9. "Regardless of the strategic factors involved and the company's orientation to market pricing, every price must be set with cost considerations in mind." Discuss.

10. "Price fixing by business is not generally viewed as an acceptable practice (at least in the domestic market), but when governments enter the field of price administration, they presume to do it for the general welfare to lessen the effects of 'destructive' competition." Discuss.

11. Do value-added taxes discriminate against imported goods?

12. Explain specific tariffs, ad valorem tariffs, and compound tariffs.

13. Suggest an approach a marketer may follow in adjusting prices to accommodate exchange rate fluctuations.

14. Explain the effects of indirect competition and how they may be overcome.

15. Why has dumping become such an issue in recent years?

16. Cartels seem to rise, after they have been destroyed. Why are they so appealing to business?

17. Discuss the different pricing problems that result from inflation versus deflation in a country.

18. Discuss the various ways in which governments set prices. Why do they engage in such activities?

19. Discuss the alternative objectives possible in setting prices for intracompany sales.

20. Why do governments so carefully scrutinize intracompany pricing arrangements?

21. Why are costs so difficult to assess in marketing internationally?

22. Discuss why countertrading is on the increase.

23. Discuss the major problems facing a company that is countertrading.

24. If a country you are trading with has a shortage of hard currency, how should you prepare to negotiate price?

25. Of the four types of countertrades discussed in the text, which is the most beneficial to the seller? Explain.

26. Why should a "knowledge of countertrades be part of an international marketer's pricing toolkit"? Discuss.

27. Discuss the various reasons purchasers impose countertrade obligations on buyers.

28. Discuss how FTZs can be used to help reduce price escalation.

29. Why is a proactive countertrade policy good business in some countries?

30. Differentiate between proactive and reactive countertrade policies.

31. One free trade zone is in Turkey. Visit www.esbas.com.tr and discuss how it might be used to help solve the price escalation problem of a product being exported from the United States to Turkey.

32. Visit Global Trading (a division of 3M) at www.mmm.com/globaltrading/edge.html and select "The Competitive Edge" and "Who We Are." Then write a short report on how Global Trading could assist a small company that anticipates having merchandise from a countertrade.

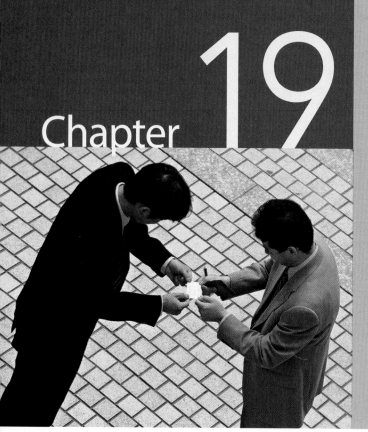

Chapter 19

Negotiating with International Customers, Partners, and Regulators

CHAPTER OUTLINE

CHAPTER LEARNING OBJECTIVES

What you should learn from Chapter 19:

LO1 The problems associated with cultural stereotypes

LO2 How culture influences behaviors at the negotiation table

LO3 Common kinds of problems that crop up during international business negotiations

LO4 The similarities and differences in communication behaviors in several countries

LO5 How differences in values and thinking processes affect international negotiations

LO6 Important factors in selecting a negotiation team

LO7 How to prepare for international negotiations

LO8 Managing all aspects of the negotiation process

LO9 The importance of follow-up communications and procedures

LO10 The basics of creative international negotiations

PART FIVE

Global Perspective

A JAPANESE *AISATSU*

It is not so much that speaking only English is a disadvantage in international business. Instead, it's more that being bilingual is a huge advantage. Observations from sitting in on an *aisatsu* (a meeting or formal greeting for high-level executives typical in Japan) involving the president of a large Japanese industrial distributor and the marketing vice president of an American machinery manufacturer are instructive. The two companies were trying to reach an agreement on a long-term partnership in Japan.

Business cards were exchanged and formal introductions made. Even though the president spoke and understood English, one of his three subordinates acted as an interpreter for the Japanese president. The president asked everyone to be seated. The interpreter sat on a stool between the two senior executives. The general attitude between the parties was friendly but polite. Tea and a Japanese orange drink were served.

The Japanese president controlled the interaction completely, asking questions of all Americans through the interpreter. Attention of all the participants was given to each speaker in turn. After this initial round of questions for all the Americans, the Japanese president focused on developing a conversation with the American vice president. During this interaction, an interesting pattern of nonverbal behaviors developed. The Japanese president would ask a question in Japanese. The interpreter then translated the question for the American vice president. While the interpreter spoke, the American's attention (gaze direction) was given to the interpreter. However, the Japanese president's gaze direction was at the American. Thus, the Japanese president could carefully and unobtrusively observe the American's facial expressions and nonverbal responses. Conversely, when the American spoke, the Japanese president had twice the response time. Because the latter understood English, he could formulate his responses during the translation process.

What is this extra response time worth in a strategic conversation? What is it worth to be able to carefully observe the nonverbal responses of your top-level counterpart in a high-stakes business negotiation?

Source: James Day Hodgson, Yoshihiro Sano, and John L. Graham, *Doing Business with the New Japan* (Boulder, CO: Rowman & Littlefield, 2008).

I (John Graham) had been in China a couple of weeks. I was tired. The fog had delayed my flight from Xian to Shanghai by four hours. I was standing in a long line at the counter to check in *again.* I started chatting with the older chap in line ahead of me. Juhani Kari introduced himself as a Finnish sales manager at ABB. He asked me what I did for a living. I responded, "I teach international business." He replied, "There is no such thing as international business. There's only interpersonal business." A wise man, indeed!

Face-to-face negotiations are an omnipresent activity in international commerce.[1] Once global marketing strategies have been formulated, once marketing research has been conducted to support those strategies, and once product/service, pricing, promotion, and place decisions have been made, then the focus of managers turns to implementation of the plans. In international business, such plans are almost always implemented through face-to-face negotiations with business partners and customers from foreign countries. The sales of goods and services, the management of distribution channels, contracting for marketing research and advertising services, licensing and franchise agreements, and strategic alliances all require managers from different cultures to sit and talk with one another to exchange ideas and express needs and preferences.[2]

Executives must also negotiate with representatives of foreign governments who might approve a variety of their marketing actions or be the actual ultimate customer for goods and services. In many countries, governmental officials may also be joint venture partners and, in some cases, vendors.[3] For example, negotiations for the television broadcast rights for the 2008 Summer Olympics in Beijing, China, included NBC, the International Olympic Committee, and Chinese governmental officials. Some of these negotiations can become quite complex, involving several governments, companies, and cultures.[4] Good examples are the European and North American talks regarding taxing the Internet, the continuing interactions regarding global environmental issues, or the ongoing WTO negotiations begun in Doha, Qatar, in 2001. All these activities demand a new kind of "business diplomacy."

One authority on international joint ventures suggests that a crucial aspect of all international commercial relationships is the negotiation of the original agreement. The seeds of success or failure often are sown at the negotiation table, vis-à-vis (face-to-face), where

---

[1]Several excellent books have been published on the topic of international business negotiations. Among them are Lothar Katz, *Negotiating International Business* (Charleston, SC: Booksurge, 2006); Camille Schuster and Michael Copeland, *Global Business, Planning for Sales and Negotiations* (Fort Worth, TX: Dryden, 1996); Robert T. Moran and William G. Stripp, *Dynamics of Successful International Business Negotiations* (Houston: Gulf, 1991); Pervez Ghauri and Jean-Claude Usunier (eds.), *International Business Negotiations* (Oxford: Pergamon, 1996); Donald W. Hendon, Rebecca Angeles Henden, and Paul Herbig, *Cross-Cultural Business Negotiations* (Westport, CT: Quorum, 1996); Sheida Hodge, *Global Smarts* (New York: Wiley, 2000); and Jeanne M. Brett, *Negotiating Globally* (San Francisco: Jossey-Bass, 2001). In addition, Roy J. Lewicki, David M. Saunders, and John W. Minton's *Negotiation: Readings, Exercises, and Cases*, 3rd ed. (New York: Irwin/McGraw-Hill, 1999) is an important book on the broader topic of business negotiations. The material from this chapter draws extensively on William Hernandez Requejo and John L. Graham, *Global Negotiation: The New Rules* (New York: Palgrave Macmillan, 2008); James Day Hodgson, Yoshihiro Sano, and John L. Graham, *Doing Business with the New Japan* (Boulder, CO: Rowman & Littlefield, 2008); and N. Mark Lam and John L. Graham, *China Now: Doing Business in the World's Most Dynamic Market* (New York: McGraw-Hill, 2007). See also http://www.GlobalNegotiationResources.com, 2010.

[2]David G. Sirmon and Peter J. Lane, "A Model of Cultural Differences and International Alliance Performance," *Journal of International Business Studies* 35, no. 4 (2004), pp. 306–19; we also note that consumers worldwide are negotiating more as the economic doldrums persist: "Let's Make a Deal," *The Economist*, February 7, 2009, p. 57.

[3]Keith Bradsher, "As Deadline Nears, GM's Sale of Hummer Faces Several Big Obstacles," *The New York Times*, February 24, 2010, p. B5.

[4]R. Bruce Money provides an interesting theoretical perspective on the topic in "International Multilateral Negotiations and Social Networks," *Journal of International Business Studies* 29, no. 4 (1998), pp. 695–710. Lively anecdotes are included in Jiang Feng, "Courting the Olympics: Beijing's Other Face," *Asian Wall Street Journal*, February 26, 2001, p. 6; Ashling O'Connor, "After 54 Years, the Olympic Clock Is Ticking," *Times of London*, February 10, 2003, p. 35; Manjeet Kripalani, "Tata: Master of the Gentle Approach," *BusinessWeek*, February 25, 2008, pp. 64–66.

not only are financial and legal details agreed to but, perhaps more important, the ambiance of cooperation and trust is established.[5] Indeed, the legal details and the structure of international business ventures are almost always modified over time, usually through negotiations. But the atmosphere of cooperation initially established face-to-face at the negotiation table persists—or the venture fails.

Business negotiations between business partners from the same country can be difficult. The added complication of cross-cultural communication can turn an already daunting task into an impossible one.[6] However, if cultural differences are taken into account, oftentimes wonderful business agreements can be made that lead to long-term, profitable relationships across borders. The purpose of this final chapter is to help prepare managers for the challenges and opportunities of international business negotiations. To do this, we will discuss the dangers of stereotypes, the impact of culture on negotiation behavior, and the implications of cultural differences for managers and negotiators.

The Dangers of Stereotypes

LO1

The problems associated with cultural stereotypes

The images of John Wayne, the cowboy, and the samurai, the fierce warrior, often are used as cultural stereotypes in discussions of international business negotiations.[7] Such representations almost always convey a grain of truth—an American cowboy kind of competitiveness versus a samurai kind of organizational (company) loyalty. One Dutch expert on international business negotiations argues, "The best negotiators are the Japanese because they will spend days trying to get to know their opponents. The worst are Americans because they think everything works in foreign countries as it does in the USA."[8] There are, of course, many Americans who are excellent international negotiators and some Japanese who are ineffective. The point is that negotiations are not conducted between national **stereotypes**; negotiations are conducted between people, and cultural factors often make huge differences.

Recall our discussions about the cultural diversity *within* countries from Chapters 4 and 11 and consider their relevance to negotiation. For example, we might expect substantial differences in negotiation styles between English-speaking and French-speaking Canadians. The genteel style of talk prevalent in the American Deep South is quite different from the faster speech patterns and pushiness more common in places like New York City. Experts tell us that negotiation styles differ across genders in America as well. Still others tell us that the urbane negotiation behaviors of Japanese bankers are very different from the relative aggressiveness of those in the retail industry in that country. Finally, age and experience can also make important differences. The older Chinese executive with no experience dealing with foreigners is likely to behave quite differently from her young assistant with undergraduate and MBA degrees from American universities.

The focus of this chapter is culture's influence on international negotiation behavior. However, it should be clearly understood that individual personalities and backgrounds and a variety of situational factors also heavily influence behavior at the negotiation table—and it is the manager's responsibility to consider these factors.[9] Remember: Companies and countries do not negotiate—people do. Consider the culture of your customers and business partners, but treat them as individuals.

[5]Constantine Katsikeas, Dionysis Skarmeas, and Daniel C. Bello, "Developing Successful Trust-Based International Exchange Relationships," *Journal of International Business Studies* 40, no. 1 (2009), pp. 132–55.

[6]James K. Sebenius, "The Hidden Challenge of Cross-Border Negotiations," *Harvard Business Review*, March–April, 2002, pp. 76–82.

[7]Nurit Zaidman discusses how stereotypes are formed in "Stereotypes of International Managers: Content and Impact on Business Interactions," *Group & Organizational Management*, March 1, 2000, pp. 45–54.

[8]Samfrits Le Poole comments on the American stereotype in "John Wayne Goes to Brussels," in Roy J. Lewicki, Joseph A. Litterer, David M. Saunders, and John W. Minton (eds.), *Negotiation: Readings, Exercises, and Cases*, 2nd ed. (Burr Ridge, IL: Irwin, 1993). The quote is from the Spanish newspaper *Expansion*, November 29, 1991, p. 41.

[9]Stephen E. Weiss provides the most complete recent review of the international negotiations literature—"International Business Negotiations Research," in B. J. Punnett and O. Shenkar (eds.), *Handbook for International Management Research* (Ann Arbor: University of Michigan Press, 2004), pp. 415–74.

The Europeans stereotype themselves. This postcard was purchased at the European Parliament gift store in Brussels. Of course, not all Dutch are cheap; there are sober Irish, and so on. Now that the European Union has expanded to 27 countries, a larger card will be required. But we're fairly certain they'll have a humorous perspective on all the new entrants.

The Pervasive Impact of Culture on Negotiation Behavior

LO2

How culture influences behaviors at the negotiation table

The primary purpose of this section is to demonstrate the extent of cultural differences in negotiation styles and how these differences can cause problems in international business negotiations. The material in this section is based on a systematic study of the topic over the last three decades in which the negotiation styles of more than 1,000 businesspeople in 17 countries (20 cultures) were considered.[10] The countries studied were Japan, Korea, Taiwan, China (Tianjin, Guangzhou, and Hong Kong), the Philippines, the Czech Republic, Russia, Israel, Norway, Germany, France, the United Kingdom, Spain, Brazil, Mexico, Canada (English-speaking and French-speaking), and the United States. The countries were chosen because they constitute America's most important present and future trading partners.

---

[10]The following institutions and people provided crucial support for the research on which this material is based: U.S. Department of Education; Toyota Motor Sales USA Inc.; Solar Turbines Inc. (a division of Caterpillar Tractors Co.); the Faculty Research and Innovation Fund and the International Business Educational Research (IBEAR) Program at the University of Southern California; Ford Motor Company; Marketing Science Institute; Madrid Business School; and Professors Nancy J. Adler (McGill University), Nigel Campbell (Manchester Business School), A. Gabriel Esteban (University of Houston, Victoria), Leonid I. Evenko (Russian Academy of the National Economy), Richard H. Holton (University of California, Berkeley), Alain Jolibert (Université des Sciences Sociales de Grenoble), Dong Ki Kim (Korea University), C. Y. Lin (National Sun-Yat Sen University), Hans-Gunther Meissner (Dortmund University), Alena Ockova (Czech Management Center), Sara Tang (Mass Transit Railway Corporation, Hong Kong), Kam-hon Lee (Chinese University of Hong Kong), and Theodore Schwarz (Monterrey Institute of Technology, Monterrey, CA).

Looking broadly across the several cultures, two important lessons stand out. The first is that regional generalizations very often are not correct. For example, Japanese and Korean negotiation styles are quite similar in some ways, but in other ways, they could not be more different. The second lesson learned from this study is that Japan is an exceptional place: On almost every dimension of negotiation style considered, the Japanese are on or near the end of the scale. Sometimes Americans are on the other end. But actually, most of the time Americans are somewhere in the middle. The reader will see this evinced in the data presented in this section. The Japanese approach, however, is most distinct, even *sui generis*.

Cultural differences cause four kinds of problems in international business negotiations, at the levels of:[11]

1. Language
2. Nonverbal behaviors
3. Values
4. Thinking and decision-making processes

LO3
Common kinds of problems that crop up during international business negotiations

The order is important; the problems lower on the list are more serious because they are more subtle. For example, two negotiators would notice immediately if one were speaking Japanese and the other German. The solution to the problem may be as simple as hiring an interpreter or talking in a common third language, or it may be as difficult as learning a language. Regardless of the solution, the problem is obvious. Cultural differences in nonverbal behaviors, in contrast, are almost always hidden below our awareness. That is to say, in a face-to-face negotiation, participants nonverbally—and more subtly—give off and take in a great deal of information.[12] Some experts argue that this information is more important than verbal information. Almost all this signaling goes on below our levels of consciousness.[13] When the nonverbal signals from foreign partners are different, negotiators are most likely to misinterpret them without even being conscious of the mistake. For example, when a French client consistently interrupts, Americans tend to feel uncomfortable without noticing exactly why. In this manner, interpersonal friction often colors business relationships, goes undetected, and, consequently, goes uncorrected. Differences in values and thinking and decision-making processes are hidden even deeper and therefore are even harder to cure. We discuss these differences here, starting with language and nonverbal behaviors.

Differences in Language and Nonverbal Behaviors

LO4
The similarities and differences in communication behaviors in several countries

Americans are clearly near the bottom of the languages skills list, though Australians assert that Australians are even worse. It should be added, however, that American undergrads recently have begun to see the light and are flocking to language classes and study-abroad programs. Unfortunately, foreign language teaching resources in the United States are inadequate to satisfy the increasing demand. In contrast, the Czechs are now throwing away a hard-earned competitive advantage: Young Czechs will not take Russian anymore. It is easy to understand why, but the result will be a generation of Czechs who cannot leverage their geographic advantage because they will not be able to speak to their neighbors to the east.

The language advantages of the Japanese executive in the description of the *aisatsu* that opened the chapter were quite clear. However, the most common complaint heard from American managers regards foreign clients and partners breaking into side conversations in their native languages. At best, this is seen as impolite, and quite often American negotiators are likely to attribute something sinister to the content of the foreign talk—"They're plotting or telling secrets."

[11]For additional details, see William Hernandez Requejo and John L. Graham, *Global Negotiation: The New Rules* (New York: Palgrave Macmillan, 2008); http://www.GlobalNegotiationResources.com, 2010.

[12]Mark Bauerlein, "Why Gen-Y Johnny Can't Read Nonverbal Cues," *The Wall Street Journal*, August 28, 2009, online.

[13]Jan Ulijn, Anne Francoise Rutowski, Rajesh Kumar, and Yunxia Zhu, "Patterns of Feelings in Face-to-Face Negotiation: A Sino-Dutch Pilot Study," *Cross Cultural Management* 12, no. 3 (2005), pp. 103–18.

Japanese negotiators exchange business cards at the front end of a meeting. Even more important than the nonverbal demonstration of respect in the "little ritual" is the all-important information about the relative status of the negotiators, clearly communicated by job title and company. Japanese executives literally do not know how to talk to one another until the status relationship is determined, because proper use of the language depends on knowledge of the relative status of the negotiators.

This perception is a frequent American mistake. The usual purpose of such side conversations is to straighten out a translation problem. For instance, one Korean may lean over to another and ask, "What'd he say?" Or the side conversation can regard a disagreement among the foreign team members. Both circumstances should be seen as positive signs by Americans—that is, getting translations straight enhances the efficiency of the interactions, and concessions often follow internal disagreements. But because most Americans speak only one language, neither circumstance is appreciated. By the way, people from other countries are advised to give Americans a brief explanation of the content of their first few side conversations to assuage the sinister attributions.

Data from simulated negotiations are also informative. In our study, the verbal behaviors of negotiators in 15 of the 21 cultures (six negotiators in each of the 15 groups) were video-taped. The numbers in the body of Exhibit 19.1 represent the percentages of statements that were classified into each category listed. That is, 7 percent of the statements made by Japanese negotiators were classified as promises, 4 percent as threats, 7 percent as recommendations, and so on. The verbal bargaining behaviors used by the negotiators during the simulations proved to be surprisingly similar across cultures. Negotiations in all 15 cultures studied were composed primarily of information-exchange tactics—questions and self-disclosures. Note that the Japanese appear on the low end of the continuum of self-disclosures. Their 34 percent (along with Spaniards and English-speaking Canadians) was the second lowest across all 15 groups, suggesting that they are the most reticent about giving information, except for the Israelis. Overall, however, the verbal tactics used were surprisingly similar across the diverse cultures.

Exhibit 19.2 provides analyses of some linguistic aspects and nonverbal behaviors for the 15 videotaped groups. Although these efforts merely scratch the surface of these kinds of behavioral analyses, they still provide indications of substantial cultural differences.[14] Note that, once again, the Japanese are at or next to the end of the continuum on almost every dimension of the behaviors listed. Their facial gazing and touching are the least among the 15 groups. Only the northern Chinese used the word *no* less frequently, and only the English-speaking Canadians and Russians used more silent periods than did the Japanese.

A broader examination of the data in Exhibits 19.1 and 19.2 reveals a more meaningful conclusion: The variation across cultures is greater when comparing linguistic aspects of language and nonverbal behaviors than when the verbal content of negotiations is considered. For example, notice the great differences between Japanese and Brazilians in Exhibit 19.1 vis-à-vis Exhibit 19.2.

Following are further descriptions of the distinctive aspects of each of the 15 cultural groups videotaped. Certainly, conclusions about the individual cultures cannot be drawn from an analysis of only six businesspeople in each culture, but the suggested cultural differences are worthwhile to consider briefly.

Japan.   Consistent with most descriptions of Japanese negotiation behavior, the results of this analysis suggest their style of interaction is among the least aggressive (or most polite). Threats, commands, and warnings appear to be deemphasized in favor of more positive promises, recommendations, and commitments. Particularly indicative of their polite conversational style was their infrequent use of *no* and *you* and facial gazing, as well as more frequent silent periods.

Korea.   Perhaps one of the more interesting aspects of the analysis is the contrast of the Asian styles of negotiations. Non-Asians often generalize about Asians; the findings

---

[14]Thomas W. Leigh and John O. Summers, "An Initial Evaluation of Industrial Buyers' Impressions of Salespersons' Nonverbal Cues," *Journal of Personal Selling & Sales Management*, Winter 2002, pp. 41–53.

Exhibit 19.1
Verbal Negotiation Tactics (The "What" of Communications)

Bargaining Behaviors and Definitions	JPN	KOR	TWN	CHN**	RUSS	ISRL	GRM	UK	FRN	SPN	BRZ	MEX	FCAN	ECAN	USA
Promise. A statement in which the source indicates its intention to provide the target with a reinforcing consequence, which the source anticipates the target will evaluate as pleasant, positive, or rewarding.	7†	4	9	6	5	12	7	11	5	11	3	7	8	6	8
Threat. Same as promise, except that the reinforcing consequences are thought to be noxious, unpleasant, or punishing.	4	2	2	1	3	4	3	3	5	2	2	1	3	0	4
Recommendation. A statement in which the source predicts that a pleasant environmental consequence will occur to the target. Its occurrence is not under the source's control.	7	1	5	2	4	8	5	6	3	4	5	8	5	4	4
Warning. Same as recommendation, except that the consequences are thought to be unpleasant.	2	0	3	1	0	1	1	1	3	1	1	2	3	0	1
Reward. A statement by the source that is thought to create pleasant consequences for the target.	1	3	2	1	3	2	4	5	3	3	2	1	1	3	2
Punishment. Same as reward, except that the consequences are thought to be unpleasant.	1	5	1	0	1	3	2	0	3	2	3	0	2	1	3
Normative appeals. A statement in which the source indicates that the target's past, present, or future behavior will conform with social norms or is in violation of social norms.	4	3	1	1	1	5	1	1	0	1	1	1	3	1	2
Commitment. A statement by the source to the effect that its future bids will not go below or above a certain level.	15	13	9	10	10	10	9	13	10	9	8	9	8	14	13
Self-disclosure. A statement in which the source reveals information about itself.	34	36	42	36	40	30	47	39	42	34	39	38	42	34	36
Question. A statement in which the source asks the target to reveal information about itself.	20	21	14	34	27	20	11	15	18	17	22	27	19	26	20
Command. A statement in which the source suggests that the target perform a certain behavior.	8	13	11	7	7	9	12	9	9	17	14	7	5	10	6

*For each, group n = 6.

**Northern China (Tianjin and environs).

†Read "7 percent of the statements made by Japanese negotiators were promises."

Source: From William Hernandez Requejo and John L. Graham, *Global Negotiation: The New Rules* (New York: Palgrave Macmillan, 2009). Reproduced with permission of Palgrave Macmillan.

Exhibit 19.2
Linguistic Aspects of Language and Nonverbal Behaviors ("How" Things Are Said)

Bargaining Behaviors (per 30 minutes)	Cultures*														
	JPN	KOR	TWN	CHN**	RUSS	ISRL	GRM	UK	FRN	SPN	BRZ	MEX	FCAN	ECAN	USA
Structural Aspects															
"No's." The number of times the word *no* was used by each negotiator.	1.9	7.4	5.9	1.5	2.3	8.5	6.7	5.4	11.3	23.2	41.9	4.5	7.0	10.1	4.5
"You's." The number of times the word *you* was used by each negotiator.	31.5	35.2	36.6	26.8	23.6	64.4	39.7	54.8	70.2	73.3	90.4	56.3	72.4	64.4	55.1
Nonverbal Behaviors															
Silent periods. The number of conservational gaps of 10 seconds or longer.	2.5	0	0	2.3	3.7	1.9	0	2.5	1.0	0	0	1.1	0.2	2.9	1.7
Conversational overlaps. Number of interruptions.	6.2	22.0	12.3	17.1	13.3	30.1	20.8	5.3	20.7	28.0	14.3	10.6	24.0	17.0	5.1
Facial gazing. Number of minutes negotiators spent looking at opponent's face.	3.9	9.9	19.7	11.1	8.7	15.3	10.2	9.0	16.0	13.7	15.6	14.7	18.8	10.4	10.0
Touching. Incidents of bargainers touching one another (not including handshaking).	0	0	0	0	0	0	0	0	0.1	0	4.7	0	0	0	0

*For each group, n = 6.

**Northern China (Tianjin and environs).

Source: From William Hernandez Requejo and John L. Graham, *Global Negotiation: The New Rules* (New York: Palgrave Macmillan, 2009). Reproduced with permission of Palgrave Macmillan.

CROSSING BORDERS 19.1   Poker Faces and Botox Injections

We often hear from American executives the complaint that their Japanese counterparts are "hard to read" at the negotiation table; that is, they use "poker faces." However, when we videotape and count negotiators' facial movements (smiles and frowns), we see no differences between Japanese and Americans. It appears that because of differences in the timing and meaning of facial expressions across the two cultures, the Americans are unable to interpret the Japanese facial expressions, so they mistakenly report seeing nothing.

Now it seems that American executives are seeking their own poker-face advantage through the new wonder of science, Botox. Shots of the new drug are being used to freeze and sculpt their faces into "semipermanent serenity." Says one American executive, "When you look strong and tough and not afraid, people respect you more . . . showing less expression really makes a statement."

Paul Ekman, a University of California psychologist who studies facial expressions, describes this trend as "very scary." Facial expressions have evolved to serve a purpose, to aid in the formation of basic human bonds through subconscious facial movements. Take those away, and how can we tell friend or foe, mate or murderer?

Rather than preparing for your international negotiations using Botox, we instead recommend a good book, a nice round of golf, or perhaps a good, old-fashioned facial!

Sources: Suein L. Hwang, "Some Type A Staffers Dress for Success with a Shot of Botox," *The Wall Street Journal*, June 31, 2002, p. B1; James D. Hodgson, Yoshihiro Sano, and John L. Graham, *Doing Business with the New Japan* (Boulder, CO: Rowman & Littlefield, 2008).

demonstrate, however, that this generalization is a mistake. Korean negotiators used considerably more punishments and commands than did the Japanese. Koreans used the word *no* and interrupted more than three times as frequently as the Japanese. Moreover, no silent periods occurred between Korean negotiators.

China (Northern). The behaviors of the negotiators from northern China (i.e., in and around Tianjin) were most remarkable in the emphasis on asking questions (34 percent).[15] Indeed, 70 percent of the statements made by the Chinese negotiators were classified as information-exchange tactics. Other aspects of their behavior were quite similar to the Japanese, particularly the uses of *no* and *you* and silent periods.[16]

Taiwan. The behavior of the businesspeople in Taiwan was quite different from that in China and Japan but similar to that in Korea. The Chinese in Taiwan were exceptional in the length of time of facial gazing—on average, almost 20 of 30 minutes. They asked fewer questions and provided more information (self-disclosures) than did any of the other Asian groups.

Russia. The Russians' style was quite different from that of any other European group, and, indeed, was quite similar in many respects to the style of the Japanese. They used *no* and *you* infrequently and used the most silent periods of any group. Only the Japanese did less facial gazing, and only the Chinese asked a greater percentage of questions.

[15]The Chinese emphasis on questions is consistent with other empirical findings: Dean Tjosvold, Chun Hui, and Haifa Sun, "Can Chinese Discuss Conflicts Openly? Field and Experimental Studies of Face Dynamics," *Group Decision and Negotiation* 13 (2004), pp. 351–73.

[16]There is a burgeoning literature on negotiations with Chinese. See Catherine H. Tinsley and Jeanne M. Brett, "Managing Workplace Conflict in the U.S. and Hong Kong," *Organizational Behavior and Human Decision Process* 85 (2001), pp. 360–381; Pervez Ghauri and Tony Fang, "Negotiating with the Chinese: A Socio-Cultural Analysis," *Journal of World Business* September 22, 2001, pp. 303–312; Vivian C. Sheer and Ling Chen, "Successful Sino-Western Business Negotiation: Participants' Accounts of National and Professional Cultures," *Journal of Business Communication*, January 1, 2003, pp. 50–64; Rajesh Kumar and Verner Worm, "Social Capital and the Dynamics of Business Negotiations between the Northern Europeans and the Chinese," *International Marketing Review* 20, no. 3 (2003), pp. 262–86; John L. Graham and N. Mark Lam, "The Chinese Negotiation," *Harvard Business Review*, October 2003, pp. 82–91; Anna Stark, Kim-Shyan Fam, David S. Waller, and Zhilong Tian, "Chinese Negotiation Practice, Perspective from New Zealand Exporters," *Cross Cultural Management* 12, no. 3 (2005), pp. 85–102.

Israel.   The behaviors of the Israeli negotiators were distinctive in three respects. They used the lowest percentage of self-disclosures, apparently holding their cards relatively closely. Yet they also used, by far, the highest percentages of promises and recommendations. They were also at the end of the scale for the percentage of normative appeals at 5 percent, with the most frequent references being to competitors' offers. Perhaps most important, the Israeli negotiators interrupted one another much more frequently than negotiators from any other group. This important nonverbal behavior is most likely to blame for the "pushy" stereotype often used by Americans to describe their Israeli negotiation partners.

Germany.   The behaviors of the Germans are difficult to characterize because they fell toward the center of almost all the continua. However, the Germans were exceptional in the high percentage of self-disclosures (47 percent) and the low percentage of questions (11 percent).

United Kingdom.   The behaviors of the British negotiators were remarkably similar to those of the Americans in all respects.

Spain.   *Diga* is perhaps a good metaphor for the Spanish approach to negotiations evinced in our data. When you make a phone call in Madrid, the usual greeting on the other end is not *hola* ("hello") but instead *diga* ("speak"). It is not surprising then that the Spaniards in the videotaped negotiations likewise used the highest percentage of commands (17 percent) of any of the groups and gave comparatively little information (self-disclosures, only 34 percent). Moreover, except for the Israelis, they interrupted one another more frequently than any other group, and they used the terms *no* and *you* very frequently.

France.   The style of the French negotiators was perhaps the most aggressive of all the groups. In particular, they used the highest percentage of threats and warnings (together, 8 percent). They also used interruptions, facial gazing, and *no* and *you* very frequently compared with the other groups, and one of the French negotiators touched his partner on the arm during the simulation.

Brazil.   The Brazilian businesspeople, like the French and Spanish, were quite aggressive. They used the second-highest percentage of commands of all the groups. On average, the Brazilians said the word *no* 42 times, *you* 90 times, and touched one another on the arm about 5 times during 30 minutes of negotiation. Facial gazing was also high.

Mexico.   The patterns of Mexican behavior in our negotiations are good reminders of the dangers of regional or language-group generalizations.[17] Both verbal and nonverbal behaviors were quite different from those of their Latin American (Brazilian) or continental (Spanish) cousins. Indeed, Mexicans answer the telephone with the much less demanding *bueno* (short for "good day"). In many respects, the Mexican behavior was very similar to that of the negotiators from the United States.

French-Speaking Canada.   The French-speaking Canadians behaved quite similarly to their continental cousins. Like the negotiators from France, they too used high percentages of threats and warnings and even more interruptions and eye contact. Such an aggressive interaction style would not mix well with some of the more low-key styles of some of the Asian groups or with English speakers, including English-speaking Canadians.

English-Speaking Canada.   The Canadians who speak English as their first language used the lowest percentage of aggressive persuasive tactics (threats, warnings, and punishments totaled only 1 percent) of all 15 groups. Perhaps, as communications researchers suggest, such stylistic differences are the seeds of interethnic discord as witnessed in Canada over the years. With respect to international negotiations, the English-speaking

---

[17]T. Lenartowicz and J. P. Johnson, "A Cross-National Assessment of the Values of Latin American Managers: Contrasting Hues or Shades of Gray?" *Journal of International Business Studies* 34, no. 3 (May 2003), pp. 266–81.

Canadians used noticeably more interruptions and *no*'s than negotiators from either of Canada's major trading partners, the United States and Japan.

United States.   Like the Germans and the British, the Americans fell in the middle of most continua. They did interrupt one another less frequently than all the others, but that was their sole distinction.

These differences across the cultures are quite complex, and this material by itself should not be used to predict the behaviors of foreign counterparts. Instead, great care should be taken with respect to the aforementioned dangers of stereotypes. The key here is to be aware of these kinds of differences so that the Japanese silence, the Brazilian "no, no, no . . . ," or the French threat is not misinterpreted.

Differences in Values

LO5

How differences in values and thinking processes affect international negotiations

Four values—objectivity, competitiveness, equality, and punctuality—that are held strongly and deeply by most Americans seem to frequently cause misunderstandings and bad feelings in international business negotiations.

Objectivity.   "Americans make decisions based upon the bottom line and on cold, hard facts." "Americans don't play favorites." "Economics and performance count, not people." "Business is business." Such statements well reflect American notions of the importance of objectivity.

The single most important book on the topic of negotiation, *Getting to Yes*,[18] is highly recommended for both American and foreign readers. The latter will learn not only about negotiations but, perhaps more important, about how Americans think about negotiations. The authors are emphatic about "separating the people from the problem," and they state, "Every negotiator has two kinds of interests: in the substance and in the relationship." This advice is probably worthwhile in the United States or perhaps in Germany, but in most places in the world, such advice is nonsense. In most places in the world, particularly in collectivistic, high-context cultures, personalities and substance are not separate issues and cannot be made so.

For example, consider how important nepotism is in Chinese or Hispanic cultures. Experts tell us that businesses don't grow beyond the bounds and bonds of tight family control in the burgeoning "Chinese Commonwealth." Things work the same way in Spain, Mexico, and the Philippines by nature. And, just as naturally, negotiators from such countries not only will take things personally but will be personally affected by negotiation outcomes. *Guanxi*, the Chinese word for personal connections, is key for negotiators working in China. Long-term reciprocity is the basis of commercial interactions there, and Western concepts like objectivity almost always take a back seat.[19] What happens to them at the negotiation table will affect the business relationship, regardless of the economics involved.

Competitiveness and Equality.[20]   Simulated negotiations can be viewed as a kind of experimental economics wherein the values of each participating cultural group are roughly reflected in the economic outcomes. The simple simulation used in our research represented the essence of commercial negotiations—it had both competitive and cooperative aspects. At least 40 businesspeople from each culture played the same buyer–seller game, negotiating over the prices of three products. Depending on the agreement reached, the "negotiation pie" could be made larger through cooperation (as high as $10,400 in joint profits) before it was divided between the buyer and seller. The results are summarized in Exhibit 19.3.

The Japanese were the champions at making the pie big. Their joint profits in the simulation were the highest (at $9,590) among the 20 cultural groups involved. The American

---

[18]Roger Fisher, William Ury, and Bruce Patton, *Getting to Yes: Negotiating Agreement without Giving In* (New York: Penguin, 1991).

[19]Flora F. Gu, Kineta Hung, and David K. Tse, "When Does Guanxi Matter? Issues of Capitalization and Its Dark Sides," *Journal of Marketing* 72, no. 4 (2008), pp. 12–28.

[20]Of course, the opposite of equality is hierarchy, and the latter is more prevalent in China. For example, see Ray Friedman, Shu-Chen Chi, and Leigh Anne Liu, "An Expectancy Model of Chinese-American Differences in Conflict Avoiding," *Journal of International Business Studies* 37 (2006), pp. 76–91.

Exhibit 19.3

Cultural Differences in Competitiveness and Equality

Source: William Hernandez Requejo and John L. Graham, *Global Negotiation: The New Rules* (New York: Palgrave Macmillan, 2009). Reproduced with permission of Palgrave Macmillan.

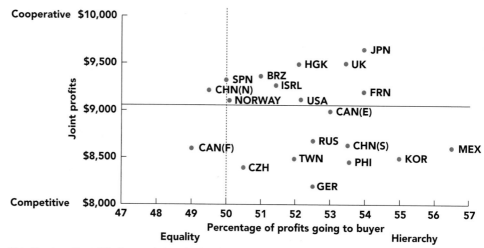

Note: Based on at least 40 businesspeople in each cultural group.

pie was more average sized (at $9,030), but at least it was divided relatively equitably (51.8 percent of the profits went to the buyers). Conversely, the Japanese (and others) split their pies in strange (perhaps even unfair)[21] ways, with buyers making higher percentages of the profits (53.8 percent). The implications of these simulated business negotiations are completely consistent with the comments of other authors and the adage that in Japan the buyer is "king." By nature, Americans have little understanding of the Japanese practice of giving complete deference to the needs and wishes of buyers. That is not the way things work in America. American sellers tend to treat American buyers more as equals, and the egalitarian values of American society support this behavior. Moreover, most Americans will, by nature, treat Japanese buyers more frequently as equals. Likewise, American buyers will generally not "take care of" American sellers or Japanese sellers. The American emphasis on competition and individualism represented in these findings is quite consistent with the work of Geert Hofstede[22] detailed in Chapter 4, which indicated that Americans scored the highest among all the cultural groups on the individualism (versus collectivism) scale. Moreover, values for individualism/collectivism have been shown to directly influence negotiation behaviors in several other countries.[23]

Finally, not only do Japanese buyers achieve better results than American buyers, but compared with American sellers ($4,350), Japanese sellers also get more of the commercial pie ($4,430) as well. Interestingly, when shown these results, Americans in executive seminars still often prefer the American seller's role. In other words, even though the American sellers make lower profits than the Japanese, many American managers apparently prefer lower profits if those profits are yielded from a more equal split of the joint profits. A new study has likewise demonstrated that Americans and Japanese have different views about fairness.[24]

Finally, the Japanese emphasis on hierarchical relationships seems to hamper internal communications; subordinates don't pass along bad news, for example. This reticence seems to have been a major problem during the Toyota product quality issues mentioned

---

[21]Concepts of fairness clearly vary across cultures; see Nancy R. Buchan, Rachael T. S. Croson, and Eric J. Johnson, "When Do Fair Beliefs Influence Bargaining Behavior: Experimental Bargaining in Japan and the United States," *Journal of Consumer Research* 31, no. 2 (2004), pp. 181–90.

[22]Geert Hofstede, *Culture's Consequences*, 2nd ed. (Thousand Oaks, CA: Sage, 2001).

[23]L. Graham, "Culture's Influence on Business Negotiations: An Application of Hofstede's and Rokeach's Ideas," in Farok J. Contractor and Peter Lorange (eds.), *Cooperative Strategies and Alliances* (Amsterdam: Pergamon, 2002), pp. 461–92. Also see Roy J. Lewicki, David M. Saunders, and John W. Minton, *Essentials of Negotiation*, 2nd ed. (New York: McGraw-Hill, 2001).

[24]Nancy R. Buchan, Rachel T. A. Croson, and Eric J. Johnson, "When Do Fair Beliefs Influence Bargaining Behavior? Experimental Bargaining in Japan and the United States," *Journal of Consumer Research* 31 (2004), pp. 181–90.

in previous chapters. These differences in approaches also have influenced interactions externally with U.S. government regulators. One analysis described Toyota's problem as follows: "Its secretive corporate culture in Japan clashed with the U.S. requirements that auto makers disclose safety threats."[25]

Time.   "Just make them wait." Everyone else in the world knows that no negotiation tactic is more useful with Americans, because no one places more value on time, no one has less patience when things slow down, and no one looks at their wristwatches more than Americans do. The material from Chapter 5 on P-time versus M-time is quite pertinent here. Edward T. Hall[26] in his seminal writing is best at explaining how the passage of time is viewed differently across cultures and how these differences most often hurt Americans.

Even Americans try to manipulate time to their advantage, however. As a case in point, Solar Turbines Incorporated (a division of Caterpillar) once sold $34 million worth of industrial gas turbines and compressors for a Russian natural gas pipeline project. Both parties agreed that final negotiations would be held in a neutral location, the south of France. In previous negotiations, the Russians had been tough but reasonable. But in Nice, the Russians were not nice. They became tougher and, in fact, completely unreasonable, according to the Solar executives involved.

The Americans needed a couple of discouraging days to diagnose the problem, but once they did, a crucial call was made back to headquarters in San Diego. Why had the Russians turned so cold? They were enjoying the warm weather in Nice and weren't interested in making a quick deal and heading back to Moscow! The call to California was the key event in this negotiation. Solar's headquarters people in San Diego were sophisticated enough to allow their negotiators to take their time. From that point on, the routine of the negotiations changed to brief, 45-minute meetings in the mornings, with afternoons at the golf course, beach, or hotel, making calls and doing paperwork. Finally, during the fourth week, the Russians began to make concessions and to ask for longer meetings. Why? They could not go back to Moscow after four weeks on the Mediterranean without a signed contract. This strategic reversal of the time pressure yielded a wonderful contract for Solar.

Differences in Thinking and Decision-Making Processes   When faced with a complex negotiation task, most Westerners (notice the generalization here) divide the large task up into a series of smaller tasks. Issues such as prices, delivery, warranty, and service contracts may be settled one issue at a time, with the final agreement being the sum or the sequence of smaller agreements. In Asia, however, a different approach is more often taken wherein all the issues are discussed at once, in no apparent order, and concessions are made on all issues at the end of the discussion. The Western sequential approach and the Eastern holistic approach do not mix well.[27]

That is, American managers often report great difficulties in measuring progress in Japan. After all, in America, you are half done when half the issues are settled. But in Japan, nothing seems to get settled. Then, surprise, you are done. Often Americans make unnecessary concessions right before agreements are announced by the Japanese. For example, one American department store buyer traveling to Japan to buy six different consumer products for his chain lamented that negotiations for his first purchase took an entire week. In the United States, such a purchase would be consummated in an afternoon. So, by his calculations, he expected to have to spend six weeks in Japan to complete his purchases.

---

[25]Kate Linebaugh, Dionne Searcey, and Norihiko Shirouzu, "Secretive Culture Led Toyota Astray," *The Wall Street Journal*, February 8, 2010, online.

[26]Edward T. Hall, "The Silent Language in Overseas Business," *Harvard Business Review*, May–June 1960, pp. 87–96.

[27]East–West differences in thinking are studied in detail in Joel Brockner, Ya-Ru Chen, Elizabeth A. Mannix, Kwok Leung, and Daniel P. Skarlicki, "Culture and Procedural Fairness: When the Effects of What You Do Depend on How You Do It," *Administrative Science Quarterly*, March 1, 2000, pp. 138–57. Most important is Richard E. Nisbett, *The Geography of Thought: How Asians and Westerners Think Differently . . . and Why* (New York: The Free Press, 2003). Also, for a discussion of related communication problems in international work teams, see Jeanne Brett, Kristin Behfar, and Mary C. Kern, "Managing Multicultural Teams," *Harvard Business Review*, November 2006, pp. 84–91.

He considered raising his purchase prices to try to move things along faster. But before he was able to make such a concession, the Japanese quickly agreed on the other five products in just three days. This particular businessperson was, by his own admission, lucky in his first encounter with Japanese bargainers.

This American businessperson's near-blunder reflects more than just a difference in decision-making style. To Americans, a business negotiation is a problem-solving activity, the best deal for both parties being the solution. To a Japanese businessperson, a business negotiation is a time to develop a business relationship with the goal of long-term mutual benefit. The economic issues are the context, not the content, of the talks. Thus, settling any one issue really is not that important. Such details will take care of themselves once a viable, harmonious business relationship is established. And, as happened in the case of our retail goods buyer, once the relationship was established—signaled by the first agreement—the other "details" were settled quickly.

American bargainers should anticipate such a holistic approach and be prepared to discuss all issues simultaneously and in an apparently haphazard order. Progress in the talks should not be measured by how many issues have been settled. Rather, Americans must try to gauge the quality of the business relationship. Important signals of progress can be the following:

- Higher-level foreigners being included in the discussions.
- Questions beginning to focus on specific areas of the deal.
- A softening of attitudes and positions on some of the issues—"Let us take some time to study this issue."
- At the negotiation table, increased talk among themselves in their own language, which may often mean they're trying to decide something.
- Increased bargaining and use of the lower-level, informal, and other channels of communication.

Implications for Managers and Negotiators

Considering all the potential problems in cross-cultural negotiations, particularly when you mix managers from relationship-oriented cultures with those from information-oriented ones, it is a wonder that any international business gets done at all. Obviously, the economic imperatives of global trade make much of it happen despite the potential pitfalls. But an appreciation of cultural differences can lead to even better international commercial transactions—it is not just business deals but highly profitable business relationships that are the real goal of international business negotiations.

Four steps lead to more efficient and effective international business negotiations. They are as follows: (1) selection of the appropriate negotiation team;[28] (2) management of preliminaries, including training, preparations, and manipulation of negotiation settings; (3) management of the process of negotiations, that is, what happens at the negotiation table; and (4) appropriate follow-up procedures and practices. Each is discussed in this section.

Negotiation Teams

LO6

Important factors in selecting a negotiation team

One reason for global business successes is the large numbers of skillful international negotiators. These are the managers who have lived in foreign countries and speak foreign languages. In many cases, they are immigrants to the United States or those who have been immersed in foreign cultures in other capacities (Peace Corps volunteers and Mormon missionaries are common examples). More business schools are beginning to reemphasize language training and visits abroad. Indeed, it is interesting to note that the original Harvard Business School catalog of 1908–1909 listed courses in German, French, and Spanish correspondence within its curriculum.

The selection criteria for international marketing and sales personnel previously detailed in Chapter 17 are applicable in selecting negotiators as well. Traits such as maturity,

---

[28]C. Leonidou, Constantine S. Katsikeas, and John Hadjimarcou, "Building Successful Export Business Relationships," *Journal of International Marketing*, January 1, 2002, pp. 96–101.

emotional stability, breadth of knowledge, optimism, flexibility, empathy, and stamina are all important, not only for marketing executives involved in international negotiations but also for the technical experts who often accompany and support them. In studies conducted at Ford Motor Company and AT&T, three additional traits were found to be important predictors of negotiator success with international clients and partners: willingness to use team assistance, listening skills, and influence at headquarters.

Willingness to use team assistance is particularly important for American negotiators. Because of a cultural heritage of independence and individualism, Americans often make the mistake of going it alone against greater numbers of foreigners. One American sitting across the negotiation table from three or four Chinese negotiators is unfortunately an all too common sight. The number of brains in the room does make a difference. Moreover, business negotiations are social processes, and the social reality is that a larger number of nodding heads can exercise greater influence than even the best arguments. It is also much easier to gather detailed information when teams are negotiating rather than individuals. For example, the Japanese are quite good at bringing along junior executives for the dual purposes of careful note taking and training via observation. Compensation schemes that overly emphasize individual performance can also get in the way of team negotiating—a negotiation team requires a split commission, which many Americans naturally eschew. Finally, negotiators may have to request the accompaniment of senior executives to better match up with client's and partner's negotiation teams. Particularly in relationship-oriented cultures, rank speaks quite loudly in both persuasion and the demonstration of interest in the business relationship.

The single most important activity of negotiations is listening. The negotiator's primary job is collecting information with the goal of enhancing creativity. This goal may mean assigning one team member the sole responsibility of taking careful notes and not worrying about speaking during the meetings. It may also mean that knowing the language of clients and partners will be crucial for the most complete understanding of their needs and preferences. The importance of listening skills in international business negotiations cannot be overstated.

Women can get the job done. Here U.S. Secretary of State Hillary Clinton meets with German Chancellor Andrea Merkel.

Bringing along a senior executive is important because influence at headquarters is crucial to success. Indeed, many experienced international negotiators argue that half the negotiation is with headquarters. The representatives' lament goes something like this: "The better I understand my customer, the tougher time I have with headquarters." Of course, this misery associated with boundary-spanning roles is precisely why international negotiators and sales executives make so much money.

Finally, it is also important to reiterate a point made in Chapter 5: Gender should not be used as a selection criterion for international negotiation teams, despite the great differences in the roles of women across cultures. Even in countries where women do not participate in management, American female negotiators are treated as foreigners first. For obvious reasons it may not be appropriate for female managers to participate in some forms of business entertainment—common baths in locker rooms at Japanese golf course clubhouses, for example. However, it is still important for female executives to establish personal rapport at restaurants and other informal settings. Indeed, one expert on cross-gender communication suggests that women may actually have some advantages in international negotiations:

In general, women are more comfortable talking one-on-one. The situation of speaking up in a meeting is a lot closer to boys' experience of using language to establish their position in a large group than it is to girls' experience of using language to maintain intimacy. That's something that can be exploited. Don't wait for the meeting; try to make your point in advance, one-to-one. This is what the Japanese do, and in many ways American women's style is a lot closer to the Japanese style than to American men's.[29]

[29]Deborah Tannen, *You Just Don't Understand: Men and Women in Conversation* (New York: William Morrow, 1990).

Negotiation Preliminaries

LO7 ▨

How to prepare for international negotiations

Many companies in the United States provide employees with negotiations training.[30] For example, through his training programs, Chester Karrass[31] has taught more people (some 400,000) to negotiate than any other purveyor of the service[32]—notice his ads in almost all in-flight magazines of domestic U.S. air carriers. However, very few companies provide training for negotiations with managers from other countries. Even more surprising is the lack of cultural content in the training of the government's diplomats. Instead, in most schools of diplomacy the curricula cover language skills, social and diplomatic skills, and knowledge specific to the diplomatic profession, including diplomatic history and international relations, law, economics, politics, international organizations, and foreign policies. Cultural differences in negotiation and communication styles are seldom considered.

Things are different at Ford Motor Company. Ford does more business with Japanese companies than any other firm. Ford owns 33 percent of Mazda, it built a successful minivan with Nissan, and it buys and sells component parts and completed cars from and to Japanese companies. But perhaps the best measure of Ford's Japanese business is the 8,000 or so U.S.-to-Japan round-trip airline tickets the company buys annually. Ford has made a large investment in training its managers with Japanese responsibilities. Over 2,000 of its executives have attended a three-day program on Japanese history and culture and the company's Japanese business strategies. Furthermore, more than 1,000 Ford managers who work face-to-face with Japanese have attended a three-day program entitled "Managing Negotiations: Japan" (MNJ). The MNJ program includes negotiation simulations with videotape feedback, lectures with cultural differences demonstrated via videotapes of Japanese–American interactions, and rehearsals of upcoming negotiations. The company also conducts similar programs on Korea and the People's Republic of China.

In addition to MNJ, the broader Japan training efforts at Ford must be credited for Ford's successes in Japan. Certainly, MNJ alumni can be seen exercising influence across and up the ranks regarding Japanese relationships. But the organizational awareness of the cultural dimensions of the Japanese business system was quickly raised as well by its broader, three-day program on Japanese business strategies. Remember the story about the Russians in Nice? Two critical events took place. First, the Solar Turbines negotiators diagnosed the problem. Second, and equally important, their California superiors appreciated the problem and approved the investments in time and money to outwait the Russians. So it is that the Ford programs have targeted not only the negotiators working directly with the Japanese but also their managers, who spend most of their time in the company's Detroit headquarters. Negotiators need information specific to the cultures in which they work. Just as critical, their managers back in the United States need a basic awareness of and appreciation for the importance of culture in international business so that they will be more amenable to the "odd-sounding" recommendations coming from their people in Moscow, Rio, or Tokyo.

Any experienced business negotiator will tell you that there is never enough time to get ready. Given the time constraints of international negotiations, preparations must be accomplished efficiently—the homework must be done before the bargaining begins. We recommend the following checklist to ensure proper preparation and planning for international negotiations:

1. Assessment of the situation and the people
2. Facts to confirm during the negotiation

---

[30]The Harvard Program on Negotiations provides a range of negotiations courses (http://www.pon.harvard.edu). Also, negotiations courses are the most popular in MBA programs around the country; see Leigh Thompson and Geoffrey J. Leonardelli, "Why Negotiation Is the Most Popular Business Course," *Ivey Business Journal* (Online), July/August 2004, p. 1.

[31]See Karrass's Web site for information regarding his programs: http://www.karrass.com. A key portal with information on negotiations in 50 different countries and links to several associated Web sites is http://www.GlobalNegotiationResources.com.

[32]Lee Edison provides an interesting description of what he calls "The Negotiation Industry," in an article he wrote for *Across the Board* 37, no. 4 (April 2000), pp. 14–20. Other commentators on training for international business negotiators include Yeang Soo Ching, "Putting a Human Face on Globalization," *New Straits Times*, January 16, 2000, p. 10; A. J. Vogl, "Negotiation: The Advanced Course," *Across the Board*, April 1, 2000, p. 21; and R. V. Veera, "MIT Preparing Students for New Millennium," *New Straits Times*, July 21, 2002, p. 5.

En los negocios no se consigue lo que se merece, se consigue lo que se negocia.

Ahora, más que nunca, la gente de éxito acude a Karrass.

La revista **Forbes** lo dijo en pocas palabras: "Claro, hay docenas de tipos -demasiados -que corren de acá para allá dando cursos, pero la lista de clientes de Karrass es de otra casta: Mobil, General Motors, Ford, IBM, General Electric, Arco, Shell, ITT, Phillips Petroleum, -9 de las 15 empresas más grandes de los Estados Unidos -y 140 más." Añadió **Forbes:**
Kaiser Aluminum & Chemical, que gastó en el transcurso de varios años, cerca de $15,000 dólares en cursos de Karrass, pidió que sus empleados identificaran ahorros específicos logrados al negociar mejor. El total sumó millones de dólares. Un ejecutivo de ventas de Boeing dijo lo mismo acerca de una sola negociación en el Medio Oriente. En General Electric, reconocida por sus programas internos de capacitación, el 90 por ciento de los empleados se

Dr. Chester L. Karrass

Continúa en la siguiente página

Through his books and training courses, Chester Karrass has taught more people to negotiate than anyone else in the world. His firm offers seminars in dozens of countries and advertises in in-flight magazines, here in Spanish.

3. Agenda

4. Best alternative to a negotiated agreement (BATNA)[33]

5. Concession strategies

6. Team assignments

Preparation and planning skill is at the top of almost everyone's list of negotiator traits, yet it seems many Americans are still planning strategies during over-ocean flights when they should be trying to rest. Quick wits are important in business negotiations, and arduous travel schedules and jet lag dull even the sharpest minds. Obviously, information about the other side's goals and preferences should be sought ahead of time. Also important are clear directions from headquarters and detailed information about market conditions.

No matter how thorough the preliminary research, negotiators should always make a list of key facts to reconfirm at the negotiation table. Information gathered about foreign customers and markets almost always includes errors, and things can change during those long airline flights. Next, anticipate that managers from other cultures may put less emphasis on a detailed agenda, but having one to propose still makes sense and helps organize the meetings.

The most important idea in *Getting to Yes* is the notion of the **best alternative to a negotiated agreement (BATNA)**.[34] This notion is how power in negotiations is best measured. Even the smallest companies can possess great power in negotiations if they have many good alternatives and their large-company counterparts do not. It is also important to plan out and write down concession strategies. Concessions can often snowball, and writing them down ahead of time helps negotiators keep them under control.

Finally, specific team assignments should be made clear—who handles technical details, who takes notes, who plays the tough guy, who does most of the talking for the group, and so forth. Also, in relationship-oriented cultures, the selection of intermediaries and the seniority of negotiators will be crucial considerations.

At least seven aspects of the negotiation setting should be manipulated ahead of time if possible:

1. Location

2. Physical arrangements

3. Number of parties

4. Number of participants

5. Audiences (news media, competitors, fellow vendors, etc.)

6. Communications channels

7. Time limits

Location speaks loudly about power relations. Traveling to a negotiating counterpart's home turf is a big disadvantage, and not just because of the costs of travel in money and fatigue. A neutral location may be preferred—indeed, many trans-Pacific business negotiations are conducted in Hawaii. The weather and golf are nice, and the jet lag is about equal. Location is also an important consideration because it may determine legal jurisdiction if

---

[33]The most instructive story we have ever seen regarding how to build one's BATNA is found in Daniel Michael, "In Clandestine World of Airplane Contracts, An Inside Look at a Deal," *The Wall Street Journal*, March 10, 2003, p. A1. It is a must-read for anyone interested in the topic of international business negotiations.
[34]Fisher, Ury, and Patton, *Getting to Yes.*

Different negotiation settings have different advantages and disadvantages. Of course, teleconferencing saves money, but meetings tend to be rushed. Golf course negotiations are perhaps the most leisurely, but thoughtful responses are more likely as golfers can consider reactions to statements made at the tee as they chase down their errant shots. E-mail also allows for thoughtful reactions in a similar way. Here an executive "negotiates" a putt at China's first golf course, the Chuan Shan Hot Spring Golf Club.

disputes arise. If you must travel to your negotiating counterpart's city, then a useful tactic is to invite clients or partners to work in a meeting room at your hotel. You can certainly get more done if they are away from the distractions of their offices.

Physical arrangements can affect cooperativeness in subtle ways. In high-context cultures, the physical arrangements of rooms can be quite a source of embarrassment and irritation if handled improperly. To the detriment of their foreign business relationships, Americans tend to be casual about such arrangements. Furthermore, views about who should attend negotiations vary across cultures. Americans tend to want to get everyone together to "hammer out an agreement" even if opinions and positions are divergent. Japanese prefer to talk to everyone separately, then, once everyone agrees, to schedule inclusive meetings. Russians tend toward a cumulative approach, meeting with one party and reaching an agreement, then both parties calling on a third party, and so on. In addition, the importance of not being outnumbered in international business negotiations has already been mentioned.

Audiences can have crucial influences on negotiation processes. Purchasing executives at PetroBras, the Brazilian national oil company, are well known for putting competitive bidders in rooms adjacent to one another to increase competitive pressures on both vendors. Likewise, news leaks to the press played a crucial role in pushing along the negotiations between General Motors and Toyota regarding a joint venture production agreement.

As electronic media become more available, efficient, and sometimes necessary (e.g., the war in Iraq or the SARS outbreak mentioned in Chapter 17), more business can be conducted without face-to-face communication. However, Americans should recognize that their counterparts in many other countries do not necessarily share their attraction to the Internet[35] and teleconferencing.[36] Indeed, recent research has shown that when using e-mail, trust is harder to build.[37] Additionally, businesspeople in Hong Kong tend to negotiate more competitively when using e-mail than in face-to-face settings.[38] A conversation

---

[35]Jan M. Uljn, Andreas Lincke, and Yunus Karakaya, "Non-Face-to-Face International Business Negotiation: How Is National Culture Reflected in This Medium," *IEEE Transactions on Professional Communication* 44, no. 2 (June 2001), pp. 126–37.

[36]Tim Ambler and Chris Styles, *The Silk Road to International Marketing* (London: Financial Times and Prentice Hall, 2000).

[37]Charles E. Naquin and Gaylen D. Paulson, "Online Bargaining and Interpersonal Trust," *Journal of Applied Psychology* 88, no. 1 (2003), pp. 113–20.

[38]Guang Yang, "The Impact of Computer-Mediated Communication on the Processes and Outcomes of Buyer–Seller Negotiations," unpublished doctoral dissertation, Merage School of Business, University of California, Irvine, 2003.

CROSSING BORDERS 19.2

The Digital Impact on International Negotiations

All in all, e-commerce is good for global marketing. It allows domestic firms to internationalize more quickly and at less cost. It allows international firms to communicate internally and externally with greater efficiency. Fax replaced telex, which, in turn, replaced the telegram. But e-mail is only partly replacing mail, fax, and phone. It is better seen as a different, more informal medium than fax and more convenient than phone. For networking purposes, e-mail is easily copied and relayed, though excess should be avoided. Many of us have learned to screen out e-mails addressed to multiple recipients.

Above all, e-mail can nurture, but not create, the long-term relationships so crucial to international marketing. The decision by Boeing to enter into an automated relationship with Dell was made not by two machines

but by personal contact between executives on both sides. The success of the Procter & Gamble–Walmart relationship rests with the personal relationships and interactions between P&G's key account team and Walmart's buyers. Although non-Thais can learn a great deal about Thailand from the Internet, they can never really understand Thai customers, the way they do business, and their feelings toward products unless they interact directly. Understanding culture requires personal experiential learning, the wellspring of social information.

Sources: Reprinted with permission from Tim Ambler and Chris Styles, *The Silk Road to International Marketing* (London: Financial Times and Prentice Hall, 2000); Guang Yang, *The Impact of Computer Mediated Communication on the Process and Outcomes of Buyer–Seller Negotiations*, unpublished doctoral dissertation, Merage School of Business, University of California, Irvine, 2003.

over a long dinner may actually be the most efficient way to communicate with clients and partners in places like Mexico, Malaysia, and China.

Finally, it is important to manipulate time limits. Recall the example about the Russians and Americans in Nice. The patience of the home office may be indispensable, and major differences in time orientation should be planned for when business negotiations are conducted in most other countries.

At the Negotiation Table

LO8

Managing all aspects of the negotiation process

The most difficult aspect of international business negotiations is the actual conduct of the face-to-face meeting. Assuming that the best representatives have been chosen, and assuming those representatives are well prepared and that situational factors have been manipulated in one's favor, things can still go sour at the negotiation table. Obviously, if these other preliminaries have not been managed properly, things will go wrong during the meetings. Even with great care and attention to preliminary details, managing the dynamics of the negotiation process is almost always the greatest challenge facing Americans seeking to do business in other countries.

Going into a business negotiation, most people have expectations about the "proper" or normal process of such a meeting, the *ritual*, so to speak.[39] Based on these expectations, progress is measured and appropriate bargaining strategies are selected. That is, things may be done differently in the latter stages of a negotiation than they were in the earlier. Higher-risk strategies may be employed to conclude talks—as in the final two minutes of a close soccer match. But all such decisions about strategy are made relative to perceptions of progress through an expected course of events.

Differences in the expectations held by parties from different cultures are one of the major difficulties in any international business negotiation. Before these differences are discussed, however, it is important to point out similarities. Everywhere around the world we have found that business negotiations proceed through four stages:

1. Nontask sounding

2. Task-related exchange of information

3. Persuasion

4. Concessions and agreement

---

[39]Sometimes these expectations are referred to as "the spirit of the deal" or the "social contract." See Ron S. Fortgang, David A. Lax, and James K. Sebenius, "Negotiating the Spirit of the Deal," *Harvard Business Review*, January–February 2003, pp. 66–74.

Exhibit 19.4
Summary of Japanese, American, and Chinese Business Negotiation Styles

Category	Japanese	Americans	Chinese
Language	Most Japanese executives understand English, though interpreters are often used.	Americans have less time to formulate answers and observe Japanese nonverbal responses because of a lack of knowledge of Japanese.	Often Chinese negotiators will understand at least some English, but will prefer an interpreter.
Nonverbal behaviors	The Japanese interpersonal communication style includes less eye contact, fewer negative facial expressions, and more periods of silence.	American businesspeople tend to "fill" silent periods with arguments or concessions.	Similar in quantities to Americans in most respects, yet difficult to read.
Values	Indirectness and face saving are important. Vertical buyer–seller relationships, with sellers depending on goodwill of buyers (amae), is typical.	Speaking one's mind is important; buyer–seller relationships are horizontal.	Relationship-oriented, guanxi, and face are key, looking for a "way" to compromise, truth is secondary.
Four Stages of Business Negotiations			
1. Nontask sounding	Considerable time and expense devoted to such efforts is the practice in Japan.	Very short periods are typical.	Long, expensive, formal, intermediaries are key.
2. Task-related exchange of information	The most important step: High first offers with long explanations and in-depth clarifications.	Information is given briefly and directly. "Fair" first offers are more typical.	Indirectness, explanations first, intermediaries.
3. Persuasion	Persuasion is accomplished primarily behind the scenes. Vertical status relations dictate bargaining outcomes.	The most important step: Minds are changed at the negotiation table, and aggressive persuasive tactics are often used.	Questions, competing offers, delays.
4. Concessions and agreement	Concessions are made only toward the end of negotiations—a holistic approach to decision making. Progress is difficult to measure for Americans.	Concessions and commitments are made throughout—a sequential approach to decision making.	Holistic approach, revisiting closed issues, goal is long-term relationship. Progress is difficult to measure for Americans.

Sources: N. Mark Lam and John L. Graham, *China Now, Doing Business in the World's Most Dynamic Market* (New York: McGraw-Hill, 2007); James Day Hodgson, Yoshihiro Sano, and John L. Graham, *Doing Business with the New Japan* (Boulder, CO: Rowman & Littlefield, 2008).

The first stage, nontask sounding, includes all those activities that might be described as establishing rapport or getting to know one another, but it does not include information related to the "business" of the meeting. The information exchanged in the second stage of business negotiations regards the parties' needs and preferences. The third stage, persuasion, involves the parties' attempts to modify one another's needs and preferences through the use of various persuasive tactics. The final stage of business negotiations involves the consummation of an agreement, which is often the summation of a series of concessions or smaller agreements.

Despite the consistency of this process across diverse cultures, the content and duration of the four stages differ substantially. For example, Exhibit 19.4 details procedural differences in Japan, the United States, and China as well as differences in language, nonverbal behavior, and values.

Nontask Sounding.
Americans always discuss topics other than business at the negotiation table (e.g., the weather, family, sports, politics, business conditions in general)

but not for long. Usually the discussion is moved to the specific business at hand after 5 to 10 minutes. Such preliminary talk, known as **nontask sounding**, is much more than just friendly or polite; it helps negotiators learn how the other side feels that particular day. During nontask sounding, one can determine if a client's attention is focused on business or distracted by other matters, personal or professional.

Learning about a client's background and interests also provides important cues about appropriate communication styles. To the extent that people's backgrounds are similar, communication can be more efficient. Engineers can use technical jargon when talking to other engineers. Sports enthusiasts can use sports analogies. Those with children can compare the cash drain of "putting a kid through college," and so on.

During these initial stages of conversation, judgments, too, are made about the "kind" of person(s) with whom one is dealing: Can this person be trusted?[40] Will he be reliable? How much power does she have in her organization? All such judgments are made before business discussions ever begin.

These preliminary nontask discussions have a definite purpose. Although most people are often unaware of it, such time almost always is used to size up one's clients. Depending on the results of this process, proposals and arguments are formed using different jargon and analogies. Or if clients are distracted by other personal matters or if the other people seem untrustworthy, the decision may be to discuss no business at all. This assessment sounds like a lot to accomplish in 5 to 10 minutes, but that's how long it usually takes in the information-oriented United States. Such is not the case in relationship-oriented countries like China or Brazil; the goals of the nontask sounding are identical, but the time spent is much, much longer. Instead of five minutes, it might take five meetings.

In the United States, firms resort to the legal system and their lawyers when they've made a bad deal because of a mistake in sizing up a customer or vendor. In most other countries, the legal system cannot be depended upon for such purposes. Instead, executives in places like Korea and Egypt spend substantial time and effort in nontask sounding so that problems do not develop later. Americans need to reconsider, from the foreigner's perspective, the importance of this first stage of negotiations if they hope to succeed in Seoul or Cairo.

Task-Related Exchange of Information.   Only when nontask sounding is complete and a trusting personal relationship is established should business be introduced. American executives are advised to let foreign counterparts decide when such substantive negotiations should begin, that is, to let them bring up business.

A **task-related information exchange** implies a two-way communication process. However, observations suggest that when Americans meet executives from some cultures across the negotiation table, the information flow is unidirectional. Japanese, Chinese, and Russian negotiators all appear to ask "thousands" of questions and give little feedback. The barrage of questions severely tests American negotiators' patience, and the lack of feedback causes them great anxiety. Both can add up to much longer stays in these countries, which means higher travel expenses.

Certainly an excellent negotiation tactic is to "drain" information from one's negotiation counterparts. But the oft-reported behaviors of Chinese, Japanese, and Russians may not necessarily represent a sophisticated negotiation ploy. Indeed, reference to Exhibit 19.2 provides some hints that differences in conversational styles—silent periods occurred more frequently in negotiations in all three cultures—may be part of the explanation. Indeed, in careful studies of conversational patterns of Americans negotiating with Japanese, the Americans seem to fill the silent periods and do most of the talking. These results suggest that American negotiators must take special care to keep their mouths shut and let foreign counterparts give them information.

Exchanging information across language barriers can be quite difficult as well. Most of us understand about 80 to 90 percent of what our same-culture spouses or roommates say—that

[40]Trust is a key negotiation concept that is receiving growing attention in diverse areas. See Alaka N. Rao, Jone L. Pearce, and Katherine Xin, "Governments, Reciprocal Exchange, and Trust among Business Associates," *Journal of International Business Studies* 36, no. 1 (2005), pp. 104–18; on the chemical basis of trust, see Michael Kosfeld, Markus Heinrichs, Paul J. Zak, Urs Fischbacher, and Ernst Fehr, "Oxytocin Increases Trust in Humans," *Nature* 435 (June 2005), pp. 673–76.

CROSSING BORDERS 19.3   Fishing for Business in Brazil

How important is nontask sounding? Consider this description about an American banker's meeting in Brazil, as recounted by an observer:

Introductions were made. The talk began with the usual "How do you like Rio?" questions—Have you been to Ipanema, Copacabana, Corcovado, etc.? There was also talk about the flight down from New York. After about five minutes of this chatting, the senior American quite conspicuously glanced at his watch, and then asked his client what he knew about the bank's new services.

"A little," responded the Brazilian. The senior American whipped a brochure out of his briefcase, opened it on the desk in front of the client, and began his sales pitch.

After about three minutes of "fewer forms, electronic transfers, and reducing accounts receivables," the Brazilian jumped back in, "Yes, that should make us more competitive . . . and competition is important here in Brazil. In fact, have you been following the World Cup *fútbol* (soccer) matches recently? Great games." And so the reel began to whir, paying out that monofilament line, right there in that hot high-rise office.

After a few minutes' dissertation on the local *fútbol* teams, Pélé, and why *fútbol* isn't popular in

the United States, the American started to try to crank the Brazilian back in. The first signal was the long look at his watch, then the interruption, "Perhaps we can get back to the new services we have to offer."

The Brazilian did get reeled back into the subject of the sale for a couple of minutes, but then the reel started to sing again. This time he went from efficient banking transactions to the nuances of the Brazilian financial system to the Brazilian economy. Pretty soon we were all talking about the world economy and making predictions about the U.S. presidential elections.

Another look at his Rolex, and the American started this little "sport fishing" ritual all over again. From my perspective (I wasn't investing time and money toward the success of this activity), this all seemed pretty funny. Every time the American VP looked at his watch during the next 45 minutes, I had to bite my cheeks to keep from laughing out loud. He never did get to page two of his brochure. The Brazilian just wasn't interested in talking business with someone he didn't know pretty well.

Source: William Hernandez Requejo and John L. Graham, *Global Negotiation: The New Rules* (New York: Palgrave Macmillan, 2008).

means 10 to 20 percent is misunderstood or misheard. That latter percentage goes up dramatically when someone is speaking a second language, no matter the fluency levels or length of acquaintance. And when the second language capability is limited, entire conversations may be totally misunderstood. Using multiple communication channels during presentations—writing, exhibits, speaking, repetition—works to minimize the inevitable errors.

In many cultures, negative feedback is very difficult to obtain. In high-context cultures such as Mexico and Japan, speakers are reluctant to voice objections lest they damage the all-important personal relationships. Some languages themselves are by nature indirect and indefinite. English is relatively clear, but translations from languages like Japanese can leave much to be understood. In more collectivistic cultures like China, negotiators may be reluctant to speak for the decision-making group they represent, or they may not even know how the group feels about a particular proposal. All such problems suggest the importance of having natives of customer countries on your negotiation team and of spending extra time in business and informal entertainment settings trying to understand better the information provided by foreign clients and partners. Conversely, low-context German executives often complain that American presentations include too much "fluff"—they are interested in copious information only, not the hyperbole and hedges so common in American speech. Negative feedback from Germans can seem brutally frank to higher-context Americans.

A final point of potential conflict in information exchange has to do with first offers. Price padding varies across cultures, and Americans' first offers tend to come in relatively close to what they really want. "A million dollars is the goal, let's start at $1.2 million" seems about right to most Americans. Implicit in such a first offer is the hope that things will get done quickly. Americans do not expect to move far from first offers. Negotiators in many other countries do not share the goal of finishing quickly, however. In places like China, Brazil, or Spain, the expectation is for a relatively longer period of haggling, and first offers are more aggressive to reflect these expectations. "If the goal is 1 million, we better start at 2," makes sense there. Americans react to such aggressive first offers in one of two ways: They either laugh or get angry. And when foreign counterparts' second offers reflect deep discounts, Americans' ire increases.

A good example of this problem regards an American CEO shopping for a European plant site. When he selected a $20 million plot in Ireland, the Spanish real estate developer he had visited earlier called wondering why the American had not asked for a lower price for the Madrid site before choosing Dublin. He told the Spaniard that his first offer "wasn't even in the ballpark." He wasn't laughing when the Spaniard then offered to beat the Irish price. In fact, the American executive was quite angry. A potentially good deal was forgone because of different expectations about first offers. Yes, numbers were exchanged, but information was not. Aggressive first offers made by foreigners should be met with questions, not anger.

Persuasion.   In Japan, a clear separation does not exist between task-related information exchange and persuasion. The two stages tend to blend together as each side defines and refines its needs and preferences. Much time is spent in the task-related exchange of information, leaving little to "argue" about during the persuasion stage. Conversely, Americans tend to lay their cards on the table and hurry through the information exchange to persuasion. After all, the persuasion is the heart of the matter. Why hold a meeting unless someone's mind is to be changed? A key aspect of sales training in the United States is "handling objections." So the goal in information exchange among Americans is to quickly get those objections out in the open so they can be handled.

This handling can mean providing clients with more information. It can also mean getting mean. As suggested by Exhibit 19.2, Americans make threats and issue warnings in negotiations. They do not use such tactics often, but negotiators in many other cultures use such tactics even less frequently and in different circumstances. For example, notice how infrequently the Mexicans and English-speaking Canadians used threats and warnings in the simulated negotiations. Others have found Filipino and Chinese

You want him on your side! Banana salespeople such as this fellow in Agra, India, are known worldwide for their negotiation skills—they're hawking a perishable product that shows the wear. In Japan they even have a negotiation strategy named for them: Outrageously high first offers are derogated as *"banana no tataki uri,"* the banana sale approach.

negotiators to use a less aggressive approach than Americans.[41] Indeed, in Thailand or China, the use of such aggressive negotiation tactics can result in the loss of face and the destruction of important personal relationships. Such tough tactics may be used in Japan but by buyers only and usually only in informal circumstances—not at the formal negotiation table. Americans also get angry during negotiations and express emotions that may be completely inappropriate in foreign countries. Such emotional outbursts may be seen as infantile or even barbaric behavior in places like Hong Kong and Bangkok.

The most powerful persuasive tactic is actually asking more questions. Foreign counterparts can be politely asked to explain why they must have delivery in two months or why they must have a 10 percent discount. Chester Karrass, in his still useful book *The Negotiation Game*,[42] suggests that it is "smart to be a little dumb" in business negotiations. Repeat questions; for example, "I didn't completely understand what you meant—can you please explain

[41]X. Michael Song, Jinhong Xie, and Barbara Dyer, "Antecedents and Consequences of Marketing Managers' Conflict Handling Procedures," *Journal of Marketing* 64 (January 2000), pp. 50–66; Alma Mintu-Wimsatt and Julie B. Gassenheimer, "The Moderating Effects of Cultural Context in Buyer–Seller Negotiation," *Journal of Personal Selling & Sales Management* 20, no. 1 (Winter 2000), pp. 1–9.

[42]Chester Karrass, *The Negotiation Game* (New York: Crowell, 1970).

that again?" If clients or potential business partners have good answers, then perhaps a compromise on the issue is best. Often, however, under close and repeated scrutiny, their answers are not very good. When their weak position is exposed, they are obliged to concede. Questions can elicit key information, the most powerful yet passive persuasive device. Indeed, the use of questions is a favored Japanese tactic, one they use with great effect on Americans.

Third parties and informal channels of communication are the indispensable media of persuasion in many countries, particularly the more relationship-oriented ones. Meetings in restaurants or meetings with references and mutual friends who originally provided introductions may be used to handle difficult problems with partners in other countries. The value of such informal settings and trusted intermediaries is greatest when problems are emotion laden. They provide a means for simultaneously delivering difficult messages and saving face. Although American managers may eschew such "behind the scenes" approaches, they are standard practice in many countries.

Concessions and Agreement. Comments made previously about the importance of writing down concession-making strategies and understanding differences in decision-making styles—sequential versus holistic—are pertinent here. Americans often make concessions early, expecting foreign counterparts to reciprocate. However, in many cultures no concessions are made until the end of the negotiations. Americans often get frustrated and express anger when foreign clients and partners are simply following a different approach to concession making, one that can also work quite well when both sides understand what is going on.

After Negotiations

LO9

The importance of follow-up communications and procedures

Contracts between American firms are often longer than 100 pages and include carefully worded clauses regarding every aspect of the agreement. American lawyers go to great lengths to protect their companies against all circumstances, contingencies, and actions of the other party. The best contracts are written so tightly that the other party would not think of going to court to challenge any provision. The American adversarial system requires such contracts.

In most other countries, particularly the relationship-oriented ones, legal systems are not depended upon to settle disputes. Indeed, the term *disputes* does not reflect how a business relationship should work. Each side should be concerned about mutual benefits of the relationship and therefore should consider the interests of the other. Consequently, in places like Japan written contracts are very short—two to three pages—are purposely loosely written, and primarily contain comments on principles of the relationship. From the Japanese point of view, the American emphasis on tight contracts is tantamount to planning the divorce before the wedding.

In other relationship-oriented countries, such as China, contracts are more a description of what business partners view their respective responsibilities to be. For complicated business relationships, they may be quite long and detailed. However, their purpose is different from the American understanding. When circumstances change, then responsibilities must also be adjusted, despite the provisions of the signed contract. The notion of enforcing a contract in China makes little sense.

Informality being a way of life in the United States, even the largest contracts between companies are often sent through the mail for signature. In America, ceremony is considered a waste of time and money. But when a major agreement is reached with foreign companies, their executives may expect a formal signing ceremony involving CEOs of the respective companies. American companies are wise to accommodate such expectations.

Tung Chee Hwa, at the time Chief Executive of the Hong Kong Special Administrative Region, consummated the deal with the Mouse for Asia's new Walt Disney World, which opened in 2005.

Finally, follow-up communications are an important part of business negotiations with partners and clients from most foreign countries. Particularly in high-context cultures, where personal relationships are crucial, high-level executives must stay in touch with their counterparts. Letters, pictures, and mutual visits remain important long after contracts are signed. Indeed, warm relationships at the top often prove to be the best medicine for any problems that may arise in the future.

    D. Legal system
        1. Organization of the judiciary system
        2. Code, common, socialist, or Islamic-law country?
        3. Participation in patents, trademarks, and other conventions
    E. Social organizations
        1. Group behavior
        2. Social classes
        3. Clubs, other organizations
        4. Race, ethnicity, and subcultures
    F. Business customs and practices

V. Religion and aesthetics
    A. Religion and other belief systems
        1. Orthodox doctrines and structures
        2. Relationship with the people
        3. Which religions are prominent?
        4. Membership of each religion
        5. Any powerful or influential cults?
    B. Aesthetics
        1. Visual arts (fine arts, plastics, graphics, public art, colors, etc.)
        2. Music
        3. Drama, ballet, and other performing arts
        4. Folklore and relevant symbols

VI. Living conditions
    A. Diet and nutrition
        1. Meat and vegetable consumption rates
        2. Typical meals
        3. Malnutrition rates
        4. Foods available
    B. Housing
        1. Types of housing available
        2. Do most people own or rent?
        3. Do most people live in one-family dwellings or with other families?
    C. Clothing
        1. National dress
        2. Types of clothing worn at work
    D. Recreation, sports, and other leisure activities
        1. Types available and in demand
        2. Percentage of income spent on such activities
    E. Social security
    F. Healthcare

VII. Language
    A. Official language(s)
    B. Spoken versus written language(s)
    C. Dialects

VIII. Executive summary

After completing all of the other sections, prepare a *two-page* (maximum length) summary of the major points and place it at the front of the report. The purpose of an executive summary is to give the reader a brief glance at the critical points of your report. Those aspects of the culture a reader should know to do business in the country but would not be expected to know or would find different based on his or her SRC should be included in this summary.

IX. Sources of information

X. Appendixes

II. ECONOMIC ANALYSIS

The reader may find the data collected for the economic analysis guideline are more straightforward than for the cultural analysis guideline. There are two broad categories of information in this guideline: general economic data that serve as a basis for an evaluation of the economic soundness of a country, and information on channels of distribution and media availability. As mentioned previously, the guideline focuses only on broad categories of data and must be adapted to particular company and product needs.

Guideline

I. Introduction
II. Population
   A. Total
      1. Growth rates
      2. Number of live births
      3. Birthrates
   B. Distribution of population
      1. Age
      2. Sex
      3. Geographic areas (urban, suburban, and rural density and concentration)
      4. Migration rates and patterns
      5. Ethnic groups
III. Economic statistics and activity
   A. Gross national product (GNP or GDP)
      1. Total
      2. Rate of growth (real GNP or GDP)
   B. Personal income per capita
   C. Average family income
   D. Distribution of wealth
      1. Income classes
      2. Proportion of the population in each class
      3. Is the distribution distorted?
   E. Minerals and resources
   F. Surface transportation
      1. Modes
      2. Availability
      3. Usage rates
      4. Ports
   G. Communication systems
      1. Types
      2. Availability
      3. Usage rates
   H. Working conditions
      1. Employer–employee relations
      2. Employee participation
      3. Salaries and benefits
   I. Principal industries
      1. What proportion of the GNP does each industry contribute?
      2. Ratio of private to publicly owned industries
   J. Foreign investment
      1. Opportunities?
      2. Which industries?
   K. International trade statistics
      1. Major exports
         a. Dollar value
         b. Trends
      2. Major imports
         a. Dollar value
         b. Trends

        3. Balance-of-payments situation
          a. Surplus or deficit?
          b. Recent trends
        4. Exchange rates
          a. Single or multiple exchange rates?
          b. Current rate of exchange
          c. Trends
   L. Trade restrictions
      1. Embargoes
      2. Quotas
      3. Import taxes
      4. Tariffs
      5. Licensing
      6. Customs duties
   M. Extent of economic activity not included in cash income activities
      1. Countertrades
        a. Products generally offered for countertrading
        b. Types of countertrades requested (barter, counterpurchase, etc.)
      2. Foreign aid received
   N. Labor force
      1. Size
      2. Unemployment rates
   O. Inflation rates
IV. Developments in science and technology
   A. Current technology available (computers, machinery, tools, etc.)
   B. Percentage of GNP invested in research and development
   C. Technological skills of the labor force and general population
V. Channels of distribution (macro analysis)
   This section reports data on all channel middlemen available within the market.
   Later, you will select a specific channel as part of your distribution strategy.
   A. Retailers
      1. Number of retailers
      2. Typical size of retail outlets
      3. Customary markup for various classes of goods
      4. Methods of operation (cash/credit)
      5. Scale of operation (large/small)
      6. Role of chain stores, department stores, and specialty shops
   B. Wholesale middlemen
      1. Number and size
      2. Customary markup for various classes of goods
      3. Method of operation (cash/credit)
   C. Import/export agents
   D. Warehousing
   E. Penetration of urban and rural markets
VI. Media
   This section reports data on all media available within the country or market.
   Later, you will select specific media as part of the promotional mix and strategy.
   A. Availability of media
   B. Costs
      1. Television
      2. Radio
      3. Print
      4. Internet
      5. Other media (cinema, outdoor, etc.)
   C. Agency assistance

D. Coverage of various media
E. Percentage of population reached by each medium
VII. Executive summary
   After completing the research for this report, prepare a two-page (maximum) summary of the major economic points and place it at the front
VIII. Sources of information
IX. Appendixes

III. MARKET AUDIT AND COMPETITIVE MARKET ANALYSIS

Of the guidelines presented, this is the most product or brand specific. Information in the other guidelines is general in nature, focusing on product categories, whereas data in this guideline are brand specific and are used to determine competitive market conditions and market potential.

Two different components of the planning process are reflected in this guideline. Information in Parts I and II, Cultural Analysis and Economic Analysis, serve as the basis for an evaluation of the product or brand in a specific country market. Information in this guideline provides an estimate of market potential and an evaluation of the strengths and weaknesses of competitive marketing efforts. The data generated in this step are used to determine the extent of adaptation of the company's marketing mix necessary for successful market entry and to develop the final step, the action plan.

The detailed information needed to complete this guideline is not necessarily available without conducting a thorough marketing research investigation. Thus another purpose of this part of the country notebook is to identify the correct questions to ask in a formal market study.

Guideline

I. Introduction
II. The product
   A. Evaluate the product as an innovation as it is perceived by the intended market
      1. Relative advantage
      2. Compatibility
      3. Complexity
      4. Trialability
      5. Observability
   B. Major problems and resistances to product acceptance based on the preceding evaluation
III. The market
   A. Describe the market(s) in which the product is to be sold
      1. Geographical region(s)
      2. Forms of transportation and communication available in that (those) region(s)
      3. Consumer buying habits
         a. Product-use patterns
         b. Product feature preferences
         c. Shopping habits
      4. Distribution of the product
         a. Typical retail outlets
         b. Product sales by other middlemen
      5. Advertising and promotion
         a. Advertising media usually used to reach your target market(s)
         b. Sales promotions customarily used (sampling, coupons, etc.)
      6. Pricing strategy
         a. Customary markups
         b. Types of discounts available
   B. Compare and contrast your product and the competition's product(s)
      1. Competitors' product(s)
         a. Brand name
         b. Features
         c. Package
      2. Competitors' prices

      3. Competitors' promotion and advertising methods
      4. Competitors' distribution channels
  C. Market size
      1. Estimated industry sales for the planning year
      2. Estimated sales for your company for the planning year
  D. Government participation in the marketplace
      1. Agencies that can help you
      2. Regulations you must follow
IV. Executive summary
  Based on your analysis of the market, briefly summarize (two-page maximum) the major problems and opportunities requiring attention in your marketing mix, and place the summary at the front of the report.
V. Sources of information
VI. Appendixes

IV. PRELIMINARY MARKETING PLAN

Information gathered in Guidelines I through III serves as the basis for developing a marketing plan for your product or brand in a target market. How the problems and opportunities that surfaced in the preceding steps are overcome or exploited to produce maximum sales and profits are presented here. The action plan reflects, in your judgment, the most effective means of marketing your product in a country market. Budgets, expected profits and losses, and additional resources necessary to implement the proposed plan are also presented.

Guideline

I. The marketing plan
  A. Marketing objectives
      1. Target market(s) (specific description of the market)
      2. Sales forecast years 1-5
      3. Profit forecast years 1-5
      4. Market penetration and coverage
  B. SWOT Analysis
      1. Strengths
      2. Weaknesses
      3. Opportunities
      4. Threats
  C. Product adaptation or modification—Using the product component model as your guide, indicate how your product can be adapted for the market.
      1. Core component
      2. Packaging component
      3. Support services component
  D. Promotion mix
      1. Advertising
        a. Objectives
        b. Media mix
        c. Message
        d. Costs
      2. Sales promotions
        a. Objectives
        b. Coupons
        c. Premiums
        d. Costs
      3. Personal selling
      4. Other promotional methods
  E. Distribution: From origin to destination
      1. Port selection
        a. Origin port
        b. Destination port

     2. Mode selection: Advantages/disadvantages of each mode
       a. Railroads
       b. Air carriers
       c. Ocean carriers
       d. Motor carriers
     3. Packing
       a. Marking and labeling regulations
       b. Containerization
       c. Costs
     4. Documentation required
       a. Bill of lading
       b. Dock receipt
       c. Air bill
       d. Commercial invoice
       e. Pro forma invoice
       f. Shipper's export declaration
       g. Statement of origin
       h. Special documentation
     5. Insurance claims
     6. Freight forwarder. If your company does not have a transportation or traffic management department, then consider using a freight forwarder. There are distinct advantages and disadvantages to hiring one.

F. Channels of distribution (micro analysis). This section presents details about the specific types of distribution in your marketing plan.
     1. Retailers
       a. Type and number of retail stores
       b. Retail markups for products in each type of retail store
       c. Methods of operation for each type (cash/credit)
       d. Scale of operation for each type (small/large)
     2. Wholesale middlemen
       a. Type and number of wholesale middlemen
       b. Markup for class of products by each type
       c. Methods of operation for each type (cash/credit)
       d. Scale of operation (small/large)
     3. Import/export agents
     4. Warehousing
       a. Type
       b. Location

G. Price determination
     1. Cost of the shipment of goods
     2. Transportation costs
     3. Handling expenses
       a. Pier charges
       b. Wharfage fees
       c. Loading and unloading charges
     4. Insurance costs
     5. Customs duties
     6. Import taxes and value-added tax
     7. Wholesale and retail markups and discounts
     8. Company's gross margins
     9. Retail price

H. Terms of sale
     1. EX works, FOB, FAS, C&F, CIF
     2. Advantages/disadvantages of each

I. Methods of payment
   1. Cash in advance
   2. Open accounts
   3. Consignment sales
   4. Sight, time, or date drafts
   5. Letters of credit
II. Pro forma financial statements and budgets
   A. Marketing budget
      1. Selling expense
      2. Advertising/promotion expense
      3. Distribution expense
      4. Product cost
      5. Other costs
   B. Pro forma annual profit and loss statement (first year through fifth year)
III. Resource requirements
   A. Finances
   B. Personnel
   C. Production capacity
IV. Executive summary
   After completing the research for this report, prepare a two-page (maximum) summary of the major points of your successful marketing plan, and place it at the front of the report.
V. Sources of information
VI. Appendixes
   The intricacies of international operations and the complexity of the environment within which the international marketer must operate create an extraordinary demand for information. When operating in foreign markets, the need for thorough information as a substitute for uninformed opinion is equally important as it is in domestic marketing. Sources of information needed to develop the country notebook and answer other marketing questions are discussed in Chapter 8 and its appendix.

Summary

Market-oriented firms build strategic market plans around company objectives, markets, and the competitive environment. Planning for marketing can be complicated even for one country, but when a company is doing business internationally, the problems are multiplied. Company objectives may vary from market to market and from time to time; the structure of international markets also changes periodically and from country to country; and the competitive, governmental, and economic parameters affecting market planning are in a constant state of flux. These variations require international marketing executives to be especially flexible and creative in their approach to strategic marketing planning.

GLOSSARY

a

administered pricing The attempt to establish prices for an entire market through the cooperation of competitors, through national, state, or local governments, or by international agreement. Its legality differs from country to country and from time to time.

advanced pricing agreement (APA) An agreement made between a company and the Internal Revenue Service covering **transfer pricing** methods used by the company. Without such an agreement, if the IRS charges the company with underreporting income through its transactions with affiliates, the burden of proof that a transfer price was fair rests with the company.

aesthetics Philosophically, the creation and appreciation of beauty; collectively, the arts, including folklore, music, drama, and dance.

AFTA ASEAN (Association of Southeast Asian Nations) Free Trade Area; a multinational trade group that evolved from ASEAN. *See* **APEC; ASEAN+3**

agent middlemen In an international transaction, intermediaries who represent the principal (home manufacturer/marketer) rather than themselves; agent middlemen work on commission and arrange for sales in the foreign country but do not take title to the merchandise. *See* **home-country middlemen; merchant-middlemen**

Amsterdam Treaty *See* **Treaty of Amsterdam**

analogy A method of market estimation that assumes that demand for a product develops in much the same way in all countries as comparable economic development occurs in each country.

APEC The Asian-Pacific Economic Cooperation; a forum that meets annually to discuss regional economic development. *See* **AFTA; ASEAN+3**

arbitration A procedure, used as an alternative to **litigation,** in which parties in a dispute may select a disinterested third party or parties as referee to determine the merits of the case and make a judgment that both parties agree to honor.

ASEAN (Association of Southeast Asian Nations A multinational regional trade group including Brunei, Cambodia, Indonesia, Laos, Malaysia, Myanmar, Philippines, Singapore, Thailand, and Vietnam.

ASEAN+3 A forum for ministers of the Association of Southeast Asian Nations plus ministers from China, Japan, and South Korea. *See* **AFTA; APEC**

b

back translation The process in which a document, such as a questionnaire, or phrase is translated from one language to another and then translated by a second party into the original language. Back translations can be used to verify that the first translation, as of a marketing slogan, has the intended meeting for the targeted audience. *See* **decentering; parallel translation**

balance of payments The system of accounts that records a nation's international financial transactions.

balance of trade The difference in value over a period of time between a country's imports and exports.

barter The direct exchange of goods between two parties in a transaction. *See* **compensation deals; counterpurchase; countertrade**

BATNA Acronym for "best alternative to a negotiated agreement," a notion discussed in *Getting to Yes*, by Fisher, Ury, and Patton.

BEMs Big emerging markets; used to describe the core group of populous nations that will account for much of the growth in world trade among developing and newly industrialized countries.

bills of exchange A form of international commercial payment drawn by sellers on foreign buyers; in transactions based on bills of exchange, the seller assumes all risk until the actual dollars are received, making them riskier for the seller than **letters of credit.**

bottom-of-the-pyramid markets (BOPM) These consist of the 4 billion people around the world with incomes of $1,200 or less per capita. They are not necessarily defined by national borders, but are rather pockets of poverty particularly concentrated in south Asia and sub-Sahara Africa.

bribery The use of funds, usually illegally, to influence decisions made by public employees and government officials. Such payments often range into the millions of dollars in international commerce.

c

capital account The portion of a **balance of payments** statement that shows a record of direct investment, portfolio investment, and short-term capital movements to and from countries.

cartel An arrangement in which various companies producing similar products or services work together to control markets for the goods and services they produce. The Organization of Petroleum Exporting Countries (OPEC) is the best known international cartel.

client followers Companies, often providers of services, that follow companies that first moved into a foreign market; for example, an American insurance company setting up in Mexico to serve a U.S. auto company that had previously opened a factory there.

code law A legal system based on an all-inclusive system of written rules, or codes, of law; generally divided into three separate codes: commercial, civil, and criminal. In the United States, Louisiana is the one state to use code law. *See* **common law**

Commerce Control List (CCL) A directory, organized by a series of **Export Control Classification Numbers,** that indicates U.S. rules for the exportability of items. Exporters must use the list to determine if there are end-use restrictions on certain items, such as uses in nuclear, chemical, and biological weapons, and determine if a product has a dual use—that is, both in commercial and restricted applications. *See* **Export Administration Regulations**

Commerce Country Chart (CCC) A directory of information that a U.S. exporter needs to consult, along with the **Commerce Control List,** to determine if the exporter needs a license to export or reexport a product to a particular destination. *See* **Export Control Classification Number**

common law The body of law based on tradition, past practices, and legal precedents set by courts through interpretations of statutes, legal legislation, and past rulings. Common law, which is used in all states in the United States except Louisiana, uses past decisions to interpret statutes and apply them to present situations. Also known as English law. *See* **code law**

common market An agreement that eliminates all tariffs and other restrictions on internal trade, adopts a set of common external tariffs, and removes all restrictions on the free flow of capital and labor among member nations.

compensation deals Transactions that involve payment in both goods and cash. *See* **barter; counterpurchase; countertrade**

complementary marketing The process by which companies with excess marketing capacity in different countries or with a desire for a broader product line take on additional lines for international distribution; commonly called *piggybacking.*

conciliation A nonbinding agreement between parties to resolve disputes by asking a third party to mediate differences. Also known as *mediation. See* **arbitration; litigation**

confiscation The seizing of a company's assets without payment. Prominent examples involving U.S. companies occurred in Cuba and Iran. *See* **domestication; expropriation**

Confusion Philosophy The 2,500-year-old teachings of Chinese philosopher, Confucius, still strongly influence cultures in East Asia today. Primary among his teachings were a deep respect for elders, rulers, and husbands.

controllable elements The aspects of trade over which a company has control and influence; they include marketing decisions covering product, price, promotion, distribution, research, and advertising. *See* **uncontrollable elements**

corporate planning The formulation of long-term, generalized goals for an enterprise as a whole. *See* **strategic planning; tactical planning**

counterpurchase A type of **countertrade** in which a seller receives payment in cash but agrees in a contract to buy goods from the buyer for the total monetary amount involved in the first transaction or for a set percentage of that amount; also known as *offset trade. See* **barter; compensation deals**

countertrade A type of transaction in which goods are imported and sold by a company from a country in exchange for the right or ability to manufacture and/or sell goods in that country. Countertrade can substitute for cash entirely or partially and is used extensively in trade between U.S. firms and the former Soviet bloc, along with other emerging markets. *See* **barter; compensation deals; counterpurchase**

countervailing duty A fee that may, under **World Trade Organization** rules, be imposed on foreign goods benefiting from subsidies, whether in production, export, or transportation; may be applied in conjunction with *minimum access volume,* which restricts the amount of goods a country will import.

creativity in negotiations The use of creative processes such as joint brainstorming in informal side-bar negotiations. This assumes a collaborative approach to negotiations rather than a competitive one, and assumes long-term, mutually beneficial commercial and personal relationships are the goal of the negotiation.

cultural borrowing The phenomenon by which societies learn from other cultures' ways and borrow ideas to solve problems or improve conditions.

cultural congruence A marketing strategy in which products are marketed in a way similar to the marketing of products already in the market in a manner as congruent as possible with existing cultural norms.

cultural elective *See* **elective**

cultural exclusive *See* **exclusive**

cultural imperative *See* **imperative**

cultural sensitivity An awareness of the nuances of culture so that a culture can be viewed objectively, evaluated, and appreciated; an important part of foreign marketing.

cultural values The system of beliefs and customs held by a population in a given *culture.* A book by Geert Hofstede describes a study of 66 nations and divides the cultural values of those nations into four primary dimensions: the Individualized/Collectivism Index, the Power Distance Index, the Uncertainty Avoidance Index, and the Masculinity/Femininity Index (which is not considered as useful as the other three).

culture The human-made part of human environment—the sum total of knowledge, beliefs, arts, morals, laws, customs, and any other capabilities and habits acquired by humans as members of society.

current account The portion of a **balance of payments** statement that shows a record of all merchandise exports, imports, and services, plus unilateral transfers of funds.

customs-privileged facilities Areas, as in international transactions, where goods can be imported for storage and/or processing with tariffs and quota limits postponed until the products leave the designated areas. *See* **foreign-trade zones**

customs union A stage in economic cooperation that benefits from a *free trade area*'s reduced or eliminated internal tariffs and adds a common external tariff on products imported from countries outside the union. *See* **common market; political union**

cybersquatters Persons or businesses that buy, usually for a nominal fee, and register as Web site names descriptive nouns, celebrity names, variations on company trademarks, geographic and ethnic group names, and pharmaceutical and other descriptors and then hold them until they can be sold at an inflated price. Sometimes called *CSQ.*

d

dealers The middlemen selling industrial goods or durable goods directly to customers; their actions are the last steps in the **distribution channel.**

decentering A method of translation, a variation on **back translation,** that is a successive process of translation and retranslation of a document, such as a questionnaire, each time by a different translator. The two original-language versions are then compared, and if there are differences, the process is repeated until the second original-language version is the same as the first. *See* **parallel translation**

derived demand Demand that is dependent on another source; it can be fundamental to the success of efforts to sell capital equipment and big-ticket industrial services.

diffusion (of innovations) The adoption or spread of products across markets by increasing numbers of consumers.

direct exporting The type of exporting in which a company sells to a customer in another country. *See* **indirect exporting**

distribution channels The various routes through which marketers must negotiate their goods to deliver them to the consumer. Distribution channel structures range from those with little developed marketing infrastructure, as found in many emerging markets, to those with a highly complex, multilayered systems, as found in Japan. Consideration for channel structure involves "the six Cs": cost, capital, control, coverage, character, and continuity.

distribution process The physical handling of goods, the passage of ownership (title), and—especially important from a marketing viewpoint—the buying and selling negotiations between the producers and middlemen and between middlemen and customers. *See* **distribution structure**

distribution structure The system, present in every country's market, through which goods pass from producer to user; within the structure are a variety of middlemen. *See* **distribution process**

domestication A process by which a host country gradually transfers foreign investments to national control and ownership through a series of government decrees mandating local ownership and greater national involvement in company management. *See* **confiscation; expropriation**

domestic environment uncontrollables Factors in a company's home country over which the company has little or no control or influence. They include political and legal forces, the economic climate, level of technology, competitive forces, and economic forces. *See* **uncontrollable elements**

dumping An export practice, generally prohibited by laws and subject to penalties and fines, defined by some as the selling of products in foreign markets below the cost of production and by others as the selling of products at below the prices of the same goods in the home market.

e

economic development Generally, an increase in national production that results in an increase in average per capita gross domestic product.

economic dualism The coexistence of modern and traditional sectors within an economy, especially as found in less-developed countries.

ELAIN Export License Application and Information Network; an electronic service that enables authorized exporters to submit license applications via the Internet for all commodities except supercomputers and to all free-world destinations. *See* **ERIC; SNAP; STELA**

elective A business custom (as in a foreign country) to which adaptation is helpful but not necessary. *See* **exclusive; imperative**

EMU The Economic and Monetary Union; formed by the **Maastricht Treaty,** which also formed the European Union.

ERIC Electronic Request for Item Classification; a supplementary service to **ELAIN** that allows an exporter to submit commodity classification requests via the Internet to the Bureau of Export administration. *See* **SNAP; STELA**

European Parliament The legislative body of the European Union, similar in concept to the U.S. House of Representatives. That is, more populous countries have more representatives.

exclusive A business custom (as in a foreign country) in which an outsider must not participate. *See* **elective; imperative**

exclusive distribution A practice in which a company restricts which retailers can carry its product; often used by companies to maintain high retail margins, to maintain the exclusive-quality image of a product, and to encourage retailers to provide extra service to customers.

expatriate A person living away from his or her own country. In international sales, expatriates from the selling company's home country may be the best choice for the sales force when products are highly technical or when selling requires an extensive knowledge of the company and its product line. *See* **local nationals**

expert opinion A method of market estimation in which experts are polled for their opinions about market size and growth rates; used particularly in foreign countries that are new to the marketer.

Export Administration Regulations (EAR) A set of rules issued by the U.S. Department of Commerce, designed to alleviate many of the problems and confusions of exporting; they are intended to speed up the process of granting export licenses by concentrating license control on a list of specific items, most of which involve national security. Exporters must ensure that their trade activities do not violate the provisions of EAR. *See* **Commerce Control List; Export Control Classification Number**

Export Control Classification Number (ECCN) Under the provisions of the U.S. **Export Administration Regulations (EAR),** a classification number that a U.S. exporter must select for an item to be exported; the number corresponds to a description in the **Commerce Control List,** which indicates the exportability of the item.

export documents The various items of documentation for an international transaction, as required by the exporting government, by established procedures of foreign trade, and, in some cases, by the importing government.

export management company (EMC) An important middleman for firms with relatively small international volume or those unwilling to involve their own personnel in the international function. These EMCs range in size from 1 person upward to 100 and handle about 10 percent of the manufactured goods exported. Typically, the EMC becomes an integral part of the marketing operations of its client companies. Working under the names of the manufacturers, the EMC functions as a low-cost, independent marketing department with direct responsibility to the parent firm. The working relationship is so close that customers are often unaware they are not dealing directly with the export department of the company.

export regulations Restrictions placed by countries on the selling of goods abroad; among reasons they may be imposed are to conserve scarce goods for home consumption and to control the flow of strategic goods actual or potential enemies. *See* **import regulations**

Export Trading Company (ETC) Act An act allowing producers of similar products in the United States to form an export trading company; the act created a more favorable environment for the formation of joint export ventures, in part by removing antitrust disincentives to trade activities.

expropriation   The seizure of an investment by a government in which some reimbursement is made to the investment owner; often the seized investment becomes nationalized. *See* **confiscation; domestication**

f

factual knowledge   A type of knowledge or understanding of a foreign culture that encompasses different meanings of color, different tastes, and other traits of a culture that a marketer can study, anticipate, and absorb. *See* **interpretive knowledge**

FCPA   Foreign Corrupt Practices Act. The act prohibits U.S. businesses from paying bribes to officials or foreign governments, openly or using middlemen as conduits for a bribe when the U.S. official knows that the middleman's payment will be used for a bribe.

foreign environment uncontrollables   Factors in the foreign market over which a business operating in its home country has little or no control or influence. They include political and legal forces, economic climate, geography and infrastructure, level of technology, structure of distribution, and level of technology. *See* **domestic environment uncontrollables**

foreign-trade zones (FTZs)   Regions or ports that act as holding areas for goods before quotas or customs duties are applied. In the United States, more than 150 FTZs allow companies to land imported goods for storage or various processing such as cleaning or packaging before the goods are officially brought into the United States or reexported to another country. *See* **customs-privileged facilities**

forfaiting   A financing technique that may be used in an international transaction in which the seller makes a one-time arrangement with a bank or other financial institution to take over responsibility for collecting the account receivable.

Four Asian Tigers   Refers to Hong Kong, Taiwan, Singapore, and South Korea as they fast achieved affluence in the 1980s and 90s.

franchising   A form of **licensing** in which a company (the franchiser) provides a standard package of products, systems, and management services to the franchisee, which in foreign markets has market knowledge. Franchising permits flexibility in dealing with local market conditions while providing the parent firm with a degree of control.

free trade area (FTA)   A type of regional cooperation that involves an agreement between two or more countries to reduce or eliminate customs duties and nontariff trade barriers among partner countries while members maintain individual tariff schedules for external countries. An FTA requires more cooperation than the arrangement known as the regional cooperation for development.

full-cost pricing   A method of pricing based on the view that no unit of a similar product is different from any other unit of a similar product and that each unit must bear its full share of the total fixed and variable cost, whether sold in the home market or abroad. *See* **skimming; variable-cost pricing**

g

GATT   General Agreement on Tariffs and Trade; a trade agreement signed by the United States and 22 other countries shortly after World War II. The original agreement provided a process to reduce **tariffs** and created an agency to patrol world trade; the treaty and subsequent meetings have produced agreements significantly reducing tariffs.

global awareness   A frame of reference, important to the success of a businessperson, that embodies tolerance of cultural differences and knowledge of cultures, history, world market potential, and global economic, social, and political trends.

global brand   The worldwide use of a name, term, sign, symbol (visual or auditory), design, or a combination thereof to identify goods or services of a seller and to differentiate them from those of competitors.

global marketing   The performance of business activities designed to plan, price, promote, and direct the flow of a company's goods and services to consumers or users in more than one nation for a profit. The most profound difference between global and domestic marketing involves the orientation of the company toward markets and planning activities around the world.

global marketing concept   A perspective encompassing an entire set of country markets, whether the home market and one other country or the home market and 100 other countries, and viewing them as a unit, identifying groups of prospective buyers with similar needs as a global market segment, and developing a market plan that strives for standardization wherever it is effective in cost and cultural terms.

global orientation   A means of operating by which a company acts as if all the company's markets in a company's scope of operations (including the domestic market) were approachable as a single global market, with the company standardizing the marketing mix where culturally feasible and cost effective.

green marketing   Consideration and concern for the environmental consequences of product formulation, marketing, manufacturing, and packaging.

green-house gas emissions   These are gases resulting primarily from the use of fossil fuels that tend to trap heat in the earth's atmosphere and are causal factors in global climate change. The main problem compounds are carbon dioxide, methane, nitrous oxide, and fluorinated gases.

h

home-country middlemen   In international transactions, the intermediaries, located in the producer's home country, who provide marketing services from a domestic base; also known as *domestic middlemen*. Home-country middlemen offer advantages for companies with small international sales volume or for those inexperienced in international trade. *See* **agent middlemen; merchant middlemen**

homologation   A term used to describe changes in a product that are mandated by local standards for product and service **quality.**

i

IMF   The International Monetary Fund. A global institution that, along with the World Bank Group, was created to assist nations in becoming and remaining economically viable.

imperative   A business custom (as in a foreign country) that must be recognized and accommodated. *See* **elective; exclusive**

import jobbers   In international transactions, business entities that purchase goods directly from the manufacturer and sell to wholesalers and retailers and to industrial customers.

import regulations   Restrictions placed by countries on the sale of goods from outside markets; among the reasons they are imposed are to protect health, conserve foreign exchange, serve as economic reprisals, protect home industry, and provide revenue from tariffs. Exporters to markets under such regulations may have to go through various steps to comply with them. *See* **export regulations**

indirect exporting   The type of exporting in which a company sells to a buyer (an importer or distributor) in the home country; the buyer in turn exports the product.

infrastructure   The collective assortment of capital goods that serve the activities of many industries and support production and marketing.

innovation   An idea perceived as new by a group of people; when applied to a product, an innovation may be something completely new or something that is perceived as new in a given country or culture. *See* **product diffusion**

integrated marketing communications (IMCs)   The collective arrangement of efforts and methods to sell a product or service, including advertising, sales promotions, trade shows, personal selling, direct selling, and public relations.

international marketing   The performance of business activities designed to plan, price, promote, and direct the flow of a company's goods and services to consumers or users in more than one nation for a profit.

international marketing research   The form of **marketing research** involving two additional considerations: (1) the need to communicate information across national boundaries, and (2) the challenge of applying established marketing techniques in the different environments of foreign markets, some of which may be strange or vexing milieus for the marketer.

interpretive knowledge   An ability to understand and to appreciate fully the nuances of different cultural traits and patterns. *See* **factual knowledge**

Islamic law   The *Shari'ah;* the legal system based on an interpretation of the Koran. Islamic law encompasses religious duties and obligations as well as the secular aspect of law regulating human acts. Among its provisions is a prohibition of the payment of interest.

ISO 9000s   A series of international industrial standards (ISO 9000–9004) originally designed by the International Organization for Standardization to meet the need for product quality assurances in purchasing agreements.

j

joint venture   A partnership of two or more participating companies that join forces to create a separate legal entity. *See* **strategic international alliance**

justice or fairness   One of three principles of ethics (the others are **utilitarian ethics** and **rights of the parties**); it tests an action by asking if the action respects the canons of justice or fairness to all parties involved.

l

Large-Scale Retail Store Law   In Japan competition from large retail stores has been almost totally controlled by *Daitenho*—the Large-Scale Retail Store Law (and its more recent incarnations).

Designed to protect small retailers from large intruders into their markets, the law required that any store larger than 5,382 square feet (500 square meters) must have approval from the prefecture government to be "built, expanded, stay open later in the evening, or change the days of the month they must remain closed." All proposals for new "large" stores were first judged by the Ministry of International Trade and Industry (MITI). Then, if all local retailers *unanimously* agreed to the plan, it was swiftly approved. However, without approval at the prefecture level, the plan was returned for clarification and modification, a process that could take several years (10 years was not unheard of) for approval.

Large-Scale Retail Store Location Act   A regulatory act in Japan, implemented under pressure from the United States in 2000; it replaced the protective Large-Scale Retail Store Law and relaxed restrictions on the opening of large retailers near small shops and abolished the mandate on the number of days a store must be closed.

letters of credit   Financing devices that, when opened by a buyer of goods, allow the seller to draw a draft against the bank issuing the credit and receive dollars by presenting proper shipping document. Except for cash in advance, letters of credit afford the seller the greatest degree of protection. *See* **bills of exchange**

licensing   A contractual means by which a company grants patent rights, trademark rights, and the rights to use technology to another company, often in a foreign market; a favored strategy of small and medium-sized companies seeking a foothold in foreign markets without making large capital outlays. *See* **franchising**

linguistic distance   The measure of difference between languages; an important factor in determining the amount of trade between nations.

litigation   The process in which a dispute between parties is contested in a formal judicial setting; commonly instigated by a lawsuit asserting one party's version of the facts.

local nationals   Persons living in their home country; historically the persons preferred by **expatriate** managers to form the sales force. Local nationals are more knowledgeable about a country's business structure than an expatriate would be, and they are generally less expensive to field and maintain.

logistics management   A total systems approach to management of the distribution process that includes all activities involved in physically moving raw material, in-process inventory, and finished goods inventory from the point of origin to the point of use or consumption.

lubrication   The use of funds to expedite actions of public employees and government officials. The payments made to minor officials may or may not be illegal and are usually of inconsequential amounts.

m

Maastricht Treaty   Treaty signed by 12 nations of the European Community creating the European Union.

Manifest Destiny   The notion that Americans were a chosen people ordained by God to create a model society; it was accepted as the basis for U.S. policy during much of the 19th and 20th centuries as the nation expanded its territory.

maquiladoras   Also known as *in-bond companies* or *twin plants*, a type of customs-privileged facility that originated in Mexico in the 1970s and provided U.S. companies with a favorable means to use low-cost Mexican labor. They operated through an agreement with the Mexican government allowing U.S. companies to import parts and materials into Mexico without import taxes, provided the finished products are reexported to the United States or another country. *See* **customs-privileged facilities**

marketing research   The systematic gathering, recording, and analyzing of data to provide information useful in marketing decision making. *See* **international marketing research**

Marxist-socialist tenets   The set of views in which law is subordinate to prevailing economic conditions. Marxist-socialist tenets influenced the legal systems of Russia and other republics of the former Soviet Union, as well as China, forcing these nations to revamp their commercial legal code as they become involved in trade with non-Marxist countries.

merchant middlemen   In international transactions, the intermediaries, located in the foreign market, who take title to the home-country manufacturer's goods and sell on their own account. Manufacturers using merchant middlemen have less control over the **distribution process** than those using **agent middlemen.** *See* **home-country middlemen**

Mercosur   An evolving South American union, also called the Southern Cone Free Trade Area, formed in 1991 with the goal of creating a **common market** and **customs union** among the participating countries. The original signers were Argentina, Brazil, Paraguay, and Uruguay; Bolivia and Chile later signed agreements with Mercosur.

merge-in-transit   A distribution method in which goods shipped from several supply locations are consolidated into one final customer delivery point while they are in transit and then shipped as a unit to the customer.

Monroe Doctrine   A cornerstone of U.S. foreign policy as enunciated by President James Monroe, it proclaimed three basic dicta: no further European colonization in the New World, abstention of the United States from European political affairs, and non-intervention of European governments in the governments of the Western Hemisphere. *See* **Roosevelt Corollary**

M-time   Monochromatic time; describing a view of time, typical of most North Americans, Swiss, Germans, and Scandinavians, as something that is linear and can be saved, wasted, spent, and lost. M-time cultures tend to concentrate on one thing at a time and value promptness. *See* **P-time**

multicultural research   Inquiry, analysis, and study of countries and cultures that takes into account differences in language, economic structure, social structure, behavior, and attitude patterns. Different methods of research may have varying reliability in different countries.

multinational market regions   The groups of countries that seek mutual economic benefit from reducing interregional tariffs and barriers to trade.

n

NAFTA   North American Free Trade Agreement. NAFTA is a comprehensive trade agreement that addresses, and in many cases improves all aspects of doing business within North America. By eliminating trade and investment barriers among Canada, the United States, and Mexico, it created one of the largest and richest markets in the world.

nationalism   An intense feeling of national pride and unity; an awakening of a nation's people to pride in their country. Nationalism can take on an antiforeign business bias.

NGOs   Large advocacy organizations, usually not-for-profit, often multinational, and run by citizens rather than companies or governments. Prominent examples are Green Peace, Amnesty International, and the Red Cross.

NICs   Newly industrialized countries; countries that are experiencing rapid economic expansion and industrialization.

noise   The term for an impairment to communications process comprising external influences, such as competitive advertising, other sales personnel, and confusion at the "receiving end." Noise can disrupt any step of the communications process and is frequently beyond the control of the sender or the receiver.

nontariff barriers   Restrictions, other than **tariffs,** placed by countries on imported products; they may include quality standards, sanitary and health standards, **quotas,** embargoes, boycotts, and antidumping penalties.

nontask sounding   The part of the negotiation process in which conversation covers topics other than the business at hand; non-task sounding is commonly a preliminary phase and precedes **task-related information exchange.**

o

open account   In U.S. domestic trade, the typical payment procedure for established customers, in which the goods are delivered and the customer is billed on an end-of-the-month basis.

Opium Wars   Two wars fought between China and Britain over the British run opium trade in China during the middle 1800s. The British navy attacked Chinese ports in retribution for a Chinese ban on the drug, and the Treaty of Nanjing signed in 1842 allowed greater European access to Chinese ports generally, a resumption of the opium trade, and ceding of Hong Kong to British control

orderly market agreements (OMAs)   Agreements, similar to **quotas,** between an importing country and an exporting country for a restriction on the volume of exports. Also known as **voluntary export restraints.**

p

parallel imports   International transactions in which importers buy products from distributors in one country and sell them in another to distributors that are not part of the manufacturer's regular distribution system.

parallel translation   A method of translation in which two translators are used to make a **back translation;** the results are compared, differences are discussed, and the most appropriate translation is used. The method addresses the use of common idioms in the languages being translated. *See* **decentering**

penetration pricing policy   A low price policy directed at gaining market share from competitors.

physical distribution system The overall network for the physical movement of goods, including plants and warehousing, transportation mode, inventory quantities, and packaging.

planned change A marketing strategy in which a company deliberately sets out to change those aspects of a foreign culture resistant to predetermined marketing goals. *See* **unplanned change**

political union A fully integrated form of regional co-operation that involves complete political and economic integration, either voluntary or enforced; the most notable example was the now disbanded Council for Mutual Economic Assistance (COMECON), a centrally controlled group of countries organized by the Soviet Union.

predatory pricing A practice by which a foreign producer intentionally sells its products in another country for less than the cost of production to undermine the competition and take control of the market.

price escalation The pricing disparity in which goods are priced higher in a foreign market than in the home market; caused by the added costs involved in exporting products from one country to another.

price–quality relationship The balance between a product's price and how well the product performs. Often the price–quality of a product is ideal if it meets basic expectations and no more, allowing it to be priced competitively.

primary data Data collected, as in market research, specifically for a particular research project. *See* **secondary data**

principle of justice or fairness *See* **justice or fairness**

principle of rights of the parties *See* **rights of the parties**

principle of utilitarian ethics *See* **utilitarian ethics**

prior use versus registration The principle, as observed in the United States and other common-law nations, that ownership of intellectual property rights usually goes to whoever can establish first use.

product buyback agreement A type of **countertrade** in which the sale involves goods or services that produce other goods or services—that is, production plant, production equipment, or technology.

Product Component Model A tool for characterizing how a product may be adapted to a new market by separating the product's many dimensions into three components: support services, packaging, and core component.

product diffusion The process by which product **innovation** spreads; successful product diffusion may depend on the ability to communicate relevant product information and new product attributes.

protectionism The use by nations of legal barriers, exchange barriers, and psychological barriers to restrain entry of goods from other countries.

PSAs Political and social activists. PSAs are individuals who participate in efforts to change the practices and behaviors of corporations and governments, with tactics that can range from peaceful protest to terrorism.

P-time Polychromatic time; a view of time, as held in "high con-text" cultures, in which the completion of a human transaction is more important than holding to schedules. P-time is characterized by the simultaneous occurrence of many things. *See* **M-time**

public relations (PR) The effort made by companies to create positive relationships with the popular press and general media and to communicate messages to their publics, including customers, the general public, and government regulators.

purchase price parity (PPP) GDP at PPP corrects GDP for differentials across countries in the costs of consumer purchases. The PPP correction allows for direct comparisons of the overall well-being of consumers across countries.

q

quality The essential character of something, such as a good or service; defined in two dimensions: market-perceived quality and performance quality. Consumer perception of a product's quality often has more to do with market-perceived quality than performance quality.

quotas Specific unit or dollar limits applied to a particular type of good by the country into which the good is imported. *See* **tariff**

r

relationship marketing The aspect of marketing products that depends on long-term associations with customers; an important factor in business-to-business contexts and especially important in most international markets, where culture dictates strong ties between people and companies.

repatriation The process of bringing a local national back to his/her home country after an assignment abroad.

research process The process of obtaining information; it should begin with a definition of the research problem and establishment of objectives, and proceed with an orderly approach to the collection and analysis of data.

reserves account The portion of a **balance-of-trade** statement that shows a record of exports and imports of gold, increases or decreases in foreign exchange, and increases or decreases in liabilities to foreign banks.

rights of the parties One of three principles of ethics (the others are **utilitarian ethics** and **justice or fairness**); it tests an action by asking if the action respects the rights of the individuals involved.

Roosevelt Corollary An extension of U.S. policy applied to the Monroe Doctrine by President Theodore Roosevelt, stating that the United States would not only prohibit non-American intervention in Latin American affairs but would also police Latin America and guarantee that all Latin American nations would meet their international obligations. *See* **Monroe Doctrine**

rural/urban migration As countries develop industrial huge numbers of agricultural workers move to cities causing major difficulties in urban infrastructure capacity and big city slums around the world.

s

sales promotion Marketing activities that stimulate consumer purchases and improve retailer or middlemen effectiveness and cooperation.

secondary data Data collected by an agency or individual other than the one conducting research; often useful in market research. *See* **primary data**

self-reference criterion (SRC) An unconscious reference to one's own cultural values, experience, and knowledge as a basis for a decision.

separation allowances Payment of overseas premiums to employees who take on short-term foreign assignments and travel without their families; allowances generally compensate for all excess expenses and any tax differential.

silent language Term used by Edward T. Hall for the non-spoken and symbolic meanings of time, space, things, friendships, and agreements, and how they vary across cultures; from Hall's article "The Silent Language of Business."

Single European Act An agreement, ratified in 1987, designed to remove all barriers to trade and to make the European Community a single internal market.

skimming A method of pricing, generally used for foreign markets, in which a company seeks to reach a segment of the market that is relatively price insensitive and thus willing to pay a premium price for the value received; may be used to sell a new or innovative product to maximize profits until a competitor forces a lower price. *See* **full-cost pricing; variable-cost pricing**

SNAP Simplified Network Application Process; an electronic service offered by the U.S. Department of Commerce as an alternative to paper license submissions that enables an exporter to submit export and reexport applications, high-performance computer notices, and commodity classification requests via the Internet. *See* **ELAIN; ERIC; STELA**

social institutions The methods and systems, including family, religion, school, the media, government, and corporations, that affect the ways in which people relate to one another, teach acceptable behavior to succeeding generations, and govern themselves.

sovereignty The powers exercised by a state in relation to other countries, as well as the supreme powers of a state as exercised over its own inhabitants.

special drawing rights (SDRs) A means of monetary measurement that represents an average base of value derived from the value of a group of major currencies. Known as "paper gold," it is used by the **IMF** to report most monetary statistics in a unit more reliable than a single currency, such as dollars.

stage of economic development A classification describing the (stage of) maturity and sophistication of a nation's economy as it evolves over time. The best known model, by Walt Rostow, describes five stages, starting with the traditional society and finally reaching the age of high mass consumption.

STELA System for Tracking Export License Applications; an automated voice response system for exporters that enables license applicants to track the status of their license and classification applications with U.S. authorities. *See* **ELAIN; ERIC; SNAP**

strategic international alliance (SIA) A business relationship established by two or more companies to cooperate out of mutual need and to share risk in achieving a common objective.

strategic planning A type of planning conducted at the highest levels of management, dealing with products, capital, and research and the long- and short-term goals of a company. *See* **corporate planning; tactical planning**

subornation The giving of large sums of money—frequently not fully accounted for—designed to entice an official to commit an illegal act on behalf of the one offering the money.

sustainable development An approach toward economic growth that has been described (by Joke Waller-Hunter) as a cooperative effort among businesses, environmentalists, and others to seek growth with "wise resource management, equitable distribution of benefits, and reduction of negative efforts on people and the environment from the process of economic growth."

t

tactical planning A type of planning that pertains to specific actions and to the allocation of resources used to implement strategic planning goals in specific markets; also known as *market planning*; generally conducted at the local level. *See* **corporate planning; strategic planning**

Taiping Rebellion The most costly civil war in human history in China during 1851–1964. Some estimates have the death toll at between 20–40 million.

tariff A fee or tax that countries impose on imported goods, often to protect a country's markets from intrusion from foreign countries. *See* **nontariff barriers; quotas**

task-related information exchange The point in the negotiation process at which nontask communication, or **nontask sounding,** is completed and substantial negotiations begin.

TCNs Third-country nationals; expatriates from one country working for a foreign company in a third country. *See* **expatriate; local nationals**

terms of sale The set of rules and costs applying to a transaction, covering such categories as price, freight, and insurance. In international trade, terms of sale often sound similar to those in domestic commerce but generally have different meanings. Also known as *trade terms*.

The Greater China Refers to both the People's Republic of China (PRC or Mainland China) and the Republic of China (Taiwan). Both political units divided in 1949, and claim the other as their territory.

trading companies Business entities that accumulate, transport, and distribute goods from many countries.

transfer pricing The pricing of goods transferred from a company's operations or sales units in one country to its units elsewhere; also known as *intracompany pricing*. In transfer pricing, prices may be adjusted to enhance the ultimate profit of the company as a whole.

Treaty of Amsterdam Treaty, concluded in 1997, that addressed issues left undone by the **Maastricht Treaty** and identified priority measures necessary to bring a single market in Europe fully into effect and to lay a solid foundation for both a single currency and an enlargement of the European Union into central and eastern Europe. *See* **Single European Act**

triangulation A term borrowed from naval charting meaning using at least three differing measures of the same concept to verify the accuracy of any one method. For example, regarding forecast of demand separate opinions of experts, sales representatives, and quantitative economic analyses might be compared.

24-Hour Rule   A U.S. requirement, part of the Cargo and Container Security Initiative, mandating that sea carriers and NVOCCs (Non-Vessel Operating Common Carriers) provide U.S. Customs with detailed descriptions (manifests) of the contents of containers bound for the United States 24 hours before a container is loaded on board a vessel.

U

uncontrollable elements   Factors in the business environment over which the international marketer has no control or influence; may include competition, legal restraints, government controls, weather, consumer preferences and behavior, and political events. *See* **controllable elements**

United States–Canada Free Trade Agreement   An agreement, known as CFTA, between the United States and Canada designed to eliminate all trade barriers between the two nations.

unplanned change   A marketing strategy in which a company introduces a product into a market without a plan to influence the way the market's culture responds to or resists the company's marketing message. *See* **planned change**

utilitarian ethics   One of three principles of ethics (the others are **rights of the parties** and **justice or fairness**); it tests an action by asking if it optimizes the "common good" or benefits of all constituencies.

V

variable-cost pricing   A method of pricing goods in foreign markets in which a company is concerned only with the marginal or incremental costs of producing goods for sale in those markets. Firms using variable-cost pricing take the view that foreign sales are bonus sales. *See* **full-cost pricing; skimming**

VERS   *See* **voluntary export restraints**

voluntary export restraints (VERS)   Agreements, similar to **quotas,** between an importing country and an exporting country for a restriction on the volume of exports. Also known as **orderly market agreements (OMAs).**

W

work councils   In Europe, work councils (that is, internal labor union committees) are very much involved in setting rules about compensation and other human resources policies companywide, even for sales people. In Austria and Germany, for example, work councils not only codetermine compensation plans, but also must approve them before implementation.

World Trade Organization   *See* **WTO**

WTO   World Trade Organization. The organization formed in 1994 that encompasses the **GATT** structure and extends it to new areas that had not been adequately covered previously. The WTO adjudicates trade disputes. All member countries have equal representation.

CREDITS

Chapter 1

Opener, p. 4: AP Photo/Aaron Favila; p. 5: AP Photo/Lee Jin-man; p. 6: AP Photo/Str; p. 8, p. 10, p. 15 (left): © John Graham; p. 15 (right): © Neil Thomas/Africa Media Online; p. 23 (top): © Robyn Beck/AFP/Getty; p. 23 (bottom left): © John Graham; p. 23 (bottom right): © The McGraw-Hill Companies, Inc.

Chapter 2

Opener, p. 29 (left): AP Photo/The Gazette, Cliff Jette; p. 29 (right): © Allstarphotos/Newscom.com; p. 40 (top): © John Graham; p. 41 (bottom left): © Sharon Hoogstraten; p. 41 (bottom right): AP Photo/Conn. Attorney General; p. 43: © John Graham; p. 44: © Tom McHugh/Photo Researchers, Inc; p. 48: "Globalization" by Gifford Myers, Altadena, CA, 2001.; p. 49 (top): © Mike Nelson/AFP/Getty; p. 49 (bottom): AP Photo/Jane Mingay.

Chapter 3

Opener, p. 58: © Dave G. Houser/Corbis; p. 65: © Frimmel Smith/PlayPumps; p. 66: © John Graham; p. 68 (left): AP/Wide World Photos; p. 68 (right): © Wolfgang Kumm/epa/Corbis; p. 70: © John Graham; p. 71: © Edro Lobo/Bloomberg News/Landov; p. 73 (left), p. 73 (right): © John Graham; p. 80: Courtesy Beluga Group.

Chapter 4

Opener, p. 99, p. 100 (Florida), p. 100 (Aalsmeer Flower Auction): © John Graham; p. 100 (Pope): AP Photo/Antonio Calanni; p. 100 (Amsterdam flower market), p. 100 (seeds): © John Graham; p. 100 (painting): © Salmer; p. 101 (inside Aalsmeer), p. 101 (flower auction), p. 101 (trucks at Aalsmeer): © John Graham; p. 101 (Rembrandt's Night Watch): © Rijksmuseum, Amsterdam/SuperStock; p. 101 (Van Gogh's Vase with Fifteen Sunflowers): AP Photo/Tsugufumi Matsumoto, File; p. 101 (Van Gogh's Potato Eaters): © SuperStock, Inc.; p. 108: © Cary Wolinsky; p. 113 (top): © Mahmoud Mahmoud/AFP/Getty; p. 113 (bottom): © Rika Houston; p. 117: AP Photo/Maxim Marmur; p. 121: © Joe McNally/Getty.

Chapter 5

Opener, p. 126: © John Graham; p. 128: © Reuters /Landov; p. 131 (left): © Michael Nicholson/Corbis; p. 131 (right): © 20th Century Fox/The Kobal Collection; p. 136 (left): © Ed Kashi/Corbis; p. 136 (right): © Andy Rain/Bloomberg News//Landov; p. 141 (left): © David Coll Blanco; p. 141 (right): AP Photo/Hasan Jamali; p. 145 (bottom): © John Graham; p. 146 (top): © Phillippe Lopez/AFP/Getty; p. 152: © Reuters/Stringer; p. 153: © John Graham.

Chapter 6

Opener, p. 160: © Eric Feferberg/AFP/Getty; p. 163: © Carolyn Cole/Los Angeles Times. Copyright 2010. Reprinted with permission.; p. 165: © Behrouz Mehri/AFP/Getty; p. 170 (all): © John Graham; p. 172 (top): AP Photo/Claude Paris; p. 172 (middle): AP Photo; p.172 (bottom): © Georges Gobet/AFP/Getty; p. 173 (top): © Klaus-Dietmar Gabbert/epa/Corbis; p. 173

(middle): © Reuters/Corbis; p. 173 (bottom): Courtesy of Sea Shepherd Conservation Society; p. 174: © Carolyn Cole; p. 175, p. 182: © John Graham.

Chapter 7

Opener, p. 188: © Derek Berwin/The Image Bank/Getty; p. 199 (top left): Photo by Rick Loomis, Los Angeles Times. Copyright 2005, Los Angeles Times. Reprinted with permission.; p. 199 (top right): © Mike Clark/AFP/Getty; p. 199 (bottom): AP Photo/Christian Schwetz; p. 202: AP Photo/Ng Han Guan; p. 205 (top left), 205 (top right): © John Graham; p. 205 (middle): AP Photo/Pat Roque; p. 205 (bottom): AP Photo/Jayanta Saha; p. 207: © AFP/Getty; p. 215: © Roger Ressmeyer/Corbis.

Chapter 8

Opener, p. 220 (left): AP Photo/Greg Baker; p. 220 (right): © Jim Watson/AFP/Getty; p. 229: © Brian Lee/Corbis; p. 232 (both): © John Graham; p. 233: © Cary Wolinsky; p. 240 (left), p. 240 (right): © John Graham.

Chapter 9

Opener, p. 253 (both): © Christopher Anderson/Magnum Photos; p. 253 (bottom), p. 261: © John Graham; p. 263 (left): AP Photo/Monica Rueda; p. 263 (right), p. 271: © John Graham.

Chapter 10

Opener, p. 276 (both), p. 282, p. 284: © John Graham; p. 286: © AFP Photo/Louisa Gouliamaki; p. 288: Courtesy of American Legacy Foundation, American Cancer Society, and Campaign for Tobacco Free Kids; p. 290, p. 291, p. 294 (left): © John Graham; p. 294 (right): AP Photo/Amr Nabil; p. 296: AP Photo/NASA.

Chapter 11

Opener, p. 307: AP Photo/Ng Han Guan; p. 311: AP Photo/Sherwin Crasto; p. 315 (left): © Ruth Fremson /The New York Times/Redux; p. 315 (right): © John Graham; p. 317 (left): © Tomas Munita; p 317 (right): © Amit Bhargava/Bloomberg News/Landov; p. 319: © Jimin Lai/AFP/Getty; p. 324: © Roger Ressmeyer/Corbis; p. 325: © Goh Chai Hin/AFP/Getty.

Chapter 12

Opener, p. 333 (all): © John Graham; p. 334: AP Photo/Richard Drew; p. 343 (all), p. 347 (left), p. 347 (right), p. 350: © John Graham.

Chapter 13

Opener, p 361: © Kenneth Garrett/National Geographic Image Collection; p. 362, p. 366: © John Graham; p. 367: Courtesy of Angelic Pretty; p. 370 (top): © Michael Edrington/The Image Works; p. 370 (bottom left), p. 370 (bottom right), p. 379 (both): © John Graham; p. 384 (both): © Kevin Lee/Bloomberg News/Landov; p. 386: © Studio 101/Alamy; p. 390: © John Graham.

Chapter 14

Opener, p. 396 (top), p. 396 (bottom), p. 397 (both): Courtesy of Microsoft Corporation.; p. 405: © John Graham; p. 410: © Adam Berry/Bloomberg via Getty; p. 413–416 (all): Courtesy of Solar Turbines Inc.

Chapter 15

Opener, p. 420: © David Pierson/Los Angeles Times; p. 421, p. 426 (both), p. 427 (both), p. 431, p. 434, p. 437 (all): © John Graham; p. 444–447 (all): Courtesy of Marriot.

Chapter 16

Opener, p. 458 (top): © John Graham; p. 458 (bottom left): © Covered Images/A-Frame; p. 458 (bottom right): © Tom Cozad/newport surfshots.com; p. 459 (top left): AP Photo/Greg Baker; p. 459 (top right), p. 462 (bottom left), p. 462 (bottom right): © John Graham; p. 464–466 (all): Courtesy of Microsoft; p. 469 (top left), © John Graham; p. 469 (bottom left): © Tom Purslow/Manchester United via Getty; p. 469 (bottom right): AP Photo/Mark Baker; p. 470 (all), p. 471, p. 474 (top): © John Graham; p. 474 (bottom left): AP Photo/Denis Doyle/File; p. 474 (bottom right): Courtesy of GE; p. 482 (all), p. 486–487 (both): © John Graham; p. 489 (top left): AP/Wide World Photos; p. 489 (top right): © Tatsuyuki Tayama/Fujifotos/The Image Works.

Chapter 17

Opener, p. 499: © David Paul Morris/Getty; p. 501 (top left): © Roger Ressmeyer/Corbis; p. 501 (top right): © John Maier, Jr./The Image Works; p. 504 (both): © David McIntyre/Stock Photo; p. 508: © Tom Wagner/Corbis; p. 514: © John Graham.

Chapter 18

Opener, p. 528: AP Photo/Greg Baker; p. 529, p. 530: AP Photo/Katsumi Kasahara; p. 531: © John Graham; p. 532: AP Photo; p. 536: © 20th Century Fox/Marvel Ent Group/The Kobal Collection; p. 542: © Dadang Tri/Reuters /Landov; p. 543: © Susan Van Etten/PhotoEdit, Inc; p. 545: © John Graham.

Chapter 19:

Opener, p. 556: © Photodisc Green/Getty; p. 565: © Ralph Orlowski/Getty; p. 567: Copyrighted and used by permission of KARRASS, LTD. Beverly Hills, CA.; p. 568 (left): © Jon Feingersh/Blend Images/Getty; p. 568 (right): © Macduff Everton/Corbis; p. 573: © John Graham; p. 574: AP Photo/Anat Givon.

NAME INDEX

Page numbers followed by n refer to notes.

Aaker, David A., 385n
Aaker, Jennifer L., 112n, 117n, 467n, 475n
Abdullah, King of Jordan, 380
Abkowitz, Alyssa, 22n
Abley, Mark, 518n
Acito, Frank, 332n
Adams, Mike, 377
Adetoun, Bolanle, 150n
Adler, Nancy J., 143n, 554n
Agarwal, Sanjeev, 341n
Aguilera, Ruth V., 339n
Ah Kheng Kau, 388n
Ahluwalia, Rohini, 475n
Ajami, Fouad, 176n
Albaum, Gerald, 355n
Alden, Dana L., 233n, 385n
Alexander, Nicholas, 426n
Allan, Graham, 264
Allen, Michael W., 116n
Allred, Brent B., 373n
Almond, Phil, 211n
Alpert, Frank, 230n, 422n
Altaras, Selin, 384n
Alum, Ian, 257
Amador, Manuel, 53
Ambler, Tim, 568n, 569n
Amine, Lys S., 389n
Ammar, Essam, 440
Anderson, Beverlee B., 139n
Anderson, Erin, 509n
Anderson, Eugene W., 361n, 406n
Anderson, Nicola, 473n
Andrews, J. C., 233n
Andrews, Michelle, 106n
Andriani, Pierpaolo, 237n
Andruss, Paula Lyon, 472n
Anita, Kersi D., 526n
Annan, Kofi, 380
Ansari, Paradis, 144n, 515n
Ansfield, Jonathan, 306n
Anterasian, Cathy, 152n, 398n
Appert, Nicolas, 63
Apud, Salvador, 515n
Areddy, James T., 206n, 359n, 498n, 518n
Armstrong, David, 254n
Arndt, Michael, 264n, 372n, 425n
Arnold, Mark J., 389n
Arnould, Eric J., 96n, 315n, 316n, 384n
Arnst, Catherine, 380n
Arregle, Jean-Luc, 356n
Asbell, Bernard, 105n
Askegaard, Soren, 334n
Asmussen, Christian Geisler, 20n
Aston, Adam, 70n
Ataman, M. Berk, 387n
Auger, James, 213n
Aulakh, Preet S., 347n
Axxin, Catherine N., 241n
Aybar, Bulent, 354n
Azevedo, Jose Sergio Gabrielli de, 70n

Baack, Sally A., 512n
Bacon, Francis, 60
Bae Yeong-ho, 119
Bagozzi, Richard P., 503n, 505n
Bailey, Thomas A., 29n
Bajaj, Vikas, 270n, 304n
Bakalar, Nicholoas, 103n
Baker, Ted, 133n

Balabanis, George, 388n
Balasubramanian, Sridhar, 428n
Ball, Deborah, 109n
Banderas, Antonio, 146
Bannon, Lisa, 145n, 453n
Banon, Lisa, 125n
Barboza, David, 303n, 429n
Bardon, Jeffrey Q., 352n
Bardsher, Keith, 304n
Barkema, Harry G., 19n, 344n, 345n
Barnes, Brooks, 386n
Barrasa, Angel, 150n
Barrett, Nigel J., 236n
Barrinuevo, Alexi, 71n
Barta, Patrick, 74n, 397n
Barzilay, (Judge) Judith M., 535
Basu, Sudita, 220n
Bate, Roger, 199n
Batra, Rajeev, 385n
Batson, Andrew, 408n
Bauerlein, Mark, 555n
Bauers, Sandy, 67n
Baum, Caroline, 42n
Baumgartner, Hans, 233n
Beamish, Paul W., 356n
Bearden, William O., 355n
Beck, Ernest, 424n
Beckham, David, 469
Beechler, Schon, 339n, 515n
Beerens, Marie, 535n
Begley, Sharon, 68n, 473n
Begley, Thomas M., 132n
Begum, Delora, 314
Behfar, Kristin, 563n
Beibei Dong, 355n
Belderbos, Rene A., 352n, 498n
Belk, Russell W., 388n, 457n, 462n
Belkin, Liuba Y., 144n, 515n
Bell, Alexander Graham, 62, 67
Bell, Simon, 121n
Bellman, Eric, 310n
Bello, Daniel C., 553n
Benedetto, Anthony Di, 368n
Benedict XVI, Pope, 146
Benito, Gabriel. R. G., 340n
Bennett, Jeff, 152n
Berg, Peter T. van den, 150n
Bergen, Mark E., 526n
Berlusconi, Silvio, 160
Berman, Paul Schiff, 190n
Berns, Sjors, 148n
Beutin, Nikolas, 401n
Bhabwati, Jagdish, 4n
Bhagat, Rabi S., 119n
Bhardwaj, Vertica, 385n
Biederman, Patricia Ward, 39n
Bird, Matthew, 521n
Birkinshaw, Julian, 354n
Bisoux, Tricia, 23n
Biswas, Somdutta, 475n
Bjorkman, Ingmar, 355n
Blackstone, Brian, 31n
Blair, Edward, 475n
Blair, Tony, 403
Blakeney, Roger N., 242n
Blasius, Jorg, 35n
Block, Lauren, 97n
Block, Robert, 179n
Block, Steven A., 165n

Bobina, Mariya, 150n
Bodur, Muzaffer, 150n
Bodzin, Steven, 168n
Boekmann, Alan, 151
Boggs, David J., 490n
Bolino, Mark C., 513n
Bolivar, Simón, 64
Bond, Michael Harris, 109n, 506n
Bond, Paul, 535n
Bono, 469
Boone, James, 380n
Boonstra, Jaap J., 506n
Booth, William, 185n
Borden, Jeff, 412n
Borzo, Jeannette, 411n
Boscariol, John W., 185n
Bovard, James, 36n
Bove, Jose, 7
Boyacigiller, Nakiye A., 339n, 515n
Bradsher, Keith, 67n, 270n, 304n, 306n, 552n
Brannen, Mary Yoko, 354n
Branson, Richard, 378
Brat, Ilan, 397n, 398n
Bremmer, Brian, 164n
Brencic, Maja Makovec, 335n
Bressman, Henrik, 354n
Brett, Jeanne M., 552n, 559n, 563n
Brewer, Geoffrey, 507n
Brewer, Thomas L., 114n, 398n
Bridson, Kerrie, 339n
Briley, Donnel A., 117n, 118n
Brislin, Richard, 118n
Brock, David M., 513n
Brockner, Joel, 563n
Broderick, Amanda J., 234n, 335n
Brodowsky, Glen H., 139n
Broekemier, Greg M., 144n
Bronnenberg, Bart J., 387n
Brouthers, Keith D., 345n
Brouthers, Lance Eliot, 345n
Brown, Donald E., 102n, 102n
Brown, James R., 341n
Brown, Philip, 541n
Brundtland, Gro Harlem, 491
Bruton, Garry D., 332n
Bryan-Low, Cassell, 403n
Bryant, Barbara Everitt, 361n, 406n
Buatsi, Seth N., 141n
Buchan, Nancy R., 119n, 562n
Buchholz, Todd G., 27n
Buckley, Peter J., 332n, 336n
Bufalini, Sam, 472n
Buffett, Warren, 331
Bulkeley, William M., 312n
Bunau-Varilla, Philippe Jean, 53
Bunkley, Nick, 364n
Burbridge, John, Jr., 147n
Burkink, Timothy J., 4n, 288n
Burroughs, James E., 230n
Burrows, Peter, 393n, 523n
Buruma, Ian, 306n
Bush, George W., 60n, 161, 165, 200, 267
Bustillo, Miguel, 424n
Byrnes, Nanette, 499n
Byron, Ellyn, 425n

Calantone, Roger J., 237n, 425n
Campbell, Nigel, 554n
Campion, Michael A., 512n